Folklore and Society

Series Editors

Roger Abrahams
Bruce Jackson
Marta Weigle

Books in the series Folklore and Society:

George Magoon and the Down East Game War: History, Folklore, and the Law
Edward D. Ives

Diversities of Gifts: Field Studies in Southern Religion
Edited by Ruel W. Tyson, Jr., James L. Peacock, and Daniel W. Patterson

DIVERSITIES OF GIFTS

DIVERSITIES OF GIFTS

Field Studies in Southern Religion

Edited by
Ruel W. Tyson, JR.,
James L. Peacock,
and
Daniel W. Patterson

UNIVERSITY OF ILLINOIS PRESS
Urbana and Chicago

©1988 by the Board of Trustees of the University of Illinois
Manufactured in the United States of America
C 5 4 3 2 1

This book is printed on acid-free paper.

Library of Congress Cataloging-in-Publication Data

Diversities of gifts.

Includes index.
Contents: A Quaker meeting and mainstream religion in
a North Carolina community / Isabel B. Terry—The sons
of God / James Wise—Finding a home in the Church /
Beverly B. Patterson—[etc.]
1. North Carolina—Religious life and customs.
2. Southern States—Religious life and customs.
I. Tyson, Ruel W., Jr., 1930-   . II. Peacock,
James L. III. Patterson, Daniel W. (Daniel Watkins)
BR555.N78D58   1988   280'.4'09756   87-22576
ISBN 0-252-01517-7 (alk. paper)

Now concerning spiritual gifts, brethren,
I would not have you ignorant. . . .
Now there are diversities of gifts,
but the same Spirit. . . .
And there are diversities of operations,
but it is the same God which worketh all in all.
But the manifestation of the Spirit
is given to every man to profit withal.

—1 *Cor.* 12: 1, 4, 6-7
King James version

Contents

Preface

In this volume we offer studies of Southern religious life, but not of the highly organized and self-publicizing denominations like the Southern Baptists, Episcopalians, Presbyterians, or United Methodists. We report instead religious traditions of groups we call "independent Protestants," although at least one of them — the Primitive Baptists — will not gladly accept the label of Protestant. These are groups that for the most part have no national bureaucracies and do not house their faiths in uptown churches. The journalist or the academic rarely hears their voices, or hearing, misunderstands. These believers deserve better. Their spiritual experience is rich, and they are often gifted to speak eloquently of it.

Our studies deal principally with independent Protestants in a single state, North Carolina, but even so form only a sampling rather than a comprehensive survey. The picture formed by these groups is a mosaic of many, many pieces, and the essays merely suggest the diversity of ecological, social, and theological terrains characteristic of independent Protestant religion in North Carolina. At the same time, the accounts are relevant to the study of religion in much of the rest of the South. In them, we treat groups in all three major geographical subregions of the South Atlantic states (the coastal plain, the piedmont, and the Appalachians), groups from varied ethnic traditions (Native American, black, white, and Asian), and groups representing several theological strains (Calvinist, Wesleyan, and Pietist). Some of these churches — Quaker, for example, or African Methodist Episcopal Zion — by their very names imply richly braided histories that stretch back several centuries and have roots in the cultures of several continents. Complex webs of relationships tie other churches to congregations with similar faiths up and down the Appalachian chain or across the Sun Belt crescent. To study the local embodiment is to learn about similar congregations throughout much of the South. If individually the congregations are small, in the aggregate they compose a significant wing of Southern — and American — religion.

The volume is arranged in four parts:

Introduction. In the introductory essay the editors discuss an approach adopted by many of the authors of these studies in carrying out their research and writing, emphasizing the metaphor of "gesture"—living forms through which the various religious traditions express themselves.

Religious Communities and Congregations. This set of essays presents descriptions of religious groups within the contexts of their various communities. The studies show varying degrees of openness and closure between these religious groups and their respective communities.

Experiences and Forms. With the second group of studies the authors illustrate the distinctive voices of particular religious traditions. The chapters display an array of aesthetic forms commanded by religious persons in the articulation of their beliefs and hopes. Each chapter demonstrates the expressive virtuosity evident in all the groups sampled in this book.

Conclusion. The final section is a summary in which the editors reflect on the variety of religious experiences and group practices explored in the book and consider common themes, their variations, and their implications for an understanding of religious traditions in North Carolina and the larger culture that frames it.

The editors shared all the tasks of assembling this volume, but each had a special assignment. Ruel Tyson drafted the Introduction and James Peacock the Conclusion. Daniel Patterson undertook the task of editing the chapters for publication.

Each study in the volume grows from an extended period of observation and inquiry with one group of independent Protestants. Our descriptions are based on some months of attending regular services and special ceremonies such as baptisms, weddings, and funerals, of touring members' work places, of talking on front porches late into the evening, and of sharing meals. Such observation and conversation are the necessary ways of learning about the faiths of independent Protestants. Although some groups can furnish an inquirer with a published denominational history or theological treatise, the fullest expression of their religious life is in the gestures they enact. We therefore tried to understand — and to enlist each congregation's help in understanding — the sermons, testimonies, songs, and ceremonies. We wanted to learn what the members themselves had to teach and to show about their religion.

Like others who before us have done field research in the region — Max Weber, Howard Odum, Guy B. Johnson, and their students and successors — we are attempting to describe and understand the diversity and richness of little-noticed traditions. We seek to fill gaps in the general knowledge of groups who choose not to conform to mainstream models. Through these field studies of Southern religion we hope to break down stereotypes, to disturb set memories and unexamined patterns of perception, and to awaken little-exercised faculties of appreciation.

The fieldwork on which these studies rest was carried out during the last decade under the auspices of the Departments of Anthropology and Religious Studies and the Curriculum in Folklore at the University of North Carolina at Chapel Hill. We gratefully acknowledge the support of these departments and the grants and other support that we have received from the University Research Council and the Institute for Research in the Social Sciences at Chapel Hill; the National Endowments for the Humanities and the Arts in Washington, D.C.; the National Science Foundation; the National Institute of Mental Health; and the Wenner-Gren Foundation for Anthropological Research. The editors thank their former students for the stimulation they have given us — and for their patience during the lengthy preparations for this volume. Above all, the editors and contributors wish to acknowledge their indebtedness to the practitioners of religion under whom we study and about whom we write. Except for members of the Golden Echoes gospel group — public performers with published record albums and a film in which they appear under their own names — we have used pseudonyms instead of the actual names of persons and congregations. And we refrain from thanking them all here by name; we trust that those who see this volume will understand that we are prevented from doing this by their great numbers and by our wish to respect their privacy. Though nameless here, they have our gratitude for sharing with us their religious experience, their time, their homes and meals — their friendship.

DIVERSITIES OF GIFTS

INTRODUCTION — Method and Spirit: Studying the Diversity of Gestures in Religion

With a Photographic Sampler of Religious Gestures by Ann Hawthorne

> *Gesture* . . . manner of carrying the body; bearing, carriage, mien, deportment; manner of placing the body; position, posture, or attitude, especially in acts of prayer or worship; in early use: the employment of bodily movements, attitudes, expressions of countenance as a means of giving effect to oratory; a movement expressive of thought or feeling.
> — Oxford English Dictionary

> The spoken word is a gesture, its meaning, a world.
> — Merleau-Ponty

A task that confronts those who do fieldwork with local religion is to discover routes from the particular gestures enacted by members of a religious group to the worlds of meaning manifested in such actions. No field-worker can fully finish this task, but the authors of the studies that compose this volume do open pathways from gestures to meanings and invite the reader to follow.

The student who studies religion in the neighborhood where it is practiced begins with gestures:

> A pair of raised arms and closed eyes . . . a hymn sung without parts in a minor key . . . the alternating light and dark colors of pews and walls . . . a Bible held in the upward arm of a preacher . . . the cadences and intonations of "Praise God!" and "Thank you, Jesus" . . . moistened faces and shaking bodies . . . stately processions, robed choirs, and organ music . . . baskets or plates, wooden or gold, passed out or set on a table in the main aisle . . . the absence of musical instruments or stained glass windows . . . a pulpit on a stage surrounded by amplifying equipment . . . the cacophony of drums and stomping feet . . . the hum of silence.

Such are some of the gestures that define a religion in the actions of its members, giving collective expression to its way of appearing in

3

time and space, inviting the appreciation of those who apprentice themselves to learning its spirit by attending to its particulars.

Before its denominational status or its theological tradition, a religion first appears in the world as gestures, which are the elementary forms of its life. Prior to the condition of individual conscience or soul and before declarations of belief by a member, a religion displays itself in the language of gesture, spoken and enacted by an individual and the congregation together. Gesture is not one thing, belief and ritual another. Gesture enfolds both beliefs and the ritual of worship. Only at the level of reflection for the believer and only at the distance of observation for the researcher does gesture fold into the abstractions of "belief," "feeling," and "ritual."

Considered only as belief systems shorn of their contexts of enactment, most Baptist and Pentecostal churches are classified "fundamentalist." They both adhere to "the fundamentals," such as the doctrines of the inerrancy of the Bible, the virgin birth, and the bodily resurrection of Jesus. Hence these churches are often grouped together both in the press and in scholarly writing. Yet any observers who visit a Baptist and a Pentecostal church will see that while holding some of the same beliefs, Baptists and Pentecostals practice their religion in distinctively different ways. Baptist preaching is different from Pentecostal preaching; Baptists sing in a different manner from Pentecostals; and it is easy to imagine that Baptist tears are different from Pentecostal tears.

To learn the gestures of a religion is to get closer to its genius than using an abstract of its official beliefs and classifying them according to some previously adopted typology. Gestures are richer than any explicit formulation of belief. Gestures are pivotal, for they are at once public and personal. They are the articulations of tacit belief and explicit feeling.

Like the contributors to this volume, any researcher who leaves the classroom and the library and ventures into a church to study religion in its own domain learns how its members live their religion by learning how they enact it in meeting together. The actions that take place in a service or in a meeting are not like a play performed in a theater. For any of the religious groups studied by the authors of this book, there is no script separate from the action. Members of the cast do not speak lines that they have self-consciously memorized; instead, as "prompted by the Spirit," they speak and act out of that second nature called memory. They do not conspire in a fiction to create an aesthetic world that members leave to return to "the real world." The meanings of the real world and how they live in it are determined for the members by the ensemble of gestures they collectively enact. "It's real!" shouts a Lumbee woman in the act of giving her testimony. Religious gestures are acknowledgments of such realities. There is also a negative mode for such acknowledgment. One young Primitive Baptist Elder said, "You know, I believe that it is good when I am not blessed to preach even though I try . . . then I know I am not just acting, that what I am doing is for real."

Members live their religion by doing it, acting its rites, restating its memories, speaking its hopes, obeying its commands, thus gaining an identity and a world to live in. In these actions members carry on by carrying out the calls and promises of their religion. Their gestures of singing and remaining silent, of praying and preaching, of listening and meditating, of weeping and smiling are not secondary means to other, primary ends. Gestures are not instruments that translate into a language understood elsewhere. These gestures, on the contrary, are the thoughts of the religion they express, the forms of the religion held by its members. Gesturing is a way of holding one's religion, gesturing is a way of being held by one's religion. By attending to gestures, the serious observer working in the field to learn a religion seeks to avoid a reductive formalization that smoothes out its singular features, the eccentric edges that render distinctive the identity of the religion.

Set beside the rich weave of bodily movement and verbal nuance, the stated beliefs and rules of a religion appear abstract, formal, and removed from the rhythms and arrests and tastes indigenous to the practices of a religion. Sacred means and ends meet and are bound together in these actions, postures, and attitudes. Gestures and their meanings are not divided as a message and its code, once sent, then to be decoded. The gesture is the message and code at once, both personal and public, with meanings unique to the person overlapping meanings commonly shared by the group.

By understanding a religion according to its gestures, the researcher learns that believing is not one activity or state of mind and belonging another activity and state. Belief and membership are not distinct cate-

Testimony, Free Will Baptist Church

Song, Free Will Baptist Church

Altar Prayer, Free Will Baptist Church

Embrace of Love, Camp Meeting

Testimony, Free Will Baptist Church

Testimony, Free Will Baptist Church

Homecoming Dinner on the Ground, Church of God

gories for members, although they may speak of membership in terms of beliefs, as well as beliefs in terms of membership, as in identifying oneself as a Baptist or as a Pentecostal.

Belief, membership, denominational type, theological tradition, and such terms as *ritual, symbol, belief system,* and *gesture* are categories that have their home in the culture of the field investigator, not in the culture of the religious group. The student of religion who leaves the academic domain, who dwells for a time in the community where a religious group has its home, and who returns to write about these visits in essays like the chapters of this book produces a cluster of formalizations based on observations, interviews, historical sources, and knowledge of theory. There is no more powerful formalization or shaper of thought than the act of writing, through which all these sources of knowledge are mediated. Whatever poetry there is in the practice of religion, it is fated to be mediated through the prose of the observer, a medium difficult for the passage of gestures from their native ground to the world of writers and readers. In addition, theories of ritual, language, belief, and action — the categories of the discipline in which the writers are schooled — affect perception as much as they affect the ways observations are translated into writing.

Within these dense mediations of category and the medium of writing, the ethnographic writer seeks a bridge term to connect the field of action in which the religion studied has its life with the world of the prospective reader. The bridge term must be appropriate to the identity and practice of the religion studied in the field — *appropriate* means at once accurate and fair, a double requirement that includes epistemological and ethical criteria. The bridge term must be conducive to making central features of the religion under study accessible to readers, who though perhaps geographically near may be culturally distant. As bridges make opposite banks of a river accessible to each other, so bridging terms in ethnographic writing allow authors and readers to acquire an approximate understanding of the religious world lived by persons within the religious community. The choice of bridge terms is the work of ethnographic judgment, whose importance it is difficult to overestimate.

The choice in our case of *gesture* as a bridge term must be judged by these criteria. The subjects of the following articles will best judge the appropriateness of particular gestures selected for presentation and interpretations offered by an author. The readers of the following essays will best judge the success of the authors' efforts to communicate about others who may be different from themselves ethnically, culturally, and especially religiously.

This last reflection acknowledges that the folkloric or anthropological student who writes of a religious group faces three groups of critics: general readers, peers, and members of the group reported in the study. Many devotees of a religion not only enact its gestures but also are skilled in judging the gestures as well. They make finely tuned judgments about the quality of their own and their fellows' gestures, judgments that are a rich blend of psychological, aesthetic, moral, and theological insights. Learning what a "sweet service" or a "moving sermon" means for the members who utter such judgments on their own rituals and leaders is as much a part of learning the way a religion works as observing its worship, studying its history, and mastering the social facts of the local community. Adept at judging their own performances, members of religious groups are equally competent to judge what has been written about them in the essays that follow.

The authors of the ethnographic reports gathered in this book also face their professional peers as critics. These readers may ask why the editors have selected the odd term *gesture* as a master emblem for the work collected here. Gesture, after all, is not a category commonly used in the disciplines of folklore, religious studies, or anthropology. Unlike *symbol, myth,* or *ritual,* it has no standing in the conventions of these disciplines. Thus our use of the term *gesture* registers our dissent from prevailing academic approaches to the study of local religions of Protestant orientation in the South. One pervasive theory is that religion is functional for needs extrinsic to its own working, that it is a collective fantasy compensating for social or economic deprivations. This theory assumes that religious action, especially ritual action, is only a secondary process in the human economy, not among primary processes like the need for status and psychological integration. In this view, religious action is either a substitute for primary needs that are not being met through other social means or a set of behaviors that can be understood through an analysis of sociological or psychological data. For this group of critics, gestures are secondary, displaced by analysis of primary levels of human behavior, such as communicative mechanisms, rather than acknowledged as having power to create a world of meaning worthy of study in its own right.

Another group of critics translates gestures not by reducing them to primary processes inherent in human behavior but by understanding them strictly in terms of beliefs or the ideas they express. If the first group of professional peer critics reduces gestures to social or organic processes, the second group of theorists reduces gestures to an item in a belief system. Both behavioral and intellectualist theories of religion limit gesture to secondary roles. While a few of the essays in this book may be grounded in one of these approaches, for most of the authors gesture is the matrix that generates the interpretation, whether it moves toward the intellectual aspects of religious beliefs or toward the personal or social aspects of religious life. Students of religion of our persuasion acknowledge that gestures evoke and sustain a world of meaning whose understanding from the outside both requires a plurality of approaches and rejects any single scheme as reductionistic. This challenges us to master ways the religious practitioners enact a gesture, to learn how they interpret its meaning, and to cast what we learn in extensive descriptions organized by appropriate bridge terms.

There is another angle of analysis that is compatible with both the behavioral and intellectualist understanding of religion: understanding a religion by classifying it according to some previously adopted scheme. Researchers who accept this form of analysis classify individual religious groups in a descending hierarchy as Christian and Protestant, followed by the appropriate subclass of denomination or sect. This device is a hallmark of various surveys of religion heavily relied upon by many students of religion. Each classification carries with it a set of typical features, so that when the final classification is made, a series of descriptive indicators is in place. But no particular group is described. Its "description" is derivative from the sequences of classification with their ideal-typical cluster of features, such as: Christian — Protestant — Pentecostal — shouting and dancing and speaking in tongues. These gestures could come at the end of the hierarchy, or they could be the occasion for invoking the various classifications that allow the student to move efficiently from the observed phenomena of shouting and dancing and speaking in tongues to a chart of religious groups. No matter which direction this analysis moves, from the highest order of generality to the most particular phenomena, the consequence is that gestures disappear into other categories.

For this kind of professional study of religion — perhaps more characteristic of sociologists and historians — no on-site observation, no local study is necessary. In this approach all references to gestures are by type and are not dependent upon particular observations. Such description by type is compatible with a variety of interpretations of religious actions; and while the approach taken by the authors of the chapters in this book cannot avoid the use of classification as a descriptive shorthand and as a necessary part of any comparative work, their bias is toward the local and the particular, a major, although not an exclusive, strategy for disturbing stereotypical thinking about religion, particularly thinking about Protestant religion in the South.

A particular version of the approach we oppose exploits the term *Southern religion,* in which the rough determinants of geography partially disguise the fact that *Southern religion* is a construct composed of a variety of types and relies on a number of pervasive images derived from the media as well as from fiction. Those who pursue this line of inquiry must, of course, exclude from their constructs those groups of Southerners who are Roman Catholics, Jews, Christian Scientists, and Mormons. This construct, Southern religion, ignores the fact that some religious groups in the South belong to national denominations with headquarters outside the South; some others belong to no national organization but have strong bonds of affiliation with churches in other parts of the country. For example, a black church in northern Orange County, North Carolina, regularly exchanges ministers, choirs, and laity with a church in Bridgeport, Connecticut. Other examples can be cited of churches in North Carolina in regular exchanges with churches in Virginia, Maryland, and Pennsylvania. A large number of Primitive Baptist churches have elders who visit up and down the valley chains of the Appalachian Mountains and beyond from Delaware to the Panhandle of Texas, and they accept an elder who broadcasts from Ohio as the closest figure they have to a national spokesman. On overlapping but different routes, large numbers of Pentecostal churches recognize and visit sister churches in a crescent from Norfolk, Virginia, to Orange County, California, with major congregations in Dallas and Phoenix. We cite these examples to contrast empirical particularities with the abstraction called Southern religion.

One misleading classification that abets the synthetic category Southern religion is *fundamentalism,* a term now used with reference to Islam as well as to Protestantism, and even occasionally with reference to some groups of Jews. Baptist churches aligned with the Moral Majority and a significant number of independent Pentecostal churches can be accurately grouped under the classification fundamentalist. As we have already noted, however, anyone who attends churches of both groups can observe that they hold and enact their fundamentals with unmistakable differences in doctrinal formulations, in tone and intensity, in the implications they draw for social policies, and in the manners of their respective religions. When this typical classification is traversed at the level of gesture and ethos, distinctive differences emerge that are hidden in a lumping category such as fundamentalist.

The deficient academic portrayal of local religious groups has its parallel in literary and journalistic depictions. Local religious groups populate novels, films, and news reports in fantastic images. Authors and producers are engrossed with the exceptional case: the snake handler, holy roller, or the itinerant faith healer. They frequently draw these figures as hypocritical sex fiends and con artists or as raving fanatics who seek financial gain from the manipulations of religious rites and rhetoric. These fictitious embodiments of wild deviancy are untamed by education or suburban gentility. The crazed stare of the street-corner evangelist as imaged in literary fiction, film, and journalism stands as a hint for the unimaginably bizarre activities suspected to occur within the storefront church or in the tent out at the fairgrounds, where hawkers regularly exhibit monsters and limbless freaks of nature. Southern novelists of great literary merit and journalists of high reputation have written of local religious groups in ways that provide the general public with images of such religious groups, which are classifications of "those others" and definitions of unacceptability.

All such images and classifications of the alien other, who may live across the tracks in the same town as the scholars and writers, are at the same time collective representations of the prejudices of the members of the academy, the literati, and the media. They are collective self-descriptions inversely expressed through images of minority others marginal to power and status. Members of "low" or folk culture do not promulgate theories of "high culture" and "low culture," nor do they run surveys of the population asking cooperative respondents to classify themselves according to class and status or to report their perceptions of the ways the society stratifies itself according to class, occupation, and religious membership. Unfortunately, researchers who leave the academy to study Southern religion on site are as unable to leave behind the assumptions and theories of the academy as they are unable to escape entirely the influence of images of religion purveyed by the dominant culture. Neither are these investigators exempt from the tacit judgments implied by the use of such terms as *gesture* or *local religion.* No terminology escapes its cultural origins or the predispositions of the audience to whom it is addressed. These are social actions that may say more than authors intend. Gestures and their interpretation by the student of religion are, like their use by the religious practitioner, not private realms of meaning solely determined by individual intention. Both practitioner and observer are engaged in cultural transactions and are therefore open to cultural criticism. The editors of this book hope, nevertheless, that they and the other authors have at least partially transcended their own constrictive terminology and that the volume can disturb the academy and the media by presenting a sampler of some gestures in religious groups in the South rather than presenting a theory or a stereotype of these groups.

We choose to describe this collection of essays as a sampler for the play of its several meanings, which offer several ways to describe the essays. One meaning of the term *sampler* refers to an illustrative or typical instance, as in a sampling of the available goods. Thus most of the studies present a characteristic instance from the cluster of gestures that compose the religious world of the group studied in fieldwork. Just as we say of someone's gait that the way he walks and talks tells of his character, so in its central place among the repertory of gestures composing the genius of the religious group, each gesture described in the essays samples the character of the local religious group. By limiting attention to particular gestures, an author also imposes limits on the license to generalize and classify. While acknowledging the need to engage in generalizing, particularly in the comparative study of several groups, the editors hope that the authors make such comparative work as difficult as possible. We contend that the diversity and the extraordinary skill and art of the practitioners of religions we have visited have been obscured for appreciation by our scholarly classifications and popular stereotyping. If we and the reader are predominantly attentive to particular trees, we make it difficult to generalize facilely about the forest.

A sampler is also an example, a pattern, a model to be imitated or used as a guide, particularly by an apprentice in the art of embroidery. Our authors in their practice of fieldwork attempt also to apprentice themselves, within the limits of cultural boundaries, tact, and skill in observation, to the religious practices of the group they study. In order to meet the requirements of the essay form, each is a limited work, itself a small and serious gesture toward understanding a limited number of gestures at work in the group chosen for study. Each imitates the particularizing character of the religion rather than its generalizing scope. In these limited and limiting ways, most of the essays are an imitation by quotation and description of the gestures the authors seek to understand.

As studies of religious groups, the essays that follow are samplers, but many of them required of their authors a second kind of learning in addition to learning about the religious actions the authors sought to describe. This second kind of learning was an unlearning of deeply ingrained ways of understanding religion acquired through formal training and through membership in various sectors of the larger American culture. In a domain where fresh perceptions of religion are rare (because the predispositions of cultural memory, structured by race and social class, remain powerful among academicians, journalists, and the general public), we hope that by focusing on gesture many of the authors can help to discipline the tendency to generalize too freely and to classify too confidently. To follow some of the routes from gesture to the worlds of meaning they elaborate is an itinerant journey in discovering the varieties of religious experience in neighborhoods otherwise adjacent. These papers are but beginnings, and much work remains to be done. The best provocation to fresh perception is "thick description" of local religions as they play in and out of regional societies. We believe others may usefully enter a field where for the student of a religion as for the member of that religion, the spoken or the written word is "a gesture, its meaning, a world."

NOTES

Several works have nurtured the orientation toward religious actions described in the introduction. The second epigraph is found in Maurice Merleau-Ponty, *The Phenomenology of Perception,* trans. Colin Smith (London: Routledge and Kegan Paul, 1962), p. 184, and following Merleau-Ponty's arguments, we have tried to make a case for an alternative course from the various brands of behaviorism and intellectualism in the study of religious practices. Another work of influence on us has been Walter Benjamin's *Illuminations,* ed. and intro. Hannah Arendt, trans. Harry Zohn (New York: Schocken Books, 1969). Benjamin, widely acclaimed as an astute literary critic and philosopher of culture, has many things to teach the ethnographer of religious practices. In "The Task of the Translator," he offers useful analogies to the task of the ethnographer and in "The Storyteller: Reflections on the Works of Nikolai Leskov" he finds gestures central to the traditional practice of storytelling. A third influence has been Ludwig Wittgenstein's *Remarks on Frazer's Golden Bough,* ed. Rush Rhees, with English trans. A. C. Miles, rev. Rush Rhees (Atlantic Highlands, N.J.: Humanities Press, 1979). Wittgenstein offers the student of religious phenomena "perspicuous" representations of ritual action as well as rich, if elusive, meditations on its meanings.

RELIGIOUS COMMUNITIES
AND CONGREGATIONS

A Quaker Meeting and Mainstream Religion in a North Carolina Community

Isabel B. Terry

Quakers, or Friends, were among the earliest European settlers of North Carolina. The Religious Society of Friends was established in eastern Carolina in 1698, the first organized religion in the state, and large numbers of Quakers settled the central Piedmont Region in the eighteenth century. Today, there are about fourteen thousand members of over one hundred local Meetings in North Carolina, where they comprise the largest Quaker population in the South and one of the three largest in the United States. These contemporary North Carolina Quakers vary in outlook and in practice. Some emphasize the Inner Light doctrine, seeking guidance from an inward God or inspired conscience, while others emphasize the Scriptures and Christ as a personal savior. Some worship in silence or speak only when they feel inwardly led to do so, while others have programmed, pastor-led services with hymns and sermons. The majority, including the community described here, tend toward an evangelical theology and programmed worship — reflecting a trend among Southern Quakers toward the Protestant patterns of the region — while adhering to reflective religion and guidance through the Spirit of God.

Meadowlane Friends Meeting, or Meadowlane Friends Church, as its members more often call it, serves about forty families in a rural community in the North Carolina Piedmont. Settlement in the area is dispersed among farmlands, with a crossroads center a few miles from the Meadowlane neighborhood. A number of other small churches, mostly Friends, Baptist, and Methodist, dot the landscape. Like the Meadowlane Meeting, they are family-oriented churches in which most members are related by descent or marriage.

Several of the Meadowlane Friends have farms and a few have small businesses in the locale, but the majority are employed in a wide variety of jobs outside the area, including teaching school and secretarial work, skilled labor or management in furniture factories and textile mills, computer programming, trucking, sales, and more. Members of the Meeting are white, and most enjoy a rural, middle-class way of life.

Although Quakers constitute a sizable proportion of the community's population and most inhabitants count Quakers among their fore-bears, only the oldest people remember a time when the Quakers were markedly different from their neighbors, and most of their memories are of their parents' or grandparents' recollections, or of a group of quietist Conservative Friends in the vicinity. A vestige of Quaker plain speech does remain among the Meadowlane and other local Quakers, however, in the practice of using first names where others in the region use titles and surnames. Community members are aware that the Quakers have a special history in the area, but the Friends are regarded as much the same as others in the community; their daily lives are like those of their Methodist and Baptist neighbors.

Devotional services in Meadowlane Friends Meeting are also in many ways like those of other Protestant churches in the community. Sunday worship takes place in the sanctuary of the church building, in which rows of pews with a center aisle face a raised platform with pulpit and facing bench and a picture of a moonlit, meditating Christ. There is no altar; choir pews and a piano and small organ are situated to one side of the front platform.

On most Sundays, a choir of small children sings from the choir pews as the congregation gathers for worship. After the children have finished and have run down the aisle to sit with their families, the organist begins the prelude and the adult choir takes its place without ceremony. The choir and the pastor are dressed as the others, with-out robes. Except for special services, worship does not follow a set or printed program. The pastor begins with a personable greeting and with a prayer of thanksgiving to God. Early in the service a passage from Scripture is read, and the pastor or choir director announces a hymn selected from the Meeting's nondenominational hymnal, after which there may be, at this point in the service or at another time, a few seconds of silence that provide opportunity for reflection. As the service proceeds, the pastor offers additional prayer or asks a mem-ber to pray from the pews. The music director leads the weekly choral hymn and may then turn to the congregation to ask if anyone has a favorite hymn to request. On many Sundays, the pastor announces a period of silent or open worship. This may be a time of meditation or the sharing of thoughts given by the Lord. At some time during the first half of the service, announcements of church activities are made by the pastor, and the offering is taken. Before the pastoral sermon, small children join one of the mothers in the Meeting at a front pew, where she engages them with a children's sermon about the importance of Christ in their lives. The second half of the service is given to a pastoral sermon, whose content varies considerably according to the individual pastor's style and theological concerns but which often culminates in a statement of the need for forgiveness and dedication to Christ. Occasionally, an invitational is given or the pastor asks the congregation to stand with heads bowed and eyes closed and for anyone among them who feels a need for God's Spirit in his or her life simply to raise a hand. If a person goes to the front of the church in response to an invitational, he or she prays quietly, sometimes with the pastor or another member, as the service is closed. Most often, there is no call, and the service is closed with a prayer or benediction by the pastor or an elder.

In contrast to the services of other churches in Meadowlane, those of the Friends do not include sacramental rituals. The Friends believe that such outward rituals are unnecessary for spiritual commitment and communion with God. They are not, however, militant about this belief. "Baptists immerse; Methodists sprinkle; Quakers dryclean" is the way they put it, with the implication that these varied forms represent the same basic experience. Although their services are programmed, they follow a varying order, and members regard this flexibility, as well as lay participation in planning and leading some segments of the service, as particular to Quaker practice. Occasionally, but not as often as in many Quaker services, events are bounded by a few seconds of silence; these moments for reflection or inward preparation for the next event are distinctively Quaker (and often quite disconcerting to non-Quaker visitors accustomed to uninterrupted performance). The pastor, who as a coequal is addressed by his or her first name, generally provides the overall direction of the service, but he neither announces and carries out all events nor remains at the pulpit for all events. In the Monthly Meeting for Worship and

Business, the Meeting's administrative body to which all members belong, a lay clerk, not the pastor, oversees the traditional consensual decision-making process, in which a matter is acted upon only after opinion has been carefully elicited and approval is unanimous. Thus the Quaker ideal of lay responsibility in church affairs is deliberately maintained.

The most distinctive devotional practice of the Meadowlane Quakers is one that not only derives from traditional form but also reflects a synthesis of the Inner Light doctrine and the Southern Protestant emphasis on a personal, experiential relationship with God or His Spirit. This is the period of silent or open worship incorporated into most services. The congregation sits in silence, and any member feeling led to do so stands to speak a few words, often of thankfulness to God. These words, which are given in a prayerful cadence or a more conversational tone, rarely contain personal detail, although the membership understands that they reflect heartfelt experience. Members do not usually look at the speaker but rather maintain prayerful or meditative attitudes. Frequently no one stands to speak, in which case the congregation remains in silence for several minutes. Some members value the silence itself as a medium of worshipful group reflection; a few see it as successful only when it gives rise to testimonies. The Meeting does not indoctrinate its members on how or why they are to participate in open worship, and people ascribe many meanings to it. Although most Meadowlane Friends are Bible-oriented Quakers rather than adherents of the Inner Light, some members are familiar with the concept and sometimes speak of the Light. Most members believe in inspiration and guidance through leadings of the Spirit of God, in daily life as well as in worship; although differently derived, this belief does not in practice conflict with mainstream Protestant belief and has become meshed with it, while the traditional Quaker form is maintained.

The Meadowlane Quakers do not emphasize the differences between their beliefs and those of their non-Quaker neighbors. "We are Christians first and Quakers second" is an often-repeated sentiment. It is important to belong to a church — church membership is still an important aspect of social identity as well as of respectability in the community — but the choice of church is a matter of family relations, proximity, and individual conscience. An elderly member who has attended the Meadowlane Meeting all of her life expresses the ideal in these words: "The denominations, I don't think they have much to do with it. It's your heart; whether you're a Quaker or Baptist or whatever, so long as your heart is right. I want to be a good neighbor and love people, not hate folks, to be a blessing as I go through life, and to be kind." A younger woman who was reared a Baptist and transferred her membership to the Meadowlane Meeting upon marriage to a Quaker explains: "It's a personal thing. A person's relationship with God is what's important, not the church one goes to. To me, if you have a really close relationship with God, your religious life is not separate from other aspects of life. Instead of having religion here, this here, that there, and so on, it's all interwoven. This is more true in the South. . . . You have to understand that it is partly a cultural thing."

Meadowlane Friends describe themselves as nondoctrinal. While being Quaker is part of their religious identity, they do not constantly instruct in their creed. When new members join the Meeting, most of them youths who have been reared there or people who have married members, they are seldom given lessons in Quaker doctrine, nor are children in their Sunday school classes indoctrinated with Quaker history or denominational practice. They learn most of the particulars of their religion through participation and as members of their family and community.

Meadowlane Friends Meeting is, like many rural Southern churches, a family church. It is comprised of interrelated family groupings descendant from the founding generation; and in the minds of its people attachment to the church is associated with attachment to family. Individual Meadowlane Friends also have multiple kinship ties with members of other churches in the area through intermarriage. Kinship strengthens church affiliation; however, unlike in the days when the Quakers married only within their sect, kinship is not an isolating factor, but rather has contributed to de-emphasis of differences between the Quakers and their non-Quaker neighbors.

Of the adults who attend the Meadowlane Meeting, almost three-fourths carry surnames of the Meeting's founders or those who joined soon after its inception as an independent Monthly Meeting. Two-thirds of the adults and most of the children are direct descendants of the founding group. The remainder are almost all related through marriage and fully entrenched in the Meeting's kinship network. Individual Meadowlane Quakers are further related through marriage between the descent lines. As one young bachelor observed, he will not find a wife among the young women who attend the Meadowlane Meeting, because he is already related to almost all of them. The association between family and church is fundamental to members. "Ever since it's been started my people have gone there, so naturally it's important to me. And I have people buried there," a young member explained. An elderly widow expressed the same sentiment, "Meadowlane is my home church, where I've gone since childhood, where my parents are buried, and my husband." Parents, whether reared in the Meeting or not, speak of the importance to them of bringing up their children in the church, mostly of the religious values they learn there but also of the warm kin and friendship bonds they experience. Not all people share appreciation for the family/church connection—some attend out of family obligation and some do not attend despite it— but on the whole the association is a positive one. An active member who joined the Meeting in adulthood when he married a Meadowlane woman chose these words in speaking of their involvement in the church: "The church feels a part of us, a family, really."

The family ties that strengthen, even underlie, identification with the church do not have the same effect upon denominational identity. This is because the ties extend to other churches in the area. Quakers have intermarried with Methodists and Baptists and other non-Quaker Protestants over several generations. Not only were nearly a third of the Meadowlane Quakers reared in other churches, but also most of the members have relatives belonging to other churches in the community and people buried in other cemeteries. A Meadowlane Quaker might have a Quaker father, a Baptist-turned-Quaker mother, Quaker, Baptist, and Pentecostal siblings, and a Methodist-turned-Quaker spouse. A child might marry out and a grandchild back in. It is not unusual in the area for an individual to remain upon his or her home church's roll even after years of regular attendance at another church, and the association between respect for family and respect for family churches is illustrated by the handling of children's memberships when this occurs. If both parents of a child are official members of the Meeting, the child is listed on the roll as an associate member; if one parent is on the roll and the other is not, the child is not listed as an associate member (although fully included in the church community). Associate status can be obtained for the child by request, and sometimes a pastor suggests this be done. Most of the Meadowlane Quakers, however, feel it would be insensitive to solicit for membership the child of a parent, even a faithful church attender, who has chosen to remain on the roll of his or her home church.

The degree of interrelatedness among members of the community's congregations is evident during their annual homecoming services. As is the custom in the rural South and many other places, former members or children who have grown to adulthood and moved away or joined other churches return for one Sunday to their home church for the worship service and a sociable meal afterward with relatives and old friends. At the Meadowlane Meeting the homecoming is held on Memorial Day Sunday, when the return of former members and their families is combined with remembrance of those who have died. The church is always full, even crowded, on this Sunday. Most of the visitors are from churches in the community whose parents or grandparents attend or attended the Meadowlane Meeting. Their churches, too, have homecoming or memorial services. When a nearby Methodist church holds its gathering, over one-fourth of the Meadowlane Meeting's families attend it. Family reunions are also held at the church. These do not have as long a tradition as the homecomings, but in recent years they have been expanding collaterally as well as by generational addition. In contrast to the pattern of attendance at homecomings, more people come from outside the community to attend reunions and appear more socially diverse (not all are church-affiliated). The growth of reunion attendance may be related to mobility and appreciation for roots in family and locale. The Memorial Day homecoming, on the other hand, is more an affair of the community, a function of the exchange of church members through marriage in a locale where church membership is an important facet of social identity. It is a social expression of the coexistence and interdependence of like units of affiliation within the larger community, as well as the more personal return of individuals to the church of their childhood.

A representative family history of a sister and brother from the Meadowlane Meeting illustrates well the denominational admixture that has occurred in the locale. She is in her eighties and he in his late seventies, and both have attended the Meadowlane Meeting since childhood. They have remarkably sunny and lively dispositions; their Christian witness, they explain, is to "let their light shine through." Both are faithful churchgoers and often speak in open worship. As is the Quaker custom, others address them by their first names as Molly and Johnny, but sometimes, in deference to their age, by their first and last names.

Their mother was apparently a birthright Quaker whose family was associated with the Meadowlane Friends who met for worship before the Meeting was formally established in the first decade of the twentieth century. Their father, the son of a Civil War veteran, transferred his membership from a Methodist church to the Meadowlane Meeting during the time of its establishment. The family also regularly attended a nearby Holiness church (now a Wesleyan Methodist church). Molly and Johnny have relatives there and frequently attend its annual revival, as well as those of a Baptist church and two neighboring Friends Meetings in which they have friends or kin. There were nine children in the family, not all of whom remained Quakers. An older sister, infirm and unable to attend services, is a member (and honorary elder) of the Meadowlane Meeting and has progeny in three of the family groupings in the Meeting.

Molly married a member of a Christian church in the locale. She and her husband joined the Meadowlane Meeting; but upon moving to an industrial city within an hour's drive of Meadowlane, where they lived for many years and where Molly was employed in a mill, they transferred to a Methodist church there. Molly's daughter married a Methodist and belongs to that denomination today. Her son attended a Presbyterian church after marrying a woman of that denomination (who now attends a Baptist church). Molly and her husband eventually returned to the Meadowlane area to live in her family's home place, which incorporates the family's original nineteenth-century log cabin. She renewed her Meadowlane Meeting affiliation and, now widowed, is an active and beloved member of the Meeting. Although Molly's two children did not become Quakers, one of her several grandchildren did. This grandson and his Presbyterian-reared wife moved from the city to the Meadowlane area, where they situated their mobile home on family land across the road from Molly. They commute daily to mill jobs in the city and plan eventually to build a permanent house near Molly. They and their two small children have close relations with Molly, whom they see daily, and have joined Meadowlane Friends Meeting. The young wife is a recent recording clerk, or secretary, of the Monthly Meeting.

Molly's brother Johnny, whose energies have enabled him to continue his employment in a furniture factory beyond the usual retirement age, has always lived in the Meadowlane area and with his late wife reared two children there. He now lives alone adjacent to his grandson and family, and his son and his wife live nearby on the same road. The structures fit the generations they house: Johnny's older wooden farmhouse; his son's post– World War II brick gabled house; and his grandson's modern brick ranch-style house. Johnny was reared in the Meeting, as was his late wife, and he became a member in youth following a revival held there. His son, who has been the clerk of the Meeting's body of elders, married a woman whose family has long been associated with an older and larger Friends Meeting in the area. She transferred her membership to the Meadowlane Meeting in the year following her marriage. Johnny's son and his wife regularly attend special services, revivals, and homecomings at her home church. Johnny's daughter also married a local man, a Baptist who joined the Meadowlane Meeting for a few years after their marriage. Later this couple transferred their membership to the husband's Baptist church. (In the past it was usual for the wife to join the husband's church, but today the husband is as likely to join the wife's church.) The adult children of Johnny's son, both members of the Meadowlane Meeting, married non-Quakers, one a Methodist and one associated in childhood with a Holiness church. The latter joined the Meadowlane Meeting and is a Sunday school teacher in the Meeting.

This family history, which is typical for the Meadowlane Meeting (and other churches in the area), makes two things clear: that the Meeting has been open to non-Quaker Protestant influence through in-marrying members over a long period of time, and that a network of reciprocal obligation or association has emerged, through common kinship, among Quaker and non-Quaker churches in the area. From this network has also emerged emphasis on common beliefs.

The accommodation of in-marrying members has made a major contribution to the emphasis on likeness of beliefs and the process

31

of synthesis. The family histories suggest that many, if not most, of the children's Sunday school classes at the Meadowlane Meeting are taught by in-marrying wives, most of whom have not received indoctrination in Quaker tradition and theology. In-marrying members are often asked to fill positions in the Meeting soon after they have joined, as Molly's granddaughter-in-law was asked to serve as recording clerk. This is partly because everyone is expected to share in responsibility and partly to ensure belongingness, or as a hospitable gesture of inclusiveness. In-marrying members rarely make an effort to subvert Quaker practices; in fact, a few of those who have familiarized themselves with the reasons for them are sometimes more conscientious about upholding such practices than those reared in the Meeting (who, of course, are most often themselves products of denominational admixture). In-marrying members are most comfortable, however, with the beliefs they hold in common with the Quakers. When new members do retain beliefs counter to those of the majority of the Meadowlane Quakers, they are still usually accepted as members of the community, even if their beliefs are not accepted, and the value and exercise of tolerance is reinforced. A few, for example, tend toward belief in the "once saved, always saved" doctrine that is promoted by a few religious groups in the locale but rejected by the Quakers, who stress continual dedication. Whereas the Meeting rejected for employment a potential pastor who held to this tenet, its members tolerate it in individuals, especially when they are respected as persons and they and their families are valued for their participation in the church. Although it is highly unlikely that the Meeting as a whole will come to accept this belief through the influence of its adherents, some mainstream beliefs or attitudes have, over time, gained increasing acceptance this way.

Sometimes an in-marrying member may hold and act upon a non-Quaker attitude shared by many or most members of the Meeting (or even by a high proportion of American Quakers), and thus contribute to its ascendance. An instance of this took place several years ago, during the Vietnam War era, when a member named Don, who was on the Meeting's largely inactive Committee on Peace and Morals, attended a workshop on conscientious objection held at a Quaker Meeting in a nearby community. Like most but not all of his church-fellows, Don has reservations about the Society's Peace Testimony, and at the workshop he said so. He especially objected to the pacifist principle of not killing even to protect the lives of one's family and community. By voicing in the workshop context an opinion held by most men in the region, he was instrumental in discouraging the efforts of the Society's peace committee to reach conscientious objectors in the area. Putting the comfort of his conscience above the lives of valued people is as clearly wrong to Don as the killing of a human being is to another Meadowlane Meeting member who adheres to the Peace Testimony. A few of the Meadowlane Quakers have wrestled with this paradox, generally politely respecting each other's conscientious considerations in the matter. Meanwhile, the nonpacifist attitudes prevalent in the larger community have come to be accepted by probably the majority of its Quakers, partly through events like that involving Don.

Often, in-marrying members accommodate themselves to Quaker practices by reinterpreting them in terms of the religious practices of the churches of their upbringing or adjust to them by seeking rationales based on common belief. In this, they are generally encouraged by members of the church. Over time, synthesis results. In-marrying members, when asked in what ways they find the beliefs and practices of the Meadowlane Quakers different from those of their upbringing, remark most often upon the absence of baptism and communion and upon open worship. (Also among the differences they mention are the less-fixed order of worship or greater spontaneity and, depending partly upon the individual's former church, greater simplicity, belief in goodness in every person, and less biblical education.) Most express a liking for the periods of open worship. This is a form that is not only compatible with the mainstream Protestant experience of personal relationship with God but also symbolically underscores its ultimate importance in a region that is both traditionally egalitarian and increasingly open. (It is interesting that this Quaker practice is now being incorporated into services of a few non-Quaker churches in the area.) The understanding brought to this form varies greatly and among in-marrying members especially often reflects mainstream theology. A former Baptist, for example, spoke of her appreciation of open worship when she joined the Meadowlane Meeting, and she added, "I believed in the importance of being filled with the Holy Spirit before then." One woman especially missed participation in the

Lord's Supper. This rite had been deeply meaningful to her, so she purposively came to experience open worship as an opportunity for personal communion. A few new members have found the absence of the sacraments initially disturbing but agree with the others that baptism of the Spirit and felt communion are of the essential importance, not participation in outward rituals. In this process of agreement in shared faith, the Quaker testimony of not having outward rituals also becomes de-emphasized. A few former Baptists retain their belief in baptism, although most do not consider it necessary for salvation. For those who do, the Society, which was not so long ago adamantly antisacrament, will now allow baptism upon request, officiated by a Quaker pastor or performed in another church. The request is rarely made, but attitudes have been changed through this accommodation of felt individual needs.

For most in-marrying members the adjustment to Quakerism is not at all difficult. As one member said, comparing the nondenominational, evangelical church of her upbringing with the Meadowlane Meeting, "Both have the same basic sound doctrine. . . . Both are biblical." Virtually every member, whether reared in the Meeting or married into it, emphasized the likeness of their faith to that of other mainstream churches in the vicinity even when expressing an infrequent criticism or taking sides over points of doctrine. "I'm proud to be a Quaker, but denomination isn't important. Basically, we believe the same."

Patterns of visiting and friendship among individuals often reveal the social dimensions of interactions important to people, and in the Meadowlane locale kinship governs visiting relations among individuals to a considerable extent, even though, with increasing mobility, most members of the Meeting associate with many different people. Denominational affiliation apparently affects friendship and visiting little. A number of the Meadowlane Meeting's members name close relatives, especially siblings and siblings-in-law, as among their closest friends. Adult children who live near their parents often gather with their families at the parents' or grandparents' house for Sunday dinner, and a few speak with family members in person or on the telephone every day. With many, proximity accounts for much of the time spent with relatives, but neighbors who are not kin are not visited nearly as regularly. Rather, neighborly ties are kept active through participation in community organizations such as the Ruritans, garden clubs, and fire department, and through interchurch activities and children's play groups. Although many mention Meadowlane Meeting's members or other Quakers among the people they see most often or whom they count among their personal friends (comembers of the adult Sunday school classes are most often mentioned), kinship, generational affiliation, and joint participation in church activities account for many of these interactions. Only infrequently is there a trace of denominational coidentity expressed. Most, like Johnny, stress the opposite: "I spend some time, visit around, with older folks like I am. I make it a point to visit folks who can't get out. . . . I spend some time with relatives, some who go to [the] Meadowlane [Meeting] and some who don't—visit anybody, Quakers or what-not, also non-Christians. . . . It doesn't matter if they're Quakers or whatever they might be, doesn't make a speck of difference." The closest friendships of Meadowlane Quakers with people of the same sex, although frequently reflecting kinship bonds, follow no denominational pattern. These friends, defined by them as people they can fully confide in, are more often non-Quaker than Quaker, reflecting the denominational ratio of members' acquaintances. They extend throughout the community and beyond.

While tolerance about religious or other matters does vary among the membership, individuals occasionally make explicit statements for tolerance in public settings. For example, shortly after a certain pastor (a recent arrival in the community) refuted in a sermon the biblical interpretations of an established sect located in a nearby community, a member of the Meadowlane congregation rose during open worship to speak of the value of personal commitment to God and of her respect for commitment itself, including "the sincerity of the [established sect] and others with different beliefs when they have deep commitment." When such statements are made, the subject is almost always specific (as when the clerk of the Meeting's board of elders spoke in worship of experiencing the presence of God in a neighboring Baptist church) rather than about the abstract virtue of tolerance, and the mode is usually exemplary ("I feel . . .") rather than imperative. These public statements, although individual, reflect and contribute to ideal attitudes and standards in dealing with others of different beliefs. Mainly, however, tolerance is advanced by stressing likeness.

Among non-Quakers in the area, too, denominational allegiance tends to be downplayed, whereas specific church affiliation and the commonalities of faith are emphasized. Pastors of local Methodist and Baptist churches remark upon the relative denominational tolerance in the community. (Possibly this is more true within the Piedmont Region than in other areas of the South that do not have the Piedmont's history of religious diversity.) Some of the oldest people are among the most deliberate in de-emphasizing differences. An elderly Methodist woman assured me with typical care that she had never known a time when the Quakers were different from their neighbors. She then recalled that she knew nothing of her grandmother's family and added, "I always wondered if she might have been a Quaker." It is possible that unhappy experiences of past generations with family schisms in the days when Quakers disowned members for marrying non-Quakers have contributed to the relative tolerance in the locale. The traditional Quaker respect for individual conscience may also have made its contribution. It is difficult to substantiate these suggestions, but the network of kinship linking the locale's churches is readily observable, and the people themselves attribute their common beliefs and attitudes to common kinship.

Intermarriage and common kinship with mainstream Protestants in a community where family ties are strong have nurtured the blending of Quaker and Southern Protestant traditions at Meadowlane Friends Meeting, but the synthesis stems ultimately from evangelical movements of the nineteenth century. The Quakers who settled the Piedmont from eastern Carolina, Virginia, the northern colonies, and the British Isles during the latter half of the eighteenth century were independent small farmers, quietist — and insular — in their faith. They did not all share in the affluence of many Quakers elsewhere, but these Southern Quakers were especially conscientious in the care of their needy.[1] Elders were especially watchful over members' lives, and disownments for deviating from plain dress, marrying out of the faith, or participating in the military were numerous. North Carolina's Quakers stalwartly maintained their Peace Testimony. As the Civil War neared, Quaker opposition to slavery intensified the sect's isolation in an increasingly hostile environment, and they lost many of their number to western emigration.

The decades following the Civil War, however, saw the transformation of a large body of North Carolina's Quakers from isolationist sectarians to evangelicals. This was a time of evangelical crusade in the South, and Quaker evangelists who journeyed to the region to help rebuild the Society and to promote Bible study were especially successful among the young and the returning western émigrées. Public revivals came to be held in common cause with Wesleyan Methodists, and in meetings for worship the silence of seeking came often to be filled with hymns and testimonies and preaching. With the reemphasis on individual salvation, the oversight of the elders was undermined and the practice of disownment all but discontinued. Intermarriage between Quakers and non-Quakers became common. Eventually, many Meetings came to support pastors with food and housing, and then to employ them—at first, perhaps, to shepherd converts made from the general population.[2]

These changes were not welcomed by all Quakers. Some withdrew to form separate organizations of unprogrammed Meetings emphasizing the Inner Light or quietist ways and a few began to affiliate with more doctrinaire evangelical alliances in the West. In 1902, after the evangelical fervor had subsided, the majority adopted a Uniform Discipline as affiliates of the North Carolina Yearly Meeting of the Religious Society of Friends (Friends United Meeting). The Uniform Discipline, while generally avoiding creedal pronouncement, merged or accommodated quietist and evangelical beliefs, Inner Light mysticism, and Wesleyan belief in individual salvation through the historic, atoning Christ.

Southern evangelicals emphasized the subjective and voluntaristic, rather than corporate, nature of religious experience and salvation. They interpreted moral behavior in terms of personal prohibitions. Although they encouraged personal kindness and service in relations with individuals, their ethic was less socially oriented than that of the quietist Friends. This Southern evangelical tradition was not entirely at odds with that of the Quakers, however. Each stressed the inward experience of God or His Spirit (although Southern Protestants conceived of God as more of a personal being), and in fact, this common experiential emphasis had common roots among nonconformists of the sixteenth and seventeenth centuries. With this experiential focus, neither Quakers nor evangelical Southerners had developed a consistently systematic theology. The Inner Light and the Bible each

37

allowed selective interpretation in the respective traditions. The quietist Quakers, too, maintained strict personal prohibitions, including those that separated the saved from the unsaved. As the evangelical influence gained strength in the Society, its proponents easily found precedents in the movement's beginnings. The individualist-corporate tensions in Quakerism from its inception and the common origins of Quakerism and Southern Protestantism among European and English sectarians, who stressed above all the direct accessibility of God to the individual, must be taken into account in understanding compatibilities between the two traditions.

Nineteenth-century revivalism instituted many changes in manner of worship and oversight among North Carolina's Friends. It introduced ceremonial and educational activities for which the Friends had no tradition at all; borrowed outright were the appointment of full-time pastors and the use of Bible study aids and evangelical hymns. An even more important change was the removal of strictures against marrying out of the faith, which made intermarriage and common kinship major factors in the accommodation of mainstream and evangelical beliefs and practices among many Meetings in the region, such as the Meadowlane Friends. It is family, more than socioeconomic activity — the field in which social scientists have been inclined to look for explanation of sectarian compromise with the world — that has been a major locus of this accommodation. Thus children have often been reared to, or have internalized, a synthesized religious worldview before (or even without) institutionalization of synthesis in a formal, public, or group sense. Because of this and ongoing family and community considerations, the process of accommodation has been a relatively smooth one at the Meadowlane Meeting, seldom marked by doctrinal clash among members and unmarked by schism.

The Quakers who established Meadowlane Friends Meeting were among those touched, perhaps even gathered, by revivalism, and the subsequent history of the Meeting has been one of ongoing synthesis. But because members of the Meeting have not, for the most part, self-consciously perpetuated Quaker belief and practice for the sake of identity in opposition to other churches or to advance special interests, the ways in which traditional Quaker social attitudes and modes of worship have been retained deserve some comment.

Although the Meadowlane Quakers have a southern regional identity, their view of their social order conforms less in some ways to the regional view described by students of the South than do the views of other denominations. Region of birth — in the South or outside it — is an important dimension of classification, but, overall, oppositions of race, class, and sex are less dramatically observed among the Meadowlane Quakers than among other Southerners. The Meadowlane Quakers are not social reformers, and they tend, with exceptions, to cherish the value "that one individual should not interfere in the affairs of another, and that radical change based on abstract ethics is dangerous."[3] They do not, however, appear to share the hierarchical view of society that stems from the aristocratic feudalism of the early South, although this view and the manners that accompany it are observable among residents in towns nearby. Relations among the Meadowlane Friends and between Friends and outsiders may best be described as cordial or personable, but characterized neither by extreme ritualistic politeness nor by extreme folksiness. Their continued use of first names underscores a practical kind of egalitarianism. The division of the sexes is much less apparent among Quakers than among many other groups of Southerners, including some living in similar, non-Quaker rural communities not far away.

Similarly, while the basic beliefs of the Meadowlane Friends are those of mainstream Southern Protestantism, their practice does not reveal all of the traits attributed to it.[4] Their religion does not have Southern Protestantism's episodic, dramatic quality, at least not among the majority of members. The sustained and sustaining faith the Quakers emphasize may ebb and flow and require renewal, and the Society as an institution provides encouragement and opportunity for this, but renewal is largely continuous and private, even for those individuals who occasionally accept the invitational in church. This emphasis on the whole rather than on the religious episode is epitomized in the prayer of a member who asked that his life in itself might be a testimony "even if I don't say a word." In the same way, services give more emphasis to worship of God than to individual religious experience.

While many of the hymns sung at the church — many of them Methodist hymns — are centered on the individual or tell of personal salvation, often in the first person, speaking in open worship does not usually contain the personal detail of testimonies given in many evangelical churches. Because worship is open, the observer might expect the influence of Southern Protestantism upon the religious belief and practices of the Meeting to be revealed especially clearly in it; but although this may have been so during the period of revivalism, it is not the case today. The tone of the silence that contains the speaking and the postures of its participants in waiting upon the Lord is distinctly Quaker and much like that of most other Quaker Meetings, programmed or unprogrammed. The form tends to preclude most personalistic expression and to contain that which is given within a frame of group worship. The Southern Protestantism of the Meadowlane Quakers, then, is one based in a common tradition of experiential religion and modified by forms of Quakerism evolved in containment of individual expression in corporate worship and an integral faith.

As the South becomes increasingly open and the diversity within it becomes less contained by a regional uniformity, one might expect a reemphasis of the identity of the several groups that make up the religious diversity of the North Carolina Piedmont. Among the Quakers, there are signs that this may happen. The North Carolina Yearly Meeting has been strengthening its affiliation with its national association. At the Meadowlane Meeting, members have recently, as a group, subscribed to a Quaker publication. When the sign in front of the church that gives its name and times of worship needed rebuilding recently, the name "Meadowlane Friends Church" was replaced with "Meadowlane Friends Meeting." Whereas members tend primarily to characterize their Quaker predecessors by their strictness or even by their oddity, some now show more awareness of the national regard of (if not agreement with) the Quaker history and ethic (and, one might add, mystique). In the Yearly Meeting, at the same time that evangelicalism is becoming more predominant, more instruction is being offered in Quaker history. In association with the growing professionalism of the ministry, church growth and extension are becoming major concerns. Among the Quakers, however, these concerns are not sectarian. Rather, kinship and neighborliness have overridden sectarian separateness in communities like Meadowlane, letting the Quaker Meeting take its place among other mainstream churches of the community. Quakerism in North Carolina is stepping into its place among the denominations of regional Protestantism.

NOTES

This analysis grew from fieldwork undertaken between 1975 and 1980, with support from the National Institute of Mental Health, and reported more fully in my doctoral dissertation, *A Programmed Quaker Meeting in the North Carolina Piedmont* (Chapel Hill: Department of Anthropology, The University of North Carolina, 1980). The Quaker Collection at Guilford College and the executive offices of the North Carolina Yearly Meeting also provided research resources. Key scholarly works useful to the study but not directly cited in individual notes are: Hugh Barbour, *The Quakers in Puritan England* (New Haven: Yale University Press, 1964); Fernando Cartland, *Southern Heroes or the Friends in War Time* (Cambridge: Riverside Press, 1895); C. Dwight Dorough, *The Bible Belt Mystique* (Philadelphia: Westminster Press, 1974); Elbert Russell, *The History of Quakerism* (New York: Macmillan, 1942) and *The Inner Light in the History and Present Problems of the Society of Friends* (Greensboro, N.C.: North Carolina Friends Historical Society, 1946); Stephen B. Weeks, *Southern Quakers and Slavery: A Study in Institutional History* (Baltimore: Johns Hopkins University Studies, 1896); and Bryan Wilson, *Religious Sects: A Sociological Study* (New York: McGraw-Hill, 1970) and *Religion in Sociological Perspective* (New York: Oxford University Press, 1982). Several denominational publications have also been helpful: *Faith and Practice: Book of Discipline* (Greensboro, N.C.: North Carolina Yearly Meeting of the Religious Society of Friends, 1979); Francis C. Anscombe, *I Have Called You Friends: The Story of Quakerism in North Carolina* (Boston: Christopher Publishing House, 1959); Edwin Bronner, ed., *American Friends Today* (Philadelphia: Friends World Committee, American Section and Fellowship Council, 1966); Seth B. Hinshaw, *Walk Cheerfully, Friends: The Essential Optimism of the Quaker Faith* (Greensboro, N.C.: The Publications Board, North Carolina Yearly Meeting of the Religious Society of Friends, 1978); and Seth B. Hinshaw and Mary Edith Hinshaw, eds., *Carolina Quakers: Our Heritage, Our Hope, Tercentenary 1672–1972* (Greensboro, N.C.: North Carolina Yearly Meeting of the Religious Society of Friends, 1972).

1. Rufus M. Jones, *The Quakers in the American Colonies* (London: Macmillan, 1911), p. 308.

2. Errol T. Elliott, *Quakers on the American Frontier* (Richmond, Ind.: Friends United Press, 1969), p. 124.

3. James L. Peacock, "Secular Ritual in Archaic but Changing Society: Java and the American South," unpublished paper presented at the Wenner-Gren Foundation Symposium No. 64 at Burg Wartenstein, Austria, on August 24–September 1, 1974.

4. Samuel S. Hill, *Southern Churches in Crisis* (New York: Holt, Rinehart and Winston, 1967).

The Sons of God   2

James Wise

The Sons of God — a Christian millenarian movement — appeared in the western half of North Carolina in the mid-1970s. A faith developed and transmitted wholly by oral processes, it showed evidence of an origin in faith healing. With other Protestant bodies, such as Holiness and Pentecostal churches, and with the Charismatic Renewal movement, it shared a belief in the baptism of the Holy Spirit and practices such as glossolalia. However, the Sons of God was a non-denominational ministry, expressed in the services of loosely organized, independent churches with no formal membership.

The Rocky Top House of Prayer was a building that once had been a filling station, squatting on a country roadside on the eastern slope of the Blue Ridge Mountains in North Carolina. On Sunday afternoons, meetings were held there of a kind called "open pulpit," which had no prescribed order of worship or formal sermon, but rather a pulpit open to all who cared to testify, sing, or preach, however the Holy Spirit moved them. The preacher was little more than a master of ceremonies.

Inside, the building was recognizable as a church. There were rows of pews with seating space for about eighty people, arranged on both sides of a central aisle with walk space along the walls. The pews faced an open area partially covered with a gold-colored rug draped over a small, low platform supporting a lectern near the back wall. The walls were cinder block painted institutional green. Before the open pulpit meetings began, the walls had been completely bare except for the motto "Jesus Came to Give Us Life" lettered behind the pulpit in red and black wedding script; but on June 6, 1976, when the open pulpit meetings had been going for a couple of months, the walls behind the lectern and to the stage left of it were hung with posters: a diagram of the Hebrew tabernacle, explanation of the symbolism of five-, six-, and eight-pointed stars, newspaper cartoons depicting the ascendance of the Soviet Union's military, one captioned "The Westward Trek" which traced the movement of Judaeo-Christian tradition from the Middle East, across Europe, and to North America.

Sunday the sixth of June was unusual. A shirtsleeved congregation of about twenty adults and uncounted unquiet children had taken seats when Brother Conway, the preacher for the Sunday-afternoon meetings, came in with three strangers. Here was a special guest speaker, Conway told the congregation, who had come a long way with his wife and a friend "to feed a lot of hungry folks" at Rocky Top. There were a lot of people there with ministries to share, Brother Conway knew, but he wanted to let Brother Ness go first and for him to feel free to take all the time he needed, because he had come a long way.

A man with a guitar led the worshippers in several songs, singing out of *Songs for Eagle Saints,* a paperback songbook from an evangelical center in Missouri.[1] A quartet performed one song, a woman was called up from the congregation for a solo, then Conway said that it was time for Brother Ness to come forth. Some joking went back and forth about whether Conway meant for Ness to sing; then Ness, Conway, and Ness's friend went about setting up an overhead projector and screen.

Ness started by introducing himself, standing beside his projector in the central aisle. He was a native Canadian who had lived in Florida for twenty years — "So we're not Yankees" — and a former teacher of salesmen. Once an Episcopalian, he had also been a teacher in the Charismatic movement. Striking an informal and easy tone, he began to explicate history from biblical times to the present as fulfillment of biblical prophecy and the working out of a divine plan. The coming of the Kingdom of God on earth was imminent, he said, and there were two agents working to bring it: the Holy Ghost, preparing people like these at Rocky Top to rule in the Kingdom, and Jesus Christ, "working in the world, preparing a kingdom."

Ness went along, showing pictures of mock-up newspaper stories from the distant past and of real ones from the recent. The road-building of the Roman Empire, the invention of the printing press, the American Revolution, were all manifestations of the divine plan, handwork of a sovereign God. So were the American interstate high-ways and the Lebanese civil war that was currently going on. A time of catastrophes was upon the world, as prophesied in Revelation to precede the Kingdom — earthquakes, religious wars, depressions, and conspiracies. A Zen Buddhist was running for the presidency of the supposedly Christian United States — "And he just might get it" — and another candidate was in league with the current vice president in a plot for world government.

Turning from the projector, Ness began explaining the fulfillment of biblical prophecies and his own revelations in events of the recent past. A passage from Isaiah had come true in the form of the Aswan Dam and Egyptian politics. He pointed out a distinction between the biblical Houses of Israel and Judah and went on to discuss the identity of the true Israelites, and how modern-day Egyptians were really the good guys and modern-day Israelis, the bad.

The light and comfortable mood that had filled the church at the start of the meeting had dissolved into one of general boredom after two hours of Ness's talking. Conway was the only remaining evidence of the enthusiasm and responsiveness that had characterized the group at first. What Ness was delivering was not a spontaneous testimony nor even a planned sermon, but a practiced lecture — if not a sales pitch.

The true Israelites, Ness was saying, were the literal "seed of Abraham." And they existed in the world in the twentieth century as the Caucasian race, which carried the root of God's covenant in their biological heritage, which alone could sustain the true word of God in a pagan world.

Ness's friend spoke up from his seat at the back, pointing to the enrichment of the world by the spread of European technology and civilization and calling it fulfillment of scriptural prophecies that "They [Israelites] shall establish the earth" and "Wherever Israel is, the world shall be blessed."

"May I say a word?" asked another man in the congregation.

"Yes, brother," Ness said.

Brother Avery stood up — a man who had grown up nearby on a mountain farm and had worked in orchards and a car garage and as a part-time farmer — but he did not move away from his place among the worshippers. "Let's go back into our Bibles and find out what a true Israelite is," he said, facing Ness. "It's one that God has reached down and touched his heart with the Holy Spirit, and knows God. When you come into the knowledge of God, you're a true Israelite, don't make no difference what color. We can't build up color. And, we've built Babylon up, everything that's been taught here today is building Babylon, Babylon, Babylon!"

His voice strained, Avery talked on, fast as though his jaws could not keep up with his words and feelings. And the church changed. Where listlessness and boredom had been everywhere apparent, suddenly there were expressions of joy and excitement and the room was filled with a sensation of energy. Building up race and nations was building Babylon, Avery said, and Babylon was doomed to pass away before a spiritual realm that would be "holy and pure just like God" and hold no distinctions of color nor nation nor anything of man. He finished and a second man jumped to his feet and began reading Scripture to affirm what Avery had said; then Avery stood and testified some more.

"Them that are led by the Spirit shall become the Sons of God," he said. "He ain't give you no color line! . . . They's a spiritual world, that we've got to enter into! And all this stuff about who we are or what we are, we'll know who we are and what we are! We'll either be childs of God, or we'll be pushed back 'til we come in subjection and is a child of God."

When he finished his voice had cracked and his face was streaked with tear trails. Ness and his friend, the former suddenly nervous, began to quote Scripture in refutation of the two testimonies. Eventually Conway added his opinions to theirs, but by that point the meeting had broken into a steady stream of departures. Conway, Ness, and Ness's friend became defensive, Conway assuring people that he wanted them to come back, Ness and his friend asking people if they had been offended; then an argument started between Ness and Avery over what the Kingdom was going to be like. People kept leaving, the visiting folklorists started packing up their tape recorders, Ness started packing up his equipment and trying to get people to take the printed handouts he had brought along, and Conway snatched up a collection plate and ran after the folks who had already gone outside. He came back in a minute or two with the plate still empty.

The congregation was standing around outside the building, talking about what had just gone on, about meetings to be held and revelations that had been given lately. Avery was at the center of a group. "It's what I've said to them," he said, "that as long as they let the Spirit just move in these meetings, they'll go on, but as soon as they try to raise one up, they're gonna die." The group watched Ness and his wife and friend drive away. A few other people, who had long rides ahead of them, headed home. The rest went back inside and had another meeting.

The refutation of Brother Ness's ministry at the Rocky Top House of Prayer was an expression of an original, distinct vision of the world and the shape of things to come being voiced in the mid-1970s in meetings of a number of small, nondenominational churches in North Carolina. The adherents applied various names to this idea, among them the Sonship, the End-Time Message, and the Sons of God Message.

The Sonship was a local faith. While some Sons expressed a spiritual affinity with the Missouri-based Overcomer organization of evangelist Bill Britton, there were no organizational ties and no sense of evangelical mission among the Sons. One Son mentioned the ministry of one William Brandon, a midwestern faith healer who preached in North Carolina soon after World War II, as the germ of the Sonship, but the idea developed in an oral process of testimony and worship, and its origins and history became hidden along the way.

Sonship ministry spread at least as far east as the Piedmont industrial town of High Point and west into the mountains past Asheville. It was particularly strong in the interface region of mountains and Piedmont roughly triangulated by Wilkesboro, Statesville, and Lenoir. Much of the area is part of the greater southern Appalachian region, sharing its heritage of traditional mountain culture, but it has undergone considerable social and economic change in the last thirty-five years. Relatively isolated and predominantly rural at the time of World War II, it has been increasingly urbanized, industrialized, and opened to outside influence by the growth of local commerce, mass communication, and improved transportation. An example is Wilkes County, labeled "Bootleg Capital of America" by Vance Packard in a 1950 article in *American* magazine, and in the early 1980s a regional center for manufacturing and home of a large retail hardware chain and one of the largest banks in the state.

Traveling in the region, one is struck by the sheer number of churches of all kinds, in the country and in towns. Historically, the area's religious life has been characterized by small, rural, informal churches, with Southern Baptists overwhelmingly dominant among scattered congregations of Primitive Baptists, Methodists, Adventists, Presbyterians, and Episcopalians. The Sons expressed a sense of community with all Christians, all religionists, and all mankind, even as they went on living conventional lives among their neighbors. But they also thought of themselves as separate from the rest of humanity, as living in another reality. They had, nevertheless, no tests for membership or continued affiliation, other than expression of belief in some or any essential parts of the Message and association with other believers by going to church or simply discussing religion during personal visits. A church's congregation could only be taken as the particular group present at a particular time. Allegiances were fluid. Individuals did tend to regularly attend particular churches, but they attended others, too, including denominational ones, however they were moved. Some tended to follow certain preachers from church to church. Church meetings were open to outsiders. Who was and was not a member was a matter of opinion for any member. When Sons spoke of their coreligionists, "those who hear this" or "them who can eat this" were their common expressions.

Similarly, a *preacher* was one who called himself or herself a preacher and was called a preacher by others. Preachers might or might not have charge of a church building, might or might not be formally ordained (by Sons or by an orthodox church), could be male or female, or any adult age. Preachers who had their own churches often visited others to worship or to speak. Even when a preacher was the customary leader of services at a particular place, actual charge of the building — housekeeping, arranging for meetings, paying rent — was often in the hands of another, a *pastor*. Pastors were usually women. They might take pronounced roles in services, or none at all. There were also *evangelists,* itinerant preachers without churches of their own, who were commonly called to lead services and to preach at different churches.

If the Sonship had no organization to speak of, neither did it have a fixed body of doctrine. It had a text, the Bible, and Scriptures were often invoked, chapter and verse, to support statements of belief. But it had no written creed, no bylaws or articles of faith, nothing that distinguished it from Christianity at large except ideas in the minds of its believers that were expressed in song, testimony, preaching, and the ritual forms of the services. The Sonship existed more as an unofficial consensus than as a formal code. It was re-created, renewed, and changed a little bit each time it was expressed.

The absence of organization and fixed belief lent a particular significance to the Sonship's church meetings. Its structure became apparent only in them. Those meetings were not all alike, but after attending a number of them, at different times and places, one perceived a pattern in the worship and a governing logic in the beliefs expressed.

The Sonship meetings could be held at any time, but were most common on Friday and Saturday nights and Sunday afternoons. Sunday night services were also common. Attendance ranged from six people one Sunday afternoon to more than one hundred at one Saturday night service preached by a healing evangelist. People in the congregations were generally middle-aged or older and came dressed in ordinary clothing. There were a few younger adults, teenagers only when they had prescribed roles as singers or musicians, and almost always young children brought by their parents or grandparents. The services were invariably oriented to adults who understood and accepted the Message. What was said developed acknowledged themes or commented upon and updated premises already familiar.

The interior decoration of each church was minimal. An area at one end would be set off like a stage by carpeting or by being raised a few inches above floor level. In one church, a large watercolor of a mountain landscape hung behind the stage. In another, there was a fabric wall hanging of Jesus as a shepherd; during one service, the pastor pointed to the hanging, said, "We're not worshipping that kind of a God, but we're worshipping God in the spirit," and took it down.

The music of the services varied from occasion to occasion. In one church worshippers sometimes used the Overcomer hymnal. In others there were no books. The songs were sometimes popular gospel music such as "One Day at a Time," sometimes standards such as "Sweet

Hour of Prayer," and sometimes Message songs, either from the Over-comer book or locally composed, such as "New Day A-Dawning," with lines like

> For we're in the Resurrection morning
> And we'll never die.

Message songs were usually performed a cappella or accompanied by a single acoustic guitar. Popular-style songs were usually accompanied by rock music from electric guitars, electric organs, and pianos. What kind of music was used and how it was performed varied from church to church: one might use a cappella Message songs exclusively, another some of those and some rock, another all rock. Whether music was customarily congregational or done by a performer or group also varied from place to place. If it was done by performer, it was customary for the congregation to take part by clapping, shouting, or singing along.

The Message was expressed in two types of meetings. One may be called "standard," for its similarity to conventional Protestant services. The other was the "open pulpit," in which the order of worship was left to the moving of the Holy Spirit. Both types were more free than the services of most other groups. At one church, a bell was rung to announce the start of the meeting. At the others, the pastor or some other person simply went onto the stage area and began to talk or sing. If the pastor was on stage, he might take part in the singing, and singers would commonly deliver short testimonies between songs. At some point early in the meeting, someone might be called out of the congregation to lead a group prayer—which might take the form of one leader talking for a room of bowed, silent heads, or of the entire congregation praying out loud, each person saying his own prayer. In a standard meeting, someone might offer a testimony after the music was finished, which could serve to introduce the preaching as well as to express a personal feeling. The actual preaching followed, much like the sermon in an orthodox service—only usually much longer. There might be more than one preaching, by different speakers. A preacher might interrupt his sermon to sing—alone or with others called out of the congregation—picking up again or quitting after the song, and might call for others to "obey the Lord" when he finished. In an open-pulpit service there was no preaching as such. The pulpit would be available for anyone wishing to testify or to sing, with the pastor or a preacher calling people up and offering commentary and bits of personal testimony between the others. Open-pulpit services were less common than standard ones, but they were considered a deeper form in that they allowed the Holy Spirit the greatest freedom to manifest as it would, with a minimum of fleshly tampering. Both types of meeting were usually closed by taking up the collection, which was always announced for a specific purpose such as paying the rent or subsidizing an evangelist. If an offering was not taken, the preacher or pastor closed by announcing the time of the next meeting. A central feature of both kinds of services was that the line between stage and seats, performer and audience, was constantly being crossed. People on stage would call to people in the congregation by name. People would call out from the congregation, and performers — including pastors — took seats in the congregation when their time on stage was done.

Preachings and testimonies were statements of belief, developed apparently by free association for as long and as far as speakers were led to go. Speakers commonly disclaimed responsibility for what they said, affirming they were merely instruments through which the Spirit worked. As one speaker explained:

> I heard a preacher preach one time. He said, "A lot of preachers has preached so long," he said, "they learnt how to preach." Well I grabbed that right quick, I was sitting in the pews, I said, "God, I thank you I have never learned how." I never learned how to preach. If you preach by the Spirit and the revelation of Jesus Christ, you ain't learned how to preach. Because it ain't you doing it nohow. It's not you doing it. You can't memorize the Spirit of God and get up and begin to quote that to save your life. You can't do it. You got to get up and be a willing and a open mouth, a open vessel for God to speak through.

As here, when a speaker mentioned something personal he would quickly move on to generality or abstraction. Personal experiences were used only to illustrate and were always subordinate to statements and explications of belief. During testimonies, there would be exclamations of "Amen!" and "Praise the Lord!" and so on, as people felt the Holy Spirit in what was said. The exclamations could be shouted or spoken quietly. They might come at points when the speaker was emotionally stirred or calm. Audience response was also part and product of each separate testimony. It did not mount toward a cathartic climax as the meeting went along, and while some particularly moving point might produce a chorus of response from all over the church, at other points response came at random from different hearers, moved in their own ways. Audiences were most moved to respond by statements of particular points of belief, however emotional or flat their expression.

The outside world entered Sonship testimony almost exclusively as signs of the coming of the Kingdom. Oil shortages, economic recessions, the anticipated swine flu epidemic, and other events were taken as fulfillments of biblical prophecies and signals that the end of the world was at hand. But the concern was with here, now, and us. For the Message was that the Kingdom of God was coming on earth, today, and in his people, the Sons of God themselves: "we're just now beginning to see daylight, I mean the light coming, it's just now beginning to come to us and . . . what we're doing is waking out of sleep, waking out of, we're waking out, you see, because we've come to the time that now is." That Message, in some form or extension, made up every preaching and testimony. Expressed in various individual styles and with different words, the Message was a theme upon which speakers improvised and the meetings a genre in which they performed.

The Sons of God believed that God existed within every person, singly and collectively. God was simultaneously present in every man's spirit — that part of God contained in each human — and as an omnipresent, all-inclusive whole. No distant, uninterested being enthroned in a supernatural heaven, he was a close presence in the tangible world of everyday living. Further, the God present in men was in the process of manifesting himself in the physical, carnal world. The present time, the end of the second millennium after Christ, was interpreted as being the dwindling of the second day of the Crucifixion into the dawn of the third — Resurrection morning. Manifestation of the Holy Spirit in the carnal world was preparation for the carnal world's passing away, and the manifestation would take place in the bodies of the Sons of God.

Their flesh, their carnal bodies would be transmuted into spiritual matter. God, in them, would take on human form and flesh. They would become spirits in flesh, just as Christ had been. The Sons would assume leadership of the Kingdom of God on earth and would guide the rest of mankind into the spiritual state before — after a thousand years — the earth and the flesh were abandoned totally for the spiritual and union with God.

The Sons expressed an ambiguous attitude toward the flesh. On one hand, it was the enemy of the spirit, that which held men back from knowing God and their own godly nature. But it was in the flesh God would be manifested, and the transformation of flesh into spirit would be demonstration and proof of God's power. With divinity taking over human flesh, there would be no graves, no death for the Sons of God. They would gain immortality without dying. But along the way, their flesh had to be made into a fit tabernacle for God. As one preacher put it, "He's coming in this old body. But it's going to be a new body. He ain't going to come in this *old* body, He's going to come in this *new* body. Do you know this thing's getting newer all the time, Fred? No wonder the wrinkles is leaving. No wonder my hair's coming back."

Orthodox Christianity taught that perfection could only be attained in heaven, after death. The Sons, believing "Jesus Christ has told me that I will never die," saw themselves in opposition to the passing-away realms of orthodoxy. They did not consider orthodoxy false, however, merely limited. It had a place in God's plan, because not all men were ready to receive the Message. The church and the carnal realm were thought of as stepping stones toward eventual universal salvation. Similarly, the Sonship itself was thought of as a process, or as part of the universal process of movement from carnality to spirituality. The preacher's body was "getting newer."

Hearing the Message was realizing the fact of one's own godly nature, but once that was recognized, attaining the final spiritual state could only be accomplished through a long process of learning, understanding, and spiritual growth. The process was described both as growth and as return toward "what Adam let get away." The idea of conversion or conventional salvation, therefore, had little meaning in Sonship, since ultimate salvation was the result of a process over time. The Sons regarded Jesus not as the Savior himself, but merely as a type of the Sons to come. The salvation Christ represented was the realization of godliness in flesh; Christ was an example of what men would be, but not an actor in the salvation process.

The route to heaven, and oneness with God and knowledge of him, lay in a spiritual realm, but the spiritual realm itself was not heaven. Rather, it was described as an unseen, parallel universe. Approaching it was difficult and fearsome. One Son put it this way:

> There's no time of trouble for God's people except one thing. And that is fear of the unknown. You've got to enter in a spiritual realm that this flesh has never walked in before. And you don't fear anything that you know all about, it don't make no difference how dangerous it is, if you know all about it, you don't fear it. You got a fear of deep, dark water or dark places that you haven't been and you know nothing about, and that's the only fear that God's people's got, is afraid of the unknown, something we've never been preached, something we've never been taught, that's the reason he said, "Them as would become Sons of God is led by the Spirit." Because we'll go anywhere [that the Spirit] we're following . . . wants to take us. If we're following man or flesh, we're gonna back down when we get to going into this spiritual realm.

For men, God's guidance was the only chance of safe passage.

One came to know God and the shape of things to come by being touched by him, by Bible study, by prayer, and by revelations given directly by God. Thus, while the Bible was often cited as support for points of belief and was held the final and ultimate source of knowledge, authority for an idea could be claimed for God himself. Sons of God spoke of the freedom to be found in hearing and accepting the Message—"Where I'm at, everybody's free"—which was by implication contrasted with bondage in the church realm. They regarded the church realm as a product and servant of the flesh, an attempt on the part of men to order and regulate the knowledge of God and God's presence in the physical world. The Sons, on the other hand, were disposed to "let the Spirit manifest"—a disposition they followed in all levels of their belief and practice.

From Sonship oratory a set of oppositions and mediations seemed to emerge, as will be seen in the table on the following page. These lists could be extended, and some terms might be moved from one column to another. Sonship, transformation of the flesh, and the Message itself could function as mediators in some contexts rather than as positives; so could church, female, or grave rather than as negatives. The scheme is a description, not a definition.

I see in the structure of oppositions a logic behind the Message's

Negative	Mediator	Positive
hell		heaven
religion		salvation
sickness		health
flesh		spirit
orthodoxy		the Message
science	Sons of God	faith
human law	the Word	God's law
death	Jesus	life
past	now	future
church		Sonship
female		male
child		adult
grave		transformation
bondage		freedom
incompletion		wholeness

development, one suggested by the fact that some people traced the origin of the Message to faith healing and by the frequent references in testimonies to healing by faith, such as: "I thank the Lord for being here tonight and I thank him for what he means to me. I thank him most of all for healing my son because they was two doctors give him up, he had that spinal meningitis. You know Jesus touched him and healed him."

In faith healing, physical health is associated with belief in God. Physical health requires wholeness and purity of the body. Testimonies often associated the beginning of belief in God with an experience of miraculous healing, so that physical and spiritual health become interconnected states and ideas. An improving, "new," body correlates with an improving, "new," spirit, one growing closer to and more like God.

The idea of development toward, rather than immediate achievement of, perfection correlated the evident fact that the Sons were not divine with the belief that their physical and mental health was being improved. In cases of actual healing and conversion, the improvement would be a tangible reality. As life was maintained by physical health, aligned with Sonship, so death became aligned with church.

The "Sons" image in all likelihood derived from Christ's biblical title Son of God and implied a masculine nature to the Sonship. The masculine nature was reinforced by the traditional identification of God with maleness (Our Father), by biblical images of the female nature as that which draws men away from God (Eve, Delilah), by the fact that humans, flesh, are borne and nurtured by women, and by the historical association of the church with women — that is, home and stability and order which oppose the randomness and insecurity and danger associated with the male realm.

The Sons identified the church as female, referring to it as "the womanhood" or even as the Whore of Babylon. Orthodoxy, one could infer, tamed God into fleshly, graspable terms; similarly, women in the traditional scheme tamed men by marrying and raising families around them. Such a tamed state opposes the liberty of the Sonship. Sons of God did not have to reach God by way of the grave — and there is no stronger image of antifreedom, stasis, unhealth, and death than a grave.

Leaving the church world was spoken of as being separated from the womb. In the Sonship, the holy relationship was that of sons to their father. The only place for the female — mother — was with the unholy. The Sons were expressly sensitive to this male-female relation and its implications, and they expressly separated the literal from the imagistic. Women were said to be equal with men in God's eyes, equally likely to hear the Message and equally qualified to preach it. Concern with physical sexual identity was considered a trait of the flesh. However, the fact that the pastor role was usually filled by a woman replicated the spiritual dichotomy. Maintaining a church building and arranging services were elements of church which necessarily persisted in the Sonship.

The male-female dichotomy and the equation of womanhood with the church were matters of description and metaphor, but had little to do with what the Sons saw as the real point of their faith. In doctrine, the most important implication of the Sons image was that of inheritors. The father-son relation was spoken of far more often than the church-woman theme. As sons grow into adulthood — as Sons grow into spirit — they inherit the things of their fathers. As the Sons said: "You know, a lot of people don't know it, but he's my inheritance, praise God. Lot of people don't know it, but he's their inheritance, praise God. He's my inheritance, praise God. He was promised to

56

me, praise God, the Promised Land, praise God, I might inherit this, praise God. That's what was given unto me, praise God."

The male-female dichotomy and concern with inheritance suggest a link between this western North Carolina faith and greater Appalachian traditions, and hint that in the Sonship there was a reaffirmation of traditional Appalachian culture in the face of modernism that tamed the wild high country, replaced faith with medicine, and brought the church. A visible sign of the continuity was the seating pattern in Sonship meetings. People generally favored seats to the left of the central aisle. With a small group, the right side might be empty. Response to what was said or sung on the stage was always louder and more frequent from the seats on the left. This was reminiscent of the practice in Primitive Baptist and some other older churches which were prevalent in the region in times many of the Sons were old enough to have known, in which the left side of the church (the right side of the minister, or by extension the right hand of God) was reserved for men.

Traditionally, the home was the woman's province and the outside world the man's. But the rough-and-tumble world outside the home and the agrarian economy that encouraged individualism have been tamed by the coming of outside culture. The new order has little place for the traditional male role. The organized churches have often been leading, or at least highly visible, agents in that taming process. Church membership has risen dramatically in the mountains in the twentieth century, and the new membership has been predominantly female.[3]

On the other hand, the Sonship also offered mediation between the old way and the new. To people feeling dislocated by social change, the Message brought word that the modern world which had done the dislocating was already on the way out and that it would be replaced by a new order in which the formerly dislocated would have the leading role. A Sonship meeting was thus a mediating point itself: between church and the free move of the spirit, between past and present, flesh and spirit. It was held in a church that was not a church, almost barewalled and stripped of most of the "fleshly" trappings of established Christianity, and attended by a group that was not a congregation. Being "separated from the mother's womb" was a hard and fearsome thing, and the Sons retained the tangible form of a church, almost like a crutch, as a support from which to move on, to help them learn to walk in the spiritual realm. That crutch was gradually being dispensed with, as the pastor demonstrated when he removed the wall hanging of Jesus during a service. As God was said to be not bound by walls or bounded time, so the meetings were fluid and open-ended, held any day of the week, open to anyone, affording any spirit a chance to manifest. The interchangeability of roles in meetings, performers becoming spectators and vice versa, and the constant crossing of the artificial boundaries that separate clergy and functionaries from laity, dramatized the egalitarianism of the Message that was made explicit in testimony and preaching, those impersonal statements of belief; and in the call of the Message to dispense with one's fleshly identity, all that was human, mortal, and earthly, and move toward a totality in God. In the meeting, one entered — or at least approached in metaphorical and ritualistic form — a subtotality that was itself a type of the complete transformation to come. And in the "ritual" of a meeting, the Sons' belief system was embodied and enacted.

However demonstrative or extrasensory it may have been, a "community relationship" of joint participation by performer and audience was integrally a part of the Sonship's oral "literature." In such performances, the performer (distinct from the participating audience) had to conform to what was expected of him or the performance did not work.[4] The audience was informed of what type of performance to expect by certain generic clichés, which at the same time informed it of its part in the performance; for the performance to work, there had to be a consonance between the situation, what kind of performance was expected, and the enactment.

On the occasion of Brother Ness's visit to the Rocky Top House of Prayer, there was no consonance but a harsh dissonance, which was rectified only when Brother Avery began to speak. Ness's racial ideas, offensive as they may have been to people who include all mankind in God's elect — and expressly include blacks — were also offensive as an attempt to define an identity for the people at the Rocky Top church. Such a definition, it has been seen, is a quality of the church world and was contradictory to essential Sonship assumptions. Concern with self-identification, in terms of fleshly qualities, was not only alien to the Sonship, but also constituted backsliding into the church.

As academic, mass-cultured outsiders, the folklorists immediately noted the refutation of Ness's racial ideas and attention to worldly matters that were expressed in Avery's testimony. But within the context of Sonship meetings there were other and more important factors involved. Avery objected to Ness's attention to the "natural," but even more to Ness's manner of presentation and to what was happening to the Rocky Top church and its open-pulpit meetings.

The Rocky Top church had been altered that afternoon, its previously bare walls hung with posters — fleshly matter — dealing primarily with worldly matters: politics and human history. The place was more mindful of a schoolroom than a church, and Ness even went so far as to tell his audience that it needed teachers — when the action of a typical Sonship meeting involved breaking down such specific, elevated roles and essential Sonship belief held that God is the only teacher. Ness talked about the omnipotence of God and surrendering to his will, but Ness's surroundings and behavior belied these words.

Sonship preaching and testifying were usually emotional and always free-associative. Ness's performance was obviously planned, seemingly practiced, and bolstered by gadgetry — a performance out of consonance with the invocations given by both Conway and Ness for the Spirit to move as it would in the meeting. The audience, entering with particular expectations that were reinforced by the early phases of the service, became lethargic and bored when the performance turned out to be not an impersonal, free-moving series of testimonies in which members could take an accustomed part, but a mechanistic sales pitch full of personal anecdotes. When Ness was finally broken off by performances like those the people had come for, the mood of the group immediately and dramatically changed, and energy suddenly filled the building. The Spirit was moving; the fleshly order was being overturned. The Sons were feeding on the Spirit, and the congregation took on a joy and unity of which Ness was not a part. As a Son would say, "Thank You, Jesus, hallelujah. Praise God, we're practicing, brother, just exactly what we believe in."

NOTES

Fieldwork for this essay was conducted in 1975 and 1976 in preparation for my master's thesis, *The Sons of God Message in the North Carolina Mountains: An Exercise in Thick Description* (Chapel Hill: Curriculum in Folklore, University of North Carolina, 1977). The research was also part of a documentary film project supported in part by the National Endowment for the Arts and jointly undertaken by the University of North Carolina Curriculum in Folklore and Tom Davenport Films. Scenes from Sons of God services appear in this 58-minute, color, 16-mm film, *Being a Joines* (Delaplane, Va.: Tom Davenport Films, 1981). I have phrased this essay in the past tense, not having continued the investigation of this unfolding religious movement after completing work on these projects; the Sons of God do continue to practice.

In addition to works cited in individual notes, the study is indebted to Peter Berger, "Some Second Thoughts on Substantive versus Functional Definitions of Religion," *Journal for the Scientific Study of Religion* 13 (1974): 125–35, and *A Rumor of Angels: Modern Society and the Rediscovery of the Supernatural* (Garden City, N.Y.: Doubleday, 1969); Clifford Geertz, *The Interpretation of Cultures* (New York: Basic Books, 1973); and Charles Hudson, "The Structure of a Fundamentalist Christian Belief-System" in Samuel Hill, Jr., ed., *Religion and the Solid South* (Nashville, Tenn.: Abingdon Press, 1972).

1. Bill Britton, *Songs for Eagle Saints* (Springfield, Mo.: The Overcomer Ministry, n.d.).

2. My terminology for categories of Sonship clergy is taken from Bruce Rosenberg, *The Art of the American Folk Preacher* (New York: Oxford University Press, 1970).

3. See Linda Johnson, "The Foot-Washin' Church and the Prayer-Book Church," *The Christian Century,* November 3, 1976: 952–55; Emma Bell Miles, *The Spirit of the Mountains,* facsimile reprint (Knoxville, Tenn.: The University of Tennessee Press, 1967); Harry K. Schwarzweller, James S. Brown, and J. J. Mangalam, *Mountain Families in Transition: A Case Study of Appalachian Migration* (University Park, Penn.: The Pennsylvania State University Press, 1971); W. D. Weatherford and Earl D. C. Brewer, *Life and Religion in Southern Appalachia* (New York: Friendship Press, 1962); Jack E. Weller, *Yesterday's People: Life in Contemporary Appalachia* (Lexington, Ky.: The University of Kentucky Press, 1965).

4. Roger Abrahams, "The Complex Relations of Simple Forms," *Genre* 2 (June 1969): 105–6.

Finding a Home in the Church: 3
Primitive Baptist Women

Beverly B. Patterson

The oldest of the Primitive Baptist churches along the North Carolina–Virginia border, beyond the first crest of the Blue Ridge Mountains, date their founding to the 1790s, the generation of the first white settlers in the region. When Baptists split in the 1830s over the issue of missions, these churches hewed to the more conservative position, based on a predestinarian interpretation of the doctrines of grace and election, and took the name Primitive or Old School Baptist. Throughout the nineteenth century they remained a leading denomination in the region. Even today, although increasingly outnumbered by their evangelical Methodist, Southern Baptist, or Pentecostal neighbors, Primitive Baptists continue to vigorously support numerous small churches averaging about twenty-five members each.

The one-room church, a plain white frame building with green shutters, was already open. Wanting to hear all of the half hour of singing that would precede the preaching, I arrived early for a Primitive Baptist service. The preacher and his wife were already there and had opened both front doors of the church that led directly onto the two aisles of the meeting room. It was Saturday, time for the first of two services to be held that weekend at the church, and the late afternoon sunlight streamed through a window behind the pulpit, highlighting the straight-backed wooden pews and a wood stove that stood between pulpit and pews.

As a small congregation gradually assembled, one older couple, probably in their seventies, caught my eye. They got out of their late-model car and walked toward the front of the church. I expected them to come in together, but they separated. The woman came in the door that was the entrance for the right aisle and her husband walked farther to the parallel door and aisle on the left. Originally built as separate entrances for men and women, the two doors still served to guide at least some in the congregation to their customary places inside, a seating arrangement traditionally separated by sex.

The service was also traditional, composed entirely of hymns so familiar to the congregation that they could have been sung without the hymn books, of prayers voiced by the pastor, and of a sermon that the preacher delivered extemporaneously to the extent he felt "liberated" to preach. The sermon was low key and it defended, as Primitive Baptist sermons generally do, the Calvinist themes of election and grace. At its close, as we stood and sang the final hymn, we extended the hand of fellowship to those nearby; then in a line women followed the men to shake hands with the preacher. I went with the women as they continued walking to the men's side to shake hands during the hymn. These handshakes were solemn, keeping the dignity and warmth of the service, and they acknowledged the shared fellowship among the small gathering of husbands and wives, parents and children, friends, and visitors. Finally, we returned to our places for a closing prayer.

I thought about the women in this church who, for generations, have participated in similar Primitive Baptist services in this mountain region. In modest but steady numbers, they continue to come and, eventually, to request membership by asking their pastor and congregation for a home in the church. I wanted to understand something of the power that still attracts women to an old-time religion that, on the surface, delegates to them not only a separate but also an unequal place.

The church's separation of male and female, marked by two entrances in some of the older churches and by separate seating in virtually all of the churches I visited, is carried further by a total male dominance in the formal church polity — a dominance that Primitive Baptists believe is authorized in the scriptures. As one preacher explained, "Sarah obeyed Abraham. . . . Of course that didn't mean that she called him lord in heaven, but she recognized him as her authority, you know, over her."

The preacher quickly acknowledged that some of the women in his churches were very bright and perceptive: "And I'm not saying that [women] don't have a certain knowledge of the Scripture, and things of that sort. Maybe sometimes even more than some men, as far as that's concerned. I talk to sisters and members of the church that's very well blessed to understand some things in the Scripture. Sometimes even more than some men you talk to for that matter." Nevertheless, he maintained that ability in itself did not qualify women to be leaders of men. "Men," he declared flatly, "oughtn't to be governed by them."

And men are clearly in charge. Interpreting their duties in accordance with their understanding of the King James translation of the Bible, men assume full responsibility for conducting all worship and business or conference meetings of the church. With very few exceptions, women are expected to sit quietly and listen attentively while men speak. Only those men who have been liberated by the church may lead the church by introducing the worship service, praying aloud in public, and preaching, but while women must always observe a rule of silence, any man may make announcements and take part in conference discussions.

Occasionally, preachers publicly commend women on their silence in church, reminding them that they are expected to ask their husbands or another male spokesman to communicate any of their concerns to the church. The strictness with which this rule of decorum is enforced varies somewhat from one congregation to another, but members believe that church elders would and should correct any woman who speaks out and thus exceeds appropriate limits. Situations that require this kind of intervention are rare. Said one elder, "I've never had no problem with [women speaking] here in my churches but . . . back over through the years they ventured [twice] to speak in conference, and when . . . they'd get sort of run down where I could get in a word, . . . I just ask them to be seated."

Women often told me that they share this view of proper decorum and referred to scriptural authority to support their opinion. A deacon's wife, when asked how she felt about the rule of silence, simply stated, "That's exactly the way I believe, that [women] are supposed to keep quiet. And if they have any questions, or anything that's worrying them, and bothering them, they're to ask their husbands, at home. And it says in the Bible, I don't remember just where it's at, for the women to keep silent. And I firmly believe that they should."

Even a widow whose husband had never been a Primitive Baptist spoke in favor of complete male authority in the church:

> We're not allowed to bring up any policy, or change policy, or offer things of that sort, because we think we have Scripture to oppose that. You know St. Paul says if a woman would know anything, to ask her husband, and if she doesn't have a husband then she can ask one of the brethren, but for her to be quiet in the church. . . . It all boils down to the fact that the man is the head of the woman the same as Christ is head of the church . . . and so to put a woman up and let her be in authority over the men, in any capacity, would be . . . going against . . . the man as the head of the woman the same as Christ is head of the church. . . . We like it this way.

A woman who confessed feeling some ambivalence about having to keep silent in church meetings still supported the practice because it was traditional. "Back when [my mother] was younger, if [women] wanted something said [in church], they got around to their daddy or a deacon or somebody and talked to them before preaching time. . . . Really, if I hadn't been brought up that way, I'd say I didn't like it. But my mother was real strong about that. And there've been times when out here in my home church that I would have spoke up and said something when I didn't because of that."

That women cheerfully uphold and strongly support the traditions of a church in which their participation is so limited and narrowly defined is a remarkable feature of Primitive Baptist life and one not easily understandable in a contemporary American social and political climate where feminist issues command considerable attention.

At a practical level, it is not surprising that the practice of separate seating is strictly observed during the annual communion and foot-washing services. In the churches I visited, men do not wash women's feet nor do women wash men's feet, and naturally men sit together so they can serve each other easily and women do the same. But the degree to which men and women continue to maintain their distance from one another during regular worship services, in the absence of a clear need to do so, is puzzling. Likewise, if women must accept subordinate roles and receive few compensations in terms of privilege or personal recognition for their contributions, why do they continue to ask for, and find, a home in the church?

Answers that rely on stereotypes of ignorance, poverty, and isolation fail to address the realities present in the church and in the lives of these women. None of the stereotypical descriptions fit. One gains more insight into the complex nature of the question from paying attention to women's action in the church and their emotional response to that action insofar as they articulate or demonstrate that, and especially from exploring the church's concept of what it means to be female. This concept is embodied not only in church architecture and the structure of the service but also in the performance and texts of the hymns, in the texts of frequently quoted Scriptures, in the often elevated language of sermons, and even in the conversational language of daily life.

Women do actively participate in the life of the church, but since there are no Sunday schools, choirs, musical instruments, missionaries, or women's societies in the church, their options for service are limited and revolve around providing hospitality, cleaning churches, and cooking for church dinners. Although many of these women have full-time jobs in local businesses, textile industries, and schools, some regularly open their homes to welcome preachers and other out-of-town church visitors who may stay as long as a week for special meetings. Primitive Baptists are proud of their long tradition of hospitality and make every effort to house and feed these visiting church friends who would otherwise have to pay for public accommodations. Several women can show long lists of visitors' names in guest registers they have kept over the years.

Some women also help clean the churches and most decorate family graves in the cemeteries. Deacons' wives launder the cloths and sterilize the pans used for foot washing, and they make the bread and wine for the communion table, which is set once a year. Aside from attending church meetings, preparing and serving food is the most visible and substantial service that all women perform for the church. Both women and men view food preparation as the woman's duty. After citing a passage of Scripture, an elder interpreted a phrase to make his point about this duty: "This word 'faithful in all things' don't just

mean being a faithful wife to a husband. . . . 'In all things' here is
pertaining to the church. And back to making bread . . . [women]
do the cooking in other words."

And "doing the cooking" is no small job. Two refrigerators, a large
freezer, and a well-stocked pantry are standard in many homes. In
homes occupied by only two people, some kitchens or dining rooms
are still furnished with cloth-covered tables that will seat twelve, and
two homes I visited even had two kitchens. Although only deacons'
wives prepare the ritual foods—the unleavened bread and homemade
wine used in annual communion services —every woman who is able
cooks large family-style meals to take to church for dinner on the
ground at these all-day meetings. And women who have house guests
cook even more, often daily producing a fourth meal (sandwiches or
snacks) for their guests after evening church services.

In short, women put in many hours on food preparation for church
gatherings, often at times when they are already tired from a day's
work or not feeling well. They do not deny this and yet they speak
persuasively of cooking for the church as a pleasure. "No one minds,"
one woman insisted. "It's worth it for the fellowship." She, like most
of the women, spoke of fellowship as the most rewarding feature of
these communal meals. I heard variations of this sentiment from both
men and women. One of the preachers interpreted the women's attitude about cooking, saying, "These people feel that when they cook,
they cook just exactly what they want to . . . and you'll notice, every
one of them brings a complete meal. . . . And they all set it on the
table together and everybody eats whatever they want to. . . . In our
church, as you notice, the women don't have much say in the church.
According to the Bible they ought not to have. And I think this is
one part that they feel free."

Even though food has important consequences in strengthening the
church fellowship that women value so highly, one woman typically
insisted that the food she and others prepared could only partially
feed a "hungry" congregation: "In our church here we're strict . . .
and people come to be fed. It's spiritual food you go for, it's not to
be entertained. . . . And of course you have to have this desire, you've
got to be hungry, you've got to be thirsting after righteousness before
you are satisfied, before this has any meaning for you. . . . If this

were taken away from me, I'd be of all people most miserable, really I would."

Implicit in her statement is the idea that "spiritual food" strengthens one's understanding, that women who think and reason can find more food for thought in the Primitive Baptist church than in other churches. And these Primitive Baptist women do show intellectual energy. One has kept a notebook for years, recording data from every service she has attended—names of preachers present, hymns, Scriptures, sermon topics, and quotations from sermons. At first she kept these records as references for family discussions with an elderly parent at home who could not attend services, but later she continued the practice for her own benefit. She says it helps her to pay attention during the service and also to recall things she wants to think more about later.

Another woman expressed a strong preference for doctrinal sermons that offer detailed explication of Scriptures rather than less-weighty, anecdote-filled sermons. She says that "stories" in sermons interest her only when they clearly illustrate a point of doctrine. And if a preacher gets off the familiar doctrinal track, or stops in mid-journey, she is among the first to notice and to express disapproval or disappointment.

These women have found intellectual stimulation in their church and have acquired a confidence in their own beliefs and in their ability to defend them thoughtfully that, they feel, sets them apart from women of other churches. A Primitive Baptist woman who works in an office with local women of various other denominations says that, although she and her co-workers occasionally talk about religion, the others "don't seem to think for themselves—just accept whatever the preacher says."

Women freely discussed church customs, their own church-related activities, and their interest in doctrine, but were more reticent when talking about their "experience," or how they came to join the church. In their brief comments, however, they revealed something of the emotional dimension of their place in the church.

Like Primitive Baptist men, women wait for some evidence of God's grace to be manifested in their lives before they ask to join the church. They may wait for years and endure long periods of self-doubt and feelings of unworthiness, having both a great desire and a great reluctance to join the church. Their spiritual struggles occasionally reveal themselves in vivid dreams or visions. Some of these are reassuring, but others are disturbing, such as the following dream that an elderly woman recalled having in her youth.

> Now you know a lot of people say there's no hell, but I've seen that. I guess it was in a dream, it don't seem like to me it was. But I seen my soul and it looked like just a black . . . crow or something, you know just a-flying around. And this smoke was coming up out of that pit, and there was just a lot of them birds a-flying around, and once in a while one would go down in there. And I was one in the crowd now, I just knowed I was. And it just . . . bothered me to death. . . . And I woke up and I got up and went out on the porch, and it still yet seemed like to me that I could just see that, you know.

Their religious experiences often begin during childhood, but Primitive Baptist women do not usually join the church until they are adults, and often not until after marriage. Even after going through years of spiritual doubts and struggles, women say that when they finally present themselves to the congregation requesting "a home in the church" it feels like a spontaneous act.

> I had wanted to go ahead and join when my husband did, but I was backward I guess. And I just kept putting it off. I had thought about it, and went a time or two planning to join. And [I'd] come back, and I'd study on it, and talk to him about it. . . . So the day that I joined I didn't have any intentions of joining when I went. I sure didn't. And it just seemed like there was just the awfulest burden on me, after I got in the church you know, it was just, I can't explain it to you. But after I went up there and joined, seemed like that lifted that burden, but it wasn't gone until after I was baptized. Now that was my experience. And after I was baptized then it just all left me, seemed like, and I just felt relief.

Other women remembered experiencing similar feelings, especially that of carrying some burden until the moment of baptism. One said, "You've heard people say a great burden was lifted after they were baptized. That's how it was for me. And I immediately began to feel at home among Primitive Baptists."

In addition to feeling relieved of a burden upon joining the church and being baptized, women also feel they have become part of a larger, loving family. For many of these Primitive Baptists, the concept of "family" properly belongs only to life in this earthly, physical world. Only here can family life exist and here it must be nurtured, for there will be no recognition of one's family members in heaven.

Family life is not necessarily limited to one's kinship group, however. Seeing and experiencing the church itself as a family in its ideal form is one of the more pervasive themes in women's accounts of their religious experience. One said, "I would go [to church] and seemed like I just felt like I was one of them . . . all the members there . . . felt just like they was one of my family. I just felt so relieved and good with them. And seemed like they just loved me, and just wanted to be with me. I don't know if all, if anybody else has that experience like I did or not." For one woman, the feeling of being among family seemed to develop more slowly after joining the church: "Well, I'll be honest, I didn't notice people until I joined the church. To me life was to get rich, to get ahead, to progress. . . . People didn't mean that much to me. . . . But after I joined the church, they became my family . . . and as time goes on you know more about them, and you understand them, and . . . they just become closer." Another woman stressed the acceptance and trust she feels within her church family:

> And I think of myself back prior to my being involved in the Primitive Baptists. . . . And at that time I thought to myself, if I needed to confide in somebody . . . that I could respect and know that my confidence . . . was respected. I couldn't think of many people that I could turn to, if any. And now, there are so many, so many people that I could turn to and would feel . . . that I'd be understood and loved for it, even if it was something that was bad. I think I'd be understood . . . there's so many that I feel I could go to within the ranks of this association. . . . It's a sense of kindredship, brothers and sisters in Christ Jesus. That's what we're supposed to be. You know if I feel that my sins have been forgiven, and you feel that yours have been forgiven . . . well then, aren't we kindred, don't I belong in the family of God. . . . To me, this is what it's all about. It's a . . . resting place. . . . There's a definite saving in this time-world for me, in the gospel church, as I believe the Primitive Baptist to be."

Another woman, a poet, whose work is frequently published in a Primitive Baptist journal, makes a similar statement in verse:

> Come be with those who understand
> The trials you must face —
> Oh, bring your burdened, weary heart
> Unto its resting place.[1]

Women may experience the church as a "resting place" not only in hearing sermons that are compatible with their view of the world and in sensing themselves in the midst of sympathetic and supportive family, but also in singing and hearing the hymns in Primitive Baptist meetings. At first, congregational singing seems as male dominated as the rest of the service — men lead and women take secondary roles, sometimes by providing an alto part to harmonize with a male lead, but often by just singing the melody with less volume than men. Two women who have strong voices that naturally stand out have, on occasion, apologized privately to me for not being able to "hold it down" more, whereas men have apologized in public for not being able to sing out stronger.

From another perspective, however, congregational singing validates women in the church in several ways. Hymn singing is the one part of the service where women may fully participate. Even though preaching constitutes the core of Primitive Baptist meetings and may last more than an hour, especially if the congregation hears more than one preacher, church meetings begin with a full half hour of singing during which women may request hymns. Calling out numbers of their favorite texts, women often take the opportunity to direct the course of a service that is otherwise led by men.

The performance style itself may be interpreted as feminine. In a culture that has encouraged the development of competitive and individualistic males, the song style of the church remains unaccompanied, communal, and cooperative, giving no opportunity for men to display any musical gifts in solo performances comparable to opportunities that exist outside the church. Even though the most able male singer serves as the song leader, he typically remains seated to give the congregation its starting pitch and quickly becomes indistinguishable from the rest of the congregation once the singing begins. The only approved departures from this practice occur when a song leader "lines out" the hymn for his congregation, calling out each line of text in an improvised chant to which the congregation responds by setting the same line of text to its tune.

70

And the hymn texts themselves conform to a theology in which men and women alike are powerless to affect their own salvation and must wait, wholly dependent on God to reveal signs of grace in their lives. These Primitive Baptists have chosen hymns consistent with the Calvinist concept of the unworthy sinner saved only by grace and chosen by God before the foundation of the world, pilgrims and strangers suffering hardships and doubt in the natural world but hoping for the full joys of an eternal, spiritual world to come — texts paralleling the religious experience reported by both men and women.

It is not surprising that a search through the hymn texts yields far more masculine than feminine images, particularly those referring to God, such as Father, Jehovah, Savior, King, and Redeemer. Of the 321 texts in the *Primitive Baptist Hymn Book,* only twenty-six contain direct references to female figures, and these references occur either in the form of the nouns *woman, Mary, bride, mother, sister,* and *daughter,* or the pronouns *she* and *her.* [2] Of the twenty-six hymns that contain these references, probably fewer than ten are actually being sung now, making any inferences about women from texts alone highly speculative. Nevertheless, the existence and approval of such references makes them possible indexes to Primitive Baptist views of women, to women's images of themselves, and to women's experience in the Primitive Baptist church.

In keeping with the doctrinal view of the human as sinful and unworthy, the few hymn texts that refer to women present them as unfortunate or unhappy (a "weeping widow") or as subject to human failings ("Mary's stains," "doubting sister").

There is not a single reference to the Virgin, and there is no sentimentalization of the mother in the hymn repertory. The following stanza, for example, quite unsentimentally emphasizes a mother's weakness rather than her strength:

> Can a woman's tender care
> Cease toward the child she bare?
> Yes! She may forgetful be,
> Yet will I remember thee! (Hymn 185)

Primitive Baptists do honor mothers in sentimental songs they write and sing, but they keep this repertory separate from that used in the church. An elder explained that they do not use songs about mothers or other kin in worship because the church must avoid any appearance of placing mothers above God. However, men often speak of their mothers as the persons who usually brought them to church services when they were children. And it is not unusual to hear singers attribute their love of music and singing, as well as their extensive knowledge of hymns, to their mothers, who often sang at home.

Preachers do sometimes include stories about their mothers in their sermons, and I have seen such stories move a whole congregation to tears — men and women alike. One preacher told of his mother's devotion to the church and of her strength and courage shortly before she died. He confessed to a sympathetic congregation, "I'd rather have an old mother in Israel praying for me than anything else in this world, I'll tell you that brother. I'll tell you, their prayers goes a long way." And then he spoke directly to the women. "So you mothers in Israel, don't think that you're not needed in the church."

On hearing this comment, I glimpsed the senior women in the church as both human and symbolic figures, prone to doubt as humans are, but granted spiritual power by virtue of being "mothers in Israel" through which they serve the congregation as nurturers and mediators. The nurturing function is clearly visible in the food they bring for communal meals. And the meals, in turn, reinforce the church's fellowship. As the older women cheerfully and consciously maintain Primitive Baptist traditions of hospitality, they encourage and inspire their own daughters and other young women in the church.

Seeing how women function as mediators is more difficult. Prayer, which would be the most visible form of mediation, is a private and personal activity for women, not open to observation. But even if it were, the question of what gives these "mothers in Israel" special mediating power would still remain. Clearly, at the human level, men and women alike are sinful and unworthy in Primitive Baptist eyes. Even much-loved mothers are not the perfect creatures a child might want. For women to function effectively as mediators, therefore, they must be conceptualized in some way that moves beyond their human frailties. And there is some evidence that the woman, traditionally a symbolic figure for the Christian church, remains a powerful symbol for Primitive Baptists. In its most indirect form, this symbolic evidence occurs as gender references in the feminine pronouns used in Primitive Baptist hymn texts and sermons.

Apparently deriving their language from the King James translation of the Bible, hymn writers used and Primitive Baptists have retained feminine pronouns to assign gender to some words that we may no longer think of as feminine. Not only do *earth* and *nature* take on a familiar feminine gender in these hymn texts, but so do *moon, hand, soul, love, mercy, faith, conscience, reason, Zion,* and *church.* Some of these associations are simply suggestive. The concept of soul as feminine, for instance, is loosely supported in hymn texts. Out of numerous references to the soul, only a few assign to it any gender at all:

> (1) My soul stands trembling while she sings
>   The honors of her God. (Hymn 3)
> (2) My favored soul shall meekly learn
>   To lay her reason at thy throne. (Hymn 5)
> (3) My willing soul would stay . . .
>   And sit and sing herself away. (Hymn 49)
> (4) My soul looks back to see . . .
>   And hopes her guilt was there. (Hymn 64)

Primitive Baptists, in interviews and conversations, do not suggest that the concept of soul is necessarily feminine, but neither do they exclude the possibility. Mercy and wisdom likewise have tentative gender associations in both hymn and biblical texts used by Primitive Baptists. An elder alluded to the feminine nature of mercy in an interview when he was asked, "Which [hymns] do you think speak the experience most truly?" He noted that there are "a whole lot of them" and then read the full text of one he thought fit his experience pretty well, which included the following lines:

> And Mercy's angel-form appeared;
> She led me on with gentle pace. (Hymn 199)

This same elder discussed "one of the most glorious times" he experienced in the pulpit. He could not recall what he said, but remembered his text clearly: "Wisdom hath builded her house, she has hewn out her seven pillars, she's killed her beast, she's mingled her wines, she's furnished her table."

Although none of the several hymn texts that mention wisdom assign to it any gender identity, one text does speak of a role for wisdom that, among Primitive Baptists, is clearly feminine.

> Come all ye hungry starving souls,
>   That feed upon the wind,
> And vainly strive with earthly toys
>   To fill an empty mind.
>
> Eternal wisdom has prepared
>   A soul-reviving feast,
> And bid your longing appetites
>   The rich provision taste. (Hymn 122)

Any tentativeness in gender associations rapidly diminishes when the language shifts to images of the church, however. Here the identification with the feminine becomes strong and pervasive. For example, Zion, the city of God and church of the heavenly world, is feminine according to hymn texts, Scriptures, and sermons. At least one hymn about Zion, "Glorious things of thee are spoken," is a congregational favorite. Preachers reinforce the female metaphor in their sermons. In his explication of such a scripture, an elder draws together past and present, earthly world and heavenly world, reminding his congregation once more of Zion's meaning for them:

> This particular spot was in the southwestern part of Jerusalem, Zion . . . and David the king took possession, and actually lived there himself . . . but in spite of David's, you might say prestige, or wanting to be honored by having it named after him, the "City of David," — the word Zion, the old poets, the songs we sing here [at church] many times, the Old Testament writers — seemed like Zion somehow held on. . . . And so it describes here . . . a type of sacred capitol. . . . She's the city of the great king. . . . She's exalted there, the house of God."

But it is in the self-image of the local church network that the most pervasive feminine identification appears. In identifying the church as feminine, Primitive Baptists are not unique. They share this traditional image and the hymns that stress the image with many churches. One widely sung hymn, for example, begins, "I love thy church, O God," and continues through lines such as:

> Her walls before thee stand . . .
> For her my tears shall fall;
>   For her my prayers ascend;
> To her my cares and toils be giv'n . . .
>   I prize her heav'nly ways;

Her sweet communion, solemn vows,
    Her hymns of love and praise. (Hymn 266)

If Primitive Baptists are not unique in identifying the church as feminine, they do appear to be unique in the strength with which men in particular weight the identity of the church as feminine. This identity is reinforced not only in hymns, but also in daily language, Scripture, sermons, and narratives of personal experience.

Virtually all lay members and elders talk informally about their "sister" churches, at once revealing and underlining their strong sense of the church here in this world as feminine. Elders strengthen the identity by consistently using feminine pronouns when paraphrasing and explicating Scriptures that refer to the church, such as the following interpretation of a passage from chapter 16 of the book of Ezekiel:

"And I saw thee polluted in thine own blood, and I said unto thee . . . 'Live.' And he placed a skirt on her and washed her." There's a mutual love here between Christ and his church. He condescended because of God's eternal love for her.

Another preacher wove an account of his experience of seeing the church for the first time into his sermon:

I can remember . . . sitting in that church pew one day as a little child, and that preacher began to preach about the church and about this woman and the jewel that was in her forehead and all those things. And I believe — I'm serious beloved, I'm not saying this to boast — if I hadn't restrained my very little frame, I'd a leaped through that building. From that day forward, I'll tell you this, there was nothing the same about the church. Because then, I could see her, high and lifted up, above the things of this earth.

The bride, another traditional Christian symbol of the church, expands the feminine image. One hymn contains a single direct reference to the church as bride:

Then, in his love and his decrees,
    Christ and his bride appeared as one,
Her sin, by imputation, his,
    Whilst she in spotless splendor shone. (Hymn 244)

Another hymn supports the bride image by referring to Christ as "bridegroom of your souls." Again, a symbol which is shared by many churches appears to be unusually active in the thought and experience of Primitive Baptists. One elder, for example, chose to refer to the church as bride in an original poem that, in part, reads as follows:

> Then out of Adam's poor fallen race
> The Father gave his son a bride
> He promised to save her by his grace
> He then agreed for her to die.
>
> He found her polluted in her own blood
> In the ruins of the fall did lay,
> He raised her up from where she fell,
> By his loving hand was raised to stay.[3]

During an interview, another elder told about receiving the image of the church as bride in a dream: "I had a dream or a vision one night and I saw the most beautiful woman that I've ever saw. She was up in the sky, just up above the earth. I thought she was dressed like a bride adorned for her husband. I think the Lord revealed that to me, that that was his church, she's above the world, she's not of the world."

More surprising is yet another elder's acount of seeing the church for the first time in which he not only uses the bride as a symbol of the church, but also acknowledges that, doctrinally speaking, he has a husband: "I remember the first time that I saw the church, the bride of Christ. And the most beautiful bride—one of the most beautiful women that I ever looked upon or ever expect to look upon. At that time I didn't even know I had a husband. Brethren, we have a husband—the Lord Jesus Christ. He's the husband of the bride. And how wonderful to look upon these things."

In these comments and personal experience narratives, Primitive Baptist elders reveal to their congregation the extraordinary power with which traditional symbols of the church act in their lives. This elevation of feminine images operates freely alongside, and in sharp contrast to, the restriction on women's roles in the church. Often, however, only the restrictions are visible to an outside observer who may simply see women in this church as inappropriately submissive. Primitive Baptist women then appear to be unduly bound by religious traditions that require them to sit separately from the men, to serve the church in the traditional womanly activities of cooking and cleaning, and to keep silence in the church—recipients of scriptural exegesis but never themselves allowed to interpret Scripture publicly or to preach or to hold any prominent leadership roles. Primitive Baptist women are conscious of being seen in this limited way.

Nevertheless, this is not how these women see themselves, and it is not how they experience their church. The Primitive Baptist woman typically finds in her church a scripturally-grounded religion, replete with human imperfections but firm and predictable in doctrines, and practices that are compatible with her interpretation of the Bible and with her religious beliefs. She has often looked for a church home in other denominations, but the Primitive Baptist church is the one that best satisfies her. Where formal structures are restrictive, she sees and uses informal channels to exert her influence and thus avoids a sense of powerlessness. Through listening to the Scriptures and sermons, singing the hymns of the church, and grounding her actions in her own religious beliefs and experience, a Primitive Baptist woman realizes her power to affect the course of church life and fellowship. She is modest, but sees a vital place for women in the church and finds significance and meaning in those activities that nurture her church family. In turn, she feels supported by the church. Although she may criticize the preacher in her protectiveness of church doctrine, she listens attentively as he reminds her and the rest of his congregation that women are not just a part of the church but are, in fact, a type of the church. She hears the language of the Bible carried over into the expression of the church and translated into the experience of the church, and it becomes a powerful affirmation of the female as the chosen and beloved. Even the existence of the Bible itself can be a reminder of this care, according to one elder, who says, "I call it a love letter—from Jesus to his bride."

NOTES

This paper is based on team fieldwork carried out by the author with James L. Peacock, Ruel W. Tyson, Jr., and Daniel W. Patterson, chiefly in the summers of 1980 through 1983, supported by grants from the National Endowment for the Humanities and the Wenner-Gren Foundation. Sound recordings of the singing, services, and interviews have been deposited in the University of North Carolina Library. See the notes for Brett Sutton's essay (chapter 9) for references to key historical studies of Primitive Baptists and to his ethnographic essay for the album, "Primitive Baptist Hymns of the Blue Ridge." Robert Paul Drummond's dissertation *A History of Music Among Primitive Baptists Since 1800* (Greeley, Colo.: Department of Music, University of Northern Colorado, 1986) provides a comprehensive overview of Primitive Baptist singing and hymn books as well as an extensive bibliography of related Primitive Baptist and scholarly publications. Little other substantial scholarship deals with the group. Melanie L. Sovine's "Been a Long Time Travelin': Three Primitive Baptist Women" is an edited radio transcript of recorded interviews, without analysis. Standard works on Appalachian religion give little attention to these churches. I have found provocative, however, the feminist perspective in "Women and Religion," special section in *Signs: Journal of Women in Culture and Society* 9 (Autumn 1983). Of particular pertinence to my essay is Daniel N. Maltz, "The Bride of Christ Is Filled with His Spirit," in Judith Hoch-Smith and Anita Springs, eds., *Women in Ritual and Symbolic Roles* (New York: Plenum Press, 1978), pp. 27–44.

1. June Hawks Goins, *Children of Comfort: A Collection of Poems* (Cincinnati, Ohio: Baptist Bible Hour, 1968), p. 7.

2. D. H. Goble, *Primitive Baptist Hymn Book for All Lovers of Sacred Song* (Greenfield, Ind.: D. H. Goble Printing, 1887; still in print).

3. From an unpublished poem written by a Primitive Baptist elder whom I interviewed.

The Devil Sits in the Choir   4

John Forrest

Potuck Missionary Baptist Church, founded in 1893, has 151 registered mem-
bers — nearly half the white population of the town — though a much smaller active
membership. A Methodist and a Disciples of Christ Church in the town have
been defunct for several decades. The 100 blacks in the community are served
by an A.M.E. Zion church. One of numerous congregations in eastern North
Carolina affiliated with the Southern Baptist Convention, Potuck Missionary
Baptist Church has nevertheless frequently been at odds with the Convention on
doctrine or on policies like racial integration. It is very largely an autonomous body.

It is a truism that the church in the South is a force for social unity.
Yet this apparently simple, easily comprehended social fact is actually
complex and frequently misunderstood. Often it is conflict within a
church that itself creates social cohesion, and the aesthetic expressions
of a church, the enactment of its unity, may both promote and resolve
this conflict. An illustrative case is a schism in the membership of
Potuck Missionary Baptist Church, which began ostensibly because
of the quality of the singing in the choir but rapidly spread to a number
of other issues.

The town for which the church is named is a small, predominantly
white community in the southern reaches of the Great Dismal Swamp
in northeastern North Carolina. The town's economy rests very heavily
on family farming and freshwater fishing. The whole region is exclusively rural: there are no incorporated towns in the county, and there
is not a single stop light in the entire county. The Potuck Missionary
Baptist Church, granted a charter in 1893, began with a membership

of only eighteen people (nine married couples). The families of these founder members still form the core of the church. When it was constructed the church building was a simple edifice. The land was donated by the local doctor, who was the prime mover in organizing the church in the first place. Materials and labor were contributed by local people. Wood for the frame came from logs cut from the swamp, and rip cut and dressed at a local sawmill. The interior of the sanctuary was designed by an itinerant boat builder and consists of a lathlike paneling on walls and ceiling stained and finished with hard oil (a special palm oil used on boats). The members particularly like the look of the interior of the church and are proud of the fact that it has never been refinished yet retains its original lustre. The original floor was made from roughly hewn boards sawed from drift lumber salvaged from a nearby canal.

The first furniture was handmade by local craftsmen. The pulpit, which is a simple Bible stand, was made by the local blacksmith, and the pews by various members. At the outset pulpit and pews constituted the total inventory of furniture in the church. The church was, and is, largely without ornamentation on the interior. The pews were severely functional with no beads or molding. Only the pulpit was carved.

Only one major alteration has been made to the church interior. In the early 1950s a regular choir was formed. They originally sat and sang from a special area on the preacher's left, but soon found this arrangement unsatisfactory. Thus a choir loft was built for them. This was effected by moving the pulpit away from the back wall, fitting a tier of benches behind it, and enclosing the benches with a guard rail.

From its founding until the late 1950s the church was on a circuit because it had insufficient income to support a full-time preacher. For most of this time there were four churches on the circuit, and Potuck had services on one morning and one evening per month. While the church was on this circuit there was no serious upheaval among the membership. However, since having a full-time preacher, the church has gone through a number of crises, usually involving the preacher as a prime mover or as a leading figure on one side of the dispute.

Wherever dissension may start in the church, it always comes to a head at business meetings, and one way or another, it is resolved there. According to the rules of discipline of the church a business meeting must be held every quarter. Extraordinary meetings may also be held if there is pressing business to be discussed. For the most part these meetings are uneventful, with little more than a quorum (seven) present. Matters discussed are generally uncontroversial, and even though there are members noted for their ability to talk at length on any issue, there is little debate. Such matters include the dates for the annual chicken supper and revival, choice of preacher for the revival, and the like. Issues that require planning or multiple decisions are handed over to ad hoc or standing committees for investigation or for implementation. In the case of an investigation, the committee reports back to the full body for a decision to be made. The standing committees also handle the day-to-day business of the church, such as maintaining the property, paying bills, and so forth. This means that the bulk of the secular business of the church is handled in committee, and in reality, most of the decisions are made there too because in the great majority of cases the congregation accepts the recommendations of the committees. This is not to say that all business meetings are pro forma. The church may, in the end, accept the decisions of committees, but there is sometimes a considerable amount of discussion concerning the implications of the decisions and about the precise wording of the matter to be voted on. In all of these dealings strict parliamentary procedure is followed.

The meetings, which are usually held on a Wednesday evening at 8 p.m., open with a hymn or Scripture reading, followed by a short prayer. The hymns and readings are mostly concerned with unity, but the preacher may read something of seasonal interest if he feels so inclined. One of the most commonly used hymns opens:

> Blest be the tie that binds
> Our hearts in Christian love;
> The fellowship of kindred minds
> Is like to that above.

The minutes of the previous meeting are read, amended if necessary, and approved. The business of the day is then conducted, and the meeting closes with a prayer of dismissal. When there is nothing of any great moment to be discussed, the whole meeting can be concluded within thirty minutes.

When radical disagreements arise in the church, the members first try to resolve the conflict through open debate. When this does not work, one side will try to outmaneuver the other using the committee structure of the church or manipulation of parliamentary procedure. For example, in 1962 it was unanimously decided to replace the old handmade pews, but there was disagreement as to what would go in their place. The preacher wanted to paint the stained paneling white and purchase pews with white ends, to brighten up the sanctuary. The idea of painting the walls was met with utter coldness from the members and displayed a startling failure on the preacher's part to understand the aesthetic values of the local people. However, his choice of pews was favored by a significant minority and informal debate on the issue stretched over several months. At the first business meeting at which the pews were discussed the white-ended ones were eliminated from further discussion by a narrow margin. At the next meeting this motion was rescinded, again by a narrow margin. Finally a resolution was passed to hand the matter over to an ad hoc committee for a decision and implementation of it. This was a coup for the opponents of the white-ended pews, although this was not readily apparent. Committees are always chosen from a coterie of established members of the church who are considered to be hard workers and to have the best interests of the church at heart. Normally they can be relied upon to give every point of view a fair hearing. However, in this case all of the members of the coterie were opposed to the white-ended pews and immediately dropped them from consideration. The pews they chose were plain oak, very much like the older ones.

In this case major conflict was diverted by skillful manipulation of the system. Proponents of the white-ended pews felt that they had been given a fair hearing (even though they had not), and opponents got their own way without appearing to be domineering. The only person who fared badly was the preacher, who was forced to resign shortly thereafter. Sometimes, however, feelings over an issue run too high to be soothed by subtle tactics. A disagreement concerning the choir and a different preacher turned into an open and hostile feud between rival factions.

The regular choir was established in the early 1950s by a trained musician who, as it happens, was a member of the family that helped found the church and gave the land on which the building was erected.

She taught the choir to sing in a controlled manner, with particular emphasis on clear enunciation and on singing softly and sweetly. However, after about ten years she became ill and another director was chosen to substitute until she was well enough to continue. The new director favored music of the Pentecostal or camp-meeting style, that is, songs with an antiphonal verse and chorus sung raucously. At about the same time a new preacher was hired, who coincidentally preferred camp-meeting music.

With the new preacher and the new music director working together, the music of the church was altered to that of the style of the camp meeting over the period of a year. This caused an undercurrent of dissent, although few openly complained. The older choir members gradually stopped singing in the choir, and volunteers who preferred the latest developments filled their places. After the end of another year dissension was so strong that the preacher decided to preach a sermon on church music entitled "World Upside-Down." He even went to the extent of printing up the text of the sermon and distributing it to all church members. The following is taken from one of these printed texts, which is bound with the church records:

> The present lack of co-operation that is giving the Church much concern is that of the music program of our church. With all Godly and due respect to all persons of our Church, only lately have we had a leader for our music program who participates in the full program of our church. This is as it should be, but it seems that many of the choir members who co-operated at least half-heartedly before do not seem to want to co-operate at all now. It falls out that we have a relatively new choir of volunteers at this point. Praise the Lord for that! I don't see anyone "Taking over" the music program of the Church. I see a worker, working and inspiring others to take part in the wonderful ministry of singing the gospel.
>
> Some do not like the style of the music used lately. Keep in mind, there are those who would not like mine or yours either. We all have individual tastes for music developed over the years. And this being true, we need to have respect for the styles of others as well as our own.
>
> Some do not like the quality of the music presentation. There are those who desire and require "Note Perfect music" for our Church. Also a choir of "Trained Voices" to sing.
>
> I'm sorry. This is not a Conservatory.
>
> This is a CHURCH

Psalm 66:1&2 reads: "Make a Joyful Noise unto God, all ye lands: Sing forth the honor of His name; make His praise Glorious."
Did the psalmist say: "All ye trained choirs."
No. He said, "All ye lands."
As important as musical quality is (because shoddy music is not a good offering to the Lord) SPIRITUAL QUALITY is still and ever will be most important in the Church.

Then let the choir consist of those who are willing to make their "Joyful Noises unto the Lord." Let the choir consist of every one who prays earnestly to be used to sing the Gospel.

The best choir member is not necessarily the best trained voice but the *best trained Soul,* singing the very best he or she can.

In the course of the sermon the preacher referred to the missions of Paul and Barnabas. He suggested that the Jews, especially of Thessalonica, were outraged at Pauline teaching, not because of its moral content, but because it radically conflicted with the teachings of "their fathers." But, the preacher suggested, Christians must not be bound by tradition, but must do what is morally right. He illustrated this point by referring to a part of the Potuck Baptist Church covenant where it is stated that the members are not opposed to the *temperate* use of alcohol. (Baptists in the United States are opposed to *any* consumption of alcohol, and standard church covenants express this fact unequivocally.) He suggested that the members were blindly following the lead of their "fathers" rather than doing what they knew was morally right. As such they were just like the Jews of Thessalonica.

Needless to say, this sermon raised a furor in the church. In the first place the members do not like being taken to task, whatever the cause. In this case the preacher had offended two powerful groups. He had injured the pride of the original choir director, the organists whom she had trained, and the members of the original choir. He had also struck out at the families of the founder members, many of whom were influential members of the church.

What had begun as a defense of the new choir quickly turned into a vehement attack on the use of alcohol and on all of those members who condoned drinking. The preacher launched a crusade to change the wording of the covenant. He preached three sermons on the nature of covenants in general and on that of the Potuck Baptist Church in particular, and he distributed copies of the sermons to the members.

His ultimate aim was to send a referendum form to all the members asking whether they wished the covenant to remain the same, or whether they wanted it changed so that it explicitly forbade the use of alcohol as a beverage. This referendum was to be presented at the next business meeting, and the sermons were designed to sway opinion. However, opinion in the church had already been polarized over his stand on church music, and the same sides remained drawn up for and against the preacher on the alcohol issue.

The preacher's draft for the referendum was presented for discussion at a regular business meeting. There was a heated debate on the issue, but when it was clear that the tide was turning against the preacher, members voted to table the motion to try to salvage some unity out of the meeting. It was felt that if the discussion continued, there would be a serious split in the church. Most opponents of change thought that tabling the motion would quietly settle the issue, but three months later, at the next business meeting, both the referendum and the question of who was to be the permanent choir director were brought to the floor. Only fifteen members were present, none of whom was fully conversant with parliamentary procedure. By the end of the meeting two motions had passed. The first (nine votes for, six against) changed the wording of the covenant, and the second called for the reconstituting of the nominating committee to select nominees for permanent choir director. As it happens, in the matter of the covenant parliamentary procedure was not followed. The motion to change the covenant had been voted on without first removing it from the table. Therefore the vote was invalid. The recording secretary, who was opposed to the change, realized after the vote was taken that proper procedure had not been followed and so made sure that the minutes were accurate and detailed. The next day when the parliamentarian among the opponents learned of the vote, he went to the preacher with the minutes and explained that the changes that he desired could not be effected.

A special meeting was called a week later to resolve the question. This time the opponents of change packed the meeting and quickly voted against removing the motion from the table (sixteen votes for, twenty against). At this point the major proponents of the change left the meeting. Next the nominating committee gave its recommendation that the original choir director be responsible for music and choir practice on the first and second Sundays in the month, and that the temporary director be responsible for the third and fourth Sundays. A third organist would take care of fifth Sundays when they occurred. One member, the husband of one of the substitute organists trained by the original director, moved that the suggestion of the nominating committee be put aside and that the church choose a permanent full-time music director. The committee's suggestion was designed to pour oil on troubled waters, but because the supporters of the camp-meeting style of music had all left the meeting, there appeared to be no reason for compromise. Consequently the motion was accepted and the original choir director was nominated for the position. She was accepted without dissent.

After this meeting the vocal supporters of the preacher joined churches in nearby towns, and three months later the preacher resigned. The choir, under the tutelage of the original director, returned to its old style of singing, and those members who had left in protest of the camp-meeting music quickly came back.

When the major events of this schism are generalized, a clearer and richer picture of what happened emerges. The lines in the dispute were clear cut and the membership was completely polarized. One side consisted of the members of the original choir and the members of the founding families. They not only formed a simple majority of the membership but also held all of the principal offices in the church. The other side was made up of the preacher, the new choir members, and members of families that did not live in Potuck when the church was founded. It should come as no surprise that the factions in the issue of the pews were fundamentally the same (even though the preachers were different men) and that other disputes have involved the same personnel on the same sides. Even though there is no evidence that the inevitable losers, that is, the preacher's side, harbored grudges about their losses in past disputes, it is equally clear that the schism over the choir and the covenant was the culmination of a long-standing ideological division in the church community.

The division in the membership can be characterized in a number of ways. The most all-embracing labels, though, for the two parties are the "outsiders" (the preacher and his followers) and the "insiders." The outsiders are so named because they are relative newcomers to the town, because they do not hold powerful offices in the church, and because they are not consistently involved in church activities. This is as true of the preacher as it is of other outsider members. That he counts for but a single vote at times of decision making is patent in the following story told to me by an insider: "We had some problems when we put the air conditioning in. The contractor he made such a mess of it. And he came here to be paid, and several of the members told me not to pay him until he got it right. So he came and he got so mad with me 'cause I wouldn't pay him. He said, 'Well, I'll go see the preacher.' I said, 'Go right ahead. He's got no authority whatsoever.'" Most preachers do not even participate in general church activities, such as fund-raising events, because they do not believe in them. They feel that were the members to tithe, there would be adequate funds for all reasonable ventures.

The dispute over the choir music made the social and political division between the insiders and outsiders patent, and for that reason alone it was extremely troubling to the members. After all they are as convinced as any social scientist that the church is a force for unity. When this apparently axiomatic fact is called into question, the profoundest principles of the church are attacked. In response to my question "Why do people go to church?" informants replied "for fellowship" or "because if you take away the church you take away morality." The latter answer was very common and was the reasoning behind such statements as "There'd be more order in schools if you put Christianity in the curriculum," and "Kids that take drugs and steal were never sent to church." I take these statements to imply that they believe that humans are by nature disorderly and that it is the church which acts as a force to organize them. The business meetings start with the hymn "Blest Be The Tie" to remind members that the "fellowship of kindred minds" is the model of Christian behavior. To be a force for order and unity, the church should presumably be orderly and unified itself. Yet it clearly is not, and excuses and solutions have to be found.

The simplest remedy for dissent in the church is to fire the preacher. He represents the outsiders both as an advocate and as a symbol. Firing him is always the last act in the course of a problem that has divided the members and is taken by both sides in the dispute to symbolize the end of disharmony and a desire to be unified. Yet the differences between the two sides do not evanesce because of this act. In fact they will probably never vanish. The founding families always seek to maintain the status quo because their claims to power rest solely on tradition. That is, they are powerful because their parents and grandparents were powerful. The outsiders seek to change the status quo because they can never gain power under the old order.

The simple cycle of harmony and schism at the Potuck Missionary Baptist Church might have gone on for a long time were it not that the choir became a major feature in the conflict. It is commonly said in the church that "the devil sits in the choir," meaning that the choir is a breeding ground for dissent and a mighty foe when roused. The choir is a powerful force for a number of reasons. First, it was formed and trained by a member of the principal founding family. Second, belonging to the choir is a significant commitment to the church. It involves giving up one night per week to practice, and it means attending church regularly, as well as attending all of the special services that require a choir. Third, the members are *seen* to be working for the church. Weekly they are on display in front of the whole congregation. This commitment can also be seen in another way. On the Wednesday night of the annual revival that I observed, a choir of adolescents sang in place of the regular choir. After they had sung their special music, the revival preacher had them leave the choir loft and sit in the front row of the church. He then directed his entire sermon at them and urged them to come forward to be baptized. That is, they were the most likely candidates for conversion because they had already shown a measure of loyalty to the church inasmuch as they were willing to form a youth choir. Fourth, choral music is important for the structuring of all church services. Regular services, for example, begin with a sung call to worship and end with a sung response to the benediction. These choral pieces not only signal the temporal boundaries of especially sacred time, but also define appropriate behavior. The words of the call to worship are taken from Habakkuk 2:20: "The Lord is in his holy temple: let all the earth keep silence before him."

The real paradox is that while choir members are evidently strong workers for the church whose avowed aim is unity and harmony, they are also most likely to stir up trouble. One explanation for this paradox is that unity is only an avowed end and that the members enjoy a certain amount of strife and rancor. Another explanation is that they are a constant threat, and so the rest of the church tries to maintain an air of peace and tranquility. Thus they work for order through negative reinforcement. It is certainly true that the choir is treated extremely circumspectly by all other church members. The special choral music is always praised lavishly, and no one ever openly criticizes choir members. During the schism the preacher bluntly attacked the musical output of the choir and accused the choir members of working only "half-heartedly" at the best of times. This stung them deeply and set in motion a battle that could not end simply with the preacher packing his bags. Greater damage had to be inflicted on the opposition, to keep it in its place and to assert the power of tradition. Thus their choir director was fired and forced out of the church, and many of her followers were forced out with her.

At heart, then, the harmony and unity that exist at Potuck Missionary Baptist Church are created out of a cyclic tension between the forces of tradition (insiders), on the one hand, and of innovation (outsiders), on the other. The values of the insiders are essentially conservative because they have something to conserve. The outsiders are on the side of change because they have nothing to gain by being conservative and nothing to lose by promoting change. That is, they have no political power to gamble with, but by attempting to bring about a new order they might possibly gain some by being in the vanguard of the movement. Consequently, the insiders favored a general aesthetic continuity when the pews were replaced, while the outsiders sought a break with the past. The insiders preferred the old soft music, and the outsiders liked a raucous style new to the church at Potuck, however old it may be elsewhere in the South.

Tradition within the church is maintained in several ways. The old families hold a simple majority, so that if democratic principles are used they always win. To ensure that democracy prevails, they keep themselves versed in parliamentary procedures and insist on their strict enforcement. Furthermore, they control all of the key political offices (secretary, treasurer, Sunday school president, deacons) so that there can never be an effective challenge to the parliamentary way.

When a battle is brewing the insiders can muster sheer numbers by virtue of their deep kin ties in the community. Over half of the church members are related to the founding families, and most of them can claim kinship to each other by blood or by marriage. These families also own almost all of the land in Potuck and considerable tracts elsewhere in the county. The outsiders are not related to the key families, nor are they related to each other. For the most part they rent their houses and land from insiders. Thus they cannot readily marshal support for democratic attacks on the opposition and must employ other tactics. Their choice tends to be to take a moral stance. In a way they try to be better Baptists than the insiders by invoking the spirit of revival with its attendant desire to throw over complacency and tradition and to replace them with moral fervor. Theologically such a position is difficult to challenge, but the insiders do not meet it with theological arguments. In fact they are not disposed to argue at all, and when their hand is forced they call for a vote.

Unity in the church at Potuck has to be striven for regularly and is sometimes wrought at great price. It is a unity that is created out of tension and dissension. Ironically, also, it is a unity that is created at the expense of established Christian values. Challenges to unity take the form of innovation in the guise of moral rectitude, but unity is preserved by purging the church of such forces. Therefore, unity is not equivalent to stability. There are cycles of tension and repose, with the forces of change testing and thereby strengthening the forces of tradition. Thus, unwittingly, the outsiders who seek to turn the world upside-down help to keep it right-side up.

NOTES

The fieldwork for this essay was conducted between February and December 1978 and formed the basis of my doctoral dissertation, *Sights of the Sound: An Ethnography of an Aesthetic Community* (Chapel Hill: Department of Anthropology, University of North Carolina, 1980). Influential upon my seeking the cultural functions of aesthetic forms were Conrad M. Arensberg and Solon T. Kimball, *Culture and Community* (New York: Harcourt, Brace and World, 1965) and Robert P. Armstrong, *The Affecting Presence: An Essay in Humanistic Anthropology* (Urbana: University of Illinois Press, 1971). Useful background on the aesthetics of rural churches in the state appears in Eliza Davidson's "North Carolina Country Churches: Explorations in the Mountains and the Tidewater," in Doug Swaim, ed., *Carolina Dwelling: Towards Preservation of Place: In Celebration of the North Carolina Vernacular Landscape,* Student Publication of the School of Design, vol. 26 (Raleigh: North Carolina State University, 1978).

"Going Up to Meet Him": Songs and Ceremonies of a Black Family's Ascent

Daniel W. Patterson

Black gospel song is an interdenominational movement. Music that has developed in the tradition is performed in black religious services, but much of its activity takes place in religious concerts held in churches, school and municipal auditoriums, and community centers. Its stars become nationally known recording artists, but the movement rests on the base of extremely active local music making in virtually all communities with a strong black presence. A community as small as Creedmoor, North Carolina, will have five or more groups that perform weekly. One branch of the movement with a distinctive history is the male gospel quartet. A fusion of barbershop-quartet singing with religious song, quartet singing came into its own in the 1940s, from which time it has evolved from unaccompanied "jubilee" singing, through performances with acoustic guitar, to performances by groups that may have six singers, with electric guitars, percussion, and even electronic keyboard instruments.

For the sultry fourth Sunday evening of every August, the Golden Echoes—an amateur male black gospel quartet—will book the auditorium of an elementary school just outside the small North Carolina town of Creedmoor. This is the night of the Echoes' anniversary concert, an occasion to which the Golden Echoes give careful thought and planning. The members must invite a popular and well-spoken figure—usually the D.J. of a gospel radio station— to serve as master of ceremonies. They must invite four or five other singing groups to appear on the program, and these they select with care to keep old friendships intact and to meet standing obligations, while at the same time drawing in the followings of groups from a ring of nearby towns and cities: Roxboro, Hillsborough, Durham, Raleigh, Louisburg, or Wake Forest. They must see that large yellow, black, and white posters describing the concert get printed and tacked to telephone poles at crossroads and street corners. They must have the concert announced at church services throughout the region. They must sell tickets to family and friends. They must arrange for soft drinks and get members of their families to act as vendors and ticket takers. They must have folding chairs set up for the audience on the floor of the basketball court that doubles as the school auditorium. They must arrive early to set up their own sound equipment and to help other groups install sound systems they may have brought.

The concert will begin around 6:30 p.m. and lasts until nearly midnight, and the Golden Echoes schedule themselves to appear between eight and nine — prime time, after the audience has fully gathered and been warmed up by other groups but before the departure of those with weary children or early-morning jobs. At the close of the evening the Echoes will go to the home of their leader to settle financial accounts and to celebrate the success of the evening.

The members of the Golden Echoes, in short, go to considerable effort to organize a concert in their own honor, they star in it, and they keep most of the proceeds of the gate. Some might believe the occasion to be inspired by vanity or by a desire for gain. But the ticket sales for an audience of five hundred or so will hardly compensate the singers for the time, labor, and expense required to mount a concert. They have printing bills, and fees to pay to the school for electricity and janitorial service, telephone and travel costs, and honoraria to give to the other participating groups, and expenditures for new clothing — all to come from a gate of about $1,500. And while they enjoy performing in public as much as other gifted musicians do, their commitment to the concerts has survived a quarter of a century and a number of changes of personnel. Even more important, the support of their audiences has never flagged during this period. Despite the ease with which their friends could now find television entertainment at home or motor to Durham for a movie, they still choose to pay to hear the anniversary concert. And not merely to come, but to give the Golden Echoes a standing ovation when they enter the hall for their turn in the program and to rise again to their feet, clapping in time with the music, when the Echoes sing one of their more stirring

92

numbers, "Trouble of this World" or "Going Up to Meet Him in the Air."[1] Clearly, neither hope of profit nor egotism can explain why the Echoes' audience sustains the group in this ceremony. It has deep meaning for them, as it does for the singers.

The most apparent meaning is of course religious. The Golden Echoes' anniversary concert is a religious songfest. An invited minister opens the program with a prayer. All the music performed is religious — either hymns, spirituals, or gospel songs. Some women in the audience grow so deeply moved by a song that they "shout." The performers intermix brief testimonies with their songs, and occasionally a singer who has recently gone through a spiritual crisis will also be moved to exhort vigorously, to shout, and even to leave the stage overcome. With an occasional rare exception the singers also try to "live the life they sing about." The members of the Golden Echoes are active members of local churches, and several are ordained deacons. They will in fact play only sacred music, and they see their performances as spreading the gospel. The song texts bear them out:

> One day, I said, I'm going where my Jesus is,
> One day, I said, I'm going where my Jesus is,
> One day, I tell you, I'm going where my Jesus is,
> Ah, I'm going up to meet him in the air.

> Oh, bye and bye, said, I'm going on a chariot ride,
> Oh, bye and bye, said, I'm going on a chariot ride,
> Oh, bye and bye, said, I'm going on a chariot ride,
> I'm going up to meet him in the air.

> Jesus, how you saved my soul one day,
> Jesus, how you saved my soul one day,
> Jesus, I never will forget it how you saved my soul one day,
> Oh, I'm going up to meet him in the air.

Nevertheless, the concerts are not denominational, and one interviewer a dozen years ago was struck by the absence of dogma in the religious professions of the members of the Golden Echoes. The only definition they gave him of being a true Christian was "trying to do the right thing."[2] In concert one or two of their members give testimonial introductions to the songs, but these are sincere and modest rather than evangelistic. Their testimony comes not in the spoken word but in the song performance itself.

93

The testimony delivered in song, however, seems both religious and something more than religious. The additional meanings began to suggest themselves at one of the Golden Echoes' periodic rehearsals at the home of the leader, "Big John" Landis. The men were practicing "Going Up to Meet Him," which John Landis heard in church as a child and recently revived for the group. It is one of a large number of black spirituals in their repertory, all of them learned traditionally, by ear, as no one in the group reads music. Their musical performance pointed to an even older stream of black singing. "One day," sang John Landis, and the three back-up voices answered, overlapping his last note, "One day." "One day," he sang again, and they answered him again, "One day." "Said, I'm," he sang, and they joined in for the remainder of the line, "going where my Jesus is." The form was call and response, and one pattern or another of responsorial singing appeared in virtually every other piece the Echoes practiced. As the men sang "One day," they also clapped — on the upbeat. And behind them a young percussion player thumped his bass drum and ran intricate rhythms over his snare drum and cymbal. All three of these stylistic features — the responsorial singing, offbeat accenting, and cultivation of rhythmically complex percussion — showed the music to be rooted in West African traditions. Listening to the Golden Echoes rehearse, then, one heard a Christian message, but its medium was the language of the black ethnic heritage, with all its wealth of felt associations.

At the same time, the men sang in harmonic patterns derived ultimately from conventional church hymnody, and the drummer played a factory-made percussion set. The two guitarists had electric instruments. The singers had four microphones. The drummer listened to the singers over a monitor. An amplifier and a mixer and a set of large speakers completed the equipment. In the confines of the chamber the volume of the music was overpowering. Doubtless every neighbor could enjoy the music — and also get the message that the Echoes possessed a large set of electronic instruments over which they had full mastery.

This happy marriage of traditional music and technological modernity had a striking parallel in the setting within which the Echoes were rehearsing. The room was the two-car garage at the rear of John Landis's home. The automobiles had cleared way for the instruments,

which now filled much of the space. But the garage was neatly finished
and decorated. On the rear walls hung two store-bought pictures
vividly printed on black cloth. One showed a woodland scene and
game birds and the other a group of dogs, some wearing hats and
smoking cigars, who were playing pool. These marked the garage as
a male recreational area. But in addition the garage had more significant appointments. Hanging along the three walls were a crosscut
saw, a single tree, a horse collar made into a mirror frame, and an
assortment of other farming tools, all decoratively arranged. Juxtaposed to these were two air conditioners, two refrigerators, and a push-
button-operated garage door. As in the music, past and present stood
not in confrontation but in combination. The implements and the
music seemed to symbolize continuation, roots nourishing distant
branches.

The same meaning seemed replicated in the larger setting within
which this rehearsal took place. The garage is in the rear of John
Landis's home, a neat brick one-story house with white trim, standing
in a large well-kept lawn. A quarter of a mile west down the country
road stands another neat brick house in another well-kept lawn beside
a vegetable garden. This is the home of John's brother Claude Landis,
the baritone singer of the Golden Echoes. Midway between the two
homes, an unpaved driveway runs back past the brick home and the
upholstery shop of their sister Priscilla Daniel and past the long yellow
mobile home of her son Kenneth, the lead guitarist of the Golden
Echoes, to a modest white frame house shaded by maples and crepe
myrtles. This is the Landis "home house," where the matriarch of the
family lives, Mrs. Bertha Mangum Landis. This was the heart of the
farm on which the Landis children grew up.

The history of the Landis farm has a bearing on the meaning of
the music of the Golden Echoes. When the children were small Bertha
Landis and her husband were farming as tenants a few miles to the
east. "But I told my husband," she says, "we needed a farm of our
own, with all these boys":

> He'd say, "Well, we can't buy no farm now, 'cause we got so many
> children and trying to send 'em to school." So, one day I was reading
> the paper — I think it was the *News and Observer* from Raleigh — that you
> could buy a farm through the Farm Security Administration, and the
> more children you had, the quicker you could get the farm, or the better

you could get the farm. I told him, I said, "We can put our application in." So we went and put our application in, and we passed. Out of ten, it was six whites and four blacks, and we were one of the blacks that passed. But when they come down to the house to interview us, they had to take an inventory of everything we had, and I had a whole lot of canned fruit upstairs, a big circle of it, and they went and took an inventory of everything we had, and went back. And we didn't hear no more from 'em for a month, and when we heard from 'em, we passed. That was 1939.

Mr. Landis was a skillful farmer and a tireless worker and a disciplinarian. On coming of age, all of his children left the farm in search of a better life in the North or in a local economy that was beginning to expand in the 1950s. Of the members of the Golden Echoes, Claude Landis works with retarded children in a hospital at Butner; John Landis is retired, but on disability from a manufacturing plant where he suffered an injury to one arm; the nephew who plays lead guitar with the Echoes works as senior computer operator at the Liggett and Myers Tobacco Company in Durham. The nephew and his brother, who graduated with a degree in electrical engineering from North Carolina State University, have planned to set up an electronics store in Creedmoor, one of four black-operated businesses in the town. The success of the family members is in part owing, of course, to the general improvement of opportunities for blacks brought about by economic growth in the region and by the civil rights movement. But the Landises' upbringing had equipped them to use their opportunities well. Their parents had taught them initiative, hard work, adaptability, concern for others, cooperativeness, and family loyalty.

As the Golden Echoes rehearsed "Going Up to Meet Him" in John Landis's garage, then, the setting as well as the songs and the performance style seemed to state not only the religious beliefs but also the social achievements of this black family and also its strong awareness of its heritage. This interpretation is in fact corroborated by three celebrations the family enacts each August.

The first of these occasions takes place on the afternoon of the third Saturday: the Landis family picnic. Members gather at the homeplace, some coming from nearby homes and communities, others from as far away as Akron, Ohio, or Bridgeport, Connecticut. Under a large tent set up in the front yard they share a dinner-on-the-ground and much news, reminiscence, and laughter and receive congratulatory visits from old friends. The second event takes place on the following Sunday morning, and here the circle widens. The family members gather at the Rock Spring Baptist Church (which back in the 1940s was the home church of the first black male gospel quartet in the community), together with the members of four other interrelated black families for a joint family reunion service. Founded by Mrs. Landis and her mother-in-law, the reunion was in 1986 meeting for its fifty-second year. This service opens with a small number of women reading Scriptures, offering a prayer, and then attracting the rest of the gathering into the church with their spontaneous singing of, mostly, old spirituals like "Come and Let's Go to That Land." Officers delegated by the families welcome the assembly and recognize guests, the newlyweds and new parents, and the elderly. They conduct a memorial tribute to all members of the families who have died in the preceding year. They read a eulogy of the families. The service does also include a prayer, a short sermon, and a benediction performed by guest preachers, but it is a family-centered service, and it is followed by a picnic lunch served in the church basement and an hour or more of visiting with relatives and old friends. The third event is the Golden Echoes' anniversary concert, held the same night for a still wider community in the auditorium of the neighborhood's predominantly black school. In 1986, this was the twenty-fifth year in which the community had supported this event.

Two statements by John Landis tie these three events together and point up the meanings that accrete to the religious meanings of the songs. One is that the people want to hear familiar songs at the concerts. The Echoes normally work up at least one new piece for each anniversary concert, but the group also tries to meet the demand for old favorites by performing numbers requested by word of mouth before the concert or even honoring requests sent up on slips of paper while the Echoes are on stage. These requests are normally for well-known staples in the Echoes' repertory, like "Trouble of This World." The Echoes find it hard to stir up the audience with a new piece, but audience participation during a familiar and favorite piece is strong.

Those moved by these pieces when sung at the concert or at the reunion service are responding to their Christian message, but this message is also clearly bound up with the community's sense of its identity. The 1982 reunion service for the five families climaxed, significantly, when Claude Landis on a sudden impulse took a microphone and began to sing, "There's a union up in heaven and—", whereupon the congregation burst forth, "I belong"—the opening call and response of an old spiritual that is virtually a theme song of the Landis family. The congregation rose to its feet and erupted into vigorous singing and swaying. One by one the Landis brothers seized a turn at the microphone to sing a stanza of the song, while the others embraced each other, their mother, and other family members, many of them weeping sweet tears:

> Sometimes I'm up, sometimes I'm down—
> I belong to the union band
> Sometimes my soul feels heavenly bound—
> I belong to the union band.

John Landis's second point was that many of the people who attend the anniversary concert come not only to hear the music but also to see the new "uniform" in which the Golden Echoes will appear: "Fifty percent of your singing or how far you'll ever get in singing is the way you dress. They're not curious over who you get [to perform with you on your program], or what's going on in there, or how many songs you're going to sing, or what songs you're going to sing, or whatever. They're curious of what you have on when you come through the door." At other programs in which the men appear virtually every week, they will wear any of their dozens of older outfits, fitting the color and the style to the informality or solemnity of the occasion. But for their anniversary they buy a new set of matching coats, vests, trousers, shirts, ties, stockings, and shoes. They guard the secret of the handsome new uniform until the actual moment of their entry for their section of the program. They will not have revealed the secret even to their wives. They will wear another uniform to the auditorium, changing quickly into the new one just before they come in, like football champions, as the master of ceremonies one by one calls each name. The crowd, standing to give them an ovation, claps and cheers, as each man strides down the aisle and mounts the stage.

Why this unveiling of the uniform was such a peak of the evening for the audience became clear in the family stories of hard times in the thirties and forties. Two of the Landis men tell, for example, of owning but one pair of shoes between them, when they were young children. On Sunday only one of the two could go to church, and the one who stayed home would out of shame lie about why he did not come. "And it wasn't because Mama and Daddy didn't work," says one; "it wasn't because they didn't work like slaves." "Didn't have no money to buy them!" interjects the other. "And we wasn't the only ones!"

For everyone of their generation memories of hard field labor are all too vivid, as are memories of deprivation. Most people in their community share these memories, and many have succeeded less well than the Landises in rising above the hard times. When the Golden Echoes come upon the stage, they stand as resplendent embodiments of the material blessings for which the entire community longs. When the songs proclaim, "You know that I soon will be done, trouble of this world" and "I'm going up to meet him in the air," in the venerable tradition of the Afro-American spiritual, the lines are this-worldly as well as other-worldly statements.

Some comments by members of the Landis family show their awareness of a range of such functions in the gospel singing. Bertha Landis says that as her boys grew up she "saw that they had a talent for singing . . . I saw that they had this singing stream. And then I come to thinking, wondering why they all were involved in trying to sing when they were small, even though they couldn't talk too good. And then I'd begin to think back about my father and my relatives. On both sides, my mother's and my father's, they were music teachers and singers. My father was a music teacher. He had a brother that taught music. My mother had two brothers that taught music. And I began to put that together and I began to realize that they had a singing stream coming from both sides of the family, so I began to teach them." The gift that Mrs. Landis saw as a musical stream from her parents through her to her children, she can now see flowing on to her grandchildren. One played guitar for the Golden Echoes and two others sang with their own gospel groups at the most recent of the Echoes' anniversary concerts. Mrs. Landis sees the songs as representing not only religion, then, but also family tradition.

She also describes other values she saw in the musical training she tried to give her children. Music would "bring them joy and happiness as they grew up in years." She saw it as helping them "be involved in something that was worthwhile." She says, "I think singing is what held them together, encouraged them to stay at home because they had brothers they could sing with." She used music to give them aspirations. When her husband would sometimes complain because the boys kept him awake at night after a hard day's labor, patting their feet and singing back and forth between the bedrooms, she would say, "Don't get after them. They may grow up to be great singers some day."

Moreover, as members of singing groups her children later gained experience in public appearance and group cooperation. John Landis frequently comments on the tact necessary, for example, to hold a singing group together. The Echoes themselves are made up of two sets of singers who had belonged to earlier groups. One set, the Landises, come from Creedmoor. The other set lives a few miles to the north in Kittrell. To avoid favoring either party, the Echoes describe themselves as from a third nearby town, Franklinton. John Landis serves in many ways as the leader, but he acts only in consultation with the others, being especially careful to touch base in all matters with the leader of the Kittrell group, Wilburt Malone. Such cooperation is essential to the actual musical performances. The members have hand and eye signals to cue each other when to switch parts, when to pick up the tempo, or when to end the piece. Much of their ability to sing together is the product of two decades of working together, knowing even each others' unexpressed intentions. In 1983 the new man in the group had been with it five years and was felt to need a few more years' experience in order to be completely at one with the group.

Performances by the Golden Echoes, then, seem dense with meanings additional to the evangelical Christian one that they bear on their surface. The singers affirm an ethnic identity, a family tradition, and a community history. They enact the values of cooperation, discipline, and unity. They are a visible and attractive symbol of the aspirations and achievements of their community. Perhaps even more important, they are proof to their family and neighbors that success does not require a rejection of the self one has for an alien self. As they "go up to meet Him in the air," they can undergo not a substitution but a transfiguration.

NOTES

The paper is one product of a documentary film project jointly carried out by the University of North Carolina Curriculum in Folklore and Tom Davenport Films in the summers of 1981 through 1985. Members of this project team were Tom Davenport, Allen E. Tullos, Barry Dornfeld, and me, with Tom Rankin, Beverly B. Patterson, Brett Sutton, and others, and the paper is indebted to the insights and fieldwork of all the participants. The film, entitled *A Singing Stream,* was completed in 1986. Outtakes and sound recordings from the project are on deposit in the University of North Carolina Library. Since the Golden Echoes and other members of the Landis family perform publicly and appear under their own names in this film and on albums, their names remain unchanged in this paper.

Study of the black male gospel quartet tradition is a fairly recent development. Tony Heilbut's short account in *The Gospel Sound* (New York: Simon and Schuster, 1971) opened the exploration. It has been succeeded by more weighty studies of individual groups or regional traditions, such as Kerill L. Rubman's Master's thesis *Jubilee to Gospel in Black Male Quartet Singing* (Chapel Hill: Curriculum in Folklore, University of North Carolina, 1980) and Christopher Lornell's Ph.D. dissertation *Happy in the Service of the Lord: Afro-American Gospel Quartets in Memphis, Tennessee* (Memphis: Department of Ethnomusicology, Memphis State University, 1983), soon to be published by the University of Illinois Press, and his "Happy in the Service of the Lord: Memphis Gospel Quartet Heritage—The 1980's," High Water Records LP-1002 (Memphis: Memphis State University, 1983), and Doug Seroff, "Birmingham Quartet Anthology, Jefferson County, Alabama (1926–1953)," Clanka Lanka Records LP-144,001/2 (Stockholm: Mr. R&B Record Sales, n.d.) and "Birmingham Quartet Scrapbook: A Quartet Reunion in Jefferson County . . . October 12, 1980" (n.p., n.d.). An exploration of musical features that he believes lift an audience to a possession state at a black gospel quartet performance is found in Morton Marks' Ph.D. dissertation *Performance Rules and Ritual Structures in Afro-American Music* (Berkeley: University of California, 1972). I am specifically indebted to an undergraduate paper written by George Holt, "Hillbilly Gospel: A Brief History of the Golden Echoes" (Ms. on file in the University of North Carolina Southern Folklife Collection). A good study of another family gospel group is Burt Feintuch's "A Noncommercial Black Gospel Group in Context: We Live the Life We Sing About," *Black Music Research Journal* 1 (1980): 37–50.

1. The Golden Echoes have two published long-playing albums: "Ride Away to Jesus" (Savoy MG-14091) and "Heaven on My Mind," ed. Vic Lukas (Rounder 2002). These two songs, however, appear only on locally issued

45-rpm discs sold at their concerts: "Trouble of This World" (GEM Golden Echoes Music 908008) and "Going Up to Meet Him" (GEM Golden Echoes Music 109051).

2. Wes Hitchison, "Theoretical Aspects" in "Notes on the Making of an Ethnographic Film, Heaven on My Mind: The Golden Echoes" (paper submitted as a team project for Anthropology 194 at Duke University, May 1, 1972), p. 8 (Ms. on file in the University of North Carolina Southern Folklife Collection).

EXPERIENCES AND FORMS

The Testimony of Sister Annie Mae   6

Ruel W. Tyson, Jr.

Pine Grove Holiness Church is an independent Protestant Christian church in Robeson County, North Carolina. Its membership is composed entirely of Lumbee Indians. The Lumbees, the fifth largest Indian tribe in the United States, have never known life on a reservation. In Robeson County the Lumbees were reported in 1980 to number 35,528 persons, while the white population totaled 39,994 and the black 25,600. The Lumbees work in mills, own small farms, or hold blue-collar jobs. They support many churches in this rural county. Some of their churches belong to national organizations like those of the Methodists and the Assemblies of God, while others like the Pine Grove Holiness Church remain independent, largely relying for their existence on the pastor and his following within the church. Many, perhaps most, of the testimonies given in the Pine Grove Church are rendered by members of its pastor's circle of followers.

The testimony of Sister Annie Mae was given during a service in the Pine Grove Holiness Church on July 6, 1979. This particular service was one in a series held in the mornings and the afternoons at Pine Grove during its annual revival week. It is customary for this church to hold revival services during the week of the Fourth of July, the traditional week for mill closings and vacations in this area. The church schedules these revivals during this week in explicit recognition that it is going against the habits of people who are more interested "in going to White Lake and to Carolina Beach," as the pastor expresses it, than in attending church.

The white frame church with a tin roof, built by its members, stands on an infrequently traveled country road in Robeson County, North

Carolina, in the upper reaches of the Cape Fear Valley, not far from Interstate 95. Like the county at large, the land on which the church stands is flat and sandy. The fields surrounding the church are waist high with beans and head high with corn in early July.

If you stand in the center aisle of the church and look west through the front door of the church, you will see across the road a large family burial ground, well kept by one of the largest families in the county. The cemetery entrance is defined by two brick columns from which rise a black wrought-iron archway spanning the white, sandy, one-lane path leading into the grounds. Between the bands of the archway the family name is spelled out sharply against the cloudy blue sky of the July morning already glistening with a moist brightness. The pastor's name is identical with the name above the cemetery entrance. He is a contractor and carpenter who leads a country gospel group in addition to pastoring three churches in different parts of the county. Each church is independent of the other two and from any denominational affiliation. The pastor, like everyone in his church at Pine Grove, is a Lumbee Indian.

The morning services begin about ten o'clock, Monday through Friday. Members "stand at ease" about one o'clock for dinner brought and served by members of the church. The dinner is served in the Fellowship Hall, a forty-by-eighty foot, framed, one-story structure, like the church, built by the members. It stands a hundred yards behind the church on a grassy plot with three sides bordered by a corn field. The building is largely given over to a dining room with long tables end on end. Across the back of the room is the serving and cooking area. To the north side of this area the pastor has his office and a studio where his musical group practices. The afternoon service begins about 2:00 p.m. — "come on back when you hear singing in the house" — and usually lasts until three or four o'clock. The times for beginning and ending these services are not regulated by the clock. This particular revival began on Sunday July 1 and ended on the sixth, the day this testimony was given.

This morning the humidity was already high at ten o'clock, and the temperature was to reach the low nineties by noon in the church cooled by two portable window fans. By the time the singing began about two dozen persons had arrived; thirty adults were eventually present by the middle of the morning service. The majority of the adults were women accompanied by a number of children ten years old or younger. The service began with hymn singing, initiated variously by two or three women, with the congregation singing while sitting in rows of wooden pews on either side of the pulpit area and on the first several rows in front of the pulpit.

Eight hymns were sung prior to Sister Annie Mae's testimony, with members intoning "A-men," "Praise the Lord," and "Yes, Jesus" between hymns. There was piano accompaniment with the sound of tambourines, clapping, and shouting out above the music. Between the seventh and eighth hymn there was a short testimony by a woman who appeared to be about fifty years old. The titles of the hymns disclosed the themes that filled the air with their echoes as Sister Annie Mae began to speak: "Press Along"; "How Beautiful Heaven Must Be, Happy and Free"; "On the Far Away Shore is the Beautiful Home of Jesus"; "We Will Never Grow Old"; "As I Travel Through this World"; "Hold Me by Thy Side, Help Me Walk in Paradise"; and just prior to Sister Annie Mae's testimony, which she began on the last notes of the hymn, "Crossing Over in the Light of Home."

The Testimony of Sister Annie Mae

1. Praise God. You know those old songs we used to sing . . . but I still feel just like they did back then . . . singing. I thought about an older person, you know, their hair is turned white, praise God. And you know, I seen some, and I heared about some, when they are just about to cross over, praise God, and some of 'em say they could see angels, and they could hear the angels sing, and ask one that was standing by, "Could you see the angels?" And they tell 'em "No," they couldn't see the angels. But, praise God, they are so near home they could see the angels. Praise God in glory. They were just about to take them over.

2. Praise God. Hallelujah. . . . You know, it's real! It's wonderful! You don't have to fear, praise God, when you come down to the end of life's journey, you don't have to be afraid, praise God. Because you got something inside that'll take you home. Praise God! Hallelujah! You know, it's going to be wonderful!

3. You know one time I was in the studio, praise God, and the power of the Holy Ghost fell on me, and it just shook me all over the place, praise God. And you know it seemed like . . . I just felt as if I was in heaven, praise God! Hallelujah!

4. And, you know, I could speak through faith, or through a vision, or something or other. Jesus don't want us to cry when his children go to heaven. Oh God, go go home, it's wonderful!

5. And you know, when you are around them, you can feel it too — Oh thank you Jesus! I remember Miss Martha up here the night she went to meet the Lord, we was there, praise God. And you know, I walked in there and looked on her face, a-laying there, praise God. She did not know she was in the world. And I stood there, and I looked at her, and I just see her going home, I could just feel it, you know. I felt the spirit of God just run all over me, praise God. And I surely felt like she went home, praise God.

6.   I thank the Lord today for being saved.
       I thank him for being sanctified.
       I thank him for the power of the Holy Ghost.
       Praise God! It's real, people. It's real, praise God.
       And if you don't have it, you need to seek for it.
       Praise God. Because you can have it. The Bible says you
           can have it, praise the Lord!
       It's wonderful! Praise God!

7. You know, I tells some of 'em one time that it's just like a new dish of food. If you would come to my house, and I had fixed something you had never tasted, you might look at it, with all different things in it, and say, "It don't look good," or maybe "I wouldn't like it," or something. But you will never know until you taste it. You will never know until you eat some of it, praise God. And that's the way it is with the Holy Ghost. You will never be able to know about the Holy Ghost until you received it, praise God, and then after you receive it, then you know what somebody else is talking about. You know what someone else feels, praise God! It's wonderful! I just wouldn't take nothing for it. And I am so glad that I was raised up in it. And I've known it ever since I was a little child . . . like this one and these over here. Praise God.

8. You know, I used to go to Evergreen [Church] down there. That's where I was raised, praise God. And you know, them older women they wore dresses a-dragging the floor. You couldn't see their shoes, praise God. And my grandmother, she wouldn't wear nothing but cotton stockings, and she dyed them black. They had to be black. And that's what she wore. And you know, I was a little child . . . I come yesterday evening to thinking about it . . . I was a little child. I could see them older people a-shouting and a-praising God. And the place was filled with the spirit of God. I just feel it too, praise God. Some of it come over my head and all over me when I was a little girl, and I knowed it was real from that moment on. And I'll tell you, nobody can't change me. They just come *too late,* and I've been in it *too long,* and I know *too much* about it. For that I praise God.

> I got it!
> I got it!
> I got it! [speaks in tongues]
> It's real, praise God! [speaks again in tongues]
>
> It's real!
> Oh yes, Jesus!
> Thank you, God.
>
> It's real.

9. Some people say that the healing days are over. My God is a-healing people. God is a-healing people right on. Praise God! The ones that got saved, the ones that has touched the hem of his garment. Praise God. They are being made whole. Praise God.

10. You know, in these last days the devil is trying to take peoples' minds. He's a-making 'em nervous. He's a-gettin' to where they can't hold jobs. He's a-gettin' them to where the doctor cannot help 'em. And he's recommending 'em go to the psychiatrists! Praise God! But you know what? When we go to the psychiatrists, we are lowering the standard of holiness. We are letting Jesus down, praise God. When we do it and stand in this church and tell somebody "God will heal you," then go to such a man as that, what do Jesus think about us when we do that? Praise God.

11. And you know what? The spirit of God took me over that night at that service, Brother Everett was there. And I was ashamed of it, I wasn't going to tell nobody about it, praise God. And the Spirit got me aholt, and I had to get up there and tell these people, praise God. It was as if I weren't even talkin'. The spirit took over, and I said I wouldn't go to save my life, praise God. When I did that, there weren't no way I would go to a psychiatrist then, praise God. I'd been back-slid, praise the Lord, and I couldn't go then. And from that moment on that I said that, I don't know where them headaches went, I don't know where them pains went. But they went, praise God,

> Oh praise God!
> I'm healed,
> I'm healed,
> I'm healed, praise God.
> He's a healer,
> He's a healer, praise God!
> And he will heal you.
> He'll do for you what he'll do for me. Praise God!
> Hallelujah!

12. And about a year ago. I don't know, I hadn't kept account of it, I had sugar, praise God. God healed me *instantly* here one Sunday. Right *there!* He healed me *instantly!*

> People, he's a healer!
> He's a healer, praise God.
> Aha . . . he's a healer, praise the Lord!
> And he loves you just as good as me.
> He'll heal you, praise God.

13. Pray for me that I'll stand because we are in the last days. Praise God. I dreamed last night, praise the Lord, that one of those beasts had come. Praise God, hallelujah! Praise the Lord. You know, he came to our house, and it was trying to get in, and it had disturbed the cats, and the cats were trying to get in, and I was trying to push the cats out, and that thing clawed me on the arm, and it had claws that long and about as sharp as a razor blade. Praise God. And I went running down into the room where Lonnie was, and I got him to come up there, and he couldn't . . . and that

thing was a-cuttin' its way in, it was coming *in* . . . and he couldn't do a-nothing with it. And we left and went to a woman's house, and either it was the same or another one, and it was trying to get in there. And we left there and went to Brother Sermon's house, praise God, way up there in Doke County. And Brother Sermon was sleeping and Sister Evelyn was sleeping, and we tried to get them up and tell them about it. Sister Evelyn was sleeping so and we couldn't do nothing with her. And so Brother Sermon did get up, and he come in there, and he had a box about *that* big and about *that* high, and it had that little teenie wire on it. And him and Lonnie got that thing in that box. And you know what it did? It just busted it in several hundred pieces about the size of a seed, a string bean seed, and there was lights on that thing, and ever one, a light on it, and that thing was trying to get on our skins, trying to cling to our bodies, and it could sting you, great God! . . . And my little boy woke me up, and I said, "Lord, thank the Lord, I'm glad you woke me up. I was dreaming about one of the beasts that's coming in the last days!

14. Praise God! People! We are near, we are nearer these things than we think we is, praise God. People is so concerned about living, so concerned about preparin' to live. My God, I feel like we are almost to the end, praise God. And I tell you we are not close enough to God to feel these things and see these things. If we would, we would forget about our jobs sometimes. We would forget about our housework sometimes. And we would go and obey God and try to get somebody saved. Praise God!

15. I want you all to pray for me, and I don't know what this dream means unless it is referring to Revelations [*sic*] when it says these things are going to come and take place. And I tell you, I feel a need in my heart to get closer to God, to get more humble.

16. And you know, I told Brother Runyon out there today, people's going to come down, we are going to come down. We are drifting away from the old landmarks, and we've got to come back. We are going to come down. People are up so high. They are going to fall down. Praise God. I told 'em this church at the beginning of the year, I felt like things were going to happen this year that

never happened. And we are just in the beginning of it, praise God. And all this gas problem, all this fruit problem, and all this here. But it's going to get worse and worse, and it will get worse. And I believe that we are going to see Jesus coming. I don't think the times are going to get any better. It's going to get worse, and we are going to have to adjust to it. We're to serve the Lord, and we are going to have to obey the Lord.

17. I want you all to pray for me because God wants to use me, cause he's got more, something else for me to do. I don't know what it is. Sister Harmony said one night that she dreamed that the Lord had given me the gift of healing, praise God. And you know I told her, "if the Lord would give me that gift, I would be glad to have it." Praise God.

But you know, we've got to be in a position where we can obey God anytime and anywhere to have these gifts. We cannot have these gifts and do what *we want* to do, but we are going to have to do what *God wants* us to do. So I want to obey the Lord, I just want to go through with him.

18.   People! We are in the last days!
       People! Did you know we are in the last days?
       Did you know Jesus is just about to come, praise God?

And our children's lost. And our friends' lost. And our neighbors' lost, My God! We need to move out. We need to be more concerned! Praise God! We are going to stand around and let our children slip through out fingers and go to hell. Praise God. And I'll tell you, if we can't help our own children, how can we help anybody else? Praise God. The Bible says church starts at home and then goes abroad. We are supposed to work with other peoples' children. Praise God. We're supposed to love other peoples' children. Praise God. Pray for me, and I'll pray for you all. . . . [The next testimony began fast upon the last words of this one, and Sister Annie Mae could be heard still speaking in the background.]

Here is an instance of Merleau-Ponty's statement made good in action—"The spoken word is a gesture, its meaning, a world,"[1] for the testimony of Sister Annie Mae is raised out of a life. The several modes of description are in accord with the concords and discords in her life. She describes herself, but she also describes a world, of places and of a people — relations and neighbors — and of her time and of the times in which she lives. The testimony discloses places and times in her history, and her assertions implicate a cosmos deeply associated with her time and the times in which she lives.

The actions of the testimony, then, situate Sister Annie Mae amid the ties that constitute her world, yet she tells and shouts of a home that is heaven, known in part already. This ecstatic discourse relies upon locality and connection, yet relates in detail and episode how the speaker experiences other tongues, another world, other realms, and other beings. While unforgettably a first-person confession, narrative, and exaltation, the testimony sometimes turns personal experience into public example; and the speaker's personal history claims to be representative of her audience. Among the testifier's several voices, there is the instruction of the pedagogue and the advocacy of the apologue stirring the brothers and sisters to action.

The enactment of the testimony is an offering, according to the teaching it presents about exchanges and transformations. It practices what it advocates. The vigor of its presentation and the vividness of its representations do not obscure those aspects that are reflections of and reflections on the life of the one who speaks. Its narrative work and its confessional declarations do not exclude reflexivity. This testimony at once enacts a life and offers reflections about that life and others connected with it who share, or may share, similar experiences.

In forms appropriate to its genre, the testimony is a formalization of the religious practice of the speaker as well as of the religious understanding of the speaker; both practice and reflection find modes of articulation in the course of the testimony. The speaker is a religious virtuosa who articulates and interprets her religious practice and the world and times in which that practice thrives. Her exemplary powers reside in the examples she narrates and in the perspicuity of her interpretations of them. Like other skillful doers — for whom doing is a mode of knowing — she senses that her art can only be communicated through the persuasions of her examples. For it was through the authority of exemplary persons, so she tells us, that she acquired the gifts of art she embodies in her testifying.

I claim all these flat descriptions of Sister Annie Mae's testimony are authorized by listening to her speaking and by attempting to identify aspects of her rhetorical practice in order to gain limited access to her experience. In making her experience available to her listeners, she also provides clues for its interpretation, or as I prefer to say, for an appreciation of her testimony. In the testimony itself she provides many conditions necessary for an understanding of it.

This overall characterization of the testimony scarcely begins to plumb its depths. The text itself rewards a careful attention to its details, but even to do this requires ignoring other dimensions of its meaning. I have not, for example, referred to the lively relationships between Sister Annie Mae in the giving of her testimony and the congregation receiving it, a vital source of energy and commentary on the testimony during its enactment. Some members present in the group before which she spoke are present in her testimony, some by name, others by indirect reference. I pass over the exchange of testimonies in this service and almost all other services, including the exchange of dreams and visions in the public space of that church; the memory theater that these exchanges create; a religious pedagogy for the young; and a source of recollection and restoration for older persons present. And the other side of these exchanges: risk taking, bidding for status, contests in religious virtuosity, muted criticism of members and ministers, arguments about "right teaching"—all through the medium of testimony, which is a major mode of communal celebration and criticism, personal disclosure, and collective affirmation.

The particulars of this testimony, even severed from its ritual setting, are rich and complex. The physical gestures accompanying her delivery are themselves eloquent. Sister Annie Mae stood in her place and spoke her testimony, but she accompanied her speech with gestures that assisted its enactment: pointing—"there," "over there," "down there," "up there," "right there," "here," "about this long," "about this wide"; raising arms to shout—"Praise God, hallelujah!"; turning from one side to the other; looking up; closing eyes; smiling; and frowning. These gestures are an extension and enrichment of her speech, tying her testimony to places, making special places out of space, and making fleeting icons of memories now being made present—all this and more are the work of the body in concert with Sister Annie Mae's speech. They help create the worlds that her speech exhibits during her act of testifying.

Her gestural speech, moreover, etches places into particularity: here (where she stands); there where she stood (in this church); the studio; Miss Martha's house up "here" and Martha "a-laying there"; "Evergreen down there"; "the night of that service" (the time and place go together); "Right *there*" (the place where she once stood and was healed); her room; "down into the room where Lonnie was" (certain people, in this instance her husband, go with a certain place); another woman's house; "up there in Doke County"; Brother Sermon and Sister Evelyn's house; outside this church today, "I told Brother Runyon"—time, place, and person are all in relation to each other.

Persons inhabit her narratives and are appealed to as witnesses to her words, including all members of the congregation and others not present, such as those who have crossed over: Miss Martha, "my grandmother," Brother Everett, Lonnie, Brother Sermon and Sister Evelyn, "my little boy," Brother Runyon, and Sister Harmony. In addition to specific persons, she names groups of persons and types of persons: older persons; "some of 'em"; Jesus' children; little children; "them older women"; "some people" (that say healing days is over); "the ones that got saved, ones that has touched the hem of his garment"; "peoples' minds"; psychiatrists; doctors; nervous people; people who cannot hold jobs; people the doctor cannot help; people "lowering the standard of holiness"; "we"—those around her as she speaks; "we"—anybody doing certain things; people "so concerned about living and preparin' to live"; "people is going to come down, we are going to come down"; people "drifting away from the old landmarks"; "we are going to see Jesus coming" soon; lost children, lost friends, lost neighbors; and "our own children," other people's children. She also names other beings and powers—the angels, the Holy Ghost, Jesus, the spirit of God, Lord, God, the devil—and even animals—beasts, cats—all related to persons, groups, and Sister Annie Mae through experience, Scripture, and dream.

Between these groups and types of persons, as well as between the powers and different realms, there are oppositions, an important kind of relationship. There is some opposition in herself between the tendency and temptation to be "back-slid" and obedience to the dictates of the Spirit, as mediated through her own words: "When I did that" (saying she would not go to a psychiatrist "to save my life"), "there weren't no way I would go to a psychiatrist then, praise God. I'd been back-slid . . . I couldn't go then." Other oppositions also bind and drive her testimony: those who feel but cannot see the angels, those who see and feel the angels, namely, those who are crossing over; those who don't have the Holy Ghost and those who do; those who seek for it and those who don't; those who have tasted and those who do not; those who know what those who have received the Holy Ghost are talking about and feel, and those who do not; those who try to change me — "from that moment on . . . nobody can't change me"; those who say the healing days are over and those who are healed; "the ones that got saved," and those that are not saved; the devil and Jesus; those who let Jesus down and those who follow the devil and go to the psychiatrist; those who uphold the standards of holiness and those who lower the standards of holiness; those who can be awakened from sleeping and those who cannot; those concerned about living and those close to God; those who forget housework, jobs, and get somebody saved, and those who do not; those who do and do not know we are in the last days; and those who do and do not know Jesus is just about to come. Heaven and Hell. Saved and Lost.

The most ecstatic predications in this testimony are confessions of possession and transformation. The narrative portions of the testimony recount transitions and continuities in the life of the one who exclaims: "I got it!" or "I am healed!" Frequently, these ecstatic utterances effect a change from the narrative past to the present of immediate confession, celebration, and thanksgiving. Ecstatic prediction and personal narrative are presented in continuity with one another in the action of testifying. Ecstatic utterance rises out of recounted experience in which past and private experiences are made public and present.

The testimony begins with a recollection of old days, old people, and old hymns and ends with a charge to action on behalf of saving children, a request for prayer, and a promise of prayers for those who have listened and joined with her. In between, the listener is presented with a variety of transformations in tone, intensity, rhythm, and forms of discourse. Here are some of the particular exchanges and transformation, transitions and continuities in the action of the testimony: feeling now "like they felt back then"; crossings and endings of life's journey to home/heaven; "the Holy Ghost fell on me . . . and it seemed like . . . I was in heaven"; "It was as if I weren't even talkin'."

I must stress the transformation of speaking. The reflexive statement, a comment on her own action, follows the first narrated experience of the Holy Ghost (in testimony paragraph 3). The narrative goes like this: "You know, one time I was in the studio, praise God, and the power of the Holy Ghost fell on me, and it just shook me all over the place, praise God. And you know it seemed like . . . I just felt as if I was in heaven, praise God! Hallelujah!" And the comment, immediately following the telling of that experience, is this: "And, you know, I could speak through faith, or through a vision, or something or other." The suggestion, or hint, here is that her speaking is transformed "through vision or faith, or something," just as her experience of the Holy Ghost transformed her so that she felt as if she were in heaven. The reports of two dreams, which come later in the testimony, lend complexity to these comments by Annie Mae about how she speaks.

The transformation of speaking is an important self-description by Pentecostal people. As Annie Mae's credo of thanks says, being saved, sanctified, and receiving the gift of the Holy Ghost are the authenticating experiences that bestow Pentecostal identity. Speaking in tongues is held by many to be the necessary condition for sanctification. Indeed, later in the testimony, she said about another Holy Ghost experience, this one associated with a healing experience: "It was as if I weren't even talkin'. The spirit took over."

The concern with speaking — whether one has "the tongues" or not — coupled with the ritual actions of praying, singing, preaching, and testifying — make it necessary to describe Pentecostal persons as having a special relationship to speaking. This is a speaking religion more than a scriptural religion. And the Holy Ghost falling on persons in the form of speaking in other tongues as the Spirit gave them utterance (Acts 2:1–4) limits human speech, making it especially problematical, yet also of great value as sanctifying experience.

The Sunday following the day on which this testimony was given, the ladies Sunday school class had a lesson on "the difficulty of taming your tongue." The teaching was: the only thing that can tame your tongue is the Holy Ghost. Praying and testifying are ways of inviting the taming of the tongue as well as of affirming and of claiming those prior experiences of the Holy Ghost in which as in Sister Annie Mae's case, the Holy Ghost took over her tongue. As indicated earlier, it is quite probable that at the peak of one of her most ecstatic utterances

117

(in testimony paragraph 8), her speech was transformed into other tongues.

The statement that she could "speak through faith, or through a vision" is a self-interpretative comment which is confirmed by the narrative incidents that populate her testimony. Self-interpretative commentary caps each narrative incident she recounts, and each narrative is structured by an episode and its transformation from the ordinary to the extraordinary. For example, when Sister Annie Mae spoke of being in the presence of dying persons, those who are going home, she said, "I felt the spirit of God run all over me, praise God." One kind of transformation—going to meet the Lord—is answered by another: spirit running over the agent and narrator of the testimony, an experience that authorizes in Sister Annie Mae the belief that Miss Martha "surely . . . went home." The credo section of the testimony follows:

> I thank the Lord today for being saved.
> I thank him for being sanctified.
> I thank him for the power of the Holy Ghost.

These statements are a series of thanksgivings for past transformations and for the Holy Ghost, which made them possible. The Holy Ghost is an intrusive narrator indeed!

Sister Annie Mae makes an imperative for her listeners from these transformations: "If you don't have it, you need to seek for it."

The ways of knowing which this testimony reports and teaches are all forms of transformations: tasting and knowing; receiving and knowing; receiving and knowing that allows one so transformed to understand the words and feelings of others who likewise have undergone the Holy Ghost. These transformations are claims for modes of knowing that provide the basis for a community of interpretation, a community enacting itself in the testifying of Sister Annie Mae and in the recurrent responses by her fellow members; the exchanges between speaker and listeners, who respond in speech of their own, are exchanges that exhibit the teachings about knowing and interpretation expressed in the testimony.

Ordinary incidents in her life become transformed by the presence of the Holy Ghost, which in turn becomes evidence for the claim she makes. The cardinal claim is: "It's real!" The experience of the Holy

Ghost is real. This is followed by a praise of thanksgiving. The recounting of past experiences generates confirming experiences of a similar kind in the present. When Sister Annie Mae shouted "Praise God" in the eleventh section of her testimony, she broke into a second ecstatic chorus of utterances. While she did so, more than one person in the congregation joined her in speaking in tongues. The same was repeated after another account of healing; the claim of transformation by the testifier transforms the listeners; exchanges and transformations recur during the testimony in a variety of intensities.

There are countertransformations: the devil's taking peoples' minds, making them nervous, making them so "they can't hold jobs." And this is countered by narration of a personal experience, ending in "I am healed — He's a healer — [God's] a healer — We live still in healing days." And by recurrent claims to reciprocal and duplicating experiences: "He'll do for you, what he'll do for me"; "He loves you just as good as me"; and "Pray for me, and I'll pray for you all."

The testimony itself is an exchange, and some of its sections repeat in fine what is enacted in the whole: telling a dream, repeating the dream of someone else about the testifier. Then there are reported conversational exchanges between Sister Annie Mae and Brother Runyon, between her and members of the church, as she reports these conversational exchanges in the testimony.

Finally, there is the exchange that particularly interests Sister Annie Mae and many anthropologists: there is the exchange called gifts. For the gift of the Holy Ghost, "I just wouldn't take nothing for it." In the interpretative example of the new dish, there is the gift of food, and in Sister Harmony's dream about Sister Annie Mae's receiving the gift of healing (the ability to heal), there is the exchange of dreams in the telling about them, concluded by a conversational exchange: "And you know I told her, 'if the Lord would give me that gift, I would be glad to have it.' Praise God."

As persons are related to particular places in this testimony, so exchanges and transformations are related to time — time denominated in several modes: first there is the historical life time of the speaker, the time of her life's history; next, empirical or biological time is grasped through an image of movement toward crossing over and going home/ heaven — "when you come down to the end of life's journey." She understands her own life in the image of a life's journey. But that view itself has a history, a beginning in another kind of time related in the testimony, the turn her life took following her first baptism by the Holy Ghost: "I was a little child. I could see them older people a-shouting and a-praising God. And the place ['Evergreen down there'] was filled with the spirit of God. I just feel it too [note her shift to present tense], praise God. Some of it come over my head and all over me when I was a little girl, and I knowed it was real from that moment on. And I'll tell you, nobody can't change me. They just come *too late,* and I've been in it *too long,* and I know *too much* about it."

This initial experience established a new time for her to live in, "from that moment on." From that moment on, she entered the life's journey that she spoke about in the second section of the testimony. All the other special times partake of this original time of the Holy Ghost. The subsequent experiences of Holy Ghost and healing redound upon this first special time. The series of special times stand out in her narration and elicit in their telling her own most ecstatic utterances: from "I got it!" after telling of the first Holy Ghost experience to "I am healed!" following the accounts of the two healings she makes in this testimony. The experiences of these special times may account for her opening statement: "You know those old songs we used to sing . . . but I still feel just like they did back then . . . singing."

The repeated installments in the history of her relation with the Holy Ghost provide for continuity in the history of her feelings. The structure of the testimony is disclosed in the beginning image and the co-relative image with which it ends — older persons, their hair turned white, in the beginning, and "children" who may "slip" through our fingers and go to hell," at the end.

Individual life journeys are set in another time — a cosmological equivalent of the individual, like Miss Martha, going to meet the Lord. This cosmological time is the time of "the last days" when "we are going to see Jesus coming." The religious life of Sister Annie Mae, according to her testimony, is set not only in autobiographical time, her life's journey, but in the days of healing that continue under the power of the Holy Ghost, and finally, the most comprehensive time of all, the time of the last days. Personal history is situated in a cosmos; autobiographical temporality is informed by cosmological time of the days of healing and the last days of historical time. The cosmological framework the testifier invokes is more than a frame, it is a source for the interpretation of her dream. Or rather, the authority for her claim about the last days is the same as her authority for the interpretation of her dream of the beast, namely the Bible, and what she calls "Revelations," chapter 19 in particular.

It is striking that the description of her relation to the beast in the dream — "that thing was trying to get on our skins, trying to cling to our bodies" — is similar to the Holy Ghost experiences she relates. Yet there are distinctive differences as well. Her understanding of herself in the larger time of the cosmos enables Sister Annie Mae to render an interpretation of the dream based on the teleological direction of history rather than on an interior drama and dreams in her psyche: "I want you all to pray for me, and I don't know what this dream means unless it is referring to Revelations [*sic*] when it says these things are going to come and take place."

Just as the direction of time is employed as reference to the interpretation of her dream, so individual experiences of healing are employed to embody her claim that the healing days are not over. Sister Annie Mae's testimony has cosmological reach and autobiographical depth, and it attains these features through a series of individual experiences that become exemplary for larger claims about the Holy Ghost and about healing and about the healing days in which she lives.

In the course of the testimony she alludes to immediate past incidents from which what she is now uttering arises. These asides manage to give the hearers in brief fragments some of the history of this particular testimony: "I come yesterday evening to thinking about it"; "I dreamed last night . . ."; and "I told Brother Runyon out there today. . . ."

But these incidental times are pale beside the imperative she feels to act, to get somebody saved, particularly children, now that she and her associates live in the last days; her understanding of the time of the world requires action in it.

I end this survey of clusters of particular features in this testimony by stressing its action, the investment of the person in the many agencies at work in this total enactment. Here are some of the actions: praising, thanking, thinking, feeling, seeing, saying, looking, running, tasting, knowing, receiving, talking, shouting, healing, saving, making, getting, recommending, letting down, standing up, trying, cutting, coming, sleeping, dreaming, waking, forgetting, drifting, giving, obeying, and praying—all through the action of speaking as testifying.

I have characterized this testimony as presenting both practice and reflection, experience and interpretation. Her practice included a style of interpretation that is formalized in the utterances of the testimony and in the manner in which she spoke them. I want to turn my attention to this characterization by examining some of the particulars in the discourse.

Sister Annie Mae interprets one episode, or narrative fragment, by another episode or narrated incident—another instance of the exchange pattern I have already noted. Being in the presence of persons who are going to meet the Lord is coupled with a report of a Holy Ghost experience occurring to her. Miss Martha "did not know she was in the world. . . . I could just feel it. . . . I felt the spirit of God just run all over me, praise God. And I surely felt like she went home." On the other hand, being saved and sanctified is like going home to meet the Lord. In the first Holy Ghost experience reported in this testimony (in paragraph 3), which follows the introduction about older persons hearing angels as they cross over, Sister Annie Mae describes her experience in the studio: "And you know, it seemed like . . . I just felt as if I was in heaven, praise God! Hallelujah!"

She is mistress of the simile and the hypothetical as modes for talking about what she means when she exclaims "It's real." The centerpiece of her interpretative skill is the example, with commentary, on tasting a new dish of food—an example and commentary of interest to the student of religion in facing the unfamiliar in the field, from dishes to dreams. Preparing, hesitating, and choosing to taste a new dish are presented as an allegory for receiving the Holy Ghost, followed by an exposition. True to her style, she again engages in the use of a simile: "I tells some of 'em one time that it's just like a new dish of food." Here Sister Annie Mae turns pedagogue, with the example of tasting a new dish following quickly on the preceding section, with its performative speech of thanksgiving:

> I thank the Lord today for being saved
> I thank him for being sanctified.
> I thank him for the power of the Holy Ghost.

Then, the reiteration of her ecstatic predications: "It's real, people! It's real, praise God."

To provide the conditions presupposed in the performatives of thanksgiving and the exclamations of the "real," she recalls a particular time when she explained what it was like to receive the Holy Ghost: "It's just like a new dish of food." In her example she provides the felicity conditions for receiving the gift of the Holy Ghost and the consequences that flow from such an exchange. These consequences illuminate the basis of the community; and the bases for the community further specify the conditions that make possible the total speech action of the testimony, including most necessarily the corresponding responses by those who speak and shout in reply to the various claims and cries of the testifier.

In the commentary that follows on the example of tasting a new dish, Sister Annie Mae claims that possession of the Holy Ghost is also access to the community for those who already find it real and wonderful, those who have already tasted the new dish. Access is by gift of the Holy Ghost, usually marked by the speaking in other tongues, and it enables the recipient to understand the language of those who speak about the Holy Ghost. By this means she indicates the conditions for the understanding of her own testimony in its deepest levels and greatest reaches. The reception of the gift also enables the recipient to understand the feelings of those who shout "It is real!" or "I am healed!" or "I got it!" Within the limits of this genre and by the way she construes the example, Sister Annie Mae is performing an epistemological inquiry into the conditions of Pentecostal religion and, of course, for her own testifying. The Holy Ghost experience provides the arc between individual experience and the community, the conditions—which include testifying about the gift—for "intersubjectivity."

In her own way she knows about the hermeneutical circle, and in her own language she offers an epistemology that supports her metaphysical claim "It's real!" Tasting new dishes is a good way to think about the Holy Ghost and about the necessary conditions for knowing and not knowing about it. Here are her words: "You will never know until you taste it. You will never know until you eat some of it. . . . And that's the way it is with the Holy Ghost. You will never be able to know the Holy Ghost until you receive it, praise God, and then after you receive it, then you know what somebody else is talking about. You know what someone else feels. . . . It's wonderful!"

Next, she moves into a narration of her first Holy Ghost experience as a little child, which culminates in the first of the two great ecstatic eruptions in the testimony. Thus she repeats a pattern, what I have called her interpretative style: from performative utterance to example, followed by assertions in commentary on the example, then concluding with an autobiographical narrative. The multiple modes of presentation that compose this testimony resist any effort to classify testimony according to one genre.

I have already indicated that Sister Annie Mae tells a dream and couples the telling with an interpretation: "I was dreaming about one of the beasts that's coming in the last days!" In sections 13 and 15 of the testimony she spells out more fully the cosmological setting that had initially been implied in the imagery of crossing over in the first part. In the interpretation of the dream, she situates the dream, the dreamer, and those who hear her in a cosmic setting that has a teleological direction in time and a geography divided into this world — heaven, or home, and hell.

The utterances in this testimony — "It's real! It's wonderful!" — linger in echo the longest. In them, metaphysical and aesthetic judgments work in high harmony. How are we to understand these claims? Although they are in the ecstatic mode, they are claims to knowledge; they can be translated more prosaically as "I know."

I characterized Sister Annie Mae's testimony as the practice, or the formalization, of her religious life through the art of testifying. As a religious virtuosa, she is the mistress of the techniques I have noted in the preceding discussion. It is in attending to the various modes of presentation found in her testimony that an answer can be given to the question just raised.

Wittgenstein wrote, "'I know' often means: I have the proper grounds for my statement. So if the other person is acquainted with the language game, he would admit that I know. The other, if he is acquainted with the language game, must be able to imagine how one may know something of the kind."[2] This is what Sister Annie Mae does. She asserts or makes a claim, and as a part of unfolding that claim, she provides by narrative fragment, simile and example, a family of transactions, contexts, types of experiences, or in Wittgenstein's metaphor, a series of "games." The several episodes, closely controlled by her own commentary upon them, enable the listener to imagine how she knows what she claims to know. The offering of example and autobiographical fragment makes possible the listener's imagining something of the experience of the person who speaks. And that requires listeners to master these rhetorical modes if they are to imagine how Sister Annie Mae knows what she claims to know.

It has been the burden of my appreciation of this testimony to show that Sister Annie Mae offers some instruction in the mastery of the techniques necessary for understanding her testimony. Mastery of the speaker's rhetorical practice is the necessary condition for appreciating testimony as a form of religious action.

NOTES

Fieldwork for this essay was carried out during the summer of 1979 with support from the National Institute of Mental Health and the University of North Carolina Faculty Research Council. The political and cultural setting within which this testimony was given is described in Karen I. Blu's *Lumbee Problem: The Making of an American Indian People* (New York: Cambridge University Press, 1980) and its Pentecostal context is described in David E. Harrell, *All Things are Possible: The Healing and Charismatic Revivals in Modern America* (Bloomington: Indiana University Press, 1975). For the theoretical perspective from which this essay is written I acknowledge my debt to J. L. Austin, *How to Do Things with Words,* ed. J. O. Urmson (Cambridge: Harvard University Press, 1962); S. J. Tambiah, "Form and Meaning of Magical Acts: A Point of View," in *Modes of Thought: Essays on Thinking in Western and Non-Western Societies,* ed. Robin Horton and Ruth Finnegan (London: Faber and Faber, 1973); and Paul Ricoeur, "The Hermeneutics of Testimony" in his *Essays on Biblical Interpretation,* trans. by David Steward and Charles E. Reagan, ed. with introduction by Lewis S. Mudge (Philadelphia: Fortress Press, 1980), pp. 119–154. For a synoptic and photographic essay, see Jeff Todd Titon, "Some Recent Pentecostal Revivals: A Report in Words and Photographs," *The Georgia Review* 32 (Fall 1978): 579–610; for additional testimonies see Jeff Titon and Ken George, transcribers, "Testimonies" in *alcheringa/ethnopoetics* 4, no. 1 (1978): 69–83.

1. Maurice Merleau-Ponty, *The Phenomenology of Perception,* trans. Colin Smith (London: Routledge and Kegan Paul, 1962), p. 184.

2. Ludwig Wittgenstein, *On Certainty,* ed. G. E. M. Anscombe and G. H. von Wright (Oxford: Blackwell, 1969), paragraph 18, p. 4e.

With His Stripes We Are Healed: 7
White Pentecostals and Faith Healing

Douglas Reinhardt

In 1906 a religious revival occurred in Los Angeles from which modern-day Pentecostalism in the United States originated. A minister in Dunn, North Carolina — G. B. Cashwell — heard of this "Azusa Street Revival" and hitchhiked across the country to participate in it. He brought the "tongues" back to Dunn, which became one of the points of origin of Pentecostalism in the South. The movement gave rise to a number of closely related denominations, the three main ones being Pentecostal Holiness, Assemblies of God, and Church of God. My research with Pentecostal Holiness churches in a rural county in eastern North Carolina and a city in the western Piedmont suggests that their written creed and system of frequent rotation of pastors from one church to another produces a religious and cultural ethos more or less independent of contrasting regional subcultures.

One very dynamic Pentecostal preacher sums up the history of Pentecostalism by saying, "The Lord took the Baptist water and the Methodist fire and made that Pentecostal steam." Allowing for a bit of denominational bias, the preacher was acknowledging that the taproot of Pentecostalism goes deep into the Protestant tradition shared with both the Baptists and Methodists. Pentecostals, however, see their roots extending well beyond the Protestant Reformation, to the day of Pentecost, when the apostles gathered and "there appeared unto them cloven tongues like as of fire, and it sat upon each of them. And they were all filled with the Holy Ghost, and began to speak with other tongues, as the Spirit gave them utterance" (Acts 2:3, 4).

The essence of the Pentecostal experience is this "baptism of the

Holy Spirit," a dynamic, intimate relationship with the spirit of God. The initial, physical evidence of this relationship is "speaking with other tongues," or glossolalia, but speaking in tongues is not an end in itself—it is merely a symbol of being filled, voluntarily, by God's spirit. The baptism is usually an ecstatic, rapturous experience and is sometimes characterized by dancing, shouting, convulsive movements of the body, and perhaps even rolling in the floor—hence the unflattering term *Holy Rollers,* a stigma to some Pentecostals, a badge of persecution worn proudly by others.

The jocular aphorism and the capsule history, however, conceal the complexity of Pentecostal relations to successive waves of American revivalism. And the stereotypes that outsiders often extrapolate from the manifestations of the baptism of the Holy Spirit are belied by many of the facts about Pentecostals. For example, while others may think of them as laborers or small farmers with little education or means (which in the early days they may have been), the Protestant work ethic has been very strong in this group, with its emphasis on clean living and strict discipline of children. For this reason, second- and third-generation Pentecostals are better educated, and many have joined the ranks of white-collar and professional occupations. Studying Pentecostals in a county in eastern North Carolina, I found only twenty-five percent to be blue-collar workers. Twenty-seven percent did clerical or sales work, and surprisingly (if one identifies Pentecostalism with the proletariat), thirty-one percent were at the managerial or professional level. In fact, the wealthiest man in the community I studied was a member and strong supporter of the Pentecostal Holiness church. A number of non-Pentecostal charismatics of higher status have also joined a Pentecostal church as a result of opposition encountered in their home churches. One example is a "spirit-filled" physician who switched his affiliation from Baptist to Pentecostal Holiness. Another is a very successful realtor who shifted his membership to the same church.

Faith healing—a key emphasis in Pentecostal religion—rewards an effort to get behind the outsider's stereotypes, to explore the worldview disclosed in Pentecostal healing practice, in the preaching and writings of Pentecostal ministers, and in the opinions of lay Pentecostals as expressed in interviews and answers to questionnaires. I have chosen the term *healing practice* rather than *healing ritual* because there are in fact so many ways that healing occurs among Pentecostals that it seems restrictive to classify it as a ritual. From my observations of healing episodes it is possible, however, to construct a prototype of a healing service.

Since Pentecostals are fundamentalists, they try to follow the Bible as literally as possible. Thus the prototypical healing practice derives from this verse: "Is any sick among you? Let him call for the elders of the church; and let them pray over him, anointing him with oil in the name of the Lord; And the prayer of faith shall save the sick, and the Lord shall raise him up; and if he have committed sins, they shall be forgiven him" (James 5:14–15). The laying on of hands, another important aspect of the practice, derives from the example of Christ who laid hands on the sick. Likewise the apostles laid hands on the sick while ministering to them.

Against the background of these examples from the New Testament, I examine a typical sequence of events that is associated with prayer for the sick. Prayers for the sick typically take place in the context of a religious service. Before prayer for the sick is offered, however, there is an intensification of emotion brought about by prayer, glossolalia, shouting, music, and preaching. Pentecostals believe that miracles are most likely to occur while the "waters are troubled" or while the "spirit is moving." For example, one evangelist I observed aroused her congregation to the point of spiritual ecstasy before attempting to pray for the sick. She accomplished this through an inspiring sermon on conquering problems and by singing and speaking in tongues. All these activities tend to build the faith of seekers. Another source of strong support for the faith of the members was her "gift of discernment," which allowed her to tell some people what their problem was before asking. Discernment is practiced by other healing evangelists as well. For example, one preacher said: "Woman, face this audience." He talked very firm and he said: "Audience, God revealed this woman's face to me today while I was praying. . . . God has heard your prayers and he's going to heal you tonight."

Once the atmosphere is charged, the sick, if they are able, come forward and stand before the altar. This is the initial act of faith and obedience on their part. Afflicted persons state to the preacher the nature of their illness, or they may simply state that "God knows the nature of my illness." It is not necessary for the name of the malady to be stated because God is omniscient and he does the healing, not man. After this, the pastor may ask "some of the brethren and sisters" to gather round the sick person and to touch the afflicted as the prayer is being offered. When they have so assembled, others may form an outer perimeter touching those who are touching the sick.

The pastor takes from his pulpit a small vial of oil and pours some on his fingertips. Then he "anoints the person's head with oil" as the prayer is being made. Prayers ensue, led off by the minister with everyone praying simultaneously. The prayer is very loud, characterized by sudden jerking movements of the body of the minister and others. The preacher prays in a commanding voice, not toward God, but toward Satan or the demon that has afflicted the person. This tone is sometimes alternated with a tone of supplication toward God. The following are typical phrases heard in these prayers: "Father, in the name of Jesus, right now, I rebuke the devil, and I command him to loose them . . . in Jesus name that your healing virtue will come through. . . . I rebuke those ulcers in the name of Jesus. . . . Loose him and set him free and make him every whit whole."

Before or during the prayer, the seeker may be asked to do something to demonstrate faith. This is reminiscent of the story of Naaman in the Old Testament who was asked to dip in the muddy Jordan River seven times to receive healing for leprosy. This gesture may be something as simple as raising the hands: "Raise your hands as a sign of surrender unto him." Or it may involve simple repeat-after-me type phrases such as "By his stripes, I claim healing," and "I receive my healing, *right now.*"

Sometimes an evangelist in a special healing service may set up a demonstration of the healing so that the congregation can witness it. In one such service, the evangelist set a chair on the stage and asked each seeker with a back problem to sit down in the chair with a straight back. Then the evangelist had the seekers hold out their feet with their knees locked to see if their legs were of even length as indicated by whether their heels came together. Several appeared to have one leg longer than the other, which the evangelist saw as the cause of the back or spine problem. She ministered to her supplicants in this manner: "I want you to look at her heels . . . alright, look at that; look at the heel [one leg appears longer than the other]. I don't have to pray because God is already . . . doing it . . . there it is. . . . Father, it has been done [the legs appear to even out as the heels come together, which action elicits a chorus of Amens and Hallelujahs from the audience].

As the healing touch is received, the supplicant may be "slain in the spirit." Being slain in the spirit usually involves a sudden jerk or convulsing on the part of the minister, followed almost instantaneously by a similar reaction by the seeker. The seeker then seems to relax and to fall backward to the floor, sometimes being assisted by "catchers" assigned this duty. The supplicant then lies motionless on his or her back for several minutes in an unconscious or semiconscious state. One seeker reported to me these sensations that she experienced: "I felt a light, cool touch on my forehead, and then I was down on the floor. It was a warm secure feeling. I did not feel afraid in the least, only totally warm and as if I was feather light. I kept praising God inwardly as I remember, and the warm feeling intensified. I did not wish to move from that spot. . . . my husband guessed [that I was on the floor] five to ten minutes."

After the healing prayer and other ministrations, the seekers may be subjected to a test of faith. They may be told to launch out and act as if the healing were a reality, for example, "take up your bed and walk." Old-time Pentecostal preachers would command their charges to throw away crutches, and to get up out of wheelchairs.

What I have described is a prototypical public healing, but there exists another form of healing among Pentecostals, a private healing, which we can know only through personal accounts, like the following one given in an interview:

> I have had two heart attacks: one in June of '78 and one the following year in July '79. Since then, I had gone back to work. . . . I was taking medicine for it—glycerin, [but] I began to get depressed about my condition. [There was] pain in the left side of my chest, [and] I felt bad in general. I went to Dr. F and asked: "Can I do some more exercise, jog, or something?" He said: "I'll send you to a specialist in Raleigh. [He'll] give you a stretch [stress] test [and] catherize your heart." I was afraid of that—I was against that.
>
> I went for a year and all at once I decided to do this; so I went and told Dr. F. This was in March 1980. He said he'd set up an appointment in April. He set it up for me to go in on Wednesday. Dr. D in

Raleigh was the man I was supposed to see. On Tuesday night [over a] week before my appointment with the specialist in Raleigh, about three o'clock in the morning, I woke up and sat up in bed with this on the tip of my tongue: "Healing, claim healing." I was right by myself there — of course, my wife was in the bed asleep — apparently I was saying this over and over. It came to me later on — this is the Lord speaking to me — in my words. There was no audible voice. . . . I rolled over and went back to sleep. . . . I didn't mention it to no one.

Interviewer: That's when it was done?

Yes, but it took time to unite this so far as man is concerned . . . I went to the doctor that afternoon [Wednesday]; my wife went with me. . . . I went up there to be examined but the doctor said: "Well, [Mr. L] I'm going to put you in the hospital and run some tests on you. . . . We're going to run you through some strenuous tests, and we're going to run a catherization of your heart. . . . It must be done now. [Mr. L wanted to go back home, but the doctor insisted that it must be done right away.] Well, that scared me.

The examination started the next day and nothing turned out. It didn't make no sense to them. They hadn't never seen me up there. . . . They thought I was up there to take a rest or stay out of work or something. . . . Well . . . my healing was being manifested. I knew that I didn't have no pain. . . . The doctor came to see me three times a day, but I had no pain. But I'd had it previous to that about every day. I mean nothing bad to where I'd have to go to the hospital, but it would be uncomfortable, but then it would stop. . . . I knew then that I'd been healed, and I wanted to relay this, and so I stayed there Friday, Saturday and Sunday. I was supposed to go home after they'd catherized me on Monday.

They x-rayed me, they ran cardiograms on me. . . . They said: "Are you sure about this?" Everything was all right. . . . I was still dreading the catherization on Monday.

Interviewer: They were going to go ahead and do it even though there were no symptoms?

Yes, because you see they wanted to know. . . . They had to find out what was clogging up. But the doctor said: "I want to cancel that catherization and do a stress test, and then we'll see about this." So Monday afternoon, they run me over. . . . Dr. C told me then that they'd do this [a stress test] first and then have the catherization on Tuesday. They put me on that treadmill, and I ran nine minutes. . . . He didn't have no idea I'd go three minutes. . . . And unbeknowing to me [at the time] Dr. S [the heart specialist] had called Dr. F [the family doctor who referred Mr. L] and told him, "I want you to show me some proof that this man has ever even had a heart attack."

I didn't ever have the catherization, but I know that he healed me — Jesus Christ. . . . God is just as alive today as he ever was when he walked the streets of Palestine.

Whether it occurs in private or in a public service, underlying the Pentecostal healing is a system of beliefs. For Pentecostals, healing is a part of the total experience of salvation, and its manifestation is closely connected with the Pentecostal experience of the baptism with the Holy Spirit. This special experience, which goes beyond salvation, gives the Christian access to a special supernatural power to deal with sickness and other human problems: "Ye shall receive power after that the Holy Ghost is come upon you" (Acts 1:8).

Most Pentecostal denominations have their own statement of faith that spells out this belief in faith healing. The constitution of the Assemblies of God states under Tenets of Faith: "Divine Healing is an integral part of the Gospel. Deliverance from sickness is provided for in the atonement, and is the privilege of all believers." Similarly, the *Faith and Practices of the Pentecostal Free Will Baptist Church, Inc.,* states "We believe that the Bible [teaches] that the healing provided in the atonement is both spiritual and physical."[1]

This same document further declares that "sickness and suffering are the result of sin"; and since Christ's death paid the penalty for sin, he also paid for the effects of sin: death and sickness. The Scripture which is used to support this belief in healing is from the Old Testament: "But he was wounded for our transgressions, he was bruised for our iniquities: the chastisement of our peace was upon him; and *with his stripes we are healed*" (Isa. 53:5).

The cause of sickness, in the Pentecostal view, is sin — not necessarily the sin of the person who is afflicted, but original sin that exists in the world as a result of the fall of man. When man fell out of harmony with the laws of God in his behavior and attitudes, sickness and death were the result. However, Pentecostals do not conceive of sin as an abstract principle. They see it personified in the form of Satan and his demons. To them Satan is more than a metaphor; he is a real spiritual being with personality and will. David E. Harrell, in his book *All Things are Possible,* indicates that Pentecostals believe in a great variety of demons, for example, demons of lies, fornication, and sickness. In his earlier years, Oral Roberts emphasized demon possession as the cause of sickness and was noted for casting out evil spirits.[2] This does not mean, however, that the afflicted person is necessarily demon possessed, since Christians can be sick. Demonic possession is more often identified with mental illness, and demons may cause physical illness without possessing the afflicted one.

If healing is provided for in the atonement, how does one appropriate this divine medicine in a specific case of sickness? The answers that Pentecostals find in the Scriptures are "Ask and ye shall receive" and "Ask in faith believing." These underlie the steps that Oral Roberts outlines in his book *If You Need Healing Do These Things,* to help the seeker to release his faith for healing: know that it is God's will to heal you; remember that healing begins within; use a point of contact; turn your faith loose now; close the case for victory; and join yourself to a companion of faith.[3]

The vital role of individual faith is given humorous expression by Kenneth Hagin in one of his sermons: "You can lay your hands on folks like that [unbelievers] until you're worn every hair off the top of their head, and all they're going to get out of it will be a bald head."[4] It is the faith of the individual supplicant that heals. However, one minister in a sermon entitled "Whose Faith Heals?" stated that "some are healed because they have been brought by someone with faith. Matthew 8:13 says 'And Jesus said unto the Centurion, go thy way; and as thou hast believed, so be it unto thee. And his servant was healed in the selfsame hour.'" This is sometimes termed *intercessory faith* and would seem to be appropriate in a prayer for a sick infant who does not understand what faith is or for a sick person who is in a comatose state and cannot have faith for himself.

The preacher went on to state that "some are healed because of the faith of the person who prays [because] Mark 16:18 [says]: 'They shall lay hands on the sick, and they shall recover.'" However, the minister moderated his own opinion on this issue: "But, friend, if you do not believe in healing, if you do not believe Jesus *will* heal you, we doubt that it will do much good for anyone else to pray for you."

If faith is the condition for healing, will everyone who has faith be healed? Two schools of thought have emerged on this issue. One is called *positive confessionalism* by Pentecostal writers, and the other I have termed *divine discretion*. Positive confessionalism is identified with the Arminian school of thought, emphasizing the will of the individual; divine discretion is aligned with Calvinist thought, which emphasizes the will of God. David Nunne, one of the healing revivalists of the 1950s, stated emphatically a major tenet of what has come to be known as positive confessionalism: "God wants to heal you. Some of these people keep praying: 'If it be thy will, oh God, heal me!' If they want to pray that way — that old faith paralyzing prayer: 'If it be thy will,' they ought to submit to it by not taking any medicine."[5]

Taken to the extreme, Arminian positive confessionalism puts God under a kind of contract whereby he is obligated to heal if the Christian meets the conditions. To meet the conditions, all the Christian has to do is claim what has been purchased by the blood of Christ. The phrase "claim your healing" or "confess your healing" is quite often heard in Pentecostal circles.

The authors of *The Believer and Positive Confession* state "the believer who refrains from acknowledging the negative and continues to affirm the positive will assure for himself pleasant circumstances. He will be sick only if he confesses he is sick. Some make a distinction between acknowledging the symptoms of an illness and the illness itself. . . . If a person wants healing, he is to confess it even though it is obviously not the case."[6]

There are several corollaries of this belief: the sick who confess their healing will always be healed (Mark 9:23, "If thou canst believe, all things are possible to him that believeth"); those who confess positive expectations should never be sick to begin with; if one does not get healed, it is because of lack of faith; God has promised man at least seventy or eighty years of life;[7] and one does not have to be sick in order to die.

There are many Pentecostals who disagree with positive confessionalism. A preacher I have already quoted is one of these. In a sermon entitled "A Study of Sickness and Healing," he said, "Now there is a new approach to the subject, which in my opinion, is unscriptural and dangerous to the cause of Christ. It is the belief and statement by some that you are healed when you 'confess' it even if you still have the symptoms. I hope to show you this position — and the position you will never be sick — is unscriptural!" He continued, giving biblical examples of what I have termed *divine discretion*, that it is in God's will and plan to heal some but not others and that some purpose may be served by pain and sickness. "A key example is Paul's thorn in the flesh . . . which was not healed on the three times he prayed" (2 Cor. 12:7–9). Later Paul was healed, but according to this sermon, it was not "confessed" until after the fact. The preacher went on to say that positive confessionalism "puts man in the position of 'ordering' God around."

Most, if not all, Pentecostals recognize the principle that it is God, not the minister, who heals. The healer is merely the instrument through which healing power flows, not the source of that power. Neither is it the faith of the "healer," but rather the faith of the supplicant that brings about a miracle in the view of most Pentecostals.

What then is the role of the healer? Some are spoken of as having the "gift of healing," while others may have the "gift of tongues" or the "gift of discernment." This belief is based upon the concept of spiritual gifts referred to in 1 Corinthians 12:8, 9: "For to one is given by the Spirit the word of wisdom; to another the word of knowledge by the same Spirit; to another faith by the same Spirit; to another the gifts of healing by the same Spirit." The gift of healing means that one possesses special charisma to influence the minds of other people. This influence can lead to a bolstering of faith, which in turn brings about the healing.

Medical science and faith healing have from time to time found themselves to be uncomfortable companions in the Pentecostal ranks. Two schools of thought have emerged in this controversy. The conservative school, which is more characteristic of the old-line Pentecostals, teaches that seeking medical help shows a lack of faith in God. The conservative group is generally characterized by an attitude that is antiscience in general and antimedical science in particular. The other school of thought, which I have termed the liberal school, is characteristic of the more modern Pentecostals. It conceives an essential complementarity between medicine and faith, science and religion. The key concept expressed here is that all healing is of God and therefore a sharp line cannot be drawn between natural healing and supernatural healing. Thus the conservative school tends to be more dualistic in thought; the liberal school, more holistic and integrative. Most, if not all, of the present-day Pentecostal churches in the eastern North Carolina county I studied have followed Oral Roberts's lead in merging prayer with medicine. The creed of the Pentecostal Free Will Baptist church explicitly states: "While it is God's highest will to anoint, lay hands on and pray for the healing of the sick, we do not believe that the Bible teaches that there is anything morally wrong with taking medicine, or receiving human aid, if one is not able to fully trust the Lord."[8]

Official Pentecostal statements of faith and the pronouncements of leading ministers clarify the premises of public and private Pentecostal healing. But the diversity of Pentecostal views and practices emerges more clearly in the opinions of lay Pentecostals, and the relative importance of particular viewpoints shows best in answers to my questionnaire.[9] A logical starting point in describing these opinions is the Pentecostal definition of faith healing. The Pentecostal is confronted with a battery of "healing" definitions in our scientific society. There is the natural healing of the body, cultural healing by medicine, mind healing, and supernatural healing that transcends all these kinds of healing. Most Pentecostals see miraculous healing as something that is supernatural, thus transcending the other levels of healing. About seventy-five percent of the respondents selected the response category "God's supernatural intervention"; however, a significant number saw healing as a combination of natural, cultural, and supernatural forces. The rationale here is that all healing comes from God and is thus divine or supernatural; therefore there is no distinction between natural and divine — all healing is one. One Pentecostal told me in an interview: "Many of our healings are psychosomatic — now I might be shot for saying that — but to me that's just as great a miracle as anything else because that is the healing of the *mind.*" However, when the point is pressed, most Pentecostals will acknowledge that there is a distinction between gradual, natural healing, and instantaneous supernatural healing.

When asked what the level of consciousness was at the moment of healing, the modal response was that they were fully awake (eight of twenty). Two said they were wide awake or hyper-alert. Five, however, said they were in a semiconscious state. Three of these were asleep when they received their healing touch. Two said they were completely unconscious or in a trance state. (The trance state is associated with complete unconsciousness or semiconsciousness and quite often occurs after one is "slain in the spirit" or completely surrenders to the Holy Spirit. As one surrenders control of the body to the Holy Spirit, the muscles give way and one collapses, falling to the floor. Some lie motionless on the floor; others twitch, convulse, or roll.) During the trance state, one may experience visions or very warm sensations. The diversity of other psychological factors associated with healing includes a focusing of attention or concentration on the idea of healing (reported by fourteen of nineteen), passivity (twelve of eighteen), lying down praying (nine of eighteen), and being alone at home (nine of twenty).

Healing testimonies and interviews confirm that healing may take place in an altered state of mind that would be distinguished by the believer as nonordinary or sacred reality. Such a state of mind might take the form of a trance following being slain in the spirit, a vision, a voice, a transcendent meditative state involving prayer, or an over-powering emotion or presence. I discovered from my interviews that three out of twelve saw visions at the time of their healing. The vision may involve seeing Christ, or it may involve seeing Satan or demons, or perhaps even a spirit guide. One person said, "I kept seeing a little vision: a little angel would come to me at night and brought me a little white bowl. She had long blond hair. She brought me this little bowl and said: 'Take this and drink it. . . . This is eternal life from Jesus.' It looked like sweet milk to me." Although only three of the twelve reported visions, nine reported an overpowering emotion or presence that made them forget the things and people around them.

Although this kind of "fire and smoke" often accompanies dramatic Pentecostal experience, many Pentecostals insist that it is faith, not feeling, that counts. Sometimes the believer has to act well on faith even though the feeling is not there and the symptoms persist. This would be especially true for gradual healing. One respondent confessed: "He [the minister] prayed for me but I didn't feel a thing but I took my glasses off by faith in Jesus Christ. . . . But I confessed the promise [that] . . . I was healed." This is generally borne out in my data, although not in every case. Of twenty-one persons, fifteen reported having faith for their healing. But three others reported a neutral attitude, and surprisingly, two reported an unbelieving attitude at the time of healing. Hence faith is usually the precondition for healing, but not always. One recipient reported that he was not even praying for healing when his knees were healed; he sees the healing as a gift from God for which he did not even have to ask. Moreover, a woman recipient said that she felt so unworthy at the time of her healing that she was not really expecting to be healed.

My study did not show that faith healing is usually associated with perceived expiation of sins. Only two of the twenty reported that healing was a part of a conversion experience; but eleven of twenty said that healing occurred as a singular experience, that is, not associated with any other type of experience. Most of those healed regarded themselves as Christian and did not see their sickness as punishment for sin. To the Pentecostal, sickness came into the world because of original sin, but the believer's sickness is not necessarily caused by his own sin. It is caused by Satan's power in this world.

When healing is associated with conversion or a forgiveness experience, it is often described as a "healing of the memories." Healing of the memories involves a kind of self-forgiveness and absolution of guilt. Ironically, much of the guilt is fostered by Pentecostal mores, which are very strict, and thus many "fall short of the glory of God." This point is borne out by Mr. X. Mr. X was reared as a Pentecostal, but when he was "sowing his wild oats" as a young man, he became obsessed with guilt and a sense of unworthiness that probably contributed to his attempted suicide. His suicidal tendencies were not resolved until he experienced a dramatic healing and exorcism. Thus it appears that what the group mores imposed with the one hand, they took away with the other.

Significant differences were observed between the two major theological orientations, positive confessionalism and divine discretionism. More positive confessionists reported a high rate of healing success than did divine discretionists. When healing failure occurred, however, divine discretionists interpreted this experience as an expression of divine will, whereas positive confessionists tended to see failure as a shortcoming of the individual. About an equal proportion of both groups saw healing success and healing failure to be an interplay between the will of God and the will of man. Hence we found some synthesis between the Arminian-Methodist tradition and the Calvinist tradition.

The North Carolina survey also suggested that more spirit-filled Christians will experience healing than non-spirit-filled Christians. Some hypothetical relationships that were not supported by our data are: those with "holistic" healing concepts show more favorable attitudes toward doctors—in fact, most Pentecostals of all orientations in our sample showed favorable attitudes; older Pentecostals show less favorable attitudes towards doctors; those with holistic orientations will report more healings than those with purely supernaturalistic orientations; and charismatics will report a higher rate of healing than noncharismatics.

With regard to the length of time required to complete the healing, over half (eleven of twenty-one questioned) reported that the healing occurred instantaneously, and only two of twenty-one reported that it took more than six months. As to whether the healing was partial or complete, there seems to be, from the outsider's point of view, some inconsistency. Whereas the overwhelming majority (twenty of twenty-one) reported that their healings were complete, only ten of nineteen reported that they had no recurrence of symptoms, and eight of nineteen indicated that there were recurrences of symptoms.

Several of the believers (four of eighteen) did not return to the doctor after their healing because they felt no need to do so. The attitude seemed to be, Why pay a doctor to tell you something you already know? This is one area of potential conflict with the medical profession, since doctors who have these patients on regular medication or treatment feel that they should be consulted before termination of the medication. The usual response of those returning to the doctor was that their doctors could not explain the healing. As indicated in the analysis of the physician's questionnaire, however, many doctors say that they go along with the belief system or try to avoid confrontation with it. This might account for some, but probably not all, of the patients' reports of favorable reaction by their doctors.

While I had originally supposed that most healings would be preceded by ecstatic, jubilant states, I found that the usual state was either calm or a normal state of mind. I likewise expected that many would be excited and jubilant after their healing; however, only eight of nineteen persons I questioned were elated or excited about the healing, whereas ten, a slight majority, felt calm and peaceful. Actually, then, about the same number reported a calm state as an ecstatic state. Some described the post-healing experience as a deep, peaceful feeling; others (especially those healed of external injuries of the limbs or joints) continue to enjoy the new freedom of movement and do quite a bit of running, jumping, and leaping. Those healed of internal problems, however, tend to be more quiescent. Another factor that seems to be of influence is whether the healing occurred in a private setting or a public setting. Private experiences tend to be characterized by a calm quiescence, whereas public experiences tend to be characterized by contagious emotional excitation.

I have already noted that the modal setting for healing was private, not public. In my sample of healing testimonies, nine out of twenty-one testified that their healing occurred while they were alone at home. Another four said that they received their healing in a hospital; most were alone at the time. However, many of those who received their "touch" privately had already been prayed for in the public setting of the church but had not received their touch at that time. Furthermore, being alone does not mean that the person was socially isolated, for he or she usually knew that fellow church members were offering intercessory prayer. Mr. L, whose testimony was quoted earlier, is an example of a person whose private healing occurred during sleep after an intercessory prayer at church. When he went to bed that night, he was praying for his healing. He was awakened in the middle of the night by these words going over and over in his mind: "Claim healing, claim healing."

Since most healings in our sample were private, there was no human healer involved at the moment. Fewer than half—nine of twenty healings in the sample—involved a healer at the moment of healing, and only six of those healed said that the healer actually laid hands on them. So while the element of social support is definitely a reality in the psychology of the believer, it is not always immediate and physical. Pentecostals have a proverb for this: "There is no distance in prayer."

What does one learn from a close inquiry into faith healing within Pentecostal Holiness churches in an eastern North Carolina county? The first lesson is that simply to observe the public gestures of the healing is surely to misunderstand the practice. Healers who seem charismatic feel themselves, and are seen by fellow believers, to be merely channels for a power not their own. The gestures of healing, moreover, occur less commonly in public than in private. They take place less often in emotion-charged contexts than public healing suggests and are followed less often by the experience and expression of ecstasy. Pentecostals report a great diversity of experiences with healing and many contrasting interpretations of their experiences. Above all, my study has shown that Pentecostalism is a total experience permeating the life of the believer and that healing has a key place in its system. The Pentecostal preacher is speaking of more than bodily health when he urges the seeker: "Be whole from the crown of your head to the soles of your feet."

NOTES

The fieldwork for this paper was undertaken between 1976 and 1979 for my doctoral dissertation, *Faith Healing: Where Science Meets Religion in the Body of Believers* (Chapel Hill: Department of Anthropology, University of North Carolina, 1982). In addition to works cited in the notes, some key studies of Pentecostalism are Robert Anderson, *Vision of the Disinherited: The Making of American Pentecostalism* (New York: Oxford University Press, 1979); Walter J. Hollenweger, *The Pentecostals: The Charismatic Movement in the Churches,* trans. R. A. Wilson (Minneapolis: Augsburg Publishing House, 1972); and Grant Wacker, "The Function of Faith in Primitive Pentecostalism," *Harvard Theological Review* 77 (June 1985): 353–75. For a psychiatric approach, see E. Mansell Pattison, "Faith Healing and Glossolalia," in Irving I. Zaretsky and Mark P. Leone, eds., *Religious Movements in Contemporary America* (Princeton: Princeton University Press, 1974), pp. 418–455; a somewhat different view is given in James L. Peacock, "Symbolic and Psychological Anthropology: The Case of Pentecostal Faith Healing," *Ethos* 12 (1984): 37–53. Another North Carolina field study of this subject was prepared by Christopher H. Walker, "The Ritual Context of Healing by Faith," Master's thesis (Chapel Hill: Department of Anthropology, University of North Carolina, 1979).

1. Herbert F. Carter et al., *Faith and Practices of the Pentecostal Free Will Baptist Church, Inc.* (Dunn, N.C.: Denominational Publication, 1977), p. 31.
2. David E. Harrell, *All Things Are Possible* (Bloomington: Indiana University Press, 1975), p. 88.
3. Oral Roberts, *If You Need Healing Do These Things* (Tulsa, Okla.: Oral Roberts Association, 1956).
4. Quoted in Harrell, *All Things Are Possible,* p. 86.
5. Ibid., p. 87.
6. Anon., *The Believer and Positive Confession* (Springfield, Mo.: Assemblies of God Gospel Publishing House, 1980), p. 7.

7. Kenneth Hagin, "How to Make the Dream God Gave You Come True" in *The Word of Faith* (Tulsa, Okla.: Kenneth Hagin Ministries, 1981), p. 7.

8. Carter, *Faith and Practices,* p. 31.

9. Douglas Reinhardt, *Faith Healing: Where Science Meets Religion in the Body of Believers,* Ph.D. dissertation (Chapel Hill: Department of Anthropology, University of North Carolina, 1982), appendix B.

Your Daughters Shall Prophesy: Women in the Afro-American Preaching Tradition

8

Catherine L. Peck

The African Methodist Episcopal Zion Church grew from a black congregation that formed in New York City in 1796 and separated from the white Methodist Episcopal Church in 1820. Excluded from the slave-holding South, it was one of the first Northern churches to send missionaries to the emancipated slaves. North Carolina was the scene where it opened its southern work, and the denomination is still strong in the state. Four of its churches in the central Piedmont — two in rural and two in urban communities — with women as preachers aided the following study.

> And it shall come to pass afterward that I will pour out my spirit on
> all flesh; your sons and your daughters shall prophesy, your old
> men shall dream dreams, and your young men shall see visions.
> Even upon the menservants and maidservants in those days, I will
> pour out my spirit (Joel 2:28–29).

This passage from the prophet Joel, which includes women as well as men in God's vision, has proven valuable for women whom God has called to preach the Gospel. For although God's authority leads women towards the pulpit, men's authority often stops them at the altar rail. I have met in North Carolina a number of black women who have received the divine calling. Every Sunday morning these women assume the pulpits in churches that they have either established themselves or to which they have been assigned by their denominational boards. Many of them are women who are called not only to preach, but also to be pastors — heads of their churches. Their callings

143

are authentic according to the way people have experienced the call since the Afro-American preaching tradition began. And yet women regularly are challenged to prove their calling in ways that men are not. Scripture is both for them and against them, and every woman preacher can quote the chapters and verses that justify her, just as she can refute the verses that admonish her to be silent in the church.

To show the extent of the challenge women face, a well-known evangelist in Durham, North Carolina, with her Bible in her hand, recalled the large number of men who have handed her their Bibles saying, "Prove to me that God called you to preach." She demonstrated how they pound the book to drive home the point. Her reply is typical of women so challenged: "I'd take the Bible and I would say, 'Prove to me that He didn't.' And I would extend it to them and say, 'Prove to me that He didn't call me.'"

In such a debate, people who wish to deny women the right to preach most often use Paul's first letter to the Corinthians. In Chapter 14, verse 34 and following, Paul writes, "As in all the churches of the saints, the women should keep silence in the churches. For they are not permitted to speak, but should be subordinate, as even the law says. If there is anything they desire to know, let them ask their husbands at home. For it is shameful for a woman to speak in Church" (RSV).

All the women preachers I know have grappled with this passage, and all have a ready response. When I told Reverend Sudi Long, for example, that I had heard many people refer to Paul's letter as a reason why women should not preach, I barely had the words out when she replied:

> But they don't go and talk about what them Corinthian women were doing. Them women were trying to run that church. And they were trying to get their husbands to get passed what they wanted to get passed. That's why St. Paul told them men that. "Now if you women want to ask your husbands then you wait 'til you get home and ask 'em."
>
> But the prophet Joel said, "In the last day" — don't get me wound up, now — "I will pour out my spirit on all flesh, and your sons and your daughters shall prophesy." That's Bible. Peter talked about it on Pentecost that day. He quoted Scripture.
>
> Then St. Paul went on a little further and he said, he told his brother

not to forget Aquilla and Priscilla, those ladies who labored with men and God. He said that. 'Course they don't say nothing about that.

All these biblical references come immediately to Reverend Long's defense, and she and the other women have other references available to help them argue their cause. Less historically objective, perhaps, but equally poignant is a rebuttal I heard from several women. As Evangelist Gail Davis put it when asked how she dealt with detractors who hauled out Saint Paul's verses to refute her calling: "The Lord just gave me to tell them that if God could trust a woman to carry the *living* Word, He can use me to carry the *written* word. Mary carried the living Word inside of her body, and if God could trust her, he can trust me."

Every woman preacher I have met has faced opposition, sometimes bitter opposition, to her calling. But what is remarkable and important is that, in spite of the obstacles facing them, women do continue to find their way into the pulpits of black churches. And once established there, they often are able to overcome prejudices against their sex on the strength of their skills and talents as verbal artists. As preachers, they not only become accepted, but also are lauded because they are, as much as their male counterparts, exemplary tradition-bearers. They are skillful at delivering the best the folk preacher has to offer. The Afro-American poet-orator, so well defined by Bruce Rosenberg, is no less present among women who preach than among men.[1] If a woman is a good preacher, her style is emotionally charged, formulaic, and personal. She seeks and gets enthusiastic responses from the congregation. Most important, she develops a message for her parishioners that is rooted in Scripture and shaped by her own personality and perception.

Inasmuch as their own personalities shape their preaching and pastoring styles, there is in the experiences of the women preachers I have known something that sets them apart from men. In their capacity as the foremost members of their churches, they exhibit the strength of character and stamina associated with all religious leaders. But in their response to their parishioners' needs, in their response to their calling, and in the imagery they choose as the foundation for their sermons, their perspective as women comes through.

There are, then, two themes to develop here. One is that women are skillful and talented bearers of the Afro-American preaching tradition. The other is that women make a mark on the established tradition by bringing into the pulpit their essential feminine personalities. A look at the courage and passionate intuition with which one woman conducts her services will serve to demonstrate how she distinguishes herself as a tradition-bearer, and a brief examination of the imagery and narratives that illustrate these women's sermons will show how the tradition is enhanced by the feminine perception.

The Reverend Sudi Long—a woman about forty-five years of age—is a prodigious preacher, tall and commanding in appearance but soft and compelling in her attitude towards her profession. She understands a good deal, too, about the problems a woman faces as she goes into the pulpit. She knows, for example, that there is among blacks a stigma attached to women preachers: They only know how to "get up, holler 'GloryHallelujahAmen' and sit back down." But she and others have shown that, having absorbed since childhood all the elements of traditional preaching, they have the means to overcome this stigma.

Long has at her disposal a large repertory of traditional religious forms that she uses to meet the spiritual needs of her congregation. I remember in particular being impressed one Sunday by the spontaneous way Reverend Long altered the course of a floundering service by creating a spiritual event in the final moments of the service, which subtly led her congregation to a level of emotional intensity I had never before seen in her church. Although the service that day was to all purposes over, Reverend Long was not satisfied. Even I could tell that the parishioners had not been moved by songs, sermon, or prayers. The sermon had been good, as typically Long's are, and the music was led by the excellent male choir, but few in the church felt the spirit moving, and Reverend Long did not want to end the service with the congregation's desultory mood unchanged.

After the altar call, she asked for "Amazing Grace," her personal favorite in the male choir's repertory. Everyone picked up the tune, of course, and she would not let it stop. After going through several verses, some twice, Reverend Long said quietly, "Oh, let's moan it one time—let's just moan it now." Then she and her assistants left the pulpit and walked to the rear of the church amidst all the people "moaning" the tune again and again. The results were profound.

Parishioners stood for a long period of silence, some in tears, before they began leaving the church.

In essence, Reverend Long took the prevailing mood that day and deepened it as a way of moving the people. Mr. Leroy Johnson, the leader of the male choir, explained in an interview how this moaning or humming, as he calls it, works: "You know this is something that'll really get to me. Now, I can just hum; you don't hear the words, you just hum, and it seems like to me those words that I'm humming— they are words there, but you're not saying them. Seems like it really goes down inside, really down in there, when you're humming. And somehow or another that brings a feeling that nothing else brings to me. We hummed a song on that last third Sunday and it looked like the spirit just was moving around during that humming. It really gets down there."

At the moment in her church, then, when Reverend Long felt that something needed to happen, she chose a course that she knew would touch her congregation at a deep level. That she knew the moaning "really gets down there," attests to her skill as a traditional preacher. Any black preacher, or for that matter any black churchgoer, will explain that this ability is God-given, that this is what the call is all about. Reverend Long's timing is almost flawless, a quality Bruce Rosenberg considers to be among the most important aspects of the "spiritual" preacher's art—timing, keeping up with the emotions of the audience, and knowing when to sit down: "Everything is in flux: the congregation and its moods, the rhythms, diction, syntax, and emotions of the preacher, and his message for the day. If the preacher is skillful he will take all, or nearly all, of these considerations into account, however unconsciously. . . . The end result should be the movement of the Spirit of God in the church."[2]

Reverend Long understands implicitly what Rosenberg describes here. If the spirit of God is going to move in the church, somebody has got to facilitate its movement, and she recognizes her mandate as well as her gift:

> When something goes wrong in the church, you can feel it. And I say to 'em, "We're not together this morning. The choir's not half singing. The piano playin's gone out. What's the matter? Let's find out what's wrong."
>
> You get up; you say, you know—just visualize the church I pastor.

You have those people, and those people come out of all kinds of circumstances. . . . And this is why I say every Sunday morning, "We've met again, and a lot of things have happened since we met last. And some we talk about and some we don't. But God has blessed us to come back together." These people, when they come on Sunday morning, they are looking for something . . . to comfort their souls, and somebody had to give it to 'em.

I feel like when a person comes to church and leaves different, something has to happen to you. If I don't hear something that moves me through the song, I want to hear it through a prayer. And if I miss it through both of them, then I got to pick it up in the sermon someway. And when I go to church and come away empty, to me, something didn't happen — somebody doesn't have something to give.

When she uses her gift for reading her congregation's moods and for saving a floundering service, Reverend Long demonstrates that there are heiresses as well as heirs to her preaching tradition. Spontaneous expression is an earmark of Afro-American religion, and Long never hesitates to draw upon her repertory of traditional religious forms and to offer them to her church when, as she says, something goes wrong.

Reverend Sudi Long learned the art of conducting a successful service in the traditional way through a succession of preachers. She grew up as a Baptist in rural Randolph County, North Carolina, and rarely did her family miss going to church. Every other Sunday, when her own church did not have a service, Long spent all day in the Holiness church nearby, where the pastor was a woman.

In sermons, Reverend Long and the other women in this study give witness to the fact that they have absorbed and preserved the traditional hortatory techniques as faithfully and precisely as men have. One may discern many traditional elements in their sermons: direct references to people in the congregation, stock phrases such as "I heard somebody say . . ." or "They tell me that . . ." preceding a biblical passage. That these sermons, like those Rosenberg recorded, are "composed in language that is largely formulaic" seems clear.[3]

In form and style of delivery, the sermons follow the formulas that any student of the folk sermon will recognize. In the content of their sermons, too, these women follow tradition. They exemplify the traditional artist whose material arises organically from his or her personality, experience, and culture. In fact, if the genius of the traditional artist is the capacity for drawing upon locally available materials, then nowhere does this commonplace of folklife studies seem any more apparent than in these women's sermons.

Like other traditional preachers, none of the women in this study considers the choice of subject an arbitrary decision she may make. The text comes from the Lord, and each pastor has given accounts of how every week she will pray for and be directed to a subject, usually a passage of Scripture. But the material the preacher chooses to illustrate the point the Lord assigns her to make is another matter altogether. "You get sermons from people, places, and things," says the Reverend Annie Johnson. "You need those experiences to illustrate with." She is not speaking of the subject of the sermons, but of the extraordinarily rich imagery that distinguishes the Afro-American folk sermon.

Appropriately Reverend Johnson illustrates her point with a story: She had gotten sick at a conference. She had dizziness and achiness, and everyone convinced her to take blood pressure medicine. "But it went against what I had. You see, they was diagnosin' my case," she told me. She went to the doctor and found out that her blood pressure was normal, and she returned to the conference: "I went back and told 'em, 'Now you was diagnosin' my case. And there's a message in this. Just like when you're saved. You know you're saved, and God knows you're saved, and if somebody wants to tell you you're not, you better just go on knowing you are.' I went to someone who knew what the problem was — to an expert — and it's the same with salvation. There's a sermon in it. I haven't got it yet, but it's one there."

The Reverend Sudi Long is a delightful storyteller whose freewheeling personal narratives give her congregation as much pleasure as they give instruction. Most of the experiences Reverend Long tells in her sermons are her own; some she has taken from others and told as her own, like many a good narrator working in the oral tradition. In her sermon, "It's Coming Up Again," for example, Reverend Long's point is that at Judgment Day our sins will be revealed, and we will have to account for them. To illustrate she tells of an event, ostensibly from her childhood:

You know, my daddy used to farm. Billy Thompson said the other
    night, "You can tell Rev'nd Long came from a farm," and I did.
He farmed his land and everybody else's land he could rent.
And when we got older we asked him, "Daddy, why?"
And he said, "To keep y'all fed."
Never cracked a smile or nothing.
But he used to plant corn. And when the corn didn't come up
This space between the corn—they used to call it "skips" then,
I don't know what they call it now. And he would tell us to
    go over. (Congregation: Go ahead, Reverend, go ahead.)
He gave us a whole bag of one of these knapsacks of peas to carry over
    and plant in the skips, so the peas would be in the corn field.
And we went over there—my brother was too little and we had
    to carry him 'cause I don't know what my mama was doing, but we
    had to carry him, anyway, and we planted and we planted.
He said, "Put two to a hill." So everytime you dig that's a hill.
He said put two in that hill.
And and, uh   we planted peas.
And you know Delsey, most of you know her, she's the most
    mischievous one of us. She said, "Now, y'all, I think we've
    planted long enough." You know, we agreed because she was
    older. And she said, "Let's go down and dig a hole to put these
    peas in." (Laughter.)
We went like she said, and you talk about some children digging.
It was ten of us.
We dug a hole.
And we poured them peas in that hole.
We got home and mama said, "You all back mighty early."
Said, "Why you children back so early? Did you plant all them peas?"
"Yes, Mama, we planted every one of 'em."
AND WE DID! Every one of 'em. (Laughter.)
She said, "That's strange because I thought your daddy had a
    hundred pound of peas."
"He did, Mama, but we planted every one of 'em."
Children *by* and *by* (laughter)
Rain started falling,   and the *sun* came out,
And that *hole* got DAMP   and got hot.
And those PEAS
Came up again! (ALL RIGHT, laughter.)
And we had to *stand*
Before the judge   who was an *un*just judge (laughter)

And give an account of our stewardship.
What are you trying to say? I'm trying to *say* regard*l*ess as to
  what you put *down,*
It's gonna COME UP again (yes, yes)
GOOD — it's coming up. . . .
If it's *bad,* it's coming up.

Though Reverend Long tells this story in the first person, I have heard one other preacher use the same story in another sermon to illustrate a similar point. Like any good tale generated in a setting where the oral transmission of information is the essential method of communication, this one has begun to circulate. That Reverend Long is quick to assimilate this kind of story into her sermons, again, places her squarely in the Afro-American narrative tradition.

As a traditional preacher, Reverend Long succeeds in her church on every level. She orchestrates her services to elicit the maximum response and emotion, and she delivers sermons in a style and with a content guaranteed to please. Reverend Long is beloved of her large congregation because she possesses the power to move her people in the old, old ways.

She possesses something else, as well, which is an asset to her as a pastor. Evangelist Gail Davis explains: "We are the softer sex. We have a way of doing things that is altogether different from a man. We take up more time with — with souls. We tend to handle them with kid gloves. We tend not to tire. Because we have the motherly instinct in us, and because we are *made* to *be* mothers, we treat a soul just like they're children. So that's the difference between most men preachers and women preachers." Some men, including Reverend Richard Saunders of the Church of God of Prophecy, which does not ordain women, agree with Gail Davis. He remarked that it makes more sense, in a way, for women to minister than for men. All of Christianity is about love and compassion, and women just naturally have the compassion of Jesus. "Men have to work at it more," he said.

How do women incorporate their feminine perspective into traditional forms and techniques? A further look at the imagery they use in sermons will serve to answer the question.

The illustrative material used by preachers is not necessarily original; most preachers I have talked with will admit this. But what appeals to the individual pastor from among all the possible sermon ideas, as well as from her own imagination, reveals a good deal about her experience and personality. One might expect, then, that images which blatantly reflect the feminine experience will pervade women's sermons, and they do.

When the Reverend Jane Saunders preached on the story of Rebekah and her twin sons, for example, she focused a great deal of attention on the physical details of Rebekah's bearing those children. The Bible says merely that the babies struggled within her, but Reverend Saunders provided much more elaborate detail to the story. Here is what she said:

> But I *believe* that Rebekah as time went on she discovered that
>   the children was struggling together within her.
> And went back and she went and she inquired to the Lord.
> Now in today's time if something was going on with one of us,
> Something was going on inside that so much disturbed me that
>   we couldn't understand why that baby was kicking too much,
> Instead of us going to inquire to God,
> We'd GO to the *doctor*. (That's right.)
> And we'd say, "Now doctor, it is something going on here in my
>   body.
> (shouting:) AND I DON'T KNOW WHAT IT IS, I KNOW THAT I HAVE
>   A BABY BUT IT LOOK LIKE TO ME IT'S MORE THAN ONE BECAUSE IT'S
>   A LOT OF *STRUGGLING* GOING ON IN ME. AND I CAN'T SLEEP AT NIGHT."
>   AND AS SHE INQUIRED TO THE LORD, I BELIEVE THE LORD TOLD HER,
>   "NOW, YOU HAVE TWO NATIONS IN YOUR BODY, IN YOUR WOMB.
>   *ONE* OF THEM'S GOING TO BE RULER OVER THE OTHER ONE."
> And as time went on and as she got in labor and she had
>   those children.

The imagery that appears in these women's sermons has frequently to do with children, and also with food or with feeding people. When Reverend Johnson preached on the "Wedding Guests and the Bridegroom," she dwelt at length on the preparations for the wedding — the food and the invitations. Once Reverend Long delivered an entire sermon on getting ready for heaven in which the central metaphor was a detailed description of her breakfast preparations that very morning.

I was not present on the day when Reverend Long preached a sermon on "God's Leftovers," but she told me about it later in an interview. It is a sermon that illustrates better than any other these women's use of feminine imagery to underscore the meaning of their messages. "I don't know what I was saying," Reverend Long told me, "but it was in essence to that whatever was left over, God can use that. If you will commit that that you have to him, he can take and make something out of it."

As always, Reverend Long creates for her parishioners concrete and eminently recognizable images to help them see her point. She elaborated for me upon the examples she used in this sermon:

> Well, when you think about all the wrong that you've done and then God preserves you. I talked about how my mother used to make petticoats. And what was left as a result of her cutting, we used 'em for bath rags. And that that was too small for the bath rags, she put it in the quilt. That's where I started, that's where I based it from. And then I came on to tell the story of when Assyria and Jerusalem were at war with each other, and where Isaiah had gone down and spoke to 'em and that here were a few good people left over. And he wanted them to go get their kingdom. And that's where I ended it.

I asked Reverend Long if she talked about leftover food as well, and she explained how that image worked into her theme: "Yes, that you can preserve it, but you can't continue to heat it because if you continue to heat it, it becomes spoiled. What I meant by that was that when our lives are such—after while God doesn't leave us but he seems to forget where we becomes spoiled, and we're not mighty careful, we won't be any good for anything. I said that."

In the same conversation, Reverend Long spoke of her intention to preach on "The Balm in Gilead." In the sermon, she would elaborate upon the fact that the balm tree was not native to Gilead, that it had been transplanted, just as Jesus was not a native of this world. She would talk about the unusual bark and the shape of the leaves and show how they also relate to Jesus. I was perplexed by her attention to these details, until Reverend Long showed me her backyard. It was a garden of flowers and trees, each of which had obviously been placed by Long herself. "I would rather mess with these flowers than do just about anything else," she said, and that explained to me why she took the trouble to look up the balm tree in her encyclopedia.

153

Less elaborate themes and short phrases reflecting a feminine perspective on religion and morality pervade these women's sermons and their spontaneous prayers. When Reverend Long, for example, enumerates sins in the world today in her sermon "It's Coming Up Again," abortion is near the top of her list. But her discussion of the problem is not merely a righteous condemnation; it is based on compassion for the children. True to the Afro-American oratorical style, she lets the babies speak for themselves:

> And we go   before him.
> There gonna be some little unborn BABIES   up there.
> That's gonna say,
> "Jesus, I would have been a preacher,
> But my mama
> Wouldn't let me be born.
> I would-a been a missionary
> But my mama couldn't afford me.
> I would-a been a PEACE   maker,
> But I didn't have a chance   to be BORN."
> I'm here to TELL YOU that it's comin' up again.
> These little fetuses.
> If my mama took care of *ten*   eating beans and bread,
> You can take care of *one* or *two*   eating steak and potatoes.

Long dwells on the sinfulness of legalized abortion, but she also emphasizes how sad it makes her that the children will not have a chance to live.

In the last sermon I heard her preach, Reverend Long finished with a most provocative statement. The sermon was at its highest level of intensity, and Reverend Long was on the move, down in front of the altar, proclaiming the power of God to help us in our lives. Finally she shouted, "GOD can help in every need, ain't that right? He's a FATHER to us when we need a father. He's a MOTHER to us when we NEED a mother, ain't that right?"

The statement seems unquestionably to imply a vision of an androgynous God. This vision is not Long's alone. Indeed it finds expression in popular black gospel tunes. It has also found favor among feminist theologians and philosophers. But only the most liberal clergymen accept it as a theological reality. In the context of the sermon,

I doubt that Reverend Long intended to make a political or social statement. It seems instead that her reference to God as a mother comes very naturally to her, as naturally as do the images of domestic life she uses to illustrate her sermons. For Reverend Long to embrace the implications of a God with feminine qualities seems a logical extension of the notion that much of the content of the folk sermon proceeds from the personality and experience of the preacher. That her statement is also a major philosophical argument seems on a conscious level unimportant to Reverend Long and to her congregation.

The decision to preach has taken no small toll upon the women described here, who are all raising families and working full-time while they follow the pastorship. Responding to God's call to preach has a significance for them unknown to most men. Men are encouraged to preach in black churches. When women reveal their callings to families and friends, they often meet with disapprobation and doubt. To place themselves in visible positions as the heads of their churches has required courage.

Once ordained, women have established their authority in church by adhering to traditions of Afro-American preaching that have been honed and tempered for over two hundred years. They have acquired the stamina to maintain all their roles as mothers, wives, breadwinners, and pastors. And they have continued, in their male-dominated profession, to foster the feminine qualities, which provide a different perspective on the religious life for women pastors and for their congregations.

This feminine perspective cannot be submerged. The women in this study have shown how they bring it to bear upon their preaching tradition through the compassionate attitude that Evangelist Davis remarked upon, and through the way they perceive the world; for how women perceive the world must come through in their oral ministries.

The feminine perspective cannot be submerged, and yet Reverend Long has said, "When it comes to the ministry, I don't think of myself as a lady minister. I think of myself as a minister." In so saying she recognizes that the foremost qualities which inform her career are those she has gained from the predominantly male line of black preachers she has followed into the pulpit. To the extent that she and the others can incorporate their experiences as women into traditional Afro-American preaching styles and religious values, they succeed as pastors.

As Afro-American preachers, the women in this study have tapped the source of power that moves black church congregations. The wellspring of traditional black preaching is as accessible to them as to the thousands of men who have drawn from it. They freely use proven formulas which do not cease to delight and inspire their church members. And they add to the old formulas fresh images and fresh emphases reflecting an underlying sensibility which the women bring to the pastorate simply because they are women.

NOTES

The field data for this study were gathered between 1980 and 1983 for my master's thesis, *Your Daughters Shall Prophesy: Women in the Afro-American Preaching Tradition* (Chapel Hill: Curriculum in Folklore, University of North Carolina, 1983). The essay is also indebted to denominational histories such as Daniel Payne, *History of the African Methodist Episcopal Church* (New York: Johnson Reprint, 1968) and William J. Walls, *The African Methodist Episcopal Zion Church: The Reality of the Black Church* (Charlotte: A.M.E. Zion Publishing House, 1974), and to scholarly studies such as Judith Ochshorn, *The Female Experience and the Nature of the Divine* (Bloomington: Indiana University Press, 1981); C. Eric Lincoln, *The Black Experience in Religion* (Garden City, N.Y.: Anchor Books, 1974); and Don Yoder, "Symposium on Folk Religion," *Western Folklore* 33 (January 1974).

1. See Bruce Rosenberg, *The Art of the American Folk Preacher* (New York: Oxford University Press, 1970).

2. Ibid., p. 43.

3. Ibid., p. 47.

Speech, Chant, and Song: Patterns of Language and Action in a Southern Church

9

Brett Sutton

Black Primitive Baptist churches on the eastern slope of the Blue Ridge Mountains date from the last third of the nineteenth century, when blacks withdrew from racially mixed but white-dominated congregations. In their Articles of Faith and their polity they remain very like their white sister churches. But the expressive forms in the black churches are now in many ways distinctive, shaped by an Afro-American aesthetic and the particular needs and values of the black community.

> For although the best prayers are sometimes without utterance, yet when the feeling of the mind is overpowering, the tongue spontaneously breaks forth into utterance, and our other members into gesture.
> —John Calvin, *Institutes of the Christian Religion*

In matters of religion the power and elegance of simplicity have great appeal. The architects of the Protestant Reformation worked to purge the church of centuries of accretions that they thought lulled the senses and isolated the heart from God, and thus to lead believers away from an ecclesiastical complexity that was of human making and therefore corrupt. A similar desire to return to the purer church of Jesus and Paul seems to motivate those modern Christians who insist that "all you need is Jesus." Even though Christian experience, in practice, often turns out to be somewhat more complex than that, the quest for simple faith is a major theme in the history of the church. The Primitive Baptists of the rural South, whose orientation is in many ways very close to that of the sixteenth-century reformers, especially

157

Calvin, have made the effort to stick to fundamentals a centerpiece of their doctrine. The denomination actually began as a reaction to the liberalization in Christianity occurring during the first half of the nineteenth century, and its members are strict predestinarians who seek above all to follow in structure and practice the original "primitive" church of the New Testament.[1] The conservatism of the Primitive Baptists is broad: they have little or no centralized ecclesiastical organization; they refrain from liturgical use of the printed word other than the Bible; their preachers are qualified only by the inspiration of the Spirit and receive neither seminary training nor salary; they repudiate organized missionary efforts and formal religious education, refusing even to conduct Sunday schools for their own children; and they emphasize at all points direct personal experience of God over formalism and routine. One could hardly convict them of popery.

There is a strong element of freedom among the Primitive Baptists, especially in their use of spoken language. Unlike the liturgy-dependent High Church tradition, Primitive Baptist worship is not determined by print, but by a durable oral tradition that finds expression, often with great intensity and spontaneity, during church meetings. And certainly on one level this provides a measure of protection from rigidity and excessive organization. Without a prescribed written liturgy to govern what is said and done in church, worshipers are better able to respond to the inspiration in their own hearts. Yet a closer analysis reveals that the spoken language of the church is hardly as open-ended as it seems, or even as church members sometimes claim. There are in fact patterns, conventions, and rules of great complexity governing language and the action that accompanies it to which all worshipers are in some sense bound. That there are forces which shape and constrain expressive behavior, even among congregations where formality is minimal and spontaneity encouraged, becomes evident when one takes a close look at the actual meetings of such groups. These features are present with particular clarity in the meetings of the subjects of this essay, a group of black Primitive Baptists from the southeastern United States.[2]

The members of these churches, like most Primitive Baptists, believe that the words of the Bible are "dead," that is, without spiritual significance, except for the elect, who are given the understanding, the grace, to perceive their mysteries. There is among these Primitive

Baptists a general distrust of all religious language that is written down, and it is widely accepted among them that language spoken extemporaneously out of religious inspiration is by far the purer and more trustworthy mode of sacred communication. Spontaneity is a key element. For preachers to write out a sermon or to speak from notes, even if they are only mental notes, is to betray a coldness of spirit, a lack of faith, and ultimately the absence of a divine calling to preach. One Primitive Baptist elder rejected the sermon of a seminary-educated pastor of a large urban church of another denomination with the words "that ain't no more than a dog barking out there!" Public worship is largely an application of the principle that the purest form of sacred language is spontaneous and divinely inspired. A central purpose of the black Primitive Baptist meeting is to provide a context in which individual experiences of transcendent communion with God can be converted into language (preaching, prayer, testimony) and shared with fellow worshipers. Members should be receptive to that inspiration and obedient if it comes, but since God is the source, no one knows who will preach or sing or lead prayer with spiritual eloquence on a given day; that is in God's hands alone.

Language is important in the worship services of all Primitive Baptists. But it is characteristic of the black Primitive Baptists that language is juxtaposed to and blended together with other nonverbal forms of expression—there are strong musical, physical, and tactile elements as well. To the visitor unaccustomed to the tradition, the typical meeting has the appearance of a disorderly, even chaotic mixture of words and actions, but the sense of disorder is more apparent than real. Under closer scrutiny, patterns emerge; these various forms become components of a single expressive order, a continuum of action loosely divisible into three general expressive modes. Each of these modes is exemplified by a particular linguistic form—speech, chant, and song—and each is accompanied by its own characteristic nonverbal elements.

By the term *speech,* I refer generally to the everyday language of the community—that is, the typical regional variant of spoken English used by the members of these churches in both secular and sacred contexts. This base form of spoken language is, of course, adapted for use in the church in various ways (intonation, lexicon, accompanying gestures), just as all spoken language is fitted to its social

159

context. Most forms of sacred speech, although oriented towards the sacred setting, are also appropriate outside the church. A few are more specialized and tend to be used only in church. For example, a member's response to the question, "How you doing, brother?" spoken in greeting in the church before the formal beginning of the service might be conventional ("Right well, sister.") or perhaps jocular ("'Bout to give out!"), both of which are also appropriate to the secular context. But given the setting, the brother might also respond in a sober tone of voice with a shake of his head, "Well, sister, sometimes I'm up, sometimes I'm down." The phrase is a formulaic one that also appears in a number of traditional spiritual songs and contains theological significance for Primitive Baptists: sometimes God's people are elevated by grace, but other times they sink into a valley of gracelessness from which they are helpless to extricate themselves. The point is not that church members would not express this idea outside the church, but that they would not typically use this particular phrase, which derives much of its meaning from the context in which it is spoken.

These formulaic varieties of sacred speech also occur in more formal settings, when a single speaker addresses the entire group (a situation much more common in the church than face-to-face conversation). Stylized utterances occur, for example, during opening announcements, personal testimonies, reading and explication of Scripture, and sermons. One pastor, for example, likes to open the service from the pulpit with the words, "Feel yourself at home. If the Spirit say sing, you sing; if he say shout, you better shout; if he say jump, you jump, but walk right when you hit the ground." But whether the words are conventional or formulaic, private or public, in most ways sacred speech is very close to that of the secular world.

The second general class of linguistic forms is *chant,* or as it is sometimes described, "heightened speech." Here I refer to spoken language that takes on some of the melodic and rhythmic regularity of song, while retaining the open-endedness of speech. Chant occurs most commonly in the form of chanted preaching, which can be considered a form of oral poetry. The melodic element of chant, which varies widely in pattern among different speakers, is generally very prominent and sometimes contains a relatively stable key center, or tonic, around which the speaker improvises modally, using a four- or five-note scale. Chant differs from speech structurally as well; the phrases of chant are shorter and more uniform in length and meter and are expressed using regular rhythmic patterns uncharacteristic of speech. It is also syntactically simpler than conventional speech. Grammatical elements that alter the meaning of phrases (such as conjunctions like "however"), embedded clauses, and complex sentences are fewer.

There is little ambiguity as to the boundary between speech and chant. Church members, even though they do not recognize these specific differences as formal categories, always know which form is in use at a given time. They are, in fact, keenly aware of the implications of the use of chant rather than speech. "Preaching," in their terms, is a less self-conscious act in which the speaker becomes a passive vessel for the Spirit, and in which chanting is typical; but "teaching" or "talking" is a product of the speaker's own mind, employs the structures of conventional speech, and is not chanted. The latter is the work of the speaker himself; the former is the work of God. The difference is clear, too, to the outside analyst and constitutes an instance of linguistic code-switching. Most preachers who chant actually alternate between the two forms in the course of a sermon.

Chant can be distinguished from speech not only by its linguistic elements, but also by the paralinguistic and kinesic elements that accompany it. When a speaker moves into the chanted mode, the facial expressions of conventional speech tend to give way to a less self-conscious, sometimes almost masklike facial set. The appearance of loss of self-awareness is consistent with the reports of preachers that the feeling of being outside oneself often accompanies preaching. The speaker also becomes more active physically during chant and may gesture more broadly, pace, march, or jump and occasionally even act out the message of his words mimetically. Such actions are normally coordinated with the rhythms of the spoken component of the performance. Just as chant occupies a medial position between speech and song, the stylized gestures that accompany chant are midway between simple movement and dance.

Another distinctive feature of chanted discourse is that it is simpler in the cognitive sense, being generally more expressive and less analytic, more personal and less objective, better suited for praise or the expression of joy and power than for exegesis or argumentation. In linguistic terms, the emphasis in chant is less strictly referential or denotative and becomes more strongly affective or poetic. That the message be formally well ordered is as important as the cogency of its reasoning. There are usually more abstractions, more formulaic phrases, and more repetition (of both words and whole sections) than in spoken passages. Chanted speech is not the medium best suited for leading to a conclusion or for developing a narrative. It is more firmly anchored in the present, expressing the "now" of the speaker's divinely inspired state. When a speaker does occasionally employ chant to deliver a narrative message, such as in the recounting of a personal conversion experience, the story loses much of its detail and linear integrity, and the speaker is more likely to wander from his subject or to shuffle the order of events. The insertion by the chanting preacher of asides, formulaic spacers, and stock descriptive phrases serves to brake rather than to propel the flow of ideas.

Chanting, in short, tends to celebrate rather than to explain. It is one of its central purposes to celebrate the gift of grace by exercising it. For the congregation, the expressive eloquence of the chant is proportional to the intensity of divine inspiration that motivates the speaker. Primitive Baptist preachers, no doubt in violation of classical principles of homiletics, do not preach primarily in order to argue particular points or to get to the end of a sequence of ideas, any more than the congregation sings a hymn for the purpose of reaching the last line.

Here is an unedited excerpt from a sermon that illustrates most of these points. I have written out the "spoken" part of the address as normal prose and the chanted passages as poetry, with each line corresponding to a single phrase. A full pause follows each line, regardless of punctuation, which I have used here only to clarify the syntax.

> Oh, they tell me
> There was a woman
> That had a little child
> By the name of Moses.
> Oh, ain't that right.
> Oh, Lord.
> And they tell me
> That, ah,
> Ah, Pharoah's
> Soldiers

Was slaying every little child.
Ah, ain't that right.
Oh, brethren.
If you
Be able
To see Jesus' face in peace,
You gonna have
Ah, hard trials
And great tribulations,
As sure as you're born.
Because these hard trials
And great tribulations
Make you go down
On your bended knee,
Make you
Call on
The name of the Lord.
Ain't that right, children.
Oh, sometime,
Oh, I can thank Jesus
For my tribulation.
I can thank him
For my downsetting.
I can thank him
For my uprising.
I can thank him
For my troubles.
Because he knows
Ah, what it takes
For to keep his people.

Ain't that right, children. He knows what it takes to keep his children. You know, they, uh, begun to slay every child, new male child that was born. You know, the things that are happening today have happened before. But just in a little different manner. Now you find today that they're destroying the human population because they have passed laws for abortion. But, uh, it's not pleasing, pleasing in the sight of the Lord. Ah, and you take Pharoah — he was trying to cut down on the population, because he was afraid that they would grow strong, and they would bind together and be a strong army.

Oh, one thing
He didn't know,

That they was God's
Chosen people.
Oh, Lord.
And God
Was suffering them
To be
Put under bondage.
Then he suffered them
To suffer
430 years,
That his name
Might be
Declared
Ah, throughout
All generations.
Oh, brethren.
If I
Have to suffer
For God's sake
That his name
Might be declared
Throughout
All generations,
It's all right.
Ain't that right, brethren.
It's all right.

The speaker has been retelling and commenting on the events of Exodus 1, Pharoah's attempt to counter the military threat of the Hebrews by having the male children killed. As the excerpt begins, the preacher is repeating points he has already made several times, using almost identical words. Such repetition is characteristic of chanted preaching. Notice that as long as the speaker is chanting, he does not stick to a straight narration of events, but in each chanted segment drifts in and out of personal commentary on those events. Only in the section in which the preacher takes up an analytical issue — comparing ancient genocide to modern abortion — does he employ regular spoken prose rather than chant. The longer, more complex sentences here require a level of listener attention and recall of previous sentences that would be less attainable during the more abstract, intermittent passages of chant.

There are rare moments in chanted preaching when the linguistic element vanishes altogether. Preachers commonly insert nonverbal vocal sounds into their chant as spacing elements (hah!, ummmm, well), but occasionally a speaker chants several lines in what are essentially nonsense syllables. At such moments, even though the congregation is receiving no verbal information at all, the effectiveness of the preacher is usually undiminished (as long as the nonverbal preaching is not sustained too long). A similar effect occurs when the volume of sound generated by a particularly lively congregation renders the preacher's words unintelligible. This is not to say that cognition is an irrelevant factor in the chanted sermon. On the contrary, the best preachers are not only able to chant effectively, but also have something to say. The point here is that a congregation can be moved emotionally by an apt phrase at one moment and by a pure chanted sound the next. Utterances in the form of speech that lack verbal information may thus still possess "eloquence." Speech becomes as music. This function of language is not restricted to the Primitive Baptist church. The inspirational effect of glossolalia in Pentecostal churches and the Latin mass among Catholics provides further evidence that effective linguistic expression in a religious setting may not depend totally on the transmission and accurate reception of the cognitive portion of the message.

An instance of verbal communication must involve not just the speaker but also those spoken to—it is, after all, the relationship between speaker and listener that constitutes communication. In the Primitive Baptist church meeting, significant changes in the relationship between speaker and congregation occur with the shift from speech to chant. The responsorial principle, in which the congregation answers the words of the speaker with words of its own, is a familiar feature of the black church (as well as secular black culture and some white churches) and occurs here in conjunction with most forms of formal speech. But the responses are not always of the same order. As the speaker moves into the chanted mode, the congregation becomes more active, and the verbal responses on the part of the congregation also change, becoming louder and more frequent, and involve a larger percentage of the group. During the spoken portion of a sermon, members who respond do so more or less routinely, answering "yes" or "that's right" in a conventional way that suggests what Malinowski called "phatic" communication — words that "fulfil a function to which the meaning of its words is almost completely irrelevant. . . . a type of speech in which ties of union are created by a mere exchange of words."[3] Such response seems to help maintain communication between preacher and congregation (the absence of congregational response during preaching is distressing for both) and is perhaps distantly related in a functional sense to the secular speech form known as "small talk." Even the least-inspired preacher will be accorded the courtesy of a minimal level of congregational response. But with the onset of chant, the congregation begins to respond with more animation and conviction. As the excerpt above shows, chant abounds with phrases that invite response. This speaker uses "Oh, brethren" and "Ain't that right, children"; other speakers use different ones.

Congregational responses themselves may sometimes take on, during chant, the features of heightened speech. Members, for example, may pick up the phrases, pitches, characteristic melodic units, or rhythms of the preacher and echo them in such an intricate and harmonious way that chanted preaching without the responses seems aesthetically incomplete. Further, as the pace of the chanting quickens, congregational responses begin to occur, not just at the pauses between chanted phrases but during them, as a kind of counterpoint. Finally, individual members of the congregation, if sufficiently motivated by the Spirit during the chant, may jump from their seats and shout energetically around the church, perhaps producing extended chanting of their own, apparently entering what some analysts would call an altered state of consciousness.

A major change in the structure of communication occurs with the shift from speech to chant. During formal but nonchanted speech events, the bulk of communication flows in one direction. Even though members of the congregation may punctuate the speaker's discourse with verbal responses, they remain relatively passive. With the onset of chanting and the sudden increase in congregational response, however, the congregation's share of the event becomes proportionally larger, and communication is decentralized. Not only does the congregation respond to the speaker, but the speaker himself becomes subject to the influence of the congregation. The preacher may even be momentarily displaced as the principal object of attention by a member engaged in an even louder performance. If a sister moves about with great animation in the open area in front of the pulpit while chanting, "He's so good! I know He's so good!" over and over, some of the attention of the congregation is inevitably drawn away from the preacher. Yet this is not in itself a matter of concern. Indeed, it is the inspired preacher's role, as the vessel through which the Spirit flows, to produce just this sort of divinely inspired intensity in his hearers. As long as it falls within the general range of appropriate response and does not violate standards of decency or safety, congregational activity is welcomed as a sign that a transcendent level of interaction with God has been reached and that the Spirit has granted a collective blessing to the assembled members of the church. Those most subject to criticism are not members who become audibly enthusiastic during the service, but those who appear to do so out of self-conscious egotism and showmanship rather than divine inspiration, which ideally obliterates the ego.

These kinds of changes are not limited to linguistic channels. The decentralization of the context during chanting is also dramatized nonverbally in the form of increased physical activity and interpersonal contact among members. As the chanting grows more heated, members of the congregation begin to nod and sway more vigorously, pat their feet, raise their hands in assent, or clap excitedly. Some, as I have already mentioned, may begin to shout and move vigorously about the church, dancing and jumping with an apparent loss of physical self-control. When that happens others will usually come to their feet to protect those who are shouting from injuring themselves or others in their enthusiasm. During moments of peak spiritual intensity the preacher himself will often come down from the pulpit and walk out among the congregation, shaking hands with first one, then another member, preaching to each directly for a moment before moving on. Other members may approach the chanting preacher and help him remove his coat or glasses or mop his face with a handkerchief while he labors under the Spirit. At such moments of heightened religious emotion members may reach out to one another, testifying privately or expressing agreement with the preacher, shaking hands, and embracing. Thus, increased enthusiasm and individual activity

167

reduce the isolation of speaker and individual worshiper in three ways: verbally, as the congregation becomes more vocally active; physically, as members begin to move around and make contact with each other; and spatially, as the preacher moves from his isolated and elevated position in the pulpit, where he faces the congregation, down onto the floor, where he becomes a part of it.

At the high points of particularly spirit-filled meetings, the emotional intensity and activity can be overwhelming. With perhaps five members in various stages of shouting, a dozen more out of their seats, and the majority of those present creating with their voices and bodies a virtual curtain of sound, the sermon itself may indeed become unintelligible and be reduced simply to one part of the total sonic texture. Perhaps it is not incorrect to say that at such points the medium of expression is no longer linguistic in the usual sense, but has become a contrapuntal juxtaposition of motion, sound, and voices — a multichanneled existential whole in which many participants take, at some point, a leading role and in which the cognitive linguistic component is drastically reduced. Whoever wishes to follow the preacher's words at such a climactic moment will be disappointed. John Calvin himself would probably have had his reservations about the burying of the preacher's words beneath what both communication theorists as well as unsympathetic observers would call noise. Even though Calvin accepted nonverbal spiritual expression as legitimate in principle, he also argued for the use of the vernacular in church so that worshipers might approach God with understanding as well as awe.

But for these worshipers, polyphonic enthusiasm is neither noise nor a barrier to communication, but a true outpouring of spiritual feeling in ways that go beyond cognitive understanding. The obscuring of the words does not necessarily mean the suppression of the Word, *Logos,* the knowledge of God. The successful meeting is a profoundly moving experience that constitutes an affirmation, not an obscuring, of truth. In short, the loss of the linguistic mode does not necessarily diminish the overall effect. It seems the very opposite is true, that orderly linear speech is sometimes itself a hindrance to full spiritual communion (hence, for example, the Primitive Baptist preacher's rejection of the written sermon). This is not to say simply that the medium is the message. McCluhan's phrase implies that the message is relatively empty but that the medium is high in informational content. What seems to occur at peak moments in the Primitive Baptist service is that the message is dispersed across several media, rather than limited to words, and that medium and message are collapsed into a single entity, experience.

We come now at last to the third category of sacred language, *song*. Singing is a major part of the church meeting, occurring at many points, but it tends to reach peak emotional intensity during and following sermons. Just as in the case of speech and chant, the difference between song and the other categories is one that is both easily observed by outsiders and recognized by church members themselves. Included here are both lined hymns and spirituals, all sung in unison by the whole congregation without instrumental accompaniment. The Primitive Baptist hymnbook contains nearly 700 texts, and the singing of hymns thus contains a strong verbal component. Since there are no musical instruments in the church, all music is vocal; there is no music "for its own sake." But as with chant, the significance of the song, or rather the act of singing, goes beyond the text itself.

What I want to emphasize here is not the category of song as a discrete form, but ways in which song is a special elaboration of speech and thus part of the linguistic continuum speech/chant/song. The switch to song involves several kinds of changes. In the most obvious change, the musical element that began to influence speech during chant becomes with song fully expressed. Musical vocalization becomes vocal music. The pitch modulations of speech are subordinated to the melodic requirements of the tune, and clarity of musical mode, pitch stability, firm key-centeredness, regularity of rhythm and phrase, all become strong. Song is more prescribed in form than either speech or chant, and both melody and words are specified; this reduces somewhat the possibilities for innovation but makes possible the coordinated, collective expression of a predetermined form. This sets singing apart from the more individualistic and unique products of speaking and chanting. While preachers follow the biddings of the Spirit in their choice of words and in the style and intensity of their chant, the singers respond to the Spirit only in the enthusiasm with which they sing a standardized text and melody. They have little power to shape personally the linguistic component of the sung message.

Singing, besides achieving a final formalization of language and melody, may also contribute on occasion to a formalization of movement (which as we have seen increases with chant). This occurs especially in the ceremonial exchange of the hand of fellowship, a popular activity that members practice frequently in conjunction with the singing of lined hymns. In this exercise, members move about the church as they sing, shaking hands with fellow members in time to the music in a traditionally patterned way. The prescribed movements of the hand of fellowship might be classified as a form of organized sacred dance, a phenomenon rare in Protestant Christianity, which tends to de-emphasize bodily forms of expression.[4]

The standardization that accompanies song has a sociological dimension. During speech, the bulk of the communication flows from the speaker to the audience. During chant, even though the preacher and his message remain the enduring focal point of the context, members of the congregation become more active in the expressive processes of the event and individuals share the stage with the preacher by enthusiastic response or shouting. An element of exchange enters the context. With group singing, the heterogeneous characteristic of the chanting context gives way to a level of coordination and cooperation unmatched anywhere else in the meeting: the individual worshipers come together as a group to sing a single song. It does not weaken this point that some of the songs are responsorial—that, for example, during a lined hymn the leader chants out the lines of the text singly or in pairs before they are sung by the group; or that, in some spirituals, a leader sings a line of verse and the congregation responds with a refrain line. First, these call-and-response elements are fully specified components of the song and are not functions of individual creation (except to the minimal degree that the leader of a spiritual selects at a given moment one rather than another stock verse). Insofar as there is specialization of role, it is because of the common submission of all to the structured "rules" of singing, which are not contingent on the creative leadership of the song leader. Second, members of the congregation continually breach the divisions of the responsorial structure of song by joining in with the leader in what are technically his own lines. The performer, in effect, is the singing congregation, as a unit rather than an aggregation of individuals, and the aspect of personal performance or expression that is so evident in speech and chant all but vanishes. In singing the congregation achieves formal union, to accom-

pany the emotional union achieved through the accumulating enthusiasm of the service.

Song, as I said, is formally distinguishable from chant. But there
are moments when the two categories appear to overlap.[5] For example,
preachers occasionally use fragments of hymns and spirituals in the
place of their own words, incorporating them into the characteristic
patterns of the ongoing chant. Indeed, the phrases are ideally suited
for this purpose. When members of the congregation join in and chant
the familiar lines along with the preacher, chant takes on, momentarily, some of the textual formality of song. In other instances, preachers occasionally push their chant one step closer to song by improvis-
ing songlike phrases of regular syllabic length and setting them to a
series of nearly identical melodic figures that are also songlike. The
result is a simple litany that resembles some of the spiritual songs
already in the repertory. Chant becomes even more songlike if members of the congregation find ways to join in. In these ways chant
becomes incipient song that could, if conditions were right, break
through into true song and thus constitute, in theory, a point of origin
for new songs in the Primitive Baptist repertory. Although I did not
observe any such instance of communal creation myself, it has been
reported in similar circumstances by others. Odum and Johnson, writing in 1925, found that, in certain black churches of North Carolina,
"Worshipers often follow the preacher through his sermon in a mental
state of song and when he has finished they burst out into song, singing
no other than an elaborate sentence which the preacher has used in
his sermon. When this is joined to a familiar chorus and tune, and
then varied, a song has originated."[6] The point is a complex one, however. It is possible that an inexperienced observer might be unable
to distinguish a litany chant that became a new, reproducible song,
from a previously existing song text or refrain line that happened to
be used in a chanted sermon.

I have used a rather simple model of linguistic form with three components (far simpler than the reality) to describe aspects of behavior
and communication in the black Primitive Baptist church meeting,
and in particular to make certain observations about the relationship
between form, religious behavior, and affective state. One fact that
emerges is that the Primitive Baptist meeting is organized, and its

171

disorderliness is only apparent. Members are told not to refrain from doing whatever the Spirit bids them to do, but the ensuing behavior is culturally consistent and patterned. Further, there is an orderly correlation of expressive forms. The mode of speech is associated with a subjective state of relative spiritual quiescence—one not driven by the force of the Spirit. In the context of speech, a principal speaker commands the attention of the congregation and receives only moderate and routine verbal responses. Physical movement and physical contact among participants are low, as is musicalness that goes beyond the pitch, rhythm, and phrasings of casual speech.

The mode of chant is associated with the penetration of the self by an external spiritual force and with outgoing, enthusiastic behavior. Chant itself consists of speech that becomes songlike through the addition of melodic and rhythmic elements not found in speech and is usually accompanied by increased physical activity on the part of the speaker and a reduced cognitive element in the words. Effective chant generates a higher level of interaction among the worshipers, eliciting enthusiastic and occasionally chanted responses from the congregation, and it stimulates increased motion and physical contact among individuals. The communicative context during chant tends to be multicentered and somewhat diffuse: even though the principal speaker remains the ongoing focal point of the scene, others may momentarily supersede him. The chant context is thus one of harmonized interaction and coordination of activity, but every act remains that of an individual. Each member, however, is affected by the combined enthusiasm of the others.

During song, language and movement have become fully musical and formalized. Most of the elements of song are prescribed, leaving small room for innovation or spontaneity on the part of the singers. Even style, which is the feature most open to individual variation, is strongly constrained by tradition. Divine inspiration is said by members to be the main source of good singing, and shouting often accompanies it, but there are fewer instances of altered states during singing than during chanting. It seems that the heightened spiritual emotions that are generated during the service, when channeled into song, are more fully contained by the form and less likely to generate scattered ecstatic behavior. As with speech and unlike chant, song has a strong cognitive element; the text carries important ideas in a linguistic medium. Also like speech, there is a greater continuity of thought. But in contrast to speech and chant, individuality is reduced during song, and all members are more equally involved in the performance. None, not even the nominal leader, has special control over the singing.

These various expressive forms do not appear at random, but in patterned sequences of rising and falling emotions and shifting activities. Most meetings can be charted as successions of cycles of various sizes and dynamic range. As the verbal forms move from speech, through chant, to song, congregational participation in the service increases and becomes more stylized, mobility and spiritual excitement increases, and the cognitive aspects of language, as well as the physical and emotional distance between speaker and audience, become smaller. At first, the role of speaker and listener is clearly marked, but with chant the boundary between those roles begins to break down, and during song disappears altogether. The endpoint of the cycle is union — union among fellow worshipers and collective union with the Spirit, which is the primary goal of the meeting. Activity that is at first individualistic, and then responsorial, coordinated, and contrapuntal, becomes at the end of the cycle simultaneous, as everyone joins in a spiritual or hymn. Thus the meeting achieves a kind of closure, as the boundaries between humans that pertain in the secular world are temporarily broken down. The ecstasy of spiritual union cannot, of course, be sustained indefinitely. What the church meeting achieves is the process of reaching it, and every step in that process is important. Only the process can achieve a transcendence of differences. Singing, for example, is associated with union, but it is not enough just to sing — the congregation must achieve that state by going through the sequence that culminates in song. Informal singing, begun cold before the service, is far less intense than that which comes at spiritual peaks. It is important to note that a satisfying level of spiritual experience does not always materialize. In some meetings the preaching falls flat, singing is lackluster, and the members are frustrated. Other services achieve union and transcendence only fleetingly. Primitive Baptists accept the intermittent nature of spiritual ecstasy, for such is the evanescent nature of the divine will.

Christianity, especially in its Protestant and fundamentalist forms, is a personal religion: members must enter into their own individual relationships with God. But the structure of these meetings indicates that, at least in the case of public worship, the religious experience of the individual is incomplete until it becomes coordinated and harmonized with that of other members. The successful worship service is not a matter of an inspired sermon here or an inward spiritual emotion there, but depends on the organized simultaneous activity of a number of persons. Individual action remains important (members regularly have solitary experiences of grace outside the church meeting), but only in a context of harmonized collective action does one fully become a Primitive Baptist.

Spoken language is a focal point of the ritual action that constitutes public worship. Although it resembles the language of the secular world, sacred language is specialized and occurs in a variety of forms. At certain points, such as during the exegesis of Scripture or a lecture on Christian ethics, the cognitive function of language is central. At other moments, during chanted praise for example, the cognitive function gives way to the affective function. Aesthetic or poetic features become prominent, and the mode of speaking becomes more important than the content. An inspired preacher can generate high enthusiasm and shouting while chanting the most mundane passages of Scripture, a genealogy for example. Inspired language remains potent even when it nears or crosses the border into pseudo-language. Nonsense words or unintelligible phrases are not necessarily without spiritual value, but are simply a link in the chain of spiritual vocal expression. This is perhaps one reason why Primitive Baptists continue to resist the introduction of musical instruments into the church: to do so would detract from the smooth movement among the basic vocal forms of speech, chant, and song and would displace the central position of language in the service. Language in the Primitive Baptist church is not just spoken, but enacted.

One might well object that this study has violated the integrity of the Primitive Baptist service by analytically isolating forms that do not in fact exist independently of their context. This, however, is precisely my point. By showing that the expressive behavior of Primitive Baptists in their meetings undergoes changes of state in regular patterns and that those expressions have a cumulative meaning owing to their relations to one another, I have tried to show that the forms therefore constitute an indivisible expressive whole. To describe the service functionally, in terms of the standard genres (sacred formula, testimony, Scripture reading, prayer, sermon, song) is inherently interesting, but as an analytical approach is too atomistic to reveal much about this expressive continuum. In order to better understand the genres as communication and to do justice to the expressive depth and complexity of the service, one must regard them in terms of their linguistic form, the various kinds of activity that accompany them, and the processes of which they are a part. Here, perhaps, is the essential liturgy of the Primitive Baptist church.

NOTES

The material for this paper was gathered from several different Primitive Baptist associations across a twelve-county area during several periods of research between 1976 and 1980. This research was supported by grants from the National Endowment for the Humanities and the National Institute for Mental Health and led to my doctoral dissertation, *Spirit and Polity in a Black Primitive Baptist Church* (Chapel Hill: Department of Anthropology, University of North Carolina, 1983) and to my album "Primitive Baptist Hymns of the Blue Ridge" (Chapel Hill: The University of North Carolina Press, 1982). Tape recordings of singing and services are on deposit in the Southern Folklife Collection of the University of North Carolina Library.

1. A dense and detailed defense of the church, written by two of its most articulate spokesmen, is Elder Cushing Biggs Hassell and Elder Sylvester Hassell's *History of the Church of God from the Creation to A.D. 1885* (Middletown, N.Y.: Gilbert Beebe's Sons, 1886; reprint, Conley, Ga.: Old School Hymnal Company, 1973). For a more detached account of the historical origins of the sect, see Byron Cecil Lambert, *The Rise of the Anti-Mission Baptists: Sources and Leaders, 1800–1840* (New York: Arno Press, 1980).

2. My analysis applies especially to the churches that are the subject of this essay. The cultural differences between Primitive Baptists of different regions and particularly between black and white Primitive Baptists make generalizing from the group to others uncertain at best.

3. Bronislaw Malinowski, "The Problem of Meaning in Primitive Languages," supplement 1 in C. K. Ogden and I. A. Richards, *The Meaning of Meaning*, 8th ed. (New York: Harcourt, Brace, 1947), pp. 313, 315.

4. Another example in American Christianity is the singing of the Shakers, who used individual mimetic gestures to accompany song ("motioning") and organized collective movement ("laboring"). See Daniel W. Patterson, *The Shaker Spiritual* (Princeton: Princeton University Press, 1979).

5. An ethnomusicological model for classifying vocal expression along the continuum from speech to song is presented in George List, "The Boundaries of Speech and Song," in *Ethnomusicology* 7 (1963): 1–16.

6. *The Negro and His Songs* (Chapel Hill: University of North Carolina Press, 1925), p. 31.

Like My Husband's Shadow: The Religious Experience of a Japanese Warbride in North Carolina

10

Yutaka Yamada

The years after World War II saw a substantial increase in the number of Asians living in the southern United States. Excluding Texas, the southern states had, for example, but 417 Japanese in 1940 and only 1,520 in 1950. By 1980 the Japanese population had grown to 26,176. In North Carolina the number of Japanese increased from 21 in 1940 to 3,286 in 1980. The Southern Baptist churches responded to the influx of Asian immigrants with an active program of evangelism. In the early 1960s they initiated Korean and Japanese fellowship groups and in the 1970s extended these to the Vietnamese as well. Another kind of Christian endeavor among the Asian immigrants was the organization of fellowships for warbrides, who were a large part of the migration following the American occupation of Japan. One such group—composed of approximately fifty persons and led by a Japanese woman—is located in a North Carolina city adjacent to a military base. The following paper explores the religious experience of the leader of this group as a way of comprehending the situation and viewpoint of one kind of Asian Southern Baptist.

Of the participants in a Southern Baptist fellowship group for Japanese warbrides in a North Carolina city, very few consider themselves converted. Few attend church services regularly. Speaking in terms of the Southern Christian tradition, only a handful are Christians, the rest only nominal ones. Most of them do not hold membership with a particular church, and most have not claimed that they "have received Jesus Christ as their personal savior." The majority of the warbrides in this town are members of Sokka Gakkai rather than Christians.[1]

One of the reasons for this pattern is the syncretic nature of the Japanese religious tradition from which most warbrides derive. One woman summarized this syncretism as follows: "*Kami* [God] take[s] many forms. It does not matter whether it is Buddha or Jesus Christ. They are different forms of the same Kami." This statement expresses the general religious belief of the Japanese. In Japan, only a small percent of the population belongs to Christian groups. The rest adhere to Buddhism, Shintoism, and other beliefs (including various forms of folk beliefs and New Religions). Except for some Japanese New Religions and Japanese fundamentalist Christians, any principle that dictates loyalty to a single church or denomination is foreign to the Japanese population. This polytheistic and syncretistic religious tradition makes it possible for individuals to hold multiple membership or multiple commitment to different sects. As the Japanese woman said, different beliefs are often considered as different forms of the same Kami. The Japanese word, in fact, is closer in meaning to the English word *spirit* than to the word *God.* It has a different connotation from that of the monotheistic word *God* in Western society.

It is therefore no surprise that there are very few dedicated Christians among the Japanese warbrides. For most warbrides, the major emphasis is the mutual aid and group support received during their participation in the fellowship rather than a dramatic and personal form of salvation. Thus another cause of warbrides' divergence from the Southern Christian tradition derives from the fact that instead of being a Christian Bible study, the fellowship becomes an important place to receive group support in times of crises.

The Japanese warbrides gather on Friday nights. They hold their fellowship meetings at the home of the woman who is the leader of the group. The meeting is a combination of informal chatting, a pot-luck meal, Bible study, and singing of hymns. But the major portion of the meeting is spent discussing and sharing the daily problems that warbrides encounter.

Warbrides share a common set of problems, especially the language barrier and their relationships with their husband and children. Their problems arise in the context of the bicultural situation in which the warbrides live. They are caught between the two cultures in their interpersonal relationships with husband and children or with the outside world, the extrafamily sphere. This particular situation has led these women to provide mutual aid. The fellowship serves as a social expression of such a reciprocal system of support. Instead of offering only Christian Bible study, the meeting also includes the informal interaction of the individuals working on solutions to their problems.

During the fellowship meeting, each participant speaks of her own experiences and troubles. By talking to the participants, the leader and the senior members of the fellowship try to provide solutions to each individual's problems. Although they do not always succeed, their major efforts are directed toward converting the others, but they often tell their listeners that by joining the church they would gain access to such benefits as nursery programs, English lessons, and job opportunities. They emphasize that by joining the church, group members will be able to overcome their problems both spiritually and socially.

In the group discussions recurrent themes reveal additional motives for commitment to the fellowship. Each woman's relationship to her husband is especially important to her because he mediates between herself and the outside world. Loss of a husband by death or divorce, or temporary loss of a husband during overseas duties, are recurrent crises that warbrides encounter. In such a situation women are required to stand on their own and need to learn to live independently. The experience of becoming a Christian — of actually going through a "born again" experience or joining a fellowship group — thus becomes an important initiation into becoming independent from the husband as the main link to the extrafamily sphere.

This transition or move from bonds with the intrafamily sphere to ones with the extrafamily sphere is sometimes expressed in the form of religious visions and dreams. Although this type of dramatic religious experience is rare among the warbrides, some do have them. The leader of the group, whom I shall call Mrs. M, was one who did, and her case illustrates well the family crises that the warbrides encounter and how they overcome them through religious means.

Mrs. M is fifty-three years old and came to the United States from her native Japan in 1954. She was born in Sendai-shi, Miyagi Prefecture. Presently, she is separated, but she met her husband while working in a restaurant near the American military base in Miyagi Prefecture. Her first encounter with Christianity was made in the United States when she met a Nisei minister who was serving at the military base near the fellowship. Since her story presents one example of warbrides' religious experience, I would like to examine her own account in detail. Her experience divides into three periods: a presalvation period, a transitional one, and a salvation period.

In the presalvation period Mrs. M's religious commitment was first triggered by the despair and loneliness that she experienced after her husband went to Okinawa for his fourth overseas assignment. Later she found out that her husband had a girlfriend there, and that fact ultimately led to her decision to divorce him. The incident left her in a state of desperation. One night after a day of reading her Bible at home, she had a dream. The starting point of her commitment to Christianity was marked by this dream. She described it as follows:

> In the dream, I was standing on an open path. I was looking at the sky and it was blue. And there was a white cloud. On that cloud there was somebody like Jesus Christ or Angel sitting dressed in white. In his right hand, he had a scroll. On the scroll, there were blue ribbons strapped. There was something written on it. But, next, I could see clearly that that person on the cloud was throwing the scroll to me with his right hand. It looked as if it was falling to earth. But when I started running to catch it, there was somebody running with me. At first I didn't know somebody was running with me. When I looked to left, I saw something like my husband's shadow. That was my husband. He was running by my side. I tried to run, but it was so hard to run. You know in the dream, you keep trying to run but you can't. I wanted to get [to the scroll] to see what was written, as quickly as possible before somebody else got it. Finally, I got there and the other figure disappeared. I was about to pick it up, then the thing broke in front of me like shattering rocks. It was like rock dust and there was about as much left as you can put in a bowl. When that happened, I felt so sad I just felt like crying. I was so sad. And suddenly I woke up.

Mrs. M searched for the meaning of her dream for several months. Finally, she found her answer in the Book of Ezekiel. She interpreted her dream of God in the plain as a command from God to speak to others or to engage in missionary activities. In chapter 1 of Ezekiel, the prophet sees a vision of God in the plain (1:1), and in chapter 2 God reveals a message to Ezekiel by giving him a scroll (2:9–10). Ezekiel 2:10 describes the scroll as being "written within and without; and there was written therein lamentation, mourning, and woe." Further, in 3:1–3, God tells Ezekiel to eat the scroll and go speak to Israel: Ezekiel 3:10 states, "Son of man, eat that thou findest; eat this scroll, and go speak unto the house of Israel." In discussing these passages Mrs. M particularly refers to Ezekiel 3:5–6, which says, "For thou art not sent to a people of a strange speech and hard language, but to the house of Israel." She said that the message that was revealed was not to speak to the people of "strange speech" or "hard language," which meant English-speaking Americans, but to her fellow Japanese, who speak her own language. Therefore, she interpreted the message as a directive to engage in ethnic missionary activities for the Japanese.

She then quotes Ezekiel 3:16–21, which gives us a clue why she needed to engage in the missionary activities — the act of saving souls. This illustrates more the general significance of the missionary activity. Ezekiel 3:18–19 reads: "When I say unto the wicked, Thou shalt surely die; and thou givest him not warning, nor speakest to warn the wicked from his wicked way, to save his life; the same wicked *man* shall die in his iniquity; but his blood will I require at thine hand. Yet if thou warn the wicked, and he turn not from his wickedness nor from his wicked way, he shall die in his iniquity; but thou hast delivered thy soul."

After quoting this passage, she talked about her husband's wrongdoings in Okinawa and her eldest son's consorting with hippies, taking drugs, and eventually going to prison. She claims that because of their wicked acts, she suffered tremendously. But through her suffering she realized the need of saving them. The dream gave her the clue that she could save her family and herself by engaging in missionary activity.

Further, Mrs. M quotes Ezekiel 3:24–27, a passage in which God spoke to Ezekiel and said, "Go, shut thyself within thy house," and "they shall put bands upon thee, and shall bind thee with them, and thou shalt not go out among them." Here, God and the Israelites have bound Ezekiel and disabled him so that he cannot move. In Mrs. M's case, this seems to symbolize her bond to her intrafamily sphere, and it symbolizes also the obstacle in the way of her going out to the extrafamily sphere. She elaborates on how she was bound to the intrafamily sphere and tells how hardship finally led her to become a member of the Baptist church:

> It was only these past couple of years that I started to work as a missionary for these Japanese women. Before that, I was sort of tied up.

I couldn't go anywhere, and I couldn't meet anybody. It is very strange. In those years, my children were small. But, now, my youngest son goes to college. In those years, it was just like doing tightrope walking. If something were to go wrong, I would fall straight into the ravine, to the deep darkness. In there, there were demons waiting with pitchforks. It was very dangerous. But my eyes were fixed straight from here to the cross of Jesus Christ. I didn't look right or left. I looked straight to the Lord. In those days, the people of Sokka Gakkai also visited me. No matter how many times they came to me, they couldn't persuade me to convert. After my husband left, I had five children and I had debts of approximately $2000. The house was mortgaged. Everything was dark. I prepared myself to suffer for this for at least seven years. But it took only five years to make it. I didn't live luxuriously, but I never became sick in those days. I worked all night but I didn't become tired. It's real strange, but God always protected me. Sometimes I didn't feel like working. I felt bad. I got hot-tempered. But when I prayed and sang a hymn, Scripture started popping out. I never knew that I knew so much. When I prayed to God, or just worshipped him or praised him, it became a joy, peace and [a] wonderful [thing]. Even in this dangerous place no one broke into my house. I know that God has blessed me.

Several episodes are worth noticing in this period. I believe that among them, the dream is most critical because it provides the key in understanding the meaning of entire episodes of her narrative. In the dream, she was unable to run because her husband's shadow held her. Here, her act of running to get the message and the difficulties caused by her husband's shadow are contrasted. The former is a move to the extrafamily sphere, and the latter is a restriction on such a move. Although the shadow takes the form of her husband, it seems to symbolize her social and psychic ties to the family and the difficulty of liberating herself from it. If one uses the psychoanalytical term, it is the unconscious counterpart of self that restricts her to the family. The presalvation period is one of crises, and the shadow seems to symbolize her crises. It stands for her domestic suffering and for the force that binds her to the intrafamily sphere.

The divine figure dressed in white throws a scroll to her. This is a figure that she describes as "Jesus Christ or Angel" and that possesses supernatural characteristics. This seems to symbolize the extrafamily sphere or something transcending the crises of the intrafamily sphere.

It is this divine figure's right hand which throws a scroll. Further, the divine figure is situated above the earth. Its height is suggestive of heaven. In contrast, the shadow was running with her — by her left side — and situated on earth. Thus the shadow and the divine figure are contrasted as heaven/right and earth/left.

In addition the scroll is interpreted by her as a message that she should engage in ethnic missions. However, the scroll in this episode is also a symbol of her link to the extrafamily sphere. It is a positive link that bridges the two spheres; it is an important key to a resolution to her crises. The destruction of the scroll may represent her link to the extrafamily sphere, which is still fragile. Further, this shows that the resolution of her intrafamily crises must wait until later in her salvation experience. In the dream, contrast between intrafamily sphere and extrafamily sphere appeared as contrast between earth/shadow/left and heaven/divine figure/right. The scroll became the link or mediator between the two spheres.

The meaning of this dream and the key to the resolution of her intrafamily crises are clarified by the passages from Ezekiel. Here also the scroll becomes the important element in understanding the meaning of the dream. In her biblical interpretation, the scroll embodies two meanings. First, in the scroll "lamentation, mourning, and woe" seem to symbolize her domestic suffering. But second, the scroll is also a message from God to engage in the missionary activity. It is mentioned that God asked Ezekiel to eat the scroll and to speak for Israel. This could be considered an internalizing of the domestic suffering and makes it a motive for the act of saving others. Thus the suffering becomes the motive for her missionary activity.

Two meanings underlying the missionary activity are revealed by the verses she quotes. First, Ezekiel 3:16–21 shows the first strategy for overcoming the suffering, that of saving the wicked — her husband and children. Second, Ezekiel 3:4–6 suggests the more specific theme of ethnic missionary activity. The second strategy for overcoming the suffering is to save her own ethnic group, the Japanese.

Ezekiel 3:16–21 tells us the general underlying meaning of the missionary activity. It suggests that if one does not attempt to save the life of the wicked through warning, one will have committed sin, will suffer from death and will be lost. Furthermore, it also conveys that, if one does attempt to save the wicked through warning, and if he does not turn away from sin, the wicked will be lost, but one will save one's soul. In the former, it is revealed that when another's soul is lost, it is the responsibility of those who did not save him. The verse tells us, "He is lost *because* you have not saved him." On the other hand, in the latter, it is noted that the act of saving others is the act of saving oneself. What is stressed is the primary importance of the act of saving the wicked—the sinner—which is the general meaning of the missionary activity. What is also represented in the wicked is her family—her husband and children—and here it is suggested that saving them was a way of saving herself and transcending her intra-family crises.

Ezekiel 3:4–6 suggested to Mrs. M that she engage in ethnic missions to her fellow Japanese, for she drew parallels between the people who are not of strange speech and hard language and the Japanese. Saving other Japanese or other warbrides who have gone through crises similar to hers is an activity that reaffirms her own ethnic identity as Japanese. In the previous passage, saving the others was saving oneself; here saving fellow Japanese was her way of saving herself. Therefore the dream and the biblical interpretation of it suggested that her missionary activities would achieve three objectives: salvation of herself, salvation of her family, and salvation of fellow Japanese.

This resolution, however, was only hinted at, since as suggested through Ezekiel 3:24–26, she was still bound to the intrafamily sphere. In the actual social scene she is in fact still bound to the intrafamily sphere. Conversely, the dream suggested a symbolic resolution. But the complete resolution was postponed until Mrs. M became a member of a church and received salvation. This resolution took place in a later phase of her experience.

In the transitional period Mrs. M attended a revival meeting at the Baptist church when invited by a friend. She described the episode as follows:

> When I first went to that church, I thought that it was so hard and strict. I felt like I was bullied with words. I thought they were so cruel. They treated me like I was a criminal. They say "this is wrong" and "that is wrong" and beat me up with their words. I thought they were rude. But, I wanted to know what the minister had to say, and I wanted to go the next night too. So I went there for three nights. I went there

every day. But the more I went, the more I came to like it. I was astonished and surprised too.

Mrs. M wanted to attend another church, but she thought it was dishonest to visit another denomination. She thought that Japanese are loyal people and they stick to it or are one-track minded. Further, she said that whatever denomination one attends, the priest or preacher would say, "we are the best" and she came to the point where "I could no longer believe in man, whether it is priest, preacher, or anybody. I needed God to be convinced."

One night before going to bed, she knelt by the bed and prayed to God to give her assurance by showing some sign to her. Most of the night brought an uneventful sleep. But just before she woke, she dreamed of a bronze serpent: "I saw a blue sky again and in that sky, there was a bronze serpent. It was upper half of the body and it was floating in the air. It was just like I was seeing a slide. I can still remember it now. For quite a while, I took a picture of it in my heart. And then suddenly, it disappeared and I woke up."

She interpreted this vision by referring to the Book of Numbers, chapter 21. During the time of Moses, the Israelites spoke against the Lord; he sent serpents to bite them to death, and many Israelites died. But when the people of Israel repented, the Lord told Moses that if he would make a bronze serpent and set it upon a pole the people would be restored to life and health. Mrs. M reasoned that although she had sinned like the Israelites, she was forgiven and allowed to attend the church. Further, she considered this to be the sign of assurance from God that she should attend this Baptist church. The day after the dream, she wrote to the pastor of the Baptist church and asked permission to attend the church and receive the pastor's teaching, promising to dedicate herself to God. She also wrote that she wanted to receive courage, wisdom, and strength from the Lord.

In the previous period, the dream symbolically expressed breaking her emotional ties to her "husband's shadow," or her intrafamily sphere, by suggesting that she accept the message of God telling her to engage in missionary activity. This hinted at the resolution of her family crises and also suggested a way to break from the intrafamily sphere to the extrafamily sphere. However, in this previous period, it only remained as a potential resolution. In the transitional period, the breaking away moved progressively into the actual social scene. Her decision to attend the church after certain negative experiences and skepticism is an indication of this. She also went through the repentance and acceptance process symbolized in the bronze serpent. Here the serpent, which is often a symbol of sin, has a double meaning. One meaning is that it is God's punishment; another is that of healing and redemption. The transitional character of this period is illustrated by this marginal symbol, the serpent, and its multiplicity of meanings.

In the final period—that of her experience of salvation—Mrs. M was given an invitation one Sunday morning to join the church. She stated that she did not know what to say and just stood at the altar trembling. The pastor asked her, "Do you want to believe in Jesus Christ as your personal savior?" She answered, "Yes. Of course, I know him, that's why I came." She first wondered why the pastor would ask such a question, but later she found that he asked that for assurance. She was also asked to work at the church and later that day attended the Sunday school for the first time.

As an epilogue to her conversion experience, she related a dream of her own funeral.

I dreamt of my own funeral. In this dream, I was in some country town. I saw a band of people. Some friends were there. I was in the casket. But do you know that I was also out of the casket? I was looking at myself there. And there were so many friends. I felt strange there and I also felt good. And the next scene, guess what? Several people carried my casket on the dusty country road on their shoulders, all four dressed in black. I went to the other side of the road. Then, I saw an open field. Above the open field I saw a gray sky. It could have been just after the rain. Or, it may have been the late afternoon about four o'clock. A gray sky, but one part was open in the gray sky. Guess what? The sun ray was reaching down to the ground from the opening. And I was there feeling like I was twenty-one years old. I was young. It was wonderful and I gave a last glance to my casket and to my body. To say goodbye to myself. And, all I had to do was to go there and then lie down and bang!—shut the casket. But I woke up before I went to heaven. All I knew was that I had assurance that that's the way.

The salvation experience is a critical rite of passage toward becoming a truly dedicated Christian. Mrs. M's account presents the episode of her invitation and attending Sunday school as an integral part of this initiation ritual. In the dream of the funeral, her departure from the old self who was unable to run in the first dream is dramatically expressed. Notice that the scene of the funeral is again the open field, which is a setting similar to one in the first dream. Nevertheless, it is characterized by gray sky, whereas the first dream was blue sky. This might indicate that her old self in the open field with a blue sky was prepared to die at the next scene, the funeral. It is a symbolic expression of the birth of a new self through the death of the old self, a truly "born again" experience. By going through the experience in this dream, she was also departing from the old self that was restricted to the intrafamily sphere and she was entering the extrafamily sphere.

When we analyze this last dream together with the first one, we realize that Mrs. M's religious experience was in essence the process of the quest for her own individual and ethnic identity. The beginning of the episodes started with the intrafamily crises, while the first dream gave her the key to solve the crises. But in the first dream, this solution was only hinted at because socially Mrs. M was still restricted to the intrafamily sphere. The actual resolution had to be postponed until her salvation, when she finally completed her departure from this intrafamily sphere. In the first dream, she found the calling to engage in the missionary activity, which demonstrated the need of saving her family and her fellow Japanese. Here the message was that in order for her to transcend her intrafamily crises, she must realize the universal significance of saving souls and then find the meaning of ethnic missions. The latter, the theme of being called to an ethnic mission, also became her process of realizing and reaffirming her ethnic identity. This realization was an important component of the process of breaking away from the intrafamily sphere.

This break could, however, be completed only when Mrs. M received salvation and went through a rebirth ("born again") experience to gain new identity as a Christian. The salvation would accomplish both the social and psychic rebirth; the last dream symbolizes this process. Here, it depicts that after symbolically dying as non-Christian, she will resurrect as Christian. She has now truly liberated herself from the intrafamily sphere and can go on to the extrafamily sphere. This process of salvation entailed her own discovery of her

Japanese identity, and this allowed her gradually to engage in activities leading the Japanese mission. About ten years ago, she started the present fellowship group under the support of the Baptist church.

I have focused primarily on Mrs. M's experience and have not touched upon the other cases. But I should note that in some other cases (especially among the fellowship leaders), visions or dreams become an important component of the religious experience. The other leaders show a pattern similar to that of Mrs. M.[2]

When observing the form of Mrs. M's religious experience, one realizes that certain features of it are shaped by the Southern Christian tradition that Samuel Hill characterizes as including religious experience of a personal and dramatic quality, Bible centeredness, and evangelism.[3] Several aspects of Mrs. M's religious experience show the influence of this tradition. For example, her emphasis on dreams as a major form of her religious experience may reflect the rather "personal" nature of Southern Christianity. The "dramatism" is expressed in the last dream, which expresses Mrs. M's "born again" experience. Her constant reference to the Bible in interpreting her dreams fits the Bible-centered nature of Southern Christianity. Finally, her strong commitment to the missionary activity also fits this tradition.

We should realize, however, that although several of the "forms" of Mrs. M's religious experience can be seen as southern, the major theme that runs through the experience is distinctive to the Japanese warbride. As mentioned previously, the major crisis of the warbride appears when she temporarily or permanently loses her husband. At such a time, she needs to learn to live independently — to break the bond of the intrafamily sphere and move to the extrafamily sphere. Commitment to a fellowship or conversion is an important part of this process, and this group support reaffirms and reinforces her ethnic identity. These themes appear in Mrs. M's experience. For her, one way of overcoming her family crisis was through the act of "saving" her fellow Japanese. The theme of saving one's ethnic group supplements the quest for a merely personal salvation.

It has been suggested by such writers as Hill that the core of Southern Christianity is in the salvation experience, which is focused on forming a one-to-one relationship with God and accepting Jesus Christ as one's exclusive or personal savior. This is a very "individualistic" form of religious experience. Mrs. M's religious experience is not limited to such individualistic salvation. Instead, it stresses group salvation, the salvation of the fellow Japanese. It could be said, then, that the Japanese warbride Christian experience is different from the typical Southern Christian experience. The former emphasizes a reaffirming and reinforcing of ethnic group identity, the latter a searching for individual identity. I believe that these differences partly lie in the deep-seated differences between the Southern Christian tradition and Japanese religious tradition, as well as in the sociocultural foundations of these traditions.[4]

NOTES

The fieldwork for this essay was carried out from July to December 1979 for doctoral work in anthropology at the University of North Carolina at Chapel Hill. Other studies of the warbride experience are John W. Connor, *A Study of the Marital Stability of Japanese War Brides* (San Francisco: R and E Research Associates, 1976); Yukiko Kimura, "War Brides in Hawaii and Their In-Laws," *American Journal of Sociology* 63 (July, 1957): 70–76; G. J. Schnepp and A. M. Yui, "Cultural and Marital Adjustment of Japanese War Brides," *American Journal of Sociology* 61 (July, 1955): 48–50; Anselm L. Strauss, "Strain and Harmony in American-Japanese War-Bride Marriages," *Marriage and Family Living* 16 (May, 1954): 99–106; and Leon K. Walters, "A Study of the Social and Marital Adjustment of Thirty-Five American-Japanese Couples," unpublished Master's thesis (Columbus, Ohio: Ohio State University, 1953). A collection of life histories of Japanese warbrides was published by Tsuneo Enari in *Dokyument, Taiheiyo o musubu ai, Hanayome no America* [The Love Beyond the Pacific: Japanese Warbrides in America], Asahi Camera Special Issue (Tokyo: Asahi Shinbunsha, 1980). On the Japanese-American religious experience, see Keiichi Yanagawa, ed., *Japanese Religions in California: A Report on Research Within and Without the Japanese-American Community* (Tokyo: Department of Religious Studies, University of Tokyo, 1983). Other useful (though psychologically slanted) studies of religious experience of Japanese-Americans in the Japanese New Religions are a number of works by Takie Sugiyama-Lebra, including "Religious Conversion as a Breakthrough for Trans-Culturation: A Japanese Sect in Hawaii," *Journal for the Scientific Study of Religion* 9 (1970): 181–196, and Winifred L. Dahl's *Religious Conversion and Mental Health in Two Japanese American Groups*, Ph.D. dissertation (Berkeley: Department of Anthropology, University of California, 1975). My own doctoral dissertation continues the investigation of this area: *Purifying the Living and Purifying the Dead: Narratives of the Religious Experience of Japanese-American and Caucasian Members of the Church of World Messianity, Los Angeles, California,* Ph.D. dissertation (Chapel Hill: Department of Anthropology, University of North Carolina, 1984). A basic source on Japanese religion is H. Byron Earhart, *Japanese Religion: Unity and Diversity* (Belmont: Dickenson Publishing, 1969).

1. Sokka Gakkai, an offshoot of the Nichiren sect of Buddhism, was founded by Tsunesaburo Makiguchi (1871–1944) in 1930 at Tokyo. It has grown intensively since World War II and has become the largest New Religion in contemporary Japan. Presently, it claims sixteen million members in Japan. In the United States, Sokka Gakkai is known as the Nichiren Shoshu Academy (NSA). It arrived in this country in the late 1950s and already in the early 1960s, using the aggressive street-conversion tactics called "shakubuku," had started an intensive evangelization program. Japanese warbrides played a very important role in establishing the NSA in the early years and up until the late 1960s the majority of the members were warbrides. Although some warbrides still hold firm leadership among the national and local chapters, the majority of the members are now Caucasian. Their increase was noticeable from the later 1960s to the early 1970s, when the NSA attracted large numbers of Caucasian youths. It is one of the largest Eastern Religions in the United States and is estimated to have approximately 200,000 members. For the activities of Sokka Gakkai in America, see James A. Dator, *Sokka Gakkai, Builders of the Third Civilization: American and Japanese Members* (Seattle: University of Washington Press, 1969); Robert S. Ellwood, *The Eagle and the Rising Sun: Americans and the New Religions of Japan* (Philadelphia: Westminster Press, 1974); David A. Snow, *The Nichiren Shoshu Buddhist Movement in America: A Sociological Examination of Its Value Orientation, Recruitment Efforts and Spread,* unpublished Ph.D. dissertation (Los Angeles: University of California at Los Angeles, 1976); and Vicki R. Holtzapple, *Sokka Gakkai in Midwestern America: A Case Study of a Transpositional Movement,* Ph.D. dissertation (St. Louis, Mo.: Washington University Press, 1977).

2. Space limitations prevent me from offering transcripts from accounts of visions given by two other leaders interviewed.

3. Samuel S. Hill, *Southern Churches in Crisis* (New York: Holt, Rinehart, and Winston, 1966), pp. 25–26, 80, 89–90.

4. Japanese religions — with the partial exception of certain New Religions like Sokka Gakkai and Dancing Religion (Tensho-Kotai-jingukyo) — lack the stress found in Southern Christianity on a dramatic rebirth experience,

aggressive evangelism, and an ultimate textual authority. These differences are apparently ethnic as well as religious. My doctoral research with the Japanese religious sect called the Church of World Messianity (Sekai-kyuseikyo) in Los Angeles revealed that Caucasian members stress an individualistic quest rather than the group solidarity sought by Japanese-American members.

A Pentecostal Account of   11
Spiritual Quest

James L. Peacock

A Pentecostal church I shall call "Mount Pisgah" happens to be pastored by a minister from Dunn, North Carolina, one of the places from which Pentecostalism spread through the South. But this church is found in a town north of Dunn, in the Piedmont Region. Mount Pisgah, in a working-class section on the edge of this town of 100,000, is a modern, air-conditioned building centered on a sanctuary that prominently displays acoustical equipment necessary for the music and preaching aimed at "raising the spirit" of the congregation to a level of excitement encouraging some to "get the Holy Ghost." Direct experience with the Holy Ghost is perhaps the most distinctive objective of this Pentecostal church, and that experience is not only an act of public worship, but the Holy Ghost is also sought privately by the individual. An account of such a quest is given by a member of Mount Pisgah whom I name Rutledge.

Rutledge, a tall, erect, well-built man in his thirties, with a strong face, thinning blond hair, and a direct gaze, is employed as a front-end mechanic in a garage. He is also a Sunday school teacher in Mount Pisgah Pentecostal Church. The pastor of the church had given us permission to attend and record services and to interview the members. After he had introduced us to the congregation, we found Rutledge (like most others) hospitable to our efforts to understand something of Pentecostal beliefs and experience.

At Rutledge's house we began an interview by asking him, "Will you tell us the history of how you came to be a member of the church?" He asked, in turn, "Do you want me to begin with my childhood?" "Sure, any way you want," we invited. He replied, "I was not raised in a Christian home at all. My parents are not Christian, neither were my brother and sister. . . . I wasn't spiritual at all when I was a young man. I was vain in the world of the devil." This was all Rutledge said about his childhood and family.

Now he moved straight to his spiritual quest. One Sunday, when he was twenty-five years old, his wife tried to get him to go to church. He replied, "I don't want no part of it," so she left him at home. Rutledge recalls: "That Sunday she went I was sitting on the porch and became real miserable all of a sudden for some reason, as if something was drawing me — spiritual. I'll never forget the experience of that, the leaves on the trees were weeping, and it's amazing how nature spoke to me. I began to think on the lines of the Creator. . . . I remember praying, I never prayed any, so I asked God in a simple way to have someone invite me to church and I'll go."

He did go, for six nights straight. "I would stand there and shake in the pew, I would not give in to it . . . it was a force pulling at me. The sixth night was when I accepted it . . . the burden was lifted, I felt new, I felt clean." Thus Rutledge experienced being saved. He tells us, "The Church I was saved at is just right up the road here." This is a Free Will Baptist Church.

The experience of being saved was not sufficient for Rutledge: "I became hungry for deeper things. . . . I said, 'Lord, if you will manifest yourself to me it will help me to believe and be strong in the things of the spirit.' This is what I began to seek after, a manifestation of the spirit of God. I wanted to see him in a vision."

While off in the woods at a place called Timberlake, about a year after being saved, Rutledge had such an experience: "A force, it just drew me to him, it anointed me all over, it was joy that I had never experienced." Rutledge called the pastor of his Baptist church, then called a deacon to tell them about his ecstasy. The pastor had not had the experience, and discounted it; the deacon had, but thought such experiences came from a demon.

These interpretations disturbed Rutledge "for seven long years. This was such an experience, there was so much glory, and so much joy. . . . But I had never heard of the baptism of the Spirit, or nothing. All I had ever heard was get saved, sit in the church, and go through the rituals of every day and every Sunday service."

In the ensuing seven years, Rutledge taught in the Baptist Sunday school, telling about the Holy Ghost: "How God could manifest himself in the third Person." Finally, the church condemned Rutledge's experience and his teachings, but Rutledge stood firm in his commitment to the experience, regardless of how the church chose to see it: "Although my pastor told me it was an evil spirit, I said, 'If the devil has something this good to offer me, then I'm worshipping the wrong one.'"

He left the church. Leaving the church, Rutledge also left his job. Three new opportunities were "sent by God," and he emphasizes that he chose the job which on rational grounds was least desirable. But this proved to reflect the mysterious workings of God, for this job led to his second experience with the Holy Ghost. This occurred at the body shop.

He met a Pentecostal, Billy, at work. Rutledge now explains that he had always thought of Pentecostals as "Holy Rollers [who] jump pews and swing from the lights." Rutledge went with Billy to a Pentecostal service, which he found "really funny. A woman threw a leg up on a table and talked about how God had healed it. . . . I went home and me and my wife laughed about it for several hours."

One day everything was going wrong: "It seemed as if a force was fighting me." Finally, about 4 p.m., Rutledge went to the body shop to see Billy: "Billy, I'm about to give up and be like I used to before I got into religion at all." But at 4:15, Rutledge had another experience: "I just looked up and, for some reason, said, 'Father,' and the Holy Spirit moved me, praise God, I can feel it now. It moved on me and it seemed like everything changed . . . and I spoke in tongues." Rutledge then described the force that was in him, how he touched a policeman, Frank, who had come to pick up his car. Frank "threw both hands up in the air, and began to confess to the Lord. . . . The power that was on me at the time was unbelievable."

Thus Rutledge experienced the Holy Ghost again. Still, he had no church. He continued to look for one, and as he looked he saw many strange things. He describes what he saw with a certain detached disdain — not unlike that of an Enlightenment philosopher or old-fashioned traveler who witnessed savage rites, or like moralist David Hume, who looked askance at "superstition and enthusiasm," or Lord Monboddo, who wrote on "Men living in Brutish State, without Arts or Civility."[1] Rutledge went among snake handlers, but stood aloof: "I got by the door, and said, 'If they bring out snakes, I'm gonna be gone.'" He went to a service where they carried his friend Ruth to the altar, "screamed in her ears and spit in her face . . . trying to beat the Holy Ghost into you." Finally, he came to Mount Pisgah church, where his wife, Ruth, and he himself received the Holy Ghost again.

"The history of how you became a member of the church" is what we requested of Rutledge. This was the standard question we had adopted to solicit individual histories of members of the church. Since we were now attending the church, this helped justify our right to ask about their lives. The primary justification from their own point of view is that of testimony: the believer is committed to testifying to whoever listens.

Rutledge replied to our request by asking if we wanted to hear about his childhood. Told "yes," he proceeds to skip most of that period and deny the relevance of what he does mention of it. He also omits from his background the two primary facets of human community traditional to the species: kinship and residence. Rutledge could, as some religious autobiographies and biographies do, begin with ancestry. He does not. He mentions no kinfolk farther back than parents or farther out than siblings. The influence of parents and siblings is then denied by his stating only one fact about them, that most relevant to his Christian belief: they were not Christians.

Rutledge thus neatly brushes aside features of origin: family, place, and religious background. He has given himself a tabula rasa on which to depict the significant experience of his life, the Holy Ghost. Within a few minutes of starting his account, he is ready to present that experience.

Opening the account of his salvation, Rutledge recalls "sitting on the porch"—a typical Southern, quasi-rural way to relax and reflect. It is Sunday, his wife is at church, and he, the nonchurch independent, is presumably alone (although there are doubtless other porch-sitters up and down the street). He recalls feeling miserable, but it was not he but "the leaves on the trees" that were weeping. "Nature spoke to me," he says. Through nature, he came to reflect on the Creator; later he will go beyond "the natural," as he later puts it, to follow the Spirit.

Rutledge decides that if someone asks him to go to church, he will. A friend does invite him, to "make up" after an argument. Rutledge goes to a revival service at a Free Will Baptist church. That a Free Will Baptist church should enter at this point in the narrative is singularly appropriate, for the main contrast between this church and the Pentecostal is that the Free Will Baptists emphasize salvation, the Pentecostals the sanctification that follows salvation. Thus for Rutledge, as for some other Pentecostals, being "saved," the first stage of spiritual growth, was provided through the Baptists, while sanctification, the second stage, came after a move to Pentecostalism.

Emphasizing salvation, the Free Will Baptist church orchestrates its services, especially revival services, to draw the unsaved toward accepting the Lord and becoming saved. This is achieved through powerful sermons, followed by persuasive and cogent invitations by the preacher to the unsaved to come to the altar. There, one is invited to do nothing less than surrender oneself to God, to accept God's control over one's life.

Rutledge relates that at this Free Will Baptist revival, the gospel "had the power of the Spirit"; he would "stand" there and "shake in the pew" resisting that power. (The word "stand" instead of the expected "sit" was perhaps chosen to emphasize his resistance, as in "Here I stand"). But finally he accepted it at the altar call.

Rutledge then enjoyed a spurt of intellectual interest, studying "everything I could find to study." He was trying to interpret his experience: "Was this thing real, this thing that happened to me?" His answer was found in the Bible. "Everything would turn right back to the Scripture."

Here would seem to be the classic sequence — first, the experience; second, the effort to interpret it; third, the answer, by some scriptural formulation. But it would be a mistake to think of that answer as strictly intellectual. The Bible is hardly abstract theology; it is itself narrated experience, which can be reexperienced by the reader. Rutledge says, "I got my joy and my spiritual food from the Bible."

This food, however, did not fill him. Instead, he says, "I became hungry for deeper things." What Rutledge sought was a "manifestation of the spirit of God," perhaps in a vision or dream. What he found was his first experience of sanctification.

196

Lest it be thought that the search is sensationalist, note the base on which he grounds his search: (1) the Bible, (2) loving Christ, and (3) keeping his commandments. The book, love, and the law are the conditions necessary for the experience.

Finally, at Timberlake, while sitting quietly with his wife listening to gospel music, Rutledge did experience something, though he was not sure at the time what. He says it was frightening to his wife but a joy to him, that nothing compares with it, not even "being intoxicated." He felt possessed by some force that set him apart and is contagious: "I wouldn't allow my wife to touch me. I didn't understand it and didn't know if it would leave me and get on her, or what." Wondering what the experience meant, he called first "my pastor," then a deacon of his Free Will Baptist Church. Neither accepted the experience. The pastor dismissed it, not having had such an experience himself. The deacon, who had, attributed it to a demon.

This bothered him, he says, for "seven long years" (his repetition of "seven years" at several points suggests a special symbolic meaning of that number, perhaps scriptural, as in "seven years of famine"). "This was such an experience, there was so much glory and so much joy," that he found it hard to accept the attribution of that experience to a demon.

"But I had never heard of the baptism of the Spirit. . . . All I had ever heard was get saved, sit in the church, and go through the rituals of every day and every Sunday service." Here he succinctly contrasts the Pentecostal and the Baptist; the former affirms the Holy Ghost experience, the latter the routinizing pattern of settling down to rites once one is saved by accepting Christ.

His experience, then, brought not peace, but a time of confusion: "After that I began to hunger more and more after the deeper things of God. During this seven years the church began to notice that I was more spiritual than some of the others."

He taught about the Holy Ghost, "how God could manifest himself in the third Person." To the contrary, the Free Will Baptist Church wanted to confine the Spirit to the day of Pentecost, to deny that the Spirit could still manifest itself today. Thus the conflict moved to a head, as the Free Will Baptist preacher came to oppose Rutledge. Rutledge elaborated this opposition: "Now let me tell you about how he went about trying to get me to resign. I knew I had God with me, that God had anointed me. That he had put me there for a purpose. O.K. I can tell you what that purpose was in a little bit."

"Now" refers to his present in the narration, "in a little bit" to his future. "Now" (present) locates the schism; "in a little bit" (future) locates God's purpose. This distinction in narrative language parallels the phenomenological distinction between the situation in which he found himself — the schismatic church — and the transcendent purpose God had set for him. Even in the midst of that human situation, which he later characterized as "an awful experience," I *"knew"* God's purpose, he states, emphasizing his conviction.

He then reports two seemingly enigmatic actions by the Baptist preacher: the presentation of pieces of jewelry and the cutting of nine pieces of cake. These pieces the preacher calls "gifts of the Spirit," in doing so apparently ridiculing Rutledge's teaching by reducing the gifts to ludicrously inadequate symbols. However this message was intended, Rutledge took it as rejecting his teaching. He continued to teach in the spirit for six weeks until finally he was directly asked to leave the church and did so.

The sociology of the schism would need to be understood in order to assess the severity of Rutledge's conflict and the intensity of his commitment; we know little about this. We do know that Rutledge lives in a pluralistic community where alternatives to this particular Free Will Baptist Church are readily available; the town boasts hundreds of churches, dozens of which are in Rutledge's vicinity. However, this particular church is the one in which he was saved and which he had attended for seven years, so he had doubtless a strong investment in this church. In any case, when he left he took with him at least two couples who have now joined Mount Pisgah Pentecostal Church with him. He and his wife seemingly feel one of these couples to be their closest friends, and it was noteworthy that at one of the business meetings of the church (a men's breakfast at Shoney's Restaurant) Rutledge and the two men who had left the Baptist church with him sat together and formed a kind of opinion bloc.

Rutledge paused to summarize his life as twenty-five years without knowing God, seven years in confusion, and the last two years at Mount Pisgah. He expresses his discontent and his faith that his search will achieve its object. He then returns to this schism, signaling the shift back through the adverb "anyway." Then he points toward the next episode by the phrase "getting to": "But anyway, getting to Mount Pisgah church. . . ."

Getting there takes Rutledge through more obstacles and adventures—but it leads toward a spiritual home. After his ecstatic afternoon at the body shop, Rutledge "hungers" and asks Billy where to go to get "filled." This search takes him to at least two religious groups that he describes as somewhat bizarre, misguided, and brutal, although not without their mysteries and exoticism. The first boasts at least one snake handler. These people put their hands on him, shaking him and jerking him. Rutledge, a man of refinement, self-possession, and pride, says this "offended him." He would not return. The second (which is a Holiness congregation, one of the largest in the town) tried the same physical manipulation of the wife of his best friend; this couple had left the Baptist church with him on the same search.

The third church he mentions is Mount Pisgah Pentecostal Church, which he came to by accident (or divine intervention), and there he remains.

We see then something of the logic and psychology of Rutledge's quest for a Holy Ghost experience. But what of the way the tale is told? Only by some attention to the style of the narration do we begin to grasp the subtlety by which such "gestures" project their power.

Especially striking in Rutledge's narration is the relationship between secular and religious language. A certain dualism in his language reflects a dualism not only in Western culture but also in his distinctive subculture. Rutledge fits many of the patterns in what could be termed, broadly, a working-class, male, southern subculture. Like the acceptable male in this subculture, Rutledge demonstrates prowess in the material world. He is capable in working with machines (a front-end man in a body shop), he likes the outdoors (his first Holy Ghost experience was at a lake), and one would guess that he fishes, hunts, follows sports, and is an able athlete. Around his male friends, he behaves appropriately—asserting strength but in a muted way, teasing roughly but gently. His voice is baritone, clear and confident but not theatrically (and suspiciously) macho. In short, Rutledge is a man's man, a good fellow—phrases he himself would not use but which perhaps convey meaning to the reader. Yet he is more; he is also an intensely religious person. This dualistic tension between his religiosity and his ordinariness—especially in his male role—is reflected in his language.

Rutledge's narration borrows authenticity from the genre of the story of fact. In this, it contrasts with testimonies proper, which announce themselves more ostentatiously as performances. In fact, a few of those interviewed chose the performance mode, signaling to the interviewer that they were to give a performance for the tape recorder by saying, "I'm ready; turn it on," then delivering a testimonial, with rapid speech and religious ejaculations. Rutledge begins with a quiet question of fact, "Would you like me to tell about my childhood?" His manner of speech, at least in the beginning, is in a style, perhaps a kind distinctive in this region, of remembered facticity.

The beginnings with reference to the world of ordinary experience are however soon transformed through the language of the spirit. Note Rutledge's words: "I was vain in the world of the devil . . . I began to consider the things of creation . . . The Spirit moved on me . . . It's amazing how nature spoke to me. Christ said . . . if you love me, you'll keep my commandments, and we will come and make our abode in you, and manifest ourselves to you." Such words are spoken in the calm, matter-of-fact way that Rutledge describes the rest of his life, uttered fluently, although (I sense) with a faint hint of embarrassment, signaled sometimes with a downward look or stumbling rhythm often replaced by a more evangelical upward look and fluency, but tempered by a gentle sarcasm, as when he refers to his old life "back there in the world."

Rutledge alternates such spiritual language with the colloquial expressions of the world. Speaking of the Baptist preacher who rejected his first experience: "He'd roll up his sleeves and ask you if you want to fight." Describing his reaction when he went to the meeting where the lady had a snake: "So I got by the door, and said, 'If they bring out any snakes, I'm gonna be gone.'"

Whether the preacher would actually roll up his sleeves or Rutledge actually got by the door may or may not have been true. The point to note is that this is accepted male secular narrative style for Rutledge's region and milieu. He dramatizes emotional reactions by images of action. When he refers directly to inner experience, for example, Christ's love or the Holy Ghost experience, the tone changes, and this is where one senses embarrassment, sublimated into the fluency and eloquence of the evangelical language.

Persons who are outside the fellowship of the Spirit are treated bluntly by Rutledge. The preacher who rolled up his sleeves, the snake handlers, the woman at the Holy Roller meeting who "threw her leg on the table" — these are described in the accepted male style of secular dramatization, where the "other" is characterized by external action that is exotic, exaggerated, not fully human, and rather outlandish. Contrast this to "I said, 'Father' . . ." spoken reverently, in a hushed tone.

The following passage, describing Rutledge's experience at the garage, combines the practical and spiritual languages: "Frank came in and was asking me had I repaired his car. I had, I had finished it. . . . He was not saved and I touched him . . . he began to run from me and he stayed away from me for over eight months, he wouldn't come around, scared. . . . [Today] he's saved, and he's chief of police at Caxton. He's doing real good. The power that was on me at the time was unbelievable." Rutledge here reports the secular actions, that he fixed the car, and the spiritual experience, the power within him, and his touching Frank. He then retreats from this power by the ordinary-life cliché, "He's doing real good."

What is displayed in these passages and throughout the narration is the epistemological problem of connecting the spiritual and the worldly. The languages are different, the culturally accepted presentations of self and others different. The male, especially in this regional subculture, has a special problem in that acceptable male narration and presentation of self must stress action rather than feelings, depicting others unsentimentally and attaining drama by exaggeration of actions; it must also temper any dramatization by toned-down facticity that, however, must not be overly technical (asked if he repaired the car, Rutledge simply says he had, not spoiling the effect by the intellectual's explication of technical detail). This language of the everyday world must be connected to spiritual language, which treats inner experience, dependency on others, and spiritual powers that by doctrine and belief cannot be treated demeaningly, so must — albeit awkwardly — somehow be honored.

Diversities of Gifts

NOTES

This essay is based on fieldwork carried out during the summers of 1977 through 1979, in company with Ruel W. Tyson, Jr., and with support from the National Institute of Mental Health and the University of North Carolina Faculty Research Council. The interview on which this essay is based was one of many with members of the church we call "Mount Pisgah," to whose pastor and congregation we are deeply grateful for their friendly hospitality and willingness to participate in our research.

1. David Hume, "Of Superstition and Enthusiasm" in *Essays,* eds. T. H. Green and T. H. Grose (London: Longmans Green, 1875), vol. 1, pp. 144–50; James Burnet, Lord Monboddo, "Examples from Ancient and Modern History of Men Living in the Brutish State, Without Arts or Civility" in *Of the Origin and Progress of Language* (Edinburgh, 1774), vol. 1, pp. 236–69.

202

CONCLUSION — Independent Protestants in North Carolina and the Study of Living Religion

The studies that comprise this book seek to understand a religion not simply as a creed or denominational organization, but as living experience embodied in what we have termed *gestures*. Encountered through the sermons, songs, narrations, and other forms, the religious traditions described here display aesthetic, intellectual, and moral power that moves outside the systematized doctrine and bureaucratized organization of the larger churches. Through their own distinctive forms and experiences these traditions can contribute humanistic as well as religious understanding not sufficiently recognized in the accepted teachings of mainline religion and mainstream culture of our society.

Independent Protestants in North Carolina

Long recognized as distinctive in contrast to the state church pattern of Europe, the American pattern of pluralism permits a variety of religious groups, no one of which is allowed dominance over others. North Carolina exemplifies this American pluralism more fully than many southern states. It has not only the leading Protestant quartet — Methodist, Southern Baptist, Presbyterian, and Episcopalian — that characterizes much of the South outside Catholic strongholds, but is also rich in other religious heritages: several strands of Quakerism, German populations represented by the Moravians, Lutherans, and Church of the Brethren, together with Pentecostal and Holiness groups and a great variety of Baptists — Missionary, Union, Primitive, Free Will, and Independent. In this list, doctrinal diversity is crosscut by ethnic diversity; in addition to the German and Anglo-American, North Carolina has rich Afro-American and native American Protestant traditions and even a growing population of Oriental and Hispanic extraction. It now has the Japanese or Korean Protestant.

This kind of religious pluralism undercuts the hypothetical "solid South." There remain Southern Baptists as an advertisement of a regional identity, but highland Primitive Baptists identify less with their fellow southerners in the lowlands than with fellow mountaineers up and down the spine of Appalachia, or with coreligionists in Texas, Ohio, or Delaware. Pentecostals of North Carolina have always maintained strong links to California, Oklahoma, Chicago, and elsewhere, and Presbyterians and Methodists have formally submerged their regional identity into national and international structures. Certainly it would be wrong to stereotype the groups described in this volume as expressions of some monolithically southern culture.

Recognizing variation even within the limited sample of North Carolina religions represented here, we feel it is not wise to attempt to construct a type. Still, we can point out some qualities shared by these diverse groups. All of the groups studied here are of the historic Protestant tradition, and they maintain the standard beliefs and practices of that tradition.[1] They profess belief in God and Christ; they worship in churches, through sermons, songs, and prayer; they baptize and hold communion; and in what is perhaps the cornerstone of Protestantism, most members actively study the Bible. They are literate, reading and writing religious literature. In short, they are bearers of one great tradition, Protestantism. Within this tradition, however, most of the groups described in the essays in this book stem from the British Separatist heritage rather than from the Anglican or the Lutheran, and Catholic and Orthodox traditions represented by immigrants from central, eastern, and southern Europe. African and other influences have of course entered the practices of some of these groups, but the British Separatist background is shared by most of them as well as by most of the Protestants in the American South.

Beyond having a Separatist heritage, the Protestant groups sampled here could be termed *independent*. Most of them are independent of the numerically and socially dominant Protestant denominations of the region, and they differ from these denominations in certain ways. The mainline United Methodists, Southern Baptists, Presbyterians, and Episcopalians are characterized by certain features: their location typically in the center of towns and cities; their sponsorship of colleges and universities; their tendency to attract the wealthy, established elite as well as aspirants to such status; and their large-scale hierarchical or associational organization. While the line between these and other groups should not be drawn too sharply — the independent churches may have educated and wealthy members and in some instances sponsor colleges and seminaries — these characteristics are not salient in their endeavors. Membership in an independent church certainly does not confer status in conventional circles of upper- and middle-class society. One infers that upper- and middle-class people who join an independent church do so for reasons other than status. The independents further tend to favor preaching inspired by God directly and hence are suspicious of education in seminaries (which some call "cemeteries," referring to what they see as their deadening effect on religious life). The independents tend to locate on country roads, mountain ridges, or side streets rather than on the main street or in wealthy suburbs. The independents are not organized into large, centralized organizations.

One who presumes too simple an historical or sociological type is often brought up short, but given their Separatist and independent orientation, many of these groups do resemble a sectarian pattern the sociologist might expect.

Architectural Simplicity and Focus

The church buildings of these groups are simple and adorned by little or no religious imagery. They contrast, therefore, with Catholic churches, which have more elaborate imagery inside, and they also contrast with the great cathedrals of the Catholic tradition in their external plainness. In this, they conform to Protestantism generally, but they are at the extreme end of the spectrum. Primitive Baptists, for example, eschew even a steeple on their meeting houses, as well as stained glass windows and replicas of the cross. Such a view is at the extreme even within the independent group, but simple one-room structures with plain wooden pews and perhaps only a stand or book board rather than pulpit and altar are characteristic in the countryside, and even the more modern air-conditioned churches of the cities still tend toward plainness of interior and exterior. Where images are present — a cross or pictures of Christ — these are concentrated at the front of the church, behind the pulpit, stand, or altar. The effect is to focus attention on this front space and what happens there, such as sermons, rather than on any ritual (such as a ceremonial procession), that diffuses attention throughout the sacred space.

Verbal Color and Physical Vigor

Paralleling this architectural simplicity and focus are simplicity in forms of worship. Rare are the robes, candles, or other material accoutrements that go with the elaborated ritual complex of the Catholic mode; again, the independents tend toward the extreme of Protestantism in this respect. However, they accompany the simplicity of their rituals with a rhetorical power and color in preaching and a vigor in physical expression. The Primitive Baptists' chanted sermon and the Pentecostal testimonies demonstrate rhetorical power. Pentecostals lay on hands, shake, hug, lift, dance, run, and swoon. Primitive Baptists are quieter, but even among them one finds the solemnly clasped hand of fellowship, the washing of feet, and accompanying such moving actions, a restrained shedding of tears. In such actions, gesture comes vigorously alive.

The Centrality of Congregational Singing

John Forrest's account of the dispute about a church choir reminds us of the importance of song in these groups. Choirs and soloists are optional among them, but congregational singing is always present and important. The very independence of the congregations ensures wide diversity in their musical performances. Instrumental accompaniment may be prohibited (as by the Primitive Baptists) or elaborated to include trumpet, guitar, and drum as well as organ and piano (by Pentecostals). The music ranges from the slow, unaccompanied modal melodies of the Primitive Baptists to the upbeat rhythms and modern harmonies of the Pentecostals. Song texts vary from seventeenth- and eighteenth-century English and early to modern American hymns. They do not, however, draw much upon either the European classical tradition of Bach, Beethoven, Buxtehude, and Handel, or upon the genteel nineteenth-century hymns of Lowell Mason heard in the dominant churches. Here, too, these groups signal independence from a self-designated high culture. They sustain musical forms compatible with congregational participation as opposed to virtuoso performance. (The gospel performers are an exception to this characterization, but they have moved outside the church to the stage.)

Emphasis on Inner Experience

Most of these independent church groups emphasize subjective experience as a referent for religious symbols. A Pentecostal song puts the point vividly: "If God is dead, what is this in my soul?" The song describes God as acting upon the spiritual self in ways apprehended directly from the emotions. Pentecostals crave the Holy Ghost experience, which may manifest itself in outward signs — speaking in tongues, dancing in the spirit, healing or being healed — but is seen as located inside the person whom the Holy Ghost enters and possesses. Quakers seek inner light even above scriptural revelation. Although Primitive Baptists reject the salvation experience — the dramatic surrender of the self to Christ in order to be saved — they too treasure "impressions," manifestations of God in one's emotional and reflective life that can be interpreted cautiously as evidence encouraging hope that one is a "child of God," one of the elect recipients of grace. Thus although the particular form and understanding of the inner experience may differ, a subjective emphasis characterizes all these groups.

Scripturalism

Independent churches are not liturgical groups in the manner of Episcopalians, who in their worship read from a Book of Common Prayer or other books than the Bible. For these groups, the Bible is the work read during services, although they may read and write theological and historical works for study. In significant ways they place the Bible at the center of their religious lives. (It is often also at the center of their daily lives, too, as symbolized by the place of the Bible on the table in their homes.) Their approach to reading the Bible is somewhat fundamentalist, in that they take the text as reporting the true message of Christianity, but they vary in their styles of interpreting this mes-

sage. In preaching, for example, Primitive Baptists are highly scriptural, weaving arguments out of the biblical text, whereas A. M. E.
Zion preachers tend toward the liberal Protestant use of nonbiblical
metaphors as themes for sermons, with Scripture cast in a supporting
role. Pentecostals tend to draw more on experience, to preach in the
style that Primitive Baptists, using an older terminology, term *experi-
mental* as opposed to scriptural. Such labels as "Bible Belt" or "fundamentalist" are obviously inadequate to capture the complex patterns
of scriptural use among these groups, but it seems fair to label them
"scripturalist" in light of their generally strong emphasis on the Scripture. Scripturalism supports subjectivism by providing an authorita-
tive definition for individual experience and a common idiom for sharing of experience.

The Place of Independent Protestantism in the Lives of the Community and the Individual

For the individual, especially where alternative institutions are not
available, the church defines milestones in the life cycle. Joining it
signals coming of age in adolescence, rejoining after backsliding or
simply going away often signals resumption of familial and social responsibilities, and remaining active in it (as in the case of Johnny
detailed by Isabel Terry) is a way of staying vigorous and alive in
old age. Conflicts and doubts that secular society and the liberal
churches might call adolescent or mid-life crises entailing psychological
problems these independent Protestants see more as issues of sin and
salvation, morality and immorality. To solve such spiritual or ethical
problems, one studies the Scripture, seeks the inner light, or goes to
the mountaintop—in short, pursues a spiritual path rather than
psychological therapy. (Note the explicit contrast Sister Annie Mae
draws between religion and psychiatry.) The independent Protestants
more completely frame their lives in religious terms than do the liberal
or mainline Protestants in the South.

Most of the independent Protestant groups could be termed *sects*
in that they rebel against hierarchical organization as exemplified by
the established church; they reject both hierarchical ecclesiastical systems maintained by the Methodists, Presbyterians, and Episcopalians
and the centralized associational network of the Southern Baptists.

Thus they are independent. They are not, however, isolated. Most of them are organized in formalized or informal associations with other churches, sometimes thousands of miles away, and they participate in far-flung networks of exchange of ministers, meetings, and other social relationships. Some of them show a movement toward a more formal ecclesiastical bureaucracy.

Whatever bureaucratization occurs among the independent Protestants differs from that of the established hierarchies in one important respect. Because the established hierarchies draw on the social elite, their leaders — whether clergy or laity — usually occupy leadership positions outside the church as well as in it. Leaders in the independent Protestant churches tend to concentrate their leadership inside the church. The independent Protestants are less anchored in the power structures of society.

The social situation of the independent Protestants is reflected in their social doctrines. All groups except the Primitive Baptists encourage missionary activity and evangelism. But most of these churches stop short of reaching out in a material rather than spiritual way; they do not, on the whole, actively organize and reform the larger society or even the economic and political lives of their members. Economic activity is not prominent as a church-organized activity except in matters directly related to the church, as in cooperative labor of men to repair the building or of women to cook dinners. The church does not organize stores, cooperative farms, or factories, for example, as some other religious groups do. Nor is secular education a prominent focus of church activity, in comparison to the schools, colleges, and seminaries maintained by some denominations; and the Primitive Baptists even forbid Sunday school.

Nor are the churches politically active. Even though some of the churches are found among minorities, such as blacks, native Americans, and Appalachians, religious messages far overshadow political ones in their sermons. Black power, red power, or the preachments of the Christian Right are not prominent themes in these sermons. Instead, religious and personal issues, such as the evils of drink, fornication, and unkindness, and a concern with salvation, sanctification, and other spiritual or moral concerns are stressed. Even the Quakers of the Meadowlane church, despite the traditionally radical social posture of Quakerism, have gone far in following this supposedly southern and fundamentalist pattern of emphasizing personal morality and spirituality over social issues.

Types and Varieties of Religious Experiences

The independent Protestants do, then, share certain characteristics. They may at first glance seem merely to confirm some well-established types, such as Troeltsch's "sect," Hill's "central theme" in Southern religion, or "fundamentalism" as elucidated by Barr—or perhaps simply to confirm that these are Protestants.[2] Here are groups that eschew architectural and ritual ornamentation together with hierarchical bureaucracy, but who preach powerfully and seek experience that is emotionally stirring and physically energizing yet scripturally grounded, and who favor an individualistic rather than bureaucratic relation of the church to their lives. Such a group would seem to exhibit North Carolina's esteemed tradition of yeoman-farmer democracy, an element that in Rhys Isaacs's term comprised a kind of "counter culture" challenging an hierarchical Anglican aristocracy having its strongest base in tidewater Virginia.[3]

Typologies have their uses, but the variation within type is as noteworthy as its generalized features. An example is the conception of the role of women; whereas all the groups studied here may be said to favor biblical and traditional values that emphasize the distinction between men and women rather than their similarities, considerable variation is apparent. Sons of God and the Primitive Baptists both categorize the church as female, but in the Sons of God this is negative (the whore of Babylon), whereas the Primitive Baptists view the church positively (the bride of Christ). Correlatively, the Sons have female pastors, the Primitive Baptists do not—a seeming paradox, since one might expect pastors to represent the positive. The groups show still other variety. Where outward display of emotion takes prominence, so do women, sometimes as preachers as among the Pentecostals and A.M.E. Zion. Among Quakers, women speak out as do men and are quiet and tactful mediators. Among the Japanese Baptists, women are missionaries. Yet despite the variety of roles they may take in these groups—whether pressing for greater scope as an A.M.E. preacher or accepting the more restrictive and traditional place accorded women within the Primitive Baptist churches, the women may find rich fulfillment in their religion. No simple recipe for the liberated or patronized woman suffices to type the woman's role among these groups.

The variety among the groups could, of course, be exemplified by other comparisons, but the concrete richness of their experience is best perceived by attention to the particular persons and forms described in each essay. Who, for example, would have thought Quakers would evolve in the path sketched by Isabel B. Terry? Our stereotype of the heirs of George Fox as persons combining austere quietism in worship with radical political stubbornness is shattered by the friendly folk of the Meadowlane church, who have accommodated so adaptively and comfortably to their small-town southern setting. Hardly accommodative are the Sons of God portrayed by James Wise. They draw fiercely radical inferences from basic Protestant premises. The comfortably compromising mainline Protestant may well feel discomfort if he permits himself to ask what it would mean in one's life to work out the logic of his faith in so radically nonconformist a way.

In the particular forms or *gestures* of these groups we also encounter a variety of performative modes and strong, but contrasting views concerning which are appropriate ones: A Southern Baptist church that experiences conflict over the style of the songs its choir and accompanist offer; black performances that range from the unaccompanied lined-out congregational hymnody of the Primitive Baptists to the Baptist gospel quartet with electric guitars and percussion; Primitive Baptist services that alternate song, prayer, and sermon; and Pentecostal services that give scope for testimony and healing. And the forms may be practiced outside as well as inside the service, as when the Japanese convert recounts her spiritual dreams or the Pentecostal offers a history of his spiritual quest.

The objective of this sampler, then, is to report and to highlight a few of the myriad religious experiences that these several fieldworkers have been privileged to discern through what is termed antiseptically *participant observation*. So doing, they attend at least to gestures, which, as we stated in the introduction, is about as close as the outsider can get to the meaning of a living religion. In her testimony Sister Annie Mae said: "If you would come to my house, and I had fixed something you had never tasted, you might look at it, with all different things in it, and say, 'It don't look good,' or maybe

'I wouldn't like it,' or something. But you will never know until you taste it. You will never know until you eat some of it, praise God!" This collection does not serve up real spiritual food; the readers cannot directly taste or eat. They can, however, taste vicariously, joining with the authors in a struggle to capture a sense of "diversities of gifts."

NOTES

1. Although the statement that these groups are in the Protestant tradition may seem accurate from the standpoint of the historian who traces their origins and orientations, not all of the groups would so classify themselves. Leading Primitive Baptists, for example, have claimed direct and unbroken descent from the Primitive Christian church rather than an ancestry in the reformation movement that grew out of Catholicism.

2. Ernst Troeltsch, *The Social Teaching of the Christian Churches,* trans. Olive Wyon (Chicago: University of Chicago Press, 1981); Samuel S. Hill, *Southern Churches in Crisis* (New York: Holt, Rinehart, and Winston, 1966), pp. 25–26, 80, 89–90; James Barr, *Fundamentalism* (Philadelphia: Westminster Press, 1978).

3. Rhys Isaacs, *The Transformation of Virginia, 1740–1790* (Chapel Hill: University of North Carolina Press, 1982).

Notes on Contributors

JOHN FORREST is associate professor of anthropology at the State University of New York, College at Purchase. He is interested in the traditional aesthetics of communities in England, Mexico, and the American South. His field study on North Carolina's coastal plain is in the Cornell University Press series Anthropology of Contemporary Issues. He received the Ph.D. (1980) in anthropology from the University of North Carolina at Chapel Hill.

ANN HAWTHORNE studied art history from 1968 to 1972 at the University of North Carolina at Chapel Hill. She is currently a free-lance photographer wandering in China and elsewhere, but considers the western North Carolina mountains as home.

BEVERLY B. PATTERSON, M.A. (1975) in ethnomusicology, SUNY-Binghamton, is a Ph.D. candidate in anthropology at the University of North Carolina at Chapel Hill. Her research interests include religion, music, and women, in the American South. She is the joint author, with Daniel W. Patterson, of *An Index of Selected Folk Recordings,* a guide to recordings in the university's Southern Folklife Collection.

DANIEL W. PATTERSON is Kenan Professor of English at the University of North Carolina at Chapel Hill and chairs the Curriculum in Folklore. The author of several books and articles on the Shaker spiritual and project director of a series of documentary films, the "American Traditional Culture Series," he is also general editor of the American Folklore Recordings Series, published by the University of North Carolina Press.

JAMES L. PEACOCK is Kenan Professor of Anthropology at the University of North Carolina at Chapel Hill. His research interests include the

213

symbolic and social-psychological aspects of proletarian drama and Islamic reformist movements in Indonesia and, more recently, the religious experiences of independent Protestants of the Appalachian Mountains. His most recent book is *The Anthropological Lens: Harsh Light and Soft Focus* (New York: Cambridge University Press, 1986).

CATHERINE L. PECK received the M.A. (1983) from the Curriculum in Folklore, the University of North Carolina at Chapel Hill. Her essay here is adapted from her thesis *Your Daughters Shall Prophesy: Women in the Afro-American Preaching Tradition.* She lives and works at George School, Bucks County, Pennsylvania.

DOUGLAS REINHARDT, formerly an associate professor of anthropology at Campbell University, Buies Creek, North Carolina, is now a self-employed photographer. His essay is adapted from his Ph.D. dissertation in anthropology (1982), the University of North Carolina at Chapel Hill.

BRETT SUTTON, M.A. (1976) in folklore and Ph.D. (1982) in anthropology from the University of North Carolina at Chapel Hill, is interested in ethnomusicology, the anthropology of religion, and cultures of the American South. He is the author of several articles on aspects of Primitive Baptist religion and is the editor of an album, *Primitive Baptist Hymns of the Blue Ridge* (Chapel Hill: The University of North Carolina Press, 1981).

ISABEL B. TERRY received her Ph.D. (1980) in anthropology at the University of North Carolina at Chapel Hill and has taught for several years at the North Carolina State University. Currently a Fulbright Fellow, she is conducting research in Belize.

RUEL W. TYSON, JR., is associate professor and former chair of the department of Religious Studies, the University of North Carolina at Chapel Hill, where he teaches courses on the rhetoric and interpretation of religion. The author of numerous articles combining his interest in religion with anthropological topics, he is currently writing a book on the Primitive Baptists of North Carolina.

JAMES E. WISE is arts and entertainment editor and primary theater critic with the *Durham Morning Herald* newspaper of Durham, North Carolina. A former editor of *Tar Heel: The Magazine of North Carolina,* he received his M.A. (1977) in folklore at the University of North Carolina at Chapel Hill.

YUTAKA YAMADA received the Ph.D. (1984) in anthropology at the University of North Carolina at Chapel Hill. Currently teaching in the Department of Japanese, Monash University, Clayton, Victoria, Australia, he is studying the leisure and life-cycle patterns of the Japanese in Australia.

Index

215

Landis, John, 94
Language game, 124
Laying on of hands, 128
Logos, 168
Long, Reverend Sudi, 146-55 passim
Lumbee Indians, 105-25

Male-female dichotomy, 56-57, 62-63
Malinowski, Bronislaw, 166
Malone, Wilburt, 100
Mason, Lowell, 207
Membership, 5, 13
Memorial Day, 29
Merleau-Ponty, M., 3, 112
Metaphysical judgments, 124
Methodists, Wesleyan. *See* Wesleyan Methodists
Millenialism, 44, 52
Ministry, professionalism of, 40. *See also* Pastors
Missionary Baptists, 79-90, 97, 203
Moaning, 146-47
Molly (a Quaker), 30-31
Monboddo, Lord, 194-95
Moral Majority, 17
Music: meaning of, 99-100; performance of, 70, 83, 84, 98, 146-47, 170; rehearsal of, 95

Naaman, story of, 129
Native Americans, 105-25
Ness, Brother, 44-59 passim
Nunne, David, 134

Odum, Howard, xiii, 171
Old School Baptists. *See* Primitive Baptists
Open pulpit, 43-44, 50-51
Open worship. *See* Worship, silent
Oppositions, 54
Oral tradition, 94, 151, 158
Original sin, 132
Overcomer organization, 47; hymnal, 50

Packard, Vance, 47-48
Participant observation, 211
Pastors: female, 155-56; status of, 25; support of, 37. *See also* Ministry
Peace testimony (Quaker), 32-33, 36

Pentecostals, 4, 16-17, 43, 117, 123, 126-42, 192-202, 203, 207, 210
Performance, 58
Politics, 45
Positive confessionalism, 133-35, 138
Possession, 116
Prayers, 159; invitational, 25; mother's, 72; for the sick, 128
Preaching, 144, 161; inspired, 5, 51, 159; responsorial, 165-67
Predestination, 158
Primitive Baptists, xi, 5, 16, 57, 203, 205, 207-8, 210-11; black, 157-76
Protestant work ethic, 127
Protestantism, Independent, xi, 203
Protestantism, Southern, 36, 39; traits of, 26, 203-12 passim
Psychiatry, 109, 115-16, 208
Psychoanalysis, 182-89

Quakers, 23-42, 203, 209-11; history, 36-38; plain speech, 24; quietist, 38

Race, 46, 94
Raleigh, N.C., 92
Rebekah, story of, 152
Religion, Southern, 16-18, 188-89; portrayals of, 17; evangelical, 37
Religions, study of, 13; theories of, 14-16
Responsibilities, lay, 26
Reunions, 98
Revivals, 37-38, 127, 184-85, 196
Rituals, 25. *See also* Baptism; Communion; Foot washing; Hand of fellowship; Laying on of hands
Roberts, Oral, 133, 135
Robeson County, N.C., 105-6
Rock Spring Baptist Church, 97
Roles: female, 57, 62-65, 144, 151, 210; interchangeability of, 58; male, 57, 62-65, 70, 199-201; traditional, 57
Rosenberg, Bruce, 145, 147-48
Roxboro, N.C., 92
Ruritans, 35
Rutledge (a Pentecostal), 192-202

Salvation, 53, 189, 196; attitudes toward, 32; experience, 186-87, 207
Sampler, 18-20, 211

217

CH
GER

Lex Donaldson

The Contingency Theory of Organizations

Foundations for
Organizational
Science
A Sage Publications Series

Sage Publications
International Educational and Professional Publisher
Thousand Oaks ■ London ■ New Delhi

Copyright © 2001 by Sage Publications, Inc.

For information:

Sage Publications, Inc.
2455 Teller Road
Thousand Oaks, California 91320
E-mail: order@sagepub.com

Sage Publications Ltd.
6 Bonhill Street
London EC2A 4PU
United Kingdom

Sage Publications India Pvt. Ltd.
M-32 Market
Greater Kailash I
New Delhi 110 048 India

Printed in the United States of America

Library of Congress Cataloging-in-Publication Data

Donaldson, Lex
    The contingency theory of organizations / by Lex Donaldson
        p. cm. — (Foundations for organizational science)
    Includes bibliographical references and index.
    ISBN 0-7619-1573-7 (cloth: alk. paper)
    ISBN 0-7619-1574-5 (pbk.: alk. paper)
    1. Contingency theory (Management) I. Title. II. Series.
    HD30.4 D65 2000
    302.3'5--dc21

                                                            00-010586

01   02   03   04   05   10   9   8   7   6   5   4   3   2   1

Acquiring Editor:	Marquita Flemming
Editorial Assistant:	MaryAnn Vail
Production Editor:	Denise Santoyo
Typesetter/Designer:	Denyse Dunn

To Derek Pugh,
Leader and Supervisor

Contents

Introduction to the Series

The title of this series, **Foundations for Organizational Science** (FOS), denotes a distinctive focus. FOS books are educational aids for mastering the core theories, essential tools, and emerging perspectives that constitute the field of organizational science (broadly conceived to include organizational behavior, organizational theory, human resource management, and business strategy). Our ambitious goal is to assemble the "essential library" for members of our professional community.

The vision for the series emerged from conversations with several colleagues, including Peter Frost, Anne Huff, Rick Mowday, Benjamin Schneider, Susan Taylor, and Andy Van de Ven. A number of common interests emerged from these sympathetic encounters, including: enhancing the quality of doctoral education by providing broader access to the master teachers in our field, "bottling" the experience and insights of some of the founding scholars in our field before they retire, and providing professional development opportunities for colleagues seeking to broaden their understanding of the rapidly expanding subfields within organizational science.

Our unique learning objectives are reflected in an unusual set of in-structions to FOS authors. They are encouraged to: (a) "write the way they teach"—framing their book as an extension of their teaching notes, rather than as the expansion of a handbook chapter; (b) pass on their "craft knowledge" to the next generation of scholars—making them wiser, not just smarter; (c) share with their "virtual students and colleagues" the insider tips and best bets for research that are normally reserved for one-on-one mentoring sessions; and (d) make the com-plexity of their subject matter comprehensible to nonexperts so that readers can share their puzzlement, fascination, and intrigue.

We are proud of the group of highly qualified authors who have embraced the unique educational perspective of our "Foundations" series. We encourage your suggestions for how these books can better satisfy your learning needs—as a newcomer to the field preparing for prelims or developing a dissertation proposal, or as an established scholar seeking to broaden your knowledge and proficiency.

—*DAVID A. WHETTEN*

—SERIES EDITOR

Acknowledgments

I should like to thank those who have helped me with this project. First, thanks to Dave Whetten who asked me to write this book. I am glad Dave gave me the opportunity to lay out contingency theory and its future.

I should like to thank those who taught me and provided an early introduction to the intellectual excitement of contingency theory: John Child, Jerald Hage, and David Hickson. Also thanks to Derek Pugh, who headed the research group at London Business School where I conducted my first contingency analyses. Other helpful contingency research colleagues there were Roger Mansfield and Malcolm Warner. More latterly I have received support in my contingency endeavors from American colleagues, including Alfred Chandler, Paul Lawrence, Nitin Nohria, and Mike Tushman.

Thanks also to my generous hosts, especially to Janine Nahapiet, at Templeton College, Oxford University, where part of this book was written. Templeton College combines high levels of efficiency and friendliness and proves to us all that this is possible.

Other parts of this book were written at London Business School and I should like to thank my hosts there: Nigel Nicholson and Paul

Willman. London Business School combines professionalism with sociability, so thanks also to my companions there: Pino Audia, Patrick Barwise, Julian Birkinshaw, Ian Cooper, Sumantra Ghoshal, Rob Goffee, Lynda Gratton, John Hunt, Andrew Likierman, Constantinos Markides, Peter Moran, Tim Morris, Anand Narasimhan, Maury Peiperl, Henri Servaes, Ken Simmonds, John Stopford, and Chris Voss.

Thanks to Peter Dodd, former Dean of the Australian Graduate School of Management, and Greg Whittred, the Acting Dean, for support throughout the writing of this book. Thank you again to June Ohlson, my ever-enthusiastic editor, whose efforts have resulted in a clearer book.

—LEX DONALDSON

AUSTRALIAN GRADUATE SCHOOL OF MANAGEMENT,
UNIVERSITIES OF NEW SOUTH WALES AND SYDNEY

Preface

This book began when Dave Whetten approached me to contribute a book to the Foundations for Organizational Science series. He wanted each book to make its topic accessible to newcomers to the field, to stimulate their interest in the possibility of joining in its research. The readers would include doctoral students and also faculty and research colleagues who were unfamiliar with the topic. Each book would provide an overview of the literature, the critical issues, and the future possibilities. I enthusiastically agreed to write a book on contingency theory that would match that agenda.

I have been involved in contingency research for almost thirty years now and so felt equipped for the task. Indeed, since I have now written four books on organizational theory, the reader might well ask: "What's new here?" Most of the book is new and does not repeat material from my earlier books. Of course, there is a thematic continuity with my previous books on organizational theory in that throughout them I have argued for contingency theory.

While I have written about contingency theory fairly extensively, much of this has been in the context of critiques of other organizational theories that challenge contingency theory. In contrast, in this book there is little (though some) critique of other theories. This book is an exposition and critical discussion of contingency theory and its research. The present book is a far more comprehensive treatment of contingency theory than any I have previously attempted. It is broader in the range of theories considered under the contingency umbrella. It is also much deeper in its analysis of the theories, evidence, and methodological issues. This allows more appreciation of the coherency of contingency theory overall. It also involves frank recognition of some of the deficiencies in contingency theory research. The coherent underlying model provides the platform from which to make good some of the deficiencies through a series of improvements in theory and method that chart a course for future research.

In keeping with a book intended to explain contingency theory, Chapters 2 and 3 lay out the foundations by reviewing the pioneering contributors to theory and empirical research. I have tried to give an accurate account of the received body of contingency theory as it comes down to us, in order to pass on this tradition to scholars who are new to it.

However, more personal views are offered also at many places. The opening chapter presents a theoretical integration to provide the reader with an overview that makes sense of what is a large literature. It also argues that there is an underlying core paradigm that renders contingency theory coherent. Chapter 4 makes an in-depth examination of the causal models in the received bureaucracy research literature and finds them to be deficient and attempts to put them on a more truly contingency theory basis. Chapters 7 and 8 examine in detail the concept of fit and its relationship with performance, including the empirical research studies.

Chapter 9 presents possible new developments for contingency theory, to make it more coherent and, it is hoped, valid. These new developments include the concepts of disequilibrium, quasi-fit, and hetero-performance. All three are novel concepts that, I believe, substantially revise and improve contingency theory. In particular, the hetero-performance concept may be of particular interest to those seeking to advance contingency theory. Chapter 10 offers suggestions on how to operationalize the ideas in this book in terms of hypotheses for future empirical research. Thus most of this book is making arguments that I have not presented previously.

In order to provide the reader with a rounded treatment of contingency theory in this one book, however, I have restated some arguments made in some earlier books. Thus sections of Chapters 5 and 6 draw upon defenses of contingency theory made in Donaldson (1995a, 1996a). To have omitted this material in its entirety could have left a reader confused about whether contingency theory can reply to certain criticisms. Similarly, a section of Chapter 9 draws upon organizational portfolio theory from Donaldson (1999) to present the implications of the idea that organizational change is performance driven. Hopefully, the condensed summaries offered in these sections may help make this material more accessible to a wider audience.

Throughout much of this book a unifying idea is that the dynamics of organizational change in contingency theory are best captured by the structural adaptation to regain fit (SARFIT) model. This is integral to the core paradigm articulated in the opening chapter. The SARFIT model recurs in the discussion at many places, such as about organizational change, bureaucracy theory, functionalism, and in the operationalization of fit for future research.

Thus this book has a triple agenda: to pay homage to a rich tradition and pass it on, to advance a coherent interpretation of the array of theories and research within it, and to set signposts to what may be fruitful avenues for future research. In these ways it seeks to fulfill the intention of the **Foundations for Organizational Science** series.

1 Core Paradigm and
Theoretical Integration

The contingency theory of organizations is a major theoretical lens used to view organizations. It yields many insights and has substantial empirical support. Contingency theory contains much of importance in the history of organizational science. Its research forms the basis of much that is taught today. Moreover, contingency research is actively pursued by scholars in the contemporary era and it is being projected into the future in a series of exciting theoretical and empirical developments. The aim of this book is to introduce the reader to the rich tradition of contingency theory research, indicate the potential for future developments, and offer guidance on how to proceed in research both in theory and empirical practice.

The essence of the contingency theory paradigm is that organizational effectiveness results from fitting characteristics of the organization, such as its structure, to contingencies that reflect the situation of the organization (Burns and Stalker 1961; Lawrence and Lorsch 1967; Pennings 1992; Woodward 1965). Contingencies include the environment (Burns and Stalker 1961), organizational size (Child 1975), and

1

organizational strategy (Chandler 1962). Because the fit of organizational characteristics to contingencies leads to high performance, organizations seek to attain fit. For this reason, organizations are motivated to avoid the misfit that results after contingencies change, and do so by adopting new organizational characteristics that fit the new levels of the contingencies. Therefore the organization becomes shaped by the contingencies, because it needs to fit them to avoid loss of performance. Organizations are seen as adapting over time to fit their changing contingencies so that effectiveness is maintained. Thus contingency theory contains the concept of a fit that affects performance, which, in turn, impels adaptive organizational change. This results in organizations moving into fit with their contingencies, so that there is an alignment between the organization and its contingencies, creating an association between contingencies and organizational characteristics (Burns and Stalker 1961; Woodward 1965; Van de Ven and Drazin 1985).

Some of the more important contingency theories of organizational structure involve the three contingencies of the environment, organizational size, and strategy. The environmental stability contingency affects mechanistic structure (Pennings 1992). The rate of technological and market change in the environment of an organization affects whether its structure is mechanistic (i.e., hierarchical) or organic (i.e., participatory; Burns and Stalker 1961). The mechanistic structure fits a stable environment, because a hierarchical approach is efficient for routine operations. Given the routine nature of operations, the managers at upper levels of the hierarchy possess sufficient knowledge and information to make decisions, and this centralized control fosters efficiency. In contrast, the organic structure fits an unstable environment, because a participatory approach is required for innovation. Knowledge and information required for innovation are distributed among lower hierarchical levels and so decentralized decision making fosters innovation. An organization that has the misfitting, mechanistic structure in an unstable environment is unable to innovate and so becomes ineffective (Burns and Stalker 1961).

The size contingency affects bureaucratic structure. The size of an organization, that is, the number of its employees, affects the degree to which its structure is bureaucratic, for example, rule-governed, and is decentralized (Pugh and Hickson 1976; Pugh and Hinings 1976). The bureaucratic structure fits a large organization, because large size leads to repetitive operations and administration so that much decision making can be by rules, rendering decision making inexpensive and efficient (Child 1975; Weber 1968). In contrast, an unbureaucratic, or simple, structure, which is not rule-governed and is centralized, fits a small organization, because top management can make almost all the decisions personally and effectively (Child 1972a). A large organization that seeks to use the misfitting, simple structure will find top management overwhelmed by the number of decisions it needs to make, so that the organization becomes ineffective.

The strategy contingency affects divisional structure. The functional structure fits an undiversified strategy, because all its activities are focused on a single product or service so that efficiency is enhanced by specialization by function (e.g., departments of production, marketing, etc). In contrast, the divisional structure fits a diversified strategy, because it has diverse activities serving various product-markets, so effectiveness is enhanced by coordinating each product or service in its own division (Chandler 1962; Galbraith 1973). An organization with a diversified strategy that seeks to use the misfitting, functional structure will find top management overwhelmed by the number of decisions and also suffer lack of responsiveness to markets, so that the organization becomes ineffective.

Thus structural contingency theory argues that organizational structure needs to fit the three contingencies of the environment, size, and strategy. As seen, each of these contingencies affects a particular aspect of structure: organic, bureaucratic, and divisional, respectively. Change in any of these contingencies tends to produce change in the corresponding structural aspect (Burns and Stalker 1961; Chandler 1962; Child 1973a). In this way the organization moves its structure into alignment with each of these contingencies, so that structure and contingency tend to be associated (Child 1973a; Hage and Aiken 1969; Rumelt 1974). There are other contingencies of organizational structure, as we shall see, but these preliminary remarks serve to exemplify contingency theory.

Contingency theory is to be distinguished from universalistic theories of organization, which assert that there is "one best way" to organize, meaning that maximum organizational performance comes from the maximum level of a structural variable, for example, specialization (Taylor 1947). Classical management is an earlier organizational theory that argues that maximum organizational performance results from maximum formalization and specialization (Brech 1957), and it is therefore a universalistic type of theory. Similarly, neo-human relations is also an earlier universalistic type of organizational theory, which argues that organizational performance is maximized by maximizing participation (Likert 1961). Contingency theory differs from all such universalistic theories in that it sees maximum performance as resulting from adopting, not the maximum, but rather the appropriate level of the structural variable that fits the contingency. Therefore, the optimal structural level is seldom the maximum, and which level is optimal is dependent upon the level of the contingency variable.

Much of contingency theory research has studied organizational structure (Donaldson 1995a, 1996a; Lawrence 1993), and this tradition is referred to as structural contingency theory (Pfeffer 1982). In this book we will focus on structural contingency theory research because it is a large and complex body of work. There are, however, contingency theories of many different organizational characteristics, such as leadership (Fiedler 1967), human resource management (Delery and Doty 1996), and strategic decision-making processes (Frederickson 1984). There are many common issues that run across the various contingency theories of the different organizational characteristics. Hence by providing a discussion that focuses on structural contingency theory we may also illuminate contingency theories of other organizational characteristics.

Contemporary organizational researchers are seeking to build upon the structural contingency tradition and make new contributions to it. For example, some contemporary contingency researchers are concerned to show the effect of fit on performance that contingency theory postulates (Gresov 1990; Hamilton and Shergill 1992, 1993; Hill, Hitt, and Hoskisson 1992; Jennings and Seaman 1994; Keller 1994; Kraft, Puia, and Hage 1995; Mahoney 1992; Marsden, Cook, and Kalleberg 1994; Palmer, Jennings, and Zhou 1993; Powell 1992; Schlevogt and Donaldson 1999). Other researchers are investigating the contingency factors and identifying which aspects of organization they effect (e.g., Anderson 1996; Birkinshaw 1999; Jarley, Fiorito, and Delaney 1997). Others again are studying the contingency adaptation processes (e.g., Priem 1992, 1994). Still other researchers, whose primary allegiance is to a theory other than contingency theory, nevertheless find in contingency work elements that may helpfully be incorporated into their own projects (e.g., Fligstein 1985).

The foregoing, brief definition of structural contingency theory raises several questions. Is there a unifying structural contingency theory paradigm, or just a loose agglomeration of vaguely related theories? Is it correct to say that contingencies cause organizational structure or are there other causal patterns, such as the structure causing the contingency? Do contingency factors determine organizational structure or is there choice? Is there really an underlying fit of organizational characteristic to contingency that drives causality, as contingency theory argues, or is the whole idea of fit just an exercise in tautology? These are some of the questions we must consider in discussing the contingency theory of organizations.

In order to begin our discussion, let us first clarify exactly what we mean by contingency theory by offering a definition in formal terms. The next step will be to consider whether there is a contingency theory paradigm that unites the disparate contingency theories. We will seek to show that there is for structural contingency theory. We will then move to consider the more specific contingencies and structural variables in structural contingency theory. It will be shown that many of them fall into two groups: organic theory and bureaucracy theory. These are seen as being theories that are to some degree in conflict, but that may be brought together, rendering structural contingency theory coherent—and not overly complex. The remainder of this chapter provides a conceptual and theoretical integration, and an introduction to the issues and material in the body of this book. In this way it puts in place some major building blocks and provides an overview for what is to come. The process therefore is to move from contingency logic, to the most general contingency theory, to contingency theories, and then in the ensuing chapters to concrete findings and methods.

A Formal Definition of Contingency Theory

The contingency theory of organizations is a subset of the contingency approach in science, so let us first define the contingency approach and then the contingency theory of organizations within it.

At the most abstract level, the contingency approach says that the effect of one variable on another depends upon some third variable, W. Thus the effect of X on Y when W is low differs from the effect of X on Y when W is high. For example, it might be that when W is low, X has a positive effect on Y, whereas when W is high, X has a negative effect on Y. Thus we cannot state what the effect of X on Y is, without knowing whether W is low or high, that is, the value of the variable W. There is no valid bivariate relationship between X and Y that can be stated. The relationship between X and Y is part of a larger causal system involving the third variable, W, so that the valid generalization takes the form of a trivariate relationship. A bivariate relationship is too simple to capture the lawlike regularity connecting X and Y. Therefore a more complex causal statement is required. However, the contingency statement is just one step more complex in that it consists of only one more variable, going from two to three variables.

The third variable, W, moderates the relationship between X and Y and can therefore be called a moderator of the relationship or a conditioning variable of the relationship (Galtung 1967). However, while a contingency factor is a moderator or conditioning variable, it plays a more specific role, so that not all moderators are contingencies. In the contingency theory of organizations, the relationship is between some characteristic of the organization and effectiveness. Thus the contingency factor determines which characteristic produces high levels of effectiveness of the organization (or some part of it, such as a department or individual member). For example, a mechanistic structure produces high effectiveness when the task uncertainty contingency is low, and an organic structure produces high effectiveness when the task uncertainty contingency is high.

The reason for the focus on effectiveness in contingency theory is that organizational theory has been concerned to explain the success or failure of organizations. However, organizational effectiveness can have a broad meaning that includes efficiency, profitability (Child 1975), employee satisfaction (Dewar and Werbel 1979), innovation rate (Hage and Dewar 1973), or patient well-being (Alexander and Randolph 1985; see also Pennings 1992). Organizational effectiveness can be defined as the ability of the organization to attain the goals set by itself (Parsons 1961), or by its ability to function well as a system (Yuchtman and Seashore 1967), or by its ability to satisfy its stakeholders (Pfeffer and Salancik 1978; Pickle and Friedlander 1967). *Organizational effectiveness* and *performance* are similar concepts and will be used interchangeably in this book.

The Core Contingency Theory Paradigm

As just seen, a *contingency* is any variable that moderates the effect of an organizational characteristic on organizational performance. Given this definition of a contingency, it is clearly quite encompassing, so the open-ended nature of such a definition can prompt unease that there is no singular, contingency theory of organizations, only a multiplicity of contingency theories and hence no unifying paradigm. Therefore the criticism is sometimes made that there is no structural contingency theory of organizations, only a loose grouping of disparate theories, each of which makes a connection between its contingency and some aspect of organizational structure, for example, task uncertainty and the organic structure, or size and bureaucracy. The question, therefore, is whether there exists some more overarching framework within which the various structural contingency theories come together. Thus, at a more abstract level, are there commonalties between the structural contingency theories? We believe that there are. It is possible to create a theoretical framework that connects contingencies in the abstract with organizational structure in the abstract. The argument is highly general so that it applies to all the contingencies and their corresponding structural aspects. In this sense, there is a unifying contingency paradigm.

Structural contingency theory contains three core elements that together form its core paradigm. First, there is an association between contingency and the organizational structure. Second, contingency determines the organizational structure, because an organization that changes its contingency then, in consequence, changes its structure. Third, there is a fit of some level of the organizational structural variable to each level of the contingency, which leads to higher performance, whereas misfit leads to lower performance. This fit-performance relationship is the heart of the contingency theory paradigm. It provides the theoretical explanation of the first two points: the association between contingency and structure, and contingency change causing structural change. An organization that changes the level of its contingency tends to have been in fit when it made the change, and thence to move into misfit so that its performance decreases. The organization then changes its organizational structure to fit the new level of the contingency variable, in order to avoid further performance loss. Therefore, because of the performance lost by being in misfit, organizations tend over time to move toward fit. Thus any organization tends to adopt the structure that fits its level of the contingency. This means that a change in contingency leads to a change in structure, so that contingency determines structure. In this way the contingency and the organizational structure move into alignment and so arises the association between the contingency and the organizational structure.

Let us now examine structural contingency theory research to see that these three elements are commonalities that exist across the different contingencies and theories. We will consider each of three core commonalties in turn: (1) the association between contingency and organizational structural variable or attribute; (2) the change process that contingency change causes organizational structural change; and (3) the fit of structure to contingency that affects performance.

1. Association Between Contingency and Organizational Structure

Contingency theory research into organizational structure frequently shows an association between contingency and structure. Sometimes these associations are presented as cross-tabulations (e.g., Woodward 1965) and at other times as correlations (e.g., Holdaway, Newberry, Hickson, and Heron 1975, p. 48). Such correlations are seen for the size contingency and various aspects of bureaucratic structure (e.g., Child 1973a, p. 170, Table 2). They are seen for the strategy contingency and divisional structure (Grinyer, Yasai-Ardekani, and Al-Bazzaz 1980, p. 198). They are seen also for technology and structure (Child and Mansfield 1972, pp. 378-379). Thus there is a clear commonality across the diverse contingencies of organizational structure in that, despite differences in contingencies and their corresponding structural aspects, the contingency theories postulate theoretically an association between contingency and structure, and demonstrate this as a central part of their empirical research.

Thus a bivariate association is expected between any contingency factor and its structural variable. Often these bivariate relationships are linear, that is, as the contingency factor increases in value, so does the structural variable. However, associations do not have to be linear and may be curvilinear, as, for example, are several of the contingency-structure associations in Woodward's analysis of technology and structure. For example, as the technology contingency increases, the span of control of the first-line supervisor first increases and then decreases (Woodward 1965). Whether linear or curvilinear, there is an association between the contingency and the structure as a core component of the structural contingency research paradigm that provides a commonality across the diverse structural contingency theories.

2. Contingency Change Causes Organizational Structural Change

The use of cross-sectional methods in empirical studies that show correlations between contingency and structure is taken in some commentaries to imply that structural contingency theory is static (Galunic and Eisenhardt 1994). However, structural contingency theory deals with organizational change. It contains a theory that is dynamic, which is supported by studies of organizations changing over time. While there are differences in the contingency and structural factors, there is a similar view of organizational change. Contingency causes structure in that change in contingency leads to change in structure (e.g., Burns and Stalker 1961; Chandler 1962). The changes in contingency lead the organization out of fit with the old structure, which lowers performance. Eventually the organization resolves this by adopting a new and better structure that fits the new level of the contingency, thereby restoring performance. This model of organizational change is seen in Burns and Stalker (1961), where increasing technological and market change eventually cause the organization to change from a mechanistic to an organic structure in their empirical case studies of changes over time. Using Thompson's concepts of contingency and structure, Van de Ven, Delbecq, and Koenig (1976) show that change in the task contingency leads to change in coordination modes, so that the task contingency causes structure. Again it is seen in the way that strategy leads to structure, that is, diversifying causes the organization to adopt a divisional structure (Chandler 1962; Channon 1973, 1978; Dyas and Thanheiser 1976; Rumelt 1974).

Thus a model of organizational change exists in structural contingency theory, in which contingency changes cause change in organizational structure. This unified theory of organizational change that goes across the contingencies (e.g., environment and strategy) is one more sense in which there is *the* contingency theory of organizations. Therefore the dynamics that contingency changes cause structural changes is a second core component of the contingency paradigm.

Contingency theory depicts organizational change as an organizationally rational process of restoring effectiveness, so that is a functionalist type of sociological theory (Burrell and Morgan 1979). Several other organizational theories challenge this rationalist, functionalist account and they will be discussed further (see Chapter 6). Much of the argument that change is functional for the organization hangs on the idea that organizations changing their structures are doing so to move from misfit into fit and thereby restoring their performance, which takes us to our next point.

3. Fit Affects Performance

Contingency theories hold that there is a fit between the organizational structure and contingency that has a positive effect on performance. In formal terms, there is a trivariate relationship between structure, contingency, and performance. Where the structural variable is at the level that fits the level of the contingency, high performance results. Where the structure is at a level that does not fit the level of the contingency, low performance results. This contingency-structure-fit explains the association between contingency and structure. Thus the decisive proof of a contingency theory involves empirically demonstrating that there is a fit of structure to contingency that positively affects performance. This requires showing that the combination of contingency and structure that is held to be a fit causes high performance and that the combination held to be a misfit causes low performance. Each contingency theory specifies the structures that fit its contingency, so that the fits and misfits are unique to that theory (e.g., divisional structure fits diversification, bureaucratic structure fits large size). Despite such diversity about the exact definition of fit, these different views all contain the concept of fit. Thus, at the more abstract level, the concept of *fit* provides a theoretical commonality across different contingency theories.

Contingency theory research looks for a relationship between fit and performance, that is, searches for a trivariate relationship among contingency, structure, and performance. For example, Woodward (1965) demonstrates that fit of span of control of the first-line supervisor to the technology contingency is associated positively with organizational performance. Other examples are Child (1975) and Khandwalla

(1973), who show that fit of bureaucratic structure to the size contingency is associated positively with organizational performance. In Chapter 8 we will review studies that empirically support fits that positively affect organizational performance for a range of different contingencies. Hence the fit-performance relationship is a common element found among the diverse contingency theories and so constitutes a third core component of the contingency theory paradigm.

Structural Adaptation to Regain Fit

The core contingency theory paradigm is illustrated by research on the strategy contingency and its relationship with divisional structure. The research supports each of the three elements of the paradigm. Moreover, it supports a more particular theoretical model of how contingency change leads to structural change, namely, structural adaptation to regain fit (SARFIT).

There is an association between the contingency variable of strategic diversification and divisionalization (i.e., the distinction between the functional and the divisional structures; e.g., Grinyer and Yasai-Ardekani 1981).

Strategy contingency change causes divisional structural change. This is shown by studies across time. In the case histories of Chandler (1962), strategy leads to structure, that is, diversifying causes the organization to adopt a divisional structure. Quantitative studies of large corporations also show that diversification precedes and causes divisionalization (Channon 1973, 1978; Dyas and Thanheiser 1976; Fligstein 1985; Rumelt 1974; Suzuki 1980).

The processes involved in changing the organizational structure in response to changes in the level of the contingency variable can be specified in the theoretical model of structural adaptation to regain fit (SARFIT; Donaldson 1987). This is shown in Figure 1.1. The SARFIT model states that an organization is initially in fit, having a structure that fits its existing level of the contingency variable. Fit positively affects performance. However, the organization then changes its level of the contingency variable while retaining its existing structure, which thereby becomes a misfit with its new contingency level (thus the effect of the contingency variable on fit is shown as negative in Figure 1.1). In turn, the misfit leads to lower performance (reversing the positive effect of fit on performance shown in Figure 1.1). When performance becomes so low (because of the effects of the misfit and other causes)

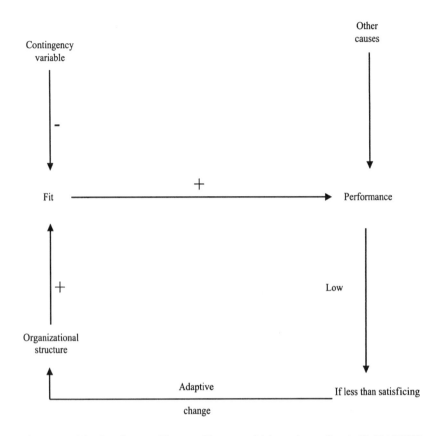

Figure 1.1. The Contingency Theory of Structural Adaptation to Regain Fit (SARFIT)

that it becomes less than the satisficing (i.e., satisfactory) level, the organization then makes an adaptive change. The adaptive change is to adopt a new organizational structure that fits its new contingency level (shown as a positive effect of organizational structure on fit in Figure 1.1). The new fit restores performance. Thus structural change occurs in response to contingency change and is triggered by the feedback effect from the low performance caused by misfit. The organization adapts its structure to changes in the contingency in order to maintain effective functioning.

To investigate whether the SARFIT theoretical model holds for the phenomena of strategy and structure, we must first operationalize fit. From Chandler (1962) it can be seen that functional structures fit undiversified firms and misfit diversified firms, while divisional structures fit diversified firms and misfit undiversified firms (Donaldson 1987, pp. 8-9). This operationalization was empirically validated by showing that firms in fit had significantly higher subsequent financial performance (growth in profit on sales and on capital), so that fit was a cause of performance (Donaldson 1987, pp. 16-17). This operational definition has been independently replicated on other firms (Hamilton and Shergill 1992, 1993).

Initially, firms are undiversified and tended to have a functional structure, so that empirically most of them were in fit (Donaldson 1987; see also Figure 1.2). Movement away from this initial position was overwhelmingly through strategic change, by diversification, while retaining their functional structure, so entering misfit. Of firms that moved from fit to misfit, 83 percent did so by increasing their strategy contingency (Donaldson 1987, p. 14). Once in misfit of structure to strategy, the firms would consequently experience reduced performance. Then, when financial performance became low, so that a crisis of poor performance occurred, firms moved from misfit into fit by adopting a new, divisional structure that fitted their diversified strategy, so making a structural adaptation. Firms in misfit were more than four times more likely to change only their structure (Donaldson 1987, p. 14), showing that misfit led to structural change. Of firms that changed only their structure, 72 percent moved from misfit to fit and only 5 percent moved from fit to misfit (Donaldson 1987, p. 14), showing that when firms made structural change it was overwhelmingly a move from misfit into fit, that is, structural adaptation. Of the firms that moved from misfit to fit by changing only their structure, 90 percent did so by adopting the divisional structure (Donaldson 1987, p. 15). Thus firms moved from misfit to fit by divisionalizing. The fit would be beneficial for their performance. Hence, overall, the firms moved from misfit into fit by adapting their structure to their strategy contingency.

The adaptation of structure to strategy is subject to time lags, however. There was no pattern of firms that diversified in one decade being more likely to change their structures in the subsequent decade, so that,

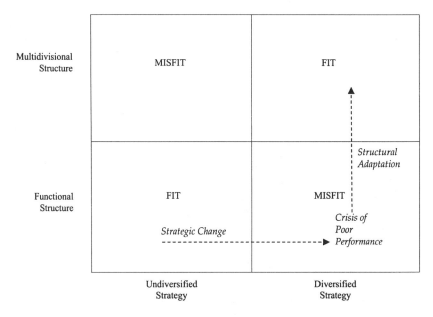

Figure 1.2. Change in Strategy Causes Change in Structure: Dynamics of Structural Adaptation

on average, structural change did not follow strategic change within ten years (Donaldson 1987, p. 13). Indeed, 77 percent of the firms in misfit had been so for ten years or more (Donaldson 1987, pp. 15-16), pointing to the lengthiness of lags of structural change to strategic change. Strategy slowly leads to structure. The reason is that performance mediates structural change, so that it occurs only when performance becomes low. For diversified firms in misfit, we can compare those that moved into fit, by structurally changing from functional to divisional, with those retaining the misfitting functional structure. The divisionalizing firms had significantly lower sales and profits, and especially earnings per share, at the start of the period than those firms that retained the functional structure (Donaldson 1987, pp. 17-18). These results show that poor performance and failure to satisfy powerful stakeholders (i.e., owners) trigger structural adaptation.

Overall, contingency change (diversification) caused structural change (divisionalization). The initial contingency change creates dysfunctions that are corrected by structural change, so that the organization starts out in fit and ends in fit. The firms went from an old fit to a new fit through the intervening stage of misfit. The effect of misfit on structural change is, however, indirect, running through performance. It is the feedback effect of low performance that is the more immediate cause of structural change. Change in the strategy contingency leads eventually to structural change, because of the need to restore performance, as the pioneers of structural contingency theory stated (e.g., Chandler 1962). While the idea that divisionalization leads to diversification is familiar, the important point is that it is through the process of misfit and low performance. This confirms the functionalist contingency theory of organizational change and, more specifically, the model of structural adaptation to regain fit (SARFIT).

Further support for the SARFIT model comes from empirical studies by Ezzamel and Hilton (1980) and Hill and Pickering (1986). Ezzamel and Hilton (1980) found that before divisionalization, firms tended to have deteriorating performance (as measured by share price), and that after divisionalization, performance tended to rise. Similarly, Hill and Pickering (1986, pp. 34-35) found that structural changes (predominantly divisionalization) of firms were seen by their top management as about equally attributable to strategic change and responding to problems. The strategic change referred to major new acquisitions and diversification (Hill and Pickering 1986, p. 35) and so is consistent with the theory that diversification leads to divisionalization. Decline in company performance was the most frequent type of problem (Hill and Pickering 1986, p. 35). Another problem was the "need to increase accountability," which probably also reflects concerns about unsatisfactory performance (Hill and Pickering 1986, p. 35). These two problems are consistent with the theory that low performance triggers structural change. Yet another problem was "intra-organizational communications," which is consistent with internal disorganization from misfit. Thus the results corroborate the theory that diversification leads to misfit that leads to low performance and divisionalization.

As we have just seen, while misfit produces a negative effect on organizational performance, structural change to a fitting structure is not usually immediate. The pioneering empirical study shows that firms often remain in misfit for some time, consequently incurring performance loss (Chandler 1962). Structural change into fit is caused by a crisis of poor performance. Chandler (1962) documents how performance crises precipitated by events such as economic recessions were required to trigger corporations to adopt the divisional structures they needed in order to fit their diversification. This low level of performance results in part from the effect of the misfit, but in part also from other causes that depress organizational performance (as will be discussed further in Chapter 9). Thus performance has to drop to a low level before the organization's management takes the corrective action needed. Organizations fail to make needed adaptive change until their performance has deteriorated substantially, so that there is a clear problem to be solved. This is consistent with the theory of Simon (1976) that managers are boundedly rational (through incomplete knowledge, etc.) so that, rather than maximize, they satisfice. As long as the organization maintains a level of performance that is at or above the satisficing level (i.e., the level judged to be satisfactory), managerial decision making is not engaged. Managerial decision making consists of problem solving, which is initiated when a problem occurs, as manifest in subsatisficing performance. It takes the form of looking for a solution good enough to return performance to the satisficing level. Therefore an organization in misfit adopts a new organizational structure and moves into fit only when performance becomes low. In these ways the SARFIT model specifies the processes whereby contingency change causes structural change, adding to the core paradigm.

In summary, structural contingency theory contains a core paradigm that generalizes across any contingency. There is an association between contingency and organizational structure. There is organizational change, that is, contingency change causing change in the structure. And there is a fit of the structure to the contingency that positively affects performance. The fit of structure to contingency explains why organizations change their structure in response to changing their contingency and thus why contingency and structure are associated.

Conceptual and Theoretical Integration of Structural Contingency Theory

The contingency theory of organizational structure may be integrated by stating that there are two main contingencies, task and size, with the task contingency being composed of task uncertainty and task interdependence. There are two main contingency theories of organizational structure: organic theory and bureaucracy theory. Task uncertainty is the main contingency of the organic theory, with task interdependence playing the role of a minor contingency. Size is the main contingency of bureaucracy theory with task interdependence, once again, playing the minor role.

There are a number of different structural contingency theories, each connecting a particular contingency to some specific aspects of organizational structure (e.g., Blau 1970; Burns and Stalker 1961; Chandler 1962; Child 1973a; Thompson 1967; Woodward 1965). However, many of the contingency and structural variables can be reduced to a few underlying constructs that compose those underlying theories. Similarly, there is considerable similarity among many of the theories so that theoretical integration is possible. We will offer a conceptual and theoretical integration of structural contingency theory. This provides an overview of many of the issues that will be discussed in detail later, in order to give the reader a map of the intellectual terrain to be navigated in the ensuing chapters. We will begin by showing how many different contingency variables can be reduced to a few underlying constructs. In the subsequent section we shall present two theories, the organic and the bureaucracy theories, that, between them, capture much of the contingency theory of organizational structure.

Contingencies

Contingencies of organizational structure include some that are within the organization and some that are outside it. Contingency factors such as task uncertainty and task interdependence are aspects of the work being performed and so lie inside the organization. Organizational size is how many people are in the organization and so is also an internal organizational characteristic. Other contingency factors are characteristics of the environment, such as environmental uncertainty. However, they affect the internal contingencies, which in turn shape other internal organizational characteristics, for example, organizational structure. For instance, environmental uncertainty affects task uncertainty, which causes the adoption of an organic structure. Thus, structure is caused by needing to fit the intraorganizational contingencies, some of which are, in turn, caused by the environmental contingencies. In this way, the organization is shaped by the need to fit its environment. Environmental contingencies indirectly shape the organization through the intervening variables of the intraorganizational contingencies.

Thus, while environmental contingencies may be more ultimate causes of organizational structure, the intraorganizational contingencies through which they work are the more immediate and direct causes of structure, so they are emphasized in this book.

Research into organizational structure has identified a number of contingencies. Task uncertainty (Gresov 1990), technology (Woodward 1965), innovation (Hage and Aiken 1967a), environmental change (Child 1975), technological change (Burns and Stalker 1961), size (Blau 1970), prospector strategy, defender strategy (Miles and Snow 1978), diversification, vertical integration (Rumelt 1974), and task interdependence (Thompson 1967) are some of the better-established contingencies. These contingency factors can be reduced to a few common, underlying concepts. We shall argue that there are three underlying contingencies: task uncertainty, task interdependence, and size.

Task Uncertainty

The set of contingencies made up of task uncertainty, technology, technological change, innovation, and environmental instability have an underlying concept of *uncertainty*. Environmental and technological change lead to uncertainty for the organization and its managers, creating uncertainty in the tasks conducted inside the organization. This task uncertainty is reinforced by the need for innovation that is part of the response to environmental and technological change (Burns and Stalker 1961; Hage and Aiken 1970). The technology used by the organization to transform its inputs into outputs also reflects differences in task uncertainty and feeds back to affect task uncertainty (Woodward 1965). More advanced technology requires greater predictability of the tasks, while also increasing task predictability (Woodward 1965). Thus task uncertainty is the core concept underlying this set of contingency factors. Moreover, the distinction between defender versus prospector strategy (Miles and Snow 1978) is, in large degree, that between cost reduction through routine operations versus innovation, and so it also relates to the underlying contingency of task uncertainty. Hence a parsimonious treatment of contingencies can reduce these contingency variables to task uncertainty, for many purposes.

Task Interdependence

A second set of contingency factors, including aspects of strategy, clusters around the underlying contingency of task interdependence. Task interdependence classifies in what way activities in an organization are connected with each other: pooled (indirect connection only), sequential (direct, one-way connection), and reciprocal (direct, two-way connection; Thompson 1967). Some of the major contingencies of strategy can be subsumed under task interdependence. Diversification—whether of products, services, or customers—is an aspect of the strategy of a firm (Rumelt 1974). It is achieved strategy that is manifested in a set of concrete activities, rather than being strategy as an intention. Similarly, vertical integration is an aspect of achieved strategy (Rumelt 1974). Diversification and vertical integration describe how far the activities of a firm are closely connected, or not, in the horizontal (diversification) and vertical (vertical integration) dimensions, respectively. Diversification and vertical integration may therefore both be grouped under the concept of task interdependence. High diversification, such as in a firm that makes unrelated products, is pooled interdependence among the products (Thompson 1967). Vertical integration is sequential interdependence between the stages of the value-added chain within the firm. An undiversified firm, such as one making a single product, will have close connections among the functional departments because all are involved with the same product, so that its interdependence is also sequential. However, there may also be reciprocal interdependence among the functional departments, if there is innovation, requiring interaction between the research and other departments (Lorsch and Lawrence 1972). Hence the strategy contingencies of diversification and vertical integration can be subsumed under task interdependence, as can the interactions between functions stemming from innovation.

Support for the idea that many contingencies are reducible to task uncertainty and task interdependence may be taken from Dess and Beard (1984). They review a number of conceptualizations of environmental contingencies and argue that they can be reduced to three dimensions: dynamism (which subsumes stability-instability and turbulence), complexity (which subsumes homogeneity-heterogeneity and concentration-dispersion), and munificence (which subsumes capacity). They show that twenty-three environmental variables that compare across fifty-two different industries reduce in a factor analysis to the three underlying factors of dynamism, complexity, and munificence. Several authors have identified dynamism as one of the major environmental contingencies of organizations (Child 1975; Duncan 1972; Thompson 1967). Dess and Beard (1984) emphasize that dynamism is not simply the rate of change, which itself could be constant, thereby rendering the environment predictable, but rather the degree of unpredictability. As they state, "Dynamism should be restricted to change that is hard to predict and that heightens uncertainty for key organizational members" (p. 56). This confirms the importance of uncertainty as a key element of dynamism. Therefore dynamism can largely be subsumed under uncertainty. Similarly, the homogeneity-heterogeneity aspect of their environmental complexity concept relates to the degree of diversification of the organization, because diversification across diverse product-markets renders the environment more heterogeneous. Given that diversification relates to task interdependence, environmental complexity relates, in turn, to the task interdependence contingency. Thus two of the environmental contingency concepts of Dess and Beard, dynamism and complexity, map onto the intraorganizational contingencies of task uncertainty and task interdependence, respectively.

The third environmental contingency concept of Dess and Beard (1984), munificence, relates to the quantity of slack resources, which we discuss below (in Chapter 9) mainly as a moderator, whereby economic stringency fosters organizational change. Similarly, the concentration-dispersion aspect of their complexity concept taps the degree of competition in the environment of an organization, which again moderates organizational change (as will also be discussed in Chapter 9). Thus the three dimensions identified by Dess and Beard in their parsimonious model of the environment are consistent with our proposal that task uncertainty and task interdependence are major underlying contingencies and that competition and lack of munificence moderate the organizational change that occurs in response to these two contingencies. Similarly, Lawrence and Dyer (1983) argue that industrial environments form two dimensions, information complexity, which taps uncertainty stemming from variations, and resource scarcity; these two dimensions relate to the task uncertainty contingency and resource munificence moderator being used herein.

Thus many of the contingency variables can be classified under either task uncertainty or task interdependence. Clearly, these two concepts can themselves be subsumed under the concept of a task contingency.

Size

A different contingency is size. Size has turned out to be a major contingency factor that affects many different aspects of structure and many of them quite strongly (Blau 1972; Child 1973a; Pugh, Hickson, Hinings, and Turner 1969). The size contingency is the number of organizational members who are to be organized (Blau 1970), determining the structure that is required. Size is therefore appropriately operationalized in empirical studies by the number of employees (Pugh et al. 1969; Pugh and Hinings 1976). However, the number of employees is conceptually and empirically closely related to other aspects of organizational membership, such as the number of members in a labor union (Donaldson and Warner 1974). The number of employees is also often closely correlated with other aspects of the scale of an organization, such as sales or assets, so that these variables may be used as indicators for size (see Child 1973a, p. 170, Table 1; Donaldson 1996b, pp. 147-156; Hopkins 1988; Lioukas and Xerokostas 1982). However, they are not always highly correlated, so that they are, at best, mere proxies for the number of employees, which remains the operational measure of size.

Organic and Bureaucracy Theories

There are two contrasting contingency theories of organizational structure that are influential in the structural contingency literature: the organic and the bureaucracy theories. Each theory has a different model of organizational structure that needs to be distinguished.

Organic Theory

Organic theory considers the fundamental dimension of organizational structure to be a continuum that runs from the poles of mechanistic to organic structure (Burns and Stalker 1961). The mechanistic structure is top-down so that top management seeks to control lower-level employees in every way possible. Top management centralizes decision making, so that it makes decisions about what should happen (Burns and Stalker 1961). It also gives subordinates detailed job assignments that define their responsibilities (Burns and Stalker 1961). Further, top management lays down rules that employees are to follow and documents they must use, such as forms that they must fill out (Weber 1968). Thus the mechanistic structure can be defined as centralized in decision making, specialized in roles and formalized (much use of rules and documents; Hage 1965; Pennings 1992). In contrast, the organic structure is decentralized (so that lower-level employees exercise autonomy in decision making) and also low on functional specialization and formalization, so that how employees should do their jobs is not prescribed by top management (Burns and Stalker 1961). Thus the organic structure neither controls employees through centralization nor through functional specialization and formalization. Instead, the organic structure relies on the initiative and expertise of middle-level and lower-level employees. Hence in the organic model of structure, lower-level employees are only lightly controlled by their organization. In sum, the mechanistic structure is centralized and high on both functional specialization and formalization, whereas the organic structure is decentralized and low on both functional specialization and formalization (Hage 1965; Pennings 1992).

The contrast between mechanistic and organic structures defines a single structural dimension. Thus organizations that are centralized are also specialized and formalized (i.e., mechanistic). Conversely, if the organization is decentralized, it will also be low on specialization and formalization (i.e., organic). Mechanistic and organic are two poles of a continuum of mechanistic and organic, with organizations distributed at points along that continuum. But if an organization is middling on centralization, then the organization will also be likely to be middling on specialization and formalization, because all three structural variable go together as part of the same dimension. According to the organic theory, the mechanistic-organic structure fits the contingency of task uncertainty (Hage and Aiken 1969). Specifically, the mechanistic structure fits low task uncertainty, whereas the organic structure fits high task uncertainty. Much of the task uncertainty comes from the environment of the organization, caused by high levels of technological and market change requiring the organization to innovate in order to remain effective and competitive, that is, to have high performance (Burns and Stalker 1961). Where task uncertainty is low, the knowledge and information possessed by senior managers enables them to exercise high control over all operations and employees so that the organization is effective. However, where task uncertainty is high, much expertise and information is distributed among employees, so that they have to be empowered to use their initiative and make decisions in a participatory manner, in order for the organization to innovate and be effective (Burns and Stalker 1961). Increasing task uncertainty over time requires an organization to change its structure from mechanistic toward organic in order to maintain fit (Burns and Stalker 1961; Hage and Aiken 1970). Thus the structural variables of centralization, specialization, and formalization go together because high levels of each provide the greater levels of hierarchical direction that fit highly certain tasks, while low levels of each also go together because they provide the participation that fits highly uncertain tasks. In this way arises the concept of the organizational structure as a single dimension from mechanistic to organic. This structural concept has been used in much contingency theory research (Burns and Stalker 1961; Dewar and Hage 1978; Hage 1965, 1974, 1980, 1988; Hage and Aiken 1967a, 1967b, 1969; Hage and Dewar 1973).

Bureaucracy Theory

In contrast, bureaucracy theory considers the fundamental dimension of organizational structure to be a different continuum, which runs from the poles of unbureaucratic, that is, simple, structure to bureaucratic structure. There exists a simple type of organizational structure that is centralized as well as being low on functional specialization and formalization (Mintzberg 1979). Conversely, there is a bureaucratic type of organizational structure that is decentralized as well as being high on functional specialization and formalization (Child 1972a; Weber 1968). Thus top management either controls employees directly through making decisions (centralization) in the simple structure, or indirectly through tight job definitions (specialization) and rules (formalization) in the bureaucratic structure (Blau and Schoenherr 1971). Top management substitutes between such direct and indirect controls, but does not try to use high levels of both simultaneously. Thus top management is applying sufficient control, rather than maximizing control. There is a continuum of degrees of bureaucratization, and an organization can lie at any point along it (Child 1972a).

A simple structure, while being low on specialization and formal-ization like the organic structure, is, nevertheless, not organic because the simple structure is centralized, rather than being decentralized like the organic structure. Similarly, a bureaucratic organization, though highly specialized and formalized like the mechanistic structure, is decentralized and so is not mechanistic. Thus the organic and bureau-cratic models of organizational structure differ according to their view about the dimension that underlies organizational structure. This dimension is composed of the two structural elements of centraliza-tion and specialization-formalization. These elements can be combined in two different ways to yield the organic and bureaucracy theories (see Figure 1.3). Organic theory sees centralization as positively correlated with specialization-formalization. Low centralization goes with low specialization-formalization in the organic structure. High centralization goes with high specialization-formalization in the mechanistic structure (Hage 1965; Pennings 1992). In contrast, bureaucracy theory sees centralization as negatively correlated with specialization-formalization. High centralization goes with low specialization-formalization in the simple structure. Low centralization goes with high specialization-formalization in the bureaucratic structure (Child 1972a).

According to bureaucracy theory, the level of bureaucratization of the structure fits the contingency of size (i.e., the number of organi-zational employees; Child 1975). Specifically, a low level of bureauc-ratization fits a small organization. Thus, for a small organization, the fitting structure is high on centralization and low on specialization and formalization (i.e., a simple structure). The limited complexity of decision making, resulting from small size, allows top management to directly control the organization through making the decisions. Conversely, a high level of bureaucratization (i.e., a bureaucratic structure) fits a large organization. Thus, for a large organization, the fitting structure is low on centralization and high on specialization and formalization. Increasing complexity and a tall hierarchy, resulting from size, requires top management to delegate many decisions. Also, size fosters the division of labor, and the recurrent nature of many deci-sions allows them to be formalized. Increasing size of an organization requires that its structure change from simple toward bureaucratic, to maintain fit and effectiveness.

There is some difference between the organic and bureaucratic theories in their concept of decentralization. Bureaucracy theory sees

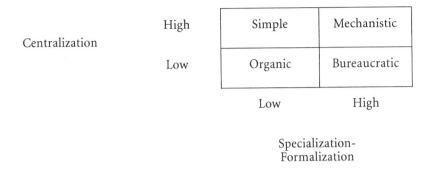

Figure 1.3. Organizational Structures in Organic and Bureaucratic Theory

increased decentralization as being mainly delegation of authority down to middle managers, with some occasional delegation to workers (Chandler 1962; Child 1973a). Organic theory includes managerial delegation, but also autonomy and participation in decision making by technical experts at low levels in the hierarchy (Hage 1980) and even by shop-floor workers (Wall, Corbett, Martin, Clegg, and Jackson 1990). Thus the real extent of decentralization is greater under organic theory than under bureaucracy theory. Similarly, the organic structure includes also lateral forms of coordination such as cross-functional project teams and ad hoc communication (Lawrence and Lorsch 1967). These nonhierarchical coordination mechanisms provide additional forums in which participation occurs.

Organic theory sees the degree to which organizational structures are organic as being driven by the need to fit not only the situational contingency of task uncertainty but also the human needs and aspirations of organizational members (Lorsch and Morse 1974). Thus the argument about replacing mechanistic with organic structures is advocating more participatory structures that not only offer effectiveness benefits through fit but also accord better with humanistic values. This creates a tension with the bureaucratization theory that tends to argue the need for bureaucratization according to a Weberian logic of subjugation of the organizational member in pursuit of effectiveness (Weber 1968).

The organic and bureaucracy theories tend to differ in their views about the direction in which organizational structures are headed over time. Organic theory sees the trend as being for task uncertainty to increase, because of increases in scientific knowledge and innovation rates, so that organizations increase over time the degree to which their structures are organic (Burns and Stalker 1961; Hage 1988). In contrast, bureaucracy theory sees a tendency toward increasing levels of bureaucratization, because of increasing concentration in fewer, larger organizations of global reach, facilitated by modern communications technologies (Weber 1968). In a formal sense both theories logically imply that an organization could move counter to the trend, if its contingencies changed in the opposite direction, such as task uncertainty reducing or size decreasing. Clearly a number of organizations have downsized in the 1980s and 1990s, so that there could be said to be something of a countertrend away from growth in certain quarters (Budros 1997; Cascio 1993; Littler and Bramble 1995). Nevertheless, bureaucracy theory tends to see increasing use of the bureaucratic structure (Blau and Meyer 1987), while organic theory depicts increasing use of the organic structure (Burns 1963; Flanders, Pomeranz, and Woodward. 1968; Hage 1974, 1980, 1988). Thus organic theory foresees decreasing specialization and formalization, while bureaucracy theory foresees them increasing. Both theories foresee increasing decentralization, though the extent is greater for organic than for bureaucratic theory. Hence organic and bureaucracy theories are optimistic or pessimistic, respectively, about the likelihood of increasing employee participation and freedom from regulation. Thus the divergence between the organic and bureaucracy theories connects with different policy prescriptions, value positions, and predictions about the future that help to animate the debate between them.

As just seen, organic and bureaucracy theories are to some degree in conflict, making rival analyses about structural trends. This conflict becomes played out as a controversy in the structural contingency literature about the role of task versus the size contingency. Organic theory seeks to promote task as the major contingency, so that task strongly and pervasively shapes organizations, leading them to take on the organic structure, especially as task uncertainty increases (e.g., Burns 1963; Hage 1988). Bureaucracy theory seeks to show, in contrast, that size is the more important contingency, in terms of the number of structural aspects it affects and the strength of the relationships, leading organizations to take on the bureaucratic structure as their size increases (Child 1973a). At the extremes, bureaucracy theory argues that the task has only limited effects (Child and Mansfield 1972) or that its effects are the opposite to those that organic theory asserts (Blau, Falbe, McKinley, and Tracy 1976). These controversial issues will be discussed in the ensuing chapters (especially Chapters 3 and 5).

Thus far we have contrasted the organic and bureaucracy theories on the structural elements of centralization and specialization-formalization. However, the concept of bureaucracy is wider than just these elements and entails two other aspects of structure: structural differentiation and divisionalization. *Structural differentiation* refers to the extent to which the organization is split into separate parts, both horizontally (the number of divisions, the number of job titles, the span of control of the CEO, etc.) and vertically (the number of levels in the hierarchy; Blau 1970). Conceptually, a bureaucratic structure has a high level of structural differentiation, for example, many departments and hierarchical levels (Blau and Schoenherr 1971; Pugh, Hickson, Hinings, and Turner 1968; Weber 1968). Divisionalization can also be thought of as another aspect of bureaucracy, because it features decentralization and increased functional specialization and formalization (Chenhall 1979; Grinyer and Yasai-Ardekani 1981). Divisionalization also correlates positively with structural differentiation, both horizontally (span of control of CEO) and vertically (hierarchical levels; Grinyer and Yasai-Ardekani 1981), thereby cementing the connection between divisionalization and bureaucratic structure. The inclusion of structural differentiation and divisionalization under the concept of bureaucracy is a further way in which it differs from the organic structural concept.

Task interdependence is a minor contingency of both the organic and the bureaucratic structures. As seen, task uncertainty is the main contingency determining whether structure is mechanistic or organic. However, task interdependence determines whether coordination mechanisms are of the mechanistic or organic type, so that task interdependence is a secondary contingency of organic structure. According to Thompson (1967), where task interdependence is pooled, then the fit is standardization, that is, rules and procedures set by the hierarchy, that is, a mechanistic coordination mechanism. Where task interdependence is sequential, then the fit is planning by the hierarchy, that is, another mechanistic coordination mechanism. In contrast, where task interdependence is reciprocal, then the fit is mutual adjustment between organizational members, that is, an organic coordination mechanism (Thompson 1967). Hence lower (i.e., pooled and sequential) task interdependence requires mechanistic coordination mechanisms, whereas high (i.e., reciprocal) task interdependence requires organic coordination mechanisms. Combining both task contingencies, low task uncertainty and low task interdependence are fitted by mechanistic structures, while high task uncertainty and high task interdependence are fitted by organic structures.

The task interdependence contingency also affects bureaucratic structure in that task interdependence affects divisionalization. Increasing diversification decreases the task interdependence between product-markets, so that the fitting structure is divisional rather than functional (Chandler 1962; Rumelt 1974). Given that divisionalization is a minor component of overall bureaucratic structure, then task interdependence is a minor contingency of bureaucracy. Task interdependence is a minor contingency relative to size, which strongly affects many of the other aspects of bureaucratic structure (e.g., formalization). Overall, increasing task interdependence leads from divisions coordinated mechanistically to functions coordinated organically.

Thus, whereas organic and bureaucracy theories differ in emphasizing the task uncertainty and size contingencies, respectively, both theories can be extended in a way that incorporates task interdependence as a contingency, thereby constituting a commonality between the organic and bureaucratic models of organizational structure.

Using the three contingencies and the two theories, we can cross-classify them, as shown in Table 1.1. The rows are the three contingencies: task uncertainty, task interdependence, and size. The columns are the two theories: organic and bureaucracy. The cross-classification yields six cells and into each cell is placed the names of some of the major authors.

Synthesis of Organic and Bureaucracy Theories

It is possible to synthesize the organic and bureaucracy theories in an integrated model of organizational structure. This shows that structural contingency theory, while it contains tensions (as discussed above), is

TABLE 1.1 Key Authors in Structural Contingency Theory Research

CONTINGENCIES	*THEORIES*	
	Organic	*Bureaucracy*
Task Uncertainty	Burns & Stalker Hage Lawrence & Lorsch Perrow Woodward	
Task Interdependence	Lawrence & Lorsch Thompson	Chandler Grinyer & Ardekani
Size		Aston Group Blau

not fragmented or inchoate. Combining the size and task contingencies we can say the following (see Figure 1.4). As organizations grow in size they increase specialization-formalization, structural differentiation, and decentralization. As task interdependence decreases because of diversification, this causes divisionalization, so that decentralization increases, as does specialization-formalization (e.g., creation of profit reporting) and structural differentiation (e.g., the number of levels), beyond that which would exist for its size alone. Conversely, increasing task interdependence leads to a functional structure, which implies less specialization-formalization, structural differentiation, and decentralization, as shown by the negative effects of task interdependence on these three structural variables in Figure 1.4. As task uncertainty increases, for example, through increased innovation in products or services, there is a reduction in formalization and an increase in decentralization. The reduction in formalization from increasing task uncertainty offsets to a degree the increase in formalization coming from size increase. However, the reduction in formalization from increasing task uncertainty reinforces the decrease in formalization that comes from any increase in task interdependence. The decentralization from increasing

Contingencies	Organizational Structure		
	Specialization-Formalization	Structural Differentiation	Decentralization
Size	+	+	+
Task Interdependence	−	−	−
Task Uncertainty	−		+

Figure 1.4. Overall Contingency Theory Model of Organizational Structure

task uncertainty adds to that coming from increasing size. However, the increase in decentralization from increasing task uncertainty offsets to a degree the decrease in decentralization coming from any increase in task interdependence. As will be seen below (Chapters 2 and 3), much of the reduction in formalization and increase in decentralization resulting from task uncertainty is localized in specific parts of the organization, but for the present we are discussing overall structural levels of the organization as a whole.

Synthesizing the bureaucratic and organic theories in this way gives a sense that it is possible to integrate structural contingency research into a model that is theoretically coherent and only modestly complex. However, the view of the two theories is highly condensed and so requires a great deal of explanation and justification regarding the theory and the supporting empirical research. We will consider first the organic theory and its supporting research (in Chapter 2) and second, bureaucracy theory and its research (in Chapter 3).

While task uncertainty and size are treated as independent contingencies in the literature, the possibility nevertheless arises that they may be brought together causally, so that one causes the other. This would constitute a causal synthesis in structural contingency theory, which would further increase its integration. A derived question is whether this causal integration would lead to theoretical integration of the organic and bureaucratic theories. These issues will be discussed in Chapter 3.

Plan of the Book

In Chapter 2 we discuss organic theory and its supporting empirical research.

In Chapter 3 we discuss bureaucracy theory and its supporting empirical research. We also attend to the issue of reconciliation between the organic and bureaucratic theories in two ways. A model that synthesizes both the organic and the bureaucratic theories is presented. The possibility of a causal relationship between task and size, the two major contingencies of organic and bureaucratic theories, is then discussed.

In Chapter 4 we consider the prevailing causal models among size and the bureaucratic structural variables. These are seen to be problematic from the viewpoint of contingency theory. They are reformulated so as to have causality work through fit, as contingency theory holds. Also discussed are reasons why some size and structural relationships are curvilinear rather than linear. A further issue that receives attention is the relationship between the systems functionalism of contingency theory and the actions by people that create causation at the systems level.

In Chapter 5 we consider some of the controversies in and around contingency theory that reflect the ongoing tension between the organic and bureaucratic theories. The rival claims of these two theories regarding the technology and size contingencies have led to controversy about their relative strengths as determinants of structure and also to what is the effect of technology on structure. These issues will be critically discussed. The idea that bureaucracy is made inevitable because of determination by contingencies such as size has been considered repellant enough by some scholars to lead to questioning of determinism. Critics have asserted that there is strategic choice, opening up the possibility of choice in favor of more participatory, organic structures. The arguments for choice will, in turn, be critically examined. Again, the causal theory that contingencies cause structure has been questioned by proposing that contingency is not a cause but just a correlate of structure, or that structure causes contingencies. Either way again escapes from structures, such as bureaucracy, as being inevitable, so opening the door to a choice of alternatives, such as participatory, organic structures. Therefore we shall need to critically examine the issues of causality and reverse causality. Concepts and variables from contingency theory research are sometimes used within the framework of configurations. This posits that there are only a few types and that they need not fit any contingencies, so removing contingency determinism. Moreover, organizational change is held to be problematic and therefore infrequent and sharply discontinuous. We will critically examine configurations. There is a stream of contingency theory concerned with organizational power, which has attracted some criticism, so this is also discussed in Chapter 5.

In Chapter 6 we examine explanations alternative to contingency theory that come from other organizational theories such as institutional, organizational economics, political, and population ecology theories. We show that contingency theory offers a sound explanation despite the challenge posed by these theories.

A central idea in contingency theory is that the fit of organizational characteristic to the contingency factor leads to higher organizational performance. The question thus arises as to whether this is just a tautology. This raises the issue of what is a fit, how to identify it, and how to show empirically that it raises performance. These philosophical, conceptual, and methodological issues are discussed in Chapter 7.

In Chapter 8 we review studies of the relationship between fit and performance. We show that there is a body of empirical work that validates the idea that contingency fits positively affect performance. However, there are also technical problems that can obscure the strength of the effects of fit on performance and so need to be corrected in future research. The discussion identifies eight lessons that can help make future research more valid and reveal more fully the importance of contingency fit.

In Chapter 9 we identify some theoretical problems within contingency theory and suggest how they may be overcome. This new theory construction makes contingency theory more coherent. The proposed theoretical reformulation also makes contingency theory more dynamic, through the concept of a disequilibrium theory, so that it becomes a more comprehensive theory of organizational adaptation and growth. A central idea is that organizational change is performance driven, and this insight is formalized through organizational portfolio theory. Again, problems in structural adaptation to changes in the contingency are addressed through the concept of quasi-fit. Furthermore, it is suggested that the concept of fit itself may be improved through reconceptualizing fit in a way that is consistent with the model of organizational adaptation dynamics that is being used in this book. Some of the new theorizing in this chapter draws upon ideas from economics and finance and so benefits from cross-fertilization from those disciplines.

Finally, in Chapter 10 we identify some possible future opportunities and challenges for contingency theory in organizational science. The preceding theoretical discussion is drawn upon to suggest hypotheses that might be used by scholars in future organizational research. The new concepts and theories presented as part of neo-contingency theory, such as disequilibrium, organizational portfolio theory, and quasi-fit, are discussed and suggestions are made on how to test them in future empirical research. A new operational definition of the effect of fit on organizational performance is also presented as a guide to future investigation into this key topic.

2 Organic Theory and Research

In the previous chapter we introduced the organic theory of organizational structure. The organic theory states that the mechanistic (centralized, formalized) structure fits situations of low task uncertainty, whereas the organic structure (decentralized, unformalized) fits situations of high task uncertainty, such as innovation. In this chapter we present the theory in greater depth together with the empirical research.

The studies that originated the organic theory of organizational structure mostly involved field studies of actual organizations, so that this branch of structural contingency theory had a strong grounding in empirical reality at its inception. This chapter will review the main studies and then bring out their theoretical connections to provide a discussion of how closely they can be integrated into a coherent theoretical model. It will be seen that organic theory constitutes a coherent theory that is supported by empirical research.

Organic Theories and Research

The point at which the contingency theory approach was invented cannot be stated with any exactitude. The first theory of organizational structure to use the term *contingency theory* is that by Lawrence and Lorsch in 1967 (p. 156), which made an early contribution to organic theory. This contribution in macro-Organizational Behavior (OB), however, was at least simultaneous with a contribution in micro-OB that bore the title of a contingency theory of leadership by Fiedler (1967). This in turn was predated by research of a contingency type, in which social psychologists conducted experiments on decision making in groups. The experiments contrasted groups using a hierarchical structure of communications with those using a participatory structure (Leavitt 1951). Where the task involved innovatory problem solving, the participatory structure produced superior decisions, but where the task was routine, the hierarchy was superior. Hence task uncertainty was a contingency factor that moderated the effectiveness of group structures. Thus the idea of contingency relationships was established in leadership and group studies by the late 1960s and this may have conditioned its acceptance in organizational structural research. More specifically, the social psychological experiments on group decision making contained within them the key idea of organic theory: Tasks low on uncertainty are most effectively managed hierarchically and tasks high on uncertainty are most effectively managed participatorily. Thus effective group structure varies from hierarchical to participatory and each fits a level of the contingency of task uncertainty.

The organic theory of organizational structure was laid down in a series of pioneering contributions. They can be divided into two sets: those that related organizational structure to the contingency of task uncertainty, often as influenced by the environment, and those that related organizational structure to the contingency of technology.

Task Uncertainty

There are three key contributions that show how organizational structure relates to the contingency of task uncertainty and the environment of the organization: Burns and Stalker (1961), Hage (1965), and Lawrence and Lorsch (1967).

Burns and Stalker

The most fundamental contribution to organic theory was provided by Burns and Stalker (1961), who offered an elegant theory that has proved to be compelling for many subsequent scholars. They distinguish between two organizational structures, the mechanistic and the organic (Burns and Stalker 1961, pp. 119-122). The mechanistic structure emphasizes hierarchy, with the task of the organization being divided into specialized roles whose occupants remain dependent upon their superordinates, who retain much of the knowledge and information. The image of a mechanistic organization structure is of a hierarchy with centralized decision making that tightly prescribes lower-level roles. In contrast, in the organic structure, understanding of the task is widely shared among employees who use their initiative, accept joint responsibility, and work flexibly. The image of an organic organization is a network in which experts collaborate in fluid and ad hoc ways. Burns and Stalker (1961, pp. 119-122) identify several other distinguishing characteristics of the organic structure, such as commitment to the "technological ethos" (p. 121), but these wider features were not often used by subsequent scholars, so that the mechanistic versus organic distinction has come to refer to structural characteristics internal to the organization.

Burns and Stalker (1961) make the contingency argument that mechanistic structures are effective only in conditions of low rates of technological and market change, whereas high rates of such change require the organic structure for the organization to be effective. With low rates of change, the top managers possess adequate knowledge to specify the work roles of their subordinates. In contrast, with high rates of change, the top managers lack much of the knowledge and so must rely on the expertise of their subordinates, who can organize the work among themselves. The mechanistic organization is not only a structure but also a culture, in which subordinates are psychologically dependent upon their superordinates (Burns and Stalker 1961). The mechanistic structure corresponds to the structure prescribed by the classical management school, with its emphasis on centralized control, job specialization, and clear job descriptions (Brech 1957; Taylor 1947). In contrast, an organic structure encourages and legitimates the exercise of discretion by employees. The organic structure corresponds to the structure prescribed by the neo-human relations school, with its emphasis on employee empowerment, self-directed teams, and participation in decision making (Argyris 1964; Likert 1961). Instead of the universal claims to a "one best way," Burns and Stalker argued that each model was valid in its own place. Its place was given by the contingency factor of technological and market change. Accommodating the two rival, preceding theoretical schools of classical management and neo-human relations into a broader framework was an attractive feature of the contingency theory of Burns and Stalker.

Burns and Stalker (1961, p. 122) present the mechanistic and organic structures as two polar extremes. The mechanistic and organic types each mark the poles of a continuum that registers differences in degrees of mechanisticness and organicness. Organizations lie at any point along the continuum.

Burns and Stalker (1961) extend their analysis to argue that the political system is different between mechanistic and organic structures, with the looser roles definitions of the organic structure fostering more political behavior than in the more tightly defined mechanistic structure. Their exposition of the overall theory is pursued in a book that recounts extensive, comparative field studies of contrasting organizations (Burns and Stalker 1961). Their method is qualitative and anthropological. Some of their empirical claims are problematic, such as that the failure of innovations in some textile firms was due to their mechanistic structures, whereas the failure seems to have been caused by lack of top management support (Burns and Stalker 1961). Nevertheless, the mechanistic versus organic distinction has proven to be an enduring contribution, providing scholars with a ready way to characterize the differing models of the overall organizational structure. This helped raise contingency analysis from just the individual and group levels to the organizational level. Further, the contingency factor of technological and market change moved the contingency out to the environment of the organization. The elegant simplicity of their model has helped propagate the contingency approach so that this is probably, even today, the single most widely known contingency theory of organizational structure.

Hage

Hage (1965) provided an early contribution that was similar to the theory of Burns and Stalker, thereby reinforcing it (see Hage 1980). Hage (1965) argues that efficiency is maximized by a structure that is centralized in decision making, formalized (e.g., using rules), and low on complexity. This structure is similar to the mechanistic structure of Burns and Stalker (1961). In contrast, innovation is maximized by a structure that is decentralized, low on formalization, and high on complexity. This structure is similar to the organic structure of Burns and Stalker (1961). "Complexity" is a measure of the amount of knowledge available within the organization. Complexity is high when the organization employs highly educated people and fosters their knowledge through occupational specialization, so that they gain added depth. This type of specialization is to be distinguished from narrow task specialization, for example, of jobs on an automobile assembly line, or specialization by function, which is part of the mechanistic structure. The use of the term *complexity* to have this meaning is somewhat idiosyncratic to Hage and his followers.

The theory of Hage (1965) is presented as a series of abstract formal propositions. The theory holds in essence that centralization and formalization allow management to coordinate operations closely so that efficiency results through tight control of a workforce that includes many employees with low education (i.e., low complexity). In contrast, high complexity, together with decentralization and low formalization, means that professionally trained persons with high expertise (i.e., high complexity) seek to implement their ideas and values, which includes an emphasis on adopting the latest developments in their profession, so that innovation ensues. *Innovation* is the rate of new programs (such as new therapies in a medical organization) adopted in a unit of time (Hage and Aiken 1967a). Thus the organic structure provides the ideas for new innovations, while also freeing personnel from bureaucratic constraints so that they can implement them, thereby letting "a thousand flowers bloom." Stated as such it is a universalistic theory, in that each proposition gives a simple, main effect of structure on outcome. It is compatible with contingency thinking, however, by saying that if efficiency is desired, because of an environment that is competing on cost, then a centralized and formalized structure must be adopted to remain competitive (Hage and Aiken 1970). Similarly, it can be said that, if innovation is desired, because of an environment that is competing on new, differentiated products or services, then a decentralized and lowly formalized structure must be adopted to remain competitive (Hage and Aiken 1970). In this way the argument takes on the logic of a fit to the environment as a contingency.

Clearly, the Hage (1965) model parallels that of Burns and Stalker (1961): Their mechanistic structure is his centralized and formalized structure, and their organic structure is his decentralized and unformalized structure. By restating the structural concepts in the abstract structural variables of centralization and formalization, Hage advances contingency theory in two ways. First, he provides a compact summary of the main ways in which the mechanistic and organic types differ. Second, his use of variables in both theoretical statements and empirical research makes it clear that these are differences of degree. Organizations vary in their amount or level of centralization and formalization rather than existing only at the two ends of these variables, that is, as being either mechanistic or organic. By using variables (derived from Hall 1963) to measure centralization and formalization, Hage also provided a methodological model for subsequent researchers. This helped to broaden the empirical research of organic theory from the anthropological, qualitative methods used by Burns and Stalker (1961) to quantitative methods.

In a series of empirical studies, Hage and his colleagues (Dewar and Hage 1978; Hage and Aiken 1967a, 1967b, 1969; Hage and Dewar 1973) showed that structure was related to contingencies and produced the expected causal outcomes. Centralization and formalization were associated positively with task routineness (Hage and Aiken 1969), that is, low levels of the task uncertainty contingency. Hage and Dewar (1973) showed that having a decentralized, low formalization structure and high complexity leads to higher subsequent innovation rates, thereby supporting the causal theory that organic structure causes innovation.

The contrary argument can also be made, however, that centralization promotes innovation, rather than preventing it, because centralized power allows top management to force through changes despite any resistance from other employees. Thus radical changes or those that require systemswide coordination to be successfully implemented may be more likely to occur where a directive approach is taken by a top management that personally makes all or many decisions (Dunphy and Stace 1988), that is, centralization. However, while centralization may foster the magnitude of an innovation, decentralization fosters the rate of innovation, that is, decentralization leads to a higher rate of innovation, that is, innovations per unit time, the aspect of innovation in the work of Hage and his colleagues. Decentralization allows many initiatives to be taken and hence many different innovations to occur simultaneously. This distinction between the magnitude and the rate of innovation may go some way to account for the mixed findings in organizational research about the relationship between centralization and innovation (Slappendel 1996).

Lawrence and Lorsch

Lawrence and Lorsch (1967, p. 156) produced a theory that is allied to that of Burns and Stalker, and of Hage, but is more complex. Because of its greater complexity, we shall have to describe it at greater length.

Lawrence and Lorsch (1967) conceptualize organizational structure in terms of differentiation and integration. The internal subunits of an organization, such as the functional departments of a firm (e.g., production, research, sales), differ from each other but also must cooperate with each other to accomplish the overall task of the organization, so the differentiated units must be integrated. *Differentiation* refers concretely to differences between departments in goal orientations, time orientations, formality of structures, and interpersonal orientations (Lawrence and Lorsch, 1967, pp. 30-38). Differentiation between departments arises because departments differ in their tasks. Lawrence and Lorsch (1967, p. 36, Figure II-1) found that task certainty is related to formality of structure, consistent with the findings of other contingency theory research. Moreover, performance was higher where greater task uncertainty was associated with less structural formality and with less centralization (Lawrence and Lorsch 1967, p. 43, Table II-3; p. 129, Figure V-2; and p. 143, Figure VI-1). Thus departments, such as research, that had highly uncertain tasks, had structures low on formality, whereas departments, such as production, that had highly certain tasks had structures high on formality (Lawrence and Lorsch 1967, p. 36, Figure II-1). In such ways there is created high differentiation of structures between departments. The greater the differentiation, the more integration that is required for effectiveness of the overall organization (Lawrence and Lorsch 1967). Integration is achieved by using integrative devices, with higher levels of integration being achieved by the more sophisticated devices, which in order of increasing sophistication are: hierarchy, rules, integrating individuals, and integrating departments (Lawrence and Lorsch 1967, p. 138, Table VI-1). Coordination is improved where centralization, the vertical distribution of influence in Lawrence and Lorsch's study, fits task uncertainty. Decisions are taken by upper hierarchical levels where tasks are certain, whereas influence is shared more with lower hierarchical levels where tasks are uncertain (Lawrence and Lorsch 1967, p. 128, Table V-5; p. 129, Figure V-2; and p. 143, Figure VI-1).

For Lawrence and Lorsch, like Burns and Stalker (1961), the contingency factor that determines the required organizational structure comes from the environment: It is the rate of new product innovation and/or changes in the market or process technology that contributes to task uncertainty in the industry. Low rates of product innovation, for example, mean that the firm needs little or no research and development and this would, in turn, reduce its required differentiation and also its need for complex integration mechanisms, none beyond hierarchy and rules (Lawrence and Lorsch 1967). Thus successful firms in low-change industries have low differentiation (Lawrence and Lorsch 1967, p. 103, Table IV-6) and employ simpler integrating mechanisms (Lawrence and Lorsch 1967, p. 138, Table VI-1). Conversely, high rates of environmental change and innovation mean that the firm needs at least some departments that deal with highly uncertain tasks (such as R and D). The result is that their overall degree of differentiation is high, and this would need to be matched by more complex integration mechanisms (such as reliance upon an integrating department). Thus successful firms in high-change (uncertain) industries have high differentiation and also achieve high integration by using a full array of integrating mechanisms (Lawrence and Lorsch 1967, p. 103, Table IV-6; p. 138, Table VI-1). Lawrence and Lorsch (1967) showed these relationships empirically in field studies of several firms from each of three industries: containers, processed food, and plastics.

Subsequent study by Lorsch and Allen (1973) of large, diversified corporations failed to find that the differentiation between divisions was accompanied by the use of complex integration mechanisms in successful corporations. Thus the simple, bivariate relationship between differentiation and integration did not hold. This led Lorsch and Lawrence (1972) to clarify their findings, using the typology of interdependence from Thompson (1967). In the first study (Lawrence and Lorsch 1967), the firms were less diversified and so their subunits were functional departments that depended upon each other, that is, marketing sells what production makes. However, in the second study (Lorsch and Allen 1973) of diversified corporations, the subunits were

divisions, which for the highly diversified corporations had very limited direct interdependence between the divisions. This clarified that
intense integration is required only where there is intense interdependence. The higher the interdependence, the higher the sophistication
of the integration needed for the firm to be successful.

Differentiation becomes less important in this reformulation (Lorsch
and Lawrence 1972). The first study had found that differentiation
across functional departments of undiversified firms was necessary for
success in innovatory industries, because they required novel problem
solving (Lawrence and Lorsch 1967). However, differentiation across
divisions was not associated with success in highly diversified corporations, because each division was self-contained and so high differentiation across them had no impact on their effectiveness or that of the
corporation as a whole (Lorsch and Allen 1973). Thus differentiation
made a contribution to organizational success only if the organization
was an interdependent system, such as a single business that needed to
innovate. There was no general positive effect of differentiation on organizations. Similarly, whereas the earlier formulation had integration
needing to match differentiation, the reformulation had integration
needing to match interdependence (Lorsch and Lawrence 1972). Differentiation played a secondary role in that it added to the integration
needed by interdependence.

As stated, integration is achieved between interdependent departments
through having the appropriate coordination devices (Lawrence and
Lorsch 1967). For highly interdependent departments these coordination devices include departments of integrators, that is, persons who
work to integrate the functional departments. Successful integrators
do not rely simply on hierarchical authority to influence decisions, but
have to match it with their expertise (Lawrence and Lorsch 1967, p. 66).
This is achieved by having the integrators reside in a department separate
from those they are integrating, in order to make them independent
and impartial. Moreover, the integrators need to have an orientation in
goals, time frame, and structure that is intermediary between the departments that they are seeking to integrate, so that they can translate
between the different departmental subcultures (Lawrence and Lorsch
1967, pp. 58-62). Further, the integrators need to use the right conflict
resolution approach: neither forcing (by power) nor smoothing (by
being evasive), but confronting (by facing the facts and solving the
problems; Lawrence and Lorsch 1967, p. 78). Confronting is the most

effective way to resolve conflict in all the situations studied, so it is a universalistic feature, contrasting with the contingency nature of the rest of the theory (Miner 1982).

We may formalize the theory of Lawrence and Lorsch, in its interdependence variant, into a causal model (Figure 2.1). The innovation, that is, degree of novelty and number of new products per unit of time, that is intended by the management increases the interdependence between the functional departments involved in making the innovation occur. The novel problem solving entailed by innovation requires that the functional departments transfer information back and forth between themselves in an unpredictable way. Thus the greater the innovation intended, the more intense the interdependence between functional departments. The interdependence raises the degree of integration that is required. If the actual integration matches the requisite integration, then fit results and, consequently, there is high achieved integration and so high performance. A high level of actual integration is provided by having integrators. Their requisite character is that they be intermediary in their orientation between the functional departments. The degree of difference between departments that the integrators must span is greater, the greater the differentiation between departments. Therefore the requisite character of the integrators is determined by differentiation. The differentiation is in turn determined by the degree of task uncertainty as caused by the intended innovation. Greater innovation causes greater task uncertainty in some functional departments (e.g., research) but not others (e.g., production), thereby creating greater differentiation. The greater gap between departmental subcultures that the integrators have to span increases their work and so tends to increase the number of integrators required, so that differentiation adds also to requisite integration.

To illustrate the theory of Lawrence and Lorsch, consider their two most contrasting industries: containers and plastics. The container industry had low rates of new product innovation (Lawrence and Lorsch 1967, p. 86, Table IV-2), limiting the amount of novel problem solving required, so that firm differentiation was low. The interdependence between departments was medium, in that marketing collects customer orders that are passed to production, which delivers to the customer. In Thompson's (1967) terms this is "sequential interdependence" that can be managed by planning and was accomplished by the CEO, that is, coordination by the simple device of hierarchy, plus some rules and

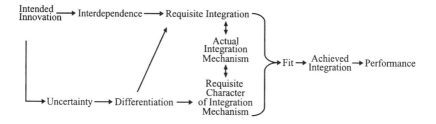

Figure 2.1. A Causal Model of Interdependence, Integration, and Differentiation of Functional Departments

procedures as additional, only slightly more sophisticated, coordination devices. Thus successful firms in the low-innovation industry of containers could be run hierarchically because of the simplicity of their structures and medium level of their interdependencies. The more successful firms conformed to this pattern, providing evidence that matching their structure to the requirements of low innovation led to higher performance.

In contrast, the plastics industry had high rates of new product innovation (Lawrence and Lorsch 1967, p. 86, Table IV-2), so successful firms required research departments pursuing novel scientific ideas in projects with long time frames using permissive cultures with low structure. These research departments differed from the sales and production departments (Lawrence and Lorsch 1967, p. 48, Figure II-2), contributing to high firm differentiation. The interdependence between departments was high, in that much novel problem solving was required, and so a considerable amount of information had to pass back and forth between the functional departments. In Thompson's terms this is "reciprocal interdependence," which requires mutual adjustment, that is, ad hoc coordination between the functional departments, achieved through cross-functional project teams facilitated by integrators. Thus the greater interdependence within plastics firms called for more sophisticated coordinating devices that involved creating the additional roles of integrators. In turn, these integrators had to have orientations (in goals, etc.) intermediary between the functional departments and to use confrontation to resolve conflicts between these departments (Lawrence and Lorsch 1967, pp. 58-62, 78). Thus successful firms in the high-innovation industry of plastics were not able to run purely hierarchically because of the complexity of their structures and high level of their interdependencies. To be successful in this innovatory type of industry, firms had to adopt more participatory structures (Lawrence and Lorsch 1967, p. 138, Table VI-1; and p. 143, Figure VI-1). The more successful firms conformed to this pattern, providing evidence that matching their structure to the requirements of high innovation led to higher performance (Lawrence and Lorsch 1967, p. 80, Table III-6).

Thus in the theory of Lawrence and Lorsch (1967), the contingency is the intended level of innovation that the organizational structure needs to fit in its differentiation and integration. Innovation leads to differentiation and interdependence, which in turn lead to integration. The language of Lawrence and Lorsch (1967) stresses the idea of an optimal defined by the contingency to which the actual must be fitted to attain high performance. This is expressed by talking about the contrast between "requisite" (i.e., required) and "achieved" (i.e., actual), for example, the requisite integration and the achieved integration. For low innovation the most effective structure is centralized, using planning and formal procedures. Thus where the environmentally given task has low uncertainty, a structure of the type prescribed by classical management is the most effective (Brech 1957). In contrast, for high innovation the most effective structure is decentralized, using participation (Likert 1961). Thus where the environmentally given task has high uncertainty, a structure of the type prescribed by neo-human relations is the most effective. Each of classical management and human relations are correct in their own place, thus making a synthesis of these two theories. The contingency factor, innovation, is similar to the technological and market change contingency of Burns and Stalker (1961): both originate in the environment and condition the uncertainty of the organization's task.

Structurally, Lawrence and Lorsch (1967) note that the high participation in organizational decision making in their innovatory firms is similar to the organic structure of Burns and Stalker (1961). However, unlike the cohesion of the organization through shared values in the organic type of Burns and Stalker, Lawrence and Lorsch have the more sophisticated concept of differentiation between departments. Only in the research and development department is the structure low on formalization and permissive in the manner of the organic concept.

By contrast, the production department is structured and directive, that is, mechanistic. These differences between functional departments in innovatory firms are shown empirically by Lawrence and Lorsch (1967). The cross-functional project teams would be expected to be more organic, as is consistent with their integrators being facilitators rather than authority figures. Thus Lawrence and Lorsch's theory is similar to Burns and Stalker's but is more complex and more realistic. Probably because of its complexity it is not as widely known as Burns and Stalker's; however, Lawrence and Lorsch's theory is well known. It was very important in the development of contingency theory and remains a major contribution.

Subsequently, Lorsch and Morse (1974) further developed the contingency theory by an empirical study that brought in the predispositions of organizational members as an additional contingency of an individual psychological kind. They showed that, for high organizational performance, fit is required among environment, organization, and member predispositions (Lorsch and Morse 1974, p. 114). More specifically, where the environment was low on uncertainty, this was fitted by a mechanistic type of structure and short-term time orientation with employees who were comfortable being controlled, liked to work with others, and had low tolerance for ambiguity (Lorsch and Morse 1974, p. 112). Conversely, where the environment was high on uncertainty, this was fitted by an organic type of structure and long-term time orientation with employees who preferred autonomy and had high tolerance for ambiguity (Lorsch and Morse 1974, p. 112). Fit led to higher feelings of competence and higher unit performance (Lorsch and Morse 1974, pp. 114-115). The interpretation was that fit depended upon members' psychological predispositions matching the structure required by the environment, which produced higher performance that created feelings of competence that in turn motivated continuing higher performance (Lorsch and Morse 1974, pp. 114-115).

Tosi, Aldag, and Storey (1973) criticized the measures of the environment used by Lawrence and Lorsch (1967). Lawrence and Lorsch's theory about differentiation and integration being shaped by the contingency of innovation has received few replication attempts, probably because it is so complex. Miner (1982) criticized it as not having been replicated. However, elements of it have been replicated. Tung (1979, p. 691) investigated environments and structure and concluded in support for Lawrence and Lorsch (1967). A study in Holland replicates portions of their model, thereby showing that aspects of the theory generalize geographically (Faas 1985). An unpublished study by Crawford (1983) of twenty diverse Australian organizations, which improved on the methods of Lawrence and Lorsch, corroborated several of their findings. Thus there is some support for Lawrence and Lorsch's theory from subsequent research. Nohria and Ghoshal (1997) have developed a contingency model of the structure of multinational corporations that uses the terms of differentiation and integration; however, there are some differences in the meaning of these terms, and their work will be discussed below (Chapter 3).

Technology

Part of organic theory consists of scholars who argue that the need for organizations to adopt organic structures follows from the contingency of technology. Three main contributors may be distinguished: Perrow, Thompson, and Woodward.

Perrow

Perrow (1967) was a pioneering theorist of technology as a contingency. For him, technology refers not to hardware or layout of equipment but to the cognitive processing involved in completing a task, that is, the perceived nature of the raw materials and the search behaviors involved in treating it. He distinguishes two dimensions: task analyzability and the number of exceptions. The cross-classification of these two dimensions creates four different situations (Perrow 1967, p. 196, Figure 1). Analyzable tasks with few exceptions are termed *routine technology*, exemplified by mass production steel mills. Analyzable tasks with many exceptions are termed *engineering technology*, for example, heavy machinery. Unanalyzable tasks with few exceptions are termed *craft technology*, for example, specialty glass. Unanalyzable tasks with many exceptions are termed *nonroutine technology*, for example, aerospace. The two situational dimensions (analyzability and number of exceptions) relate to the uncertainty of a task, and so the theory may best be thought of as a refinement of the task uncertainty contingency theory. Thus the technology contingency of Perrow may be subsumed under the previously discussed task uncertainty contingency rather than constituting a separate contingency.

The four different technologies, created by the cross-classification of the two dimensions, each require a particular type of organizational structure to fit it. Analyzable technologies require centralized structures, while unanalyzable structures require decentralized structures (Perrow 1967, p. 199, Figure 3). The greater the number of exceptions, the more flexibility that is required (Perrow 1967, p. 199, Figure 3). Thus routine technologies (analyzable, few exceptions) require formal, centralized structures (Perrow 1967, p. 199, Figure 3). Engineering technologies (analyzable, many exceptions) require flexible, centralized structures (Perrow 1967, p. 199, Figure 3). Craft technologies (unanalyzable, few exceptions) require decentralized structures (Perrow 1967, p. 199, Figure 3). Nonroutine technologies (unanalyzable, many exceptions) require flexible, polycentralized structures (Perrow 1967, p. 199, Figure 3).

Perrow (1967, p. 199) states that the formal, centralized structure is closest to the mechanistic structure (Burns and Stalker 1961) and the flexible, polycentralized structure is closest to the organic structure. Thus his structural concept can be classified as part of organic theory. In routine technology, reliance is placed on planning. Technical experts direct those supervising production operations, and there is little discretion over coding of cases (Perrow 1967, p. 200). In engineering technology, the many exceptions are handled by the technical experts, who exercise considerable discretion and adjust to feedback, whereas the operational supervisors receive direction from them and run operations to plan (Perrow 1967, p. 200). In craft technology, the unanalyzable nature of the material means that the workers have to exercise discretion and power, relying on feedback (Perrow 1967, p. 200). In nonroutine technology, the perceived nature of the raw material is such that there are many exceptions that have to be dealt with through "experimentation and 'feel'" (Perrow 1967, p. 199). Reliance has to be placed on adjustment to feedback rather than on planning. Technical experts and those supervising production operations exercise discretion over coding of cases and use high power in close collaboration with each other (Perrow 1967, pp. 199-200). Thus the theory of Perrow may be subsumed under the organic theory that low task uncertainty requires a mechanistic structure and high task uncertainty an organic structure. The four technologies also lead to differences in identification and goals (Perrow 1967, pp. 200-202).

Perrow (1967, p. 198, Figure 2) illustrates his discussion with examples drawn not only from industry but also from people changing organizations. Routine technology is exemplified by custodial institutions. Engineering technology is exemplified by a programmed learning school. Craft technology is exemplified by socializing institutions. Nonroutine technology is exemplified by elite psychiatric agencies. Perhaps because the contingencies refer to generalizable cognitive processes rather than specific types of industrial equipment, the technology contingency constructs of Perrow have been used widely, especially to study people-processing organizations, such as hospitals (e.g., Alexander and Randolph 1985). This brings out the extent to which "technology" is something of a misnomer, because it carries connotations of hardware, whereas Perrow (1967) is distinguishing different approaches to problem solving based on the perceived nature of the case situations and the degree of development of knowledge. Thus it is best classified as a refinement of the task uncertainty contingency idea.

Thompson

Thompson (1967) argues that task and technology are major contingency factors of organizational structure. He offers a typology of types of technology and their respective organizational structures. Three different types of technologies are distinguished: mediating, long-linked, and intensive. These correspond to three types of task interdependence between organizational subunits: pooled, sequential, and reciprocal, respectively (Thompson 1967).

Mediating technology refers to the linking of customers, such as a bank linking lenders and borrowers, and involves pooled interdependence. *Pooled interdependence* means that two organizational subunits (e.g., branches of a bank) have no direct connection, so that their interdependence is indirect, residing in their both drawing resources from some central pool. Another example of pooled interdependence is the relationship among divisions in a conglomerate: there is no direct connection between them because each business is unrelated to the others, but they all draw funds from the common, corporate pool of new capital (Lorsch and Allen 1973). This low degree of interdependence can be effectively structured by rules and procedures (Thompson 1967).

Long-linked technology refers to sequential interdependence where task A is the input to task B, for example, stages along an assembly line. *Sequential interdependence* means that the subunits have a direct connection, so that the output of one subunit is an input to the other subunit. Another example of sequential interdependence is the relationship among divisions in a vertically integrated company, such as in forest products: One division produces the raw materials of paper and cardboard that are then processed by the packaging division and sold to customers (Lorsch and Allen 1973). This medium degree of interdependence can be effectively structured by planning (Thompson 1967).

Intensive technologies use varying techniques according to feedback from the object worked upon, for example, a hospital using various diagnostic and treatment techniques according to the condition of the patient, and involve reciprocal interdependence. *Reciprocal interdependence* means that the subunits have a two-way connection, in which the output of each subunit is an input to the other subunit, so that they transact back and forth in an unpredictable manner. Another example of reciprocal interdependence is the relationship between the research and the production departments in a functionally structured company that is innovating new products: the novel, complex problem solving requires much information to be passed back and forth between the two departments in an unpredictable fashion (Lorsch and Lawrence 1972). Reciprocal interdependence can be effectively structured by mutual adjustment, that is, each organizational subunit will try to attain its objectives, but then receive feedback about how successful it has been, and other subunits have been, leading to reformulation of its objectives for the next time period (Thompson 1967). Thus each of the three types of interdependence requires a particular coordinating structure. (This is the theory that Lorsch and Lawrence, 1972, draw upon in their reformulation of their original study, as discussed above.) Thompson (1967) also theorizes about organizational politics, discretion, assessment, and cooperation between the organizations and its environment. There are theoretical relationships running across these topics connecting them with technology.

In terms of linkages with other structural contingency theories, coordination by rules and procedures is associated with the classical management school (e.g., Weber 1968) and may be classified as a mechanistic structural device. Coordination by planning would also seem to be quite mechanistic, albeit somewhat more flexible because it allows for the plan to be modified as the task situation changes. Coordination by mutual adjustment is associated with the neo-human relations school (e.g., Likert 1961) and entails employees agreeing among themselves their next actions, and so may be classified as an organic structural device. Hence the three types of interdependence (pooled, sequential, and reciprocal) are each fitted by varying degrees of mechanistic or organic structures. Thus task interdependence can be considered to be a contingency of organic structure.

Thompson's technology theory led to subsequent empirical research, such as the study by Gerwin and Christoffel (1974) of Thompson's theory of task interdependence. Thompson had illustrated his theory by his own study of the maintenance function of a USAF bomber wing. Gerwin and Christoffel (1974) found that a computer program based on Thompson's theory was able to predict correctly the structure of an engineering factory from the task interdependencies. This replicated Thompson and showed that his theory generalized empirically from a governmental to a private-sector organization. Other research has confirmed Thompson's theory of the relationship between task inter-dependence and coordinating structures, including in social service agencies (Van de Ven, Delebecq, and Koenig 1976; Van de Ven and Ferry 1980).

Woodward

Another path-breaking contingency theory study was by Woodward (1958, 1965). She examined the structures of one hundred companies distributed across different industries. She studied various aspects of the organizations, quantitatively and qualitatively. The quantitative measures included the number of levels of management, the spans of control of the chief executive and first-line supervisor, the ratio of managers and supervisors to total personnel, the percentage of costs allocated to wages, and the ratio of direct to indirect workers (Woodward 1965). She interpreted her measures as indices of the extent to which each company was following the prescriptions of classical management. Woodward concluded that the classical management prescriptions were being followed in some but not all the firms and that there was an association with operations technology. She distinguished stages of advance in technology, of which the three main stages are: unit and small batch production, large batch and mass production, and process production (examples would be the manufacture of musical instruments, automobiles, and oil, respectively). As firms move to more advanced technology their production becomes smoother and more continuous, associated with more automation and capital investment.

Woodward's (1965) key finding was that the classical management model was found in large batch and mass production but not in unit and small batch nor in process production. Thus she identified a historical sequence whereby advance in technology from small batch to mass production required the adoption of classical management prescriptions, but further technological advance required their abandonment. Before and after the classical management phase, the prescriptions of human relations, with their emphasis on participation and flexibility, were appropriate and tended to be followed. Drawing on Burns and Stalker (1961), she stated that the technological imperative led first to the organic structure, then to the mechanistic, and finally to the organic. Woodward's book contains many quantitative findings, showing that the means on many structural variables vary according to technology. It also included evidence that firms that were away from the mean had poorer performance (Woodward 1965, p. 69, Table 4). This provided the first quantitative depiction of the contingency idea that the firm had to fit its structure to the contingency factor in order to have high performance.

Woodward (1965) lacked a well-developed theory of why all of the structural variables are associated with technology. However, she has the broad argument that mass production renders the task more predictable so that it can be formalized and proceduralized, whereas process technology furthers task predictability but embodies the predictable elements in automation, leaving the unpredictable elements to the human operators who must be sophisticated problem solvers.

Woodward's contingency factor was internal to the organization, whereas Burns and Stalker's was environmental, but both involved technology. They mutually supported each other in the thesis that the concrete task facing the organization decisively affected the structure that it needed. Both Woodward (1965) and Burns and Stalker (1961) argued that the mechanistic structures were appropriate for firms in traditional industries with older technologies but that modern technologies forced the adoption of organic structures in order to maintain effectiveness.

Partly because Woodward's model is more complex than Burns and Stalker's model, it is not quite as well known. However, its influence upon contingency theory researchers has probably been greater than Burns and Stalker's because of the quantification. It has become an exemplar of contingency theory research at the macro-level, that is, where the unit of analysis is the organization. The argument that technology is a contingency of organizational structure has stimulated much subsequent research, with mixed findings. Woodward (1965) found relationships between operations technology and many organizational structural variables, and some subsequent studies have replicated some of these relationships (e.g., Zwerman 1970); however, other studies have found weaker and fewer relationships (e.g., Hickson, Pugh, and Pheysey 1969; Child and Mansfield 1972) or opposite relationships (Blau, Falbe, McKinley, and Tracy 1976). These issues will be discussed in detail below (see Chapter 5).

Woodward (1970) and her colleagues conducted further research that led to somewhat different concepts to analyze the management systems of firms. They argued that the technological imperative (meaning the firm has to obey it or suffer performance loss) was tempered in some situations where managerial ideology had some influence (see also Dawson and Wedderburn 1980; Reeves and Turner 1972). However, this later work has had less influence than the earlier work and so Woodward's name is synonymous with the idea of a technological imperative.

Technology may be imagined to be a hard, concrete material factor of the organization. Imagery invoked may be of smokestacks, assembly lines, and oil refineries. However, the technology variable measured by Woodward (1965) consists of two aspects: type of products produced and how many. The type of products produced is about whether they are integral, that is, discrete items that can be counted (e.g., 12 trumpets), or in a form, such as a liquid or gas, that has to be measured by volume (e.g., liters) or weight (e.g., tons). Within the manufacturing of integral products, the distinction is drawn as to how many products are produced in a batch: unit, small batch, large batch, and mass. This captures batch size and relates to the continuity of the production process. Thus Woodward's technology variable ranges from single product to many products to continuous flow, that is, from lumpy to flowing, and has been termed *production continuity* (Hickson, Pugh, and Pheysey 1969). While the products produced are a material fact, they are the result of numerous factors, such as available hardware and skills, including managerial decisions about layout and batch size (Ayoubi 1981). The production continuity may be a given for lower-level employees, but is to some degree a choice for management. Hence production continuity is partially the result of a decision about social organization, not wholly a material factor. Thus the technology thesis of Woodward is to some extent about how one aspect of organizational structure affects other aspects (Burrell and Morgan 1979, p. 223 n. 30). This places a qualification against any tendency to interpret Woodward's technology work as being about how hard impersonal technology molds the soft human organization.

Underlying Connections in Organic Theory

Burns and Stalker (1961), Hage and Aiken (1970), Lawrence and Lorsch (1967), Perrow (1967), and Woodward (1965) all argue that structure is contingent upon the uncertainty of the task facing the organization, and that this uncertainty relates to technology. The task uncertainty results from either the environmentally induced innovation, for Burns and Stalker, Hage and Aiken, and Lawrence and Lorsch, or raw materials for Perrow, or the internal organizational production set-up for Woodward. The uncertainty of the tasks facing organizational members is raised by innovation, unanalyzable raw material with many exceptions, or automation. Thus these studies have in common the contingency factor of task uncertainty related to technology. Moreover, the studies argue that low task uncertainty requires a centralized, formalized structure of the mechanistic type, whereas high task uncertainty requires a participatory structure of the organic type. Thus the studies all conclude that high task uncertainty requires an organic structure, so that they subscribe to the organic theory. The task uncertainty contingency and required structure of these organizational-level studies echoes that of the group decision-making studies in micro-OB (Leavitt 1951), so providing a connection between the macro-OB and micro-OB contingency theories.

However, not all contingency theories of organizational structure connect task uncertainty and organizational structure. As seen above, Thompson (1967) argues that the linkages among the tasks being performed by the organization, that is, the task interdependence, constitute another contingency. There is, however, a commonality between Thompson and these other authors. For all of them the contingency factor is the task: task uncertainty for Burns and Stalker, Hage and Aiken, Lawrence and Lorsch, Perrow, and Woodward, and task interdependence for Thompson. Thus there is considerable unity here.

These contributions to the contingency theory of organizational structure are all discussing one contingency factor, the task, that has two dimensions, uncertainty and interdependence. In this way, far from being a plethora of theories with no unifying connections, the stream of contingency theory research flowing from the seminal work of Burns and Stalker, Hage and Aiken, Lawrence and Lorsch, Perrow, Thompson, and Woodward can be seen as a highly coherent theory.

Indeed one might go farther with this conceptual synthesis by suggesting that task interdependence may be mainly reducible to task uncertainty. A closer examination of each of three types of task interdependence reveals that they require their corresponding coordination mechanism because of task uncertainty. The reason why reciprocal interdependence cannot be coordinated through planning and requires mutual adjustment (i.e., ad hoc coordination) would seem to be implicitly because the future interactions cannot be predicted (Thompson 1967). The crucial aspect is thus not that the interdependence is reciprocal (i.e., two way) or that it may be frequent, but that it is uncertain. Hence a reciprocal interaction requires mutual adjustment because it is highly uncertain rather than because it is reciprocally interdependent. Similarly, the distinction between pooled and sequential interdependence is really just whether there is an indirect or a direct relationship between two organizational subunits (Thompson 1967). If there is a direct relationship between them, then that flow needs coordination by planning, so that one subunit can efficiently deal with inputs it receives from the other. But this assumes that the flow is fairly predictable and that task uncertainty is at least moderate. Again, Thompson (1967) states that pooled interdependence requires coordination through rules and standardization, but this assumes that the (indirect) relationship between subunits is highly predictable, so that task uncertainty is low. If the relationship is unpredictable, then coordination by rules is not possible and so other means of coordination would be required, such as discussion, so the theory breaks down. Thus the three modes of interdependence and coordination mechanisms that Thompson posits are based on the assumption that the three interdependencies correspond to a scale of increasing task uncertainty. If they do not, then the three coordination modes (pooled, sequential, and reciprocal) specified by the theory would not be fits. Hence the theory is better stated as progressively greater uncertainty in the task interaction between two organizational subunits that leads to coordination by standardization, planning, and mutual adjustment, respectively. Thus the theory of task interdependence and coordination mechanisms is better formulated as a theory about task uncertainty and coordination mechanisms. This component of the task interdependence theory can then be subsumed under task uncertainty theory.

Another component of the theory of task interdependence is that each type of task interdependence should be located at different levels in the hierarchy, thus giving the definition and grouping of organizational subunits: pooled at the top, sequential in the middle, and reciprocal at the bottom (Thompson 1967). Yet this conclusion can be reached by stating that the types of interdependence correspond to degrees of intensity of interaction: pooled (nil or low), sequential (medium), and reciprocal (high). The theory is that activities that need intense interaction should be placed near to each other organizationally. The more intense the interaction, the organizationally closer the activities should be in order to facilitate their interaction. Therefore activities with low interaction are placed in different divisions, which become the primary organizational subunits at the top of the hierarchy. Activities with medium interaction are placed within the same divisions, as adjacent departments or sections, which become the subunits in the middle of the hierarchy. Activities with high interaction are placed within the same sections, as adjacent jobs, which become the subunits at the bottom of the hierarchy. Thus intensity of interaction governs position in the hierarchy. Hence task interdependence can be reconceptualized into task uncertainty and intensity of interaction.

For instance, consider again the argument of Lorsch and Lawrence (1972) that greater task interdependence between departments increases the coordination required and so leads to the use of coordination mechanisms additional to hierarchy, contacts between departments, and planning. In the container firms, the sequential task interdependence between functional departments was handled effectively through planning by the hierarchy (Lorsch and Lawrence 1972). But this rests on the uncertainty of the task being low: customer demand is predictable for the upcoming period, manufacturing resources are stable, and upper management possesses adequate knowledge of technical processes because of low innovation. Similarly, in the plastics firms the reciprocal task interdependence between functional departments was handled effectively by mutual adjustment, through cross-functional project teams facilitated by integrators (Lorsch and Lawrence 1972).

But this rests on the uncertainty of the task being high, so that many novel problems had to be solved through discussion between the functional departments, involving intense interactions between them that could not be completely scheduled because interactions could not be predicted. Therefore cross-functional project teams were required so that representatives of each functional department were brought together to foster intense interaction. Internally these teams organized themselves by mutual adjustment because the uncertainty precluded planning of their task interactions. Overall, where task uncertainty is low (e.g., container firms), the interaction between functions is of low intensity, so that their effective coordination is achieved by hierarchical planning. Conversely, where task uncertainty is high (e.g., plastics firms), the interaction between functions is of high intensity, so that effective coordination is achieved by mutual adjustment. Thus for Lorsch and Lawrence (1972), like Thompson (1967), the task interdependence contingency decomposes into task uncertainty and intensity of interaction.

Decomposing task interdependence into task uncertainty and intensity of interaction gives a clearer theory. It also means that task interdependence becomes largely subsumed under task uncertainty, thus increasing theoretical coherency and parsimony. Task uncertainty is a contingency of coordination mechanisms. Interaction intensity is the contingency of location in the hierarchy.

Conclusions

The key idea in the organic theory of organizational structure is that mechanistic structure, which emphasizes hierarchy, is effective for low task uncertainty; and organic structure, which emphasizes participation, is effective for high task uncertainty. The pioneering organic theories have this idea as an underlying theoretical commonality, which their empirical studies support.

A major source of task uncertainty is innovation, much of which comes ultimately from the environment of the organization, such as technological and market change. The mechanistic organizational structure is shown to fit an environment of a low rate of market and technological change. Conversely, the organic organizational structure is shown to fit an environment of a high rate of market and technological change. Increasing environmental uncertainty increases differentiation, so that some parts of the organization deal with much of the uncertainty that is entailed by innovation and become organic, while other parts are mechanistic.

Similarly, contingency research into operations technology held that advances in operations technology lead from organic to mechanistic and then organic structures. At the highest levels of task certainty, operations could be automated so that the human organization mainly dealt with the residual uncertain elements and had to be participatory.

The main other contingency factor to emerge from organic theory research into organizational structure was a second dimension of the task: task interdependence. Innovation leads to reciprocal interdependence between functional departments, which requires integration by means of cross-functional project teams using open problem solving, that is to say, organic elements added to the overall structures. While task interdependence is usually treated as a separate contingency from task uncertainty, a closer examination reveals that much in the task interdependence contingency is reducible to task uncertainty, thereby marking an even greater coherency to the organic theory.

The organic theory of organizational structure produces a consistent theoretical model. There is considerable empirical research support for organic theory overall. The link between task uncertainty and organic structure is well established. The connection of organic structures with higher innovation rates is empirically supported. The connections among task uncertainty, differentiation, integration, and performance are also empirically supported. The relationship between task interdependence (or interaction intensity) and position of organizational subunits in the hierarchy is also empirically supported. Only for operations technology is the empirical evidence such as to engender doubt about the validity of the theory (as will be discussed in Chapter 5).

In sum, organic theory is a cogent and coherent theory that is supported by empirical research, so that it constitutes a major component of the contingency theory of organizational structure and a significant part of organizational science.

3 Bureaucracy Theory
and Research

D espite the success of organic theory research, it is challenged by
bureaucracy theory, which has a different model of organizational
structure and its contingencies. Bureaucracy theory argues that structural formalization is accompanied not by centralization, but by
decentralization. For bureaucracy theory the main contingency is not
task but organizational size. Bureaucracy theory research has been at
least as successful as organic theory. In this chapter we will discuss
bureaucracy theory and its attendant research. The success of this challenge to organic theory poses the question of the relationship between
these two theories. We will argue that both may be brought together in
a parsimonious model of organizational structure. Moreover, the key
contingencies of each, task uncertainty and size, may be causally
connected, thereby furthering the coherence of structural contingency
theory as a whole.

As we saw in Chapter 1, bureaucracy theory holds that there are
three interrelated aspects of structure: bureaucratic structure (specialization-formalization, decentralization), structural differentiation,

and divisionalization. We will now examine in greater detail bureaucracy theory and research. We will begin with outlining the theory and research on bureaucratic structure, then that on structural differentiation and on divisionalization. Throughout much of this discussion size will be the main contingency, with task (i.e., task interdependence) a minor contingency. We will then discuss whether certain other causes of organizational structure are contingencies or not, in the process defining the criterion for a cause to be a contingency. Finally, we will attend to the issue of synthesizing the bureaucracy with the organic theory, in a way that follows on from, but goes farther than, the brief synthesis offered at the end of Chapter 1.

Bureaucracy Theory

Bureaucracy theory (Blau, 1970, 1972; Child 1973a) in its modern form emerged from a series of empirical studies. However, from the outset of modern research, thinking about bureaucracy was strongly influenced by the Weberian model of bureaucratic organizational structure, which omitted the idea of participation that is so central to organic theory.

Weber (1968) held that there was a general, historical tendency for administration to move toward the bureaucratic type. The bureaucratic structure features full-time, salaried, career administrators who are appointed on merit, technically qualified, arranged in a hierarchy, and subject to rules and discipline (Weber 1964, pp. 333-334). Bureaucracy possessed several advantages including efficiency, predictability, reliability, and the "stringency of its discipline" (Weber 1964, p. 337). The development of bureaucratic structure is promoted by a number of factors, including size and communications technologies (Weber 1964, pp. 338-339). Bureaucratic theory led to a number of empirical studies that used qualitative methods to make case studies of organizations (Crozier 1964; Gouldner 1954; Selznick 1949). In contrast to Weber, these studies identified negative consequences of bureaucracy, thereby questioning the superior effectiveness that Weber attributed to bureaucracy.

Weber (1968) advanced his theory in terms of ideal-types, that is, comparison of real organizations by contrasting them with types so pure that they do not exist. The ideal-types of authority structures included bureaucracy, charisma, and traditionalism. The ideal-types yield imaginary continua that run between each of two ideal-types so that an actual organization is located somewhere along this line. Given more than two ideal-types, with imaginary lines running between each pair, each actual organization is really positioned in a multi-dimensional space. However, in the absence of measurement of these dimensions, the location of the organization in the space cannot be stated precisely and analysis becomes vague. For organizational analysis to become scientific it needed to develop multidimensional measures (Price 1972, 1997). Therefore researchers sought to develop measures of each of the aspects of Weberian bureaucracy (Hinings, Pugh, Hickson, and Turner 1967).

The Aston Group (named after the University of Aston, in Birmingham, England) identified four main aspects of organizational structure, for each of which they developed a multi-item measurement scale (Pugh et al. 1963; see also Donaldson 1997). The variables are specialization, standardization, formalization, and centralization (Pugh, Hickson, Hinings, and Turner 1968). *Centralization* is how far up the hierarchy decisions are taken. *Specialization* is the division of labor in the administrative work of the organization; it is measured by a scale of functional specialization that assesses the degree to which administrative work has been specialized by functions. There is also a scale of role specialization that examines specialization within each function, which correlates with functional specialization. *Standardization* is the degree to which work is governed by rules, procedures, and scientific methods. *Formalization* is the extent of paperwork, such as for defining procedures and jobs, recording performance, and passing information. Child (1973a) later called this variable "documentation," which is more descriptive. Moreover, other researchers, especially in the United States, use *formalization* to refer to documentation and standardization together (e.g., Hage and Aiken 1967a). Therefore we will call the Aston formalization variable by the term *documentation*, and use *formalization* to refer to both documentation and standardization.

The Aston Group also gathered data on what they termed *configuration*, which is a variegated assortment of measures of reporting relationships, such as the number of levels in the hierarchy, which they termed *vertical span*, and the span of control of the CEO, together with the proportion of employees in each specialism. Most variables of configuration are measured by single indicators, rather than the multi-item scales used for the main structural variables (Pugh et al. 1968).

The Aston Group took each of the aspects of bureaucracy in the Weberian ideal-type, measured it, and then looked to see which variables went together empirically to form the dimensions of a multi-dimensional space (Pugh et al. 1968). The Group compared the structures of a sample of organizations through a quantitative analysis. The Aston Group and their later colleagues conducted numerous empirical studies, of which the original one is called the Aston Study. This study compared the organizational structures of fifty-two diverse work organizations, including manufacturing, retail, and governmental (Pugh et al. 1968). It found that specialization, standardization, documentation, and vertical span were strongly, positively correlated. In a factor analysis these three variables formed one factor called *structuring of activities.*

Centralization was in a second factor, *concentration of authority,* which was independent of structuring (see also Pugh, Hickson, and Hinings 1969). However, in a subsequent, nationally representative sample (the National Study), Child (1972a) found that centralization and structuring were not independent dimensions but rather opposite poles of the same dimension. He stated that Weber's theory posited bureaucracy as containing delegation so that structuring and decentralization should be expected to be positively correlated and form part of the same factor in factor analysis. Studies subsequent to the Aston and National Studies have investigated the underlying factorial dimensions of organizational structure (e.g., Reimann 1973, 1974), though Starbuck (1981) has noted that this question received less importance after the initial studies (see also Pugh 1981a, 1981b). But even without factor analysis, the positive correlations between specialization-formalization and decentralization in later studies (e.g., Donaldson and Warner 1974; Grinyer and Yasai-Ardekani 1980; Hinings and Lee 1971; Routamaa 1985), as is confirmed by a meta-analytic review (Wagner, Buchko, and Gooding 1988), tend to support the view of Child that structuring and decentralization are part of the same dimension.

In summary, the Aston Group found that bureaucratic structure is composed of specialization, formalization, decentralization, and vertical span.

The Aston Group studied the context of the organization, which was a large number of variables including contingency factors, some inside the organization and others in its environment (Pugh and Hickson 1976; Pugh and Hinings 1976; Pugh and Payne 1977). The main finding to emerge from the Aston Group studies of organizational context is that size (meaning the number of employees) is a contingency of organizational structure. Size is positively correlated with the structuring of activities (i.e., specialization and formalization; Pugh, Hickson, Hinings, and Turner 1969). Size is also positively correlated with vertical span, that is, the number of levels in the hierarchy. The major replication of the Aston Study, the National Study by Child (1973a), also found size to be an important correlate of organizational structure, as did numerous subsequent studies (Pugh and Hinings 1976). Bureaucratic structuring, such as specialization, formalization, and decentralization, increases as size increases, but at a decreasing rate with respect to size (Child 1973a). Thus while size growth increases bureaucratization, the rate at which it does so decreases with successive size increments. Hence while large organizations are more bureaucratic than small ones, they are much less so than would be the case if the difference was proportionate to their size differences. This curvilinear relationship becomes linear if size is transformed logarithmically, which is a reason why size is usually transformed in bureaucracy research (other reasons are to reduce the effects of outliers and to make the size distribution less skewed and more normal; see Blau and Schoenherr 1971; Child 1973a).

Child (1972a) argued that larger organizations have taller hierarchies down which authority is delegated, but such delegated authority is circumscribed by the increasing structuring of activities. Size growth weakens the direct control over lower levels by top management, which instead relies more on the indirect controls provided by bureaucratic structure, such as written job descriptions, rules, and procedures. Thus middle- and lower-level managers exercise more authority in large, than in small, organizations, but they are hedged around by tight job definitions, rules, procedures, and paperwork that limit their discretion. Thus centralization and structuring may be thought of as *substitute means of control* (though Child 1972a preferred to call them "alternative means of control"). There is a trade-off between the two means of control: centralization and specialization-formalization (Zeffane 1989a).

In sum, size leads to a taller hierarchy, decentralization, and structuring, thereby shifting top management control over employees from centralization (i.e., direct means) to specialization-formalization (i.e., indirect means).

The relationship of size and most of the major Aston structural variables, that is, specialization, standardization, and documentation, were replicated in subsequent, empirical field studies (Donaldson 1996b, pp. 137-143) that covered organizations in diverse countries and of diverse types. (The data from many of these studies are available in the Aston Data Bank; Richards 1980.) For example, size has been shown to correlate positively with specialization in forty studies that used the Aston scale. These include sixteen countries: Algeria, Canada, Egypt, Finland, France, Germany, Hong Kong, India, Iran, Japan, Jordan, Poland, Singapore, Sweden, the United Kingdom, and the United States. They include also the following different types of organizations: banks, churches, colleges, governmental, labor unions, manufacturing firms, and hospitals (for details see Donaldson 1996b, pp. 138-139). These studies are reported in Ayoubi (1981), Azumi and McMillan (1981), Badran and Hinings (1981), Blau, Falbe, McKinley, and Tracy (1976), Bryman, Beardsworth, Keil, and Ford (1983), Child and Kieser (1979), Clark (1990), Conaty, Mahmoudi, and Miller (1983), Donaldson and Warner (1974), Glueck (unpublished, in Aston Data Bank), Greenwood and Hinings (1976a), Grinyer and Yasai-Ardekani (1981), Heron (unpublished, in Aston Data Bank), Hickson, Hinings, McMillan, and Schwitter (1974), Hinings and Lee (1971), Hinings, Ranson, and Bryman (1976), Kuc, Hickson, and McMillan (1981), Payne and Mansfield (1973), Pugh and Hickson (1976), Reimann (1977), Routamaa (1985), Shenoy (1981), Tauber (1968), Wong and Birnbaum-More (1994), and Zeffane (1989b; some sources report more than one study).

A meta-analytic review concluded that the size-specialization relationship generalizes and has a positive, mean correlation of .53 across twenty-seven studies, totaling 1,066 organizations (Miller 1987, p. 317, Table 2). Another meta-analysis of a slightly different set of studies (35, totaling 1,241 organizations) calculated a similar, positive correlation of .61 and showed that, correcting for the reliability of the specialization scale, the true correlation is .82 (Donaldson 1986, p. 90, Table 9), which is considerable. For standardization, its mean correlation was .55, across nine studies (309 organizations; Donaldson 1986, pp. 80-81), which corrected is a true correlation of .69 (Donaldson 1986, p. 90, Table 9). For documentation, its mean correlation was .42, across twenty-four studies (834 organizations) in Miller (1987, p. 317, Table 2) and .51 across twenty studies (595 organizations) in Donaldson (1986, pp. 82-83), which corrected is a true correlation of .59 (Donaldson 1986, p. 90, Table 9).

In summary, the general relationships are: size and specialization are correlated over .8, size and standardization are correlated almost .7, and size and documentation are correlated almost .6. Size and specialization are very closely related, while size and formalization (i.e., standardization and documentation) are closely related. Thus increasing organizational size leads to greater bureaucratic structuring, that is, specialization, rules and procedures, and paperwork, in organizations of many types around the world, consistent with Weber (1964).

The main exception is centralization that is not consistently correlated with size in the replication studies (Donaldson 1986; Miller 1987). There probably is a general relationship between size and decentralization, but technical problems in the measurement of decentralization obscure it in many studies (Greenwood and Hinings 1976b; Grinyer and Yasai-Ardekani 1980; Lincoln, Hanada, and McBride 1986; Mansfield 1973; Marsh 1992). Moreover, size effects on decentralization can easily be confounded by public accountability because that can have an effect of similar magnitude as size. A more thorough understanding of the relationships among size, public accountability, and decentralization needs to be attained through future research.

Public accountability measures the distinction between private-sector firms and public-sector (i.e., governmental) organizations. Private-sector firms are traditionally free to pursue profitability, whereas public-sector organizations are traditionally exposed to demands for compliance with a broad range of public concerns for which they are held accountable through their board of directors (Pugh et al. 1969). Thus publicly accountable organizations are more centralized, whereas private-sector firms are more decentralized because they give more discretion to the managers as long as they produce acceptable performance on a limited range of measures, for example, profitability. The positive correlation between public accountability and centralization is quite important and is at least as important as size across a number of studies (Pugh et al. 1969; Richards 1980).

The main scales used by the Aston Group, such as specialization and standardization, were constructed from items that were conceptually closely related. These are the most useful scales and are those involved in the main findings for which their research has become known, such as the positive correlation between size and structuring. However, some of the scales derived after data collection by factor analysis are not always so conceptually meaningful. For example, they identified a factor of context that they called dependence, which was composed of an assortment of scales (Pugh et al. 1969). The conceptual coherence of this factor has been criticized (Mindlin and Aldrich 1975).

Fit and Performance

The Aston Study is written in a primarily descriptive way, reporting associations among variables; however, there is a sense that the structures studied are playing a constructive role, without claiming them to be the most effective (Pugh and Hickson 1976; Pugh and Hinings 1976). The interpretation is vaguely functionalist but without much causal theory. Child (1972a, 1973a) provides more of a theoretical interpretation. This includes theory of the contingency type. Organizations of larger size needed to adopt more structuring in order to provide more indirect control over employees, because direct control was being diluted by decentralization (Child 1972a, 1973a). This led to the expectation that organizations of larger size would have higher performance if they had greater structuring, whereas they would have lower performance if they had less structuring. The underlying logic was of the contingency theory type. There is a fit between size and structuring such that larger organizations require more structuring than smaller organizations (Child 1975). Organizations that are in fit (e.g., a large organization with high structuring) will consequently have higher performance than those in misfit (e.g., a large organization with only medium structuring). Child (1975) showed empirically this relationship between fit (of structuring to size) and performance (see also Khandwalla 1973). Thus the Aston Group revealed that size is a contingency of organizational structure.

Structural Differentiation

The idea of size as a contingency of organizational structure received considerable support also from the work of Blau and his colleagues. Blau advanced an argument that size increase led to pervasive changes in organizational structure. Some of these are that increasing size leads to more bureaucratic structuring such as specialization, rules, and documents, and more decentralization (Blau and Schoenherr 1971). This aspect of his theory closely parallels the arguments of the Aston Group and helps support the idea that size causes bureaucracy, understood as structuring with decentralization. Blau and Schoenherr (1971) argue that size causes a shift from direct to more indirect forms of control, again similar to the Aston Group. However, in regard to the specialization aspect of structuring Blau made a much more in-depth argument. The specialization of roles, as studied by the Aston Group, is part of the more encompassing concept of structural differentiation advanced by Blau (1970).

Structural differentiation refers to the breaking up of the organization along any dimension (Blau 1970). As instances, the number of divisions, the number of sections in each division, the number of occupational job titles, and the number of levels in the hierarchy are all aspects of structural differentiation. Structural differentiation refers to the shape of the hierarchy rather than to the differences in the attitudes of the employees and controls in different departments that Lawrence and Lorsch (1967) term *differentiation* (which was discussed in the previous chapter). Blau (1970) presents a highly abstract formal theory of the effect of size on structural differentiation. The theory is rigorously deduced from a few basic axioms. The main ideas are as follows.

Structural differentiation increases with size, but at a decreasing rate with respect to size (Blau 1970). Thus structural differentiation increases as size increases, but its slope becomes shallower at larger size, so that the curve flattens out somewhat from initially being steep at smaller sizes to being shallow at larger sizes (see Figure 3.1). Initial increments in size produce greater increases in structural differentiation than increments of the same magnitude when the organization is larger in size. The rate at which structure becomes more differentiated as size increases, decreases with increasing size. This relation with size is shown empirically for many aspects of structural differentiation,

Structural Differentiation

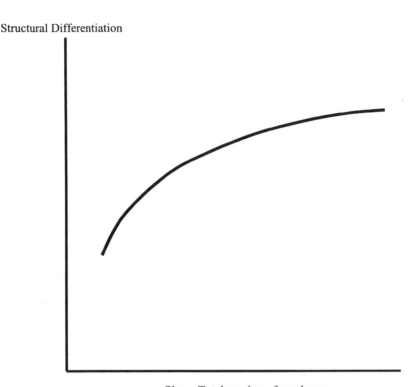

Size = Total number of employees

Figure 3.1. Size and Structural Differention

such as the number of divisions, the number of job titles, and the number of levels in the hierarchy (Blau and Schoenherr 1971). Another related theoretical proposition is that the average size of an organizational component, for example, a division, grows larger as the size of the overall organization increases. Again, the average span of control (the number reporting directly to a manager) increases as organizational size increases (Blau 1970), at a decreasing rate with respect to size. This proposition leads in turn to one of the most unexpected parts of Blau's theory.

The conventional wisdom is that as organizations grow in size they become top heavy. The increasingly tall hierarchy visible as organizations grow in size, leads, it is widely believed, to a rapid growth in managers and their associated administrative staff relative to the increase in operating personnel. Critics assert that there is a disproportionate growth in managers and administrators to workers as organizations grow in size (Parkinson 1957), leading to excessive overhead cost and loss of speed and effectiveness. Thus, in this view, the proportion of total employees who are managers and administrators would be expected to rise with increasing organizational size. However, Blau (1970) showed empirically the opposite: that the proportion of total employees who are managers and administrators decreases with increasing organizational size. Thus, far from being top heavy, large organizations enjoy economies of scale in administration. This challenges the standard economic doctrine, which is that large organizations have economies of scale in production and procurement, but diseconomies in administration.

Blau's theory explains the economies of scale in administration in the following way (Blau 1970). Because the number of levels in the hierarchy increases with increasing size, if the span of control remained constant with increasing size, then the ratio of managers to workers would rise as size increases. However, as noted above, the span of control actually increases with increasing organizational size, sufficiently that the ratio of managers to workers actually decreases as size increases, producing the economies of scale in administration. The span of control increases with increasing size for two reasons. First, organizations use more bureaucratic structuring (e.g., rules) as they grow larger and this relieves managers of having to make decisions, so permitting their spans of control to widen. Second, as organizations grow larger, jobs become more specialized, hence jobs within a work group become more homogenous, making supervision easier, so that, again, the spans of control of supervisors and managers widen. These two factors are only partially countered by an opposite tendency: the increasing complexity of the more structurally differentiated larger organization makes its coordination more difficult, so consuming managerial time and reducing their spans of control. The former two factors combined are stronger than the latter single factor, so that increasing organizational size leads to wider spans of control and thus produces economies of scale in administration.

The proportion of total employees who are managers and administrative staff may be referred to as the *administrative intensity* of an organization. As just discussed, the relationship between size and

Administrative Intensity

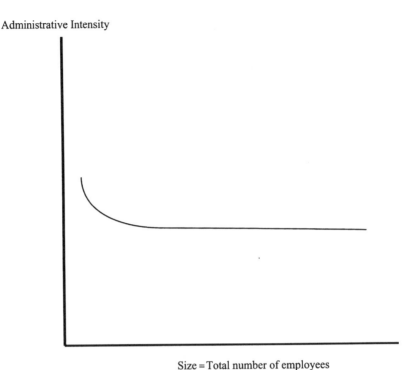

Size = Total number of employees

Figure 3.2. Size and Administrative Intensity

administrative intensity is negative. Moreover, it is curvilinear, rather than linear (see Figure 3.2). *Administrative intensity* decreases with size at a decreasing rate with respect to size (Blau 1970). Thus, while economy of scale is greater for larger than smaller organizations, its rate of increase tapers off as size increases (Blau 1970). This negative curvilinear relationship between size and administrative intensity is rendered linear by transforming size logarithmically (see Blau and Schoenherr 1971). As just seen, administrative intensity decreases with increasing size because formalization and span of control increase with increasing size. However, as also seen, both formalization and span of control increase at a decreasing rate with increasing size. Therefore the rate at which economies of scale in administration increase as size increases, decreases as size increases.

There are other aspects and subtleties to Blau's theory of structural differentiation. Here we have discussed some of the main points for which his theory is best known. Blau's theory of structural differentiation gives us a clear theoretical model of how the hierarchy develops as the organization grows in size. The theory encompasses many aspects, both vertical (e.g., hierarchy) and horizontal (e.g., number of divisions), that are applicable across work organizations of all types. Thus the theory gives us the fundamental anatomical structure (i.e., reporting relationships such as shown on an organization chart) onto which other variables can be added, such as the distribution of decisions (centralization) or the use of rules and procedures (structuring). The combination of this model of structural differentiation together with bureaucratization captures many of the important features of how organizational structure changes with increasing organizational size.

The relationships between organizational size and numerous aspects of structural differentiation that Blau and Schoenherr (1971) found have been replicated in many empirical studies (see Blau 1972), including private-sector organizations (e.g., Goldman 1973) and labor unions (Jarley, Fiorito, and Delaney 1997, p. 852, Table 2). Also, the relationships hold in countries other than the United States, for example, Britain (Child 1973a) and Germany (Child and Kieser 1979). Thus the size-structural differentiation relationship generalizes. Argyris (1972) argues that the relationships between size and structural differentiation found by Blau are created by U.S. civil service regulations. Yet, as we have just seen, these same relationships are found in commercial organizations and in those outside the United States, supporting Blau's original interpretation that there is a general causal connection between size and structure. Blau's theory has attracted a considerable critical literature (Childers, Mayhew, and Gray 1971; Hummon 1971; Mayhew, James, and Childers 1972; Meyer 1971; Sprecht 1973), some of which has stimulated response from Blau (1971). Meyer (1979) found in a study over time that there was also a substantial effect of the time of founding of the organization, additional to that of size. Daft and

Bradshaw (1980) show that while administrative differentiation in universities is caused by size, differentiation of academic departments is much less so and is more caused by the rise of new specialisms in the wider academic community related to the growth of knowledge and student demand. Thus there are limits to the generalizability of Blau's theory. There have been other criticisms of Blau's theory (e.g., Marsh and Mannari 1989), some of which have been rebutted (see Donaldson 1996b, pp. 58-107), while others (e.g., Freeman and Hannan 1975; Freeman and Kronenfeld 1973) will be rebutted in Chapter 6.

The negative relationship between size and administrative intensity that Blau and Schoenherr (1971) found empirically and explained theoretically is found also in subsequent empirical studies (Goldman 1973; Hickson, Pugh, and Pheysey 1969; Hinings and Lee 1971; Van de Ven and Ferry 1980). There is some variation in findings, with a study finding no relationship (Holdaway et al. 1975) and some studies a positive relationship that contradicts the theory (Al-Jibouri 1983; Ayoubi 1981; Marsh and Mannari 1981). However, a meta-analytic review finds that the average correlation between organizational size and the proportion of managers is −.45 (for details see Donaldson 1996b, pp. 104-105). Thus on balance the bulk of evidence supports Blau's theory that increasing size leads to a lower proportion of managers and staff to total employees (see also Marsden, Cook, and Kalleberg 1994). While this encourages the view that bureaucratization is functional, this really requires some closer examination of the economics. For declining proportions of managers and staff to directly raise efficiency, the cost of these personnel must also be declining. Yet larger organizations have more hierarchical levels and each level tends to receive higher salary and other benefits, so that the average cost per manager could possibly rise with increasing size. Therefore the question arises as to whether the decline in the proportion of managers as size increases is sufficient to more than offset the rise in their average costs. Yet personnel costs are not the ultimate yardstick, because even if the average costs of managers were increasing as organizations grew, this could be more than counteracted if managers increased organizational performance by enhancing effectiveness. Thus the question becomes whether the performance per manager is rising as size increases. Thus there is a need for future inquiry to examine in more detail issues of personnel costs and performance relative to the size of the managerial component, to address more definitively the issue of economies of scale in administration.

As we have seen, the Aston Group found that bureaucracy was composed of specialization, formalization, decentralization, and vertical span. Clearly, vertical span is a vertical aspect of structural differentiation in Blau's terms. Moreover, conceptually the Aston functional specialization variable would be subsumed under structural differentiation, as a horizontal aspect (Child 1973a). Thus the Aston model of bureaucracy can be said to be composed of formalization, decentralization, and structural differentiation. This accords with the model of bureaucracy that emerges from Blau's research (Blau and Schoenherr 1971). Thus both the Aston Group and Blau find that bureaucracy is composed of formalization, decentralization, and structural differentiation, with the complementarities being that the Aston Group had a fuller set of measures of formalization, while Blau measured a fuller set of aspects of structural differentiation.

The work of the Aston Group and Blau has been confirmed in a large study of a diverse range of establishments in the United States (numbering more than 600). This found that size was positively related to the number of departments and vertical levels (Marsden et al. 1994, p. 914), that is, to structural differentiation. Also, size was positively related to formalization and decentralization (Marsden et al. 1994, p. 914). Furthermore, the structuring cluster was extended by showing that internal labor markets correlate positively with formalization, as Weber theorized, and with size (Marsden et al. 1994, p. 914). Size was also negatively related to administrative intensity, showing economies of scale. The findings are synthesized into a causal model (Marsden et al. 1994, p. 914, Figure 1), in which (simplifying) size causes departments that cause formalization, which reduces administrative intensity; size also causes vertical levels that cause decentralization, which reduces administrative intensity (the causal model will be further discussed in Chapter 4). In this way the Aston and Blau elements of structure are integrated into one causal model that empirically validates the theory that size causes formalization, decentralization, and structural differentiation.

Both the Aston Group and Blau argue that size is an important determinant of organizational structure. Moreover, both are at least broadly compatible with contingency theory in that effective structures for large organizations are different from effective structures for small organizations, so that size moderates the relationship between structure and performance. Thus the contingency theory of organizational structure includes also a recognizable school of thought in bureaucracy theory, which argued the importance of size as a contingency of organizational structure. This bureaucracy theory school had a unity to its work in the same way that the organic theory had a unity. Clearly each school championed a different model of organizational structure and a different contingency factor (size or task) as being the more important.

There was a further theoretical significance of the Aston Group and Blau. As noted above, Weber (1964) asserted the positive functions of bureaucracy; however, later studies argued that bureaucratic structure produced dysfunctions, such as rigidity, low output, and even subversion of organizational goals (Crozier 1964; Gouldner 1954; Merton 1949; Selznick 1949). This offered a counter to Weber and argued the recalcitrance of human beings subject to attempts at top-down controls and that human organizations to some extent have a life of their own, that is, the emergent view of organization (Scott 1992). The dysfunctions of bureaucracy were shown empirically by case study methods (Crozier 1964; Gouldner 1954; Selznick 1949). In contrast, the Aston Group and Blau instead used quantitative comparisons across organizations and produced a far more positive account of bureaucracy. They lent support to Weber by arguing that bureaucracy, a top-down organizational structure, is effective for large organizations and even produces economies of scale in administration. While there may well be dysfunctional consequences to bureaucracy, as the case studies revealed, bureaucracy has positive functions that more than compensate for them. By comparing whole organizations and their overall performances, the bureaucracy theory research of the Aston Group and Blau was able to show the overall positive effect of bureaucracy that the case studies could not examine. Further, while bureaucracy theory measured centralization and formalization, that is, some aspects of organic structure, there is no measurement in their research of other aspects of the organic structure, such as participation or lateral communications (Pugh et al. 1968). This displays the lack of adherence to the organic model by the followers of bureaucracy theory and the extent to which they focused on Weberian bureaucracy theory.

Divisionalization

As argued in Chapter 1, *divisionalization* is a component of bureaucratic structure. It refers to the structure at the apex, that is, the way the work of the organization is divided among the senior managers who report to the CEO. In a functional structure the work is divided into different functions, such as manufacturing and sales, so that these are the major groupings in the organization (Child 1984). In contrast, in a divisional structure the work is divided into different divisions, such as by products or customers or regions, so that these are the major groupings in the organization (Child 1984). Divisionalization is mainly caused by the need to fit strategy, such as diversification, which is its major contingency. The diversification contingency is, in turn, part of the more abstract contingency of task interdependence. Related structural types, such as multinational and matrix structures, are also components of bureaucratic structure that are affected by the task interdependence contingency.

Divisionalization should be considered to be a part of the bureaucratic type of structure. It is positively related to bureaucracy. Divisionalization is associated with greater levels of bureaucratic structuring: functional specialization, professional qualifications, documentation, and vertical span (Grinyer and Yasai-Ardekani 1981, p. 478). Moreover, divisionalization is also associated with decentralization (Chenhall 1979; Grinyer and Yasai-Ardekani 1981, p. 478), empirically confirming that the divisional structure is a decentralized organizational structure (Chandler 1962). Thus when a large firm divisionalizes, this is not a move away from bureaucracy but rather increases bureaucracy. The decentralization of the divisional structure does not imply that it becomes less bureaucratic, rather it is displaying the familiar general pattern of the bureaucratic model of becoming more bureaucratically structured while becoming more decentralized. Thus divisionalization is just a further stage in the process of gradual change over time from a simple (i.e., unbureaucratic) structure to a highly bureaucratic structure.

Chandler (1962) argued that strategy leads to structure so that diversification leads to divisionalization. He showed that corporations that diversified needed to adopt the divisional structure that matched their diversified operations, so that there is a fit between divisionalization and strategy as a contingency. In this way Chandler contributes to contingency theories of organizational structure, though being a historian he did not state it as a contingency theory. Chandler (1962) intensively analyzes the histories of four large U.S. corporations. He concludes that there is a pattern whereby after changing their strategy they eventually changed their organizational structure, so that strategy led to structure. In particular, firms diversified and so changed from functional to divisional structures because the latter allowed more effective management of diversified corporations. In a broader survey of seventy other large U.S. firms he finds the same pattern (Chandler 1962). Thus, for Chandler, undiversified firms can be effectively managed by a functional structure, but diversified firms need a divisional structure to operate effectively. Subsequent writers have formalized these insights to argue that the greater information-processing requirement posed by diversified operations makes imperative the adoption of a structure in which each separate product-market operates as a self-contained business by being an autonomous division (Galbraith 1973). This marks a formal contingency theory of the connection between structure at the apex of the firm and strategy as the contingency factor. Whereas departments of a functionally structured firm are treated as cost and revenue centers, the divisions in a divisionalized firm are profit centers. This is a shift from control over means to control over ends (Mintzberg 1979). The separation of the corporate head office from divisional management separates strategic from operational decision making, which helps make strategic decisions more objective and beneficial for the long-run interests of the overall firm (Chandler 1962).

Chandler's seminal study has led to a considerable body of work that confirms the original thesis, shows its generality beyond the United States and extends it in various ways. Whereas Chandler (1962) conducted case histories and classified them to reveal patterns, subsequent researchers have measured strategic and structural variables and used statistical analyses to test for connections. Such studies have confirmed Chandler's insight that diversification is a major cause of divisionalization among large U.S. corporations (Fligstein 1985; Mahoney 1992; Palmer, Friedland, Jennings, and Powers 1987; Palmer, Jennings, and Zhou 1993; Rumelt 1974). Studies of large corporations in other countries have shown that strategy leads to structure in those countries also. This holds true for Australia, Canada, France, Germany, Italy, Japan, New Zealand, and the United Kingdom (Capon, Christodolou,

Farley, and Hulbert 1987; Channon 1973, 1978; Chenhall 1979; Dyas and Thanheiser 1976; Hamilton and Shergill 1992, 1993; Khandwalla 1977; Pavan 1976; Suzuki 1980). Thus the causal connection between diversification and divisionalization is well established.

The contingency theory explanation of the connection between diversification and divisionalization is the fit between these two variables that affects performance. For an undiversified firm a functional structure is the fit, whereas for a diversified firm a divisional structure is the fit. Conversely, for an undiversified firm a divisional structure is the misfit, and for a diversified firm a functional structure is the misfit. This theoretical model receives support from empirical studies of strategy-structure fit and performance (Donaldson 1987; Hamilton and Shergill 1992, 1993). The contingency fit effect on performance holds when controlling for possible universalistic effects of divisional structure (Hamilton and Shergill 1993).

There is a correspondence between the analyses of Chandler (1962) and Thompson (1967). In Chandler's case histories, the undiversified firm is composed of functional departments that are interdependent with each other; indeed Chandler (1977) documents the rise of the modern business firm by the vertical integration of supply, manufacture, sales, and distribution functions. Subsequently, diversification creates multibusiness firms in which the activities of one division are connected only loosely or not all with the other divisions. This corresponds to the decrease in task interdependence in moving from sequential to pooled interdependence found in Thompson's schema. For Thompson (1967), the organizational subunits connected only by pooled interdependence become the major organizational units, that is, divisions, at the highest level in the hierarchy, corresponding to Chandler's thesis that diversification leads to divisionalization. Hence both Chandler (1962) and Thompson (1967) discuss the contingency factor of task interdependence, albeit implicitly in the case of Chandler, and see it as leading to divisionalization.

In discussing task interdependence in the context of organic theory (Chapter 2), we concluded that it could be decomposed into task uncertainty and interaction intensity. Here, too, diversification leads to divisionalization through decreasing task interdependence because intensity of interaction between the activities dealing with each of the different product-markets decreases. The shift from sequential to pooled interdependence as the organization diversifies highly means that the activities of the product-markets go from being directly connected to having no direct connection, that is, from moderate to nil interaction intensity, and so from functional to divisional structures. Thus the reformulation of task interdependence as interaction intensity regarding the explanation of grouping of activities and their colocation applies also to divisionalization and its variants. Hence the task interdependence explanation of divisionalization can be reinterpreted as interaction intensity, consistent with our reformulation. However, in discussing the literature we will continue to use the term *task interdependence* because that is more familiar and is embedded in the literature. Nevertheless, the influences attributed to the task interdependence contingency can be reinterpreted, with some gain in clarity and precision, as being due to the intensity of task interaction.

The task interdependence contingency can also be applied to distinguish different types within the divisional structure. The greater the task interdependence, the more centralized the coordination. The distinction is drawn between unrelated product or service companies and those where the products or services are related or are vertically integrated (Rumelt 1974). Where divisions are unrelated (i.e., low task interdependence) they are highly autonomous, have little contact with the head office, and few managers transfer between them (Lorsch and Allen 1973; Pitts 1974, 1976, 1977). Also the head office is small, and the division and its manager are appraised and rewarded according to profitability of the division (Lorsch and Allen 1973; Pitts 1974, 1976, 1977). In contrast, the more the divisions are related, the less autonomous they are, they have more contact with the head office and more managers transfer between them (Lorsch and Allen 1973; Pitts 1974, 1976, 1977). Also the head office is large, and the division and its manager are appraised according to their contribution to overall company profitability (Lorsch and Allen 1973; Pitts 1974, 1976, 1977).

While task interdependence caused by strategic diversification is the main contingency of divisionalization, size also leads to divisionalization, additional to the effect of diversification (Grinyer and Yasai-Ardekani 1981). This size effect may be interpreted as due to the need to curb managerial opportunism, which increases as functional organizations grow larger and more complex (Williamson 1970). However, the size effect may also be interpreted as due to optimal plant size placing limits on the size of functions (Khandwalla 1977). Again, the size effect may be interpreted as due to the need to decompose the organization into small enough pieces that a manager can supervise each division without exceeding his or her cognitive capacity (Jaques 1976). Each of these different interpretations is a contingency theory, because divisionalization needs to fit size in order to produce higher performance, albeit for different reasons in each case. Studies of the relative effects of strategy and size have been mixed (Chenhall 1979; Donaldson 1982a; Fligstein 1985; Grinyer and Yasai-Ardekani 1981; Grinyer, Yasai-Ardekani, and Al-Bazzaz 1980; Khandwalla 1977; Palmer et al. 1987; for discussion see Child 1982; Donaldson 1986; Grinyer 1982). However, studies of organizational change support strategy more than size as a cause of divisionalization (Donaldson 1987; Fligstein 1985; Hamilton and Shergill 1992, 1993; Mahoney 1992; Palmer, et al. 1987; Palmer, Jennings, and Zhou 1993), so that, overall, size is secondary to strategy (for details see Chapter 6).

Hence, while divisionalization is a component of bureaucratic structure, it differs in its causation. Whereas size is the major contingency of bureaucratic structuring, particularly of specialization and formalization, and also of structural differentiation, task interdependence is the major contingency of divisionalization. Nevertheless, there is some overlap of causality between divisionalization and bureaucratic structure in that size has a minor effect on divisionalization, while diversification increases bureaucratic structure (Grinyer and Yasai-Ardekani 1981). Also, decentralization, which is part of both divisionalization and bureaucratic structure, is positively affected by both size (Pugh and Hinings 1976) and diversification (Grinyer and Yasai-Ardekani 1981). Despite these commonalties, the distinctive feature of divisionalization is that it is a component of bureaucratic structure whose cause is mainly task interdependence, rather than size, whereas size is the main cause for the rest of bureaucratic structure and is the central contingency in bureaucracy theory.

Structures of Multinational Corporations

One area of organizational structure that has received extensive study is *multinational corporations* (MNCs). This has followed a task contingency approach by arguing that as firms go from just operating domestically to operating internationally, they need to change their organizational structure (Stopford and Wells 1972). In particular, more geographically extensive operations can lead from the appropriate structure being functional to it being an area or geographical divisional structure in which divisions are specialized by regions or countries of the world (Davis 1972). Greater diversification by product or service can also lead to product or service divisions that control operations worldwide (Davis 1972). The research supports the contingency theory that task interdependence determines the required organizational structure: diversification of product or service tends to lead to worldwide product or service divisions, whereas diversification by area tends to lead to worldwide area divisions (Channon 1973; Rumelt 1974; Stopford and Wells 1972). The decisive point is on what basis self-sufficient divisions can be formed, given the task interdependencies (Galbraith 1973; Thompson 1967). An intermediate stage between purely domestic and extensively multinational operations may see the use of an international division to which overseas subsidiaries report, leaving the domestic operations organized separately (Davis 1972). This is something of an anomalous structure and there is evidence that U.S. corporations have used this structure more than European corporations (Franko 1974), and in a more prolonged manner (Daniels, Pitts, and Tretter 1984, 1985). Egelhoff (1982, 1988a, 1988b) has developed quite a comprehensive contingency theory of MNC structures from the information-processing requirement posed by various contingencies, building upon Galbraith (1973).

Bartlett and Ghoshal (1989) analyze MNCs in terms of the tension between local responsiveness and global integration. Their conclusion is that increasingly MNCs will converge on the transnational strategy, which has some tinges of a universalistic argument applied to strategy. However, Ghoshal and Nohria (1993) offer a sophisticated contingency theory of the organizational structure of multinational corporations. The main idea is that each strategy requires a certain degree of control over the global units in the MNC and also of local responsiveness, which requires that subsidiaries vary in their structures. These controls and complexities are expensive so that they should be avoided if not required. *Strategy* refers specifically to the multinational strategy being pursued by the corporation. It varies on two dimensions: forces for global integration and forces for local responsiveness. Each of these two dimensions is dichotomized, and their cross-classification yields four strategies: international (low global, low local), global (high, low), multinational (low, high) and transnational (high, high). The structure required to fit each strategy is: ad hoc variation structure fits international strategy, structural uniformity fits global strategy, differentiated fit structure is the fit to multinational strategy, and integrated variety structure fits transnational strategy.

Structure is the degree of control exercised by the multinational over its parts through centralization, formalization, and normative integration (shared values of managers; Ghoshal and Nohria 1993). In the *international strategy*, the MNC is attempting neither global integration of its subsidiaries nor to make them locally responsive (instead it may emphasize exporting from the domestic plants). Therefore it needs little control over its subsidiaries and hence is low on all three means of control (i.e., centralization, formalization, and normative integration), so that its subsidiaries can vary in their internal structures in an ad hoc manner, thus the MNC overall has the "ad hoc variation" structure. In the *global strategy*, the MNC is attempting global integration of its subsidiaries without encouraging them to be locally responsive. Therefore it needs substantial control over its subsidiaries and thus it is high on at least one of the three means of control (i.e., centralization, formalization, and normative integration), so that all its subsidiaries have uniform internal structures, hence the MNC overall has "structural uniformity." In the *multinational strategy*, the MNC is not attempting global integration but rather encourages its subsidiaries to be locally responsive. Therefore it needs each of its subsidiaries to fit its environment, specifically the local resources and level of complexity, which is termed "differentiated fit." In the *transnational strategy*, the MNC is attempting simultaneously global integration of its subsidiaries and to make them locally responsive. Therefore it needs substantial control over its subsidiaries of structural uniformity, together with fitting each subsidiary to its environment, as in differentiated fit, hence the overall structure of the MNC is "integrated variety."

In an empirical study of forty-one MNCs, seventeen were found to be in fit between their strategies and structures, while twenty-four were in misfit (Ghoshal and Nohria 1993). The MNCs in fit had higher performance on average in return on assets, growth in return on assets, and growth in revenues, thus providing validation of the fit model (Ghoshal and Nohria 1993). The fact that most organizations in the study were found to be in misfit, and so had reduced performance, helps dispel any illusion that contingency research always describes organizations as being in fit and so is irrelevant to practice. Examples of MNCs in fit are: Baker International (ad hoc variation structure fitting international strategy), Air Products and Chemicals (structural uniformity fitting global strategy), British-American Tobacco (differentiated fit matching multinational strategy), and Volvo (integrated variety fitting transnational strategy; Ghoshal and Nohria 1993). An example of a misfit is Kodak, which had an ad hoc variation structure, featuring weak integration and differentiation, that failed to provide the strong controls and systematic local structural variations needed to successfully pursue its transnational strategy. Another example of a misfit is Siemens, which had an integrated variety structure, featuring strong controls through centralization, formalization, and normative integration, as well as differentiated fits of subsidiaries to their local environments, which was excessive given its international strategy (Ghoshal and Nohria 1993). Thus MNCs need to invest in structures that provide the degree of central control and local variation that match their strategy, while avoiding the unnecessary expense and structural complexity of structures that are overelaborate for their strategy (Ghoshal and Nohria 1993).

In review, Ghoshal and Nohria (1993) offer a sophisticated contingency theory that has fits at two levels: the overall MNC structure to its worldwide strategy and the subsidiary to its local environment. While using the Aston concepts of centralization and formalization, the theory adds to these elements of structure the concept of normative integration, which is control through corporate culture, a dimension of organizational structure different from the more traditional aspects and one that focuses on the shared values of managers. This reflects an increasing interest among organizational theorists in organizational culture (Martin 1992) and a long-standing question in sociology about how far social systems are normatively integrated (Durkheim 1964) and how far this substitutes for bureaucratic controls (Lockwood 1964). Ghoshal and Nohria (1993) adopt the view that normative integration can substitute for centralization and formalization and hence that cultural controls are effective substitutes for these structural controls (Ghoshal and Nohria 1993). Moreover, the study places cultural controls in a contingency framework, in that shared values are seen as beneficial only where strategies require structural integration (i.e., global and transnational strategies).

Ghoshal and Nohria (1993) state that the four structures provide varying levels of integration and differentiation, because global integration requires structural integration, while local responsiveness requires differentiation. Cross-classifying the four structures on integration and differentiation, respectively, they are: ad hoc variation (low, low), structural uniformity (high, low), differentiated fit (low, high), and integrated variety (high, high). Thus the study by Ghoshal and Nohria (1993) draws on the language of Lawrence and Lorsch (1967), that is, differentiation and integration, but uses the terms in ways that are different enough to require comment. As we have seen, for Lawrence and Lorsch (1967), an organization differentiates and then integrates because the differentiation splits up the organization while the integration makes these parts work in concert. Thus for Lawrence and Lorsch integration must accompany differentiation, so that a successful organization is either low on both differentiation and integration or high on both. In contrast, in Ghoshal and Nohria (1993), their four cell model makes clear that a successful organization can be high on integration, while also low on differentiation (structural uniformity) and also can be low on integration while also being high on differentiation (differentiated fit). Thus two of the four cells in their model are contrary to Lawrence and Lorsch. This shows that for Ghoshal and Nohria, differentiation and integration are not two sides of the same coin that need to match each other, as they are for Lawrence and Lorsch. For Ghoshal and Nohria, differentiation and integration refer to structural aspects at different levels of the organizational hierarchy. Differentiation is structure at subsidiary level (and the different relationship of each subsidiary to the head office), whereas integration refers to the control achieved by the MNC over its subsidiaries through its overall structure (centralization, formalization, and normative integration). Thus differentiation here is the difference between subsidiaries that may or may not need to be integrated, depending upon the strategy. The multinational strategy requires differentiation, but not integration. Similarly, the global strategy requires integration, despite the lack of differentiation between subsidiaries. Therefore while the study uses the concepts of Lawrence and Lorsch, they are not embedded in the same theory.

The study by Ghoshal and Nohria (1993) has elements of both the bureaucracy and organic theories. It draws upon bureaucracy theory for the structural variables of centralization and formalization (Pugh et al. 1968). It draws upon organic theory for integration through normative integration, that is, through shared values, communications and interpersonal networks (Burns and Stalker 1961). Indeed, Nohria and Ghoshal (1997) use the term *differentiated network* to refer to the modern MNC, which displays affinities with the organic structure. High local responsiveness requires fit to the contingencies of resources and complexity in the environment of the subsidiary. This in some ways echoes the theory of Lawrence and Dyer (1983) that environments vary on two dimensions: resource scarcity and information complexity, which reflects resource dependence (Pfeffer and Salancik 1978) and organic theories (Burns and Stalker 1961), respectively.

The main contingency of Ghoshal and Nohria (1993) at the corporate level is strategy, with the degree of global integration being sought implicitly determining the degree of task interdependence between subsidiaries. Overall, the research on MNCs supports the idea that task is a contingency of organizational structure.

Matrix Structures

Many MNCs use a matrix structure (Egelhoff 1988a; Galbraith and Kazanjian 1988), though this structure may also be used by organizations that operate purely domestically (Burns 1989; Davis and Lawrence 1977; Kolodny 1979). Three main types of matrix may be distinguished: functional-product (or project), functional-area, and product-area (instead of product there may be a differentiation by service or customer). The essence of matrix is that an employee within the matrix has two bosses, who in turn report to a common boss. Below this common boss there are two dimensions, for example, one of various functions and one of various products, with each function and product headed by a separate manager. The matrix is an intermediate structure, so that, for instance, the functional-product matrix combines elements of both a functional and a product divisional structure. There is differentiation both of functions and products, with managers in charge of each at the same level. Therefore the product unit is less than a complete division, because functional specialists within it are reporting also to functional managers outside it, so that the product unit has less autonomy than it would if it were a division.

Matrix structures are appropriate where there is dual focus (Davis and Lawrence 1977). This corresponds to an intermediate level of task interdependence (Donaldson 1985, pp. 167-171). For instance, each product or project is a separate entity in order to facilitate its internal coordination, but certain resources are drawn from central functions (Corey and Star 1971, pp. 61-107). Thus the task interdependence between the products is less than for a functional structure yet more than for a product divisional structure. Similarly, a *functional-area matrix* fits a situation where areas are diverse enough to be required to be managed separately, but some sharing of central functions is sought, so that again task interdependence is medium. Again, a *product-area matrix* fits a situation where both products and areas are diverse enough to be required to have each their own managers, with resource units that report to both, so that again task interdependence is medium. Thus the task interdependence contingency determines where the matrix structure, and what type of matrix, is a fit (Donaldson 1985, pp. 167-171).

The issue arises as to whether matrix structures should be seen as part of organic theory or of bureaucracy theory. Matrix structures are, in the main, just a more complex form of hierarchy, rather than being inherently organic structures. They have been discussed by proponents of organic theory such as Lawrence (Davis and Lawrence 1977) and are sometimes described as being decentralized. Yet having two dimensions of managers at a level in the hierarchy increases the number of managers at that level rather than delegating decision making down from that level. Managers from each side of the matrix may have to confer because neither possesses complete authority over a subordinate, but this is really just complexity in a hierarchy, rather than being a nonhierarchical structure. Again, the subordinate has two superiors, and this violates the classical school of management prescription about unity of command (Brech 1957). However, having two bosses is not less hierarchical than having one boss—indeed it could considered more hierarchical—and so is compatible with a mechanistic structure. The functional-project subtype of the matrix structure features a cross-sectional project team, which is temporary and which is intended to have an organic structure internally, in order to facilitate interaction among the various specialists to promote problem solving. However, the other subtypes of the matrix, such as functional-area or product-functional, have subordinate units that are permanently reporting up to their two bosses and so are not temporary arrangements (Child 1984) nor necessarily organic in their internal operations.

Research identifies the enhanced potential for conflict in a matrix because of subordinates having two bosses (Fisher and Gitelson 1983; Joyce 1986; Knight 1977), so Davis and Lawrence (1977) recommend that matrix structures need to be supported by a matrix culture of openness and problem solving, which is organic in nature. However, not all structures will necessarily implement such a culture. Moreover, a culture of openness and problem solving could be adopted by organizations that lack a matrix structure. Therefore, overall, matrix structures in general (the functional-project subtype excepted) do not seem to be inherently organic. They seem to be just a more complex type of hierarchy. Hence they can be subsumed within bureaucracy theory as part of the subsection of that theory that deals with the task interdependence contingency, as a variant of the distinction between functional and divisional structures.

Thus the stream of research connecting strategy with structures such as functional, divisional, and matrix is compatible with the contingency theory of task interdependence.

Other Possible Contingencies

Are there other possible contingencies of bureaucratic structure in addition to organizational size? All contingencies are causes of organizational structure, in that organizations change their structures to attain fit and performance. However, a variable could be a cause of organizational structure without it being a contingency. In such a case the variable causes change in organizational structure but not because there is some underlying fit that the organization seeks to attain in order to gain performance. There are two steps involved in showing that a variable is a contingency of organizational structure. The first step is to show that the variable is a cause of structure. The second step is to show that the cause is a contingency. We will discuss here four possible contingencies of bureaucratic structure: public accountability, environmental hostility, CEO personality, and national culture.

As seen above, public accountability is positively correlated with centralization (Pugh et al. 1968) and appears to be one of its causes.

Accepting that it is a cause, is it a contingency? If public accountability raises centralization because the government refuses to delegate certain decisions below the board of directors (or equivalent body), then the organization is subject to a causal force. However, if there is no fit between public accountability and centralization that raises performance, then public accountability is not a contingency. In this way public accountability could be a cause of centralization without causation being of the functionalist kind, that is, driven by the search for some beneficial outcome.

Whether a factor is a contingency of organization depends on whether aligning the structure and the contingency produces higher performance. Hence a contingency factor is always embedded in a contingency theory that specifies performance as resulting from a fit of the organizational structure to the contingency. Demonstrating that a cause is a contingency involves showing that the fit posited by the theory is empirically valid, that is, that fit affects performance. In the absence of theory and evidence about why centralization fits public accountability and with what beneficial consequences for performance, then public accountability would not be a contingency of centralization. Similar considerations apply to environmental hostility, CEO personality, and national culture.

Khandwalla (1977) identified a factor of environmental hostility that is positively correlated with centralization of decision making. Environmental hostility would be a contingency of centralization if centralization fits hostile situations, in that, for example, top management can act more quickly and decisively to meet a threat by centralizing. Here the outcome of centralization under hostility would be functional and positive, that is, performance would be raised. In contrast, hostility could be just a cause of centralization, due, for example, to threat-rigidity (Staw, Sandelands, and Dutton 1981). In this case, hostility causes senior managers to feel threatened and become defensive, so they move to making all decisions themselves and no longer trust their subordinates to exercise delegated authority. The enhanced centralization resulting from hostility creates rigidity, which is dysfunctional, negatively affecting performance. Therefore there would be no underlying functionalist type of fit between hostility and centralization, so hostility would not be a contingency. Which of these views is sounder needs to be established through empirical research.

Turning to CEO personality, consider, for instance, the need for achievement of the CEO. This is positively correlated with centralization (Miller, Droge, and Toulouse 1988). If there is some fit between having a CEO with high need for achievement and centralization that raises performance, then that CEO personality need is a contingency of centralization. For example, it might be that high need for achievement causes CEOs to work very hard and effectively, but only if they can see themselves as the cause of the resulting gains in organizational performance. In such a case, centralization fits a CEO with high need for achievement, so that need for achievement is a contingency. Instead, however, it could be that a CEO with high need for achievement has a need always to be center stage in the organization and so uses his or her power to withhold delegation down to subordinates, even though this is counterproductive. In such a scenario, CEO need for achievement is a cause of centralization but not a contingency of centralization. Hence again, whether the causal factor, CEO need for achievement, is also a contingency depends on whether there is a fit of it to centralization that raises performance. Lewin and Stephens (1994) argue that CEO personality causes organizations to adopt a structure that is a misfit. In this case, CEO personality is a cause of structure but not a contingency factor that can improve performance.

National culture has become a factor that has attracted an increasing number of contingency theory researchers (Hickson and McMillan 1981; Lammers and Hickson 1979). Early structural contingency theory focused on contingencies that were presumed to have universal effect, such as technology or size (Blau 1970; Pugh et al. 1969). Later research examined whether some national cultures led to different relationships between contingency and organizational structure (e.g., Hickson, Hinings, McMillan, and Schwitter 1974; McMillan, Hickson, Hinings, and Schneck 1973; Zeffane 1989a). Initially the method was to see whether relationships found in countries such as the United Kingdom and the United States held elsewhere, with contrary findings being explained by the nationality of the organizations studied. This approach has been criticized as the "sociology of residual variables" approach, because it presumes that nationality is the cause of any differences in findings, whereas there are many potential other causes (Lammers and Hickson 1979). A preferable approach is to deduce from theory about national cultures, hypotheses that are stated prior to the research (Tayeb 1987), or to show that variations in organizational characteristics are correlated with variables that directly measure national culture. National culture could be extended in future to include language differences and differences in national political structure that may affect organizational structure. There could be other new contingency variables added in this way. To be established as a contingency of structure, it needs to be shown that there is a fit of structure to national culture that affects performance and that this is the reason why national culture causes structure. There is evidence that the centrally planned economies of the former Soviet block countries, such as Poland, had organizations that were more centralized than organizations in the West (Kuc, Hickson, and McMillan 1981). However, this could be due to the public accountability effect, that is, to the government centralizing organizational decision making, so that the reservation made earlier applies, that is, it could be a cause but not necessarily a contingency.

Thus one should not presume that every variable that is a cause of organizational structure is also a contingency. An underlying fit model has to be specified theoretically. Every time some empirical research shows that a factor is a cause of an organizational structural variable and this is interpreted as it being a contingency, then further research opens up to show whether the hypothesized fit affects performance in the way claimed.

Synthesizing the Size and Task Contingencies

Thus far, in this and the preceding chapter, we have kept both the bureaucracy and the organic theories separate, as theories that are independent of each other. Some scholars have sought to synthesize the two theories as essentially separate but equal (Collins and Hull 1986; Dewar and Hage 1978; Hage 1980; Hull 1988; Hull and Collins 1987). However, there are other scholars who seek to assimilate either task or size into the other, thereby leaving size or task as the dominating contingency. Astley (1985) sought to show a pervasive effect of size on organizational structure, reinterpreting in terms of size some aspects of structure that are normally attributed to task. In contrast, some proponents of task seek to assert a larger role for it. In particular, Gerwin (1979a, 1981) has argued that the task interdependence contingency has pervasive effects across many aspects of organizational structure.

Doubtless the size and task contingencies will each continue to have champions who will push their frontiers, to some extent at cost to the other contingency. Is it possible, instead, to reconcile the organic and bureaucracy theories of organizational structure, so that each is accepted as illuminating different aspects of structure and thereby complementing the other?

Reconciling Bureaucracy and Organic Theories

As discussed above, the bureaucracy and organic theories are somewhat opposed in their structural models. Bureaucracy theory states that both specialization-formalization and decentralization increase with size. Organic theory states that both specialization-formalization and centralization decrease with task uncertainty. As we have seen, each theory has supporting bodies of empirical research. Both the bureaucracy and organic theories deal in a broadly similar set of structural variables of specialization, formalization, and centralization, thereby creating the contradiction in their two views. However, there are differences in their measures that resolve the seeming contradiction between their findings.

Bureaucracy research measures of specialization, formalization, and centralization address the overall organizational structure rather than local variations. Moreover, they tend to focus on the administrative core of the organization, such as accounting and personnel structures (Pugh et al. 1968). In order to be comparable across widely differing sorts of organizations, the structural measures avoid the work flow, that is, the operations whereby inputs are transformed into outputs, which would involve details that are specific to technologies and competencies used in particular industries (McKelvey and Aldrich 1983; Pugh et al. 1963). It is this overall structure, relating to the administrative core, that becomes increasingly bureaucratized with increasing size, so that functional specialization (e.g., different kinds of accountants), formalization (e.g., procedures for hiring employees), and decentralization (e.g., delegation of financial decisions down the hierarchy) increase with size (see Figure 3.3). Moreover, the Aston Group studied organizations that vary in size, which brings out the true strength of the relationships between size and bureaucratic structure (e.g., Child 1972b; Pugh et al. 1969).

Figure 3.3. Reconciling Bureaucracy and Organic Theories

Organizational Level	*Theory*	*Contingency*
Administrative Core	Bureaucracy Theory Bureaucratic Structure: • Functional specialization • Formalization • Decentralization	Size
Workflow	Organic Theory Organic Structure: • Occupational specialization • Lack of formalization • Participation	Task Uncertainty

In contrast, organic theory measures tend to focus on the actual work done in the organization, so that they reflect the task contingency more. Further, some of the organic theory research is conducted on samples of smaller organizations in which the influence of the task on structure would be more pervasive, as well as restricting the size range and so attenuating the correlation between size and structure (e.g., Dewar and Hage 1978; Hage and Aiken 1967a, 1967b, 1969). There are also differences in the conceptual definitions of some of the structural measures. Specialization in bureaucracy research refers to functional specialization (Pugh et al. 1968), whereas in organic research it is occupational specialization (Hage and Aiken 1967a). Again, decentralization in bureaucracy research refers to delegation down the hierarchy mainly among managers (though supervisors and workers are not excluded; Pugh et al. 1968), whereas in organic research it is participation, including that by employees low in the hierarchy (Hage and Aiken 1967a). Thus bureaucracy research captures how the overall administrative superstructure elaborates with size. Organic research, in contrast, captures how, as task uncertainty increases, specific jobs become less bound by rules, procedures, and paperwork and become more subject to the discretion of their technologically expert incumbents, who also exercise some upward influence through participation.

Thus both the bureaucracy and the organic theories are valid in their own domains, which are different arenas within the organization, macro and micro, respectively.

Size primarily determines the macro-structure in the sense of the level of bureaucratic structuring and decentralization of the overall organization. Task primarily determines the micro-structure within this picture, that is, for each department, section, or role. This micro-structure can vary across the organization so that some sections are mechanistic and others are organic. Thus size determines the macro-structure and task determines the micro-structure. As organizations grow larger they become more bureaucratic (higher on structuring and decentralization of the overall structure). If the organization needs to innovate, it will become more organic in those roles involved in innovation, such as in the R&D department or in cross-functional project teams, with the remaining roles being more mechanistic. If the innovatory activity is large in the organization, then it will become internally differentiated into units that will be partly coordinated through formal means such as hierarchy and formalization.

This reconciliation receives empirical support in that the relationships between size and bureaucratic structuring hold across industries that are innovative such as electronics, similar to industries that are not innovative, such as confectionery (Child 1973a). The research on innovation shows effects at the more micro levels and variations within organizations in organicness (Lawrence and Lorsch 1967). While organic structures may be found in specific parts of the organization, hierarchy still exists as an overarching coordination mechanism (Lawrence and Lorsch 1967). In a study of research units, Tushman (1979) found that, while interdependence of work within units led to more organic structures, interdependence between units led to more mechanistic structures because supervisors coordinated through hierarchy. Hence the requirement for coordinating units led to hierarchy superimposed over the organic research units (see also Tushman 1977). Product development of IBM mainframe computers involved large numbers of people who were organized into several departments. The project flowed from one department to another with formal sign-offs signaling satisfactory attainment of project targets and transfer of authority (Corey and Star 1971).

A Parsimonious Model

Having reconciled both bureaucracy and organic theory as each being valid at particular organizational levels, we now need to bring both theories together into one model. There are two structural dimensions and three contingencies in the contingency theory of organizational structure, making it a parsimonious model. Organizational structure is composed of two main dimensions: bureaucratic structure and grouping. Organizational structure is molded by the contingencies of size, task uncertainty, and task interdependence.

As we have seen, bureaucratic structure includes structuring (specialization, formalization, and decentralization) and structural differentiation. Bureaucratic structure is strongly affected by the contingency of organizational size. As organizations increase in size, they increase their structuring (including decentralization) and structural differentiation. However, the total level of the structuring variables is affected to a degree by task uncertainty. Innovation reduces formalization and centralization, independent of size effects, thereby affecting structuring. Grouping defines the organizational subunits and their colocations (Child 1984). It involves whether differentiation is by functions, products, services, customers, or geographical areas. Task interdependence is the contingency that affects grouping, including divisionalization. Divisionalization is conceptually related to bureaucratic structure and has here been subsumed under bureaucratic structure. However, while bureaucracy is determined primarily by size, divisionalization is determined primarily by task interdependence. Therefore divisionalization is somewhat separate from bureaucratization. Moreover, task interdependence determines also the type of divisional structure (e.g., by product or area), so that again it has an effect on divisionalization that is separate from size.

In summary, bureaucratic structuring is increased by size and reduced by task uncertainty. Task interdependence increases divisionalization and defines the nature of the organizational subunits. In this way, a highly parsimonious model can be abstracted of how contingencies shape organizational structure, helping to stem the fear that the contingency theory literature is so complex that it defies comprehension (Bourgeois 1984).

Causal Connections Between Size and Task Contingencies

As we argued above, bureaucracy and organic theory are each valid in their own domains, which correspond to the macro-structures and micro-structures, respectively. This reconciliation leaves each of size and task as independent contingency variables, each with their own separate effects. The next question is whether size and task are causally connected so that their effects are related.

It may be the case that size causes task. Size is the antecedent cause of structure, with task the intervening variable. Thus the immediate effects on structure of task are actually caused by size. Size is the distal cause of structure and task is its proximal cause. Let us now consider some of the relationships discussed above and see if they can be placed into the causal model that size causes task, which causes structure. We will examine, in turn, the formalization, divisionalization, and organic aspects of organizational structure.

As has been seen, two major effects of organizational size are specialization and formalization. Size causes specialization, in that as size increases the division of labor, so each job becomes narrower in scope. The same few operations are done repeatedly by the incumbent and this combines with the narrow scope of the job to reduce its task uncertainty. This allows the job to be codified into rules and standard operating procedures, which can be written into detailed job descriptions and manuals. Thus size leads to specialization, which leads to lower task uncertainty and hence to formalization. Size is the ultimate cause of formalization, but task uncertainty is the intervening variable that connects size and formalization. Hence task uncertainty is the immediate cause of formalization. Moreover, task uncertainty explains *why* increasing size leads to increasing formalization. Thus a major size effect on structure in bureaucracy theory can be explained by the task contingency.

One may go farther and say that formalization, through job descriptions and manuals of procedures, reduces the uncertainty for incumbents, so that formalization feeds back to lower task uncertainty, fostering further formalization, tightening the causal connection between task uncertainty and formalization. Hence a more extended causal model is that size leads to specialization that reduces task uncertainty that increases formalization that reduces task uncertainty that increases formalization.

We can also bring diversification into the synthesis. As seen earlier, diversification leads to divisionalization. However, diversification by business organizations usually occurs when they are large in size, because the industry has matured, leaving the firm large but with limited expansion opportunities in its industry. Therefore, while diversification is the immediate cause of much divisionalization, size can often be the more ultimate cause of diversification. Here size causes task interdependence (i.e., diversification) that causes divisionalization.

There may also be an effect of size on innovation. There is some evidence that size is positively related to the extent of innovation activity, though not necessarily to more innovative outputs (Cohen and Levin 1989, p. 1071; Damanpour 1992). Given that the theory being discussed here is primarily about innovative activity, size is an ultimate cause of such innovative activity and thereby of the organicness of parts of the organizational structure that result from the task uncertainty entailed by innovation.

Hence size is the more ultimate cause of many aspects of organizational structure: formalization, divisionalization, and organicness. These effects of size are because size affects task that, in turn, produces the effects on organizational structure. As we have seen, size affects bureaucratization through reducing task uncertainty. Size can affect divisionalization through reducing task interdependence by diversification. Size can increase the level of organicness through increasing the level of innovation that is sought and thereby the task uncertainty. In all these cases size causes task that causes the organizational structure. Thus size and task can be brought together in the same causal process, so that the bureaucracy and organic theories are causally connected.

Hence contingency theory is revealed to have a deeper coherence in that the disparate effects claimed of size and task can be reconciled in a model in which they are causally linked. To the extent that they are connected, their effects on structure are no longer independent, because the level of size is not independent of the level of the task contingency. Thus organic and bureaucracy theory merge. Size causes increasing bureaucratization, which means increasing structural differentiation, formalization, and decentralization. It also causes increasing diversification, which causes divisionalization, that is, additional decentralization and formalization. Further, size also leads to innovation being sought that creates organic structures in some parts of the organization, thereby offsetting to a degree the tendency induced by large size toward minute specialization and formalization in those parts and also prompting participation in them.

This is a merger in which bureaucracy theory is the dominant partner in the sense that the overall structure conforms to bureaucracy theory, and size is the ultimate cause with pervasive influence. However, the key arguments of organic theory are retained, so that organic and participatory structural elements are given a role, albeit localized to certain parts of the organization, with task being the immediate cause of many of the structural elements, both organic and bureaucratic. Such a synthesis of two of the major streams of contingency theory research, organic and bureaucracy, is a further step toward integration of contingency theory. It continues the move toward integrating contingency theory that we began in Chapter 1.

Conclusions

The bureaucracy theory of organizational structure holds that bureaucratization is composed of structuring (formalization and decentralization), structural differentiation, and divisionalization. The level of bureaucratization is strongly affected by size.

Bureaucracy theory took as its point of departure the model of bureaucracy that was originally advanced by Weber. Contingency theory research moved from his ideal-type to a multivariate framework that was used in quantitative studies comparing across organizations. The resulting view is that a bureaucratic structure has many departments and hierarchical levels, is highly specialized and formalized, but also highly decentralized. Bureaucracy increases with size, but at a decreasing rate with respect to size, so that bureaucracy grows proportionately less than size. Furthermore, the ratio of managerial and administrative staff to total employees decreases as size increases, thereby creating economies of scale in administration. In this way, and through improving organizational performance, bureaucracy theory argues that bureaucratization is functional (i.e., effective), in contrast to earlier case studies of bureaucratic dysfunctions. The level of bureaucratization needs to fit size, and larger organizations with more bureaucratic structures have performance superior to those with less bureaucratization, consistent with the fit idea of contingency theory.

Divisionalization is a component of the bureaucratic type of organizational structure in that divisionalization increases formalization and decentralization. Strategy affects this aspect of structure in that diversification increases (and vertical integration decreases) divisionalization. Thus diversification reduces the level of the task interdependence contingency and in this way causes divisionalization. Matrix structures fit intermediate levels of the task interdependence contingency due to medium levels of either product or area diversity. Thus the structures of functional, divisional, and matrix, together with their subtypes, can be assimilated within bureaucracy theory. Size also affects divisionalization, both directly, and indirectly through diversification. Thus divisionalization is subsumable under bureaucratic theory in that it is part of the bureaucratic structure and has some affinity in causation with bureaucratization more generally.

Public accountability also affects bureaucratization by increasing centralization and formalization, though whether it is a contingency is open to discussion at the present time. Similarly, environmental hostility and CEO need for achievement increase centralization, though whether they are contingencies is also open to discussion. National culture effects structure, though whether it is a contingency is also an open question. For any contingency, it needs to be shown that there is some fit of some organizational characteristic to the contingency that positively affects performance. Otherwise it is just a cause without being a contingency.

The main accomplishment of bureaucracy theory has been to identify how macro-organizational structure in many aspects is shaped by needing to fit the contingencies, principally size. The organic theory school can be reconciled with this picture. Innovation, and hence task uncertainty, leads certain parts of the organization (e.g., departments, sections, or roles) to be more organic (i.e., less formalized and more decentralized), while the other parts are mechanistic. Thus size determines bureaucracy at the macro-structural level, whereas task has more localized effects on parts of the organizational micro-structure.

Much of the empirical literature on the contingency theory of organizational structure can be distilled into a parsimonious model of three contingencies and two structural dimensions. Moreover, the size and task contingencies can be brought together in the causal model that size causes task, which in turn causes structure. Thus much of contingency theory and research can be combined into a highly coherent theory.

4 Causality and Contingency
in Bureaucracy Theory

While bureaucracy research has established numerous empirical regularities and offers theoretical interpretations of them, there are some thorny theoretical issues pertaining to bureaucracy theory. What exactly are the causal relationships between the components of bureaucratic structure, such as formalization, decentralization, and structural differentiation? What is the theoretical reason why so many of the observed relationships between variables in the causal model are not linear? Causality is being discussed in terms of an impersonal, functionalist organizational system, but how do people actually make this happen—what is the role of human action? Is the causal model really a contingency theory? We will deal with such questions in this chapter.

By way of overview, the following several issues may be distinguished. The effect of one variable on another, such as size on an element of bureaucratic structure, could be direct or indirect. Thus, rather than assuming that size directly causes structure, we need to consider the possibility that size affects some other variables that then cause structure. The second issue is that of functionalism, which would hold that the structural variables in the model raise organizational performance. Such an effect of structure on organizational performance could be either a main effect, so that structure increases performance, or a contingency effect, so that it is the fit of structure to the contingency that increases performance. Whether a main or contingent functionalist effect, these benefits could be anticipated so that structure is increased immediately following a size increase, or there could be a process whereby structural adjustment lags and so lowers performance, leading eventually to structural change. If there is such a lag, then the effect of size on structure is indirect through misfit and lower performance. The structural adaptation to regain fit (SARFIT) model holds that structure is functionalist, that is, has positive performance consequences that result from fit of structure to contingency and that change is lagged so that the effect of size on structure is indirect. This is a complex theoretical model, and indeed the most complex of the theoretical alternatives just briefly outlined. In order to make the case for it we will go through the simpler alternatives and show their limitations. In so doing we shall move from simple to complex models of causality.

We shall attend first to direct causal models of size and bureaucratic structure, which are not functionalist in that they make no postulation that the structure is beneficial in its consequences. Subsequently, we shall examine functionalist theories of size and bureaucratic structure, beginning with universalistic variants that posit functionalist consequences of structure that are main effects, not involving contingencies. Next we shall examine contingency functionalist theories that nonetheless do posit direct causation of structure by size. Then we shall consider a contingency functionalist theoretical model that posits indirect cause of structure by size, with lags and feedback effects of misfit on performance, in the SARFIT manner. Finally, we shall attempt to bring all the lessons of the discussion together in a synthesis that is based on SARFIT but also draws selectively on other approaches.

The Causal Model of Size and Bureaucratic Structure

As seen in the previous chapter, the bureaucratic model contains three main aspects of organizational structure: formalization, decentralization, and structural differentiation. What is the causal

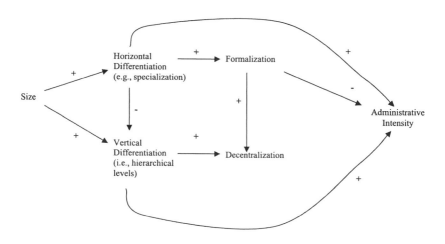

Figure 4.1. A Causal Model of the Relationship of Size and Bureaucratic Structure

relationship among these aspects of structure? Child (1973a) concludes from his empirical study that (simplifying) size causes specialization and the level of specialist qualifications (that together he calls "complexity"), which cause formalization that, in turn, causes decentralization, while size also, directly, causes decentralization. The explanation is that size leads to more specialists, who are trained to bring in new management systems that increase formalization (Child 1973a, pp. 181-183), which promotes relinquishing of direct control by the center, while large size makes direct personal control difficult, forcing decentralization. Similarly, Marsden, Cook, and Kalleberg (1994) find the causal model that (simplifying) size causes departments that cause formalization, which reduces administrative intensity, while size also causes vertical levels that cause decentralization, which also reduces administrative intensity. Thus size affects the horizontal aspect of structural differentiation that affects in turn formalization, which reduces administrative intensity. Size also affects the vertical aspect of structural differentiation that affects in turn centralization, another vertical aspect of structure, which also reduces administrative intensity. Thus in seeking a more exact causal relationship among the components of bureaucratic structure, it may be fruitful to decompose the effect of size on the horizontal aspects from the effect of size on the vertical aspects.

Drawing selectively on both causal models, together with the causal theory of Blau (1970, 1972), we may posit the causal model of the relationship among size and the bureaucratic structural variables in Figure 4.1.

Size positively affects horizontal structural differentiation in all its aspects (divisions, departments, specialization, etc). Horizontal differentiation narrows the scope of each job and so increases task certainty, which allows jobs to be codified into written job descriptions and manuals of procedures, so that formalization increases. The specialization aspect of horizontal differentiation also fosters formalization because greater administrative expertise leads to the adoption of new management systems. The narrowing of the scope of jobs also increases the span of control at each level in the hierarchy, because it is easier to supervise a less diverse set of jobs. This causes a negative effect of horizontal differentiation on vertical differentiation, that is, the number of hierarchical levels is lessened (Figure 4.1).

Size also increases the vertical aspect of structure: the number of hierarchical levels and decentralization. Increasing size leads to greater hierarchical levels in order to avoid excessively wide spans of control. This positive effect of size on hierarchical levels is offset to some extent by the increasing span of control (part of horizontal differentiation), so that hierarchical levels increase as size increases, but at a more modest rate than they would if span of control remained constant. Having many hierarchical levels isolates top management from the lowest, operational, level, so that management lacks knowledge about operations. Moreover, the elongated hierarchy prevents speedy and effective communications. Therefore, top management is forced to delegate. Also, the increasing number of middle managerial and supervisory levels provides an increasing depth of managers to whom decision authority can be delegated. Top management can have increased confidence that delegation will not be abused, because of the indirect controls over lower-level personnel provided by formalization, so that formalization has a positive effect on decentralization. Hence formalization substitutes for centralization, so that indirect, impersonal control replaces direct, personal control by top management.

Administrative intensity is raised by the complexity of coordination required through having more departments and other subunits, so that horizontal differentiation positively affects administrative intensity. However, administrative intensity is reduced by formalization, so that formalization negatively affects administrative intensity. In addition, more hierarchical levels increase administrative intensity, so that there is a positive effect of vertical differentiation on administrative intensity. However, the increasing span of control negatively affects the number of hierarchical levels, so that span of control (i.e., horizontal differentiation) has an indirect negative effect on administrative intensity through vertical differentiation. Thus administrative intensity is affected positively by differentiation (both horizontal and vertical) and negatively by formalization. While size increases horizontal differentiation, this indirectly increases formalization and also increases the span of control, which reduces the increase in vertical differentiation due to size. Thus the positive effect of horizontal differentiation on administrative intensity is offset by the indirect, negative effect of formalization. Similarly, the positive effect of vertical differentiation on administrative intensity is offset by the moderating effect of span of control on hierarchical levels. Jointly these two offsetting causations are stronger than the effects of horizontal and vertical differentiation on administrative intensity, so that the overall effect of size on administrative intensity is negative.

In sum, size positively affects both horizontal and vertical differentiation. Horizontal differentiation positively affects formalization. Horizontal differentiation negatively affects vertical differentiation. Vertical differentiation positively affects decentralization. Formalization positively affects decentralization. Horizontal and vertical differentiation both positively affect administrative intensity. Formalization also negatively affects administrative intensity. This causal model specifies the relationships between each of the components of bureaucratic structure: formalization, decentralization, structural differentiation, and administrative intensity. It is consistent with the causal models and empirical results of Blau (1970, 1972), Child (1973a), and Marsden, Cook, and Kalleberg (1994). However, while this causal model of size and bureaucratic structure is informative, it leaves open some deeper theoretical issues. The first issue is explaining why the relationships in the model are not linear.

The Curvilinear Relationship of
Size and Bureaucratic Structure

A theoretical issue in bureaucracy theory is that the empirical relationship between size and bureaucratic structure is curvilinear, so that structure increases with size at a decreasing rate with respect to size. For smaller sizes, structure increases steeply with increases in size, but at larger sizes structure increases only modestly with size increases. Thus the slope of structure is initially steep where size is small, then steadily decreases, so that it is shallower at large size. Blau (1970) shows that this holds for all the aspects of structural differentiation he studied. The Aston Group shows similar curves for its measures of hierarchical levels and specialization (Child 1973b, p. 172-173) and Marsden, Cook, and Kalleberg (1994, p. 916, Figure 2) show them for some, though not all, of their structural variables. Blau's (1970) theory of structural differentiation treats the curvilinearity explicitly. The curvilinear relationship between size and the many different aspects of structural differentiation is deduced from the basic proposition that size causes structural differentiation at decreasing rates with respect to size (Blau 1970, p. 204).

The reason why the rate of structural differentiation decreases with size is because of increasing pressure caused by the greater difficulty of coordination resulting from differentiation (Blau 1970, pp. 207, 212-214; but see also Meyer 1972, p. 439). This increased pressure means that there is a negative feedback on structural differentiation from the cost of increasing administrative overhead (Blau 1970, p. 217). However, increasing administrative overhead is accompanied in the model of Blau (1970, p. 218, Figure 6) by increasing administrative economy (as discussed in the previous chapter), so the increasing structural differentiation produces economies as well as costs. Therefore any economic constraint should be driven by the net effect of increasing administrative economy and overhead (i.e., savings and costs). Hence the feedback arrow in the causal model (Blau 1970, p. 218, Figure 6) should come from the joint effect of increasing administrative economy and overhead, not overhead alone. Moreover, given that, empirically, size increases are continuing to create economies even at large size (Blau 1970), there seems no reason for organizations to reduce the rate of structural differentiation as size increases. Thus the logic of this aspect of Blau's theory is unclear. The reason for the curvilinearity between size and structural differentiation must be sought elsewhere. We will consider first vertical structural differentiation and then its horizontal aspect.

Abdel-khalik (1988) argues that there is a mathematical relationship between size and the number of levels in a hierarchy, which accounts for the negative geometric relationship. Assuming that the span of control is the same at each level of the hierarchy, let us say seven, then in a two-level hierarchy there is a boss and seven workers, so that size of the organization is eight. In a three-level hierarchy, there is a boss, 7 supervisors, and 49 workers (7 x 7), so size is 57. In a four-level hierarchy, there is a boss, 7 managers, 49 supervisors (7 x 7) and 343 workers (7 x 7 x 7), so size is 400. Hence, every new level that is added increases size by a number that takes the number of existing workers and multiplies it by seven. Thus, mathematically speaking, every additional level adds to size the number seven raised to another power. This means that size increases by the span (of control) being raised to its next power. Thus size of the organization is equal to a series composed of 1 plus the span plus the span squared plus the span cubed, and so on, to span to the number of hierarchical levels minus one. Thus size is an increasing geometric series. Hence increases in the number of hierarchical levels correspond to geometrically increasing size. This means that geometrical increases in size are required to produce successive increases in the numbers of levels. Therefore each successive level of the hierarchy requires a greater size increase than the previous level. Thus hierarchical levels are a negative geometric function of size, in that size must increase geometrically for levels to be added. The relationship is geometric, but negatively so, in that the curve of levels on size becomes shallower as size increases. Hence hierarchical levels increase with size at a decreasing rate with respect to size, the observed empirical relationship (Blau and Schoenherr 1971).

Hence the insight of Abdel-khalik (1988) is essentially that organizational hierarchies are pyramidal structures, so that adding one more level at the base always involves adding many more employees than the present number of workers. The scenario is that all the old workers become supervisors and each supervises the number of new workers given by the span of control. Thus the number of new workers is the number of old workers multiplied by the span of control. Abdel-khalik (1988) assumes that hierarchies are symmetric in his mathematical model, so that all spans are the same and all managers and supervisors have the same number of subordinates. Neither of these conditions applies to real organizations (Blau 1971, p. 306; Blau and Schoenherr 1971). However, variations in spans and in the length of hierarchical chains to some extent cancel each other out. Thus while the elegant mathematics no longer strictly apply, the argument remains valid that any organization that approximates a pyramid must show a negative geometric curve of levels with size. Moreover, any organizational structure that seeks unity of command must approximate to a pyramid because all managers must report up to one top manager. Hence the rate of increase in structural differentiation declines with increasing size because the pyramidal shape of the hierarchy means that many more employees must be added to generate successive increases in levels as size grows. In that sense, size growth is pushing against the inherent barrier of a pyramid so that its effects on levels must become weaker as it increases. The barrier comes from the geometry of a pyramid, so that successively higher levels taper off with fewer persons at each level. The question arises as to whether other curvilinear relationships between size and other aspects of structural differentiation, such as the horizontal, can be explained similarly by some inherent limitation.

One aspect of horizontal structural differentiation is the division of labor, which conceptually is the narrowness of the scope of each job. Imagine a production process of assembling a pen. If the firm is minimally small, there is only one worker, who makes the whole pen. If the firm is larger, so that there are two workers in pen production, then each could specialize on some of the operations of assembling a whole pen. Thus now each worker does one half of the whole task, that is, specialization has doubled. If the firm is larger again, so that there are three workers in pen production, then specialization increases so that each worker does one third of the whole task. If there are four workers, each does one fourth. For five workers, each does one fifth. As size increases linearly (from 1 to 5 workers), specialization (as indexed by the proportion of the whole task being performed by each worker) increases in the series: 1, .50, .33, .25, and .20, respectively. Hence each additional worker increases the specialization index by .5, .17, .08 and .05, respectively. Thus, specialization increases at a less than proportionate rate to the increase in size. Specialization increases as size increases but at a declining rate with respect to size—a negative geometric relationship. As differentiation increases, that is to say, the work of the organization becomes split up among its members, the process of division means inherently that a negative geometric relationship with size is involved. Thus as specialization increases with size increase, it must do so at a declining rate with respect to size. This is inherent in splitting up a single entity into more and more pieces. Thus for an organization whose task is constant, such as making the same type of products or services, adding employees must lead to specialization that is progressively smaller in its increments. By implication, any basis of structural differentiation must increase with size, but with successive increments being less than the earlier ones because the same set of tasks is being split up progressively more finely. Thus the number of occupational titles, the number of divisions, the number of sections per department, and the degree of specialization by function should all increase with size at a declining rate with respect to size, the empirically observed relationships (Blau and Schoenherr 1971; Child 1973a). In this way the relationships between size and horizontal structural differentiation can be explained.

The curvilinear relationship between size and other measures of bureaucratic structure can be derived from this curvilinear relationship between size and structural differentiation. The relationship between structural differentiation and formalization is positive and linear, as is seen from the regression of overall documentation on overall role specialization and qualifications (Child 1973a, p. 182, Table 9). Thus a unit increase in specialization produces a unit increase in formalization. Given that size has a curvilinear effect on specialization, then increasing size would flow through specialization to produce the same curvilinear relationship of size with formalization. In this way the negative geometric relationship between size and formalization is explained. The specialized experts in administration, which are recorded in the Aston scales of functional and role specialization, together with the level of their qualifications (Pugh et al. 1968), produce new management systems, procedures, rules, regulations, and accompanying paperwork (Child 1973a). Each new type of specialist adds its new systems. But because the rate of addition of new types of specialists declines as size increases, the rate of increase in formalization also declines as size increases. Thus the curvilinear relationship between size and formalization can be explained, in addition to that between size and structural differentiation. Can the vertical aspect of structural differentiation and its relationship with decentralization be explained in a similar way?

As seen above, the pyramidal shape of the organizational hierarchy means that there is a negative geometric relationship of size and vertical structural differentiation (number of hierarchical levels). Therefore, if the number of hierarchical levels has a positive relationship with decentralization, then the curvilinear effect of size on levels flows through to produce a curvilinear relationship between size and decentralization. The explanation is that if levels cause decentralization because of lack of information among top management, then the declining rate at which levels are added with size increases, means that decentralization will also increase at a declining rate with respect to size.

Thus the negative geometric relationships between size and many aspects of bureaucratic structure can be explained by size necessarily having such relationships with specialization and hierarchical levels. These structural variables, in turn, have linear effects with formalization and decentralization, respectively, so that size has negative geometric relationships with formalization and decentralization. This is based on a simple kind of determinism of bureaucratic structure by size that inherently must have declining marginal effects on the vertical and horizontal structural differentiation that, in turn, affect decentralization and formalization.

Functionalist Explanations

The foregoing explains why the relationships between size and the bureaucratic structural variables are curvilinear, but it overlooks a deeper and more troubling issue. Arguing that size causes structural differentiation because of inherent limitations in differentiation can explain the form of the relationships, but it is not a functionalist explanation because it does not explain structure by its consequences for performance. Further, it is not a contingency type of functionalist theory because the explanation omits reference to a fit that affects performance. We will now discuss functionalist explanations of the relationship of size and bureaucratic structure, distinguishing between universalistic and contingency forms.

Functionalism explains that structures are adopted because they are beneficial for the organization. This may occur through organizational managers guiding the organization to adopt a more effective structure and thereby acting on behalf of the organization. However, another possibility is that organizational change may be driven by actors pursuing their own self-interests. As noted above, Child (1973a) argues that specialization causes formalization because this accords with the occupational ideology of administrative experts and furthers their self-interest. This political explanation answers the questions of how and why action occurs to increase formalization. However, the political explanation is not necessarily incompatible with functionalism, in that the politically motivated increases in formalization could be functional in their consequences for the organization (i.e., increasing its effectiveness). In such cases, the new systems that the specialists are pushing to create are needed by the organization. This would also further their career future, by being seen to help their organization. Such an interpretation appears to be empirically valid in that the increases in formalization that accompany size increases are positively related to performance, consistent with it being functional for the organization (Child 1975). Thus politics helps explain how action occurs and yet the increases in formalization are functional. Hence it is possible in this way to combine political explanations of action with functionalism. This gives an account of how beneficial systems change is brought about by actors, that is, it ties the levels of a system and action together (Giddens 1984; Parsons 1951; Silverman 1970). Here a causal relationship (specialization causes formalization) has been rendered functionalist by suggesting that positive performance consequences may flow from formalization. Other aspects of structure may be explained by functionalism if they have positive performance consequences.

Functionalism holds that organizations adopt structures that raise their performance. This means that a consequence (higher performance) becomes a cause. How is this accomplished? This question has occasioned weighty discussion (Isajew 1968; Silverman 1968). Three answers may be distinguished. The first is to say that the organization anticipates the benefits of adopting the new structure and this ideal image of the future in the minds of decision makers causes the adoption of the new structure (Etzioni 1968). The second is to say essentially that managers lack foresight, but experience problems with the existing structure and react by adopting a new structure that will restore performance (Child 1972b). The third is to say that organizations lack knowledge of better structures and so are culled by the environment and replaced by organizations with superior structures (Etzioni 1961; Hannan and Freeman 1989). We will discuss this population adaptation in Chapter 6 when considering population-ecology theory (Hannan and Freeman 1989). Thus for the moment we shall focus on anticipation or reaction to problems as the two mechanisms by which organizations adopt structures that are functional. We will consider size and bureaucracy first as explained by universalistic, functionalist theories. Next we will consider contingency functionalist theories that involve direct causation of structure by size. Then we will consider contingency functionalist theories that involve causation of structure by size indirectly, through misfit and performance, as SARFIT holds.

Universalistic Functionalist Explanation

In the case of Blau (1972), there are grounds for doubting whether his theory of structural differentiation is a contingency theory. He argues that organizations increase structural differentiation because specialization leads to greater efficiency, in that homogeneous tasks are "easier" (Blau 1972, p. 14) and reduce costs while increasing expertise: "The division of labor consequently has a double advantage. It makes it possible to fill many positions with less trained personnel, which facilitates recruitment and achieves economies, and to fill the most difficult jobs with more highly trained experts, which improves the quality of performance" (Blau 1972, p. 15).

Thus his theory is universalistic, in that maximum efficiency would result from maximum specialization. However, the highest level of specialization that an organization can attain is set by its size, that is, the number of employees available for specialization. Thus specialization causes efficiency, with size acting as a constraint on how much specialization is possible for a given organization: "the degree of feasible differentiation in an organization is limited by its size ... differentiation's instrumental contributions create the pressures that promote it to the degree size permits" (Blau 1972, p. 16). This is a universalistic theory with a situational constraint: size. It is not a contingency theory because there is no notion of fit. In particular, there is no concept that an organization could have too much specialization for its size and so be in misfit. Similarly, an organization that is too little specialized for its size is not in misfit, but rather is losing some of its potential performance because it has not specialized as much as it could given its size. Thus the optimal level of specialization for an organization is not one that fits its size, but rather the maximum it can attain given its size constraint.

In contrast, in contingency theory the organization does not strive to attain the maximum possible level of a structural variable, only to attain its optimal level, that is, the level that fits the contingency. Thus, in bureaucracy theory, the organization attains its highest performance by adopting the level of bureaucratic structure, for example, specialization, that fits its size (Child 1975), rather than by adopting the maximum level of the structural variable.

The way action creates structural differentiation in Blau's theory is consistent with it being a universalistic theory. Managers try to specialize as much as possible because they believe that specialization produces efficiency (Blau 1972, pp. 13, 16, 22). Thus the managers are following the universalistic theory. Given that universalistic theories are simpler and therefore easier to follow than contingency theories, which involve complexity and notions of fit, it is feasible to hold that managers follow universalistic theories. There is empirical evidence that the fit between structure and contingency may arise more because managers follow universalistic than contingency theory beliefs (Priem 1994). While this evidence pertains to organic theory rather than bureaucracy theory, it cautions that bureaucracy may also arise because of universalistic beliefs of managers. It suggests the need to inquire empirically into the beliefs of managers regarding bureaucratic structure to see whether they are universalistic or contingent. Universalistic beliefs of the classical management type would support Blau's theory of how organizational structures change over time. (However, universalistic managerial beliefs do not, of course, prove that universalistic theories about the objective relationship between structure and performance are correct and contingency theories incorrect, which is why continued research at the objective level is also needed.)

The functionalism in Blau (1972) is therefore of a universalistic kind: Organizations specialize as much as possible for their given size. Therefore, when an organization grows in size, the managers increase specialization up to the level allowed by its new size. This produces the causal connection between size and specialization. Given that specialization is enhanced by an increase in any of the horizontal aspects of structural differentiation, the implied causal model can be stated more generally as size causes horizontal aspects of structural differentiation that cause efficiency. The explicit causal model of Blau (1970, p. 218, Figure 6) is that size causes the structural differentiation that causes administrative intensity, with the reduction in administrative intensity being the main evidence of functionality in Blau's research (Blau 1970, 1972; Blau and Schoenherr 1971). The implicit and explicit causal models are of main effects between size and structure, and structure and functional outcomes. There is no contingency effect of structure on functional outcomes that depends upon a fit to size. Neither are there feedback effects of misfit on lower performance causing adaptations to attain new fits, as in the contingency theory of organizational change.

It seems unlikely, however, that the causal connection between size and hierarchical levels is a universalistic main effect. If it were, that would mean that management believes that performance is maximized by maximizing hierarchical levels, which runs counter to the prevailing social antipathy toward tall hierarchies as being ineffectual and wasteful. It would also mean that upper-level managers were seeking to add as many subordinate levels as possible, given the size constraint. Multiplying high status subordinates by adding new intermediary levels could be seen as aiding the self-interest of upper managers, by boosting their status and pay, consistent with a political explanation of their behavior (Parkinson 1957). However, this is contradicted by the observation that the span of control tends to increase as size increases (Blau 1970, 1972), so that management is adding new levels more parsimoniously as size and levels increase, arguing against political self-interest as a predominant causal process. Thus for the vertical aspect of structural differentiation (i.e., the number of hierarchical levels), it seems unlikely that this is caused by size in a universalistic fashion. By extension, this places a caution against accepting universalistic explanations of the horizontal aspects of structural differentiation.

Contingency Functionalist Explanation of Direct Causation

Another variant of functionalism, however, is consistent with the contingency theory that positive performance outcomes flow from the fit of structure to the contingencies. This contingency functionalist explanation would say that managers know the fits and so at the same time as increasing size they also increase the structural variables to attain new fits, thereby anticipating, and so avoiding, the performance loss that would have flowed from misfit. Thus there is no feedback effect of misfit through low performance. Instead, in this model there is a direct, if not instantaneous effect of size on structure. Thus this functionalist model is compatible with the causal model that size directly causes structure (as in the model in the first section of this chapter). Thus direct effects of size on the variables of bureaucratic structure can be consistent with contingency fit theory, if the adaptation is through anticipation, rather than feedback from lost performance due to misfit.

While the anticipation of fit is a logically possible type of contingency functionalism, and an appealing image of proactive management, it has difficulties. Management would need knowledge of the fits, which involves knowing contingency theory and also the scores on both the contingency and the structural variables that constitute the fit for their organization. Yet the structural variables are abstract quantities, such as specialization by function (Pfeffer 1997), that are assessed by arcane measurement scales (Pugh et al. 1968). Moreover, the fits are contained in mathematical formulas that are recorded in the esoteric research literature (e.g., Child 1975). Thus it is unlikely that the fits between size and the bureaucratic structural variables would be identified by the management for their organization. Hence it is more feasible that the organization moves into misfit and that the management then recognizes the problem and takes corrective action. Also, the low performance resulting from misfit provides the impetus to management to give priority to taking corrective action by adopting the new structure that fits the contingencies. For these reasons, anticipatory change is expected to be a less frequent occurrence than reactive change, which will now be discussed.

Contingency Functionalist Explanation of Indirect Causation

As seen, we can consider bureaucratic structure to consist of four components: horizontal differentiation, formalization, vertical differentiation, and decentralization. To be classed as a contingency theory, there must be fits between each of these components of structure and size that positively affect performance. The effect of misfit on performance feeds back to alter the structural variables. Thus the organization might increase in size, thereby creating a degree of misfit with the existing levels of the structural variables, which causes lower performance. The managers then seek to avoid this lost performance by increasing the structural variables to a new level that fits the new size, thereby regaining performance. This is the structural adaptation to regain fit (SARFIT) model. This functionalist explanation relies on causal connections between size and misfit, misfit and performance, and the feedback effect of performance on structure and thence of structure on fit. However, it does not entail a direct causal effect of size on any of the structural variables, nor of any structural variable on the other structural variables. Thus the contingency fit theory requires causal connections with fit, but not between the contingency and the structural variables that compose fit.

The contingency fit model would, of course, mean that size positively affects structure, but indirectly through the feedback effect of misfit on performance. Similarly, there would be a correlation between size and structure, because increases in size eventually cause increases in structure, but not because size directly causes structure. By implication, the theoretical rationales for a direct causal effect of size on structure, or of one structural variable on another, would not apply because there are no such causal relationships. Size does not increase specialization at a decreasing rate with respect to size, because of inherent limitations in dividing up the same task into smaller and smaller pieces. Specialization does not raise formalization because of experts utilizing their knowledge to create new management systems. The correlations among structural variables, such as the components of bureaucracy, would arise because each of them separately needs to fit with size. In this way, contingency fit theory explains why these associations exist without holding that the structural variables cause each other.

Figure 4.2 shows the causal relationships between size and bureaucratic structure and among components of bureaucratic structure. For convenience only two components of bureaucratic structure are shown: horizontal structural differentiation and formalization. The causal connection between size and each structural variable is indirect through misfit and performance as contingency theory holds. Looking first at horizontal structural differentiation, size has a negative effect on fit, because increasing size moves the organization into misfit with its existing level of horizontal structural differentiation. This misfit reduces performance. Therefore the low performance that results from

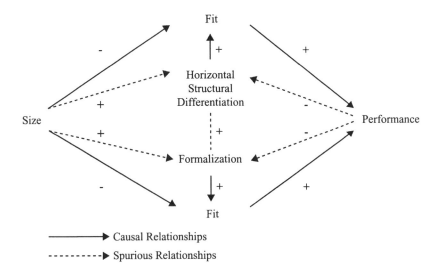

Figure 4.2. A Contingency Theory of Structural Change Caused by Feedback From Performance

the misfit feeds back to cause an increase in horizontal structural differentiation, which creates a new fit. Thus the effect of size on horizontal structural differentiation is indirect, through misfit and performance. Size affects fit negatively, while fit affects performance positively, and performance negatively affects horizontal structural differentiation. Algebraically the result of this multiplication of a negative sign by a positive sign and then a negative sign is a positive sign. Hence size has a positive correlation with horizontal structural differentiation, which could be misinterpreted as a direct positive effect on horizontal structural differentiation. However, such an interpretation is fallacious; the correlation is spurious because the effect of size on horizontal structural differentiation is indirect. While it is true to say that size causes horizontal structural differentiation, it is not because of some property of size that directly causes an increase in horizontal structural differentiation. Instead, it is because the size increase has created a misfit that adversely affects performance, which causes horizontal structural differentiation to increase in order to regain fit and performance.

A similar process occurs for formalization. Again, change in formalization in response to size increase occurs because of misfit and the feedback from the reduced performance. Thus the effect of size on formalization is indirect. The correlation between size and formalization is spurious. Size causes formalization, but through misfit and performance rather than from a property of size alone. Similar remarks would apply to vertical structural differentiation and decentralization. Thus the causal relationships between size and each component of bureaucratic structure are wholly indirect, mediated by fit and its effects on performance.

Given that size (indirectly) causes both horizontal structural differentiation and formalization in Figure 4.2, size increases simultaneously with both these structural variables, so that these structural variables are positively correlated. This might be interpreted as a causal connection between them, such as horizontal structural differentiation causing formalization. Yet this would be fallacious on the logic of Figure 4.2, because there is no direct causal connection between horizontal structural differentiation and formalization (though an indirect one). Thus, from the viewpoint of the contingency theory of structural change as driven by fit and the feedback of performance, there is no relationship between horizontal structural differentiation and formalization. Similar remarks apply to vertical structural differentiation and decentralization. Thus there is no causal connection among the four components of bureaucratic structure (horizontal structural differentiation, vertical structural differentiation, formalization, and decentralization).

Thus the SARFIT variant of contingency theory holds that the effect of size on bureaucratic structure is indirect and there is no direct causation among the components of bureaucratic structure. This gives a very different interpretation to bureaucracy theory from the traditional one. Thus the causal models of Blau (1970), Child (1973a), and Marsden, Cook, and Kalleberg (1994) are really very different from those required by contingency theory properly appreciated. The kind of simple, direct effects between size and components of bureaucratic structure that their causal models contain are to be distinguished from the contingency fit functionalism that is integral to contingency theory.

A Contingency Theory Causal
Model of Size and Bureaucracy

A conclusion may be made to the foregoing discussion by offering the following model that is based upon reactive contingency functionalism but that allows some role for anticipation and that includes other elements in a synthesis.

Size affects structural differentiation in the manner of contingency fit theory, on both the horizontal and vertical aspects of structural differentiation. On the horizontal aspect, increasing size adds employees, who initially stand idle or duplicate and interfere with the task execution of other employees, until the work is reorganized so that old and new employees each have a specialized role, so that specialization increases. Until specialization is increased to fit the new size, the disorganization lowers performance. Thus size leads to misfit and then to the increase in specialization that restores fit and performance. Thus size causes increases in specialization, that is, horizontal structural differentiation, indirectly through misfit and lower performance.

Similarly, on the vertical aspect, increasing size widens the span of control of a manager to the point where it becomes too wide and so performance suffers, which means that the span no longer fits the size. To avoid further performance loss, a new level in the hierarchy is created, which restores fit and performance. Thus size causes increases in hierarchical levels, that is, vertical structural differentiation, indirectly through misfit and lower performance. Thus size causes both the horizontal and vertical aspects of structural differentiation through the feedback of the contingency effects of misfit on performance. The effect of size on structural differentiation, however, is not linear, but curvilinear. Structural differentiation increases with respect to size at a decreasing rate with respect to size because of the inherent limitations of specializing work and adding levels to a pyramidal hierarchy (as explained above).

In some organizations, management may avoid misfit by adjusting the level of structural differentiation immediately after increasing size. As examples, specialization would be increased immediately new employees are recruited, or a new intermediary hierarchical level would be created immediately the span of control of a manager exceeds its optimal. In such cases there is no feedback effect of performance and so the effect of size on structure is not indirect but direct. The reason why the structure is changed is because of the contingency fit, so that the direct effect of size on structure is accompanied by the contingency fit effect on performance and is consistent with it.

Specialization leads to formalization because the specialists seek to have new systems adopted. This reflects their professional training and ideology and their political self-interest. However, while many new systems are likely to be advocated by various specialists in the organization, only some are adopted. New systems are most likely to find acceptance where they offer to resolve problems, and such problems will tend to exist where the organization has low performance because of being in misfit. Thus specialization increases formalization of those aspects of the organization that are in misfit because size increase has outstripped the level of formalization. The increase in formalization is due to the new administrative specialists, created by the recent size increases, who promote their management systems. Thus, formalization is increasing through adaptation to regain fit and performance, as SARFIT holds, so that the causal effect of specialization on formalization is accompanied by the feedback effect of misfit and lower performance.

Vertical structural differentiation, that is, the number of levels in the hierarchy, affects decentralization in a similar manner to the way horizontal structural differentiation (specialization) affects formalization. An increase in the number of levels in a hierarchy impedes the flow of information to the upper levels and so renders central decision making less effective while also slowing the response of the organization to changes "down on the firing line." Therefore the existing degree of centralization becomes a misfit to the new size because of the number of hierarchical levels that size induces, with adverse consequences for performance. This causes management to increase the degree of decentralization and thereby restore the fit of decentralization to size and regain performance. Thus the effect of hierarchical levels on decentralization depends upon misfit and performance and so, is indirect. The management of some organizations may avoid misfit by increasing levels and decentralization concurrently. Thus, immediately a new intermediary hierarchical level is created, it is delegated authority to make some decisions. In such a scenario there is a direct effect of levels on decentralization, because of anticipation of fit and its benefits for performance.

Thus, overall, there can be causal connections between each of size and specialization, specialization and formalization, size and hierarchy, and hierarchy and decentralization. This would be consistent with the causal models that arise from empirical research (Blau 1970; Child 1973a; Marsden, Cook, and Kalleberg 1994). Yet each of the causal connections between these pairs of variables could be indirect, involving contingency misfit and the feedback from low performance, as SARFIT holds, rather than direct effects. In some organizations, on some occasions, management might correctly anticipate the need to adopt a new structure to fit the new level of the contingency. However, such proactivity may well be rare because it requires knowledge of fits that are complex and subtle, which may be lacking, and also the will to change, which may also be lacking in the absence of performance problems. Thus there are grounds for holding, theoretically, that the causal connections among size and the bureaucratic structural variables are primarily indirect effects that occur because of misfit and low performance.

It is possible that in some of these linkages universalistic beliefs might play a role, in the manner of Blau (1972). For instance, management might believe that specialization increases performance and so will immediately increase specialization as employees are added, which increases the specialization level up to that which fits the new size. In this way, each time size increases, the organization moves into fit and gains beneficial consequences for its performance. Thus the objective relationship is between fit and performance, but fit is achieved because management is guided by a subjective belief of the universalistic type. The result is that size directly causes specialization. Thus there may be some role for universalistic beliefs even if universalistic functionalism is invalid objectively. The role of universalistic beliefs and direct causation by size may be limited to specialization and formalization, as they are most consistent with the Tayloristic scientific management principles that may undergird such management beliefs.

Overall, the relationship among the size and bureaucratic structure variables is held to be mainly explicable by reactive contingency functionalism. A secondary mechanism is anticipatory contingency functionalism whereby causation occurs directly among size and the bureaucratic structural variables. A third ranking mechanism is anticipatory universalistic beliefs whereby causation occurs directly among size and the bureaucratic structure variables. However, all three of these mechanisms are functionalist, involving beneficial outcomes for the organization. This is the view that emerges from seeking to explain the relationships among size and bureaucratic structural variables by contingency theory, with its functionalist emphasis on the consequences for performance and the crucial roles of fit and misfit. It takes us beyond the simpler causal models of size and bureaucracy in a direction that entails more complexity but thereby attains more theoretical coherence within the contingency paradigm.

This model is to be taken as a theoretical statement, so that the task for future empirical research is to inquire into its validity, relative to other, perhaps simpler models. Do the relationships between size and bureaucratic structure, and among the components of bureaucratic structure, arise because of contingency misfit and performance feedback, as contingency theory in its SARFIT variant holds? Or do they arise because managers correctly and expeditiously anticipate the need to fit structure to new size levels? Or do they, rather, arise because managers cleave to erroneous universalistic beliefs that nevertheless create contingency fits? These are some of the questions for future empirical research to emerge from the theoretical discussion herein.

Conclusions

In terms of a causal model of the relationship between size and the components of bureaucratic structure, the following can be postulated, building on previous theoretical and empirical research. Size causes structural differentiation that causes formalization and centralization, with formalization also being a cause of centralization. The effect of size on structural differentiation is a negative geometric function, so that size also shows this same curvilinear relationship with formalization and centralization. The negative geometric function of structural differentiation on size means that structural differentiation increases with respect to size at a decreasing rate to size. Such curvilinearity may reflect inherent physical barriers, in that specialization becomes progressively finer as it increases with size, and the pyramidal shape of a hierarchy means that progressively more employees are required to build each hierarchical level.

In contradistinction, functionalism stresses that structures are adopted because of their beneficial outcomes. Action may be driven in part by political self-interest of organizational members, but nevertheless still be functionalist in outcomes. Universalistic functionalism provides a simple model whereby size directly causes bureaucratic structure; however, this is considered to lack generality as a causal mechanism. Contingency theory holds that positive organizational performance results from the fit of structure to size. Where management correctly anticipates the new fit, then a size increase could directly cause an increase in bureaucratic structure. However, the complexity and subtlety of contingency fits makes this less feasible. Moreover, the impetus to structural change is impelled more strongly by low performance. Therefore structural change in response to increasing size is held to be primarily indirect through misfit and low performance as SARFIT holds, that is, reactive contingency functionalism. Thus the feedback effect of lost performance from misfit could bring about the observed associations among size and the bureaucratic structural variables, without size having a direct effect on structure. Anticipatory contingency functionalism may play a more restricted secondary role to reactive contingency functionalism. A smaller role again may be played by universalistic beliefs that unwittingly impel structural change into fit. Hopefully, the theoretical model articulated here will lead to a more incisive analysis of the role of contingency theory fit caused relationships of size and bureaucracy in future empirical research, through inquiry into the various mechanisms discussed herein.

5 Controversies in Contingency
Theory Research

W ithin the contingency theory literature there have been a number
of controversial issues. There have been debates over the relative
importance of rival contingency factors such as technology and size.
Also there is criticism of the determinism in contingency theory, and
moves to replace it with strategic choice. Again the inference that contingency causes structure has been challenged by the rival interpretations
that the contingency variables are mere correlates rather than being
causes, or that structure causes the contingency. These intellectual moves
offer an escape from the idea that contingencies make some structure,
such as bureaucracy, inevitable for an organization and open the door
to alternative structures, such as the organic. Again, some scholars have
sought to replace the multivariate contingency approach by configurations based on consistency theory. Contingency theory has been used
to explain power distributions within and between organizations, but
these explanations have been criticized in various ways. These six controversial issues of technology, strategic choice, causality, reverse causality,
configurations, and power will be considered in this chapter.

The criticisms of the original variant of contingency theory and attempts to revise its component parts have led to deeper examination of these issues. This deeper examination has tended to support the original contingency theory and to disconfirm the revisionist views. In particular there is support for the idea that contingency determines organizational structure. Thus much of this chapter is an argument for contingency theory in its original form. More specifically, the discussion of several of these issues provides support for bureaucracy theory.

Technology Versus Size

Despite the reconciliation between the organic and bureaucracy theories that we offered in Chapter 3, there is still a tension between these theories that is played out partly as an argument about the roles of the task and size contingencies. This has led to a long-running debate about the relative importance for organizational structure of task, in terms of technology, and size, that continues down to the present. The debate between technology and size has fueled an extensive discussion that has raised many issues of theory and method. The resulting literature is complex. Almost any statement made about this literature requires several qualifications and exceptions. However, we shall try to offer an overview of some of its main points.

The debate considered here is about whether technology determines overall organizational structure, relative to the explanation provided by size. The variables being explained are overall aspects of organizational structure, such as the number of levels in the hierarchy, the spans of control at the top and bottom of the hierarchy, the percentages of administrative support staff, and the mechanistic versus organic structures. Thus the interest is in the effect of technology on the overall shape of the organizational structure and management system as a whole. This macro-level focus is to be distinguished from the micro-level issue of whether individuals' roles (i.e., jobs) are affected by characteristics of the task being performed, such as uncertainty. There is considerable evidence that greater task uncertainty leads to less structured roles (Gerwin 1979b). Again, task interdependence between jobs affects role structures such as formation of teams and autonomous workgroups (Trist and Bamforth 1951; Wall et al. 1990). Such effects are part of the way that task affects the micro-structure, and in Chapter 3 we suggested that we can reconcile bureaucracy and organic theories by accepting that task shapes the micro-structure and size shapes the macro-structure. However, the issue being discussed here is whether technology shapes the macro-structure. Thus the debate is about whether technology has grander effects than the modest one attributed to it in the reconciliation in Chapter 3.

In outline, proponents of organic theory have sought to show that technology leads away from mechanistic toward organic structures (Woodward 1965). In contrast, proponents of bureaucracy theory have sought to show that technology has only weak effects relative to size (Child and Mansfield 1972; Hickson, Pugh, and Pheysey 1969). An implication is that the reduction in bureaucracy flowing from technology would be swamped by large increases in size, or nullified by more moderate increases in size. Again, other bureaucracy theorists have argued that technology actually leads to more bureaucracy, so that advances in technology reinforce the effects of size increases, rather than diminishing bureaucracy (Blau, et al.1976).

Woodward (1965) found empirically that technology affected organizational structure and that size was not associated with organizational structure. The Aston Study carefully sought to replicate Woodward's study. Its authors measured her operational technology construct with a scale that they called production continuity (Hickson, Pugh, and Pheysey 1969). They measured many aspects of organizational structure that differed from Woodward's, but also had several the same as hers, for example, the span of control of the first-line supervisor. The Aston Study found few of the relationships that Woodward had found between her technology measure and her structural variables (Hickson, Pugh, and Pheysey 1969). The subsequent study by the Aston Group, the National Study, found even fewer of her relationships (Child and Mansfield 1972). Moreover, the Aston and National Studies found little relationship between Woodwardian technology and their many other (non-Woodwardian) structural measures (Child and Mansfield 1972; Hickson, Pugh, and Pheysey 1969). Further, these studies measured other aspects of production technology, different from Woodward, and these also had few, mainly weak relationships to organizational structure (Child and Mansfield 1972; Hickson, Pugh, and Pheysey 1969). In contrast, size had relationships with many different aspects of organizational structure, often strong and almost always stronger than technology. Therefore in multivariate analyses, size rather than technology emerged as the underlying contingency factor (Child and Mansfield 1972; Hickson, Pugh, and Pheysey 1969). The Aston Group challenged Woodward, and their different findings cannot be explained away by methodology.

The cross-sectional nature of the Aston Study was seized upon by some commentators who advanced other causal interpretations. These included that technology, as measured by a construct other than Woodward's, caused size and also structuring, which in turn also was a cause of size—thereby turning the Aston interpretation on its head (Aldrich 1972a, 1972b; Heise 1972; Hilton 1972). Pugh and Hickson (1972) pointed out that in the absence of longitudinal data, causal interpretations are hazardous. However, even with cross-sectional data, reasoning can be used to clarify causality. If technology is the cause of structure, then organizations that have the same technology would be expected to have the same structure. Yet Donaldson and Warner (1974) found that in labor unions, organizations that have little difference in technology, there were nevertheless wide variations in structure that were strongly correlated with size. This is consistent with size rather than technology being the cause of structure.

Many studies have continued to investigate the relative roles of technology and size, using various definitions of technology: Grinyer and Yasai-Ardekani (1981); Khandwalla (1974); Lincoln, Hanada, and McBride (1986); Marsh and Mannari (1976, 1980, 1981), Reimann (1977, 1980); and Singh (1986). But debating the relative strengths of technology and size assumes that there is an effect of technology on structure and that it is of the Woodward (1965) kind, that is, promoting the organic structure. It may therefore be fruitful to focus on just the technology effect on structure, to verify that it exists and to ascertain whether its nature is that which Woodward (1965) argued.

Returning to the Woodward measure of technology, Zwerman (1970) reported replicating Woodward's findings that the fit between technology and structure led to higher performance. However, a secondary analysis of the study by Donaldson (1976) showed an absence of such relationships. Moreover, Donaldson (1976) also showed that none of the relationships between technology and structure found by Woodward (1965) replicated consistently across the subsequent studies that had used the same technology and structural variables as Woodward (Child and Mansfield 1972; Hickson, Pugh, and Pheysey 1969; Zwerman 1970). He concluded that there was no valid generalization connecting Woodwardian technology and organizational structure. However, the method employed, requiring each finding to be significant, has now been superseded by meta-analysis. We shall therefore turn to the results of meta-analyses to form a more definitive conclusion about the technology-structure relationship. However, at the time, the critique of Woodward was seen as damaging (Eilon 1977), so that the immediately subsequent contributions had to deal with this highly negative evaluation.

Reimann and Inzerilli (1979) countered on behalf of technology. They argued that there was a level-of-analysis problem in that some studies that found little relationship between technology and structure failed to measure both technology and structure at the same level, that is, the level of the overall organizational system. Reimann (1980) also argued that at the systems level, that is, the overall organization, where much work is administrative, structure was affected by the technology at that level, that is, office automation through computerization and information technology. Thus we need to consider whether the aspect of technology that is the contingency for organizational structure, and that thereby constitutes an imperative, is actually computerization.

Whisler, Meyer, Baum, and Sorensen (1967) argued that computerization facilitated the movement of information around the organization, horizontally and vertically, that is, from department to department and between bottom and top. This was held to lead to a reduction in structural differentiation so that computerization would reduce the number of departments and levels in the hierarchy, leading to a re-centralization of decision making. In an empirical study of computerization in the insurance industry, Whisler et al. (1967) found evidence supporting their theory. However, computerization reduced the numbers of employees and this alone could produce the observed structural changes. Given that size causes structural differentiation and decentralization, a size reduction would decrease structural differentiation and also lead to recentralization. Thus organizational structural change caused by computerization may flow through the intermediary variable of size. Hence size would be the key to structure and there would be no independent effect of computerization reversing bureaucratization in the absence of size change.

Indeed, contrary to Whisler et al. (1967), Blau and Schoenherr (1971) and also Blau et al. (1976) argue that computerization has effects similar to those of size, namely, that computerization increases structural differentiation, both horizontally and vertically. It also leads to more decentralization of decision making in that top management knows that lower-level employees are being forced to follow standard procedures that are now programmed into the computers and are subject to computer surveillance. Thus computerization provides another indirect control over lower-level employees that enables top management to relinquish its direct control to a degree, thereby increasing delegation. Thus computerization is really another aspect of bureaucratization. Moreover, it feeds back to raise the levels of other aspects of bureaucratization (more structuring and decentralization). Blau et al. (1976) see office automation as part of bureaucratization that reinforces the effect of size in pushing organizational structure to be more bureaucratic. Computerization can be considered to be part of the wider trend toward formal rationality that Weber (1968) saw as characterizing modern society and that produces bureaucracy.

Blau's theory receives support from a meta-analytic review of technology that shows that computerization is positively related to organizational structure (Caufield 1989). Specifically, computerization is positively related to structuring variables, though not to decentralization, showing that Blau's theory mostly generalizes across the studies. Thus focusing on office automation reveals an effect of technology on organizational structure, but it is weak and secondary to size, and promotes bureaucratization.

The meta-analytic reviews also reveal similar effects for operations technology, whether measured by the Woodward or other measures. Operations technology has linear relationships with organizational structural variables (Caufield 1989), rather than the curvilinear relations claimed by Woodward (1965) and others (including Blau et al. 1976). The relationships are positive between operations technology and organizational structure. More specifically, operations technology is associated with the structuring variables, but the correlations are weak (around +.3). Operations technology has similar relationships with organizational structure to those between computerization and organizational structure. It does not matter whether operations or office technologies are examined, the technology effects are the same. The technology-structure relationships (including those with operations technology) are unaffected by the size of the organizations studied, thus casting doubt on the idea that technology has more impact on macro-structure in smaller organizations than in larger ones (Hickson, Pugh, and Pheysey 1969).

The meta-analysis by Miller, Glick, Wang, and Huber (1991) also found that the relationship between technology and structure was robust and unaffected by some potential moderators, including several often cited in the literature, such as different definitions of technology and organizational size, though some moderators were found. However, their method is not a complete meta-analysis in that it does not examine how much of the variation in findings between studies is due to artifacts and therefore is spurious variation. Caufield examined the issue of artifacts, producing evidence of the robustness of the general relationship between technology and structure. Much of the variation, 70 percent, in findings from study to study is due to sampling error, that is, to small sample size. Range restriction explained another 17 percent, so that artifacts explain 87 percent of variation across studies (Caufield 1989, p. 150). Thus any role for moderator variables that conditions the technology-structure relationship is, at best, limited.

Advances in technology, whether operational or administrative, lead to more bureaucracy, reinforcing the effect of growth in size. Thus, in our view, the technology-versus-size debate may be resolved by saying that size is the more important contingency of organizational structure than technology, though both have the same type of effects. Technology, like size, increases the bureaucratization of the macro-structure, rather than reducing it as organic theory claims. This marks a major restriction in the validity of organic theory, so that its domain becomes limited to the micro-structure. It supports the reconciliation between bureaucracy and organic theories proposed in Chapter 3.

Determinism Versus Choice

As we have seen, structural contingency theory holds that change in the contingency leads to change in organizational structure, because of the need to regain fit and performance. Therefore contingency theory is deterministic (Astley and Van de Ven 1983). The organization responds to changes in the contingencies and thereby to the environment that in turn shapes those contingencies. Disquiet has been expressed about this determinism, especially where contingency theory argues that given certain contingencies, the organization has no choice but to adopt centralized or bureaucratic structures that lack participatory or democratic features (Schreyögg 1980). Therefore those who favor participatory, organic structures have been motivated to argue against contingency determinism or to show that contingencies have only weakly constraining power so that choice of organic structures is possible regardless of the contingencies.

Some scholars have argued strenuously against the idea that the organization is determined by its situation and have instead asserted that managers have free choice and are thereby to be held morally accountable (Bourgeois 1984; Whittington 1989). Contingency theory appears to some critics to be a managerially convenient ideology that justifies as inevitable organizational characteristics that are not really inevitable, because they are not really required for organizational effectiveness, and that injure the interests of employees (Schreyögg 1980). Thus contingency theory is opposed by free choice.

An intermediate position within this debate is that propounded by Child (1972b), which he terms "strategic choice" (though he is talking about choice regarding structure). This takes the contingency theory of organizational structure but shows that some degree of choice can nevertheless enter in at several stages in the process (Child 1972b). Organizations can have dominant economic positions and slack resources, so avoiding the need to adapt. Adaptation can be of contingency to structure, thereby avoiding an imperative to change structure. The effect of contingency is quite limited, and managerial decisions intervene between the objective situation and the structure chosen. All of these and other means increase the role of choice (Child 1972b; see also Child 1997). In these ways, perception, belief, political interests, and power are added to the contingency theory model so that human action is entered into a model that otherwise deals in impersonal variables such the environment, size, structure, and performance. The conclusion of Child (1972b) is that by embracing strategic choice, organizational theory can avoid the pessimism and fatalism that inheres in ideas that bureaucracy or other managerially favored structures are somehow inevitable. Thus strategic choice is held to open the door to choosing structures that include more democratic or participatory features.

The full strategic choice model is complex and will not be repeated here. Donaldson (1985) offers a critical examination of its logic that argues that it simply substitutes one set of determinants for another, thereby negating choice. Moreover, he argues that more emancipated choices about organizational structure come not from pursuing research into choice but rather from developing more valid models of organizational design that can better inform decision making. Thus Donaldson (1985) accepts the idea of choice but argues that reaching the objectives of making wider choices involves researching the outcomes of choice options rather than investigating how choice operates.

Subsequently, however, new evidence led Donaldson (1996b, pp. 14-40) to question how much choice really exists over structure and to argue that contingencies largely determine structure. Thus the original thesis of contingency theory, that there is an imperative on organizations to adopt the structure that is dictated by their contingencies to avoid performance loss, is truer than the strategic choice thesis of a large degree of choice over structure. Donaldson (1996b) goes through the evidence and shows that many of the propositions in strategic choice theory are not supported. He argues that the empirical evidence to date shows the validity of the deterministic contingency theory of organizational structure. For example, the average correlation between size and functional specialization, when corrected for measurement error in functional specialization, is +.82 (Donaldson 1986, pp. 86, 90; also, 1996a, p. 31). This correlation is so high that there is little scope for other factors to intervene and create choice. Moreover, as we saw in the previous chapter, functional specialization causes other aspects of structure, such as standardization and documentation (Child 1973a, p. 182 Table 9), so that these structural variables are also highly determined by the size contingency, indirectly through the effect of size on functional specialization.

As another example, whereas traditional contingency theory holds that organizations in misfit change their structure to regain fit (e.g., Chandler 1962; Woodward 1965), Child (1972b) argues that they could instead change their contingency to regain fit, thereby avoiding having to fit their structure to the contingency. In this way structure is not determined by the contingency and instead managers have a choice. However, empirical research shows that in less than 5 percent of cases organizations regain fit through altering the contingency of diversification to fit the functional structure (Donaldson 1987). Even in these few cases the reason for changing the contingencies might not be regaining fit, but rather strategic change forced by very low performance. While some dediversifying of organizations has occurred, empirical studies do not conclude that they are attempts to regain fit (Davis, Diekmann, and Tinsley 1994; Hoskisson and Hitt 1994). Thus the idea of a route to regain fit through contingency change is a theoretical notion that is seldom used in reality, so that organizations adapt their structures to their contingencies, as contingency theory holds.

Strategic choice theory draws on the image of the large organization that is so dominant that its wealth allows it to absorb the costs of structural misfit and also to control, rather than be determined by, its environment (Child 1972b). While dominant market share and other factors can to a degree offset the depressing effect on organizational performance of structural misfit, the former are not so much more important than the latter as to render the misfit ineffectual for organizational change. Hamilton and Shergill (1993, p. 79 Table 8.3) investigate the effect of industry concentration, a proxy of the degree of oligopolization, which indexes market share. They show that this affects 27 percent of growth in corporate financial performance, but that structural misfit affects it almost as much, by 23 percent. For profit, industry concentration affects 28 percent, while structural misfit affects 16 percent. Thus, while market power affects performance more than structural misfit, structural misfit is not trivial relative to the market power. Hence structural misfit will significantly degrade performance and increase the probability of adaptation. Many of the studies of organizations adapting to their changing strategy contingency are of the largest corporations in their countries, such as the largest 100 or Fortune 500, and so would possess dominant market positions (e.g., Chandler 1962; Channon 1973; Dyas and Thanheiser 1976; Fligstein 1985; Hamilton and Shergill 1992, 1993; Rumelt 1974; Suzuki 1980). Despite their large size, dominant market position, and wealth, even these organizations have, sooner or later, bowed to the dictate to adjust their structure to their strategy contingency, consistent with the observation that the performance loss from structural misfit is substantial.

Large organizations can influence their environments through lobbying governments, advertising, and other means (Perrow 1986; Pfeffer and Salancik 1978). Nevertheless, this influence of the organization on its environment can coexist with the environment influencing the organization and causing changes to certain internal aspects, such as its organizational structure (Burns and Stalker 1961; Thompson 1967). Moreover, the capacity of even large corporations to "engineer their environments" to make them more conducive can easily be overstated.

Hirsch (1975) shows that highly regulated environments (pharmaceuticals) allow firms to make higher profits than lowly regulated environments (phonograph records). However, the pharmaceutical industry is highly regulated because of public concerns about possible adverse effects of drugs, whereas much less public pressure occurs about phonograph records. Firms cannot, at will, change their environments so as to be highly regulated and profitable. General Motors (GM) is sometimes seen as exemplifying how large corporations control their environments. Notwithstanding some such capacity, GM suffered declining market share in its core market in the 1980s and profit decline to the point where its CEO was dismissed, so GM and its management were not able to control key features of its environment and their fates. Thus even GM has been forced to adapt its structure to changes in its strategic contingencies (Chandler 1962).

A number of studies have supported strategic choice theory by showing the effects on organizational form (e.g., structure) of characteristics of their managers, such as personality or functional background (At-Twaijiri and Montanari 1987; Finkelstein and Hambrick 1996; Fligstein 1985, 1991; Miller and Droge 1986; Miller, Droge, and Toulouse 1988; Miller and Toulouse 1986; Montanari 1979). However, the effect of these managerial characteristic variables tends to be secondary relative to the contingency variables such as organizational diversification or size (Donaldson 1996b, pp. 41-57). Moreover, some of these managerial characteristics are determined by contingencies, so that they are means by which contingencies indirectly affect organizational form. For instance, the functional background of the CEO affects the strategy and structure of a firm (Fligstein 1985, 1991). However, providing a CEO is a manifestation of a functional department being powerful relative to other departments, and departmental power is affected by the contingency of the critical environmental challenge facing the company (Hambrick 1981; Hickson, Hinings, Lee, Schneck, and Pennings 1971; Hinings, Hickson et al. 1974; Fligstein 1990a; Pfeffer and Salancik 1978). Thus, while some managerial characteristics research provides evidence of some degree of strategic choice, other research is revealing the determinist effects on organizations of contingencies.

Thus the best evidence to date disconfirms strategic choice and argues that it is mostly false, so that the extent of choice over structure is, at most, limited (see Donaldson 1996b, pp. 14-57 for further evidence and argument). Contingencies determine structure. Organizations change their structures to fit the existing level of their contingency factors, such as size or diversification, in order to avoid performance loss from misfit.

The adaptation of structure to contingency often has a time lag, which in some cases may be for years (Dyas and Thanheiser 1976). Whittington (1989) argues that such lags constitute strategic choice. However, such time lags occur because the crisis of low performance that triggers adaptive structural change is delayed due to the influence of other causes of performance. When the joint event of chronic misfit and the other causes of performance depress it low enough, then the structure will change, so moving the organization into fit, fulfilling the contingency imperative (Donaldson 1987). In this way, time lags in structural adaptation reflect the determinist effect of performance rather than resulting from free choice or providing occasions for its exercise.

In sum, despite the attractiveness of the strategic choice theory, it fails to withstand scrutiny. Organizational structures are determined to a high degree by contingencies, as shown by very high correlations with contingencies such as size. Organizations almost invariably move into fit through adaptation of their structure to the contingency, so that the contingency is an imperative to which structure must be molded. While organizations may affect aspects of their environment, nevertheless, the environment and contingencies determine their structure. This holds also for large organizations that enjoy dominant market positions, because of the substantial performance they lose from being in misfit. Organizational slack can lead to delays in structural adaptation, rather than its avoidance. Subjective factors affect structure, but they are minor relative to the contingencies. Some are determined by the contingencies and so are part of the way that contingencies determine structure. Managers choose new structures, and in that way add value, but choose the structure that fits the contingencies, so that the structures are situationally determined (Donaldson 1996b, pp. 50-52).

While the strategic choice idea is appealing, it has turned out to lack validity in many of its arguments. The strategic choice theory has forced a closer examination of many of the ideas that compose the original contingency theory. However, the more those ideas are inspected by empirical inquiry, the more they turn out to be valid. Latterly, Whittington has been involved in an empirical analysis of the adoption of divisional structure by European firms, and this leads him to reverse his prior view that organizations are governed by free choice and instead to accept that they are determined by diversification, as positivist theories hold (Donaldson 1996b). As he and his colleagues conclude: "... Donaldson's (1996) 'positivist' project for organization theory has again found international support, and in a normative context much less favourable than that of early divisionalization" (Whittington, Mayer, and Curto 1999, p. 546). Thus closer empirical study has led Whittington to reverse much of his earlier opposition to contingency determinism (Whittington 1989).

Size as Cause of Bureaucratic Structure

As we have seen, size is a prominent contingency in contingency theory research. There are many studies showing cross-sectional correlations between size and various aspects of organizational structure (e.g., Blau 1972; Pugh and Hinings 1976). The theory of Blau (1970) categorically states that size causes structural differentiation and other structural variables. The Aston Group was less explicit, but size is almost invariably treated as an independent variable in analyses of organizational structure in Aston program studies (Pugh and Hickson 1976; Pugh and Hinings 1976). Moreover, Child (1973a), in his theoretical interpretation of the Aston Group work, posited that size caused structure. Subsequent researchers have tended to follow this lead of treating size as a cause, so that correlations between size and structure are interpreted as size causing structure. However, this convention has been challenged as lacking theoretical justification (Kimberly 1976). Further, path analyses have been made of the Aston data in which size is caused by structure (see Heise 1972; Hilton, 1972). A diachronic analysis (i.e., comparison across time) in which changes in size are compared with subsequent changes in structure failed to support size as being a cause of structure, thereby leading to the argument that Blau's general relationships are static scale phenomena and not dynamics caused by size (Cullen, Anderson, and Baker 1986).

However, other diachronic analyses show that size causes bureaucratic structure. Meyer (1972) analyzed diachronic empirical data and found that size caused structure and that almost none of the positive, cross-sectional correlation between size and structure arose from any reverse causal effect of structure on size, thus supporting Blau's (1970) theory that size causes structural differentiation. Marsh and Mannari (1989, p. 88, Figure 1) analyzed longitudinal data from their study of Japanese manufacturing firms and found that size caused structural complexity (horizontal structural differentiation multiplied by vertical structural differentiation); moreover, the numerical estimate was only somewhat weaker than the cross-sectional association between size and structural complexity. Similarly, size caused administrative intensity, though the longitudinal estimate was about half that of the cross-sectional (for a discussion of this study, see Donaldson 1996b, pp. 98-104). Hence the Marsh and Mannari (1989) study supports Blau's causal theory that size causes structural differentiation and administrative intensity, rather than size being a mere correlate of structure. Overall, the results from studies, while having some conflicting findings, lend support to the view that size causes structure rather than to there just being a static association between scale and structure.

Reverse Causality

As we have stressed, contingency theory sees the connection between contingency and structure as being because contingency causes structure. This implies determinism of structure by contingency, which leads to conclusions about the inevitability of bureaucracy that are resisted by some scholars, as we saw in the sections above. Another way to escape the impasse is to argue that associations between contingency and structure arise because structure causes contingency. Thus, observed associations between contingency and structure lose their implication of the determinism of structure by contingency. In formal terms, the argument is that causality is retained but inverted. Therefore contingency determinism has to answer the reverse causality argument.

The issue has also been raised of whether contingency causes structure and also structure causes contingency, that is, reciprocal causality. Contingency theory would not be damaged, if, *in addition to* contingency causing structure, structure causes contingency. However, it is damaged, if, *instead of* contingency causing structure, as contingency theory supposes, structure causes contingency, that is, reverse causality. In that case, the whole imagery of organizations adapting to their contingency situation would be false.

The possibility that the causality between contingency and structure is really the reverse, that is, structure causing the contingency, contains a deeper problem for contingency theory. It raises the possibility that the contingency variable is not really a contingency, thus calling into question the fundamental basis of contingency theory. As we have seen, the strategic diversification contingency causes adoption of a divisional structure because that structure fits diversification and so its adoption restores performance, that is, the explanation is through an underlying contingency fit. However, any reverse causality of structure causing strategy may not be because of any underlying contingency fit. For instance, the argument that divisionalization causes diversification because divisional structures have more general managers and are thereby more likely to see the merits of diversification, is a universalistic theory that does not involve any contingency fit idea (Rumelt, 1974; Scott, 1971). In such a case, proving reverse causality, that is, that divisionalization causes diversification rather than diversification causes divisionalization, would disprove not only the contingency theory of change, but also the fit idea, which is at the core of the paradigm. Hence the issues raised by reverse causality can go beyond mere direction of causality.

Chandler (1962) and others (e.g., Channon 1973; Rumelt 1974) argue that strategy causes divisionalization. However, the argument has been made that structure leads to strategy (Hall and Saias 1980), and this may be taken as challenging the contingency theory idea that strategy leads to structure. As we shall show, the structure-leads-to-strategy arguments do not successfully challenge the idea that strategy leads to structure.

Amburgey and Dacin (1994) find both that strategy causes structure and that structure causes strategy, though the effect of strategy on structure is stronger than vice versa. This demonstrates *reciprocal* causation between the strategy contingency and structure, and shows that reverse causality coexists with strategy, causing structure rather than replacing it.

In the Chandlerian thesis that "strategy leads to structure" (Chandler 1962), the operational meaning is principally that diversification causes divisionalization. Studies made across time (i.e., longitudinal or diachronic studies) show that diversification precedes and causes divisionalization. This holds both for qualitative, intensive case histories (Chandler 1962) and also for quantitative studies of large numbers of big corporations (Channon 1973, 1978; Dyas and Thanheiser 1976; Fligstein 1985; Rumelt 1974; Suzuki 1980). As Pfeffer (1997, p. 161) comments of these studies: "the evidence is that firms diversified first and then changed their structure, not the other way around, as would be expected if structure caused strategy (e.g., Rumelt, 1974; Channon, 1973)." More specifically, these studies show that initial diversification causes divisionalization and that divisionalization does not cause the initial diversification (Channon 1973, 1978; Dyas and Thanheiser 1976; Fligstein 1985; Rumelt 1974; Suzuki 1980).

There is also the issue of whether, once a firm has adopted the divisional structure, that divisional structure increases *subsequent* diversification (e.g., Rumelt 1974)—with Donaldson (1982b) and Hamilton and Shergill (1992, p. 104, Table 3) finding no such effect. Even if this causal relationship is proved in future research, it does not contradict the previous one, that initial diversification causes divisional structure because each refers to different causal relationships. The initial move from being undiversified to being diversified causes the adoption of the divisional structure, which, in turn, then might subsequently raise the level of diversification. Only if divisionalization were shown to precede and cause the initial diversification would this reverse the causation of initial diversification causing divisionalization and thereby challenge the contingency theory.

In the Chandlerian thesis that "strategy leads to structure," *strategy* refers to achieved strategy, such as the level of diversification that the firm has attained. Thus, "strategy leads to structure," means concretely that firms that have achieved diversification adopt a divisional structure. However, if, instead, strategy is interpreted as strategic intention, then presumably creating a corporate planning department leads to more strategic planning, and in that sense structure can be said to cause strategy (Hall and Saias 1980). Thus one might say that "structure causes strategy" and that this is the reverse of "strategy causes structure." However, the terms *strategy* and *structure* are here being used in a highly abstract sense to mean potentially any aspect of strategy or structure. The contingency theory idea that initial diversification causes divisionalization is only challenged by reverse causation between diversification and initial divisionalization. It is not challenged by a reverse causation between other meanings of strategy or structure.

In sum, there are analyses across time that show that strategy causes structure. Attempts to date to nullify this by arguing that instead structure leads to strategy are not valid, because the evidence points to reciprocal causality so that reverse causality coexists with strategy causing structure.

Regarding size and bureaucratic structure, it could be argued that formal organization precedes size, in that management creates a new organizational department and then recruits its personnel. However, this speculative causal process would not produce some of the research results that have found the correlations between size and bureaucratic structure. Much of those studies measure structure by the structure actually in existence, rather than by a structure that exists purely formally and not in reality. Thus, for example, the Aston Group specialization is the number of distinct functionally specialized roles that exist and to which people are allocated, not officially defined roles that are not being performed because they are unfilled (Pugh et al. 1968). Therefore the correlations between size and these structural variables are due to size causing bureaucratic structure, not the reverse.

Overall, diversification causes divisionalization and size causes bureaucratic structuring, and neither relationship can be rejected on the grounds that the only evidence is correlations that are really produced by reverse causality.

Configurationalism Versus Cartesianism

Configurationalism presents two problems to contingency theory. It rejects contingency and it rejects multivariatism. First, it rejects the idea that organizational characteristics need to fit contingencies to produce high performance. Instead it argues that organizational characteristics need to be consistent with each other to produce high performance. Second, whereas contingency theory is multivariate and sees many fits, one for each level of the contingency variable, configurationalism tends to see only a few configurations.

The Aston Group studies and other contingency theory research use what has been termed a Cartesian approach (after Descartes; Donaldson 1996b). *Cartesianism* means that a multidimensional framework composed of multiple variables is used, consisting of several dimensions independent of each other, with each dimension being a continuum of fine gradations that run from low to high (e.g., ranging in levels from 1 to 10). An organization could be at the lowest end of a dimension (e.g., 1) such as specialization, and another organization could be at the highest end (e.g., 10), but other organizations could each be at different intermediary points along the dimension (e.g., 3, 5, 6, 8, and 9). An organization has a quantitative score on each of these dimensions that defines its position in the multidimensional space. Thus, if there are three independent dimensions, an organization might score 3 on the first dimension, 7 on the second dimension, and 5 on the third dimension.

In contrast to Cartesianism, some organizational researchers argue for the use of *configurations* (also known as types, gestalts, or archetypes; Meyer, Tsui, and Hinings 1993). Configurationalism enjoys a considerable following, as seen in a special issue of the *Academy of Management Journal* (Meyer, Tsui, and Hinings 1993). There is a growing literature that analyzes organizations in terms of configurations (Doty and Glick 1994; Doty, Glick, and Huber 1993; Ketchen et al. 1993; Ketchen et al. 1997). Configurationalism employs some elements of the contingency approach, such as its concepts or findings, for example, machine bureaucracy (Miller 1986; Mintzberg 1979), but uses them in ways different from contingency theory research.

Configurationalism asserts that every organization falls into one of a few different configurations, defined as a particular combination of characteristics or scores on variables. This has the appeal of parsimony in that a model composed of a few types is held to explain much of the organizational world. For example, Mintzberg (1979) discusses five configurations. The reason why there are so few configurations, Mintzberg (1979) argues, is that each one is based upon a single one of the modes of coordination given by Thompson (1967). Intermediary positions between the configurations are seen as internally inconsistent and therefore ineffective and not viable. Configurationalism is based on consistency theory, which holds that organizational characteristics need to fit each other for high performance to result (Child 1977, 1984; Khandwalla 1973); these fits become the configurations in configuration theory.

From Mintzberg (1979), Miller (1986) derives four strategy and structure configurations of business firms: simple structure, innovating adhocracy, machine bureaucracy, and divisionalized conglomerate. According to (Miller 1986), each configuration is an internally consistent bundle of characteristics that constitutes a viable and effective type. For instance, Miller (1986) argues that there is a simple structure organizational configuration, which is low on size and bureaucratic structuring, and that there is also machine bureaucracy organizational configuration, which is high on size and bureaucratic structuring. There are, however, no organizational configurations that are intermediary in size and bureaucratic structuring. Therefore an organization venturing into an intermediary position becomes vulnerable and unstable and either goes back to its previous configuration or moves rapidly to another configuration. Most organizations remain stable in their existing configuration, and when they do move this often takes the form of a quantum jump from one configuration to another (jumping over the intermediary, unviable positions; Miller 1986). Thus, because configurationalism holds that there are few fits, that is, configurations, widely separated in conceptual space, this leads to its postulate that organizational change consists of infrequent, large movements from one fit to another, that is, quantum jumps.

Some versions of configuration theory hold that the configurations need not fit any contingencies, thereby contradicting contingency theory, while other versions of configuration theory hold that the configurations need to fit contingencies for high performance to result (see Doty, Glick, and Huber 1993). This latter version is more compatible with contingency theory and with contingency determinism, in that the configuration needs to fit the situation. The main difference is that contingency theory holds that there are many fits and these form continua, for example, the line of fits between size and specialization (Child 1975). In contrast, fits of configurations to their contingencies can take the form of a limited number of ideal fits, separated in the concept space formed by the contingency and organizational characteristic (Doty, Glick, and Huber 1993). Thus configurationalism contains a variant that denies that there are contingencies and also a variant that holds that there are contingencies of the configurations.

The noncontingency variant of configurationalism lends support to strategic choice. Because there are no contingencies, the configurations need not fit the situation (see Doty, Glick, and Huber 1993). Therefore an organization can choose any one of a number of configurations and still have high performance. Thus there is more than one way to achieve high performance, which is termed *equifinality*. Equifinality allows strategic choice, so that contingency determinism is rejected.

Another variant of configurations holds that there are hybrids, so that many more than a few configurations are viable fits that lead to high performance (Doty, Glick, and Huber 1993). This hybrid configurations approach also has contingent and noncontingent variations (Doty, Glick, and Huber 1993). The contingent variant of hybrid configurations postulates that there are quite a number of configurations, each of which fits a particular value of the contingency variable. Clearly, this is closer to contingency theory. The more hybrids there are, and the nearer each is to one of the others, the more compatible with contingency theory is the concept of contingent hybrid configurations. However, if there are numerous hybrids (whether contingent or noncontingent), then configurationalism loses the parsimony and elegance that is part of its appeal. The most prominent versions of configurationalism tend to argue that there are few configurations, and so we shall give primary attention to the few configurations postulate. This is appropriate because it is such variants of configurationalism, especially where noncontingent, that are the most different from, and so pose the stronger challenge to, contingency theory.

In these ways configurationalism, especially in its noncontingent, nonhybrid form, takes elements of the preceding contingency theory literature and stands them on their head. Configurationalism is a major form of research using contingency variables and yet is antithetical to the contingency theory from which those variables arose. This antithesis exists regarding the number of configurations, whether they need to fit contingencies, equifinality, choice, separation in space, infrequency of movement, or magnitude of jumps. We will now critically examine configurationalism and argue that it is less sound than the original contingency theory.

Critique of Configurationalism

There are many problems with configurationalism, as we shall now see, so that it is a counterproductive movement in organizational theory research. The problems range from lack of theoretical coherence to lack of empirical validity.

Miller (1990) subsequently went on to write about configurations in a way that contradicted his basic argument that configurations are bundles of characteristics that together lead to high performance. He asserted instead that configurations, while initially leading to high performance, were subject to an "Icarus Paradox" in that they tend eventually to become pathological, leading to poor performance, because the configurations become so pure as to become extreme and unbalanced. This argues against the whole idea of configurations as being functional combinations that are viable positions for an organization long term.

Thompson (1967) argues that effective organizations can, and should, have several coordination devices within them. Therefore, the argument (Mintzberg 1979) that each viable configuration needs to have just one coordination mechanism contradicts the theory of Thompson (1967) and the supporting empirical research (Gerwin and Christoffel 1974; Van de Ven, Delbecq, and Koenig 1976; Van de Ven and Ferry 1980). Hence the rationale for defining the configurations and explaining why there are so few of them is unsound.

The empirical claims of configuration theory are disconfirmed by research, some of it conducted before the configuration approach was developed. For instance, most organizations are at intermediary points along the continua that make up the dimensions of organizational context and structure, such as size and bureaucratic structure. Most organizations are not confined to the end points of these dimensions that define the configurations, such as the small structure and the machine bureaucracy. The reader can easily verify this for himself or herself by looking at the scatter-plots of data in published studies (e.g., Blau 1970; Blau and Schoenherr 1971; Marsden, Cook, and Kalleberg 1994). The number of viable fits between structure and contingency is very many more than the five held to be the configurations. For example, the fits between bureaucratic structure and size are so many that they form a line stretching widely across the range of these variables (see Child 1975, p. 21, Figure 1). The fit line is a continuum of points of fit. There is a structure that fits each size level. The fits are adjacent to each other, so that an organization can proceed along the line from one fit to another, thereby growing incrementally from being small and unbureaucratic to large and bureaucratic.

Similarly, organizational change is far more common than the infrequent changes that configuration theory states, and it seldom includes quantum jumps, such as between the small structure and machine bureaucracy configurations. On the contrary, organizations frequently make changes, almost all of which are incremental, so that they gradually move along the dimensions such as size and bureaucracy. For instance, Inkson, Pugh, and Hickson (1970) studied the amount of change in fourteen organizations over a four-year period. The quantum jump theory would lead to the expectation that most organizations would not change and a few would change a lot, so that the distribution would be bimodal (zero and high), with no organizations scoring at intermediary levels. However, the percentage change scores on the structuring of activities variable are: -6, 0, 3, 5, 6, 10, 14, 14, 16, 17, 21, 50, 60, and 81 (Inkson, Pugh, and Hickson 1970, p. 322). This is not a bimodal distribution with organizations clustering at zero and a single, very high value—that is, remaining stationary or making a quantum jump. Instead the distribution is scattered over the range between highest and lowest values. Only one organization scored zero (i.e., was stationary), and eleven organizations increased, but by less than the maximum. Most organizations made only incremental changes. This study fails to support the quantum change notion and instead supports the contingency theory idea of incremental change. Similar results come from a study of the amount of change in 16 organizations by Dewar and Hage (1978). For instance, in the first of two three-year periods, the percentage change in structural complexity was: 0, 0, 0, 0, 0, 0, 0, 11, 14, 17, 17, 20, 26, 30, 59, and 66. Hence, half the organizations are distributed at intermediary values between zero and the maximum, so that most of them are changing incrementally (for further details, see Donaldson 1996b, pp. 120-121). The data from these two empirical studies refute the quantum jump idea and instead support the contingency theory idea that if an organization makes a large change in its structure over its life, this comes about gradually, as a result of a series of incremental changes.

Study Fails to Confirm Configurations

Ketchen et al. (1997) conducted a meta-analytic review of studies examining the relationship between organizational configurations and performance, and concluded that configurations had a positive effect. However, some of the studies included are of strategic groups (Cool and Dierickx 1993; Fiegenbaum and Thomas 1990), which essentially partition firms in an industry by their performance, thereby creating a tautologous relationship between types and performance, rather than investigating whether organizational structural configurations are related to performance. Thus the results of this meta-analysis are not proof of configurations. Therefore we should focus inquiry on a specific study (Doty, Glick, and Huber 1993) from their review that does examine structural configurations and performance.

Doty, Glick and Huber (1993) test Mintzberg's (1979) five configurations of context and structure and find no relationship between the configurations and performance. They also find that most organizations do not conform to one or other of the five configurations. Thus their findings challenge the whole typology of Mintzberg (1979) and those typologies derived from his typology (i.e., Miller 1986).

Doty, Glick, and Huber (1993) also test the strategy configurations of Miles and Snow (1978). They find these configurations relate to performance, supporting configurationalism. Moreover, they find no support for these configurations as needing to fit contingencies, thus challenging contingency theory. However, there are problems with their analysis. Their data do not really support the notion that there are few configurations nor that the configurations that exist relate positively to performance, as will now be shown.

Doty, Glick, and Huber (1993) find two sorts of configurations that relate to performance: ideal types and hybrid types. (We will follow Doty, Glick, and Huber in referring to their "ideal types" without a hyphen, while having used the hyphenated "ideal-types" to refer to those propounded by Weber, 1968). The ideal types mean, in the study by Doty, Glick, and Huber, that there are only three (equally effective) types that an organization may chose among, thus operationalizing the idea of few configurations. The hybrid fits mean that there are many more fits to chose among (because each hybrid is a combination of types and there are many such combinations). Regarding the central claim of configurationalism, that there are few configurations, the evidence from this study is rather disconcerting. While ideal (i.e., three) fits and hybrid (i.e., many) fits explained 24 percent of the variance in performance, the ideal fits alone explained only 1 percent and the hybrid fits explained 7 percent (Doty, Glick, and Huber 1993, p. 1236). Thus hybrid fits explained seven times as much as ideal fits, which on their own explain only a trivial amount of performance. (The bulk of the variance explained, 16 percent, may be due to some kind of interaction of ideal with hybrid fits.) Thus the central claim of configurations, that there are few viable types because only a few combinations of variables produce high performance, is not supported by the data in this study.

Turning to the findings that support the relation of ideal and hybrid types to performance, the data are again contrary. As Doty, Glick, and Huber (1993) state, neither the ideal nor the hybrid types correlate

positively and significantly with any of the five measures of performance. The evidence supporting the relationship between the ideal
and hybrid fits and performance comes from canonical analyses that
aggregate across variables (Doty, Glick, and Huber 1993). However,
the relationships included differ in sign, so that their aggregation is
problematic. Of the ten correlations between the ideal and hybrid fits
and the five measures of effectiveness, eight are positive and two are
negative. Therefore aggregating positive and negative correlations
would appear to be meaningless, because the positive correlations
support the theory but the negative correlations refute it. Moreover,
one of the negative correlations is the largest, and the only significant
correlation, so that this counterfinding should be given more weight
than the more numerous but nonsignificant findings that support the
theory. Therefore aggregating together positive and negative correlations boosts the association between fits and performance, but could
mislead, in that the strongest source of association could come from a
correlation that negates the theory that fit and performance are positively related. Disregarding sign, the average of the ten correlations is
+.078; allowing for sign, however, their average correlation drops to
only +.017, which is almost nil. Thus the canonical analyses that support
the relation of ideal and hybrid fits to performance may be meaningless. The more meaningful results are the ten correlations between the
ideal and hybrid fits and performance and, as noted already, none of
these correlations is significantly positive. The study by Doty, Glick,
and Huber (1993) should be coded as failing to support the idea that
configurations lead to high performance. By implication, their study
should not be seen as supporting the idea that there are multiple
equally effective configurations, because, in fact, no configuration
leads to higher levels of effectiveness.

   In sum, even for the Miles and Snow typology, the study by Doty,
Glick, and Huber (1993) fails to support the idea of a few types, supporting instead the existence of many hybrids. However, neither the
ideal types nor the hybrid types relate to performance. Thus the study
should be coded as not supporting configurations. Moreover, there is
no support for the idea of equifinality, that is, several, equally highly
effective types, among which choice can be made without losing
performance, because no type relates positively to performance. If

configurationalism is not really supported by their data, do their findings support contingency theory?

Doty, Glick, and Huber (1993) find no evidence that contingency formulations of their types are positively related to performance, and so contingency theory is not supported. However, Doty, Glick, and Huber (1993) themselves warn against interpreting their study as evidence against the constraints implied by contingency theory. As they caution, there may still be constraint operating within their sample in that only certain combinations of structure and contingency may be viable and so the organizations have already moved into alignment. This is a point made by Van de Ven and Drazin (1985) that, in their terms, natural selection brings structure into correlation with contingency and so eliminates deviations away from fit, making unobservable the association between misfit and lower performance. Thus lack of empirical support for contingency, in the Doty, Glick, and Huber (1993) study (and other studies) does not mean such constraint is not operating and that contingency theory is not valid.

Moreover, while the study provides no support for contingency theory, this may reflect the way that contingency fit is operationalized (Doty, Glick, and Huber 1993). Following configurational logic, contingency fit is operationalized as being the degree of fit of the structure to the ideal type closest to the contingency level of the organization. This is a procedure that only partially captures the deviation from the fit line of structure on contingency, which is the correct test of contingency theory. An organization that lies on the fit line and thereby is in fit could nevertheless be at a distance from what is claimed to be its ideal type, so that that organization would be scored as being in misfit. The problem arises because contingency theory sees every point along the fit line as a fit, whereas configuration theory, in its contingent form as used in this study, sees few points on the fit line as fits (i.e., as the configurations). To illustrate the point, if the fit line where defined as required structure equals the contingency, then there are fits at each point of structure equals 1, contingency equals 1; at 2, 2; at 3, 3; at 4, 4; at 5, 5; and so on. But contingent configurationalism would hold that there were few ideal types, such as at 1, 1 and at 4, 4, so that an organization in fit at 3, 3 would be coded as being a misfit with its nearest ideal type (4, 4). Hence the misfits could contain some fits, so confounding the empirical relationship between fit and performance. Therefore failure to support contingency theory may reflect a failure to operationalize fit correctly.

Miller (1986) observes that many theories use similar types and sees in this a verification of configurationalism. However, the similarity of types reflects that theorists have tended to draw from the same pool of ideas.

Miller (1986) also justifies configurations by reference to the typologies of organizational theorists such as Burns and Stalker (1961) with their mechanistic and organic types of structures. However, Burns and Stalker (1961) caution that organizations are distributed along the continua formed by these two extreme types, with some organizations oscillating between the two types and many organizations incorporating both types, ideas that all contradict configurationalism:

> the two forms of system [mechanistic and organic] represent a polarity, not a dichotomy; there are, as we have tried to show, intermediate stages between the extremities empirically known to us. Also, the relation of one form to another is elastic, so that a concern oscillating between relative stability and relative change may also oscillate between the two forms. A concern may (and frequently does) operate with a management system which includes both types. (p. 122)

Subsequent organizational theorists work within this tradition of viable structures as distributed along a continuum between extreme, polar types. For instance, Gresov (1990, p. 506, emphasis as in original) writes of his own work:

> The view embraced here is that unit design patterns can be conceptualized as ranging on a *spectrum* from the mechanistic (tight) to the organic (loose), in which the "pure" forms approach the endpoints. The spectrum approach has been used recently in a number of studies (e.g., Alexander and Randolph 1985; Koberg and Ungson 1987; Tushman 1979).

Thus the polar types of mechanistic and organic are part of a continuum, or spectrum, thereby contradicting the notion that they are configurations.

Critique can also be made of several of the configurations offered in the popular configurational theories, such as the "divisionalized conglomerate" configuration (Miller 1986, p. 115). Research into divisionalized corporations reveals many types other than the conglomerate, such as the related product and vertically integrated types, each of which requires their own variants of the divisional structure to fit them (Hill, Hitt, and Hoskisson 1992; Lorsch and Allen 1973). Similar critiques can be made of other configurations, such as the innovating adhocracy and machine bureaucracy configurations (see Donaldson 1996b, pp. 114-117). However, the way forward is not to amend one or more configurations nor to increase their number, but rather to abandon configurationalism in favor of Cartesianism. This entails using the kind of models of contingency, structure, and fits as continua as presented in this book.

The confusion induced by configurationalism is, however, to be distinguished from another use of configurations. Because organizational types can exist in the mind, as mental models, they can guide people and be used to evaluate actual organizations. The fact that the types may remain ideals that are never fully attained in practice need not diminish their orienting role. Moreover, people may only see a few types within their minds. Some configurations are used in this way as archetypes that provide a framework for human thinking about organizations, which, in turn, guide actions to try to change organizations to make them more like the archetypes, that is, more like the ideals. For instance, Cooper, Hinings, Greenwood, and Brown (1996) identify two contrasting archetypes in professional service firms: a traditional professional partnership model and a business management model. They chart how members of some professional service firms have sought to move their firms away from the first archetype and toward the second archetype, along various tracks and with varying outcomes, in part because some other members seek to retain elements of the first archetype. The organizations just move some way along the imaginary continuum from one archetype to another, so that the archetypes remain extreme states that are not attained in reality, that is, the archetypes are idealizations. Real organizations are distributed along the continuum between the archetypes. This use of organizational types is valid because they are abstract idealizations, which allows there to be few of them.

The archetypes part of the configurations school is legitimate and scientifically fruitful. It is to be distinguished from the doctrine that there are few organizational types or configurations in the world. We may term the archetypes as *cognitive configurations* (i.e., mental models) to distinguish them from the notion that reality is composed of a few types, which we may term *existential configurations*. As we have seen, existential configurations fail to explain the organizational world. In contrast, cognitive configurations help to explain organizational design, organizational change, and member reactions to organizational designs. However, existential configurationalism would seem to be more common in organizational theory research than cognitive configurationalism (consider, for example, the articles in the special issue on configurations in the *Academy of Management Journal;* Meyer, Tsui, and Hinings 1993). The influence of cognitive configurationalism seems to be strongest in the specialist topic of professional service firms, so that it is confined. Therefore, at present, the net effect of configurationalism would seem to be more negative than positive.

In summary, existential configurationalism has attractions of parsimony, but this is beguiling. Real organizations are widely distributed along both the structural and the contingency dimensions. There are many more fits than the few configurations postulated. Fits form continua along which organizations can move incrementally. Organizations do not change through occasional quantum jumps, but frequently and incrementally. Configurationalism, in its most developed variant, holds that configurations are unbounded by contingencies so that there are many structures that an organization can adopt and still have high performance, thereby constituting equifinality and choice. However, these ideas remain as assertions unproven empirically and contradicted by the empirically proven fits of structure to contingency (e.g., Child 1975). We must therefore reject existential configurationalism: the notion that fits are localized to being at discrete points in space with no viable intermediary fits between them (for further critical discussion, see Donaldson 1996b, pp. 108-129). Instead, we should use the Cartesian approach that contingencies and structures form a multidimensional framework within which fits are continuous. Thus the fits between a structural and a contingency dimension are a line in two-dimensional space, so that fit is a continuum. Because fit forms a continuum, each fit has an adjacent fit so that an organization can migrate between fits, forming a pathway. This explains how organizations can change over time, incrementally, from being small, structurally simple, and local to being, in extreme cases, large, structurally complex, and multinational.

Contingencies of Organizational Power

A branch of structural contingency theory is concerned with the power aspect of organizational structure. It can be subsumed under *resource dependence theory* (Pfeffer and Salancik 1978), which holds that organizations are dependent upon the environment for resources and seek various means to attain these resources while trying to maintain their autonomy from the external providers. One such means is the internal organizational structure. The external resource dependence becomes a contingency that shapes the internal organizational structure in two regards: the power of departments and the structure of the board of directors. Resource dependence theory specifies many other means for the organization to gain resources and influence its environment, but here we will focus just on internal organizational structure in keeping with the theme of this book (for a critical discussion of resource dependence theory in general, see Donaldson 1995b, pp. 129-163). If resource dependence theory is valid, then resource dependence becomes another contingency of organizational structure, additional to the task and size contingencies that constitute the main structural contingency theories. We will first discuss the strategic contingencies theory of intra-organizational power and then discuss co-optation theory.

The Strategic Contingencies Theory of Intraorganizational Power

The dependence of the organization upon external resources affects which department has the most power, thereby influencing an aspect of the power distribution within the organization. This theory is referred to as the *strategic contingencies theory of intraorganizational power*.

The term *contingency* refers here narrowly to some environmental challenge with which the organization must cope (Hickson et al. 1971). For example, in a study of breweries in western Canada, governmental regulations precluded the use of many competitive tactics such as marketing, and therefore low-cost production was the critical, environmentally defined, challenge that determined organizational performance (Hinings et al. 1974). There seems usually to be only one challenge so we will use the singular, contingency, rather than contingencies. The word *contingency* is used in this theory to refer not to the broad array of contingency variables in contingency theory (i.e., size, technology, etc.), but rather to just one factor, the critical challenge. This use of the word *contingency* differs from most of the contingency literature, but is consistent with the use of that word in Thompson (1967). While the theory of Thompson is clearly of the contingency type, specifying modes of organization as appropriate to various situations, he does not present it in contingency terms. Instead, Thompson (1967, p. 24) uses the term "contingency" more narrowly to refer to something that varies and is beyond the control of the organization, so that the organization must make varying responses. Technology and the other situational factors that later would be called contingencies are not discussed in these terms by him. Nevertheless, Thompson put forth the strategic contingency theory of organizational power, and the Thompsonian use of the word "contingency" is seen subsequently in the formal statements of that theory. Hence, in this theory we find the idiosyncratic use of the word "contingency" to refer narrowly to only one contingency, the critical challenge facing the organization, rather than the broad range of contingencies discussed in contingency theory.

Further, while the term *strategic contingencies* is used, the word *strategy* here is related to the idea of strategic behaviors, such as work groups acting to maintain their power and status (Crozier 1964). "Strategy" in the strategic contingency theory of intraorganizational power does not embrace other meanings of *strategy* found in the contingency research, such as referring to diversification or vertical integration (Chandler 1962; Rumelt 1974) or defender versus prospector (Miles and Snow 1978). For these reasons, we believe that referring to the strategic contingency theory is unhelpful. We prefer to classify the contingency referred to in the strategic contingency theory as the critical challenge. This is consistent with it being only one type of contingency, rather than being called *the* contingency (or the contingencies), which is misleading given that there are other contingencies in contingency theory (e.g., size and technology).

The strategic contingency theory of intraorganizational power holds that organizations are most effective where the department that deals with the most critical environmental challenge of the organization is the most powerful department in the organization. This idea features in early contingency theory research (Lawrence and Lorsch, 1967, pp. 142, 143; Perrow 1970). A formal model was specified by Hickson et al. (1971), in which a department has more power than its peer departments (i.e., those at the same level in the hierarchy) to the degree that it deals with the critical challenge, does so successfully, and is nonsubstitutable. This model was empirically validated by subsequent research (Hambrick 1981; Hinings et al. 1974; Kenny and Wilson 1984). However, Hambrick (1981) showed that which challenge is defined as most critical for an organization is influenced by the strategy adopted by that organization. In this way there is an element of strategic choice by management, so that complete determinism of the critical challenge by the environment is not a valid view. Thus it may not be wholly true to classify the critical challenge as an environmental challenge. This undermines, to a degree, the argument of resource dependence theory that the organization is externally controlled (Pfeffer and Salancik 1978). Thus this contingency of power should be termed the critical challenge, in recognition that it could be either the environment or the management that determines which challenge is critical.

Astley and Zajac (1990) provide an empirical critique of the theory that power resides with the department that controls the critical challenge. In a study, they test the alternative explanation that the department that is most central to the work flow is the most powerful. Their finding is that centrality, not the critical challenge, explains departmental power. Thus the contingency of intraorganizational power could be centrality, not critical challenge. This possibility places a caution against the validity of the critical challenge contingency theory and deserves attention in future research into intra-organizational power.

Co-optation

Co-optation theory states that the organization co-opts members of powerful outside organizations so that they work to further the interests of the organization that has co-opted them, thereby modifying the power relationships between organizations (Pfeffer and Salancik 1978). An important instance is the appointment to the board of directors of an organization, of persons who hold positions in organizations that have power over that organization, so that those external organizations then assist the organization by providing the resources it needs. Pfeffer (1972) argues a contingency version of this theory, consistent with resource dependence theory, by stating that organizational performance will be greater, the more that a company includes in its board directors from organizations that possess the resources that the company needs. He supports this empirically with a study that finds that the proportion of outside directors is higher for companies that have higher leverage (i.e., are dependent on more debt financing) and are more regulated (i.e., are more subject to governmental control). In particular, the higher the proportion of directors who are attorneys, the more the company relies on debt and is regulated (Pfeffer 1972). The more the company deviates from the proportion of outsiders expected from the contingencies of debt and regulation, the worse is its financial performance (controlling for industry; Pfeffer 1972). This supports the contingency co-optation theory that boards need to fit these contingencies for the company to perform at a higher level. However, whether the attorneys and other outside directors are from organizations that could provide such support to the organization and whether their being appointed to the board has led them to use their influence to benefit the company (i.e., to be co-opted) are undemonstrated (Mintzberg 1983, p. 87). Thus there is scope for more empirical research to confirm that the processes occurring are those postulated by co-optation theory.

Another study of boards of directors shows that outside directors have a negative effect on the financial performance of the firm, thereby suggesting that such appointments may not always succeed in co-optation (Muth and Donaldson 1998). This negative relationship only holds where there is high network connections, meaning that the board directors are highly linked to other firms (Muth and Donaldson 1998). Thus there may be a process of dysco-optation whereby directors use their board seats to extract wealth from the focal firm for the benefit of other economic organizations in which they have an interest. Hence board directorships could reduce, rather than increase, the resources available to an organization. Thus not all appointments of outsiders to boards are co-optation, and the reverse possibility should be considered in future studies of power and boards. It could be that some directorships function as co-optation and others as dysco-optation. Which of these interorganizational processes occur could be determined by some contingency so that it would be explicable by a new theory of the contingency type.

Thus contingency theories have been used to explain power in and between organizations. For both the critical challenge contingency theory of intraorganizational power and the contingency co-optation theory of interorganizational power, there is evidence supporting them, but also either counterevidence or methodological criticisms that render them somewhat controversial. It is hoped the disputation around both theories will stimulate more research to clarify the validity of these contingency theories of organizational power.

Conclusions

Whereas pioneering contingency theory treated technology as a major contingency factor, subsequent bureaucracy theory research argued against the technology thesis and in favor of size as the more important contingency theory of organizational structure. In response, some scholars have sought to reassert the technology thesis. However, technology is a less important contingency than size. Also, it has effects different from those claimed in the pioneering technology thesis. Instead of making structures more organic, it makes structures more bureaucratic. This holds for information technology as well as for operations technology. Thus the effect of technology parallels that of size. Advances in technology reinforce the effects of size increases, making the organization even more bureaucratic than it would be if size alone increased. On the issue of the technology contingency, bureaucracy theory is supported rather than organic theory.

Against the determinism of structure by contingency posited by contingency theory in its original version, some scholars have asserted instead that there is a substantial zone of choice. However, a closer inspection has revealed difficulties with many of the arguments for strategic choice and considerable determinism of structure by contingencies. Contingencies such as size correlate very highly with pivotal aspects of structure. Organizations in misfit have to adopt the structure that fits their contingency. This is due to the performance loss from misfit, which is substantial even for large corporations with market power. Subjective factors play a minor role in structural causation and some of them are paths by which contingencies indirectly determine structure. There is very little evidence of any substantial amount of strategic choice that allows organizations to reject bureaucracy and instead adopt the organic structure.

Critics sometimes contend that contingency research just consists of correlations between contingencies and structure, which could mean that the contingencies are just correlates of structure or that structure causes the contingencies. However, there is evidence that size is a cause of bureaucratic structure. Moreover, diachronic data and causal analyses show that the strategy contingency is a cause of structure. Some attempts to establish reverse causality have not used the same concepts of strategy and structure and hence failed to reverse the causality meant by "strategy leads to structure." Others have shown that reverse causality coexists with, rather than replaces, the causal effect of strategy on structure. Thus reverse causality fails to constitute a refutation of the contingency theory proposition that contingency causes structure. Hence arguments for reverse causality may lead toward a richer model, but they do not damage contingency theory. The determinism of structure by contingencies as stated in bureaucracy theory is intact.

Instead of studying organizations in terms of continua of contingencies and structures with many fits, some scholars have asserted few fits, or configurations. However, there are problems with configurationalism. The contention that there are few fits because each organization must use only one coordination mode contradicts the theory of Thompson (1967), so that the configuration argument lacks a coherent theoretical base. There is no compelling evidence that there are only a few fits, nor that they relate positively to organizational performance. Similarly, the contention that organizational change consists of quantum jumps, with most organizations making no change and a few making a large change, is contradicted by evidence that shows that most organizations make changes that are incremental in magnitude. A more coherent and more empirically valid view is that contained in contingency theory research. The contingency theory view is that there are many more fits than the few configurations. These fits are arranged adjacent to each other, providing migration routes for organizations to change incrementally, so that organizations may change gradually. Cartesianism, which treats contingencies, structure, and fits as continua, remains sounder. Thus modern contingency theories, whether bureaucracy or organic, should continue with the Cartesian contingency approach.

Thus, overall, the criticisms of bureaucracy theory, whether explicit or implicit, that are propounded by technology, strategic choice, reverse causality, and configurationalism fail to damage it. There are sound reasons for cleaving to contingency theory in its original form: a Cartesian framework, in which contingency causes structure deterministically. The main variation from the original version of contingency theory is to hold that size, rather than technology, is the more major contingency of structure.

Regarding power, structural contingency theories provide an explanation for its distribution in and among organizations. While support has been garnered for the critical challenge theory of intraorganizational power, later work has challenged its validity. Equally, the contingency variant of co-optation theory receives some empirical support, but has also been challenged by later research. Thus the contingency theory of power is a candidate for future research to clarify the extent of its validity. The outcome of such research might lead in some cases to new forms of contingency theory.

6 Challenges From
Other Theories

Contingency theory has been challenged by other theories, such as institutional theory. In this chapter we will consider several challenges from other organizational theories. It will be seen that the contingency theory explanations continue to enjoy validity. Competing explanations from other theories are not as valid as sometimes believed. Thus the present chapter will present rebuttals on behalf of contingency theory. While presenting a reasoned case for continuing to entertain contingency theory, some of the points remain in contention, thereby constituting issues for future research.

Much of the challenge to contingency theory is provoked by the functionalism and rationalism of contingency theory. As we saw above (in Chapter 1), contingency theory explains organizational change as a functionalist process of adaptation. The organization adopts a new structure that better fits its new level of the contingency variable. For example, the organization adopts a divisional structure to fit its diversified strategy. Or again, the organization increases its size and then increases the level of its bureaucratic structure to bring it into fit with size. In such ways, the organization replaces dysfunctional with functional (i.e., effective) structures. This is rational for the organization in that it fulfills its goal to be effective. Given that the organizational change comes about through the decisions made by its managers, they are acting in a pro-organizational fashion.

Such rationalism and functionalism, however, are quite at odds with other organizational theories. *Institutional* theory emphasizes ritual more than rationality and processes of conformity, such as those to gain legitimacy with powerful outside bodies, even without gain to internal organizational effectiveness (DiMaggio and Powell 1983; Meyer and Rowan 1977; Meyer and Scott 1983; Scott 1995). *Population-ecology* emphasizes organizational inertia, so that an organization may fail to adapt and become dysfunctional, leaving change to occur at the level of the population through death and birth of organizations because of lack of rational organizational action (Hannan and Freeman 1977, 1984, 1989). *Political* explanations hold that organizational change is rational for individuals as they pursue their self-interest, but often costly to the organization, for example, where managers "empire-build," so that many changes are organizationally irrational and dysfunctional (Child 1973b; Freeman and Hannan 1975; Parkinson 1957; Reimann 1979). Similarly, in organizational economics, Williamson (1970, 1985), in his *M-form* theory, sees this structure as adopted by organizations in an attempt to constrain the damage from managerial self-interest, so that it is an organizationally rational response to organizationally irrational, political managerial behavior. Further, the psychological theory of *threat-rigidity* sees organizational change as governed by irrational and dysfunctional processes (Staw, Sandelands, and Dutton 1981).

Thus, arising from the challenges of these other theories, we discuss in this chapter the rationalist, functionalist contingency theory, compared with the institutional, population-ecology, political, M-form, and threat-rigidity theories. These different views have prompted further work on the phenomena of strategy and structure, so that we extend our discussion of this contingency relationship to critically assess the validity of these alternative views. Also, the challenges to contingency theory have involved analyses of the relationship between size and bureaucratic structure so, again, we revisit these phenomena to see that the challenges have not succeeded in overturning contingency theory.

Divisionalization Is Not an Institutional Effect

Institutional theory holds that organizational change is less rational than contingency theory states and is not oriented toward adopting structures of superior effectiveness, rather their adoption is spurred by institutional isomorphism (DiMaggio and Powell 1983; Meyer and Rowan 1977; Meyer and Scott 1983; Powell and DiMaggio 1991; Scott 1995; Scott and Meyer 1994; Zucker 1977, 1987). The explanation of organizational change is change by coercive, mimetic, or normative processes that are oriented toward gaining legitimacy through conformity to institutionally approved organizational forms (DiMaggio and Powell 1983). Above, in presenting evidence for contingency, we used studies of divisionalization; however, there have been three studies of divisionalization that are often interpreted as supporting the institutional theory and contradicting the rational, functional view of contingency theory (Scott 1995, pp. 119-120): Rumelt (1974), Fligstein (1985), and Armour and Teece (1978). We will briefly review each and show that, at the least, a contingency theory interpretation is equally plausible, so that none of the studies provide decisive evidence for institutional theory against contingency theory.

Rumelt (1974) interprets much divisionalization in the 1960s as due to following a fashion rather than being rational and functional in effectiveness. However, his analysis lacks an examination of whether the firms studied were moving into a fit that raised their financial performance when they divisionalized. A secondary analysis of his data shows that all the firms that divisionalized in the sixties moved into fit (Donaldson 1995b, p. 90). Thus the firms studied by Rumelt should be coded as making rational, sociologically functional changes, rather than following fashion.

Fligstein (1985) presents evidence that firms are influenced in their divisionalization by whether other firms have adopted the divisional form. Yet this could be because the focal firm with its functional structure is in misfit and suffering poor competitiveness relative to its divisionalized competitors, which, as we have seen, are in fit. Therefore the influence of industry peers could be competitive pressure that makes divisionalization economically rational. Actually this interpretation is more consistent with the data, because it implies that, for any number above zero, the more industry peers that divisionalized, the greater the probability of the focal firm divisionalizing—which is what Fligstein (1985) shows. In contrast, a mimetic interpretation would hold only once the divisional structure was in the majority (which is consistent with the idea in institutional theory that mimetic processes occur only for late adoptions, when the new organizational form would be being used by most organizations [Tolbert and Zucker 1983]). Therefore proof of a mimetic process would require showing that only in those industries where more than half the firms had divisionalized was more divisionalization of industry peers increasing the probability of divisionalization of the focal firm—which Fligstein (1985) does not examine.

Again, institutional theory emphasizes that the adoption of organizational forms is not for reasons of effectiveness, so that it is ritual, not rational. While Fligstein (1985) gives this institutional theory explanation, for the purportedly mimetic effects in his data to be decisive there would need to be evidence that firms adopting divisional structures were not thus moving into fit and so raising their performance. However, Fligstein does not classify his firms into fit or misfit, so that his analysis cannot reject functionalist interpretation of divisionalization. Scott (1995, p. 120) makes the same criticism of Fligstein (1985): "the [cases of mimetically caused divisionalization] are treated as nonrational. However, without information on the effect of these decisions on performance measures, it is not possible to make this determination." As we have just seen, an examination of divisionalization among large U.S. firms (Donaldson 1987), a set similar to those studied by Fligstein, shows that overwhelmingly the adoption of the divisional form was a move into fit and therefore beneficial for their effectiveness and so sociologically functional. Hence the theoretical meaning of his study is equivocal and should not be coded as proof that institutional theory is a more valid explanation of divisionalization than contingency theory.

Future research may demonstrate, unequivocally, mimetic processes, but if firms that divisionalize are following firms whose divisionalization has brought them into fit and improved their financial performance, then the outcome could be economically rational and functional for the focal firm. By showing that firms are influenced in their adoption of structures by other firms, such as industrial peers, one of the ideas of institutional theory could be drawn upon—though calling this process mimicry would be inaccurate because it is pejorative. In this way, selected elements of institutional theory could become complementary to contingency theory, illuminating the social and psychological processes through which firms see what new structure they need to adopt to fit their new contingencies. However, this rapprochement would require abandoning the institutional theory assertion that organizational form is dictated by ritual rather than rationality (i.e., effectiveness in an instrumental sense).

The study of divisionalization by Armour and Teece (1978) found that divisionalization raised performance in an initial period, but not in later years. Institutional theory interprets this as meaning that early adoption of the divisional structure was economically rational, but that later adoptions were conforming to the norm and so mimetic. However, Armour and Teece (1978) do not examine whether their firms were in fit or misfit and so could not show that divisionalizing in the initial period was movement into fit with strategy or other contingencies, whereas for late adopters it was less economically rational by being less likely to be a movement into fit. Thus there is no decisive evidence to eliminate a contingency explanation that these firms were divisionalizing to move into fit after having diversified, in both the initial and later periods.

Moreover, the positive performance benefits of divisionalization found by Armour and Teece (1978) in the initial period and the absence of performance benefits of divisionalization in the later period could be compatible with contingency theory. Again, the issue revolves around fit and misfit. In Donaldson (1987), misfit overwhelmingly occurs empirically when firms have diversified and retained the functional structure, whereas divisionalized firms are overwhelmingly in fit (because they have diversified). It is possible that in the initial period of the Armour and Teece (1978) study the functional firms were a mixture, some remaining undiversified and so in fit and some having diversified and so in misfit, so that the average functionally structured firm was in partial misfit. In contrast, the divisionalized firms would predominantly be in fit. Therefore the divisionalized firms would perform higher than the functional firms—as was found empirically (Armour and Teece 1978). In the later period, however, sufficient time might have elapsed for the firms that had earlier diversified into misfit to have divisionalized and so moved into fit. Therefore there would be fewer functionally structured, diversified firms left in misfit, leaving the functional firms predominantly in fit. Thus the comparison in the later period would be between functionally structured firms that on average are in fit, with divisionally structured firms that also on average are in fit. Hence, in the later period, there would be no significant difference in performance between functional and divisional firms—the result found empirically (Armour and Teece 1978). Whether this interpretation of Armour and Teece is valid must await a future, secondary analysis that examines fit and misfit. For the present, their study cannot be seen as decisive support for institutional theory against contingency theory, because it is open to multiple interpretations.

Palmer, Jennings, and Zhou (1993, p. 120) found that large corporations were more likely to divisionalize if their CEO had been educated at a major graduate school. They interpret this finding in institutional theory terms as being normative isomorphism. However, an alternative interpretation of the finding is that CEOs with business education would have more knowledge of the divisional structure and so be more inclined to recognize the situations in which their corporations needed to adopt it. Hence the finding can be interpreted as showing the role of knowledge among top managers in inducing rational organizational adaptation.

Mahajan, Sharma, and Bettis (1988) investigated whether the adoption of the multidivisional structure among firms conformed to an imitation process and concluded that it did not. Thompson (1983) found that the diffusion of the multidivisional structure among firms was affected by diversification and size, that is, by contingency variables, thus supporting contingency theory.

A way that normative isomorphism could influence firms to adopt the multidivisional structure is through management consultants. Yet a survey of organizations that had undergone structural change (predominantly divisionalization) found that in only 11 percent of cases did their top management said that management consultants were the reason for the change (Hill and Pickering 1986, p. 35). This was much less than some other reasons for structural change: 50 percent for strategic change and 21 percent for performance decline (Hill and Pickering 1986, p. 35). These findings support the contingency theory idea that structural change is driven by change in the strategic contingency and the resulting performance decline from the ensuing misfit; they give little support to the normative isomorphism explanation of divisionalization from institutional theory.

Whittington, Mayer, and Curto (1999) studied large corporations in France, Germany, and the United Kingdom over the period 1950 to 1993 and conclude that the institutionalist explanations of division-alization are false and the Chandlerian functionalist explanation sound:

> ... the divisional form emerges as more than the product of American post-war political and economic domination. The divisional was not just foisted on Europe at a time of relative weakness (Djelic, 1998); it has been steadily absorbed into the European mainstream long after the waning of American hegemony since the 1970s. ... Indigenous forms of organization—such the holding or the French centralized functional organization—have generally withered, regardless of changing fashions. Institutionalist skepticism has been defeated by the robust qualities of the Chandlerian multidivisional. Against institutionalist arguments for the local construction of efficient forms of organizing (Whitley, 1994) or the fluctuations of business fashions (Fligstein, 1990), the multidivisional appears to have enduring and generalizable advantages over its major rivals. (p. 546)

Thus we conclude that attempts by institutional theorists to promote an interpretation of divisionalization that is contrary to, and would replace, contingency theory are not at present decisive. Assertions that institutional effects are a cause of divisionalization founder, mainly because studies fail to refute the explanation of divisionalization as a move into contingency fit (Armour and Teece 1978; Fligstein 1985; Rumelt 1974). Therefore there are grounds for maintaining the view of divisionalization as being rational and sociologically functional as shown empirically by contingency fit research (Donaldson 1987; Hamilton and Shergill 1992, 1993). The conflicting interpretations seen here prompt the need for future research that would resolve these rival in-terpretations and shows which is most empirically valid, or shows a more valid theoretical model of divisionalization that blends institu-tional and contingency theories. Any study that is seeking to refute contingency theory must show that firms changing their structures are not thereby moving into fit with their contingencies and so increasing their performance effectiveness. This involves empirically measuring fit and performance. To falsify any theory, it is necessary to use its concepts and measures in order to put them to the test. However, the empirical evidence to date from studies that examine fit and perfor-mance supports rather than refutes contingency theory, suggesting that future studies will not in fact refute the contingency theory of divisionalization. At the present time, it is reasonable to hold that divisionalization empirically supports the contingency theory of organizational change (in its SARFIT form), rather than supporting institutional theory. (For further critique of institutional theory, see Donaldson 1995b, pp. 79-128.)

Not Population-Ecology Effect

Another major contemporary school of organizational theory that rivals contingency theory is population-ecology (Hannan and Freeman 1977, 1984, 1989). This criticizes contingency theory for assuming that adaptation comes about by an organization changing itself (Hannan and Freeman 1977). Instead, *population-ecology* proposes that adaptation often comes about by changes in the membership of the population, so that misfitting organizations die out and are replaced by new, better-fitting organizations (Hannan and Freeman 1977). In particular, population-ecology holds that large organizations are inertial so that population adaptation is particularly strong in creating change among them (Hannan and Freeman 1984). If the organizational changes explained by contingency theory were really due to population adaptation and thus better explained by population-ecology theory, this would challenge contingency theory. We will show that the changes among large firms in their organizational strategies and adaptations in their structures of the kind discussed above are mainly caused by adaptation of ongoing organizations, as contingency theory holds, rather than by population change.

Whereas population-ecology theory holds that large organizations are inertial (i.e., unchanging), large corporations have changed their strategies and structures in adaptive ways, which invalidates population-ecology theory. Hannan and Freeman (1989, p. 79) list strategy among the core characteristics of an organization that are strongly subject to inertia and so resistant to change by an organization. Again, Hannan and Freeman (1989, p. 81) include hierarchical centralization to be subject to their theory and this is empirically linked to divisionalization (Chenhall 1979), so that divisionalization should also be subject to their theory. Thus strategy and structure are phenomena to which population-ecology theory applies and, consistent with this, Hannan and Freeman (1989) critique Chandler's (1962) account of strategy and structure.

Yet studies that follow the same large corporation over time show that the average large corporation increased its level of strategic diversification and consequently altered its structure from functional to divisional (Channon 1973, 1978; Dyas and Thanheiser 1976; Fligstein 1985; Rumelt 1974; Suzuki 1980). Most of the large corporations studied by Rumelt (1974) diversified and divisionalized so that most are changing in these regards rather than being inertial. As we have seen, the divisional structure fits diversification (Donaldson 1987; Hamilton and Shergill 1992, 1993) and so adopting it after diversifying is adaptive. While some research finds that diversification is counterproductive (e.g., Rumelt 1974), other research shows diversification to benefit organizational performance (Fligstein and Brantley 1992). Moreover, divisionalization moderates the effect of diversification on performance, so that diversification is adaptive when supported by divisionalization (Hill, Hitt, and Hoskisson 1992). Thus large corporations have changed their strategies and structures and this constitutes adaptive change by ongoing organizations, which contradicts the population-ecology theory that large organizations are inertial and do not adapt.

A population-ecologist might reply that while the large organizations that survived had adapted, other large corporations may not have adapted and so not survived, and may have been replaced in the population by newly founded organizations that were better adapted. However, there is little change in membership of the population of large corporations. Chandler (1977, p. 371) found that of the 278 largest industrials in 1917, only 14 had disbanded fifty years later. Similarly, Fligstein (1990b, p. 65) shows that among the largest 100 U.S. corporations over a sixty-year period, on average 98 percent remain at the end of each year. With so little change in the population of large corporations, there is little scope for adaptive organizational change through changes in population membership. Organizational disbandings is not a major mechanism for the elimination of maladapted large corporations because few of them disband. Equally, organizational foundings is not a major mechanism for adding well-adapted large corporations to the population because few of them are founded. (Of those corporations that enter the population of large corporations, some will have done so by growing larger, so they are not foundings, thus keeping the number of foundings smaller than 2 percent per annum.) Fligstein (1985, p. 388, Table 4) finds no significant effect of comers and leavers to the top 100 U.S. corporations as causes of divisionalization over a fifty-year period. Therefore examination of large corporations refutes the population-ecology claim that large organizations are inertial and that adaptation comes from population change. More specifically, the changes in strategy and structure among large corporations that have been used in this book to empirically support contingency theory are not really due to causal processes of the kind asserted by population-ecology theory (for more details, see Donaldson 1995b, pp. 73-74).

In sum, population-ecology theory holds large organizations to be inertial so that adaptation occurs by population change, whereas contingency theory sees ongoing organizations as adapting, including large organizations. Divisionalization is adaptive when following diversification, so that divisionalization by large corporations is adaptation by them and helps render diversification adaptive also. Hence organizational adaptation occurs even for large corporations, and has occurred in many of them. Little of the adaptation among large corporations could be attributed to population change because there is little population change. Thus strategic and structural change among large corporations fails to support population-ecology theory and instead supports contingency theory (for further critiques of population-ecology, see Donaldson 1995b, pp. 42-78, and Young 1988).

Rational Not Political Explanation

The structural contingency theory of organizations is a rational explanation in that the organization adopts a new structure to attain fit and performance. However, some scholars have asserted instead that organizations are in part shaped politically, that is, by the self-interest of their members, especially the members with most power, their managers (Child 1972b). In this way, while individual managers act rationally, organizations are not guided by an organizational rationality. Some writers hold that managers build empires, so that as organizations grow, the ratio of managers and administrative staff to total employees rises disproportionately, which unnecessarily increases costs so that organizational effectiveness suffers (Child 1973b; Freeman and Hannan 1975; Parkinson 1957; Reimann 1979). Williamson (1970, 1985) argues that in order to curb such managerial preferences for expense, organizations resort to the M-form, multidivisional structure as they grow larger, which restores discipline over managers by holding them accountable for profitability to the head office. We will explore each of these two ideas: that managers and administrative staff grow more than proportionately to organizational size and that the M-form is adopted in response to size growth to curb such opportunism. We shall see grounds for doubting both that organizations are plagued by managerial empire building and that the M-form is adopted to curb such managerial opportunism. This provides reasons for rejecting the political explanation of organizations and for reaffirming the rational, functionalist view of contingency theory.

Managers and Staff Not Growing Disproportionately

The political view of organizations is seen starkly in the writings of the popular satirist Northcote Parkinson (1957), who asserted his famous law, that managers multiply subordinates not rivals. In this way, managers are said to build empires of administrators to gratify their own power and status, at cost to the organization and its effectiveness (Parkinson 1957). (His influential satires have themselves been subject to critique [Donaldson 1996b].) The hypothesis from Parkinson is that the ratio of managers and administrators to workers increases with size, but, as seen earlier (in Chapter 3), the work of Blau (1970, 1972) and others refutes this, showing instead that the ratio tends to decrease with size.

Empirical scientific studies by Child (1973b) and Reimann (1979) into the relationship between size and administrative intensity (ratio of managers and administrators to total employment) conclude in support of Parkinson, but this has been challenged (Donaldson 1996b). Child (1973b) interprets his data as being evidence of complex causality congruent with political processes. However, a more meaningful and consistent interpretation is that administrative intensity is driven almost wholly by size (see Donaldson 1996b, pp. 69-70) and does not increase with size, thus contradicting Parkinson. Similar remarks apply to the study by Reimann (1979; see Donaldson 1996b, pp. 76-80). A meta-analytic review of studies of size and the proportion of managers to total employees (Donaldson and Caufield 1989) shows that of seventeen studies (totaling 2,218 organizations), the average correlation was negative: –.45

(Donaldson 1996b, p. 105, Table 5.1). This supports Blau's (1970) theory of increasing economies of administration as size increases.

These types of findings, however, were thrown into doubt by an influential article by Freeman and Kronenfeld (1973). They argued against correlating size with a variable whose denominator was also size, such as administrative (or managerial) intensity, asserting that this created a problem of definitional dependency such that the observed negative correlations were spurious. However, the article by Freeman and Kronenfeld (1973) contains several damaging errors (see Donaldson 1996b, pp. 88-93). In particular, they claim that curves, of the sort used by Blau to prove his theory, showing administrative intensity decreasing with size, can be produced spuriously by transforming random data into the ratio variable of administrative intensity (Freeman and Kronenfeld 1973, pp. 110-112). In their data, however, administrative intensity and size are not independent and, instead, administrative intensity decreases with size. Therefore Freeman and Kronenfeld fail to demonstrate their claim that such findings can be artifactually produced just by transforming one variable into a ratio (administrative intensity). What they actually show is that in data where the number of administrators grows less than proportionately to the number of workers, the ratio of administrators to workers decreases as the number of workers increases (see Donaldson 1996b, p. 92). Thus there is no inherent artifactual flaw introduced by using ratio variables, such as administrators to workers or managers to total employees.

This conclusion is supported by analyses by MacMillan and Daft (1979, 1984), who show that such supposedly flawed ratio variables and the supposedly sounder methods recommended by Freeman and Kronenfeld (1973) yield similar results. Thus the findings using ratio variables by Blau, and in the above meta-analysis, are not flawed and provide methodologically reliable findings. They are empirically valid tests that support the theory of Blau (1970) that administrative intensity declines with size. In contrast, there is very little reason to see Parkinson's theory of managerial empire building as supported by empirical social science (for further arguments, see Donaldson 1996b, pp. 58-107). The evidence shows increasing economies of scale in administration as size increases, supporting the rational explanation of organizational structures as growing in sociologically functional ways, rather than the political explanation of managers serving their personal interests at cost to the organization.

The case for the political explanation of organizations against the rational explanation comes also from some studies of organizational decline. These studies contrasted organizations that were growing in size with those that were declining in size (Freeman and Hannan 1975; Marsh and Mannari 1989). Freeman and Hannan (1975) found that changes in the administrative ratio differed between growers and decliners. This led them to criticize traditional contingency theory research as incorrectly presuming that growth and decline are symmetrical. Specifically, administrative intensity tended to shrink during growth in total employees but to increase during decline, because administrators were shed disproportionately less during decline. The inference made was that managerial interests came into play protecting managers' jobs and those of their staff. This was presented as evidence that organizations are shaped politically, by the interests of power-holders, rather than rationally and functionally (Freeman and Hannan 1975). Thus, supposedly, functionalist theory, such as Blau's of economies of scale in administration, held only in growth but not decline.

The theory of economies of scale in administration holds that administrative intensity decreases with size (Blau 1970). Therefore administrative intensity decreases for growing organizations and increases for declining organizations. The theory implies that the processes of growth and decline will be asymmetrical, not symmetrical. Hence the finding of asymmetry between growth and decline is consistent with Blau's theory, not a refutation of it. Thus several of the empirical findings presented as part of a critique of the theory actually confirm it. For instance, in school systems, when the number of teachers (i.e., operating personnel) decreases, fewer support staff are cut than are added when teachers increase by the same number (Freeman and Hannan 1975, pp. 222, 227). This means that administrative intensity is decreasing for growers and increasing for decliners, as Blau's (1970) theory holds (see also discussion of Montanari and Adelman 1987, and Marsh and Mannari 1989, in Donaldson 1996b, pp. 97-104). Thus, overall, the functionalist and organizationally rational explanation of organizational structure is valid, and the political explanation is not proven by studies that compare growth and decline. (For a critical discussion of other proponents of the political view of organizations such as Roy (1990) and Smith (1978), see Donaldson 1996b, pp. 58-84).

Divisionalization Not Caused by Opportunism

As noted earlier, Chandler (1962) explained the change from the functional to the divisional structure by the contingency of strategy. However, Williamson (1970, 1985) has explained it by the contingency of size in response to managerial opportunism. The affinity between the theory of managerial opportunism of Williamson, and other influential organizational economics views, such as agency theory (Jensen and Meckling 1976), has helped give the opportunism theory credibility, as has the stature of Williamson from his transaction cost theory (Williamson 1975, 1985). Earlier we have argued that divisionalization is caused by the strategy contingency, whereas Williamson is arguing that division-alization is caused by the size contingency. Thus we need also to examine his theory to assess whether the strategy contingency is the major con-tingency of divisionalization, that we have maintained thus far.

Williamson's (1970, 1985) structure, the *M-form*, is a multidivisional structure in which the general manager in charge of each division is held accountable for its profitability and is closely monitored and sanctioned by the head office managers and staff. This structural model is consistent with the concept of divisionalization we have been discussing, with Williamson choosing to emphasize the control aspects that are germane to his theory. This affinity between divisionalization and the M-form stems from the fact that both derive from the work of Chandler (1962).

Williamson (1970) argues that in large, functionally structured corporations, the managers in charge of departments are only weakly controlled by top management and so are able to act opportunistically. Such middle managers act to the detriment of corporate objectives by furthering their own self-interest through empire building and the like. Divisionalization imposes a discipline that curbs such waste by hold-ing divisional heads accountable for the profitability of their divisions. This is furthered by creating an elite staff at the corporate office that audits the divisions. For this reason corporations change from a func-tional to a divisional structure as they increase in size, according to Williamson (1970). The divisional structure confers other advantages, such as superior resource allocation and strategic decision making, but these benefits might be expected to flow from divisionalization without size increase. Thus the argument connecting divisionalization with a size contingency seems made most firmly by the opportunism argument.

Cross-sectional studies have examined whether divisionalization is related more to size or strategy, with mixed results (Chenhall 1979; Donaldson 1982a; Grinyer and Yasai-Ardekani 1981; Grinyer, Yasai-Ardekani, and Al-Bazzaz 1980; Khandwalla 1977). Moreover, studies examining changes over time support strategy as causing division-alization (Donaldson 1987; Hamilton and Shergill 1992, 1993). Also, Fligstein (1985, p. 388, Table 4) finds that strategy is a cause of multi-divisional structure in all five time periods, whereas size is a cause in only two out of the five periods, thereby supporting strategy as a more major cause than size (however, size is indexed by assets that may not capture fully the effects of size on divisionalization). Palmer et al. (1987, p. 37, Table 3) find that size has no effect on adoption of the multidivisional structure once diversity is included in the model. Simi-larly, Palmer, Jennings, and Zhou (1993, p. 118, Table 3) find that size has no effect on adoption of the multidivisional structure whereas di-versity has. Again, Mahoney (1992, p. 60, Table 5) found that diversifi-cation but not size causes adoption of the multidivisional structure. These findings lend support to Chandler's theory that divisionalization arises because of the problems of coordinating complex, diversified corporations effectively, rather than to Williamson's theory of mana-gerial opportunism.

Moreover, other theoretical explanations are available as to why size might cause divisionalization: limits to the economies of scale of plants (Khandwalla 1977) and limits to the cognitive ability of managers to cope with the complexity of large size (Jaques 1976). Clearly these explanations for an effect of size on divisionalization do not involve divisionalization being introduced to stem greater opportunism that results from size. Also, whether divisionalization does reduce empire building, that is, the addition of unnecessary administrative staff, is open to question. Grinyer and Yasai-Ardekani (1981, p. 478, Table 2) find empirically that the ratio of administrative to production workers is positively correlated with divisionalization, rather than the negative correlation that would be expected from Williamson's (1970) theory that the divisional structure disciplines managers and curbs empire building. There is scope for future research to test these various competing explanations. Nevertheless, as we have seen from the empirical evidence, it cannot be maintained that divisionalization is caused by size and not by diversification, Thus the explanation of divisional structure by strategy that we have invoked repeatedly is not invalidated by the argument that divisionalization is shaped politically.

Not Threat-Rigidity

The contingency theory model of the organization and its managers making rational adaptations differs also from the *threat-rigidity theory* (Staw, Sandelands, and Dutton 1981; for a discussion, see Ocasio 1995). This holds that threat leads to rigidity, so that organizations and their managers make stereotyped responses that fail to resolve the problem and tend to worsen the situation. While the threat-rigidity theory may apply to organizations facing a threat such as a liquidity crisis (e.g., negative cash flows and impending bankruptcy), this is a far worse level of performance than that seen as triggering organizational change in contingency theory. The low performance that is below the satisficing level (e.g., "15 percent return on capital") is considerably higher than teetering on bankruptcy (i.e., a negative return on capital). Thus low performance engendering crisis and rational adaptation is distinguishable from abysmal performance that may lead to feelings of threat and irrational, counterproductive decisions.

Studies show that low performance caused firms to adopt new strategies, such as refocusing by reducing diversification or to become more strategically rational in other ways (Cibin and Grant 1996; Donaldson 1994; Grant 1993; Johnson 1987; Mintzberg and Waters 1982; Smith, Child, and Rowlinson 1990). As we have stressed, the empirical studies of structural change in large corporations show clearly that their response to low performance is rational adaptation, that is, to adopt a new structure that fitted their strategy (Donaldson 1987). For example, when the financial crisis hit Du Pont, it adopted a divisional structure that fitted its diversified operations (Chandler 1962). Moreover, such divisionalization constitutes decentralization, which is the opposite of the centralization that is ascribed to organizations undergoing threat, in threat-rigidity theory, and provides a structural means to rigidity (Cameron, Kim, and Whetten, 1987; Cameron, Sutton, and Whetten, 1988; Cascio 1993; Khandwalla 1977; Whetten 1980). Thus the response by organizations and their managers to crises of low performance is rational, adaptive structural change, as held by contingency theory, rather than irrational, self-defeating actions, as held by threat-rigidity theory. Whether the level of performance acts as a moderator between rational adaptation and irrational threat-rigidity should be regarded as a hypothesis for future research. In particular, the levels of performance that activate the rational and the irrational responses should be identified empirically.

There are, of course, other views of organizational change. Meyer and Zucker (1989) write about "permanently failing organizations." They are referring to organizations whose performance is so low that they would be expected to have disbanded, yet that persist. The explanation of Meyer and Zucker (1989) is by politics, in that vested interests intervene to prevent the organization from taking the rational course of disbanding itself because it is not attaining adequate performance. While the organization has failed against the standards set by usually dominant stakeholders (such as owners), other stakeholders with an interest in the continuing existence of the organization are able to ensure its continuity (Meyer and Zucker 1989). The persistence of an organization despite disastrous performance is a different phenomenon from that being discussed here, the adaptation of structure to contingency. Structural adaptation in contingency theory can be thought of as being achieved by the dominant controllers, the managers playing their traditional role of managing the organization, and as occurring when the performance of their organization drops below the level acceptable to themselves or to company directors or owners. This acceptable or satisficing level is higher than the failing level, for example, bankruptcy, discussed by Meyer and Zucker (1989). We have seen that organizations may persist in structural maladaptation while their performance is above the satisficing level, but this is to be distinguished from the phenomenon of permanent failure, which involves a lower level of performance and pertains to the existence of the organization. Thus contingency theory and permanently failing organizations theories are different and may complement each other, rather than contradicting or refuting each other.

Conclusions

The organizational rationality and functionality postulated by contingency theory has come under challenge, and irrationalist and political explanations have been offered in its place. However, these explanations have been rebutted in this chapter.

Institutional theory has tried to show that new organizational structures are adopted out of conformity, but the evidence is that these structures are instrumentally effective, supporting the contingency theory interpretation. In particular, the institutional theory contention that divisionalization is a mere fashion cannot be sustained, given that divisionalization has been shown to be a move into fit and therefore beneficial for organizational performance.

Population-ecology holds that large organizations are inertial, but large corporations change their strategies and structures in adaptive ways. The changes in strategy and structure discussed in this book are not produced by changes in the population of large firms, as population-ecology would suggest, but rather by changes in ongoing organizations, as contingency theory states.

The organizational politics view stresses that managers further their interests at costs to the organization, such as by empire building. Yet empirical studies of changes in administrative intensity as organizations grow fail to find empire building and instead find economies of scale in administration, that is, changes that are organizationally rational and functional. Studies of decline find asymmetries with growth but these are compatible with economies of scale and so are not evidence of managerial empire building. While organizational economics holds that the M-form divisional structure is adopted to curb managerial empire building, other explanations are available that see the adoption of the M-form as a response not to politics but rather to coordinating complexity or to cognitive limitations.

Threat-rigidity theory holds that poor performance triggers irrational and dysfunctional managerial behaviors. However, the structural changes in contingency theory, such as divisionalizing in response to diversifying, are adaptive, not irrational. The performance level that triggers structural adaptation, while low, may not be as low as the poor level that may cause threat-rigidity. Thus both the contingency and threat-rigidity theories may hold, being activated by different levels of organizational performance: contingency theory where performance drops below the satisficing level and threat-rigidity theory where performance drops farther to a catastrophic level. In a similar vein, the theory that some organizations can be permanently failing may be complementary to contingency theory, rather than refuting it.

Thus overall, the contingency theory of organizations meets the challenge of the organizational theories of institutional, organizational economics, organizational politics, population-ecology, and threat-rigidity. It remains valid despite attempts to offer alternative explanations derived from these theories.

7 Fit Concept and Analysis

Fit is the concept at the heart of contingency theory. Contingency analysts strive to identify what constitutes fit. They seek to show the effect of fit on performance. This has been an increasing focus of contingency theory research. Because fit is so central to contingency theory and research we need to discuss it in detail. We need to ask what exactly we mean by fit. We also need to ask how we empirically establish the effect of fit on performance in terms of research design and empirical analysis.

This and the next chapter are intended to be read together. In contrast to previous chapters, they have a technical flavor by considering issues of modeling and methodology. Readers seeking a discussion of contingency theory in general terms may prefer to omit them, or to come back to them after reading the other chapters. However, those readers who want to perform contingency research will find that these chapters contain advice about how to conduct aspects of such research. Other readers who wish to evaluate the research findings in the literature will also find guidance in these chapters. We will begin with questions about the concept of fit and then move to methodological issues of research design and empirical analysis.

Philosophical Issues in Contingency Theory Research

Contingency Theory Is Not a Tautology

Contingency theory is sometimes criticized for being a tautology, that is, for being true by definition and therefore being circular reasoning. In logic, a *tautology* is an analytic statement masquerading as a synthetic statement; this means a definition presented as if it asserts something empirical about the world, whereas the statement defines the world to be that way (Ayer 1936). Because a tautology is true by definition it can never be falsified, so a tautology is not falsifiable (Bachrach 1989). The tautology criticism of contingency theory centers on the concept of fit. Contingency theory holds that fit produces high performance. Why does fit produce the highest performance? Because, by definition, fit is the combination of contingency and structure that produces high performance. At this most abstract level the fit-performance relationship is true by definition. Therefore the relationship between fit and performance is a tautology.

Yet it is a mistake to dismiss contingency theory for being a tautology, because scientific theories can contain such tautologies in some of their parts, while being logically and empirically valid scientific theories. Many of the most general scientific laws are true by definition. For example, Darwinian evolutionary theory states: the survival of the fittest. Why are they the fittest? The answer is: "Because they survive." Thus the most basic idea or high-level general law is a tautology. However, Darwinian theory overall escapes being tautologous by giving the abstract theoretical statement more specific content. Survival properties are identified for each creature, for example, the long necks of giraffes help them survive because they can eat the leaves they need for food from the tops of trees. This more specific proposition is empirically testable and falsifiable. It is a lower-level proposition derived from the higher-level theory idea that the fittest creatures survive. Being a tautology, the high-level general law is not falsifiable, but the lower-level, derived propositions are, because they are not tautologies. Thus the theory is tested empirically by testing its lower-level propositions rather than its high-level general law. Thus Darwinian theory needs to be assessed as an overall theoretical structure composed of basic laws and specific propositions to see that the theory is not a tautology and is falsifiable.

The same is true for the contingency theory of organizations. The most abstract general statement of contingency theory about fit is a tautology. However, contingency theory, like Darwinian theory, moves beyond tautology by specific propositions that give content to the abstract idea of fit. This is done when contingency theory states what organizational structures fit which contingency and why. For example, a divisional structure fits a diversified firm, because a diversified firm's greater complexity of products and markets (relative to an undiversified firm) needs more information-processing, which is better done in autonomous divisions. Thus under the contingency theory umbrella nests a series of specific theories that connect a contingency with a structure. Each combination of the varying levels of the contingency and the structure is stipulated to be either a fit or a misfit, and a reason is given. It is these lower-level, more specific contingency propositions that are nontautologous and falsifiable. They render contingency theory, as an overall theoretical structure, as not being a tautology and as falsifiable.

Fruitfulness of Research Program Not Falsification

Although contingency theory is falsifiable, should we be attempting to falsify it? To be sound, a theory should meet the criteria of being potentially falsifiable. However, adherence to this logical criterion does not mean that contingency theory research should be seeking to falsify the theory. Instead, contingency theory research should be seeking to develop contingency theory and to reveal as fully as possible its potential. Thus there is a distinction to be drawn between falsifiability as a logical criterion and the act of falsifying a theory.

Popper (1945) holds that theories should be falsifiable and that scientific work takes the form of an energetic attempt to falsify existing theories to open the door to new, superior theories—albeit avoiding premature and erroneous dismissal of theories. The doctrine of falsification was created to demarcate between science and metaphysics (Popper 1959). The doctrine of falsifiability has influenced social and organizational scientists, leading some to the erroneous view that scientific practice not aimed at falsification is improper and unscientific. However, philosophers of science subsequent to Popper have stressed that, historically, fruitful science often develops despite it being falsified. Some early falsifications of a scientific theory can be erroneous because its validity can be seen only after the creation of an auxiliary science consisting of improved methods and complementary scientific theory, which is needed to reveal the truth of the basic theory (Feyerabend 1975). The development of the auxiliary science can take a long time. For instance, early tests of the Copernican theory of the solar system found it to be false (Feyerabend 1975). If astronomers had adhered to the doctrine of falsification it would have been dismissed, wrongly. A proper test of the Copernican theory required the development of an auxiliary science that involved tools such as accurate telescopes, and complementary theory such as Newton's mechanics. It took 150 years before valid scientific evidence confirming the Copernican theory accumulated and became conclusive (Feyerabend 1975). Thus the modern philosophy of science stresses that fruitful science consists of programs of research within a paradigm whereby proponents pursue the basic theories and practices, acting as advocates for their theory (Feyerabend 1975; Kuhn 1970; Lakatos 1974). This involves development of the auxiliary sciences that are required to show the truth of the theory. For contingency theory—as for any organizational theory—the same applies.

Contingency theory will only be revealed in its true light by carefully resolving technical problems and developing complementary theory. This entails a lengthy program of research over many years, to be pursued by adherents of the paradigm who act as its advocates. Only after lengthy prosecution will the full power of contingency theory be able to be assessed. Only then can the true value of contingency theory be known relative to other organizational theories (whose adherents will also pursue their programs). Mercifully, it should not take 150 years to get an accurate assessment of contingency theory! In topics such as organizational structure, where it has been pursued now for forty years (Woodward 1958), there is already considerable evidence establishing its validity, as we have seen. But even in the case of structural contingency theory there is need for further development to reveal fully its true validity. This chapter is about pursuing the contingency theory research program, including by building on existing work to further develop the required body of auxiliary methodologies.

This is not to say, however, that structural contingency theory could not, or should never, be falsified in principle. If, even after prolonged attempts to develop structural contingency theory, empirical research failed to support its major tenet (fit of structure to contingency causes high performance), then the theory would have been shown to be false. However, the accumulating evidence is much more positive, as we shall see in this and the following chapter, so that future falsification of structural contingency theory is unlikely.

The Relationship Between Fit and Performance

As we have seen in previous chapters, contingency theory holds that if the organizational structure fits the contingency, then higher performance results. Conversely, if the organizational structure misfits the contingency, then lower performance results. Therefore organizations move toward fit to gain better performance. This explains organizational change by contingency theory. It also explains why contingencies and structures are associated empirically. The idea that underlies all these explanations is that there is a fit between structures and contingency that positively affects performance. Some combinations of the contingency and organizational structure are better than others for performance. For each level of the contingency variable, there is a level of the organizational structural variable that produces the highest performance and thereby constitutes the fit. Thus fit is central to contingency theory because it explains variations in organizational performance, organizational change, and associations between contingencies and structures.

There has been considerable discussion in organizational studies about the definition of performance. Organizations can be considered to be seeking their goals, so that performance is the degree to which an organization attains its goals, which are set by those in authority over the organization (Parsons 1961). Alternatively, an organization can be conceived of as a system, so that its performance is equated to various aspects of systems functioning (Yuchtman and Seashore 1967). Alternatively again, organizations can be considered to be composed of numerous individuals and external constituencies that constitute stakeholders so that each individual or stakeholder group has distinct criteria and organizational performance is therefore multidimensional (Pfeffer and Salancik 1978; Pickle and Friedlander 1967). Each of these views of performance could be the basis on which appropriate operational measures of performance are selected in empirically studying the relationship between fit and performance.

Meyer and Gupta (1994) point out that measures of organizational performance may be multiple and uncorrelated with each other. They argue that there is a process whereby performance measures lose variation across organizations over time, so that they are replaced by new measures, uncorrelated with the old, which restore variation. To the degree that this is true, it potentially adds complexity to the performance measurement issue. However, within a period, performance measures remain viable so that studies can use them, and also the results of one study can be compared with those of another study. Across time periods, performance measures might differ, though conceptually they might still all be considered to be measuring performance at a more abstract level and therefore be comparable. For instance, if organizational goals change, the new performance measures are still assessing the degree of goal attainment, so can be compared to the degree of attainment of different goals at another period.

Given the importance of fit-performance, it has been investigated empirically in contingency theory research on organizational structure from the earliest studies onward (e.g., Child 1975; Donaldson 1987; Drazin and Van de Ven 1985; Hamilton and Shergill 1992, 1993; Hill, Hitt, and Hoskisson 1992; Jennings and Seaman 1994; Khandwalla 1973; Lawrence and Lorsch 1967; Powell 1992; Woodward 1965). What exactly is meant by fit operationally in contingency theory research? There are two main operational concepts in the literature: congruence and interaction (Pennings 1987).

Fit as Congruence

The operational concept of fit as congruence holds that fit is a combination of the levels of the contingency and structure that produce higher performance. Other combinations are incongruent so that the level of the structure does not fit that required by the level of the contingency and hence lower performance results (i.e., lower performance than in fit). Pfeffer (1997, p. 158) refers to this aspect of structural contingency theory as the "consonance hypothesis," meaning "'that those organizations that have structures that more closely match' or fit 'the requirements of the context' will be 'more effective than those that do not' (Pfeffer 1982, p. 148)." Similarly, Pennings (1987, p. 225) refers to the matching concept of fit, which he defines as: "... a value on a structural dimension for each level of an environmental dimension which will maximize effectiveness." As we have discussed, in contingency theory the contingency includes the environment, but is a wider concept that extends to "context" more broadly, thereby encompassing intra-organizational variables, such as size.

Congruence (or consonance) is seen in the exemplar of fit-performance relationships—between technology and organizational structure in Woodward's (1965) pioneering contingency study. The structural variable of the span of control of the first-line supervisor was associated with technology in a curvilinear relationship, so that it rose and then fell as technology advanced. For unit and small batch the span was low, for mass production it was high, and for process production it was again low. Those firms that were at or about the mean span of control for their technology category performed higher than the firms whose spans of control deviated from the means (being either lower or higher). This held for each of the three technology categories. Thus, in this study, fit is having the mean structural value for the level of the technology contingency, and misfit is deviation from the mean.

This is the general idea across all studies that operationalize fit as congruence. There is some line of fit, which in Woodward (1965) is curvilinear but is usually linear. This is the line that connects all the points of fit. For each level of the contingency variable there is a level of the organizational structural variable that is the fit (i.e., yields the highest performance). Deviation from this fit line constitutes misfit and so produces lower performance. This kind of logic is seen in many contingency analyses of organizational structure. For example, Child (1975, p. 21, Figure 1) found that there was a fit whereby larger organizations were more bureaucratically structured. Organizations that lay on this fit line had higher performance. Those firms that lay off this fit line had lower performance. Deviation from the fit line is misfit.

This idea can be taken farther by conceptualizing degrees of misfit. The farther the organization is away from fit, the greater is its misfit and the lower is its resulting performance expected to be. The distance from the line at which the organization lies becomes its degree of misfit (see Drazin and Van de Ven 1985, p. 520, Figure 2[a]). The fit line may be represented empirically by the regression line of the organizational structure on the contingency variable, among the higher-performing organizations in the sample. The actual position of an organization in misfit is the residual, that is, the difference between the actual value and that expected from the regression. In other words, the degree of misfit of an organization is the amount of discrepancy between actual and ideal (i.e., the fit) scores. This allows quantification of the degree of misfit. It articulates the idea of fit as congruence between structure and contingency, and of misfit as incongruence between them.

Fry and Smith (1987) suggest that fit or congruence has many possible relationships with performance. They hold that the traditional view of the relationship between congruence and performance as positive is only one possibility. They state that congruence could have a negative or curvilinear relationship with performance. However, if more congruence leads to less performance, then it is not congruence or fit, because by definition congruence or fit leads to higher performance. Thus the relationship between congruence or fit and performance is always positive.

Again, Fry and Smith (1987) state that congruence can have positive effects on some performance outcomes but negative effects on others. But if a combination of organizational structures and situational factors has a negative effect on performance, then that combination is not a congruence or fit, instead it is an incongruence or misfit. Thus while the combination may be a congruence or fit for some performance outcomes, it is an incongruence or misfit for other congruence outcomes. It would be clearer to say that a combination is congruent for those performance outcomes on which its effect is positive and incongruent on those performance outcomes on which its effect is negative. Thus in specifying whether a combination is congruent or incongruent, there is a need to specify which performance outcomes are positively affected. There may be some other performance outcomes on which the effect is negative. In this way we preserve the meaning of a congruent or fit state as being one that always raises performance.

Further, Fry and Smith (1987) hold that congruence can have positive effects in the short run but negative in the long run. By definition, however, a congruence or fit always produces positive outcomes. Once again, it would be clearer to say that the combination that is congruent for the short run is incongruent for the long run and vice versa. This discussion brings out that congruence of fit is always embedded in a causal theory. That theory needs to be made explicit when saying that one combination of contingency and organizational structure is congruent or fitting. Thus a congruence or fit is with respect to some particular outcome over some time period. For another performance outcome or time period that combination may be incongruent. The discussion here is of logical possibilities, in the spirit of Fry and Smith (1987). Whether a congruence that raised performance would reduce some other aspect of performance, or whether congruence differs for short- and long-run performances, would need to be established empirically. The logical possibility of such differences does not guarantee that they actually exist.

Fit Is Not Interaction

There is a second operational definition of the fit concept in the literature (Pennings 1987). This is fit as an interaction between the contingency and the organizational structural variable. Specifically, fit is measured by a multiplicative interaction term, that is, the contingency variable multiplied by the organizational structure variable (Schoonhoven 1981). As Pennings (1987, p. 225) states: "it is assumed that effectiveness is high when high levels of both environmental . . . and structural . . . dimensions are present, but that it is low when either dimension is low or absent." However, the reason that such an interaction term is considered to be an operationalization of the fit concept is unclear. Fit combines the contingency and organizational structure variables. Interaction terms are customarily used for combinations of variables in multiple regression. Therefore the interaction term has been applied to test the fit concept in multiple regression analysis. However, this presumes that a fit is a multiplicative interaction (i.e., the contingency and structure variables are multiplied together to give an interaction term), and this is not necessarily so. Certainly some argument is required to justify the assumption that fit is a multiplicative interaction. Conversely, there are very many problems in operationalizing fit as an interaction term, and these will be discussed at various points in this chapter. Fit is not a multiplicative interaction in the way that the fit concept has been used in the seminal contingency theory studies. As seen above, in the seminal studies fit is congruence. For Woodward (1965) fit is congruence: High performance occurs when the structural variable matches the technological contingency. Similarly, for Child (1975), fit is congruence: High performance occurs when the structural variable matches the size contingency.

Moreover, a multiplicative interaction term does not capture the relationship between congruence (fit) and performance. Consider a model in which the structural variable, S, is shown on the vertical axis and the contingency variable, C, is shown on the horizontal axis (see Figure 7.1). The structural variable, S, needs to fit the contingency variable, C, for high performance to result. Suppose, for simplicity, that the fit is that S needs to equal C. Therefore the fit line is at 45 degrees to both the vertical and horizontal axes. When C is 2, S must be also of value 2 for it to be in fit. When C is 2, if S is 3, S is too big to fit so it is actually a misfit, so lower performance would result. However, the multiplicative interaction term would say that C of 2 with S of 3 equals performance of 6 (= 2 x 3) and so is better than C of 2 with S of 2 which equals performance of 4 (= 2 x 2). Thus the multiplicative interaction attributes higher performance to the misfit than to the fit. Clearly, the multiplicative term fails to calibrate the effect of misfit on performance. The essence of a good operationalization of fit is that organizations in misfit must score lower than those in fit. The multiplicative interaction term does not do this and so is not a measure of fit.

Another issue is that the multiplicative interaction term assumes that the fit is a straight line. However, some of the fits are not linear, but are curvilinear. For example, Woodward (1965) produced evidence that some of the fits between technology and structure were curvilinear. As we have seen, the fit of span of control of the foreman to technology was that the span first increased but then decreased as technology advanced, so that it was an inverted U-shaped curve (Woodward 1965). A multiplicative term assumes that the fit of span to technology would be a higher span at the more advanced technology than at the medium technology. The multiplicative term would therefore award a high score to a firm that had a large span and had the most advanced technology, even though that firm was in misfit. Thus the multiplicative interaction term fails to operationalize curvilinear fits.

Van de Ven and Drazin (1985) state that misfit is appropriately measured by a deviation score and advocate the Euclidean distance formula. However, they discuss this under the heading of interaction concepts of fit. This choice of language seems unhelpful, given that, as Van de Ven and Drazin (1985) argue, interaction terms fail to capture the deviation-from-fit concept. Therefore it seems preferable to use the word *congruence* rather than interaction to conceptualize fit.

Thus the multiplicative interaction term is not a correct operationalization of the fit construct. The underlying model of the relationship among the contingency, the organizational structure, and performance in the multiplicative interaction term is not that postulated by the fit

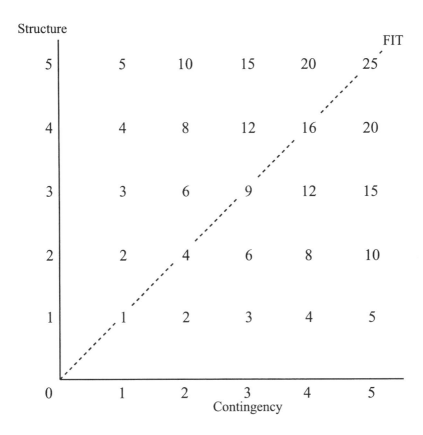

Figure 7.1. Performance From Fit and Misfit: Fit as a Multiplicative Interaction of Contingency and Structure

idea. An interaction term tells us something that may be of interest but conceptually it does not have the meaning of fit that has existed in contingency theory research. This meaning of fit is as congruence and so researchers wishing to measure the degree of fit should use measures of how close the organization is to the fit line.

However, a study by Powell (1992, pp. 127-128) finds similar empirical results from using the two different operationalizations of fit: congruence and interaction. Thus the choice between the two methods may sometimes not affect the results. Nevertheless, the two methods are not the same conceptually and so there can be no guarantee that they will always produce similar results, so research wishing to study fit in the sense that has been meant in contingency theory research should use the congruence measures, not the interaction term.

The Fit Line as Iso-Performance

In an important article that has helped define thinking about fit in contingency theory research, Van de Ven and Drazin (1985) state, *inter alia*, that the fit line is a line of iso-performance. *Iso-performance* means equal performance, so that each point on the line causes performance equal to every other point. This is seen for example in Woodward's (1965) study of the fit of span of control to technology. Those firms lying at fits were the highest performers in the whole study even though there were three different fits, one for each technology category. For instance, Firm A would be in fit with its mass production technology and Firm B in fit with its process production technology. Despite being in different fits, the two firms have equal performance ratings, that is, both are in the highest performing subgroup of all the firms in the study. Thus performance was increased by being *on* the fit line, but there is no increase in performance from moving *along* the fit line. Iso-performance means that the fit to low levels of the contingency variable produces the same performance as the fit to high levels of the contingency variable.

Hence the iso-performance concept articulates something very basic about contingency theory research: All fits are equally good. For each value of the contingency variables there is a value of the organizational structure that is a fit that produces the highest performance for that value of the contingency. This, as we have seen, is the fundamental fit, or congruence, idea of contingency theory. But the empirical research from the pioneering study of Woodward (1965) onward also contains the idea that the high performance of one fit is the same as the high performance of every other fit between that organizational structural and that contingency variable. Thus the high performance for one value of the organizational structural variable that is a fit is the same as that produced for any other value of that organizational structural variable that is a fit. Again, the high performance of a fit for one value of the contingency variable is the same as that produced by the fits for any other value of that contingency variable.

The implication is that each point of fit on the line of fit of bureaucratic structuring to size produces equal performance to every other point. Similarly, each point of fit on the line of organicness to task uncertainty produces equal performance to every other point. However, the performance effects of fit between one aspect of structure and its contingency can differ from that of another aspect of structure and its contingency. For example, the effect on performance of the fit between size and bureaucratic structuring might be different from the effect on performance of the fit between task uncertainty and organicness. Whether these two effects are similar or different is a matter for empirical research. Iso-performance means that fit effects on performance are the same *within* one structural aspect and its contingency rather than *between* structural aspects and their contingencies.

Another problem with fit as a multiplicative interaction term is that it is incompatible with fit as iso-performance. Reverting to our earlier example (Figure 7.1), if the fit line is defined as S equals C, then when S and C are both 2 then there is a fit, and when S and C are both 3 then there is another fit. According to iso-performance, both these fits would produce the same performance. However, using a multiplicative interaction term, S multiplied by C means that the first fit is 4 (= 2 x 2) and the second fit is 9 (= 3 x 3); therefore the performance of the second fit would be much greater than that of the first fit. Thus multiplicative interaction terms hold that performance is increasing as the organization goes along the fit line, which is not a line of iso-performance. This is another reason to avoid the multiplicative interaction term in seeking to operationalize the traditional contingency theory research concept of fit and showing its performance effect.

Problems With Equifinality

Some scholars argue that there is "equifinality," by which they mean several different ways to obtain the same outcome (Gresov and Drazin 1997). Doty and Glick (1994), writing as configurationalists, use "equifinality" to mean that each configuration or type is equally effective. This of course is contrary to contingency logic, which holds that the type that fits its situation is more effective than the other types that

194 THE CONTINGENCY THEORY OF ORGANIZATIONS

are misfits. We have already offered a critical observation about equifinality in configurationalism (in Chapter 5).

In discussions of contingency theory, *equifinality* may be used to mean that there are several different fits that are all equally effective in the same situation. Thus, for a given level of the contingency factor, an organization could have any one of several widely differing structures and still be in fit and have high performance. This goes against the contingency logic that for a particular level of the contingency variable there is one level of the organizational structure variable that produces the highest performance and thereby is the fit (Pennings 1987, p. 226). Where different organizational structures have been shown to be equally effective in the same industry, the firms can be seen to differ in their contingency so that each of the different structures is the fit for its situation. For example, Child (1977, 1984) has argued that, in the same industry, firms that had functional structures had equally high performance as firms with divisional structures. However, Donaldson (1985, pp. 148-151) has pointed out differences between the firms and argued that these were differences in contingencies that explain the different structures so that each firm had to adopt a particular structure to fit its contingencies, so that there was no equifinality.

Equifinality could also be taken to mean that the fit is not a line but, instead, a broad band, so that for a given level of the contingency variable, the fit is a range of values of the organizational structure. However, the existence of such broad bands of fit has yet to be shown empirically. Empirical analyses show fit to be a line (e.g., Child 1975, p. 21, Figure 1). Thus the equifinality notion is not supported to date.

Rather than equifinality being a range of fits for each level of the contingency, some authors use equifinality to mean that the fit to each level of the contingency produces the same (or similar) performance. In this meaning of equifinality it becomes the same as iso-performance, so that showing iso-performance establishes equifinality. However, equifinality carries connotations of choice, in that if there is more than one way to achieve high performance, then an organization can choose between them. The fact that there are numerous positions that produce high performance, one at each level of the contingency, does not mean that an organization can freely choose among them. An organization is confined to the fit to its level of the contingency variable, or to levels of the contingency variable that it can feasibly attain. For example, an organization has a certain size, so it is restricted to the fit to its level of the size contingency, or to fits to adjacent sizes that it could feasibly attain. Therefore to equate equifinality with iso-performance is potentially confusing because equifinality tends to be used to mean that there is choice, whereas iso-performance can exist without choice.

Jennings and Seaman (1994) found two combinations of strategy and structure that produced high performance in their empirical study: defender strategy with mechanistic structure and prospector strategy with organic structure. They interpret these findings as support for equifinality, in that the performance of the two groups in fit was similar even though each had different combinations of strategy and structure. However, this interpretation assumes that each organization was free to choose between the prospector and defender strategies. The possibility of any situational constraint was not examined, such as by investigating whether the organizations following one strategy differed in their situation from those following the other strategy. Insofar as strategies such as being a low-cost defender hang on contingencies such as size that give scale advantages (Porter 1980), then these strategies are not free choices for an organization. Thus where a study demonstrates iso-performance, such as that by Jennings and Seaman (1994), we should be cautious about accepting that there is also equifinality until the lack of determinants has been demonstrated.

Managerial Decision Not Selection Fit

Van de Ven and Drazin (1985) distinguish three concepts of fit: selection, interaction, and systems. They argue that confusion and problems in the contingency theory literature can be resolved by following their schema. Van de Ven and Drazin discuss organizational structures but say that they are applicable to other organizational characteristics. There is much to be welcomed in the concepts of Van de Ven and Drazin, but we shall argue that their three concepts of selection, interaction, and systems would be better reconceptualized as managerial decision, congruence, and multifit, respectively. We have discussed interaction fit above, arguing that it is better termed *congruence*, and will discuss systems fit in the next section. Here we will discuss the concept of selection fit.

Van de Ven and Drazin (1985) use the word *selection* to describe the process whereby organization structure comes to be correlated with the contingencies. Selection consists of natural selection through which misfitted organizations are culled and managerial selection through which managers make the decisions about structure. Drazin and Van de Ven (1985) support their conceptual arguments with an empirical analysis. They show that there are correlations between several structure variables and the contingency, which they see as supporting natural selection. Further, they show that the correlations are greater for aspects of structure and process under management control, thereby supporting the concept of management selection.

Natural selection would explain fit among firms by saying that the misfitted firms failed to survive. However, the units of analysis within the empirical study of Drazin and Van de Ven (1985) are units within a public-sector organization, so that a misfitted unit would not go bankrupt and disband, hence misfit and low performance would not necessarily lead to lack of survival. Therefore the correlations between structure and contingency in their empirical analysis would not seem to be brought about by natural selection, though their conceptual point may apply to free-standing organizations, such as firms. Thus for some organizations, none of the correlations between their structure and contingency variables are caused by natural selection and all are brought about by managerial selection. However, where referring to managerial decisions over structure it might be preferable not to use the word *selection*, which, because of the influence of population-ecology, has come to have strong connotations of natural selection in modern organizational theory. It may be better to use the term *managerial decision* to distinguish it from natural selection. This helps better recognize that almost all organizations are shaped to some degree by the decisions their managers make, without natural selection having necessarily played a part.

Combining Contingencies and Fits

The issue arises of how to combine more than one contingency to determine the fit of an organizational structure. The issue also arises of how to combine multiple fits. In our view all of these combinations should be seen as following a simple process of addition (or subtraction).

Multiple Contingencies

There may be more than one contingency for an organizational structural variable. The effect of one contingency factor is added to the effect of the second factor to determine the fit. For example, large size requires a high degree of bureaucracy, and if the task is routine, then this also requires bureaucracy, so that the fit is even more bureaucratic than it would be for just large size or routine on their own.

Sometimes contingencies may make opposing requirements for the organizational structures needed to fit each of them. In such a situation, the contingencies have "conflicting implications" (Child 1972b, p. 16) for structure, and they are termed "contradictory contingency factors" by Mintzberg (1979, p. 474). It is sometimes felt that the contradictory implications of each contingency leads to a zone of choice (Child 1972b, p.16). Yet the logic of contingency theory is that if one contingency specifies a high level of the organizational structure as the fit and a second contingency specifies a low level of the same organizational structure as the fit, then the fit is a medium level of the organizational structure. Where contingencies make conflicting prescriptions, the lower level of a structural variable that one prescribes is subtracted from the higher level prescribed by the other. This means mathematically that the effect of each contingency in determining the fit of an organizational structure that is subject to more than one contingency is additive. Hence the fit will be singular and so no zone of choice exists.

Consider the case where an organization is large and yet in an unstable environment that mandates the organization to innovate. The large size requires a bureaucratic structure while the innovation requires an organic structure, thereby creating an apparent conflict. However, the large size is dealt with by a bureaucratic macro-structure, such that the overall organization has many hierarchical levels, many departments, many administrative specialists, and many administrative rules and procedures. The requirement for innovation is dealt with by adopting organic elements in some parts of the micro-structure, that is, in those parts that innovate, for example in R&D and in project teams, leaving other parts quite mechanistic, for example, the production department (Lawrence and Lorsch 1967). Thus the opposing tendencies can coexist because some parts of the organization reflect the logic of large size and bureaucracy while other parts reflect the logic of innovation and organicness (as shown in Chapters 2 and 3). More specifically, large size requires high formalization, while innovation requires low formalization, so that the prescriptions of these two contingencies for formalization are in conflict. The overall level of formalization in the organization reflects the effects of both large size, which is pushing to raise it, and innovation that is pushing to reduce it. The administrative macrostructure has high formalization, while within this, departments that deal in innovation (e.g., R&D) have low formalization. The resulting, overall level of formalization is less than it would be for a large but noninnovative organization and higher than it would be for a small, innovative organization. Hence the lower level of formalization prescribed by innovation is subtracted from the higher level of formalization prescribed by large size. Thus the level of formalization reflects the additive effects of innovation and size. It is a single value rather than a zone of several fits that create choice.

Gresov (1989) found an empirical effect of the conflicting contingencies idea. He examined the fit of structure to both the task uncertainty and horizontal dependence contingencies simultaneously. He found that fit and performance were related where both contingencies required similar structures, but that where their requirements conflicted, the relationship broke down and units had lower performance, supporting the argument that conflicting contingencies lead to misfit. Conflicting contingencies may increase the probability of erroneous management choice and hence of misfit, rather than signifying equifinality and a range of equally effective structural choices. There is scope for replication of these results and further empirical examination of the conflicting contingencies issue.

Combining Multiple Fits

As we have seen, within the contingency theory of organizational structure there are a number of different fits between various aspects of organizational structure and their contingencies. The question arises of how to combine more than one fit to assess their total effect on organizational performance. Some analysts have suggested that the fits are additive, in that the first fit is added to the second fit to yield the overall effect on organizational performance (Randolph and Dess 1984,

Exhibit 2, p. 123). In our view, this additive model of the effects of multiple fits is sound.

Van de Ven and Drazin (1985), however, argue that the overall effect of multiple fits is not the sum of their individual effects and so is not additive. They advance a model of the combination of multiple fits as being a systems fit. In a systems fit, the effect of multiple fits on organizational performance is not just the sum of the effect of each fit on performance. Instead, there is some holistic property that is not captured by an atomistic analysis of each fit separately that then just combines them together (Drazin and Van de Ven 1985). Thus, they argue, the effect of multiple fits cannot be calculated by simply adding up the effect of each fit on performance.

Drazin and Van de Ven (1985) examine separately the pairwise fit of each structure and process variable to the contingency variable and its relationship with performance (measured by efficiency and satisfaction). They show that each fit attains only very limited support—only four out of twenty-two are significant and one of these has a sign contrary to the theory. They then show that the *systems fit* is significantly correlated with performance (both efficiency and satisfaction) in the way theoretically expected. While this is evidence that multiple fits are stronger than pairwise fits, this is no proof of systemic properties of a holistic kind whereby the whole is more than the sum of its parts. The Euclidean distance formula used by Drazin and Van de Ven to calculate systems fit sums the effects on performance of each of the pairwise fits. It is an additive model. Thus their systems fit measure is nothing more than the sum of its parts. Therefore the greater strength of the systems fit than each of the pairwise fits is caused by the summation of many small effects. Furthermore, pairwise fits suffer unreliability of measurement that reduces their observed effect on performance. Summing across the pairwise fits produces an additive index that will be less unreliable and so produce a truer correlation. Hence the superiority of the multiple fit over the pairwise fits is compatible with it being the sum of the parts and is not evidence of holistic properties.

Drazin and Van de Ven (1985) also argue, in part, by an illustration. This is a curious illustration because in it the effect of the multiple fits on overall organizational performance is calculated by simply adding up the effects of each fit on performance. Thus in the illustration the whole is simply the sum of its parts. It therefore illustrates the point against which the argument is being made. In their illustration (Drazin and Van de Ven 1985), an individual fit is often not associated with total performance of the organization. However, this is because most of the fits are negatively correlated with each other so that most of them have zero correlation with total performance. Hence each fit affects performance, but most of the fits have no correlation with total performance because of the suppressing effect of the other fits. Thus the lack of association between many of the individual fits and total performance in this illustration is no more than confounded correlation. Hence, the seemingly paradoxical result is explained through considering the correlations between each of the variables, that is, reductionism and not holism.

Thus we can see that the systems fit model really boils down to the additive model. We suggest that researchers in contingency theory use additive models to analyze the effects of multiple fits on performance. This additive model applies both to combining multiple fits of an organizational structural variable to various contingencies and to combining multiple fits of various organizational structural variables to a contingency. It also applies to more encompassing analyses that combine multiple fits of various organizational structural variables to various contingencies. Thus researchers should use the concept of multiple fits, that is, multifits.

The Identification of the Fit Line

So far we have talked about the fit line, but how do we know where it is? Conceptually it is the line of points of fit, that is, the series of values of the organizational structural variable each of which constitutes the fit for a particular value of the contingency. But how do we identify what is the value of the organizational structural variable that fits each value of the contingency? Two ways of answering this question may be distinguished: the theoretical approach and the empirical approach.

The *theoretical approach* is that for a particular organizational structure a contingency factor is identified through theoretical analysis. The specific values of the organizational structure that fits each different value of the contingency are then identified by thinking through the logic of the argument. A matrix of all the possible combinations of the values of the contingency and organizational structure is constructed. Then each combination is identified as either a fit or a misfit. One can then inspect the pattern of cells in the matrix that are fits and see whether it forms a straight line or a curve or some other nonlinear pattern.

Having generated a theoretical model on an *a priori* basis, we can test its validity empirically. This involves examining whether the combinations designated as being fits actually perform higher than those designated as being misfits. The first step may be to calculate the performances of all the cells that are fits and compare this subtotal with the performances of all the cells that are misfits (e.g., Donaldson 1987; Hamilton and Shergill 1992). This aggregate analysis has the disadvantage that some cells labeled as fits may actually be misfits and vice versa; the actual performance of the individual cell is not known, so it may be obscured by the aggregation. However, it has the advantages of larger numbers, whereas the number of cases in the individual cells may be too small to be reliable. The aggregate method allows a quick test of the overall model and if positive encourages further research, whereas a negative result is an important signal that may lead to a reassessment of the fit model or, indeed, of the theory. The second step is to calculate the performances of each cell and ascertain that each of those designated as fit actually has a performance higher than those designated as a misfit (and vice versa for the misfit cells). A negative result for a cell may indicate that it is actually a misfit rather than a fit (or vice versa) and lead to a reassessment of the theory for that particular combination of contingency and organization structure.

Conversely, instead of starting with a theory, the *empirical approach* starts with the data and then seeks to find a pattern, which is then interpreted theoretically. The analysis examines various combinations of the levels of the contingency and structures to see which produce highest performance. The high-performing combinations are the fits and the low-performing are the misfits. A theory would then be developed of why certain combinations are fits that are effective and others misfits that are ineffective.

In a completely empirical approach the contingency factor itself may be discovered empirically. Initial attempts fail to find an association between an organizational structure and organizational performance. No main effect having been found, the search is then for moderators of the relationship between the structure and performance. A frequent move is then to look for variables that are associated with the structure. Such an association would be expected if the variables were moderators of the effect of the structure on performance, that is, contingencies.

The reason for the association is that organizations would tend to move into fit to gain the resulting higher performance. Therefore variables found to be associated with the structure are then subject to an analysis to see whether they are in fact contingencies, by seeing whether these variables moderate the relationship between the organizational structure and performance.

What we have just described is an empirically based procedure (i.e., an emergent or data-driven procedure). Some would castigate it as "a fishing trip," but there is some role for it. Contingency theory research on organizational structure has quite often gone from initially seeking associations between contingency and structure to then examining the effects of combinations of contingency and structural variables on performance. This is seen in the research on technology and organizational structure (Woodward 1965) and on size and bureaucracy (Child 1975; Pugh et al. 1969).

The two different approaches for identifying the fit line, the theory-driven and empirical-driven, are extremes. Less extreme than either of these two research procedures might be the use of some mixture of theory-driven and empirically driven approaches.

Validation of the Fit Model

Once a model of what constitutes fits and misfits between structure and contingency has been created, it has to be validated empirically. This raises two methodological issues: causal inference and measurement of the relationship between fit and performance.

Contingency theory holds that the fit of structure to the contingency positively affects performance. But how can we be sure that fit is a cause of performance? Given that a cause precedes an effect, fit needs to be assessed at one point in time and performance at a subsequent time point. There is no theory that specifies the time lag, but a two-year period between fit and performance produces a positive effect of fit on performance (Donaldson 1987; Hoffman, Carter, and Cullen 1994). Thus we can have more confidence in making the causal inference that fit is a cause of performance—and that performance is an effect of fit—where fit is measured at a time prior to the point at which performance is measured. Thus a diachronic research design is preferable. However, some research designs are cross-sectional (i.e., synchronic), so that they study fit and performance at the same time. Indeed, being more exact, while some such studies collect the structural and performance data at the same time, the performance is for a time prior to that of structure (Dalton, Daily, Johnson, and Ellstrand 1999, p. 680), such as an average of several years of profitability or sales growth prior to the date for which structure is measured (e.g., Child 1974). In such cases, strictly speaking, an observed association is evidence for an effect of performance on fit, so that performance is a cause of fit. Such studies are conventionally interpreted, however, as investigations of the effects of fit on performance. Nevertheless, causal inference that fit affects performance is more certain where fit precedes performance, so that research designs should incorporate this feature. (The issue of whether performance affects fit will be discussed more fully below.)

Other causes of performance may confound the effect of fit on performance and these need to be controlled in the research design. Because in contingency theory the dependent variable is performance, which is obviously affected by many variables other than contingency fit, there is ample scope for such confounding variables. The combined effects of the causes of performance other than fit may be great and may be greater than the fit, so rendering confounding more feasible. Other causes of performance only become confounds, however, if they are correlated with fit. Sometimes such a correlation arises because the confound and the contingency fit variables are causally connected or have a systematic association, other times a correlation will exist by chance in a sample of organizations.

The appropriate procedure is to seek to control for such possibly confounding effects of other causes of performance. This may be achieved by holding constant other factors by studying only organizations that are in the same category, for example, the same industry (Dess, Ireland, and Hitt 1990). Alternatively, it may be achieved by using a control group of similar organizations that differ only in their contingency fits. However, the more usual approach is to measure each possible confounding variable and enter it into a multivariate statistical analysis that assesses the impact of fit on performance, controlling for the confounds. Such other causes of organizational performance that may be controlled statistically in analyses of fit include industry concentration, firm size, risk, and leverage (Hamilton and Shergill 1993).

Turning to the measurement of the relationship between fit and performance, there are three main ways this is done statistically in the literature: subgroup analysis, regression analysis, and deviation analysis.

Subgroup Analysis

In subgroup analysis the sample of organizations is broken into a number of groups, and their performances are compared. Typically there are two subgroups: the fits and the misfits. As noted earlier, it is an advantage that the number of cases in the subgroups can be reasonably large because the sample is being broken into only two subsamples. The comparison between the subgroups may be of various statistics: means, regression coefficients, and correlations.

Means

Perhaps the simplest form of subgroup analysis is to create two subgroups—fits and misfits—and then show that the mean performance of the fits is superior to that of the misfits. An advantage of this procedure is that the performances of organizations are aggregated within each subgroup, and this tends to produce a more reliable performance score than for organizations individually.

Regression

If there is fit between an organizational structural variable and a contingency that leads to higher performance, then organizations will tend to move into fit, leading to an association between the organizational structure and the contingency. This association produces a correlation between the organizational structure and the contingency. This in turn leads to a slope in a regression analysis of the organizational structure on the contingency. For example, size and structuring are positively correlated and structuring has a positive slope in a regression on size (Child 1975). This slope may be used as the empirical estimate of the line of fit. However, a preferable approach is to take a subsample of the best-performing organizations and use their regression slope as the estimate of the fit line. Being the high performers, more of them should be in fit than for the sample as a whole, which would contain more organizations that are in misfit, thereby lowering the performance of the whole sample.

Subgroup regression takes the regression line of the high-performing subsample, the fits, and then compares it with the regression line for the low-performing subsample, the misfits. The hypothesis is that these two regression lines will be significantly different. The regression lines are hypothesized to differ because the misfits lie away from the fit line. The regression line is therefore expected to differ in either slope coefficient, or constant term, or both. For example, Child (1975, p. 21, Figure 1) found that the regression line of the low-performing firms had a different slope and constant (i.e., intercept) than the high-performing firms in regressions of specialization on size. This shows that the low-performing firms, the misfits, lie away from the fit line. Specifically, the misfits are less specialized than the fits at large size and are more specialized than the fits at small size (Child 1975, p. 21, Figure 1). This illustrates how subgroup regression analysis can be used to show a relationship between fit and performance.

The two regression lines of the fits and the misfits, however, cross over each other at a lowish size point (Child 1975, p. 21, Figure 1). This might seem to mean that at the point of intersection fit and misfit are the same, so that the structure both fits and misfits that level of the contingency variable. Clearly that would be impossible, or would contradict the ideas of fit and misfit. However, there is really no cross over, the appearance of such is an artifact of the regression technique. The regression line creates a continuum connecting disparate data points. If the misfits to low size are above the regression line of the fits and the misfits to high size are below that line, then the regression line of the misfits will intersect that of the fits. The portion of the misfit regression line that appears to cross over the fit line is just an imaginary line achieved by connecting up the misfits on either side of the fit line. In such a scenario there is no actual crossing of a line of fits and misfits; there is no structural level that is both a fit and a misfit. There are reasons for believing the conjecture about the position of the misfits, as to where they are above and below the fit line, so that this interpretation gains credence.

Child (1975, p. 21, Figure 1) found that the regression line of structure on the size contingency for the high-performing subgroup was steeper than that of the low-performing subgroup. Moreover, the low-performing subgroup had a higher positive intercept than the high-performing group. The result was that the two lines intersected toward the lower level of the contingency variable. Yet it is reasonable to hold that positive intercepts are false. Certainly their theoretical meaningfulness is problematic. A positive intercept means that when size is zero, the organization has a structure. Thus despite having no employees, the organization nevertheless has specialized functions that are occupied by people! The functional specialization scale measures the extent to which each specialization is performed by at least one full-time person (Pugh et al. 1968), so it would have to score zero if there were no employees in the organization. Thus the fit line of structure on size is theoretically meaningful only if structure is zero when size is zero, that is, the fit line goes through the origin (0, 0). (A case could be made that structure should become positive only when there are a number of employees, so that, technically speaking, the intercept of the regression of structure on size is negative. However, for simplicity we will assume an intercept of zero, that is, the fit line passes through the origin. Even if the intercept is actually negative, the following argument holds and so the assumption being made is conservative.)

If the true fit line goes through the origin, then, at lower levels of the contingency, substantial misfits would have to lie above the true fit line due to the restricted space below the line. Similarly, at higher levels of the contingency, substantial misfits would have to lie below the true fit line due to the restricted space for misfits above it. Therefore, at the extremes of the contingencies, misfits would tend to be toward the middle of the structural variable. Regressions are very sensitive to such outliers, therefore the slope of the misfits would be shallower than the slope of the fits and also the intercept of the misfits would tend to be higher than that of fits. Thus, given that the misfits have a regression line with a shallower slope and a higher intercept than the true fit line, the low-performing subgroup would have a shallower slope and a higher intercept than the high-performing subgroup. Therefore their two regression lines would intersect, yielding the observed finding (Child 1975, p. 21, Figure 1).

While the observed differences in the regression slopes between the low- and high-performing subgroups capture the pattern of the differences between the misfits and the fits, they understate those differences. The low-performing subgroup would tend to be contaminated to some degree by fits, because the low-performing subgroup is those organizations that are only below average performance and not just the lowest performers. Therefore the true misfit line would be of even shallower slope and more positive intercept than the observed regression line of the low-performing organizations. Similarly, the high-performing subgroup would tend to be contaminated to some degree by misfits, because the high-performing subgroup is those organizations that are only above average performance. Therefore the true fit line would be of even steeper slope and less positive intercept than the observed regression line of the high-performing organizations.

Given that, as we have seen, positive intercepts of the fit line make little theoretical sense, the fit line should go through the origin, so its slope should be steeper. Therefore the observed positive intercept of the high-performing subgroup may be artifactual. The slope of the fit line could be steeper than that found in the regression analysis. Researchers should be aware of this possibility when making their interpretations of regression results. The empirical regression results should not dissuade us from theoretically meaningful fit lines, such as those that go through the origin. Similarly, if true fit lines are steeper than the regression lines of high-performing subgroups, then it becomes feasible to hold that they may have a slope of 1 as is postulated by some theoretical approaches to specifying the fit line (Alexander and Randolph 1985; Keller 1994). In summary, postulating that the fit line goes through the origin is more theoretically meaningful and explains the pattern of the misfits, including their apparent cross-over of the fits.

Also, if the fit line is steeper than the high-performance regression and the misfit line is shallower than the low-performance regression, then the comparison of these two subgroups understates the magnitude of the difference between the fits and misfits in slopes (and also intercepts). Thus the difference in slopes (or intercepts) might be found in some studies to be small and "not significant," even where the fits differ substantially from the misfits, leading to the erroneous conclusion of no relationship between fit and performance.

Another potential weakness of the subgroup regression analysis is that the misfits could all lie away from the fit line but yet there could be no difference in the regression lines. Logically, misfits can be above or below the fit line. If the misfits are both above and below the fit line, then their regression line could be identical to the fit line, that is, have the same slope and constant coefficient. In such a situation, however, the correlation coefficient of the misfit group would be lower than that of the fits, because the misfits are scattered farther away from the fit line. One might be able to confirm this interpretation by showing that the misfits can be partitioned into two groups: one with a regression line above the fit line and one below. The correlation of these two new regressions would be greater than that of the rather fuzzy line formed from all the misfits scattered on either side of the fit line. Thus if there is a fit line in the data, then subgroup regressions should be able to show that it differs from the misfits by comparing high-performing with low-performing organizations, though sometimes supplemental correlational analysis may be required to help in the verification.

Correlations

Correlations may also be used as the main tool in a subgroup analysis, by splitting the sample into low- versus high-performing organizations and correlating the contingency and structural variables within each subgroup (e.g., Khandwalla 1973, p. 490, Table 2). Again, the lower-performing subgroup is expected to have a lower correlation between the contingency and the organizational structure than the high-performing subgroup, because the misfits are scattered around the fit line. There is also the point that higher correlations indicate a higher regression slope (because correlation coefficients and regression slopes are definitionally connected). Thus higher correlations provide indirect evidence of differences in slopes and so the analysis becomes a subtle form of the subgroup regression analysis discussed above. The disadvantage of subgroup correlational analysis, however, is that if all the misfits lay on one side of the fit line, then they could have the same or an even higher correlation than the fits. In such a case, however, a supplementary regression analysis would show that the misfits had a different slope or constant than the fits. Thus correlational analysis may need to be supplemented by regression analysis.

An alternative correlational method is to split the sample into subgroups of low versus high levels of the contingency variable and then correlate structure and performance within each subgroup. Fit is supported by demonstrating that there are statistically significant differences between the subgroups, produced by the correlation being positive for one subgroup and negative for the other subgroup (Argote 1982, p. 430, Table 2).

Regression Analysis

In regression analysis, the effect of fit on performance is assessed by regressing performance on fit. Fit may be operationalized as a congruence term, so that the main effect of fit on performance is assessed. Alternatively, fit may be operationalized as an interaction term, so that a moderator effect is assessed. Either way, the effect of other causes of performance may be controlled by including them in the regression alongside fit (e.g., Hamilton and Shergill 1992 p. 106, Table 5).

Main Effect Regression Analysis

In main effect regression analysis, fit is operationalized as a single variable taking two or more values, such as fit or misfit. There may be more than one combination of the levels of the contingency and structural variables that constitute a fit, for example, a functional structure fits very low diversity and a divisional structure fits diversified strategies (Hamilton and Shergill 1992, p. 99, Figure 2). Similarly, there may be more than one combination of the levels of the contingency and structural variables that constitute a misfit, for example, a functional structure misfits diversified strategies and a divisional structure misfits very low diversity (Donaldson 1987, p. 8, Figure 4). An advantage of this approach (relative to moderated regression discussed below) is that the fit term operationalizes the idea of fit as congruency. Each of the combinations of the levels of the contingency and structural variables that constitutes a fit is a state of congruence between contingency and structure, that is, a match of a level of structural variable to a level of the contingency variable. Similarly, each of the combinations of levels of the contingency and structural variables that constitutes a misfit is a state of incongruence between contingency and structure, that is, a mismatch of a level of structural variable to a level of the contingency variable. The effect of fit on performance is empirically assessed by testing whether the fit term shows a positive effect, that is, whether there is a main effect of fit on performance.

Moderated Regression Analysis

In moderated regression analysis, fit is represented by a multiplicative interaction term, that is, the contingency multiplied by the organization structure (e.g., size times structuring). Organizational performance is regressed onto this interaction term to see the magnitude of the slope coefficient. A slope significantly different from zero is taken to indicate an effect of fit on performance (Hill, Hitt, and Hoskisson 1992; Venkatraman 1989). Alternatively, the amount of performance variance explained by the interaction term is compared with that explained by the main effects of its two constituent variables, the contingency and the structure. If there is a significant increase from the interaction, then that is taken as evidence for an effect of fit on performance (Argote 1982, p. 429, Table 1). The problem is that, as discussed above, a multiplicative interaction term does not reflect the concept of fit as congruence and so it is not an operationalization of fit as that concept has been meant in contingency theory research. Therefore researchers wishing to test for the traditional type of fit should avoid moderated regression analysis and instead use one of the other techniques, such as main effect regression or subgroup analysis.

Deviation Analysis

In deviation analysis the degree of misfit of an organization is measured by its distance from the fit line. This deviation could be from a theoretically given fit line. For instance, Alexander and Randolph (1985) and Keller (1994) define fit as a line in which the level of the structural variable equals that of the contingency variable, that is, it passes through the origin and has a slope of 45 degrees to the horizontal (see Figure 7.2). The contingency and structural variables each range from 1 to 5 in levels. A mechanistic structure (i.e., structure level 1) fits a routine level of the technology contingency (i.e., technology level 1). In contrast, an organic structure (i.e., structure level 5) fits a non-routine technology (i.e., technology level 5). For every increase of one level in technology, the structure needs to increase by one level in order for it to fit. A one-unit deviation from the fit line, that is, the mildest degree of misfit, reduces performance by one unit to −1. The greatest misfit possible is a deviation of four units, which reduces performance by four units to −4. Thus the greater the deviation, the greater the misfit, and so the lower the performance. The level of performance produced by each point of fit or misfit in the two-dimensional space is given *a priori*. In contrast, where the fit line is defined empirically

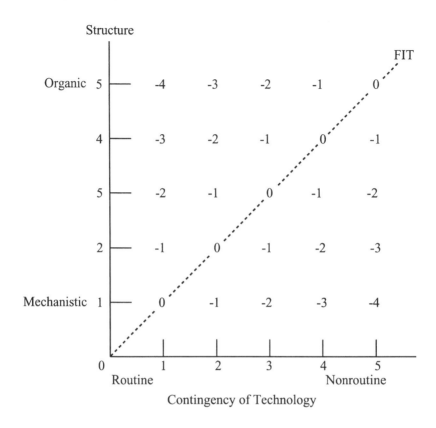

Figure 7.2. Misfit and Performance

by regression, then the misfit is a residual from that regression (Pennings 1987).

A variant of deviation analysis is to measure the degree of misfit by the Euclidean distance formula. Van de Ven and Drazin (1985, pp. 350-351) define the Euclidean distance as the distance between the actual score of an organization on a structural dimension and the ideal score that the organization would require to be in fit with its level of the contingency variable. This distance is then squared for each structural dimension and then added to the squared deviations scores of all the other structural dimensions for that organization. Finally, the square root is taken. Thus the Euclidean distance is the sum of all the deviations across all the structural dimensions. The Euclidean distance for an organization measures its degree of misfit. This Euclidean distance can be correlated with performance to test the hypothesis that misfit is negatively correlated with performance.

The deviation score has the advantage of providing a measure of misfit for each organization, which can be correlated with the performance of each organization to yield a direct estimate of the strength of the relationship between fit and performance. However, the deviation score is a difference score, between the ideal level of the organizational structure that is required to fit the contingency and the actual level of that structure. Therefore it is prone to low reliability, as will be discussed below (in Chapter 8). Thus the correlation between fit and performance tends to understate the true effect of fit on performance. Moreover, the fits are to a few ideal profiles, rather than to a line of many fits (Drazin and Van de Ven 1985, pp. 532-534). Therefore many points on a fit line would lie away from the few, ideal profile fits and so be treated as misfits, thereby contaminating the analysis of fit and performance (as discussed for configurations in Chapter 5).

Overall, the discussion of methodological issues has suggested the advantages and disadvantages of various approaches. By using more than one approach, the analyst may avoid the pitfalls inherent in any one approach and reach a sounder conclusion.

Conclusions

Fit is central to contingency theory and so is receiving increasing study in empirical research. The idea that fit raises performance moves beyond being an empty tautology by becoming more specific about which organizational structures fit which contingencies.

Fit is the congruence between the organizational structure and its contingency. The line of fit may be straight or curved. The empirical tests for fit involve showing that deviations from the fit line cause lower performance. Fit as traditionally understood in contingency theory is not captured by a multiplicative interaction term.

Fit is a line of iso-performance in contingency theory research, in that each point on the line produces the same performance as any other point. Research fails to support the notion of equifinality. Equifinality would be evidence for choice only if structures yielding the same performance exist at the same level of the contingency. If they exist for different levels of the contingency, then the organization may be constrained by its level on that contingency so that there is no choice.

Whereas it has been suggested previously that there are three concepts of fit: selection, interaction, and systems, these would be better reconceptualized as managerial decision, congruence, and multifit, respectively. Multiple fits can be combined by adding them together to produce the total effect on performance of multiple fits. Conflicting contingencies can be handled within this additive model by subtracting the structural prescriptions of one contingency from another to yield a net effect.

The process whereby fit is identified may be initially driven by either theory or data. Either way, fit needs a theoretical rationale and empirical validation. Causal inference is aided by using a research design in which fit temporally precedes performance, and other causes of performance are controlled. There are several techniques for empirically demonstrating fit. These include subgroup analyses, regression analyses, and deviation analysis. The characteristics of each have been discussed.

8 Fit Affects Performance

Contingency theory states that fit affects performance. There is overwhelming evidence that this is true. In this chapter we will review the empirical studies and see how they support the contingency idea that fit positively affects performance.

This review will be followed by a discussion of methodological issues that influence the observed strength of the relationship between fit and performance. This reveals certain pitfalls in researching the fit-performance relationship, which means that the strength of the relationship may not always be shown fully by empirical studies. We will close by extracting eight lessons that may help us surmount these potential problems in future research, so that it demonstrates the true strength of the effect of fit on organizational performance. While we will discuss these issues in the context of structural contingency research, many of them apply generally to any contingency theory.

Studies of Contingency Fit and Performance

Dalton, Todor, Spendolini, Fielding, and Porter (1980) provided a critical review of the research connecting structure and performance. They commented that despite the importance of performance there was a paucity of research, weaknesses in methods, and inconsistencies in findings, both regarding the main effects of structure and the contingent effects of structure. They called for more and better research. Two early studies of the relationship between contingency fit and performance failed to find a positive relationship (Mohr 1971; Pennings 1975). This led to the validity of contingency theory being questioned. For instance, Pfeffer (1997, p. 161) states: "This [consonance, i.e., fit-performance] hypothesis has received support in some studies (e.g., Woodward, 1965) but not in others (Mohr, 1971; Pennings, 1975)." He goes on to state that some support for the hypothesis comes also from Schoonhoven (1981) (Pfeffer 1997, p. 162). However, Pfeffer (1997) concludes about structural contingency theory that the Schoonhoven (1981) study "marked virtually the end of empirical research on organizational structure." Thus, according to Pfeffer (1997) not only is the balance of findings from studies of fit and performance not positive, but no further work has addressed the fit-performance relationship. This deficiency has occurred despite the acknowledgement by Pfeffer (1997, p. 162) that "empirical support for the consonance hypothesis has been inconsistent. But that could conceivably be remedied by more careful studies and measures." However, subsequent to Mohr (1971) and Pennings (1975), there have been other studies that have found a positive relationship between fit and performance and so support contingency theory (Alexander and Randolph 1985; Argote 1982; Dewar and Werbel 1979; Donaldson 1987; Drazin and Van de Ven 1985; Gresov 1989, 1990; Hamilton and Shergill 1993; Hill, Hitt, and Hoskisson 1992; Hoskisson 1987; Jennings and Seaman 1994; Keller 1994; Kraft, Puia, and Hage 1995; Nohria and Ghoshal 1997; Pennings 1987; Powell 1992). We have discussed some of these studies already and will now examine the other studies to draw out their findings and their implications for research into the relationship between fit and performance. Taken together, the studies of the relationship of fit and performance, overall, support the contingency theory that fit positively affects performance. More studies find for the positive relationship than find against it. Moreover, some of the studies finding for the relationship indicate that some of the earlier studies may have failed to find the relationship because of methodological limitations.

Mohr (1971) studied the fit between unpredictability of jobs and participativeness in local health departments. There was almost no association between fit and effectiveness, so contingency theory was not supported. Universalistic theory was supported in that effectiveness was higher for high participation—supporting human relations theory. Pennings (1975) studied the fit of structural to environmental variables in brokerage offices. He concluded that there was little support for such effects, and the contingency theory had to be questioned. He found support for main effects of structure, particularly power, on effectiveness, again lending support to universalism. Despite these two studies failing to support contingency theory, however, other studies have supported contingency theory.

A subsequent study by Pennings (1987) of branches of a large commercial bank found support for contingency theory. He shows that misfit is correlated with lower performance, particularly financial performance. Ideal profiles of structural (communications and power) variables for low, medium, and high levels of five environmental contingency variables (aspects of competition and customers) were identified from high-performing branches. The deviations from these ideas were then computed by the Euclidean distance formula for the remaining branches. For the three financial measures of performance, all correlations were in the theoretically expected direction and eight out of fifteen were significant. In particular, the ratio of interest income to deposits was significant in four out of five analyses with misfits and the average correlation can be calculated as −.31 (Pennings 1987, p. 231, Table 1). Canonical analyses show that the relationship between environmental contingency and structural variables is stronger for the high-performing than for the low-performing branches, which is consistent with their structures fitting the contingencies (Pennings 1987).

The degree of correlation between misfit and performance is encouraging, especially the interest to deposit average correlation of −.31. It should be noted, moreover, that these correlations underestimate the true correlation, because the highly fitting branches are not used in correlating misfit with performance, thus restricting the range of misfit. (This procedure is to avoid, perhaps unnecessarily, the seeming tautology of measuring misfit of the same organizations that were used to define fit.) A weakness of the study (Pennings 1987) is that it does

not report the main effects of environment and structure on performance, and so the extent to which these constituent variables of fit
work to create a spurious degree of misfit-performance relationship
(as will be discussed below) is unknown. Multiple structural variables
are apparently summed together to yield the misfit with each environmental contingency, in the manner of Drazin and Van de Ven (1985).
However, the misfits with each environmental contingency are not
summed together to yield an assessment of the total effect of multiple
misfit on performance. Overall, the findings of Pennings (1987) tend to
confirm the analytic approach of Drazin and Van de Ven (1985), upon
which Pennings drew. The study shows that it can be extended to different sorts of organizations (bank branches), to different structural variables, and to multiple contingencies that differ from the single one
used by Drazin and Van de Ven (1985).

Further Studies of Task Contingency

While Pennings (1987) studied the contingency of the environment,
others have studied the contingency of the task itself and in that way
examined a contingency similar to the job unpredictability that Mohr
(1971) studied. Unlike Mohr, these subsequent studies found positive
evidence supporting contingency theory. There have been four such
studies of the task contingency (Alexander and Randolph 1985; Argote
1982; Gresov 1990; Keller 1994).

Argote (1982) studied the fit of organizational coordination structures to input uncertainty in hospital emergency units. She found that
fit was positively correlated with effectiveness as measured by patient
care. These results held using both moderated regression and subgroup
analyses (i.e., correlations between structure and effectiveness for low
and high uncertainty). Thus these two methods yielded similar results.
It may be noted in passing that input uncertainty was not significantly
correlated with most of the structural variables in this study (Argote
1982). Hence a preliminary analysis looking for contingencies by
seeking variables correlated with structure would not have detected
that input uncertainty was a contingency of most of the structural variables. Therefore, while contingency relationships will often be revealed
by associations between contingency and organizational structure,
such associations are not always present. Their absence should not

forestall trivariate analyses of contingency, structure, and outcomes to test directly for contingency relationships.

Similar to Argote (1982), Alexander and Randolph (1985) found, in a study of nursing, that the fit between structure and technology (i.e., task) affected the quality of patient care. This effect of fit on patient care held after controlling for the effects of both structure and technology on patient care, that is, for the constituent variables of fit. However, this fit effect holds only for the fit of horizontal participation (structure) to variability (technology). The fit of formalization (structure) to uncertainty (technology) was significantly correlated with care quality, but the sign was opposite to that theoretically expected (Alexander and Randolph 1985). Whereas contingency theory holds that uncertainty needs less formalization, in this setting it required more. Thus the general theory connecting uncertainty and formalization may be argued to have an exception in nursing aimed at producing quality care, as Alexander and Randolph (1985, p. 856) suggest. Alexander and Randolph (1985) used, as their measure of misfit, deviation from the fit line defined as structure score equals the technology score. Thus the fit line is given *a priori.* The theory is that an increase in technology requires the same increase in structure for the organizational unit to be in fit. This contrasts with the empirical derivation of the fit line from data that are used in other contingency theory research (e.g., Pennings 1987). The positive findings attained by Alexander and Randolph for the fit of horizontal participation to variability confirm that their theoretical fit line does approximate the true fit line for these variables, because deviations from it are correlated with lower performance.

The same approach to modeling fit was used by Keller (1994), who also examined the effects of fit on performance in organizational subunits. However, in this study, the subunits were project groups from four industrial research and development organizations, composed of highly qualified professionals, mostly male. The fit of project group structure to technology was found to affect project group performance. Specifically, more information-processing structures fitted more nonroutine task technology and led to higher-quality project outcomes. Keller (1994) also found a main effect of structure (information processing) on performance, though this was weaker than fit, thereby confirming the importance of contingency. Moreover, the effect of fit on performance is not a spurious effect of the constituent variables (structure and technology) because both were controlled (as discussed below). Again, the positive findings confirm the fit line used, even though it was derived simply and on an *a priori* theoretical basis. The positive effect of fit on performance held not only for project quality measured concurrently with fit, but also one year later (which was stronger than concurrently). This means that fit affected subsequent performance, thereby providing evidence that fit is a cause of performance. This is an important finding in that most studies of the relationship between fit and performance have been cross-sectional and thereby less definite about causality. Focusing on the causal effect of fit on performance should reduce any negative effect of performance on fit (discussed below), so this may be a reason why this relationship was stronger than for concurrent performance.

In Keller (1994), however, a postulated fit of information processing to unanalyzable task technology had a weak and nonsignificant effect on project quality. The smaller variation of this fit (relative to that with nonroutineness [Keller 1994, p. 173]) may have artificially reduced the correlation below its true size. Further, neither fit had a significant effect on the ability of teams to keep their projects on budget and schedule (Keller 1994, p. 173). Both the Alexander and Randolph (1985) and Keller (1994) studies—like Argote (1982)—found positive effects of fit on quality. It may be that quality measures the enhanced ability of groups to solve problems posed by more uncertain and variable tasks. As the task becomes more uncertain and variable, so it requires more problem solving, and this need is met by more organic structures (i.e., more participation and more information processing). Thus quality may be one of the measures that is more suitable for testing the benefits of fitting organicness to task. In contrast, measures that tap administrative efficiency such as budget attainment may not tap the benefits from this fit. Future research should be sensitive to whether the measures of performance used are those that are relevant for the fit under study. It is worth noting that, in both studies (Alexander and Randolph 1985; Keller 1994), the variables called technology are really aspects of the task rather than hardware, so that the positive findings support the task contingency rather than technology.

Gresov (1990) found that the efficiency of organizational work units was related to the fit of their structures to the task uncertainty contingency and also to the horizontal dependence contingency. High task uncertainty and high horizontal dependence each required an organic rather than a mechanistic structure. In sum, the relationship of the fit of structure to the task contingency with performance is supported in four empirical studies (Argote 1982; Alexander and Randolph 1985; Gresov 1990; Keller 1994).

Fit to the Strategy Contingency

There have been studies also of the fit between strategy and structure. These are to be distinguished from studies of the main effects, that is, whether either strategy or structure each on its own affects performance, that is, universalistic rather than contingency effects (Cable and Dirrheimer 1983; Cable and Yasuki 1985; Harris 1983; Hill 1985a; Hill and Pickering 1986; Hoskisson and Galbraith 1985; Teece 1981). Rumelt (1974) investigated the effects of strategy and structure on performance (see also Channon 1978), but did not analyze the effects of fit between strategy and structure on performance. Subsequent scholars developed operational measures of fit and analyzed their effects on performance, finding nil (Grinyer, Yasai-Ardekani, and Al-Bazzaz 1980) or positive effects (Donaldson 1987; Hamilton and Shergill 1992, 1993; Hoskisson 1987; Jennings and Seaman 1994).

Hamilton and Shergill (1992, 1993) conducted a study of the largest corporations in New Zealand. They found that the fit of structure to diversification strategy led to higher financial performance. This held for both of their indices of financial performance: growth (in sales, dividends, assets, and earnings per share) and profitability (return on assets and return on equity). They also compared the variance explained by fit to that explained by the effect of strategy on its own (i.e., its main effect) and to organizational size. The results were that there was an effect of fit that held controlling for a main effect of strategy, so that its strategy constituent did not spuriously cause the fit effect. Moreover, the effect of fit on profitability was much larger than size, a variable often found to affect profitability.

Other research has tested for effects of strategy-structure fit on performance but failed to find it (e.g., Grinyer, Yasai-Ardekani, and Al-Bazzaz 1980). In order to reveal the effect of strategy-structure fit on performance, the organization needs to be in that state long enough to be definitely in fit rather than misfit and for its effects to cumulate and so be visible. In order to tap the cumulative effect it is necessary to confine the study to organizations that have been in one state, either fit or misfit, for a lengthy period, such as ten years. Both the studies that use multiple (10) year periods of fit versus misfit find effects of fit on performance (Donaldson 1987; Hamilton and Shergill 1992, 1993). In contrast, the study that fails to find such an effect (e.g., Grinyer, Yasai-Ardekani, and Al Bazzaz 1980), examines fit at only one point in time, which may mean the organization has not been in fit long enough to have produced a detectable effect of fit. Therefore, the effect of being in fit for ten years should be stronger than being in fit for a short time. In other words, the more "treatment," the greater the effect, and so the more chance of the effect being detected.

Moreover, to isolate the true effect for organizations it is necessary to ensure that an organization remains in fit for the entire period over which fit is measured. An organization that is in fit at time period 1 and then in fit at time period 2 (say 10 years later) may not have remained in that state during the intervening years if it diversifies during that period. The dynamic pattern is that an organization in fit that diversifies moves into misfit and then eventually changes its structure and moves into fit. Therefore an organization in fit at times 1 (i.e., having a functional structure) and 2 (i.e., having a divisional structure), that diversified between those times, can have spent much of the intervening time in misfit. Therefore to classify the organization as in fit is incorrect in that for most of the time period it was in misfit and this contaminates the findings. The analysis of Hamilton and Shergill (1993) is of corporations that changed neither their strategy nor their structure over the study period, in order to control for the effects of such changes. This is similar to Donaldson (1987), who excludes corporations that diversified during the study period. Hence studies of effects of fit on performance would do well to confine the organizations to those that remain in the one state for at least several years. For organizations measured at two points in time, those organizations changing strategies should be excluded to be certain that the organizations remain in the same state.

Donaldson (1987) studied the effect of being in strategy-structure-fit (for 10 years) on performance in the ensuing years. Thus the research design was not cross-sectional but rather diachronic, adding confidence that performance was an effect of fit. Hamilton and Shergill (1993) used a cross-sectional design, but, because fit at the start of the period precedes growth (in sales, dividends, assets, and earnings per share) during that period, we can make the causal inference that fit was a cause of the growth dimension of performance. Thus their study also provides evidence that fit is a cause of performance.

Hoskisson (1987) examines the performance of firms before and after divisionalizing (i.e., adoption of the M-form structure) and in this way ascertains the causal impact of divisionalization on performance. Controls were applied for annual gross national product growth, asset growth, company trend residuals, early versus late adopters, industry, and sales (Hoskisson 1987, pp. 634-635). Hoskisson (1987) finds that the effect of divisionalization on performance is moderated by strategy, consistent with the contingency idea of fit. Firms with the highest level of diversification (i.e., unrelated diversifiers) had performance increases resulting from adoption of the divisional structure (Hoskisson 1987, p. 639, Figure 1). This is explicable in contingency theory because the divisional structure is a fit with unrelated diversification, so that, by divisionalizing, these firms are moving into fit and therefore increasing their performance. In contrast, vertically integrated firms had a performance decline resulting from adoption of the divisional structure (Hoskisson 1987, p. 639, Figure 1). This is explicable in contingency theory as the divisional structure not being a fit with vertical integration, because the interdependence among the "divisions" precludes their operating autonomously as well as assessment as independent profit centers, so that the fully fledged divisional structure, that is, the M-form, is dysfunctional (Lorsch and Allen 1973). Firms with the medium level of diversification (i.e., related diversifiers) had milder performance decreases resulting from adoption of the divisional structure (Hoskisson 1987, p. 639, Figure 1). This is explicable in contingency theory as the divisional structure not necessarily being a fit with related diversification. Where innovation is sought, the greater flexibility and customer responsiveness makes the divisional structure a fit, but where cost reduction is the priority, as in a price-competitive market, then a functional structure is the fit for a related diversifier (Donaldson 1979, 1985). If more of the related diversifiers faced cost rather than innovation as their critical challenge, then these results of mild decrease in performance would be expected. The inclusion of this additional contingency factor in subsequent studies would clarify these results. Thus the findings of Hoskisson (1987) are consistent with contingency theory and illustrate a research design based on comparing performance before and after the adoption of a particular structure.

Jennings and Seaman (1994) illustrate the way in which contingency theory can illuminate the fits between innovation strategy and structure in strategic management. They studied savings and loans organizations. Some of these had a prospector strategy and high adaptation, in that they were aggressively pursuing the new opportunities made possible by deregulation. Some had a defender strategy of conducting traditional business and low adaptation. Effective implementation of these two contrasting strategies was postulated to involve adopting a fitting organizational structure: organic for prospectors and mechanistic for defenders. Among the prospectors, the group of organizations with the most organic structures had the highest performance (Jennings and Seaman 1994, p. 469). Similarly, among the defenders, the group of organizations with the most mechanistic structures had the highest performance. This shows the importance of fitting structure to strategy in order to attain high performance. Specifically, among prospectors, the most organic group had profitability over 100 times greater than the least organic group. Similarly, among defenders, the most mechanistic group had profitability over thirty times greater than the least mechanistic group (Jennings and Seaman 1994, p. 469).

These results indicate that the best fit for the prospector strategy was the highest level of organic structure, possessed by the most organic group of firms (Jennings and Seaman 1994). Of the two other groups of prospector firms, both had less organic structures, and the less organic their structures, the lower their performance. Similarly, the best fit for the defender strategy was the highest level of mechanistic structure, possessed by the most mechanistic group of firms. Of the two other groups of defenders, both had less mechanistic structures, and the less mechanistic, the lower their performance. Hence the best performing groups of both prospectors and defenders were at the extremes of the organic-mechanistic continua. This is consistent with the idea that there was a fit line running diagonally from prospector-high organic to defender-low organic (i.e., high mechanistic). The two high-performing groups were on the fit line (or closer to it than the other groups). The further an organizational group was from this fit line, the lower was its performance. Thus organizations whose structures were at an intermediate level between organic and mechanistic had lower performance because they were not in fit with their strategy. In this study the broad nature of fit of structure to strategy was given from *a priori* theory, but the level of structure that is more optimal was discovered empirically. A main limitation of the study was that fit and performance were apparently measured for the same time period, so that causal inference is less certain.

Steer and Cable (1978) investigated the effect of organizational structure on performance. Their analysis was in the contingency spirit in that they used optimal form to capture the fit of divisional structure to the firm's "operating environment" (Steer and Cable 1978, p. 17), but unfortunately the nature of this fit is unclear (see also Thompson 1981).

Other Studies of Fit and Performance

Kraft, Puia, and Hage (1995) reanalyzed the data from Child's National Study. Unlike Child (1975), who used subgroup regressions to identify fit and misfit, they measured misfits by deviations from a fit line of an *a priori* theoretical sort (the required structure equals the contingency) and also by residuals from a regression analysis. They found that the deviation method was superior in revealing fit effects, which suggests that the theoretically defined fit line was closer to true fit than the regression line. They also examined for main effects and found as many as their fit effects. Kraft et al. analyzed service organizations separately from manufacturing organizations and found more relationships among service organizations. They also used a wider set of performance measures than the financial measures used by Child (1975). Their results suggest that while fit may lead to higher financial performance, it may be at a social cost such as industrial unrest, that is, work stoppages. This study illustrates how contingency theory research can differentiate among the outcomes of fit for different stakeholders of the organization. The results of fit can be positive for one set of stakeholders but negative for others, so that a fit for one group may be a misfit for another.

Schlevogt and Donaldson (1999) examined the relationship between fit and performance of firms in China. Fit was of three structural variables (centralization, formalization, and integration) to two contingency variables (size and uncertainty), exemplifying a multistructure, multicontingency approach to fit, that is, multifit. In an analysis in which eleven other environmental and organizational causes of performance were controlled, structural fit was shown to positively affect performance. Moreover, fit was the third strongest out of the twelve causes of performance, thus suggesting the continuing importance of fit for both researchers and managers.

Overall, while the two studies by Mohr (1971) and Pennings (1975) fail to support contingency theory, other studies support contingency theory by finding a positive relationship between fit and performance (Alexander and Randolph 1985; Argote 1982; Child 1975; Donaldson 1987; Drazin and Van de Ven 1985; Gresov 1990; Hamilton and Shergill 1993; Hill, Hitt, and Hoskisson 1992; Hoskisson 1987; Jennings and Seaman 1994; Keller 1994; Khandwalla 1973; Kraft, Puia, and Hage 1995; Pennings 1987; Powell 1992; Schlevogt and Donaldson 1999). More studies support the positive relationship of fit and performance than fail to support it. Moreover, the later and more sophisticated research provides more support for contingency theory than the earlier research. This shows that the contingency approach is sound. It should receive increasing attention to attain more accurate definitions of fit and more exact estimations of the effect of fit on performance, to reveal the full potential of contingency theory.

The Empirical Estimation of the Effect of Fit on Performance

In the previous chapter we discussed how to identify the fit line and validate its existence by showing that fits differ from misfits in their effect on organizational performance. But we may also want to know how much fit affects performance. The estimation of the strength of fit on performance is prone to certain problems such that the strength is often underestimated in empirical studies. Moreover, if the fit-performance relationship is understated sufficiently, such as if it fails statistical significance tests, then the erroneous conclusion might be drawn that fit has no effect on performance and thus that the fit concept is invalid. Knowledge of the pitfalls in estimating the strength of fit on performance may enable us to avoid them. Sometimes they cannot be avoided in an empirical study, but being aware of these pitfalls assists us to make a better interpretation of the study. We may explore these issues using three methodological categories that affect the strength of empirical results: unreliability, range restriction, and confounds. These general methodological considerations have specific significance in the topic of fit and performance.

Unreliability

If two variables have a true correlation of, say, .6, this will be found only if both variables are measured with complete reliability. Any unreliability lowers the observed correlation below the true correlation, because its effect is to create random error (Nunnally 1978). Thus any unreliability in the measurement of either fit or performance leads the empirical estimate of the effect of fit on performance to understate the true magnitude of that effect.

If performance is measured by the accounting figures of a firm, say profit, then there will be some unreliability due to errors of measurement. If firm performance is measured by return on assets (ROA), that is, the ratio of profit to assets, then this is liable to be even more unreliable because of the well-known unreliability in the measurement of assets. Measuring firm performance by ROA is quite popular in studies of fit-performance of firms and so these studies are underestimates (e.g., Hamilton and Shergill 1992). Again, changes in performance, such as growth measures, are prone to be of lesser reliability because their numerator (e.g., profit now less profit 2 years earlier) is a difference score and, as such, subject to measurement error, as will be discussed below. Thus whatever the operationalization of performance, any unreliability in its measurement renders the observed fit-performance relationship conservative.

However, larger problems of unreliability occur regarding fit. Fit is a combination or congruence of two variables, the contingency and the organization structure. Therefore any unreliability in the measurement of either of these will lower the observed fit-performance relationship below its true strength. However, misfit is a difference between the level of the organization structure that is required to fit the contingency and the actual level of the organizational structure. This aspect is readily apparent by referring to measures of misfit as differences (Powell 1992) or residuals from the fit line (Van de Ven and Drazin 1985). In psychometrics, such difference scores are seen as being much less reliable than the variables of which they are composed (Johns 1981; Venkatraman 1989). The ratio of measurement error to true score is much higher for difference scores than for the variables from which the difference is calculated. (Nevertheless, Alexander and Randolph 1985 and Keller 1994 argue that their theoretically derived misfit scores are reliable despite being difference scores.)

To put it simply, if variable X is measured on a ten-point scale (from 1 to 10) and an organization scores five, the error of measurement may be one point, so that the true score could be four or six, that is, an error of measurement of 20 percent. However, the level of X required to fit the contingency value might be seven, so that the misfit is two, but with a one-point error of measurement, the error for that misfit is 50 percent. Thus, in this example, the misfit, being a difference score, has a ratio of measurement error to true score that is two-and-a-half times that of variable X, from which it is constructed.

Hence every time we estimate the fit-performance relationship, this problem of underestimation due to unreliability potentially occurs. The problem is present, for instance, whenever correlations or regressions are used that involve the misfit or fit of each individual organization being measured and then entered into the analysis separately. It is particularly a problem where we measure the misfit of each organization and then correlate this with the performance of each organization, because both the misfit and the performance measure may be low on reliability. Therefore all such findings must be regarded as underestimates and interpreted accordingly. For example, the correlation between the Euclidean distance and performance of organizational subunits by Drazin and Van de Ven (1985) will underestimate the true relationship considerably.

A solution that reduces this problem is to use aggregation. The average score on a variable of a sample is more reliable than the score of an individual organization in that sample. The errors of measurement are random and therefore combining across individuals to form a sample average cancels out much of the errors. This is achieved in the procedure discussed earlier of forming two subgroups, the fits and the misfits, and then calculating the mean performance of each. Because of the aggregation into the two subgroups, the mean performances of each subgroup are more reliable than those of their members. By comparing the differences in the means of the fit and misfit subgroups, a fairly reliable estimate of the benefits of fit may be obtained.

Such an estimate, however, is of the form: "fit raises performance by 20 percent relative to misfit." This is informative, but it is not an estimate of the fit-performance relationship of the kind that says: "fit and performance are correlated .4." Where statements of that kind are sought, correlational or regression techniques can be used, but the analyst should be aware that they are liable to yield underestimates. However, the correlations can be corrected for the unreliability of their two variables by applying a formula (Hunter, Schmidt, and Jackson 1982). If the reliability of either fit or performance (preferably both) can be calculated, then the correction formula can be applied. The correction of observed correlations between fit and performance would tend to raise their value, leading to a better appreciation of the strength of the effect of fit on performance.

Range Restriction

An observed empirical relationship can also underestimate the true relationship because of restriction in range. If two variables X and Y are correlated .6 in the real world, an empirical study of a sample of organizations will only find that correlation if the variation on X in the sample is as great as that in the world, and similarly for Y. If variable X ranges in value from 1 to 10 in the world, but only from 3 to 8 in the sample, then its range is restricted. In order to reveal the true magnitude of a correlation, a study must first attain the true variation on both the variables being correlated. Yet we often read published studies whose sample is confined to one industry or region, which may restrict the range on either X or Y, so that when they find that, contrary to their hypothesis, there is no significant correlation between X and Y, this could be a false conclusion. The general relationship connecting X and Y may hold for organizations in that industry or region, but there is not enough variation therein to reveal it. Again, a project may examine the relationship between size and bureaucratic structuring in a set of small organizations (e.g., Miller, Drogue, and Toulouse 1988), which considerably restricts the range in size, so that the resulting estimate of the size-structuring relationship will be substantially attenuated, leading to an underestimate.

In the fit-performance relationship, the problem of range restriction occurs in several forms. It occurs in the subgroup analyses discussed earlier. These dichotomize the sample into fits and misfits. Therefore some of the organizations in the fit subgroup are truly in fit whereas others classed as fits are some way off fit. Similarly, the misfits subgroup contains some organizations that are complete misfits and some that are just moderate misfits. Therefore, in comparing the mean performances of the two subgroups we are really comparing the performances of the average fitness of the fit subgroup with the average misfitness of the misfit subgroup. The sample may have the full range by containing an organization that is completely in fit and one that is completely in misfit. Nevertheless, the variation between the two subgroups is less than full because the averages of the two subgroups are toward the middle of the continuum that runs from fit to misfit. Thus the comparison is analogous to comparing the first and third quartiles, not the bottom and top of the scale. Hence if the fit group has a mean profit of $15 million and the misfit group has a mean performance of $10 million profit, the benefit of fit seems to be $5 million profit or 50 percent. But the difference in performance would be greater between the organization that is completely in fit compared with the organization that is completely in misfit, which is the more exact measure of the effect of fit on performance.

Similar remarks apply to regression and correlational methods that compare subgroups. As discussed above (in Chapter 7), the comparison of regression lines is not of complete fit versus complete misfit but only of a group in fit relative to one in misfit. Therefore the differences in slope coefficients, constant terms, and correlations understate the true effect of misfit so that no significant difference may be observed, which leads to a false conclusion of no effect of fit on performance. This could occur even if, in the sample, the organizations that are in complete misfit are very different in their position in the two-dimensional contingency-structure space from the organizations that are in complete fit. Therefore despite the reliability advantage of subgroup analyses that were discussed above, they suffer a disadvantage of range restriction that leads to an underestimate of the strength of the effect of fit on performance. This should be borne in mind when interpreting such analyses.

There is less range restriction where the analysis of the relationship between fit and performance is conducted at the level of the individual case. For instance, the fit of each organization is measured and related to the performance of that organization, with the cases in the sample being used to compute the correlation between fit and performance. If an organization is completely in fit or completely in misfit, then this value is entered directly into the analysis without the reduction in extreme values that occurs where data are aggregated (e.g., subgroup averages are calculated). Thus analyses such as correlations or regressions preserve the full range of fit that is in the sample. This helps them to reveal the true correlation. Hence they suffer less from range restriction than subgroup analyses.

Yet even correlation and regression analyses can suffer from some range restriction. To really assess the true strength of the effect of fit on performance, we need to know the different performances of cases in complete fit and complete misfit. Yet cases in the real world may not be as extreme as either complete fit or misfit. For this reason even the best sample would have less range than potential variations in fit. Empirical research can study only variations that actually occur. High misfit would be very damaging to organizational performance, so that organizations in misfit tend to change their structure and move into fit, as the SARFIT model states. Moreover, as March (1999) argues, firms tend to imitate more successful competitors, thereby eliminating variation in the independent variables (here contingency and structure) that cause performance and also performance itself. Alternatively, misfitted organizations having low performance are consequently less likely to survive; in particular, a firm may become bankrupt and disband. Thus, while above (in Chapter 6) we expressed reservations about ecological selection, any ecological selection against misfit that occurs will reduce the extremes of misfit occurring in the population (Hannan and Freeman 1989; Van de Ven and Drazin 1985). For these reasons of adaptation and selection, few actual organizations may be in high misfit at the time of study, despite some being in high misfit at other times and misfit being very damaging for performance. The empirical studies can only assess the relationship of fit and performance as revealed by variations in fit at the time of the study. If these variations are only moderate relative to potential variation, then the fit-performance relationship may be only moderate or weak. This might lead analysts, or someone reading their results, to state that fit only weakly affected organizational performance. Perhaps the observed correlation is so weak that it is not even statistically significant, leading to the conclusion that fit has no effect on performance; this in turn would tend to be construed as a refutation of the idea that there was such a fit. However, the true effect of fit on performance might be strong so that organizations avoid high misfit, thereby restricting the range of fit and leading to misleading empirical results.

The strength of a contingency theory fit may be assessed by comparing it to some other cause of organizational performance. If the correlation of fit and performance is weaker than the correlation between that other cause and performance, then the analyst may conclude that the contingency theory fit has a weaker effect than that other cause. The inference may be drawn that contingency theory fit is unimportant and can be virtually ignored by management, who should rather concentrate on using the other cause to boost the performance of their organization. Yet the contingency theory fit could actually be more important than that other cause, so much so that organizational management has adjusted its organizational structure so that there is little misfit. In contrast, they did not work on the other cause yet because that is a weaker determinant of performance, but therefore it has more actual variation and shows up as apparently a stronger cause in analyses. There is thus a paradox that organizational structures that strongly affect organizational performance may be restricted in their range, because of adaptation or selection, and possibly more so than other organizational characteristics that have weaker effects on performance. Living organizations are not unthinking experiments to allow social scientific observers to make easy inferences, but rather are dynamic, adaptive systems in which managers seek to avoid loss and increase gain. The propensity of adaptation to eliminate variation in factors affecting performance should always be borne in mind when interpreting empirical results in organizational science.

Van de Ven and Drazin (1985) argue that, rather than adopting structures that fit the contingencies, managers may follow universalistic rules that impose a standard structure regardless of the situation. Again, local managers may be more likely to tailor their structure to its situation, in contingency theory fashion, but upper-level managers are more likely to impose a standard structure in universalistic fashion. Where managerial decisions impose structural uniformity there may be fewer fits than would occur if structures were allowed to vary to match their contingencies. Once again, this could reduce the correlation between fit and performance, leading to an underestimate of its true strength. Conforming in this way to some general rule, despite it being counterproductive, is consistent with institutional theory. Therefore, isomorphic effects, by reducing variance of either contingency or structure, could lead to range restriction and hence attenuation of the correlation between contingency and structure. Thus SARFIT, population-ecology, and institutional theories all point to ways in which range restriction could occur (through adaptation, selection, and conformity, respectively), reducing the observed fit-performance relationship.

Confounds

As is widely understood in social science, the assessment of the true effect of any cause can be upset by confounds. Such confounding variables can obscure the impact of the cause, or they can lead to spurious effects that appear to be due to a factor but are really due to the confound. Such highly general considerations apply also in estimating the effect of fit on performance, as discussed above. However, there are reasons why confounds may be particularly troublesome when studying the fit-performance relationship. Confounds of the effect of fit on performance are more than just the usual idea that "other things are not equal." Instead there are liable to be systematic causal forces arising from within contingency theory itself. The variables endogenous to fit and performance can produce confounds to the relationship of fit on performance, which are additional to the more usual situation in social science of confounds by extraneous variables. There are two main systematic forces that create confounds of the relationship between fit and performance. These are the negative effect of performance on fit and the spurious effects introduced through associations of the constituents of fit with performance.

Negative Effects of Performance on Fit

There is reason to believe that there is a negative effect of performance on fit. As we have stressed, contingency theory research shows that organizations in misfit tend to adapt into fit only when the overall performance of the organization becomes low so that a crisis of poor performance occurs (Chandler 1962; Donaldson 1987). High performance tends to keep an organization that is in misfit in that state. In contrast, low performance of an organization in misfit tends to trigger adaptive change so that it moves into fit. Thus the theory of performance-driven organizational change holds that there is a negative effect of performance on fit (as will be discussed further in the next chapter). Moreover, high performance tends to cause an organization in fit to expand, for example, by using slack resources to increase in size or diversification, so that it moves into misfit. Hence a negative effect of performance on fit arises.

Thus a more fully specified contingency theory model would be that fit affects performance positively, but also that performance affects fit negatively. Thus a cross-sectional correlation between fit and performance is the net result of these two opposing causal forces. A negative effect tends to cancel out the positive effect so that the observed correlation between fit and performance could be zero. A stronger negative than positive effect would make the observed correlation between fit and performance become negative. The observed correlation registers whichever cause is stronger in a particular sample. In this way, the results of studies using cross-sectional methods to assess the effect of fit on performance could be misleading. They could lead to the erroneous conclusion that there was no positive effect of fit on performance, when it was just being masked by a negative effect of performance on fit. Even if this masking was insufficient to cause the correlation of fit and performance to become negative or zero, it would depress the magnitude of the positive correlation so that the positive effect of fit on performance was underestimated.

In fact, it is not unusual for fit at one point in time to be related to performance averaged over several prior years, so that fit is actually after performance (e.g., Child 1974). This means that the correlation between fit and performance is actually registering quite a lot of the effect of performance on fit. If that effect is negative, as held by the theory of performance-driven organizational change, then it will be masking the effect of fit on performance, so that any observed positive correlation is more likely to be a substantial underestimate. Thus the timing of the measurement of the fit and performance variables can amplify the masking of the positive fit-performance relationship by the negative-effect performance-fit relationship.

There is a benign implication of performance having an effect on fit, which can help make more correct causal inferences from cross-sectional data. Some empirical studies of the effects of fit on performance measure fit and performance at the same point in time, so that they are cross-sectional rather than diachronic. Thus they do not show unambiguously that fit causes performance, because a positive association between fit and performance could logically be due to a positive effect of performance on fit. However, as we have just seen, the theory of performance-driven organizational change holds that the effect of performance on fit is negative. Therefore, according to this underlying theoretical model, any positive association between fit and performance cannot be caused by an effect of performance on fit (because that would be negative). Hence, positive associations between fit and performance found in cross-sectional studies are not spurious. Thus, to the degree that it is true that performance negatively effects fit, this adds confidence to interpreting observed positive correlations between fit and performance as reflecting a positive effect of fit on performance. This reasoning applies also to empirical studies where performance is actually measured at a time prior to fit, which will amplify the negative effect of performance on fit, so that any observed positive correlation signifies a stronger underlying positive effect of fit on performance.

In order to control for this systematic confound it is necessary to control for the negative effect of prior performance on fit. This control can be achieved in an empirical study by measuring fit before performance, which is lagged several years after fit, while also controlling for existing (i.e., prior) performance. This helps to capture the true effect of fit on performance by controlling the negative feedback effect of performance on fit. Another method is to study only organizations with slim profit margins, such as in competitive industries, that would suffer low performance and adapt promptly when they came into misfit. In this case, the values of the other causes of performance are not correlated with fit in such a way as to mask the effect of fit on performance. Such organizations lack the slack that would allow them to be in misfit with high performance, the condition that produces the negative association between performance and fit that confounds the positive effect of fit on performance.

Notwithstanding the control on prior performance, there is still a need to control directly for other causes of organizational performance when estimating the effect of fit on performance. As we have argued, controlling for prior performance turns off the confounding, negative feedback effect from performance to fit, yielding a truer estimate of the effect of fit on performance. This control for prior performance also controls for those effects of other causes on organizational performance. However, prior performance is performance several years earlier, which reflects the effects of the other causes of performance at an even earlier time. These other causes of organizational performance could, however, affect organizational performance within the past several years. If any of these causes were themselves correlated with fit, then they would confound the relationship between fit and performance. In order to control for these possible confounds, it is necessary to control for these other causes of performance as well as to control for prior performance. This control can be achieved by the methods mentioned above (e.g., inclusion of confounding variables in statistical analyses).

The theory of performance-driven organizational change is an example of an auxiliary science. It is a body of theory that offers explanations of its own phenomenon, that is, how performance drives organizational change. Yet it also sheds light on the phenomenon considered in this chapter, that is, the empirical study of how fit affects performance. Thus, in the context of the study of the effect of fit on performance, the theory of performance plays an auxiliary role (Feyerabend 1975).

Constituents of Fit

Contingency theory is peculiarly prone to another type of confound. As we are aware, misfit is a discrepancy score between the level of the organizational structure required by the contingency and the actual level of the organizational structure. The contingency and structural variables are the constituents of misfit. There is a definitional connection between the discrepancy and its constituents that can lead to a correlation between them (see Cohen and Cohen 1983; Cronbach and Furby 1970; Edwards and Parry 1993; Johns 1981; Wall and Payne 1973; Werts and Linn 1970). Hence discrepancy scores tend to have a built-in correlation with each of their constituent variables. Where these constituents happen to be, in turn, correlated with the dependent variable, an apparent effect of the discrepancy score on the dependent variable can be spurious. Similarly, the constituent variables can have a relationship with performance that is the opposite of that between fit and performance. Then the constituent variables mask the effect of fit on performance, making its effect seem smaller than it is, or nil, or even negative. In these cases, the apparent lack of a significant positive relationship between fit and performance may be false, due to its constituent variables.

The reason why discrepancy scores tend to have a built-in correlation with their constituent variables is because of range restriction. Consider again the simple model where the fit of the organizational structure to its contingency is a line in which, mathematically, structure equals contingency. Structure is the vertical axis and contingency is the horizontal axis, and the fit line is 45 degrees to the horizontal axis. If all misfits are below the fit line, then large misfit is possible only where contingency is large; where contingency is small the misfit must also be small. Thus the level of the contingency variable determines the maximum value of misfit, and so misfit is positively correlated with contingency. By similar reasoning, large values of misfit are possible only if structure is small, so misfit is negatively correlated with structure. These relationships follow from the way that the space of possible misfits has been defined as a triangular area below the fit line. Thus these correlations between misfit and its constituents are artifactual in that they arise because fit and its constituents are not variables that are independent of each other, taking any value whatever the other; rather their possible values are linked by definition.

Because of such artifactual correlations between misfit and its constituents, if either constituent has a relationship with performance, then it could lead to a spurious relationship between misfit and performance. For instance, given that contingency is artifactually positively correlated with misfit, if contingency also has a negative effect on performance, then there will be a spurious negative effect of misfit and performance. Thus an observed negative effect of misfit on performance could be wholly due to the negative effect of contingency on performance. In that case, inferring that misfit causes lower performance would be erroneous because the real effect on performance is by the contingency. The true effect is universalistic, in that higher values of the contingency variable cause less performance, not contingency misfit. Similarly, given that structure is artifactually negatively correlated with misfit, if structure also has a positive effect on performance, then this would produce a spurious, negative effect of misfit on performance. Both contingency and structure could each contribute to a spurious, negative effect of misfit on performance, thereby making it more likely to occur. Furthermore, if contingency has a positive effect on performance and structure has a negative effect, then both contingency and structure would produce spurious positive effects of misfit on performance. These could mask any true negative effect of misfit on performance, leading to erroneous inferences, such as that misfit had a non-significantly negative effect on performance, or nil effect, or even a positive effect. In order to avoid these confounds, it is desirable to control both the contingency and organizational structure variables by including them as control variables in analyses that test for an effect of fit on performance.

The artifactual correlations between contingency and structure will not always arise and depend upon the distribution of organizations around the fit line. If all the misfits occurred above the fit line, then this also creates artifactual or in-built correlations with contingency and structure that can confound the fit-performance relationship. However, these artifactual correlations are of reverse signs to those where the misfits are all below the fit line. Thus, if misfits are scattered equally above and below the fit line, then they offset each other and there is no artifactual correlation between fit and contingency and structure. In such a situation, even if either contingency or structure has an effect on performance, the problem described of spurious effects of misfit on performance does not arise. An inspection of the scatter of misfits around the fit line should inform the analysis. Hence whether the constituents of fit spuriously affect the fit-performance relationship is determined by the scatter of data around the fit line and whether either of the constituents is correlated with performance. The safe course is routinely to include both contingency and organizational structure as controls in a multivariate analysis when testing for the effect of fit on performance.

Given that either contingency or organizational structure can be definitionally correlated with misfit, there is a possibility that any claimed effect of fit on performance could really be due to a universalistic effect of contingency or structure on performance. Controlling for contingency and structure in a multivariate analysis of the effect of fit has the advantage of showing that the effect of fit on performance is a contingency relationship, and is not really due to a universalistic relationship of the contingency or structure on performance.

While we have discussed the problem of causal effects of constituents of fit on performance confounding the effects of misfit on performance, the same holds for other associations between misfit and performance (e.g., correlations). If there is a correlation between performance and one of the constituents of misfit, then, given an artifactual correlation between that constituent and misfit, this can create a spurious correlation between misfit and performance. Such a correlation between a constituent and performance can arise for reasons other than an effect of the constituent on performance (as discussed so far): an effect of performance on the constituent, or just by an association between the constituent and performance. Thus the potentiality for confounding constituents of misfit is rather broader in the case of correlational analysis. Again, however, correlational analysis may be protected from this confound by including both the constituents as control variables.

The study by Keller (1994) provides an example of how fit measures are correlated with their constituent variables. Fit of information processing (i.e., structure) to nonroutineness (i.e., the technology contingency) is positively correlated with each of its constituent variables: information processing (.57) and nonroutineness (.52). In turn, both information processing and nonroutineness are positively correlated with performance (project quality), thereby introducing a degree of spurious correlation between fit and performance. This is dealt with by controlling for both constituent variables in the analysis of the effect of fit on performance, by including both in the multivariate analysis (Keller 1994).

In sum, confounds are liable to occur quite systematically in analyses of the effects of fit on performance. Confounds can be controlled by entering potential confounding variables in the statistical analysis. Such potential confounding variables include prior performance and also the constituent variables of fit. An alternate procedure to controlling for prior performance in the analysis is to sample organizations with little slack (such as in competitive industries). Additional controls for the other causes of performance should also be made.

Overall, the discussion has brought out a number of methodological problems. It is possible that empirical results will not always be good estimates of the underlying relationships. In particular, the magnitude of the effect of fit on performance is liable to be underestimated in empirical studies. It is hoped that the analyst will make better interpretations in the light of the considerations discussed here.

Lessons for Future Research

Because of the centrality of fit to contingency theory, empirical validation that fit leads to higher performance is important. As we have seen, however, studies of the effect of fit on performance are prone to a number of methodological problems that can obscure the true effect, leading to underestimates or to spuriously nil or negative findings. Below we abstract eight lessons from the preceding discussion. Drawing upon these lessons can reduce these methodological problems and improve the accuracy of estimates of the effect of fit on performance.

Lesson 1: Use multiple fits

As seen, there are numerous fits between various contingencies and organization structural variables. Therefore fit is more completely captured if the degree of misfit of each is measured to yield the total misfit. If only one aspect of fit is studied, then fit is in a sense underspecified and this will makes its effect understated. Moreover, multiple fits provide a multi-item measure of fit that is thereby more reliable than a single item. The unreliability of fit measures is a problem, and the construction of multi-item measures helps improve reliability.

Lesson 2: Use reliable measures of performance

Unreliability of the performance variable also lowers the correlation between misfit and performance. Performance can be measured more reliably by avoiding variables such as assets that are prone to arbitrary valuations and idiosyncratic changes. Changes in performance, such as changes in profitability, also suffer from unreliability because their numerator is a change score (e.g., profit this year minus profit last year) and so would have lower reliability than the constituent performance variables (e.g., profit). Thus measures should be used that are reliable, such as sales and profit or the ratio of profit to sales. Moreover, multi-item scales improve reliability and this could be done by combining performance measures. This is best done after establishing that they form a common factor in factor analysis so that the scale has construct validity.

Lesson 3: In contrasting the effects on performance of fits and misfits, use organizations that have remained as either fits or misfits for several years

This is in order for the effects on performance of fit to cumulate into substantial variations in performance between the fits and the misfits, which will be clearly visible differences and show the true strength of the effect.

Lesson 4: Use a diachronic research design in which fit precedes performance

This adds confidence to the causal inference that fit is a cause and that performance is its effect.

Lesson 5: Control for prior performance

In the analysis of the effect of fit on subsequent performance, include performance as a control variable. More specifically, use the performance for the same time as fit as a control variable. This switches off the negative feedback effect from performance to fit, thereby preventing a major potential confound.

Lesson 6: Use the constituent variables of fit, that is, the contingency and organizational structural variables, as control variables in the analysis of the effect of fit on performance

This is to rule out any confounding of the relationship between fit and performance that is actually due to the possible definitional connection of fit and its constituent variables. This control also demonstrates that the effect of fit on performance is independent of any main effect on performance of either the contingency or the organizational structural variables, including universalistic effects.

Lesson 7: Control for other causes of performance

This is the standard methodological procedure to ensure that causality attributed to fit in its relationship with performance is valid and not spurious. It also helps to control for any negative effects of performance on fit not controlled for by controlling for prior performance.

Lesson 8: Correct observed correlations for unreliability of measurement

Because misfit is a difference score, it is much less reliable than the organizational structure and contingency variables that constitute it. The formula for correction of unreliability should be used to obtain a more accurate estimate of the true positive correlation between fit and performance (Hunter, Schmidt, and Jackson 1982). However, if confounds are not controlled, then spurious negative correlations may be obtained and correcting them for unreliability will simply inflate the negative correlations. This shows the importance of controlling confounds before applying the formulas for correction of unreliability.

The best estimates of the fit-performance relationship will be obtained by applying all the lessons in the same research project. They should be applied in the following order:

- measure fit comprehensively and over several years, and fit and subsequent performance as reliably as possible
- then control in the statistical analysis of the effect of fit on performance for prior performance, fit constituents, and other causes of performance
- then correct for unreliability

Applying these lessons will tend to increase the magnitude of the resulting relationship between fit and performance, better revealing its true strength.

Conclusions

Overall, empirical studies show that fit positively affects performance, thereby supporting the central idea of contingency theory. Whereas two early studies of the relationship between fit and performance failed to find it, many subsequent studies have done so. The discussion of individual studies has brought out some of the methodological improvements that allow the effect of fit on performance to be seen.

The empirical estimation of the effect of fit on performance is affected by unreliability, range restriction, and confounds. These standard methodological considerations have particular meanings here. They tend to make the empirical estimates understate the strength of the effect of fit on performance. Fit is prone to unreliability because it is a difference score. Similarly, performance may be measured unreliably. The unreliability of both fit and performance makes the correlation between them lower than their true relationship. Again, range will be restricted where organizations are aggregated, such as into subgroups of fits and misfits. Also, range becomes further restricted through organizational adaptation, selection, and conformity. These sources of range restriction lower the correlation between fit and performance. Confounds of the fit-performance relationship arise in a systematic way, in that performance feeds back to mask it. Further, confounds can also arise through the definitional connection between fit and its constituent variables, which may mask the fit-performance relationship or create it spuriously. To the extent that past (and some future) research will be afflicted with some of these problems, this needs to be borne in mind in interpreting results.

Eight lessons have been identified here for avoiding methodological problems. Their use in future contingency research should help to ascertain truer estimates of the effects of fit on performance. These methodological improvements constitute the development of auxiliary techniques so that the full explanatory power of contingency theory can be revealed as its research program progresses.

9   Neo-Contingency Theory

So far we have remained within the traditional framework of contin-gency theory research. However, there are certain problems with the traditional view. In this chapter we identify these problems and suggest how to resolve each of them. This leads to a revised form of contingency theory that may be termed *neo-contingency theory.*

Contingency theory is traditionally concerned with organizational performance and in that broad sense is consistent with economics. However, contingency theory has mostly not drawn much on econom-ics and tends to remain isolated from it. Some attempts have been made to import elements of economics into organizational theory more generally, such as agency theory (Jensen and Meckling 1976) and transaction costs economics (Williamson 1975). However, these have proven controversial (Barney 1990; Donaldson 1990a, 1990b; Ghoshal and Moran 1996; Moran and Ghoshal 1996; Williamson 1996). More-over, they deploy only a narrow range of economic concepts. In our reformulation of contingency theory we shall draw on economics and the related discipline of finance, at numerous points, to gain concep-tual insights. In so doing, we will utilize aspects of economics different from those used to date in organizational theory. We hope that in this way we may break some new ground and encourage an infusion of ideas from economics and finance into organizational theory.

Problems in Traditional Contingency Theory

In the present book and elsewhere (Donaldson 1985, 1995a, 1996a) we have defended contingency theory from criticism made against it. However, there are three problems that exist within contingency theory, and these have not been widely canvassed to date.

As we have seen, traditional contingency theory holds that an organization in misfit will change its structure to move into fit with its contingency (e.g., Burns and Stalker 1961). However, the organization is in misfit because of a prior change in the level of a contingency variable, such as task uncertainty, so that the organization moved out of fit. The question arises as to why the organization changed its contingency. This is not explained by contingency theory. Such a move seems problematic because it creates misfit that lowers organizational performance. Thus there is a need to extend contingency theory to explain changes in the contingency.

Contingency theory holds that an organization in misfit will typically, eventually move into fit. The question arises as to how managers know what the fit is. If management is unsure about what structures fit their contingencies, as is quite plausible, then they cannot move decisively into fit. Thus we again need to extend contingency theory, to provide a more realistic account of how change in the organizational structure occurs so that the organization moves toward fit.

As we saw in Chapter 7, contingency theory holds that the fit line is a line of iso-performance so that each fit produces as high performance as any other fit (Van de Ven and Drazin 1985). The question arises as to why organizations move from one fit to another if there is no performance gain from so doing. We need to make revisions to the concept of the line of fit being a line of iso-performance.

These are the three problems with traditional contingency theory that this chapter will address. Their resolution will lead to the reformulation of contingency theory into neo-contingency theory. While retaining some of the building blocks of contingency theory, we will replace some of the traditional assumptions in order to produce what is, we hope, an improved theory.

Disequilibrium and Ongoing Change

Traditional contingency theory is a theory of equilibrium in that it describes organizational change as a process of regaining equilibrium (Burns and Stalker 1961). An organization in misfit moves into fit, but is then assumed to stay there. There is no theory of why the organization moves out of fit into misfit in the first place. The move into misfit by changing the contingency, such as task uncertainty or technology or size, is just a given. Contingency theory provides a motivation for an organization in misfit to move into fit: to gain the higher performance that fit produces (Burns and Stalker 1961; Woodward 1965). However, when the organization moves out into misfit it consequently loses performance, so that there is no incentive for it to move out of fit. Therefore fit is an equilibrium because once attained, the tendency of the organization would be to stay there. The equilibrium aspect of contingency theory is consistent with it being a functionalist type of theory. It is consistent also with contingency theory being a cybernetic type of theory (Hage 1974) that is focused on deficit reduction, that is, reducing misfit. Other types of theories in organizational behavior explain how deficits are created; for instance, goal-setting theory (Locke and Latham 1990; Wood and Locke 1990) explains that people set new performance targets that exceed their present performance, thereby creating a "gap" or deficit, which is analogous to a misfit. Such deficit-creating theories attribute to the individual or organization the quality of being proactive, thereby creating a tension. In contrast, deficit reduction theories, such as structural contingency theory, attribute to the individual or organization the quality of being reactive, so removing an existing irritant. Given that in contingency theory the deficit, misfit, is removed by regaining fit, the question becomes how misfit is attained, that is, how and why an organization moves into misfit, thereby creating a deficit. Why would an organization move from the comfort of fit to the discomfort of misfit?

The organization moves out of fit because of a change in the level of one or more of its contingencies, such as an increase in size or diversification. What would cause an increase in a contingency? Increases in many contingencies require increases in resources, for example, additional financial resources to hire new employees, who constitute an increase in size. An increase in the degree of technological advance (Woodward 1965) requires surplus resources to pay for the new capital equipment and employee training. Diversification involves acquiring a new business or internally generating new products or services (Rumelt 1974), so that diversification requires surplus resources to acquire firms or to pay internal development costs (Chandler 1962). Increases in the innovation rate, with its accompanying increase in task uncertainty, requires surplus resources to pay for research and development, including for the hiring of professionally qualified technologists. Thus increases in the contingencies of size, technology, diversification, innovation, and task uncertainty all require surplus resources to fund them. Surplus resources and wealth are often generated by the organization performing at a high level, such as by a firm producing high profits. An organization is more likely to perform highly if it is in fit. Therefore, an organization in fit that experiences high performance may in consequence increase its contingencies. More specifically, the greater the performance of an organization in fit, the higher the rate at which its contingencies increase. As a result of increases in the levels of its contingencies, an organization in fit moves into misfit. Thus high performance feeds back to cause an organization to move from fit into misfit. The high performance of such an organization is partly caused by its fit and partly by other causes (e.g., an upswing in the business cycle).

Thus there is a natural tendency for organizations in fit to move into misfit. The theory is no longer an equilibrium theory of changing and then staying put. The theory is now one of disequilibrium. It predicts that organizations in misfit will move into fit *and* also that organizations in fit will move into misfit. In this way it becomes symmetrical. It becomes symmetrical also in regard to the feedback effects of performance. As we have seen, traditional contingency theory holds that low performance feeds back to cause adaptation by an organization so that it moves from misfit into fit (Chandler 1962; Donaldson 1987). There is no consideration in traditional contingency theory of a feedback effect of high performance. In contrast, our revised formulation states that there is a feedback effect of high performance, causing increases in the contingencies, such as size.

The whole theory becomes more dynamic, for now change in one thing leads to change in the other, which feeds back to cause further change in the first thing, causing recurrent change. Specifically, by adapting its structure to its contingencies, the organization moves from misfit into fit, which raises its performance, which feeds back to increase its contingencies that create misfit again and so on. Thus the organization can cycle recurrently through these causal paths, moving between misfit and fit. In so doing the organization alternates in increments of increase in the contingencies, such as size growth, and in increments of change in its structures, such as increases in its bureaucratic structuring. By recurrently making incremental changes in its contingencies and structures, the organization can gradually change, growing from one form to another. For example, the organization can grow from small to large, or undiversified to highly diversified, or local to multinational. Thus the theory can explain the incremental change that many organizations display (as seen in Chapter 5; see also Donaldson 1996a, pp. 120-122). Further, some organizations will have gone through the cycle more times than others, which accounts for the wide variations in organizational contingencies (e.g., size and strategy) and also structures, which are observable in populations of organizations (Donaldson 1996a; Hannan, Ranger-Moore, and Banaszak-Holl 1990).

Thus the new theory is more complete, more symmetrical, and accounts for a change in a contingency and for the possibility of repeated changes in contingencies and structures that fundamentally alter the organization over time.

Performance-Driven Organizational Change

We are now in a position to discuss more systematically the idea that performance drives organizational change. As we have seen, traditionally contingency theory held that a crisis of poor performance was required to trigger needed adaptive change (Chandler 1962; Donaldson 1987). This is consistent with the theory of Simon (1976), that managerial decision making is boundedly rational, so that organizations do not maximize their performance, but satisfice. Managerial decision making is problem solving that is activated when organizational performance falls below the level deemed to be satisfactory (i.e., satisficing). Thus low performance of an organization whose structure misfits its contingency leads to a change in the organizational structure to bring it into fit. In addition, we have just argued that high performance feeds back to increase the contingency variables. Hence low performance tends to cause an increase in the organizational structure, and high performance tends to cause an increase in the contingency. These are the central ideas of the theory of performance-driven change (see Donaldson 1999 for a fuller version).

If organizational performance drives organizational change, then this argues that to understand organizational change we have to attend to the causes of organizational performance. As we have seen, misfit leads toward lower performance and fit leads toward higher performance. However, organizational performance is affected by many causes other than fit. Some of these causes are internal to the organization, such as diversification and debt. Other causes are external to the organization, such as the business cycle and competition. The low performance that leads to adaptive change in the organizational structure is caused by the effect of misfit being reinforced by other causes depressing organizational performance. Similarly, the high performance that leads to an increase in the contingencies, such as growth in organizational size, is caused by the effect of fit being reinforced by other causes raising organizational performance. Thus to understand organizational change we need to analyze the conjunction between fit and the other causes of performance.

Portfolio Theory

In order to analyze the way multiple causes interact to determine the overall performance of an organization, we can make use of the risk concept and portfolio theory from finance.

Organizational risk is the variation over time in the level of organizational performance. A cause of organizational performance that varies over time will thereby cause fluctuations in organizational performance, that is, will cause organizational risk. For organizational change to occur, the causes of organizational performance need to act together in such a way as to produce nontrivial organizational risk. An organization with widely fluctuating performance, when it is in misfit, will experience the low performance needed to trigger adaptive change in the organizational structure. The organization will also experience the high performance, when it is in fit, that leads to rapid growth in the contingencies (e.g., size). Thus to have repeated episodes of growth and adaptation, the organization needs to have recurrent swings of its performance from high to low and back again. Such recurrent increments in each of size and organizational structure produce long-term growth and success of the organization. Thus, for an organization to develop over time from small to large and successful, it needs to have fluctuations in its performance. Therefore the optimal organizational risk is not zero, because that would forestall organizational adaptation and growth.

Portfolio theory states that the risk of a portfolio is affected by the risk of each element and also by the correlation among the elements. If two elements have high risk but are negatively correlated (or even are only weakly, positively correlated), then they produce lower risk in the portfolio than in each of the elements (Brealey and Myers 1996). The upward fluctuation in one element is offset by the downward fluctuation in the other, so that the fluctuation in the overall portfolio is less than in either element. Organizational portfolio theory applies the portfolio theory from finance to the organization, so that the organization is considered to be a portfolio composed of the causes of overall organizational performance. Each cause of organizational performance is a factor in the organizational portfolio. Each factor has a certain degree of risk (i.e., variation over time) and correlation with the other factors. Overall organizational performance is thus determined by the risks of the portfolio factors and their correlations. If one cause of organizational performance is negatively correlated with a second, then the fluctuation in overall performance is reduced. Thus the portfolio of causes of performance determines the fluctuations in organizational performance that are necessary for organizational change. If the causes are high risk and are substantially, positively correlated, then the organization will have large fluctuations in its performance and will change frequently, recurrently adapting and growing to become successful over the long term. However, if the causes are low risk or negatively correlated, then the organization will have small fluctuations in its performance and will not change, leading to stagnation. These are the key ideas of organizational portfolio theory (Donaldson 1999). This theory complements contingency theory by giving a more articulated treatment of the way performance mediates changes in structure and contingencies.

Organizational portfolio theory identifies eight portfolio factors that are major causes of organizational performance and thereby of organizational change. Four factors tend to promote organizational change: the business cycle, competition, debt, and divisional risk. They work by either increasing organizational risk (the business cycle and divisional risk) or decreasing the organizational performance level (competition and debt). Four factors tend to forestall organizational change: diversification, divisionalization, divestment, and directors. They work by either decreasing organizational risk (diversification, divisionalization, and directors) or increasing the organizational performance level (divestment). These eight factors interact with organizational maladaptation or adaptation to determine whether a maladapted organization makes adaptive change and whether an adapted organization grows at a high rate.

Factors That Promote Organizational Change

Organizational change is promoted where the depressing effect of misfit on organizational performance is reinforced by other causes of performance also depressing it. Some organizational portfolio factors, competition and debt, work directly on the level of performance, lowering it. Other portfolio factors, the business cycle and divisional risk, are causes of performance that fluctuate highly and so contribute to organizational risk, thereby inducing episodes of low performance that promote change when the organization is in misfit.

The Business Cycle

The business cycle is a succession of changes in the level of activity in the economy, so that economic activity fluctuates up and down recurrently over the years (Kuczynski 1986). It strongly affects the sales and profitability of firms in the economy (Dotsey and King 1987). The upswing of the business cycle leads to growth in firms, so that a firm in fit will increase its size so that its new size comes to misfit its existing organizational structure. While the misfit works to reduce firm performance, the buoyant condition of the economy more than offsets the misfit so that the firm continues to prosper. At this point, the effect on performance of the business cycle is negatively correlated with the effect on performance of the misfit, thereby countering it and producing no organizational adaptive change, despite change being needed. After the business cycle turns down, however, the depressive economic conditions reinforce the depressive effect of misfit on performance. When organization performance becomes low enough, adaptive organizational change occurs, and the organization adopts the required new structure (Chandler 1962). At this point, the effect of the business cycle is positively correlated with the effect of misfit, thereby reinforcing it and producing the needed adaptive organizational change. Thus the business cycle promotes organizational growth on its upswing and adaptive change in organizational structure on its downswing. It moves the organization into misfit on the upswing and into fit on the downswing. Hence the fluctuations in the economy drive fluctuations in organizational performance that in turn drives organizational change. Some industries have deeper business cycles than others and so would be predicted to have more organizational changes in their firms (for a fuller set of theoretical propositions about the business cycle and organizational change, see Donaldson 1999).

Competition

Competition also promotes adaptive change in organizational structures. The greater the competition, the lower the profit margin of the firm (Samuelson 1980) and the more likely that misfit will force a crisis of poor performance and trigger adaptive change. Competition is affected by the number of other organizations in that industry, which in turn is affected by globalization (Dunning, Kogut, and Blomström 1990). However, competition is also affected by the quality of the competitors. Other things being equal, a firm in misfit will suffer loss of sales to competitors if those competitors are themselves in fit, because they are better organized, but not if the competitors are themselves in misfit. For example, a firm in misfit, having diversified but retained a functional structure, that has competitors that are in fit, will suffer low performance and so regain fit by divisionalizing. Whereas if its competitors are in misfit, also having diversified yet retaining a functional structure, the firm would not suffer low performance and so would not divisionalize. This introduces a relativity perspective into analyses of the effect of fit on performance and organizational change that has been lacking from the contingency theory literature.

Debt

Financial strategies also play a role in organizational change. Debt reduces the surplus profit, thereby lowering the performance level, so that a crisis of poor performance has a higher probability of occurring.

Therefore an organization in misfit is more likely to make adaptive change the more highly it is indebted, because its performance has a higher chance of becoming low. Therefore debt must be added to the portfolio factors of the business cycle and competition as factors promoting adaptive organizational change. These three factors are at the corporate level, that is, the level of the overall organization. However, there is another organizational portfolio factor that works to promote organizational change, and it is at the divisional level: divisional risk.

Divisional Risk

The risk of a division is the fluctuation in its performance; this affects divisional change in a way that parallels how organizational performance affects organizational change. Low performance of a division that has a misfit between its structures and its contingencies leads to adoption of the required structures that fit the contingencies. Conversely, high performance of a division in fit raises its rate of growth and increases its contingencies, leading the division into misfit. The higher the risk of a division, the more its performance fluctuates, creating adaptation, growth, and the long-term success of that division. Such positive developments for a division contribute to the success of the corporation as a whole. Therefore divisional risk helps corporate success.

In sum, the business cycle, competition, debt, and divisional risk all work to increase organizational change.

Factors That Forestall Organizational Change

There are, however, four organizational portfolio factors that work to prevent or delay organizational change. These are diversification, divisionalization, divestment, and directors.

Diversification and Divisionalization

It is a familiar idea in finance that diversification reduces corporate risk (Salter and Weinhold 1979). The reason is that diversification spreads the corporation across different industries so that their different cycles offset each other. This leads to more stable profits for the corporation than for its divisions. Diversification leads to divisionalization (Rumelt

1974), and this enhances the dampening effect of diversification on corporate risk, because the divisional structure reduces risk (Buhner and Möller 1985; Hoskisson 1987). The autonomy of divisions allows their profits to fluctuate independently of each other and fully reflect the divergence of their industrial cycles. Moreover, divisional heads are held accountable for the profitability of their divisions (Williamson 1970), and this leads them to manipulate their reported profits, smoothing out fluctuations in divisional profits in order to reliably attain budgeted targets. In portfolio theory terms, divisionalization increases the negative correlations between the businesses of a diversified corporation while also reducing their risk, so that corporate risk is reduced. Thus divisionalization interacts with diversification to lower the risk of the corporation (Donaldson 1999).

The lower organizational risk reduces the likelihood of crises of poor performance for the diversified-divisionalized corporation. Therefore when it enters misfit it tends to avoid making needed adaptive changes, drifting into mediocre performance in the longer term. Organizational theory has traditionally celebrated the advantages of the divisional structure, such as superior strategic decision making, resource allocation, and discipline on divisions (Williamson 1970). Contingency theory, of course, holds that a divisional structure fits diversification and thereby leads to higher performance (Chandler 1962). While these benefits inhere in the divisional structure, organizational portfolio theory points to the possibility of a longer-term disadvantage: the lack of adaptation because of insulation from crises of poor corporate performance.

Divestment

This tendency of the diversified, divisionalized corporation not to adapt may be reinforced by another factor: divestment. A corporation that is experiencing a crisis of poor performance—because it is in misfit and so needs to make adaptive change, such as to its organizational structure—may instead divest some business or businesses. The sale of these businesses will often generate large amounts of cash, raising profits and so preventing performance from becoming low, so that no needed changes are made to the remaining organization. Moreover, a highly diversified corporation with many independent divisions could divest them one by one, over an extended period, thereby keeping its profitability satisfactory and so avoiding changes to its core. Thus divestment may be a tactic that is most available to the diversified, divisionalized corporation and reinforces the tendency of such corporations to avoid adaptive change and to continue in mediocrity.

Directors

Nonexecutive directors also may work to reduce the risk of the corporations on whose boards they sit as directors or chair. Agency and transaction costs theories hold that nonexecutive directors provide a needed control on managers on behalf of the shareholders, thereby raising corporate profit and shareholder returns (Jensen and Meckling 1976; Williamson 1985). Stewardship theory states the opposite: that freeing managers from controls increases intrinsic motivations and so boards predominantly of executive directors raise corporate profit and shareholder returns (Davis, Schoorman, and Donaldson 1997; Donaldson 1990a). Research into the effect of nonexecutive directors on corporate profit and shareholder returns has been mixed (e.g., Baysinger and Butler 1985; Donaldson and Davis 1991; Ezzamel and Watson 1993; Kesner 1987). Some reviews calculate the average effect to be practically nil (Boyd 1995). Instead of focusing on the level of performance of a company as the outcome of board structure, organizational portfolio theory focuses on the fluctuation in the performance of a company.

Nonexecutive directors are less likely to approve risky courses of action for their company than are executive directors. Any decision involves balancing costs and benefits. Senior managers formulate proposals for expansion that involve risky actions such as investment in a new, large-scale plant or in research and development. Their familiarity with their company leads them to have confidence in their predictions about the future. When they sit on the board as executive directors, they carry this conviction with them and can influence other directors through their advocacy at the board meeting. However, a nonexecutive director is liable to see such executive predictions as mere promises and perhaps as self-justifications. The nonexecutive director can feel more certainty about the costs of the proposed project and accord them greater weight than the supposed benefits. Therefore nonexecutive directors lead to less risky strategies by corporations. Research finds empirically that nonexecutive directors lead to less risky corporate strategies (see Baysinger, Kosnik, and Turk 1991; Hill and Snell 1988), despite this being contrary to the assertions of agency theory.

Thus organizational portfolio theory states that nonexecutive directors reduce corporate risk and thereby forestall wide fluctuations in corporate profit (Daily and Dalton 1994a, 1994b). In this way nonexecutive directors tend to prevent the episodes of low performance that trigger needed adaptive organizational changes. Thus, unwittingly, nonexecutive directors become another factor preventing long-term organizational success.

In sum, the four portfolio factors of diversification, divisionalization, divestment, and directors combine to reduce organizational risk and so forestall adaptive organizational change, leading to long-term mediocre performance. Many large corporations are high on several, if not all, of these factors, which would tend to make their problems of adaptation chronic. These four factors tending to prevent organizational change are, as we have seen, opposed by the four factors that promote it: the business cycle, competition, debt, and divisional risk.

The risk of an organization and thereby its propensity to adapt and grow is affected by its level on each of the eight organizational portfolio factors. An organization is more likely to make needed changes and grow if it is undiversified, functionally structured, in a competitive industry with a large business cycle, and it has mainly executive directors who take on debt and do not divest. An organization is less likely to make needed changes and grow if it is diversified, divisionally structured, in industries with little competition and small business cycles, and has mainly nonexecutive directors who refuse to take on debt and who readily divest if performance becomes low. Thus by specifying factors that affect organizational performance and their interaction with misfit and fit, we can develop a systematic theory about organizational change. This builds on the insight of the pioneers of contingency theory that organizations needing to make adaptive changes often fail to do so until performance falls low enough that there is a crisis (Chandler 1962).

Quasi-Fit

We have been talking about the organization moving from misfit into fit. But how does the management know what fit is? The traditional contingency theory tends toward an implicit view that management knows what a fit for its organization would be. However, this view may be unrealistic. We shall therefore first examine the traditional view, then explain why it is unrealistic, and then propose a more realistic view.

The traditional contingency literature seems to take it as largely unproblematic that when an organization is in misfit, its management can see what would be a fit. Yet how can management know what would fit its organization in its particular situation? Perhaps, one might reason, management has been educated in contingency theory. Contingency theory holds that as size increases, an organization should increase its level of formalization. Yet few people, apart from researchers, know the regression equations that specify the level of formalization that fits size (such as that in Child 1973b, 1975). Moreover, to apply that knowledge prescriptively, management would need to know the required score of its organization on the scale used in the research to measure formalization (Pugh et al. 1968). Even if a manager knew the quantitative level, variables such as formalization are abstract and so not directly actionable (Pfeffer 1997). Thus the management of most organizations would not know exactly which level of each organizational structure it needed to adopt to move into fit with the contingencies of its organization, such as its size.

Management might more plausibly know the direction in which fit lay, and head in that direction. For example, they might realize that having grown, they need to increase the level of their formalization. But how could they know by how much they should increase it? How do they avoid increasing the formalization too little or too much, given that they do not know the exact level that is required to fit the size of their organization? It might be argued that they use trial and error, that is, undershooting and overshooting through numerous iterations, until they eventually land on the target, that is, the level of formalization that fits their organizational size. Yet that would make organizational adaptation very troublesome and protracted. Moreover, it implies numerous increments and decrements in quick succession for many organizations until the organization converges on the fit line through extensive trial and error. Yet this seems implausible. Thus we need another theoretical account of organizational adaptation.

We suggest that organizational adaptation is a move into quasi-fit. For the reasons already given, organizations in misfit will only rarely, and to a degree with luck, move into full fit. They will much more typically move toward fit, but attain only quasi-fit. That is to say, the organization will move closer to fit but not attain fit completely. The organization will adjust the level of its structure to narrow the gap between its actual level and that required to fit its contingencies, without completely eliminating the gap.

Some support for the view that when organizations adjust their structure they often enter only quasi-fit rather than full fit, is found in empirical studies of the divisionalization of large firms. There is a strong tendency for firms that have diversified to eventually adopt the divisional structure (Channon 1973; Dyas and Thanheiser 1976; Fligstein 1985; Mahoney 1992; Palmer et al. 1987; Palmer, Jennings, and Zhou 1993; Rumelt 1974; Suzuki 1980). Replacing their functional or holding structures with a divisional structure is a move away from misfit between structure and diversification, toward fit, which increases performance (Donaldson 1987; Hamilton and Shergill 1992, 1993). However, a closer examination within these divisional structures shows that many of them are incomplete, having failed to adopt all the attributes that make a fully developed divisional structure (Allen 1978; Hill 1985a, 1985b, 1988a; Hill and Pickering 1986; Steer and Cable 1978; Williamson and Bhargava 1972). For instance, some divisionalized firms fail to decentralize decision making (Hill 1985a, p. 744). Thus many divisionalized firms are only in quasi-fit to the level of their diversification contingency, rather than being in full fit. However, quasi-fit would still produce higher levels of performance than misfit, so that firms could be in quasi-fit and yet be moderately effective, sufficient to have the capacity for further growth. Moreover, given that incomplete divisionalization is so common among large firms, there is a chance that a firm with incomplete divisionalization will face competitors who are similarly, incompletely divisionalized. Therefore the firm may nevertheless be able to maintain moderately high performance and growth despite its being only in quasi-fit.

By moving from misfit to quasi-fit the organization improves its degree of fit and thereby improves its performance. This increase in performance is sufficient to feed back and commence growing again. In turn, such increase in the contingency increases the misfit and begins to reduce performance, so that eventually a further increase in the organizational structure is triggered. Hence the organization can go through the cycle of increasing the contingency and structure described in the previous section, despite not attaining full fit. The organization needs only to attain quasi-fit for the feedback effect of performance on the contingency to cause another round of the cycle of growth. Thus an organization needs only to enter quasi-fit recurrently to experience recurrent incremental increases in contingencies and structures.

The concept of the organization moving into quasi-fit is more realistic than that of the organization moving into full fit. The management of an organization does not need to know exactly what fit is, but only has to know the correct direction. It can infer the correct direction by extrapolating from past decisions. For example, when the organization grew and had problems in the past, management increased the level of formalization in the organizational structure and this reduced the problems. Now that the organization has grown again and has similar problems again, a sensible course of action is to increase again the level of formalization. This model of managerial decision making is consistent with bounded rationality. Lacking complete knowledge, managers tend to act only when there is a problem and to use a solution close at hand that is not perfect but that satisfices, that is, reduces the magnitude of the problem to an acceptable level (Simon 1976).

If managers were to move the organization into full fit, they would need to have the contingency fit model in their minds, but we have seen that this is implausible. In contrast, if managers believed in a universalistic theory, they could follow it by simply increasing whichever structural variable the universalistic theory said should be maximized. This would provide enough guidance for the managers so that they increased the level of their structure, so that they moved into quasi-fit. Priem (1994) provides evidence for organic theory that closeness to fit is more strongly associated with CEO beliefs of a universalistic than of a contingency theory type. Hence managers just increase a structural variable, which closes the gap somewhat, thereby moving the organization from misfit closer to fit, without necessarily attaining full fit, so that the organization enters only quasi-fit. By chance an organization moving toward fit will move into full fit, but this will be the occasional exception rather than the general pattern. Hence, an organization moving only into quasi-fit rather than into full fit is compatible with organizational change being guided by universalistic managerial beliefs.

Figure 9.1 shows the concept of quasi-fit diagrammatically. There is a quasi-fit line at some distance away from the full-fit line. Indeed there is a quasi-fit line both below and above the full-fit line. The quasi-fit line is the line that connects up all the points of quasi-fit. For an

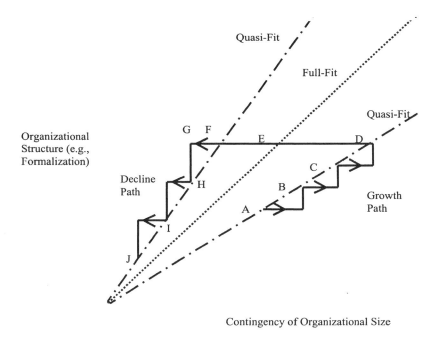

Figure 9.1. Lines of Quasi-Fit: Showing Growth and Decline Paths

organization that is below the full-fit line, if it is on the quasi-fit line at point A, then it is sufficiently in fit that its performance is high enough for it to have some surplus resources so that it grows. This increase in organizational size while retaining the existing level of organizational structure, for example, formalization, means that the organization moves from quasi-fit into misfit. The low performance from this misfit eventually causes the organization to increase its level of formalization, so that it attains quasi-fit again, this time at a new point, B. The restored performance eventually causes a further increase in organizational size, which then leads to a further increase in formalization until the organization regains quasi-fit again, this time at point C. Similarly, the organization subsequently moves to point D. The growing organization follows a zigzag path such that it moves along the quasi-fit line (A, B, C, and D) that is below the full-fit line. In this way the organization could grow over its life from very small with very low formalization, to very large with very high formalization.

If at any point in its life the organization decreases in size, that is, declines or downsizes, then initial size decreases will mean that it approaches closer to the full-fit line. It may eventually come to lie on the full-fit line at E. Further size decrease brings the organization to F on the quasi-fit line above the full-fit line. Then a further size decrease again brings the organization into misfit at G above that quasi-fit line. To attain quasi-fit, the organization must decrease its formalization sufficiently to move to H. If the organization continues to decrease its size, it again moves into misfit and must again reduce its formalization so that it attains the quasi-fit line again at I. Thus once having moved onto the quasi-fit line above the full-fit line, an organization may continuously decline by moving in a zigzag fashion down along that quasi-fit line (F, H, and I). If at any time an organization that is on the quasi-fit line above the full-fit line increases its size (i.e., reverses its decline), this initially moves it toward fuller fit and hence higher performance. Only when the organization grows further into misfit by crossing the full-fit line and then the quasi-fit line that is below the full-fit line, will the organization enter misfit that is severe enough to stop it growing. It will then increase its formalization and will move into a new quasi-fit on the quasi-fit line that is below the full-fit line. In terms of Figure 9.1, an organization at H that grows, will grow to (approximately) B and then reattain quasi-fit at C. Hence an organization that is continuously growing will move up the quasi-fit line that is below the full-fit line, while an organization that is continuously declining will move down the quasi-fit line that is above the full-fit line.

In summary, while contingency theory states that organizations adapt and move into fit, they may not move into full fit. They may move only into quasi-fit, being that level of fit that is sufficient to raise performance enough that contingencies increase again (e.g., growth). This in turn means that the organization begins to move toward a new misfit. In this way the organization can cycle toward and away from fit without ever entering full fit. Thus the organization may develop over time, in both its contingency and structural variables, without ever moving along the line of full fits. There are alternate increments of increases in the organizational structural variable and in the contingency (e.g., size). A growing organization could move along a quasi-fit line that lies below the full-fit line. Conversely, a declining organization could move along a quasi-fit line that lies above the full-fit line.

Fit as Hetero-Performance

As we have seen, traditional contingency theory holds that fit is a line of iso-performance. This holds that the performance of each fit is the same as any other fit, so that the performance produced by a fit to low levels of the contingency variable is equal to that produced by fit to the high levels of the contingency. The exemplar is the pioneering study by Woodward (1965) in which the fit for low-technology contingency (unit and small batch production) produces the same level of performance as the fit for medium technology (mass production) and high technology (process production). If this is true, what is the incentive for a firm to advance its technology from low to medium to high? More generally, what is the incentive for an organization to increase the level of its contingency beyond the lowest level? The iso-performance concept is incompatible with the observed fact that organizations increase their levels of the contingencies. Otherwise all organizations would have low technology and be small.

The reason for this theoretical hiatus lies in the fundamental nature of structural contingency theory. As we noted at the outset, contingency logic is that the performance or effectiveness of an organizational structure is moderated by some factor, which is termed the contingency. The focus is upon the organizational structure as a cause of performance. The only interest in the contingency is as a moderator of the causal effect of organizational structure on performance. There is no concept that the contingency is itself a cause of organizational performance.

Such a view is, strictly speaking, illogical. As we saw earlier (in Chapter 1), a contingency is a moderator, and any moderator is itself also a cause of the dependent variable. If W moderates the causal effect of X on Y, then this relationship means also that X moderates the causal effect of W on Y. Thus both X and W have a causal effect on Y. It is a matter of convenience whether X or W is taken as the primary cause or as the moderator. Hence, it follows that, if an organizational structure has a positive effect on organizational performance that is conditional upon a contingency, then that contingency also has an effect on performance that is conditional upon the structure. Both structure and contingency are causes of effectiveness. They are interchangeable, and each could play the other's role.

There is a kind of theoretical myopia in structural contingency theory that treats variables, such as size or technology, only as contingencies and does not consider them as having a larger role. This myopia is consistent with contingency theory being a theory of how organizational structures affect performance. It is, however, inconsistent with a more rounded theory of organizational performance. Such a broader view would have to consider the causal contribution of these contingencies to organizational performance. Where organizations are generally observed to increase their contingencies, such contingencies will often be causes of performance. This is the hypothesis from functionalism; whether a contingency does in fact raise performance is a matter for empirical validation.

An example of contingency myopia may be seen regarding the concept of strategy. In structural contingency theory, strategy is treated as being a contingency of divisional structure (Hoskisson 1987). As such, the level of strategy determines whether a divisional structure produces high or low performance. A divisional structure produces high performance when the strategy of the firm is a high level of diversification, because a divisional structure fits a diversified strategy. Thus strategy makes no contribution to performance and is merely a moderator of the effect of structure on performance, so that structure, not strategy, is the cause of performance. This is the view taken by approaching strategy from the theoretical lens of a theory of organizational structure, structural contingency theory.

However, theories within the field of strategy, naturally enough, view strategy as a cause of performance. Given that studies failed to find consistently the expected universal positive effect of strategic diversification on performance (e.g., Rumelt 1974), strategy theory research examines whether there is a moderator of the strategy-performance relationship that accounts for the variations in findings. Strategic management research shows that structure moderates the strategy-performance relationship. Hill, Hitt, and Hoskisson (1992) suggest that the effect of diversification on performance is contingent upon the organizational structure of the company. For each degree of diversification there is an organizational structure that fits it, such that high effectiveness results if the company adopts the structure that fits its diversification. Hill, Hitt, and Hoskisson (1992) argue that for a highly diversified company, producing products unrelated to each other, a highly decentralized structure is the fit. In contrast, for a medium diversified company, producing products that are related to each other, a medium decentralized structure is the fit. They show that the fit of structure to the degree of diversification positively affects performance, thus supporting their contingency theory of strategy as contingent upon structure. Hence diversification is treated as the cause of performance, with structure being the moderator. This illustrates that a variable considered by structural contingency theory to be a contingency can be considered to make a causal contribution. Thus variables treated as contingencies can also be considered as causes of performance. Whether a variable is considered to be a cause of performance or a contingency tends to be a matter of convention in a research literature, reflecting the theory that dominates therein.

Moreover, there is a theoretical reason for holding that what are customarily treated as the contingency variables in structural contingency theory have a causal impact on organizational performance. Without the contingency contributing to performance there is no reason for the organization to increase its level on the contingency variable. For example, why should a firm make the capital investment required to move from batch to mass production without some benefit flowing from that increase in technology?

If the contingency itself contributes to raising organization performance, then the fit line is not one of iso-performance, but rather is one of hetero-performance. As a line of hetero-performance, the fit line is reconceptualized so that, instead of each point on it producing the same level of performance (i.e., iso-performance), each point along it enjoys higher performance. Therefore the fits do not all produce the same performance; rather they produce different performances. More specifically, the performances of the fits increase as the level of the contingency increases. Thus the point on the fit line that corresponds to the lowest level of the contingency variable has the lowest performance. The next point on the fit line, which corresponds to the next from lowest level of the contingency variable, has a higher level of performance than the first point. Likewise the next point up from that point enjoys higher performance again. In this way each successive point along the fit line, going from low to high values of the contingency, produces higher performance. A fit to a higher level of the contingency produces a higher performance than a fit to a lower level of the contingency. Thus a hetero-performance fit line is a monotonically increasing function of performance. Hence performance rises as an

266 THE CONTINGENCY THEORY OF ORGANIZATIONS

organization goes along the fit line from the lowest to highest value of the contingency.

The fit line being a line of hetero-performance provides an incentive for the organization and its management to move along the fit line. As we have just seen, being in fit to the lowest level of the contingency variable produces less performance than being in fit to the next higher level of the contingency variable, therefore the organization has an incentive to move from the first fit to the second fit. Because each fit produces higher performance at each successive level of the contingency variable, there is incentive for the organization to move up along the fit line from low to high levels of the contingency.

This increased performance from increasing the level of the contingency variable explains why organizations increase their contingency level and do not simply remain in fit at the lowest level of the contingency. It is therefore consistent with our reformulation of contingency theory as a theory of disequilibrium. An organization in fit will tend to move into misfit because it will increase its level of the contingency variable (e.g., size) in order to gain the benefits of that higher level of the contingency. Initially, the misfit will reduce performance. But when the organization adopts a new value of the organizational structure and thereby moves into the new fit, the organization will experience the higher performance that motivated its earlier increase in the contingency variable. Thus an organization will wish to move along the fit line, increasing its contingency and its structure, so that it moves from one fit to the next, because the organization increases its performance at each step. Thus the hetero-performance concept of fit is compatible with the disequilibrium theory of organization that an organization in fit does not remain there indefinitely.

Moreover, an organization in misfit has an incentive to move into the new fit, that is, into the next fit on the line of hetero-performance, in order to reap the benefit of the enhanced performance. The organization has a disincentive to return to the old fit, because it is at a lower level on the hetero-performance line and therefore has lower performance. Thus the hetero-performance concept of fit is also consistent with the SARFIT model of structural adaptation to regain fit. An organization in fit will tend to increase its contingency, thereby moving into misfit, and then increase its structure in order to enter the new fit. The fit line being one of hetero-performance provides incentive both for the initial move away from fit and for the eventual move into the new fit. The repetition of this cycle of the organization moving into new misfits and then new fits creates successive incremental increases in the contingency and the structure. Thus the organization moves over time along the fit line, growing on both the contingency and the structural variables. Hence the hetero-performance fit concept proposed here is compatible with the SARFIT model and its explanation of the dynamics of recurrent, incremental organizational change.

The model of fit and performance also needs to state misfit and perfor-mance by specifying the level of performance that inheres in being in misfit at each location off the fit line. The concept of hetero-performance has implications for the performance of misfits relative to fits. Consider the performance produced by mild misfit, that is, being just below the hetero-performance fit line. The level of performance of a mild misfit is that it must be lower not only than the new fit but also than the old fit (otherwise it might regain fit by moving back to the old fit). Given that, as we have seen, the old fit has lower performance than the new fit, the mild misfit must be lower performance than the old fit as well as being lower still than the new fit. Thus a mild misfit has not only lower per-formance than the adjacent fit at the same level of the contingency vari-able (i.e., the new fit), but also lower performance than the fit at the next lower level of the contingency variable (i.e., the old fit). In this way the performances of misfits relative to fits can be specified.

The performances of misfits relative to other misfits can also be spec-ified by the hetero-performance fit concept. Because hetero-performance fit is a line on which fits further along the line produce higher per-formances, points just off the line, that is, in mild misfit, have different performances. A point just below the low performance end of the fit line (i.e., corresponding to the lowest level of the contingency variable) has lower performance than the adjacent fit, which itself has low performance, so that the mild misfit has very low performance. In contrast, a point just below the high performance end of the fit line (i.e., corresponding to the highest level of the contingency variable) has lower performance than its adjacent (new) fit, which itself has high performance, so that the mild misfit has quite high performance. Thus mild misfit has lower performance near the low than near the high end of the fit line. More generally, the same degree of misfit that is the same distance away from the line (i.e., deviation) has higher perfor-mance at higher levels of the fit line (corresponding to higher levels of the contingency) than at lower levels of the fit line. Thus a corollary of the fit line being hetero-performance is that the misfits are also hetero-performance. In these ways, elements of the new misfit-performance model are also derivable from the SARFIT theory, specifying the performances of misfits relative to fits and other misfits.

In summary, fit is a line of hetero-performance on which each point along the line (corresponding to each higher value of the contingency variable) is higher in performance than the one before it. Misfit is also hetero-performance, so that the same degree of misfit (i.e., deviation from the fit line) produces higher performance at higher levels of the fit line. A misfit adjacent to the fit line produces performance lower than the old fit and even lower than the new fit. In these ways an organization has incentives to move out from fit into misfit and then into a new fit, so moving along the fit line, point by point, thereby increasing in contingency and structure, as stated by the SARFIT model of organizational dynamics. The same holds for the quasi-fit line concept.

Discussion

Overall we have sought to make good several deficiencies in contingency theory. We have striven to fill in gaps and make the theory more coherent. In so doing we have created a more dynamic picture of the organization as tending always to be changing in some way or other, if not in organizational structures then in contingencies. Change feeds upon change, rather than rolling the organization into some equilibrium corner position from which it does not move. This has required attending to the fuller consequences of performance that feed back to affect not only the organizational structure but also the contingencies. The causation becomes more symmetrical, circular, and complete. The focus of the theory broadens from the organizational structures to include a more rounded appreciation of the role of the contingencies. These emerge from just being adjuncts to the organization structure, to being variables in their own right that make performance contributions, in conjunction with structure, and are in turn molded by those performance consequences. It is now a theory of organizational performance and organizational change. It may be termed a theory of organizational adaptation.

At numerous points we have drawn on economics and finance. This is seen in the concept that increases in contingencies, such as size and diversification, flow from surplus resources generated by high performance (Penrose 1959). It is seen in the use of the concepts of risk and portfolio from finance. It is further seen in the nature of several of the portfolio factors. The business cycle comes from macro-economics. Competition is, of course, central to economics. Diversification, debt, and divestment are tools of corporate finance. Finally, the fit line as a line of hetero-performance brings in the incentives that are required to impel action in economics. In these ways we hope to bring some new insights into organizational theory and to encourage a more productive exchange with economics.

Conclusions

Contingency theory may be usefully developed in a number of directions. The point of departure is to recognize difficulties in traditional contingency theory and then to devise solutions to them. Three such difficulties are recognized here, and a solution to each is offered.

First, contingency theory seems to be too static and only to discuss change as a movement from misfit into equilibrium. In particular it does not explain why the organization moved out of fit and into misfit. We propose that organizations frequently change their contingencies when in fit because of the feedback from high performance. Thus an organization in fit has higher performance as a result and this (together with other causes raising performance) provides the surplus resources that cause increases in contingencies such as size and diversification, that is, hiring new employees or adding new product lines. These increases in contingencies move an organization from fit into misfit.

The theory is symmetrical in that both low and high values of performance lead to change. Low performance leads from misfit to fit by change in the organizational structures, but high performance also leads from fit to misfit by change in the contingencies. Thus changes in both organizational structure and contingencies are affected by the feedback from performance. Hence there is a built-in tendency toward disequilibrium that counters the tendency toward equilibrium that is traditionally the focus of contingency theory. Misfit leads toward fit, but also fit leads toward misfit. Therefore there can be a cycle of perennially renewing change rather than stasis. In this way an organization can experience repeated increments of change in contingencies and organizational structure, so that it can grow large and internally elaborate over time. Thus contingency theory becomes more dynamic.

Given that organizational performance drives organizational change, there are other causes of performance than just the fit and misfit discussed in contingency theory. For the low or high values of performance to occur that are required to cause organizational change, misfit or fit must be accompanied by the right values of these other causes of performance. Misfit needs to be accompanied by other causes of performance that are depressive in order to create low performance and hence adaptation. Fit needs to be accompanied by other causes of performance that are buoyant in order to create high performance and hence high growth rates. We need to analyze the interaction between fit and these other causes of performance to understand when change will and will not occur.

Organizational portfolio theory, inspired by portfolio theory from finance, provides concepts that help this analysis. Each cause produces a certain degree of fluctuation of organizational performance and therefore constitutes a certain degree of organizational risk. The interaction of these causes with fit and with each other constitutes a portfolio that affects the risk of the overall organization and thus its propensity to change. Portfolio factors can reinforce each other and induce organizational change or they can offset each other and prevent needed organizational change. Organizational portfolio theory identifies eight portfolio factors that affect performance in addition to fit. Four of these raise organizational risk or lower performance and so promote organizational change: the business cycle, competition, debt, and divisional risk. Four of these reduce organizational risk or raise performance and so forestall organizational change: diversification, divisionalization, divestment, and directors. The interaction of each of these organizational portfolio factors with misfit influences whether needed adaptive organizational changes occur or not. Similarly, their interaction with fit influences the rate of organizational growth. An implication is that the diversified, divisionalized corporation may fail to make needed adaptive changes in a timely manner, especially if it has directors who are mainly nonexecutives who respond to performance problems by divesting. This provides a caution to the rather optimistic appreciation of the divisionalized corporation in the literature at present.

The second problem in traditional contingency theory is that it is unclear how managers know what exact organizational structures fit their contingencies. The suggestion is that, rather than having such knowledge and moving their organization into full fit, it is more realistic to say that organizations move only into quasi-fit. Managers know the direction in which to move their organization but not the amount of movement required. Therefore organizational change often stops short of full fit. However, by reducing the degree of misfit, organizational performance increases sufficiently to feed back and increase the contingencies. Thus the cycle of incremental growth in organizational structure and contingency can occur by the organization moving into quasi-fit.

The third problem in traditional contingency theory is the concept of the fit line as being one of iso-performance. This is a line of points all of which produce equal organizational performance. This begs the question of why an organization should move from one fit to another by changing its level of the contingency variable, especially when that entails incurring additional expenditure. The suggestion here is that the fit line be reconceptualized as a line of hetero-performance, so that fits vary in their performance effects. In particular, the fits to higher levels of the contingency variable produce higher performances than the fits to lower levels of the contingency variable. Thus organizational performance increases as the organization goes along the fit line. Therefore the organization has an incentive to move along the fit line by investing in higher levels of the contingencies, such as size or technology.

Overall, the modifications to contingency theory proposed here seek to make it more realistic and more dynamic. They also make it more internally coherent. In so doing, the theory broadens out from just explaining the effect of organizational structures on performance as being conditioned by contingencies. The contingencies become contributors to organizational performance in their own right. Changes in contingencies are also explained by the feedback of performance. It becomes a more rounded theory of organizational performance and organizational change. In so doing, it forges closer connections between organizational theory and the disciplines of economics and finance.

10 Future Research Opportunities

In this chapter we will consider some possible future developments for contingency theory research. These include research questions arising from the need to prove that the relationships among size and bureaucracy are caused by contingency theory fits. They include also research questions that stem from the reformulation of contingency theory into neo-contingency theory, such as those pertaining to the ideas of disequilibrium, the organizational portfolio, and quasi-fit. Further, the neo-contingency idea of fit as hetero-performance leads to a new operationalization of fit. Throughout this chapter, the emphasis is on turning the theoretical discussion in this book into future research practice by emphasizing the hypotheses that would allow the theoretical ideas to be tested empirically. The hypotheses given are illustrative of the possibilities rather than exhaustive.

Fit and Bureaucracy Theory

As we discussed in Chapter 4, the prevailing causal models of the relationships among size and the bureaucratic structural variables leave open the question of whether their underlying cause is contingency fit or some other causal process, for example, universalistic causation. In order to demonstrate that the underlying causal processes that generate the relationships among size and the bureaucratic structural variables are contingency fits, each relationship needs to be examined empirically. The relationships involved are those between size and each of horizontal and vertical structural differentiation, between horizontal structural differentiation and formalization, and between vertical structural differentiation and decentralization. For each of these four relationships the examination needs to proceed in two stages. First, show that there is fit of each of the structural variables (horizontal structural differentiation, vertical structural differentiation, formalization, and decentralization) to size that positively affects performance. Second, show that each of the structural variables comes into fit with size, after a size change, through the indirect process of misfit causing low performance and resulting structural adaptation. For formalization, the misfit between it and size allows specialization to increase the level of formalization, through administrative specialists, who are newly created by size increase(s), promoting their new management systems. For centralization, the misfit between it and size is created by the newly created hierarchical level(s), due to recent size increases, so that hierarchical levels affect decentralization through misfit. Thus the effect of specialization on formalization and of hierarchy on decentralization is conditional upon misfit leading to low performance. In this way, the apparent direct relationships among these bureaucratic structural variables are really dependent upon indirect effects of misfit of structure to size. Some specimen hypotheses are:

There is a fit of formalization to size that positively affects performance.

Size increase causes misfit between the old level of formalization and the new size level.

The misfit of formalization to size lowers performance and results in an increase in formalization to fit the new size level.

When an organization is in misfit of its formalization to its size, specialization acts to increase formalization, through newly created administrative specialists promoting their new management systems.

Researching Neo-Contingency Theory

In the previous chapter, a number of new theoretical developments for contingency theory were advanced. These ideas need to be tested in empirical study and therefore offer avenues for future research. To provide a framework for empirical investigation, these theoretical ideas need to be turned into hypotheses that can be tested. The following discussion seeks to facilitate that process by suggesting hypotheses and addressing other research issues such as the operational definition of variables implied by the newer approaches.

Disequilibrium Theory

Above (in Chapter 9), it was suggested that high performance leads organizations that are in fit to increase the level of their contingency so that they move into misfit. Donaldson (1987, p. 14) showed that organizations in fit move into misfit by increasing their contingency. In that study the contingency was diversification, so the fit was a functional structure to an undiversified strategy, and the misfit was a functional structure to a diversified strategy. There is scope for testing whether increasing the contingency causes misfit for other contingencies and their related aspects of structure. These would include, but not be restricted to, size and bureaucratic structure, task uncertainty and organic structure, and so on. Whatever the contingency and its related aspect of organizational structure, the hypotheses are:

For an organization in fit, the higher its performance, the higher the probability that it will increase the level of its contingency variable.

For an organization in fit, the higher its performance, the higher the probability that it will move from fit into misfit.

For a firm, organizational performance could be measured by profit. High profit gives surplus (or slack) resources that could be used to increase contingencies, such as size (i.e., employees), technology (i.e., new capital investments), geographic spread, vertical integration, or diversification. Wherever possible, organizational performance should be measured by the objective performance; but where this is not possible subjective estimates of performance could be used, and these have been shown to correlate quite highly with the objective measures in some organizations (Dess and Robinson 1984).

The Theory of Performance-Driven Organizational Change

A central idea of the theory of performance-driven change is that organizations in misfit fail to make the adaptive changes that would move them into fit, if they have performance above the satisficing level. As we have seen, there is case study evidence supporting this idea, in that corporations failed to adapt their structure to their new strategy until they underwent a crisis of low performance (Chandler 1962). Donaldson (1987) shows that diversified large corporations in misfit (i.e., having a functional structure) were more likely to adopt the divisional structure, thereby moving into fit with their diversified strategy, the lower their antecedent performance. There is a need to replicate these quantitative findings on samples of other corporations and establish the generality of the findings with other types of organizations, such as small firms, governmental organizations, and so on. The testing also needs to be extended to other combinations of contingencies and structure, such as size and bureaucracy and uncertainty and organic structure.

While the theory of performance-driven organizational change asserts that low performance produces an adaptive response, the theory of threat-rigidity asserts the contrary, that low performance induces rigidity and failure to adapt. The suggestion has been that both theories may be true but apply at different levels of performance. The level of performance that induces threat-rigidity is lower than that which induces adaptive change. Thus the testable hypothesis is that there is a curvilinear relationship between organizational performance and organizational adaptation:

Organizational adaptation fails to occur at higher and very low levels of performance, and occurs at an intermediate point (i.e., below the satisficing level).

The satisficing level depends upon the performance expectations held by senior managers, board directors, and owners, but for operational, research purposes it is probably performance below the industry average (Donaldson 1994; Hilmer 1998). At least that suggestion may enable empirical research to proceed, leading to a more refined location of the level of performance deemed to be unsatisfactory and thus inducing adaptive change.

Organizational Portfolio Theory

The theory that organizational change is driven by organizational performance has been formalized into organizational portfolio theory (as we discussed in the previous chapter). Organizational portfolio theory is a new theory and therefore needs to be empirically researched. There are numerous theoretical propositions that lend themselves to testing. Perhaps the most fundamental one is that fluctuations in performance are required so that adaptation and growth are triggered recurrently, producing over the long run an organization that is structurally elaborated and successful. The hypothesis is that:

Some level of organizational risk (i.e., variation over time in performance) nontrivially above zero is required for long-term success.

This is not, of course, to say that the higher the risk, the greater the success, but rather that zero or a very low level of risk will tend not to produce episodes of either adaptation or growth, so that the organization will be stable but stagnant.

Organizational performance is affected negatively by misfit and positively by fit. But it is also affected by other causes of organizational performance. Their interaction with misfit controls adaptation and with fit controls growth. Organizational portfolio theory identifies eight such causes as organizational portfolio factors: the business cycle, competition, debt, diversification, divestment, divisionalization, divisional risk, and directors. Each of these factors gives rise to theoretical propositions about adaptive change and growth that can be the basis for research hypotheses. Without being exhaustive, the following provides some illustrations of the hypotheses that might be deduced from organizational portfolio theory.

Business Cycle. The upswing of the business cycle creates growth into misfit and also buoys up the performance of a firm, so that misfit persists. The downswing creates economic stringency that leads to adaptive changes into fit. Some hypotheses are:

Organizations are more likely to go from fit to misfit in the upswing of the business cycle than in its downswing.

Organizations are more likely to go from misfit to fit in the downswing of the business cycle than in its upswing.

Competition. Competition reduces slack and so induces adaptive change. It can take many forms, including having competitors that are themselves in fit. The general proposition is:

An organization in misfit is more likely to move into fit, the greater its competition.

A specific derivation is the hypothesis that:

A diversified firm in misfit (i.e., functionally structured) is more likely to divisionalize, the more of its competitors that are in fit (e.g., undiversified and functional or diversified and divisional).

Fit applies to any combination of contingencies and organizational structures that constitute fit in contingency theory, and each deserves to be studied a hypothesis in empirical research.

Debt. Debt reduces free cash flow because of the large, periodic payments required to service it. Thus performance (e.g., profitability) is reduced that it may more easily drop below the satisficing level, thereby inducing adaptive change. A hypothesis is:

An organization in misfit is more likely to move into fit, the more it is indebted.

Diversification. Diversification spreads the firm across the business cycles of industries and thereby stabilizes corporate performance, reducing the probability of low performance and hence adaptive change when the organization is in misfit. A hypothesis is:

The more a firm is diversified, the lower the probability that it will make needed adaptive change.

Divisionalization. Divisionalization augments diversification, reinforcing its effects. A hypothesis is:

Divisionalization and diversification interact to lower the probability that a firm will make needed adaptive changes.

Divisional Risk. Divisional risk (i.e., variation in performance over time), like organizational risk, makes divisional adaptation and growth more likely. Some hypotheses are:

The higher the risk of a division in misfit, the greater the probability that it will move into fit.

The higher the risk of a division in fit, the greater its rate of growth.

Directors. Nonexecutive directors induce conservatism and reduce organizational risk, which has negative consequences for organizational adaptation. Some hypotheses are:

The higher the proportion of a board of directors who are nonexecutive directors, the lower the probability that the firm will make needed adaptive changes.

A nonexecutive chairperson of a board of directors lowers the probability that the firm will make needed adaptive changes.

Divestment. Divestment creates new, slack resources that can bolster otherwise flagging performance. The more of its assets that the firm sells and the longer the period over which it makes any serial divestment, the greater this effect. A hypothesis is:

Divestment lowers the probability that a firm will make needed adaptive changes.

The typical large corporation in many countries, such as Australia, Canada, France, Germany, Italy, Japan, New Zealand, the United Kingdom, and the United States, is diversified and divisionalized (Capon, et al.t 1987; Khandwalla 1977; Dyas and Thanheiser 1976; Pavan 1976; Suzuki 1980; Hamilton and Shergill 1993; Channon 1973; Rumelt 1974, respectively). An implication of the foregoing organizational portfolio theory is that a large firm that is diversified and divisionalized will tend to fail to make needed adaptive changes, so that the typical large firms in these countries are predicted to be becoming chronically maladapted and suboptimal performers. This is especially true if the firm has a nonexecutive dominated board and resorts to divestment. In the United States, notwithstanding the high levels of diversification among many large firms (Fligstein 1985; Rumelt 1974), there has been something of a trend in some large firms to downscope (Davis, Diekmann, and Tinsley 1994; Hoskisson and Hitt 1994), that is, reduce diversification. This means that substantial divestment is quite common in the United States, thereby reinforcing tendencies toward chronic maladaptation and suboptimal performance in those firms. This is a longer-run effect that comes into play after the firm receives the benefits of adopting a divisional structure that fits its strategy. Thus there are many testable hypotheses that flow from organizational portfolio theory (for a fuller list of theoretical propositions, see Donaldson 1999).

Quasi-Fit

While contingency theory states that organizations adapt and move into fit, they may not move into full fit. They may move into only quasi-fit, that level of fit that is sufficient to raise performance enough that contingencies increase again (e.g., growth). This in turn means that the organization begins to move toward a new misfit. In this way the organization can cycle toward and away from fit without ever entering full fit. Thus the organization may develop over time in both its contingency and structural variables without ever moving along the line of full fits. There are alternate increments of increase in the organizational structural variable and the contingency (e.g., size). Therefore, a growing organization could increase its levels on both the structural and contingency variables in a zigzag path that is parallel to, but lies below, the full-fit line. Conversely, a declining organization could repeatedly decrease its levels of organizational structure and the contingency, so that it attains only quasi-fit and follows another zigzag path that is parallel to, but above, the full-fit line. Some hypotheses are:

Organizations that move from misfit toward fit tend not to attain full fit, but rather only quasi-fit.

Organizations that are repeatedly increasing the level of their contingency move parallel to and below the full-fit line.

Organizations that are repeatedly decreasing the level of their contingency move parallel to and above the full-fit line.

An Operationalization of Fit as Hetero-performance

In the previous chapter, the fit line was reconceptualized from a line of iso-performance to one of hetero-performance. The hetero-performance concept was argued to explain organizational change more adequately and, in particular, to be compatible with the structural adaptation to regain fit (SARFIT) theory of organizational dynamics. As we have seen, the relationship between fit and performance is a key one in contingency theory. Therefore researchers need to study fit-performance for many reasons. An important reason is to validate postulated fits between contingencies and organizational structures. Another reason is to explain organizational change as adaptation into fit. Yet another motive for identifying fits is to offer managerial prescriptions. Hence research needs to have an operational definition of the hetero-performance concept of fit to use in empirical studies. Such an operationalization will now be offered.

A hetero-performance fit line would have a higher level of performance being produced by each successive point along that line. Therefore an organization has an incentive to increase the level of its contingency over time and so move along the line, thereby increasing its structure. We will first postulate the performance produced by being in fit, that is, in lying on the fit line, and then postulate the performance produced by being in misfit, that is, lying off the fit line.

Fit and Performance

For the line of hetero-performance, each point along the fit line produces a higher level of performance than the previous point, going from the lowest to the highest levels of the contingency. How much increase is produced is not given by theory and needs to be found empirically, by examining the actual performance of each point along the fit line. However, in the interest of stimulating and guiding future research, we will postulate the following.

Assume that the fit line runs through the origin (i.e., contingency variable is zero, structural variable is zero; see Figure 10.1). This is reasonable because otherwise the organization could have a positive level of the organizational structural variable when the contingency variable is zero, or zero level of structure when the level of the contingency is positive. Examples would be some formalization with zero employees, or zero formalization with some employees, respectively. Either of these scenarios seems implausible, so that it seems more sensible to posit that when the contingency is zero, the structure is also zero. Assume further that the organizational structure and the contingency variables are each measured on scales that vary from zero to ten. Assume also that the slope of the fit line is 45 degrees, so its slope is one (i.e., the ratio of a unit increment in the organizational structure to a unit increment in the contingency is 1). Thus the first point on the fit line lies at level one of the organizational structure and level one of the contingency variable. The next point on the fit line lies at organizational structure two and contingency variable two. Similarly, the successive points on the fit line lie at structure three and contingency variable three, and so on, up to structure ten and contingency variable ten. Thus for any level of the contingency variable, it is fitted by the same level of the organizational structure variable.

The key postulate is that, for a line of hetero-performance, each point on the fit line is one unit of performance greater than the next lower point. At the origin the performance is 0, so then the first fit point is 1 unit of performance (see Figure 10.1). This first fit is at level one of the contingency variable and level one of the organizational structure variable. The second fit point produces 2 units of performance and is at level two of the contingency and structural variables. The third fit point produces 3 units of performance and is at level three of the contingency and structure variables. A similar pattern holds for the fourth through the ninth points on the fit line. The final, tenth fit point produces 10 units of performance and is at level ten of the contingency and structure variables. Thus the fit points along the fit line range in their performances from 1 to 10. For a firm, performance could be measured by profit, so that the postulate would be that a high fit would be ten times greater in amount of profit produced than a low fit, *ceteris paribus*. This provides the organization with an incentive to progress along the fit line and thereby to grow through successive increments from low to high values on both the contingency and the organizational structure variables.

Misfit and Performance

What are the implications of this fit model for the relationship between misfit and performance? Clearly, an organization in misfit has lower performance than an organization that is in fit at the same level of the contingency variable. However, as we have just seen, the same degree of misfit does not produce the same performance. Because performance is greater at higher points along the fit line (i.e., those that correspond to higher levels of the contingency variable), a misfit is creating greater performance at higher levels of the contingency than at lower. Thus the performance of a degree of misfit (i.e., deviation off the fit line of one level of either the contingency or structural variables) varies according to the level of the contingency variable. A degree of misfit creates higher performance at higher levels of the contingency than at lower levels. Of course, the greater the distance (i.e., deviation) from the fit line, the lower the performance, so that each successive degree of greater misfit diminishes performance. Nevertheless, an organization that is in substantial misfit, being some way off the fit line (i.e., is several degrees in

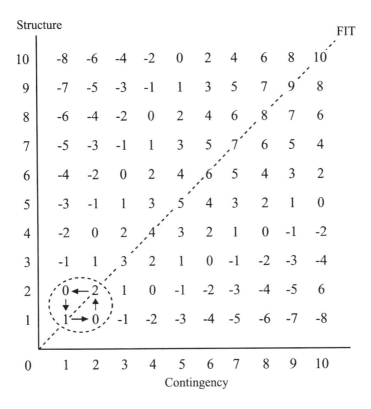

Figure 10.1. Hetero-Performance: Fit, Misfit, and Performance

misfit), at high values of the contingency, while not having performance as high as it would be if were in fit, still has quite high performance. Thus an organization in some misfit at high contingency has performance equal to an organization in fit at a medium level of the contingency.

The next step is to specify the exact performance of each of the misfits. Traditional approaches such as the Euclidean distance formula (Drazin and Van de Ven 1985) seek to specify mathematically the relationship between the degree of misfit and performance, that is, by a formula that applies to every misfit. This is not possible with hetero-performance misfit, because, as we have just seen, the performance each produces varies according to the location of the misfit, that is, to the point along the fit line, to which that misfit is nearest. Thus considering the two-dimensional space formed by the contingency and the structure variables, the performance of each point in that space needs to be defined. This can be done by following an algorithm.

Starting with the points immediately below the fit line, that is, just one space below the fit line, for each of them their degree of misfit is mild (see Figure 10.1). An organization can enter that mild misfit by increasing its level of the contingency by one unit, so that it leaves the old fit. The organization may then regain fit by increasing the level of its structure by one unit so that it enters the new fit. These two moves bring the organization to the next highest point along the fit line from the previous point, that is, an increase of one performance unit. As argued in the previous chapter, to have an incentive to make these two moves, the performance while in misfit must be less than that of the two fits, the old and the new. Given that the performance of the old fit is one unit less than the new fit, the mild misfit must be one performance unit less than the old fit and two performance units less than the new fit. Using this algorithm or decision rule we can specify the performance of the mild fits in Figure 10.1.

For example, a mild misfit exists at contingency level two and structural level one (see Figure 10.1). An organization would move into this mild misfit by increasing its contingency level by one unit, thereby moving out of the fit at contingency and structure of one that yielded a performance of 1. Thus the misfit produces a performance of 0. An organization there has an incentive to increase its structures to level two and so move up into the new fit that corresponds to its contingency level of two, because that new fit has performance of 2. A similar logic applies to each of the mild misfit points that lie immediately below the fit line. Each of these misfits has a performance that is two units less than the fit that corresponds to its level of the contingency variable. Thus these eight mild misfits (corresponding to contingency levels two to ten) range in their performances from 0 to 8 units.

A similar logic applies to each misfit point that is farther away from the fit line (below that line). Thus for any level of the contingency, each misfit that is one more degree farther from the fit line is two units less in its performance. This fulfills the condition that it be one performance unit less than the point to its left, which is nearer to the line, because it is more of a misfit and so produces less performance. The condition is also fulfilled that the focal misfit point be less in its performance than the point above it, which is less of a misfit. Thus this value of performance for the focal misfit maintains the condition that an organization moving into a higher degree of misfit by increasing its contingency level will have consequently less performance. It also maintains the condition that an organization that increases its structure will reduce its misfit. Furthermore, it maintains the condition that it will reduce its misfit by moving closer to a new fit, because there is an incentive to move to the new fit rather than to the old fit. The greatest degree of misfit occurs at level ten of contingency and one of structure, where performance is −8 units (see Figure 10.1). Thus misfit varies from +8 to −8, respectively, at levels nine and one of the structure, both for level ten of the contingency variable. The causal pattern is that misfit produces lower performance, the greater the distance from the fit line, which is possible only at the lower levels of the structural variable.

For misfits above the fit line, the logic is similar. A mild misfit above the fit line produces lower performance than its adjacent old and new fits, because it is a misfit. The organization moves out from the old fit by decreasing its contingency level and so enters the misfit. The organization may then decrease its structure so that it attains the new fit that corresponds to its level of the contingency variable. Because the organization has thereby moved down along the fit line, the new fit has less performance than the old. The new fit must produce more performance than the mild misfit, in order that there is an incentive for the organization to move into the new fit rather remaining in the misfit. Therefore the mild misfit is one performance unit less than the new fit. For example, an organization is in fit at level two of the structure and contingency variables, so that its performance is 2 units (see Figure 10.1). It then decreases its contingency by one unit, so entering misfit, which lowers its performance to 0. The organization then decreases its structure by one unit to attain the new fit (at level one of contingency and structure), which produces a performance of 1 unit. Thus the organization has followed the SARFIT model, by changing first its contingency and then adjusting its structure so that contingency causes structure. In so doing the organization has moved down the fit line.

Lower points along the fit line produce less performance than the higher point from which the organization started. Hence there is no incentive for an organization to move down the fit line. Therefore an organization will tend only reluctantly to move down the fit line, usually as a result of being forced to. This could be caused by some factor other than fit, for example, such as through cuts to its budget by a parent organization. Alternatively, the organization might be driven to reduce its contingency by ideology, such as to reduce its size because of the positive value placed on downsizing at certain historical periods (Budros 1997; Cascio 1993; McKinley, Sanchez, and Schick 1995). An organization that has declined to a new, lower level of the contingency variable (e.g., size) will have to regain fit by adopting the new structural level that fits that lower level. Given a choice, management would prefer to move back up to the old, higher level of the contingency and regain fit that way, because it would produce higher performance. However, in contingency decline that option will often be infeasible, because the reason that caused the decline may still be operative. For instance, if the decline was caused by reduction in resources, management may be unable to restore those resources. Or again, the downsizing ideology that caused shrinkage in employee numbers may be still dominant.

Because of the incentives, growth may be more frequent than decline, depending upon the economic conditions. Therefore more misfits would be expected to be below than above the fit line. However, SARFIT applies in decline as in growth and therefore contingency-driven change can occur there. Thus we have depicted the relationship between misfit and performance above as well as below the fit line.

The greatest degree of misfit above the line occurs at level one of contingency and ten of structure, where performance is −8 units. Thus misfit (above the line) varies from +8 to −8 performance units, respectively, at levels nine and one of the contingency, both for level ten of the structural variable. The causal pattern is that misfit produces lower performance, the greater the distance from the fit line, which is possible above the fit line only at the higher levels of the structural variable.

The pattern of performance for each misfit is symmetrical for the misfits above and below the line (Figure 10.1). This is to be expected given that the same theory was used to create both specifications, the SARFIT model of organizational dynamics. Combining both above and below the fit line, the greatest degree of misfit occurs at level ten of each of the contingency and structure variables, where performance is −8 units. Thus, overall, misfit ranges from +8 to −8. Performance is higher, the farther along the fit line, which is only possible at high levels of the contingency and structural variables simultaneously. Performance is lower the greater the misfit, that is, the greater the distance from the fit line, which is possible only at the lower levels of the contingency or structural variables.

We have stated the necessary relationships among fit, misfit, and performance to motivate structural adaptation to regain fit in response to contingency changes. However, there is no presumption that all organizations will actually move up and down the fit line, which is the line of full fit. For the reasons advanced in Chapter 9, many organizations will move along the paths of the quasi-fit lines that lie alongside of, but off, the full-fit line. The performances ascribed to the misfit points here provide them with incentives to adapt structure to changes in the contingency variable.

Of course, these relationships of performance to fit and misfit are theoretical postulates at present. Whether they are valid is a task for empirical research to investigate. The fit line is held to be one in which performance is higher at higher levels of contingency than at lower levels, that is, higher performance at the top and the bottom. Thus organizations lying on the fit line should be examined to see whether their performances differ in this way. The hypothesis is that:

Organizations lying at each successive point on the fit line produce higher performance at each higher level of the contingency variable than at the level immediately below.

The contrasting hypothesis from the iso-performance concept is that:

Organizations lying on the fit line produce the same performance at each level of the contingency variable.

The testing of the overall model, containing both fits and misfits, would be as follows. For each organization in the study, first find its position in the matrix (Figure 9.1) and thus its performance as predicted by the matrix. The predicted performance of that organization should correspond to its actual performance relative to the other organizations in the study. The correlation would then be calculated between the predicted and actual performances. If this correlation is positive, then some support exists for the model. The higher the positive correlation, the greater the empirical support for the model. Thus the hypothesis is that the correlation between the predicted and actual performances would be positive and substantial. Given that the model is intended to be an advance on other, more traditional measures of fit, the hypothesis would be that the correlation between the predicted and actual performances would be greater than that between other measures of misfit and actual performance. Other measures of misfit would be exemplified by the Euclidean deviation scores. These misfit-performance relationships are expected to be negative, whereas the predicted performance relationship from the hetero-performance concept is expected to be positive. Thus a hypothesis would be that:

The positive correlation between actual performance and that predicted by the hetero-performance fit concept is higher than the negative misfit-performance correlation of the Euclidean deviation method.

Clearly many factors other than fit or misfit affect organizational performance. The potential confounding affect of these can be controlled for statistically in the analyses discussed above. For example, the actual performance that is being compared with that predicted from the hetero-performance concept could be performance (e.g., profits) after controlling for other confounding variables (such as industry, etc).

Conclusions

The intention of this chapter has been to help future empirical research address some of the structural contingency theory issues that have been discussed in this book. Guidance has been offered in the form of hypotheses to be tested and the operationalization of the key relationship between fit and organizational performance.

Regarding bureaucracy, there is a need to test hypotheses empirically about the effect of fit on performance. There is also a need to show that organizational change conforms to the dynamic pattern of contingency change leading to structural change, by investigating size change and bureaucratic structural change. Moreover, it needs to be shown empirically that these changes occur through the intervening processes of misfit lowering performance.

The new theoretical developments of neo-contingency theory provide many opportunities for fresh empirical work in structural contingency theory. There is a need to test the hypotheses from disequilibrium theory that the higher the performance of a firm in fit, the greater the probability that it will increase the level of its contingency variables and so move into misfit. While such high performance of a firm in fit stimulates increases in the contingencies, low performance of a firm in misfit stimulates structural adaptation. This idea that organizational change is driven by organizational performance has been refined into organizational portfolio theory. This yields many theoretical propositions and testable hypotheses, illustrative examples of which have been provided in this chapter. Putting many individual effects together, an organization is more likely to make adaptive structural change if it is undiversified in a competitive industry with a deep business cycle and it has a functional structure, mainly executive directors, much debt, and does not divest. Each of these effects needs to be studied separately in order to establish the validity of each component part of organizational portfolio theory. Again, the new concept of quasi-fit deserves to be examined, such as by ascertaining whether organizations empirically tend to attain only quasi-fit, rather than full fit, as they structurally adapt and recommence growing.

Throughout this book we have stressed that the idea of fit is at the heart of contingency theory. Therefore it is appropriate that we should end by suggesting a new operationalization of the relationship between fit and performance that is consistent with the change dynamics that have been argued, that is, structural adaptation to regain fit (SARFIT).

Thus contingency theory continues to develop, such as in the directions considered here under the heading of neo-contingency theory. In this way work continues in the tradition that has seen so much valuable research work over the years.

Contingency theory has a rich past.

It also has a promising future.

References

Abdel-khalik, A. Rashad. 1988. "Hierarchies and Size: A Problem of Identification." *Organization Studies* 9:237-251.

Aldrich, Howard E. 1972a. "Reply to Hilton: Seduced and Abandoned." *Administrative Science Quarterly* 17:55-57.

Aldrich, Howard E. 1972b. "Technology and Organizational Structure: A Reexamination of the Findings of the Aston Group." *Administrative Science Quarterly* 17:26-43.

Alexander, Judith W., and W. Alan Randolph. 1985. "The Fit Between Technology and Structure as a Predictor of Performance in Nursing Subunits." *Academy of Management Journal* 28:844-859.

Al-Jibouri, Sadia Jabouri Joudi. 1983. "Size, Technology, and Organizational Structure in the Manufacturing Industry of a Developing Country: Iraq." Ph.D. diss. Mississippi State University.

Allen, Stephen A. 1978. "Organizational Choices and General Management Influence Networks in Divisionalized Companies." *Academy of Management Journal* 21:341-365.

Amburgey, Terry L., and Tina Dacin. 1994. "As the Left Foot Follows the Right? The Dynamics of Strategic and Structural Change." *Academy of Management Journal* 37:1427-1452.

Anderson, Stuart. 1996. "Unravelling the 'Publicness Puzzle' in Organization Theory: A New Use for the Aston Approach." Paper presented at the annual conference of the British Academy of Management. Aston University, Birmingham, UK, September.

Argote, Linda. 1982. "Input Uncertainty and Organizational Coordination in Hospital Emergency Units." *Administrative Science Quarterly* 27:420-434.

Argyris, Chris. 1964. *Integrating the Individual and the Organization.* New York: John Wiley.

Argyris, Chris. 1972. *The Applicability of Organizational Sociology.* London: Cambridge University.

Armour, Henry Ogden, and David J. Teece. 1978. "Organizational Structure and Economic Performance: A Test of the Multidivisional Hypothesis." *Bell Journal of Economics* 9:106-122.

Astley, W. Graham 1985. "Organizational Size and Bureaucratic Structure." *Organization Studies* 6:201-228.

Astley, W. Graham, and Andrew H. Van de Ven. 1983. "Central Perspectives and Debates in Organization Theory." *Administrative Science Quarterly* 28:245-273.

Astley, W. Graham, and Edward J. Zajac. 1990. "Beyond Dyadic Exchange: Functional Interdependence and Sub-unit Power." *Organization Studies* 11:481-501.

At-Twaijri, Mohamed Ibrahim Ahmad, and John R. Montanari. 1987. "The Impact of Context and Choice on the Boundary-spanning Process: An Empirical Extension." *Human Relations* 40:783-798.

Ayer, A. J. 1936. *Language, Truth and Logic.* London: Gollancz.

Ayoubi, Z. M. 1981. "Technology, Size and Organization Structure in a Developing Country: Jordan." Pp. 95-114 in *Organization and Nation: The Aston Programme IV,* edited by D. J. Hickson and C. J. McMillan. Farnborough, Hants, UK: Gower.

Azumi, K., and C. J. McMillan. 1981. "Management Strategy and Organization Structure: A Japanese Comparative Study." Pp. 155-172 in *Organization and Nation: The Aston Programme IV,* edited by D. J. Hickson and C. J. McMillan. Farnborough, Hants, UK: Gower.

Bacharach, Samuel B. 1989. "Organizational Theories: Some Criteria for Evaluation." *Academy of Management Review* 14:496-515.

Badran, M., and C. R. Hinings. 1981. "Strategies of Administrative Control and Contextual Constraints in a Less Developed Country: The case of Egyptian Public Enterprise." Pp. 115-131 in *Organization and Nation: The Aston Programme IV,* edited by D. J. Hickson and C. J. McMillan. Farnborough, Hants, UK: Gower.

Barney, Jay B. 1990. "The Debate Between Traditional Management Theory and Organizational Economics: Substantive Differences or Intergroup Conflict?" *Academy of Management Review* 15:382-393.

Bartlett, C. A., and S. Ghoshal. 1989. *Managing Across Borders: The Transnational Solution.* Boston: Harvard Business School Press.

Baysinger, Barry D., and Henry N. Butler. 1985. "Corporate Governance and the Board of Directors: Performance Effects of Changes in Board Composition." *Journal of Law, Economics and Organization* 1:101-124.

Baysinger, Barry D., R. T. Kosnik, and T. A. Turk. 1991. "Effects of Board and Ownership Structure on Corporate R&D Strategy." *Academy of Management Journal* 34:205-214.

Birkinshaw, Julian. 1999. *Contingency Theory and the Characteristics of Knowledge: Strategic, Environmental and Knowledge Predictors of International R&D Organization.* London: London Business School.

Blau, Peter M. 1970. "A Formal Theory of Differentiation in Organizations." *American Sociological Review* 35:201-218.

Blau, Peter M. 1971. "Comments on Two Mathematical Formulations of the Theory of Differentiation in Organizations." *American Sociological Review* 36:304-307.

Blau, Peter M. 1972. "Interdependence and Hierarchy in Organizations." *Social Science Research* 1:1-24.

Blau, Peter M., Cecilia McHugh Falbe, William McKinley, and Phelps K. Tracy. 1976. "Technology and Organization in Manufacturing." *Administrative Science Quarterly* 21:21-40.

Blau, Peter M., and Marshall W. Meyer. 1987. *Bureaucracy in Modern Society.*, 3rd ed. New York: Random House.

Blau, Peter M., and P. A. Schoenherr. 1971. *The Structure of Organizations.* New York: Basic Books.

Bourgeois, L. J., III. 1984. "Strategic Management and Determinism." *Academy of Management Review* 9:586-596.

Boyd, B. 1995. "CEO Duality and Firm Performance: A Contingency Model." *Strategic Management Journal* 16:301-312.

Brealey, Richard A., and Stewart C. Myers. 1996. *Principles of Corporate Finance*, 5th ed. New York: McGraw-Hill.

Brech, E. F. L. 1957. *Organisation: The Framework of Management.* London: Longmans, Green.

Bryman, A., A. D. Beardsworth, E. T. Keil, and J. Ford. 1983. "Research Note: Organizational Size and Specialization." *Organization Studies* 4:271-277.

Budros, Art. 1997. "The New Capitalism and Organizational Rationality: The Adoption of Downsizing Programs, 1979-94." *Social Forces* 76:229-249.

Buhner, R., and P. Möller. 1985. "The Information Context of Corporate Disclosures of Divisionalization Decisions." *Journal of Management Studies* 22:309-326.

Burns, Lawton R. 1989. "Matrix Management in Hospitals: Testing Theories of Matrix Structure and Development." *Administrative Science Quarterly* 34:349-368.

Burns, Tom. 1963. "Industry in a New Age." *New Society* 18:17-20.

Burns, Tom, and G. M. Stalker. 1961. *The Management of Innovation.* London: Tavistock.

Burrell, Gibson, and Morgan, Gareth. 1979. *Sociological Paradigms and Organisational Analysis: Elements of the Sociology of Corporate Life.* London: Heinemann.

Cable, John, and Manfred J. Dirrheimer. 1983. "Markets and Hierarchies: An Empirical Test of the Multidivisional Hypothesis in West Germany." *International Journal of Industrial Organization* 1:43-62.

Cable, John, and Hirohiko Yasuki. 1985. "Internal Organization, Business Group and Corporate Performance: An Empirical Test of the Multidivisional Hypothesis in Japan." *International Journal of Industrial Organization* 3:401-420.

Cameron, Kim S., M. U. Kim, and David A. Whetten. 1987. "Organizational Effects of Decline and Turbulence." *Administrative Science Quarterly* 32:222-240.

Cameron, Kim S., Robert I. Sutton, and David A. Whetten, eds. 1988. *Readings in Organizational Decline: Frameworks, Research, and Prescriptions.* Cambridge, MA: Ballinger.

Capon, N., C. Christodolou, John U. Farley, and James M. Hulbert. 1987. "A Comparative Analysis of the Strategy and Structure of United States and Australian Corporations." *Journal of International Business Studies* 18:51-74.

Cascio, Wayne F. 1993. "Downsizing: What Do We Know? What Have We Learned?" *Academy of Management Executive* 7:95-104.

Caufield, Clyde Curtis. 1989. "An Integrative Research Review of the Relationship Between Technology and Structure: A Meta-Analytic Synthesis." Ph.D. diss. University of Iowa.

Chandler, Alfred D., Jr. 1962. *Strategy and Structure: Chapters in the History of the Industrial Enterprise.* Cambridge: MIT Press.

Chandler, Alfred D., Jr. 1977. *The Visible Hand: The Managerial Revolution in American Business.* Cambridge, MA: Belknap Press.

Channon, Derek F. 1973. *The Strategy and Structure of British Enterprise.* London: Macmillan.

Channon, Derek F. 1978. *The Service Industries: Strategy Structure and Financial Performance.* London: Macmillan.

Chenhall, Robert H. 1979. "Some Elements of Organizational Control in Australian Divisionalized Firms." *Australian Journal of Management* Supplement to 4:1-36.

Child, John. 1972a. "Organization Structure and Strategies of Control: A Replication of the Aston Study." *Administrative Science Quarterly* 17:163-177.

Child, John. 1972b. "Organizational Structure, Environment and Performance: The Role of Strategic Choice." *Sociology* 6:1-22.

Child, John. 1973a. "Parkinson's Progress: Accounting for the Number of Specialists in Organizations." *Administrative Science Quarterly* 18:328-348.

Child, John. 1973b. "Predicting and Understanding Organization Structure." *Administrative Science Quarterly* 18:168-185.

Child, John. 1974. "Managerial and Organizational Factors Associated With Company Performance." *Journal of Management Studies* 11:174-189.

Child, John. 1975. "Managerial and Organizational Factors Associated With Company Performance, Part 2: A Contingency Analysis." *Journal of Management Studies* 12:12-27.

Child, John. 1977. "Organizational Design and Performance: Contingency Theory and Beyond." *Organization and Administrative Science* 8:169-183.

Child, John. 1982. "Discussion Note: Divisionalization and Size: A Comment on the Donaldson/Grinyer Debate." *Organization Studies* 3:351-353.

Child, John. 1984. *Organization: A Guide to Problems and Practice,* 2nd ed. London: Harper and Row.

Child, John. 1997. "From the Aston Programme to Strategic Choice: A Journey From Concepts to Theory." Pp. 45-71 in *Advancement in Organizational Behaviour: Essays in Honour of Derek S. Pugh,* edited by Timothy Clark. Aldershot, Hants, UK: Ashgate.

Child, John, and Alfred Kieser. 1979. "Organizational and Managerial Roles in British and West German Companies: An Examination of the Culture-free Thesis." Pp. 51-73 in *Organization and Nation: The Aston Programme IV,* edited by D. J. Hickson and C. J. McMillan. Farnborough, Hants, UK: Gower.

Child, John, and Roger Mansfield. 1972. "Technology, Size and Organization Structure." *Sociology* 6:369-393.

Childers, Grant W., Bruce H. Mayhew, Jr., and Louis N. Gray. 1971. "System Size and Structural Differentiation in Military Organizations: Testing a Baseline Model of the Division of Labor." *American Journal of Sociology* 76:813-830.

Cibin, R., and R. M. Grant. 1996. "Restructuring Among the World's Leading Oil Companies, 1980-92." *British Journal of Management* 7:283-307.

Clark, P. 1990. *Aston Programme: Describing and Explaining the Structure of Canadian Textile Firms.* Birmingham, UK: Aston University, Aston Programme Press.

Cohen, J., and P. Cohen. 1983. *Applied Multiple Regression/Correlation Analysis for the Behavioral Sciences,* 2nd ed. Hillsdale, NJ: Lawrence Erlbaum.

Cohen, Wesley M., and Richard C. Levin. 1989. "Empirical Studies of Innovation and Market Structure." Pp. 1059-1107 in *Handbook of Industrial Organization, Vol. 2,* edited by R. Schmalensee and R. D. Willig. Amsterdam: Elsevier Science Publishers B. V.

Collins, Paul D., and Frank Hull. 1986. "Technology and Span of Control: Woodward Revisited." *Journal of Management* 23:143-164.

Conaty, J., H. Mahmoudi, and G. A. Miller. 1983. "Social Structure and Bureaucracy: A Comparison of Organizations in the United States and Prerevolutionary Iran." *Organization Studies* 4:105-128.

Cool, K., and I. Dierickx. 1993. "Rivalry, Strategic Groups and Firm Profitability." *Strategic Management Journal* 14:47-59.

Cooper, David J., Bob Hinings, Royston Greenwood, and John L. Brown. 1996. "Sedimentation and Transformation in Organizational Change: The Case of Canadian Law Firms." *Organization Studies* 17:623-647.

Corey, E. Raymond, and Steven H. Star. 1971. *Organization Strategy: A Marketing Approach.* Boston: Harvard University, Graduate School of Business Administration, Division of Research.

Crawford, Michael Arthur. 1983. "The Character, Determinants and Performance Effects of Inter-Unit Interactions Within Organisations: A Disaggregated Systems Approach." Ph.D. diss. University of New South Wales, Sydney, New South Wales, Australia.

Cronbach, Lee J., and Lita Furby. 1970. "How Should We Measure 'Change'—Or Should We?" *Psychological Bulletin* 74:68-80.

Crozier, Michel. 1964. *The Bureaucratic Phenomenon.* London: Tavistock.

Cullen, J. B., K. S. Anderson, and D. D. Baker. 1986. "Blau's Theory of Structural Differentiation Revisited: A Theory of Structural Change or Scale." *Academy of Management Journal* 29:203-229.

Daft, Richard L., and Patricia Bradshaw. 1980. "The Process of Horizontal Differentiation: Two Models." *Administrative Science Quarterly* 25:441-456.

Daily, Catherine M., and Dan R. Dalton. 1994a. "Bankruptcy and Corporate Governance: An Empirical Assessment." *Strategic Management Journal* 15:643-654.

Daily, Catherine M., and Dan R. Dalton. 1994b. "Corporate Governance and the Bankrupt Firm: The Impact of Board Composition and Structure." *Academy of Management Journal* 37:1603-1617.

Dalton, Dan R., Catherine M. Daily, Jonathan L. Johnson, and Alan E. Ellstrand. 1999. "Number of Directors and Financial Performance: A Meta-Analysis." *Academy of Management Review* 42:674-686.

Dalton, Dan R., William D. Todor, Michael J. Spendolini, Gordon J. Fielding, and Lyman W. Porter. 1980. "Organization Structure and Performance: A Critical Review." *Academy of Management Review* 5:49-64.

Damanpour, Fariborz. 1992. "Organizational Size and Innovation." *Organization Studies* 13:375-402.

Daniels, John D., Robert A. Pitts, and Marietta J. Tretter. 1984. "Strategy and Structure in U.S. Multinationals: An Exploratory Study." *Academy of Management Journal* 7:292-307.

Daniels, John D., Robert A. Pitts, and Marietta J. Tretter. 1985. "Organizing for Dual Strategies of Product Diversity and International Expansion." *Strategic Management Journal* 6:223-237.

Davis, Gerald F., Kristina A. Diekmann, and Catherine H. Tinsley. 1994. "The Decline and Fall of the Conglomerate Firm in the 1980s: The Deinstitutionalization of an Organizational Form." *American Sociological Review* 59:547-570.

Davis, James H., F. David Schoorman, and Lex Donaldson. 1997. "Toward a Stewardship Theory of Management." *Academy of Management Review* 22:20-47.

Davis, Stanley M. 1972. "Basic Structures of Multinational Corporations." Pp. 193-211 in *Managing and Organizing Multinational Corporations,* edited by Stanley M. Davis. Elmsford, NY: Pergamon.

Davis, Stanley M., and Paul R. Lawrence. 1977. *Matrix.* Reading, MA: Addison-Wesley.

Dawson, Sandra, and Dorothy Wedderburn. 1980. "Introduction." Pp. xiii-xl in *Industrial Organization: Theory and Practice,* 2nd ed., by Joan Woodward. Oxford: Oxford University Press.

Delery, John, and D. Harold Doty. 1996. "Modes of Theorizing in Strategic Human Resource Management: Tests of Universalistic, Contingency, and Configurational Performance Predictions." *Academy of Management Journal* 39:802-835.

Dess, Gregory G., and R. B. Robinson. 1984. "Measuring Organizational Performance in the Absence of Objective Measures: The Case of the Privately-held Firm and the Conglomerate Business Unit." *Strategic Management Journal* 5:265-273.

Dess, Gregory G., and Donald W. Beard. 1984. "Dimensions of Organizational Task Environments." *Administrative Science Quarterly* 29:52-73.

Dess, Gregory G., R. Duane Ireland, and Michael A. Hitt. 1990. "Industry Effects and Strategic Management Research." *Journal of Management* 16:7-27.

Dewar, Robert, and Jerald Hage. 1978. "Size, Technology, Complexity, and Structural Differentiation: Toward a Theoretical Synthesis." *Administrative Science Quarterly* 23:111-136.

Dewar, Robert, and James Werbel. 1979. "Universalistic and Contingency Predictions of Employee Satisfaction and Conflict." *Administrative Science Quarterly* 24:426-448.

DiMaggio, Paul J., and Walter W. Powell. 1983. "The Iron Cage Revisited: Institutional Isomorphism and Collective Rationality in Organization Fields." *American Sociological Review* 48:147-160.

Donaldson, Gordon. 1994. *Corporate Restructuring: Managing the Change Process From Within.* Boston: Harvard Business School Press.

Donaldson, Lex. 1976. "Woodward, Technology, Organisational Structure and Performance—A Critique of the Universal Generalisation." *Journal of Management Studies* 13:255-273.

Donaldson, Lex. 1979. "Regaining Control at Nipont." *Journal of General Management* 4:14-30.

Donaldson, Lex. 1982a. "Divisionalization and Diversification: A Longitudinal Study." *Academy of Management Journal* 25:909-914.

Donaldson, Lex. 1982b. "Divisionalization and Size: A Theoretical and Empirical Critique." *Organization Studies* 3:321-337.

Donaldson, Lex. 1985. *In Defence of Organization Theory: A Reply to the Critics.* Cambridge UK: Cambridge University Press.

Donaldson, Lex. 1986. "Size and Bureaucracy in East and West: A Preliminary Meta Analysis." Pp. 67-91 in *The Enterprise and Management in East Asia,* edited by S. R. Clegg, D. Dunphy, and S. G. Redding. Hong Kong: University of Hong Kong Press.

Donaldson, Lex. 1987. "Strategy and Structural Adjustment to Regain Fit and Performance: In Defense of Contingency Theory." *Journal of Management Studies* 24:1-24.

Donaldson, Lex. 1990a. "The Ethereal Hand: Organizational Economics and Management Theory." *Academy of Management Review* 15:369-381.

Donaldson, Lex. 1990b. "A Rational Basis for Criticisms of Organizational Economics: A Reply to Barney." *Academy of Management Review* 15:394-401.

Donaldson, Lex. 1995a. *American Anti-Management Theories of Organization: A Critique of Paradigm Proliferation.* Cambridge UK: Cambridge University Press.

Donaldson, Lex. 1995b. *Contingency Theory.* Vol. 9 in *History of Management Thought Series.* Aldershot, Hants, UK: Dartmouth Publishing.

Donaldson, Lex. 1996a. *For Positivist Organization Theory: Proving the Hard Core.* London: Sage.

Donaldson, Lex. 1996b. The Normal Science of Structural Contingency Theory." Pp. 57-76 in *The Handbook of Organization Studies,* edited by S. R. Clegg, C. Hardy, and W. Nord. London: Sage.

Donaldson, Lex. 1997. "Derek Pugh: Scientific Revolutionary in Organization Studies." Pp. 23-43 in *Advancement in Organizational Behaviour: Essays in Honour of Derek S. Pugh,* edited by Timothy Clark. Aldershot, Hants, UK: Ashgate.

Donaldson, Lex. 1999. *Performance-Driven Organizational Change: The Organizational Portfolio.* Thousand Oaks, CA: Sage.

Donaldson, Lex, and Clyde C. Caufield. 1989. "Economics of Scale in Public and Private Administration: Is Market Discipline Mythic?" Sydney, NSW: Australian Graduate School of Management in the University of New South Wales (Working Paper, 89-003).

Donaldson, Lex, and James H. Davis. 1991. "Stewardship Theory or Agency Theory: CEO Governance and Shareholder Returns." *Australian Journal of Management* 16:49-64.

Donaldson, Lex, and Malcolm Warner. 1974. "Structure of Organizations in Occupational Interest Associations." *Human Relations* 27:721-738.

Dotsey, Michael, and Robert G. King. 1987. "Business Cycles." Pp. 302-310 in *The New Palgrave: A Dictionary of Economics,* edited by John Eatwell, Murray Milgate, and Peter Newman. London: Macmillan.

Doty, D. Harold, and William H. Glick. 1994. "Typologies as a Unique Form of Theory Building: Towards Improved Understanding and Modeling." *Academy of Management Review* 19:230-251.

Doty, D. Harold, William H. Glick, and George P. Huber. 1993. "Fit, Equifinality, and Organizational Effectiveness: A Test of Two Configurational Theories." *Academy of Management Journal* 36:1196-1250.

Drazin, Robert, and Andrew H. Van de Ven. 1985. "Alternative Forms of Fit in Contingency Theory." *Administrative Science Quarterly* 30:514-539.

Duncan, Robert B. 1972. "Characteristics of Organizational Environments and Perceived Environmental Uncertainty." *Administrative Science Quarterly* 17:313-327.

Dunning, John H., Bruce Kogut, and Magnus Blomström. 1990. *Globalization of Firms and the Competitiveness of Nations.* Lund, Sweden: Lund University, Institute of Economic Research.

Dunphy, D. C., and D. Stace. 1988. "Transformational and Coercive Strategies for Planned Organizational Change: Beyond the O. D. Model." *Organizational Studies* 9:317-334.

Durkheim, Emile. 1964. *The Division of Labor in Society.* New York: Free Press.

Dyas, Gareth P., and Heinz T. Thanheiser. 1976. *The Emerging European Enterprise: Strategy and Structure in French and German Industry.* London: Macmillan.

Edwards, Jeffrey R., and Mark E. Parry. 1993. "On the Use of Polynomial Regression Equations as an Alternative to Difference Scores in Organizational Research." *Academy of Management Journal* 36:1577-613.

Egelhoff, William G. 1982. "Strategy and Structure in Multinational Corporations: An Information-Processing Approach." *Administrative Science Quarterly* 27:435-458.

Egelhoff, William G. 1988a. *Organizing the Multinational Enterprise: An Information Processing Perspective.* Cambridge, MA: Ballinger.

Egelhoff, William G. 1988b. "Strategy and Structure in Multinational Corporations: A Revision of the Stopford and Wells Model." *Strategic Management Journal* 9:1-14.

Eilon, S. 1977. "Structural Determinism." *Omega, The International Journal of Management Studies* 5:499-504.

Etzioni, Amitai. 1961. *A Comparative Analysis of Complex Organizations: On Power, Involvement and Their Correlates.* New York: Free Press.

Etzioni, Amitai. 1968. *The Active Society: A Theory of Societal and Political Processes.* London: Collier-Macmillan; New York: Free Press.

Ezzamel, M. A., and K. Hilton 1980. "Divisionalisation in British Industry: A Preliminary Study." *Accounting and Business Research* 10:197-214.

Ezzamel, M. A., and R. Watson. 1993. "Organizational Form, Ownership Structure and Corporate Performance: A Contextual Empirical Analysis of UK Companies." *British Journal of Management* 4:161-176.

Faas, F. A. M. J. 1985. "How to Solve the Communication Problems on the R and D Interface." *Journal of Management Studies* 22:83-102.

Feyerabend, P. 1975. *Against Method: Outline of an Anarchistic Theory of Knowledge.* London: New Left Books.

Fiedler, F. E. 1967. *A Theory of Leadership Effectiveness.* New York: McGraw-Hill.

Fiegenbaum, A., and H. Thomas. 1990. "Strategic Groups and Performance." *Strategic Management Journal* 11:197-215.

Finkelstein, Sydney, and Donald C. Hambrick. 1996. *Strategic Leadership: Top Executives and Their Effects on Organizations.* Minneapolis/St Paul, MN: West.

Fisher, Cynthia D., and Richard Gitelson. 1983. "Meta-Analysis of the Correlates of Role Conflict and Role Ambiguity." *Journal of Applied Psychology* 68:320-333.

Flanders, Allan, Ruth Pomeranz, and Joan Woodward. 1968. *Experiment in Industrial Democracy: A Study of the John Lewis Partnership*. London: Faber.

Fligstein, Neil. 1985. "The Spread of the Multidivisional Form Among Large Firms, 1919-1979." *American Sociological Review* 50:377-391.

Fligstein, Neil. 1990a. "Organizational, Demographic and Economic Determinants of the Growth Patterns of Large Firms, 1919-1979." Pp. 45-76 in *Business Institutions,* edited by Craig Calhoun, Vol. 12, *Comparative Social Research,* Greenwich, CT: JAI.

Fligstein, Neil. 1990b. *The Transformation of Corporate Control*. Cambridge, MA: Harvard University Press.

Fligstein, Neil. 1991. "The Structural Transformation of American Industry: An Institutional Account of the Causes of Diversification in the Largest Firms, 1919-1979." Pp. 311-336 in *The New Institutionalism in Organizational Analysis,* edited by Walter W. Powell and Paul J. DiMaggio. Chicago: University of Chicago Press.

Fligstein, Neil, and Peter Brantley. 1992. "Bank Control, Owner Control, or Organizational Dynamics: Who Controls the Large Modern Corporation?" *American Journal of Sociology* 98:280-307.

Franko, Lawrence G. 1974. "The Move Toward a Multidivisional Structure in European Organizations." *Administrative Science Quarterly* 19:493-506.

Frederickson, J. W. 1984. "The Comprehensiveness of Strategic Decision Processes: Extensions, Observations, Future Directions." *Academy of Management Journal* 27:445-466.

Freeman, J., and M. T. Hannan. 1975. "Growth and Decline Processes in Organizations." *American Sociological Review* 40:215-228.

Freeman, John H., and Jerrold E. Kronenfeld. 1973. "Problems of Definitional Dependency: The Case of Administrative Intensity." *Social Forces* 52:108-121.

Fry, Louis R., and Deborah A. Smith. 1987. "Congruence, Contingency, and Theory Building." *Academy of Management Review* 12:117-132.

Galbraith, Jay R. 1973. *Designing Complex Organizations*. Reading, MA: Addison-Wesley.

Galbraith, Jay R., and Robert K. Kazanjian. 1988. "Strategy, Technology, and Emerging Organizational Forms." Pp. 29-41 in *Futures of Organization: Innovating to Adapt Strategy and Human Resources to Rapid Technological Change,* edited by Jerald Hage. Lexington, MA: Lexington Books.

Galtung, Johan. 1967. *Theory and Methods of Social Research*. Oslo, Norway: Universitetsforlaget.

Galunic, D. C., and K. M. Eisenhardt. 1994. "Renewing the Strategy-Structure-Performance Paradigm." Pp. 215-255 in *Research in Organizational Behavior,* Vol. 16, edited by L. L. Cummings and B. M. Staw. Greenwich, CT: JAI.

Gerwin, Donald. 1979a. "The Comparative Analysis of Structure and Technology: A Critical Appraisal." *Academy of Management Review* 4:41-51.

Gerwin, Donald. 1979b. "Relationships Between Structure and Technology at the Organizational and Job Levels." *Journal of Management Studies* 16:70-79.

Gerwin, Donald. 1981. "Relationships Between Structure and Technology." Pp. 3-38 in *Handbook of Organization Design: Vol. 2. Remodeling Organizations and Their*

Environments, edited by P. Nystrom and W. Starbuck. New York: Oxford University Press.

Gerwin, Donald, and Wade Christoffel. 1974. "Organizational Structure and Technology: A Computer Model Approach." *Management Science* 20:1531-1542.

Ghoshal, Sumantra, and P. Moran. 1996. "Bad for Practice: A Critique of the Transaction Cost Theory." *Academy of Management Review* 21:13-47.

Ghoshal, Sumantra, and Nitin Nohria. 1993. "Horses for Courses: Organizational Forms for Multinational Corporations." *Sloan Management Review,* Winter:23-35.

Giddens, Anthony. 1984. *The Constitution of Society.* Cambridge: Polity.

Goldman, P. 1973. "Size and Differentiation in Organizations: A Test of a Theory." *Pacific Sociological Review* 16:89-105.

Gouldner, Alvin W. 1954. *Patterns of Industrial Bureaucracy.* Glencoe, IL: Free Press.

Grant, Robert M. 1993. *Restructuring and Strategic Change in the Oil Industry.* Milan, Italy: FrancoAgneli.

Greenwood, Royston, and C. R. Hinings. 1976a. "Centralization Revisited: Further Discussion." *Administrative Science Quarterly* 21:151-155.

Greenwood, Royston, and C. R. Hinings. 1976b. "Contingency Theory and Public Bureaucracies." Pp. 87-101 in *Organizational Structure: Extensions and Replications: The Aston Programme II,* edited by D. S. Pugh and C. R. Hinings. Farnborough, Hants, UK: Saxon House.

Gresov, Christopher. 1989. "Exploring Fit and Misfit With Multiple Contingencies." *Administrative Science Quarterly* 34:431-453.

Gresov, Christopher. 1990. "Effects of Dependence and Tasks on Unit Design and Efficiency." *Organization Studies* 11:503-529.

Gresov, Christopher, and Robert Drazin. 1997. "Equifinality: Functional Equivalence in Organization Design." *Academy of Management Journal* 22:403-428.

Grinyer, Peter H. 1982. "Discussion Note: Divisionalization and Size—A Rejoinder." *Organization Studies* 3:339-350.

Grinyer, Peter H., and Masoud Yasai-Ardekani. 1980. "Dimensions of Organizational Structure: A Critical Replication." *Academy of Management Journal* 23:405-421.

Grinyer, Peter H., and Masoud Yasai-Ardekani. 1981. "Strategy, Structure, Size and Bureaucracy." *Academy of Management Journal* 24:471-486.

Grinyer, Peter H., Masoud Yasai-Ardekani, and Shawki Al-Bazzaz. 1980. "Strategy, Structure, the Environment, and Financial Performance in 48 United Kingdom Companies." *Academy of Management Journal* 23:193-220.

Hage, Jerald. 1965. "An Axiomatic Theory of Organizations." *Administrative Science Quarterly* 10:289-320.

Hage, Jerald. 1974. *Communications and Organizational Control: Cybernetics in Health and Welfare Settings.* New York: Wiley InterScience.

Hage, Jerald. 1980. *Theories of Organization: Form, Process and Transformation.* New York: John Wiley.

Hage, Jerald. 1988. *Futures of Organizations: Innovating to Adopt Strategy and Human Resources to Rapid Technological Change.* Lexington, MA: Lexington Books.

Hage, Jerald, and Michael Aiken. 1967a. "Program Change and Organizational Properties: A Comparative Analysis." *American Journal of Sociology* 72:503-519.

Hage, Jerald, and Michael Aiken. 1967b. "Relationship of Centralization to Other Structural Properties." *Administrative Science Quarterly* 12:72-92.

Hage, Jerald, and Michael Aiken. 1969. "Routine Technology, Social Structure and Organizational Goals." *Administrative Science Quarterly* 14:366-376.

Hage, Jerald, and Michael Aiken. 1970. *Social Change in Complex Organizations.* New York: Random House.

Hage, Jerald, and Robert Dewar. 1973 "Elite Values Versus Organizational Structure in Predicting Innovation." *Administrative Science Quarterly* 18:279-290.

Hall, D. J., and M. D. Saias. 1980. "Strategy Follows Structure!" *Strategic Management Journal* 1:149-163.

Hall, Richard H. 1963. "The Concept of Bureaucracy: An Empirical Assessment." *Administrative Science Quarterly* 69:32-40.

Hambrick, Donald C. 1981. "Environment, Strategy, and Power Within Top Management Teams." *Administrative Science Quarterly* 26:253-275.

Hamilton, R. T., and G. S. Shergill. 1992. "The Relationship Between Strategy-Structure Fit and Financial Performance in New Zealand: Evidence of Generality and Validity With Enhanced Controls." *Journal of Management Studies* 29:95-113.

Hamilton, R. T., and G. S. Shergill. 1993. *The Logic of New Zealand Business: Strategy, Structure, and Performance.* Auckland, New Zealand: Oxford University Press.

Hannan, Michael T., and John Freeman. 1977. "The Population Ecology of Organizations." *American Journal of Sociology* 82:929-964.

Hannan, Michael T., and John Freeman. 1984. "Structural Inertia and Organizational Change." *American Sociological Review* 49:149-164.

Hannan, Michael T., and John Freeman. 1989. *Organizational Ecology.* Cambridge, MA: Harvard University Press.

Hannan, Michael T., J. Ranger-Moore, and J. Banaszak-Holl. 1990. "Competition and the Evolution of Organizational Size Distributions." Pp. 246-68 in *Organizational Evolution: New Directions,* edited by J. V. Singh. Newbury Park, CA: Sage.

Harris, Barry C. 1983. *Organization: The Effect on Large Corporations.* Ann Arbor, MI: UMI Research.

Heise, D. R. 1972. "How Do I Know My Data? Let Me Count the Ways." *Administrative Science Quarterly* 17:58-61.

Hickson, David J., C. R. Hinings, C. A. Lee, R. E. Schneck, and J. M. Pennings. 1971. "A Strategic Contingencies Theory of Intraorganizational Power." *Administrative Science Quarterly* 16:216-229.

Hickson, David J., C. R. Hinings, C. J. McMillan, and J. P. Schwitter. 1974. "The Culture-Free Context of Organization Structure: A Trinational Comparison." *Sociology* 8:59-80.

Hickson, David J. and C. J. McMillan, eds. 1981. *Organization and Nation: The Aston Programme IV.* Farnborough, Hants, UK: Gower.

Hickson, David J., Derek S. Pugh, and Diana G. Pheysey. 1969. "Operations Technology and Organization Structure: An Empirical Reappraisal." *Administrative Science Quarterly* 14:378-397.

Hill, Charles W. L. 1985a. "Internal Organization and Enterprise Performance: Some UK Evidence." *Managerial and Decision Economics* 6:210-216.

Hill, Charles W. L. 1985b. "Oliver Williamson and the M-form Firm: A Critical Review." *Journal of Economic Issues* 19:731-751.

Hill, Charles W. L. 1988a. "Corporate Control Type, Strategy, Size and Financial Performance." *Journal of Management Studies* 25:403-417.

Hill, Charles W. L., Michael A. Hitt, and Robert E. Hoskisson. 1992. "Cooperative Versus Competitive Structures in Related and Unrelated Diversified Firms." *Organization Science* 3:501-521.

Hill, Charles W. L., and J. F. Pickering 1986. "Divisionalization, Decentralization and Performance of Large United Kingdom Companies." *Journal of Management Studies* 23:26-50.

Hill, Charles W. L., and S. A. Snell. 1988. "External Control, Corporate Strategy, and Firm Performance in Research-Intensive Industries." *Strategic Management Journal* 9:577-590.

Hilmer, Frederick G. 1998. *Strictly Boardroom: Improving Governance to Enhance Company Performance*, 2nd ed. Melbourne, Victoria, Australia: Information Australia.

Hilton, G. 1972. "Causal Inference Analysis: A Seductive Process." *Administrative Science Quarterly* 17:44-55.

Hinings, C. R., David J. Hickson, J. M. Pennings, and R. E. Schneck. 1974. "Structural Conditions of Intraorganizational Power." *Administrative Science Quarterly* 19:22-44.

Hinings, C. R., and Gloria Lee. 1971. "Dimensions of Organization Structure and Their Context: A Replication." *Sociology* 5:83-93.

Hinings, C. R., Derek S. Pugh, David J. Hickson, and C. Turner. 1967. "An Approach to the Study of Bureaucracy." *Sociology* 1:61-72.

Hinings, C. R., S. Ranson, and A. Bryman. 1976. "Churches as Organizations: Structure and Context." Pp. 102-114 in *Organizational Structure: Extensions and Replications: The Aston Programme II*, edited by D. S. Pugh and C. R. Hinings. Farnborough, Hants, UK: Saxon House.

Hirsch, Paul. 1975. "Organizational Effectiveness and the Institutional Environment." *Administrative Science Quarterly* 20:327-344.

Hoffman, James J., Nancy M. Carter, and John B. Cullen. 1994. "The Effect of Lag-Structure Identification When Testing for Fit." *Organization Studies* 15:829-848.

Holdaway, Edward A., John F. Newberry, David J. Hickson, and R. Peter Heron. 1975. "Dimensions of Organizations in Complex Societies: The Educational Sector." *Administrative Science Quarterly* 20:37-58.

Hopkins, H. Donald. 1988. "Firm Size: The Interchangeability of Measures." *Human Relations* 41:91-102.

Hoskisson, R. E. 1987. "Multidivisional Structure and Performance: The Contingency of Diversification Strategy." *Academy of Management Journal* 30:625-644.

Hoskisson, R. E., and C. S. Galbraith. 1985. "The Effect of Quantum Versus Incremental M-form Reorganization on Performance: A Time-series Exploration of Intervention Dynamics." *Journal of Management,* 11:55-70.

Hoskisson, Robert E., and Michael A. Hitt. 1994. *Downscoping: How to Tame the Diversified Firm.* New York: Oxford University Press.

Hull, Frank. 1988. "Inventions From R&D Organizational Designs for Efficient Research Performance." *Sociology* 22:393-415.

Hull, Frank, and Paul D. Collins. 1987. "High-Technology Batch Production Systems: Woodward's Missing Type." *Academy of Management Journal* 30:786-797.

Hummon, Norman P. 1971. "A Mathematical Theory of Differentiation in Organizations." *American Sociological Review* 36:297-303.

Hunter, John E., Frank L. Schmidt, and Gregg B. Jackson. 1982. *Meta-Analysis: Cumulating Research Findings Across Studies.* Beverly Hills, CA: Sage.

Inkson, J. H. K., Derek S. Pugh, and David J. Hickson. 1970. "Organization Context and Structure: An Abbreviated Replication." *Administrative Science Quarterly* 15:318-329.

Isajew, Wsevolod. 1968. *Causation and Functionalism in Sociology.* London: Routlege & Kegan Paul.

Jaques, Elliott. 1976. *A General Theory of Bureaucracy.* London: Heinemann.

Jarley, Paul, Jack Fiorito, and John Thomas Delaney. 1997. "A Structural Contingency Approach to Bureaucracy and Democracy in U.S. National Unions." *Academy of Management Journal* 40:831-861.

Jennings, Daniel F., and Samuel L. Seaman. 1994. "High and Low Levels of Organizational Adaptation: An Empirical Analysis of Strategy, Structure and Performance." *Strategic Management Journal* 15:459-475.

Jensen, Michael C., and William H. Meckling. 1976. "Theory of the Firm: Managerial Behavior, Agency Costs and Ownership Structure." *Journal of Financial Economics* 3:305-360.

Johns, Gary. 1981. "Difference Score Measures of Organizational Behavior Variables: A Critique." *Organizational Behavior and Human Performance* 27:443-463.

Johnson, G. 1987. *Strategic Change and the Management Process.* Oxford UK: Basil Blackwell.

Joyce, William F. 1986. "Matrix Organization: A Social Experiment." *Academy of Management Journal* 29:536-561.

Keller, Robert T. 1994. "Technology-Information Processing Fit and the Performance of R&D Project Groups: A Test of Contingency Theory." *Academy of Management Journal* 37:167-179.

Kenny, Graham K., and David C. Wilson. 1984. "The Interdepartmental Influence of Managers: Individual Sub-Unit Perspectives." *Journal of Management Studies* 21:409-427.

Kesner, Idalene F. 1987. "Directors, Stock Ownership and Organizational Performance: An Investigation of Fortune 500 Companies." *Journal of Management* 13:499-508.

Ketchen, David J., James G. Combs, Craig J. Russell, Chris Shook, Michelle A. Dean, Janet Runge, Franz T. Lohrke, Stefanie E. Naumann, Dawn Ebe Haptonstahl, Robert Baker, Brenden A. Beckstein, Charles Handler, Heather Honig, and Stephen Lamoureux. 1997. "Organizational Configurations and Performance: A Meta-Analysis." *Academy of Management Journal* 40:223-240.

Ketchen, David J., James B. Thomas, and Charles C. Snow. 1993. "Organizational Configurations and Performance: A Comparison of Theoretical Approaches." *Academy of Management Journal* 36:1278-1313.

Khandwalla, Pradip N. 1973. "Viable and Effective Organizational Designs of Firms." *Academy of Management Journal* 16:481-495.

Khandwalla, Pradip N. 1974. "Mass Output Orientation of Operations Technology and Organizational Structure." *Administrative Science Quarterly* 19:74-97.

Khandwalla, Pradip N. 1977. *The Design of Organizations*. New York: Harcourt Brace Jovanovich.

Kimberly, John R. 1976. "Organizational Size and the Structuralist Perspective: A Review, Critique and Proposal." *Administrative Science Quarterly* 21:571-597.

Knight, Kenneth. 1977. *Matrix Management*. New York: PBI-Petrocelli Books.

Kolodny, Harvey F. 1979. "Evolution to a Matrix Organization." *Academy of Management Review* 4:543-553.

Kraft, Kenneth L., George M. Puia, and Jerald Hage. 1995. "Structural Contingency Theory Revisited: Main Effects Versus Interactions in Child's National Study of Manufacturing and Service Sectors." *Revue Canadienne des Sciences de l'Administration—Canadian Journal of Administrative Sciences* 12:182-194.

Kuc, B., D. J. Hickson, and C. J. McMillan. 1981. "Centrally Planned Development: A Comparison of Polish Factories With Equivalents in Britain, Japan and Sweden." Pp. 75-91 in *Organization and Nation: The Aston Programme IV*, edited by D. J. Hickson, and C. J. McMillan. Farnborough, Hants, UK: Gower.

Kuczynski, M. G. 1986. "Recent Developments in Business Cycle Theory." *Journal of Economic Dynamics and Control* 10:255-260.

Kuhn, Thomas S. 1970. *The Structure of Scientific Revolutions*, 2nd ed. Chicago: University of Chicago Press.

Lakatos, I. 1974. "Falsification and the Methodology of Scientific Research Programmes." Pp. 91-196 in *Criticism and the Growth of Knowledge*, edited by I. Lakatos and A. Musgrave. Cambridge: Cambridge University Press.

Lammers, Cornelis J., and David J. Hickson, eds. 1979. *Organizations Alike and Unlike: International and Inter-Institutional Studies in the Sociology of Organization*. London: Routledge & Kegan Paul.

Lawrence, Paul R. 1993. "The Contingency Approach to Organizational Design." Pp. 9-18 in *Handbook of Organizational Behavior*, edited by Robert T. Golembiewski. New York: Marcel Dekker.

Lawrence, Paul R., and Davis Dyer. 1983. *Renewing American Industry: Organizing for Efficiency and Innovation*. New York: Free Press.

Lawrence, Paul R., and Jay W. Lorsch. 1967. *Organization and Environment: Managing Differentiation and Integration*. Boston: Harvard University, Graduate School of Business Administration, Division of Research.

Leavitt, Harold J. 1951. "Some Effects of Certain Communication Patterns on Group Performance." *Journal of Abnormal and Social Psychology* 46:38-50.

Lewin, Arie Y., and Carroll U. Stephens. 1994. "CEO Attitudes as Determinants of Organization Design: An Integrated Model." *Organization Studies* 15:183-212.

Likert, Rensis. 1961. *New Patterns of Management*. New York: McGraw-Hill.

Lincoln, James R., Mitsuyo Hanada, and Kerry McBride. 1986. "Organizational Structures in Japanese and U.S. Manufacturing." *Administrative Science Quarterly* 31:338-364.

Lioukas, S. K., and D. A. Xerokostas. 1982. "Size and Administrative Intensity in Organizational Divisions." *Management Science* 28:854-868.

Littler, Craig R., and Thomas Bramble. 1995. "Conceptualising Organizational Restructuring in the 1990s." *Journal of the Australian and New Zealand Academy of Management* 1:45-56.

Locke, E. A., and G. P. Latham. 1990. *A Theory of Goal-Setting and Task Performance.* Englewood Cliffs, NJ: Prentice Hall.

Lockwood, D. 1964. "Social Integration and System Integration." Pp. 244-257 in *Exploration in Social Change,* edited by George K. Zollschan and Walter Hirsch. London: Routledge & Kegan Paul.

Lorsch, Jay W., and Stephen A. Allen.1973. *Managing Diversity and Inter-Dependence: An Organizational Study of Multidivisional Firms.* Boston: Harvard University, Graduate School of Administration, Division of Research.

Lorsch, Jay W., and Paul R. Lawrence. 1972. "Environmental Factors and Organizational Integration." Pp. 38-48 in *Organizational Planning: Cases and Concepts,* edited by Jay W. Lorsch and Paul R. Lawrence. Homewood, IL: Irwin/Dorsey.

Lorsch, Jay W., and John J. Morse. 1974. *Organizations and Their Members: A Contingency Theory Approach.* New York: Harper and Row.

MacMillan, Alexander, and Richard L. Daft. 1979. "Administrative Intensity and Ratio Variables: The Case Against Definitional Dependency." *Social Forces* 58:228-248.

MacMillan, Alexander, and Richard L. Daft. 1984. "Inferences About Economics of Scale DO Depend on the Form of Statistical Analysis: A Reconciliation." *Social Forces* 62:1059-1067.

Mahajan, Vijay, S. Sharma, and R. A. Bettis. 1988. "The Adoption of the M-form Organizational Structure: A Test of Imitation Hypothesis." *Management Science* 34:1188-1201.

Mahoney, Joseph T. 1992. "The Adoption of the Multidivisional Form of Organization: A Contingency Model." *Journal of Management Studies* 29:49-72.

Mansfield, Roger. 1973. "Bureaucracy and Centralization: An Examination of Organizational Structure." *Administrative Science Quarterly* 18:477-488.

March, James G., with Robert I. Sutton. 1999. "Organizational Performance as a Dependent Variable." Pp. 338-353 in James G. March, *The Pursuit of Organizational Intelligence.* Oxford UK: Basil Blackwell.

Marsden, Peter V., Cynthia R. Cook, and Arne L. Kalleberg. 1994. "Organizational Structures: Coordination and Control." *American Behavioral Scientist* 37:911-929.

Marsh, Robert M. 1992. "Research Note: Centralization of Decision-Making in Japanese Factories." *Organization Studies* 13:261-274.

Marsh, Robert M., and Hiroshi Mannari. 1976. *Modernization and the Japanese Factory.* Princeton, NJ: Princeton University Press.

Marsh, Robert M., and Hiroshi Mannari. 1980. "Technological Implications Theory: A Japanese Test." *Organization Studies* 1:161-183.

Marsh, Robert M., and Hiroshi Mannari. 1981. "Technology and Size as Determinants of the Organizational Structure of Japanese Factories." *Administrative Science Quarterly* 26:33-57.

Marsh, Robert M., and Hiroshi Mannari. 1989. "The Size Imperative? Longitudinal Tests." *Organization Studies* 10:83-95.

Martin, Joanne. 1992. *Cultures in Organizations: Three Perspectives.* New York: Oxford University Press.

Mayhew, Bruce H., Jr., Thomas F. James, and Grant W. Childers. 1972. "System Size and Structural Differentiation in Military Organizations: Testing a Harmonic Series Model of the Division of Labor." *American Journal of Sociology* 77:750-765.

306   THE CONTINGENCY THEORY OF ORGANIZATIONS

McKelvey, Bill, and Howard E. Aldrich. 1983. "Populations, Natural Selection and Applied Organizational Science." *Administrative Science Quarterly* 28:101-128.

McKinley, William, Carol M. Sanchez, and Allen G. Schick. 1995. "Organizational Downsizing: Constraining, Cloning and Learning." *Academy of Management Executive* 9:32-44.

McMillan, Charles J., David J. Hickson, Christopher R. Hinings, and Rodney E. Schneck. 1973. "The Structure of Work Organizations Across Societies." *Academy of Management Journal* 16:555-569.

Merton, R. K. 1949. *Social Theory and Social Structure*. Chicago: Free Press.

Meyer, Alan D., Anne S. Tsui, and C. R. Hinings. 1993. "Configurational Approaches to Organizational Analysis." *Academy of Management Journal* 36:1175-1195.

Meyer, John W., and Brian Rowan. 1977. "Institutionalized Organizations: Formal Structure as Myth and Ceremony." *American Journal of Sociology* 83:340-363.

Meyer, John W., and W. Richard Scott, with the assistance of B. Rowan and T. E. Deal. 1983. *Organizational Environments: Ritual and Rationality*. Beverly Hills, CA: Sage.

Meyer, Marshall W. 1971. "Some Constraints in Analyzing Data on Organizational Structures: A Comment on Blau's Paper." *American Sociological Review* 36:294-297.

Meyer, Marshall W. 1972. "Size and the Structure of Organizations: A Causal Analysis." *American Sociological Review* 37:434-441.

Meyer, Marshall W. 1979. *Change in Public Bureaucracies*. Cambridge, UK: Cambridge University Press.

Meyer, Marshall W., and Vipin Gupta. 1994. "The Performance Paradox." *Research in Organizational Behavior* 16:309-369.

Meyer, Marshall W., and Lynne G. Zucker. 1989. *Permanently Failing Organizations*. Newbury Park, CA: Sage.

Miles, Raymond E., and Charles C. Snow. 1978. *Organizational Strategy, Structure, and Process*. Tokyo: McGraw-Hill Kogakusha.

Miller, C. Chet, William H. Glick, Yau-De Wang, and George P. Huber. 1991. "Understanding Technology-Structure Relationships: Theory Development and Meta-Analytic Testing." *Academy of Management Journal* 34:370-399.

Miller, Danny. 1986. "Configurations of Strategy and Structure: Towards a Synthesis." *Strategic Management Journal* 7:233-249.

Miller, Danny. 1990. *The Icarus Paradox: How Exceptional Companies Bring About their Own Downfall: New Lessons in the Dynamics of Corporate Success, Decline, and Renewal*. New York: HarperCollins.

Miller, Danny, and Cornelia Droge. 1986. "Psychological and Traditional Determinants of Structure." *Administrative Science Quarterly* 31:539-560.

Miller, Danny, Cornelia Droge, and Jean-Marie Toulouse. 1988. "Strategic Process and Content as Mediators Between Organizational Context and Structure." *Academy of Management Journal* 31:544-569.

Miller, Danny, and Jean-Marie Toulouse. 1986. "Chief Executive Personality and Corporate Strategy and Structure in Small Firms." *Management Science* 32:1389-1409.

Miller, George A. 1987. "Meta-Analysis and the Culture-Free Hypothesis." *Organization Studies* 8:309-326.

Mindlin, Sergio E., and Howard Aldrich. 1975. "Interorganizational Dependence: A Review of the Concept and a Reexamination of the Findings of the Aston Group." *Administrative Science Quarterly* 20:382-392.

Miner, J. B. 1982. *Theories of Organizational Structure and Process.* Chicago: Dryden.

Mintzberg, H. 1979. *The Structuring of Organizations A Synthesis of the Research.* Englewood Cliffs, NJ: Prentice Hall.

Mintzberg, H. 1983. *Power In and Around Organizations.* Englewood Cliffs, NJ: Prentice Hall.

Mintzberg, H., and James A. Waters. 1982. "Tracking Strategy in an Entrepreneurial Firm." *Academy of Management Journal* 25:465-499.

Mohr, Lawrence B. 1971. "Organizational Technology and Organizational Structure." *Administrative Science Quarterly* 27:420-434.

Montanari, John R., 1979. "Strategic Choice: A Theoretical Analysis." *Journal of Management Studies* 16:202-221.

Montanari, John R., and Philip J. Adelman. 1987. "The Administrative Component of Organizations and the Ratchet Effect: A Critique of Cross-Sectional Studies." *Journal of Management Studies* 24:113-123.

Moran, Peter, and Sumantra Ghoshal. 1996. "Theories of Economic Organization: The Case for Realism and Balance." *Academy of Management Review* 21:58-72.

Muth, Melinda, and Lex Donaldson. 1998. "Stewardship Theory and Board Structure: A Contingency Approach." *Corporate Governance: An International Review* 6:2-28.

Nohria, Nitin, and Sumantra Ghoshal. 1997. *The Differentiated Network: Organizing Multinational Corporations for Value Creation.* San Francisco: Jossey-Bass.

Nunnally, J. C. 1978. *Psychometric Theory.* New York: McGraw-Hill.

Ocasio, William. 1995. "The Enactment of Economic Adversity: A Reconceptualization of Theories of Failure-Induced Change and Threat-Rigidity." *Research in Organizational Behavior* 17:287-331.

Palmer, D., R. Friedland, P. Devereaux Jennings, and M. E. Powers. 1987. "The Economics and Politics of Structure: The Multidivisional Form and Large U.S. Corporation." *Administrative Science Quarterly* 32:25-48.

Palmer, D., P. Devereaux Jennings, and Xuegang Zhou. 1993. "Late Adoption of the Multidivisional Form by Large U.S. Corporations: Institutional, Political, and Economic Accounts." *Administrative Science Quarterly* 38:100-131.

Parkinson, C. Northcote. 1957. *Parkinson's Law and Other Studies in Administration.* Boston: Houghton Mifflin.

Parsons, Talcott. 1951. *The Social System.* London: Routledge & Kegan Paul.

Parsons, Talcott. 1961. "Suggestions for a Sociological Approach to the Theory of Organizations." Pp. 32-47 in *Complex Organizations: A Sociological Reader,* edited by Amitai Etzioni. New York: Holt, Rinehart and Winston.

Pavan, Robert J. 1976. "Strategy and Structure: The Italian Experience." *Journal of Economics and Business* 28:254-260.

Payne, Roy L., and Roger Mansfield. 1973. "Relationships of Perceptions of Organizational Climate to Organizational Structure, Context, and Hierarchical Position." *Administrative Science Quarterly* 18:515-526.

Pennings, J. M. 1975. "The Relevance of the Structural Contingency Model for Organizational Effectiveness." *Administrative Science Quarterly* 20:393-410.

Pennings, J. M. 1987. "Structural Contingency Theory: A Multivariate Test." *Organization Studies* 8:223-240.

Pennings, J. M. 1992. "Structural Contingency Theory: A Reappraisal." *Research in Organizational Behavior* 14:267-309.

Penrose, Edith T. 1959. *The Theory of the Growth of the Firm.* Oxford, UK: Basil Blackwell.

Perrow, Charles. 1967. "A Framework for the Comparative Analysis of Organizations." *American Sociological Review* 32:194-208.

Perrow, Charles. 1970. "Departmental Power and Perspectives in Industrial Firms." Pp. 59-89 in *Power in Organizations,* edited by M. N. Zald. Nashville, TN: Vanderbilt University Press.

Perrow, Charles. 1986. *Complex Organizations: A Critical Essay, 3rd ed.* New York: Random House.

Pfeffer, Jeffrey. 1972. "Size and Composition of Corporate Boards of Directors: the Organization and its Environment." *Administrative Science Quarterly* 17:218-228.

Pfeffer, Jeffrey. 1982. *Organizations and Organization Theory.* Marshfield, MA: Pitman.

Pfeffer, Jeffrey. 1997. *New Directions for Organization Theory: Problems and Prospects.* New York: Oxford University Press.

Pfeffer, Jeffrey, and Gerald R. Salancik. 1978. *The External Control of Organizations: A Resource Dependence Perspective.* New York: Harper and Row.

Pickle, Hal, and F. Friedlander. 1967. "Seven societal criteria of organizational success." *Personnel Psychology* 20:165-178.

Pitts, Robert A. 1974. "Incentive Compensation and Organization Design." *Personnel Journal* 53:338-344.

Pitts, Robert A. 1976. "Diversification Strategies and Organizational Policies of Large Diversified Firms." *Journal of Economics and Business* 28:181-188.

Pitts, Robert A. 1977. "Strategies and Structures for Diversification." *Academy of Management Journal* 20:197-208.

Popper, K. R. 1945. *The Open Society and Its Enemies: Vol. 2. The High Tide of Prophecy: Hegel, Marx and the Aftermath.* London: Routledge & Kegan Paul.

Popper, K. R. 1959. *The Logic of Scientific Discovery.* New York: Harper and Row.

Porter, Michael. 1980. *Competitive Strategy.* New York: Free Press.

Powell, Thomas C. 1992. "Organizational Alignment as Competitive Advantage." *Strategic Management Journal* 13:119-134.

Powell, Walter W., and Paul DiMaggio, eds. 1991. *The New Institutionalism in Organizational Analysis.* Chicago: University of Chicago Press.

Price, James L. 1972. *Handbook of Organizational Measurement.* Lexington, MA: D. C. Heath. Also, updated as, 1997. "Handbook of Organizational Measurement." *International Journal of Manpower* 18:303-558.

Priem, R. L. 1992. "An Application of Metric Conjoint Analysis for the Evaluation of Top Managers' Individual Strategic Decision Making Processes: A Research Note." *Strategic Management Journal* 13:143-151.

Priem, R. L. 1994. "Executive Judgement, Organizational Congruence, and Firm Performance." *Organization Science* 5:421-437.

Pugh, Derek S. 1981a. "The Aston Program Perspective: The Aston Program of Research: Retrospect and Prospect." Pp. 135-166 in *Perspectives on Organization Design and Behavior,* edited by Andrew Van de Ven and William Joyce. New York: John Wiley.

Pugh, Derek S. 1981b. "Rejoinder to Starbuck." Pp. 199-203 in *Perspectives on Organization Design and Behavior,* edited by Andrew Van de Ven and William Joyce. New York: John Wiley.

Pugh, Derek S., and David J. Hickson. 1972. "To the Editor: Causal Inference and the Aston Studies." *Administrative Science Quarterly* 17:273-276.

Pugh, Derek S., and David J. Hickson. 1976. *Organizational Structure in Its Context: The Aston Programme I.* Farnborough, Hants, UK: Saxon House.

Pugh, Derek S., David J. Hickson, and C. R. Hinings. 1969. "An Empirical Taxonomy of Structures of Work Organizations." *Administrative Science Quarterly* 14:115-126.

Pugh, Derek S., David J. Hickson, C. R. Hinings, K. M. Macdonald, C. Turner, and T. Lupton. 1963. "A Conceptual Scheme for Organizational Analysis." *Administrative Science Quarterly* 8:289-315.

Pugh, Derek S., David J. Hickson, C. R. Hinings, and C. Turner. 1968. "Dimensions of Organization Structure." *Administrative Science Quarterly* 13:65-105.

Pugh, Derek S., David J. Hickson, C. R. Hinings, and C. Turner. 1969. "The Context of Organization Structures." *Administrative Science Quarterly* 14:91-114.

Pugh, Derek S., and C. R. Hinings. 1976. *Organizational Structure: Extensions and Replications: The Aston Programme II.* Farnborough, Hants, UK: Saxon House.

Pugh, Derek S., and R. L. Payne, eds. 1977. *Organizational Behaviour in Its Context: The Aston Programme III.* Westmead, Farnborough, Hants, UK: Saxon House, Teakfield.

Randolph, W. Alan, and Gregory G. Dess. 1984. "The Congruence Perspective and Organization Design: A Conceptual Model and Multivariate Research Approach." *Academy of Management Review* 9:114-127.

Reeves, T. K., and B. A. Turner. 1972. "A Theory of Organization and Behavior in Batch Production Factories." *Administrative Science Quarterly* 17:81-98.

Reimann, Bernard C. 1973. "On the Dimensions of Bureaucratic Structure: An Empirical Reappraisal." *Administrative Science Quarterly* 18:462-476.

Reimann, Bernard C. 1974. "Dimensions of Structure in Effective Organizations: Some Empirical Evidence." *Academy of Management Journal* 17:693-708.

Reimann, Bernard C. 1977. "Dimensions of Organizational Technology and Structure: An Exploratory Study." *Human Relations* 30:545-566.

Reimann, Bernard C. 1979. "Parkinson Revisited: A Component Analysis of the Use of Staff Specialists in Manufacturing Organizations." *Human Relations* 32:625-641.

Reimann, Bernard C. 1980. "Organization Structure and Technology in Manufacturing: System Versus Work Flow Level Perspectives." *Academy of Management Journal* 23:61-77.

Reimann, Bernard C. and Giorgio Inzerilli. 1979. "A Comparative Analysis of Empirical Research on Technology and Structure." *Journal of Management* 5:167-192.

Richards, V. G. 1980. "Research Note: The Aston Databank." *Organization Studies* 1:271-278.

Routamaa, Vesa. 1985. "Organizational Structuring: An Empirical Analysis of the Relationships and Dimensions of Structures in Certain Finnish Companies." *Journal of Management Studies* 22:498-522.

Roy, William G. 1990. "Functional and Historical Logics in Explaining the Rise of the American Industrial Corporation." Pp. 19-44 in *Comparative Social Research.* Greenwich, CT: JAI.

310   THE CONTINGENCY THEORY OF ORGANIZATIONS

Rumelt, Richard P. 1974. *Strategy, Structure and Economic Performance*. Boston: Harvard University, Graduate School of Business Administration, Division of Research.

Salter, Malcolm S., and Wolf A. Weinhold. 1979. *Diversification Through Acquisition: Strategies for Creating Economic Value*. New York: Free Press.

Samuelson, Paul A. 1980. *Economics*, 11th ed. New York: McGraw-Hill.

Schlevogt, Kai-Alexander, and Lex Donaldson. 1999. "Eclectic Fit: Combining Theoretical and Empirical Approaches to Explain Organizational Performance." Paper presented at the annual meeting of the Academy of Management, Organization and Management Theory Division, Chicago, August.

Schoonhoven, C. B. 1981. "Problems With Contingency Theory: Testing Assumptions Hidden Within the Language of Contingency Theory." *Administrative Science Quarterly* 26:349-377.

Schreyögg, Georg. 1980. "Contingency and Choice in Organization Theory." *Organization Studies* 1:305-326.

Scott, Bruce R. 1971. Stages of Corporate Development. Boston: Harvard Business School.

Scott, W. Richard. 1992. *Organizations: Rational, Natural and Open Systems*, 3rd ed. Englewood Cliffs, NJ: Prentice Hall.

Scott, W. Richard. 1995. *Institutions and Organizations*. Thousand Oaks, CA: Sage.

Scott, W. Richard, and John J. Meyer. 1994. *Institutional Environments and Organizations*. Thousand Oaks, CA: Sage.

Selznick, Philip. 1949. *TVA and the Grass Roots*. Berkeley: University of California Press.

Shenoy, S. 1981. "Organization Structure and Context: A Replication of the Aston Study in India." Pp. 133-154 in *Organization and Nation: The Aston Programme IV*, edited by D. J. Hickson and C. J. McMillan. Farnborough, Hants, UK: Gower.

Silverman, David. 1968. "Formal Organizations or Industrial Sociology: Towards a Social Action Analysis of Organizations." *Sociology* 2:221-238.

Silverman, David. 1970. *The Theory of Organizations*. London: Heinemann.

Simon, Herbert A. 1976. *Administrative Behavior: A Study of Decision-Making Processes in Administrative Organization*, 3rd ed. New York: Free Press.

Singh, Jitendra V. 1986. "Technology, Size and Organizational Structure: A Reexamination of the Okayama Study Data." *Academy of Management Journal* 29:800-812.

Slappendel, Carol. 1996. "Perspectives on Innovation in Organizations." *Organization Studies* 17:107-129.

Smith, Chris, John Child, and Michael Rowlinson. 1990. *Reshaping Work: The Cadbury Experience*. Cambridge, UK: Cambridge University Press.

Smith, M. R. 1978. "Profits and Administrative Intensity: A Longitudinal Analysis." *Sociology* 12:509-521.

Sprecht, David A. 1973. "System Size and Structural Differentiation in Formal Organizations: An Alternative Baseline Generator." *American Sociological Review* 38:479-480.

Starbuck, William H. 1981. "A Trip to View the Elephants and Rattlesnakes in the Garden of Aston." Pp. 167-98 in *Perspectives on Organization Design and Behavior*, edited by Andrew Van de Ven and William Joyce. New York: John Wiley.

Staw, Barry M., Lance E. Sandelands, and Jane E. Dutton. 1981. "Threat-Rigidity Effects in Organizational Behavior: A Multilevel Analysis." *Administrative Science Quarterly* 26:501-524.

Steer, Peter, and John Cable. 1978. "Internal Organization and Profit: An Empirical Analysis of Large U.K. Companies." *The Journal of Industrial Economics* 27:13-30.

Stopford, John M., and L. T. Wells, Jr. 1972. *Managing the Multinational Enterprise.* New York: Basic Books.

Suzuki, Y. 1980. "The Strategy and Structure of Top 100 Japanese Industrial Enterprises 1950-1970." *Strategic Management Journal* 1:265-291.

Tauber, I. 1968. "A Yardstick of Hospital Organization." Diploma Thesis, University of Aston, Birmingham, England.

Tayeb, Monir. 1987. "Contingency Theory and Culture: A Study of Matched English and the Indian Manufacturing Firms." *Organization Studies* 8:241-261.

Taylor, F. W. 1947. *Scientific Management.* London and New York: Harper.

Teece, David J. 1981. "Internal Organization and Economic Performance: An Empirical Analysis of the Profitability of Principal Firms." *The Journal of Industrial Economics* 30:173-199.

Thompson, James D. 1967. *Organizations in Action.* New York: McGraw-Hill.

Thompson, R. S. 1981. "Internal Organization and Profit: A Note." *The Journal of Industrial Economics* 30:201-211.

Thompson, R. S. 1983. "Diffusion of the M-form Structure in the U.K.: Rate of Imitation, Inter-Firm and Inter-Industry Differences." *International Journal of Industrial Organization* 1:297-315.

Tolbert, Pamela S., and Lynne G. Zucker. 1983. "Institutional Sources of Change in the Formal Structure of Organizations: The Diffusion of Civil Service Reform, 1880-1935." *Administrative Science Quarterly* 28:22-39.

Tosi, Henry, Ramon Aldag, and Ronald Storey. 1973. "On the Measurement of the Environment: An Assessment of the Lawrence and Lorsch Environmental Uncertainty Scale." *Administrative Science Quarterly* 18:27-36.

Trist, E. L., and K. W. Bamforth. 1951. "Some Social and Psychological Consequences of the Longwall Method of Coal-Getting." *Human Relations* 4:3-38.

Tung, Rosalie. 1979. "Dimensions of Organizational Environments: An Exploratory Study of Their Impact on Organization Structure." *Academy of Management Journal* 22:672-693.

Tushman, Michael L. 1977. "Special Boundary Roles in the Innovation Process." *Administrative Science Quarterly* 22:587-605.

Tushman, Michael L. 1979. "Work Characteristics and Subunit Communication Structure: A Contingency Analysis." *Administrative Science Quarterly* 24:82-98.

Van de Ven, Andrew H., A. L. Delbecq, and R. Koenig, Jr. 1976. "Determinants of Coordination Modes Within Organizations." *American Sociological Review* 41:322-338.

Van de Ven, Andrew H. and Robert Drazin. 1985. "The Concept of Fit in Contingency Theory." Pp. 333-365 in *Research in Organizational Behaviour,* Vol. 7, edited by B. M. Staw and L. L. Cummings. Greenwich, CT: JAI.

Van de Ven, Andrew H., and Diane L. Ferry. 1980. *Measuring and Assessing Organizations.* New York: John Wiley.

Venkatraman, N. 1989. "The Concept of Fit in Strategy Research: Toward Verbal and Statistical Correspondence." *Academy of Management Review* 14:423-444.

Wagner, John A., III, Aaron Buchko, and Richard Z. Gooding. 1988. "Aston Research on Organizational Structure: A Meta-Analytic Examination of Generalizability."

THE CONTINGENCY THEORY OF ORGANIZATIONS

Paper presented at the annual meeting of the Academy of Management, Organization and Management Theory Division, Anaheim, California, August.

Wall, Toby D., J. Martin Corbett, Robin Martin, Chris W. Clegg, and Paul R. Jackson. 1990. "Advanced Manufacturing Technology, Work Design, and Performance: A Change Study." *Journal of Applied Psychology* 75:691-697.

Wall, Toby D., and Roy Payne. 1973. "Are Deficiency Scores Deficient?" *Journal of Applied Psychology* 58:322-326.

Weber, Max. 1964. *The Theory of Social and Economic Organization, translated by A. M. Henderson and Talcott Parsons, edited by Talcott Parsons*. New York: Free Press.

Weber, Max. 1968. *Economy and Society: An Outline of Interpretive Sociology,* edited by Guenther Roth and Claus Wittich. New York: Bedminster Press.

Werts, Charles E., and Robert L. Linn. 1970. "A General Linear Model for Studying Growth." *Psychological Bulletin* 73:17-22.

Whetten, David A. 1980. "Sources, Responses, and Effects of Organizational Decline." Pp. 342-374 in *The Organizational Life Cycle: Issues in the Creation, Transformation and Decline of Organizations,* edited by John R. Kimberly and Robert H. Miles. San Francisco: Jossey-Bass.

Whisler, Thomas L., Harald Meyer, Bernard H. Baum, and Peter F. Sorensen, Jr. 1967. "Centralization of Organizational Control: An Empirical Study of Its Meaning and Measurement." *Journal of Business* 40:10-26.

Whittington, Richard 1989. *Corporate Strategies in Recession and Recovery: Social Structure and Strategic Choice.* London: Allen and Unwin.

Whittington, Richard, Michael Mayer, and Francesco Curto. 1999. "Chandlerism in Post-War Europe: Strategic and Structural Change in France, Germany and the UK, 1950-1993." *Industrial and Corporate Change* 8:519-550.

Williamson, Oliver E. 1970. *Corporate Control and Business Behavior: An Inquiry Into the Effects of Organization Form on Enterprise Behavior.* Englewood Cliffs, NJ: Prentice Hall.

Williamson, Oliver E. 1975. *Markets and Hierarchies: Analysis and Antitrust Implications.* New York: Free Press.

Williamson, Oliver E. 1985. *The Economic Institutions of Capitalism: Firms, Markets, Relational Contracting.* New York: Free Press.

Williamson, Oliver E. 1996. "Economic Organization; The Case for Candor." *Academy of Management Review* 21:48-57.

Williamson, Oliver E., and Narottam Bhargava. 1972. "Assessing and Classifying the Internal Structure and Control Apparatus of the Modern Corporation." Pp. 125-148 in *Market Structure and Corporate Behaviour: Theory and Empirical Analysis of the Firm,* edited by Keith Cowling. London: Gray-Mills.

Wong, Gilbert Y. Y., and Philip H. Birnbaum-More. 1994. "Culture, Context and Structure: A Test on Hong Kong Banks." *Organization Studies* 15:99-123.

Wood, R. E., and E. A. Locke. 1990. "Goal Setting and Strategy Effects on Complex Tasks." Pp. 73-109 in *Research in Organizational Behavior,* Vol. 12, edited by B. M. Staw and L. L. Cummings. Greenwich, CT: JAI.

Woodward, Joan. 1958. *Management and Technology.* London: H.M.S.O.

Woodward, Joan. 1965. *Industrial Organization: Theory and Practice.* Oxford, UK: Oxford University Press.

Woodward, Joan. 1970. *Industrial Organization: Behavior and Control.* Oxford, UK: Oxford University Press.

Young, Ruth C. 1988. "Is Population Ecology a Useful Paradigm for the Study of Organizations?" *American Journal of Sociology,* 94:1-24.

Yuchtman, E., and S. E. Seashore. 1967. "A Systems Resource Approach to Organizational Effectiveness." *American Sociological Review* 32:891-903.

Zeffane, Rachid M. 1989a. "Centralization or Formalization? Indifference Curves for Strategies of Control." *Organization Studies* 10:327-352.

Zeffane, Rachid M. 1989b. "Organization Structures and Contingencies in Different Nations: Algeria, Britain, and France." *Social Science Research* 18:331-369.

Zucker, Lynne G. 1977. "The Role of Institutionalization in Cultural Persistence." *American Sociological Review* 42:726-743.

Zucker, Lynne G. 1987. "Institutional Theories of Organization." *American Review of Sociology* 13:443-464.

Zwerman, William L. 1970. *New Perspectives on Organization Theory: An Empirical Reconsideration of the Marxian and Classical Analyses.* Westport, CT: Greenwood.

Index

size as cause of, 102-122, 137-138
Weberian ideal-type of, 62-63
Bureaucracy theory, 23-30, 61-100, 102-122
and computerization, 129-130
and divisionalization, 27, 77-81
and fit, 24
and matrix structures, 87-88
and size, 24, 102-122
and structural differentiation, 27, 69-76
causal connections among structural variables, 102-122
contingency theory of, 115-122
future study of, 274-275
in multinational corporations, 85
merger of with organic theory, 95
reconciling with organic theory, 92-95
synthesis with organic theory, 28-30
Business cycle, 252-253, 269, 278

Cartesianism, 141-152
Causality:
of size and bureaucracy, 101-122
reverse, 138-141
Centralization, 22, 23-25, 39-40, 46, 49, 63-64
and centrally planned economies, 91
and environmental hostility, 89
and multinational corporations, 83-85
and personality of CEO, 90
and public accountability, 67, 88-89
and size, 65-67
and task interdependence, 80
fit to size, 225
Challenges to contingency theory, 161-177
Choice, 54
and equifinality, 194-195
versus determinism, 131-137
Classical management theory, 3, 38, 46, 51, 52, 53
Cognitive capacity of managers, 81, 175
Cognitive processing, 48, 50
Cognitive configurations, 151-152

Competition, 163, 239, 253, 259, 269, 278
Complexity:
environmental, 19-20
of contingency theory, 30, 95
organizational, 39, 71, 103
Configurationalism, 141-152
cognitive versus existential configurationalism, 151-152
critique of, 144-152
divisionalized conglomerate configuration, 150
Conflict resolution, 43-45
Confounds, 233-239, 288
Congruence, 186-189
Constituents of fit, 236-239
Contingencies, 2-3, 17-21
association with organizational structure, 8-9
causal connection of size and task contingencies, 96-98
cause of changes in, 247-248
causes versus contingencies, 88-91
centrality, 155
changes in, 9, 11
changing contingencies to fit structure, 133-134
contingency change caused by performance, 248
contingency change causes misfit, 248
contradictory contingencies, 197
critical challenge, 153-155
definition of, 6, 153-154
environmental hostility, 89
innovation, 18-19, 39-41, 46, 47, 94-95, 223
intensity of interaction, 57-58
interdependence, 19-21, 27-30, 42-46, 50-52, 55-58, 77-87, 95, 126
leverage, 155-156
members' predispositions, 47
multiple contingencies, 197-198
of organizational power, 152-156
personality of CEO, 90
public accountability, 88-89

and local responsiveness, 82-86
and multinational strategy, 83-85
and transnational strategy, 83-84
differentiated fit structure in, 83-85
integrated variety structure in, 83-85
structural uniformity structure in,
     83-85
Multinational strategy, 83-85
Multiple contingencies, 197-198, 225
Multifits, 196-200, 225
Munificence, 19-20
Mutual adjustment, 51, 56, 57

Neo-contingency theory, 245-271, 275-288
Neo-human relations theory, 4, 38, 46,
     51, 217
Nonroutine technology, 48-50
Normative integration, 83-86
Normative isomorphism, 163, 166

Opportunism by managers, 80, 174-176
Organic structure, 2, 37-40, 46-47, 49,
     52, 93-94
   and technology, 53
   definition of, 22, 24-25
   dimension of, 22-23
   fit of to prospector strategy, 224
   fit of to task uncertainty, 22-23, 220
   fit of to task interdependence, 27-28, 52
Organic theory, 21-30, 35-59
   and matrix structures, 87-88
   and task interdependence, 27-28
   and task uncertainty, 22-23, 28
   in multinational corporations, 86
   measures of, 93
   merger with bureaucracy theory, 95
   reconciling with bureaucracy theory,
        92-95
   synthesis with bureaucracy theory,
        28-30
   underlying connections in, 55-58
Organizational change, 1, 9-16
   and disequilibrium, 247-249

and hetero-performance, 263-268
and quasi-fit, 259-262
as performance-driven, 249-257
factors that forestall, 254-257
factors that promote, 252-254
Organizational portfolio theory, 250-257,
     277-280
Overhead cost, 71

Paradigm of contingency theory, 7-16
Participation, 23, 25, 36, 38, 46, 53, 62,
     93, 98, 132, 217, 219-220
Performance:
   affected by fit, 10-13, 53, 68, 79, 84,
        134, 215-243
   affected by fit of bureaucracy to size, 68
   affected by fit of divisionalization to
        diversification, 13, 79
   affected by fit in multinational
        corporations, 83
   affected by fit with technology, 53
   affects fit, 11, 14-16, 233-236
   and configurations, 147-149
   and effectiveness, 6
   and functionalist explanations, 110-118
   and quasi-fit, 259
   as cause of contingency change, 248
   as cause of misfit, 248
   causes of, 13, 68, 216-226, 250-257
   causes change, 177
   causes decentralization, 176
   causes rational adaptation, 176
   causes strategic adaptation, 176
   causes structural adaptation, 14-16, 176
   causes time lags, 136
   crisis of, 15, 176, 249-257, 276
   fluctuations in, 250-257
   future research of, 275-276
   hetero-performance, 263-268, 281-288
   per manager, 74
   wider measures of, 225
Performance-driven organizational
     change, 12, 14-16, 136, 233-234,
     249-257, 276-280

About the Author

Lex Donaldson is Professor of Organizational Design at the Australian Graduate School of Management, which is a joint venture of the Universities of New South Wales and Sydney. He holds a B.Sc. in Behavioral Sciences from the University of Aston (1968) and a Ph.D. from the University of London (1974). His research interests are organizational theory, organizational structure, and corporate governance.

Donaldson is the author of six books, including *Performance-Driven Organizational Change: The Organizational Portfolio* (1999), *For Positivist Organization Theory: Proving the Hard Core* (1996), *American Anti-Management Theories of Organization: A Critique of Paradigm Proliferation* (1995), and *In Defence of Organization Theory: A Reply to the Critics* (1985). He is coauthor (with Frederick G. Hilmer) of *Management Redeemed: Debunking the Fads That Undermine Our Corporations* (1996). He also edited a collection of key articles under the title *Contingency Theory* (1995).

Donaldson is on the editorial boards of *Academy of Management Review, Organization Studies,* and the *Strategic Management Journal.* He has served as a guest editor of a special issue of the *Academy of Management Review* on "Market Discipline and the Discipline of

Management" (1990). He has held visiting appointments at the Universities of Aston, Iowa, London, Maryland, Northwestern, Oxford, and Stanford.